Leaves from the Garden of Eden

BY HOWARD SCHWARTZ

POETRY

Vessels
Gathering the Sparks
Sleepwalking Beneath the Stars
Breathing in the Dark

FICTION

A Blessing Over Ashes
Midrashim
The Captive Soul of the Messiah
Rooms of the Soul
Adam's Soul
The Four Who Entered Paradise

EDITOR

Imperial Messages: One Hundred Modern Parables
Voices Within the Ark: The Modern Jewish Poets
Gates to the New City: A Treasury of Modern Jewish Tales
The Dream Assembly: Tales of Rabbi Zalman Schachter-Shalomi
Elijah's Violin & Other Jewish Fairy Tales
Miriam's Tambourine: Jewish Tales from Around the World
Lilith's Cave: Jewish Tales of the Supernatural
Gabriel's Palace: Jewish Mystical Tales
Tree of Souls: The Mythology of Judaism
Leaves from the Garden of Eden: One Hundred Classic Jewish Tales

ESSAYS

Reimagining the Bible: The Storytelling of the Rabbis

CHILDREN'S BOOKS

The Diamond Tree
The Sabbath Lion
Next Year in Jerusalem
The Wonder Child
A Coat for the Moon
Ask the Bones
A Journey to Paradise
The Day the Rabbi Disappeared
Invisible Kingdoms
Before You Were Born
More Bones
Gathering Sparks

Leaves from the Garden of Eden

SELECTED AND RETOLD BY

Howard Schwartz

ILLUSTRATIONS BY

Kristina Swarner

CALLIGRAPHY BY

Tsila Schwartz

OXFORD
UNIVERSITY PRESS

Oxford University Press, Inc., publishes works that further
Oxford University's objective of excellence
in research, scholarship, and education.

Oxford New York
Auckland Cape Town Dar es Salaam Hong Kong Karachi
Kuala Lumpur Madrid Melbourne Mexico City Nairobi
New Delhi Shanghai Taipei Toronto

With offices in
Argentina Austria Brazil Chile Czech Republic France Greece
Guatemala Hungary Italy Japan Poland Portugal Singapore
South Korea Switzerland Thailand Turkey Ukraine Vietnam

First published by Oxford University Press, Inc., 2009
198 Madison Avenue, New York, New York 10016

www.oup.com

First issued as an Oxford University Press paperback, 2010

Library of Congress Cataloging-in-Publication Data
Schwartz, Howard, 1945–
Leaves from the garden of Eden : one hundred classic
Jewish tales / selected and retold by Howard Schwartz.
p. cm.
Includes bibliographical references and index.
ISBN 978-0-19-975438-0
1. Jews—Folklore. 2. Fairy tales. 3. Legends, Jewish. I. Title.
GR98.S343 2008
398.20892'4—dc22 2008020278

1 3 5 7 9 8 6 4 2

Printed in the United States of America
on acid-free paper

For Tsila,
Shira,
Nati,
Miriam,
Ari,
and Ava

If a man could pass through Paradise in a dream,
and have a flower presented to him as a pledge
that his soul had really been there,
and if he found that flower
in his hand when he awoke
—Ay!—
and what then?

—Samuel Taylor Coleridge

ACKNOWLEDGMENTS

I have been assisted by many people over the years in my work in Jewish folklore. Foremost among these is my editor, Cynthia Read, whose insight, guidance, and support have been essential. Thanks, too, to the others at Oxford who worked on this book: Peter Brigaitis, Margaret Case, Christine Dahlin, Woody Gilmartin, Meechal Hoffman, Brian Hughes, and Marie S. Nuchols.

I owe a special thanks to my wife, Tsila, for her help and understanding. Thanks, too, to my agent, Susan Cohen of Writer's House. Without the dedicated work of the scholars of the Israel Folktale Archives, a book such as this would not be possible. I gratefully thank Dov Noy, the founder of the IFA, and Idit Pintel-Ginsberg, the director, as well as the individual collectors of the tales included here. I am also grateful to the following editors, scholars, rabbis, and friends: Evelyn Abel, Dina Abramovitch of YIVO, Marc Bregman, Deborah Brodie, Nissim Binyamin Gamlieli, Jeremy Garber, Rabbi James Stone Goodman, Avraham Greenbaum, Edna Hechal, Leah Holbrook, Arielle North Olson, Cynthia Ozick, Linda Robbins, Barbara Rush, Marc Saperstein, Peninnah Schram, Charles Schwartz, Cherie Karo Schwartz, Maury Schwartz, Miriam Schwartz, Laya Firestone Seghi, Rabbi Zalman Schachter-Shalomi, Dan Sharon, Byron Sherwin, Y. David Shulman, Ted Solotaroff, Michael Stone, Susan Stone, Rabbi Susan Talve, Shlomo Vinner, Rabbi Gershon Winkler, and Nati Zohar.

CONTENTS

FOLKTALES

SUPERNATURAL TALES

MYSTICAL TALES

APPENDICES

Leaves from the Garden of Eden

Introduction

Summoning the Patriarchs

According to Jewish folk tradition, Abraham and Sarah never died. Ever since they took leave of this world, the patriarch and his wife are said to make their home in the Garden of Eden. During the week Abraham wanders through the Garden and gathers leaves that have fallen there. And on the eve of the Sabbath, Sarah crushes those leaves and takes the powder made from them and casts it into the wind. Then winds guided by angels carry it to the four corners of the earth, so that all those who breathe in even the smallest speck have a taste of Paradise, and their Sabbath is filled with joy, for that is the spice of the Sabbath.[1]

Just from this one little tale we can learn a lot. First, Abraham and Sarah are so deeply imprinted on the Jewish imagination that they are said to still be alive, even though Genesis clearly reports their deaths.[2] So, too, is the affection for them very great. Abraham is known as *Avraham Aveinu*, "our father Abraham," and even today, most Jews still think of themselves as "descendants of Abraham."

This tale also answers the question of where Abraham and Sarah can be found—in the Garden of Eden. After all, nothing is said in Genesis about the fate of the Garden of Eden after Adam and Eve were expelled from it, and in Jewish folklore it still exists. Even Franz Kafka makes this assumption in his parable "Paradise": "We were cast out of Paradise, but it was not destroyed. Our expulsion was in a sense fortunate. Had we not been cast out, Paradise would have had to be destroyed."[3] Additionally, this legend explains why, although alive, Abraham and Sarah are still beyond our reach, as is the Garden.

From a mythic perspective, an original myth about the Garden of Eden has been created, in which Abraham and Sarah take on the roles of a new Adam and Eve. Just as the expulsion from Eden of Adam and Eve represents a fallen state, so does the presence of Abraham and Sarah in the Garden represent hope of redemption. This is consistent with the rabbinic view that history started over again with Abraham and Sarah, the first Jews. In addition, it is a Sabbath myth, providing a mythical explanation for why food seems more delicious on the Sabbath. The myth transforms a proverbial phrase, "the spice of the Sabbath," into an enchanted spice emanating from the Garden of Eden.

Abraham and Sarah are not the only figures in Jewish tradition who are said to still be alive. Similar myths exist for Adam, Enoch, Jacob, Moses, King David, and Elijah.[4] According to one interpretation, God intended for Adam to be immortal, but when he tasted the fruit of the Tree of Knowledge he lost his right to immortality.[5] That is why God exiled Adam and placed the Cherubim at the gate of the Garden of Eden with the flaming sword, *to guard the way to the Tree of Life* (Gen. 3:24). Note, however, that in the rabbinic commentaries there is an alternate interpretation of the statement that "Adam was not meant to experience death." According to this reading, Adam never died and still exists.[6] This would place Adam in the category of the great figures who never died, whose continued existence is reported in many folktales. In "The Princess and the Slave," Samuel, an old Jewish slave, is sent on an impossible quest to find Moses—and succeeds. In "The Cave of King David," a sultan sends Rabbi Rafael Recanti on a quest to find King David, and he finds him living in a cave near the fabled city of Luz, where no one dies. This folk tradition about King David is so widespread it is the subject of an ancient song with lyrics that mean "David, king of Israel, lives and exists" (*David melekh Yisrael hai hai ve-kayyam*). And it is certainly true that King David, along with Abraham and Sarah, is still alive in Jewish folklore.

The notion that the patriarchs still exist is suggested in this brief tale, "Summoning the Patriarchs," from the cycle of stories about Rabbi Judah Loew of Prague:

> During the reign of Emperor Rudolf II, the great Rabbi Judah Loew, known as the Maharal, lived among the Jews of Prague. Not only was he a master of the Torah, he was well-versed in all of the mysteries and he was a great master of Kabbalah. Now it happened that the emperor heard of Rabbi Loew's reputation and sent for him with a strange request: he wanted the rabbi to invoke the patriarchs Abraham, Isaac, and Jacob, and the sons of Jacob, to summon them from their graves. Rabbi Loew was appalled at this request, but when the emperor threatened the well-being of the Jews of Prague if he did not comply, Rabbi Loew agreed to attempt it. The rabbi warned the emperor, however, that under no circumstances must he laugh at what he saw, and the emperor promised he would not. Nor could anyone else be present.
>
> Then emperor and Rabbi Loew went to a secluded room of the castle, where Rabbi Loew pronounced a spell that summoned the patriarchs and the sons of Jacob. And to the great amazement of the emperor, they appeared one after the other in their true form, and the emperor was amazed at the size and power of each of them, which far exceeded that of men in his time. But when Naphtali, the son of Jacob, leaped with great ease over ears of corn and stalks of flax in the vision, the emperor could not contain himself and began to laugh. Suddenly the apparitions vanished and the ceiling of that room began to descend and was on the verge of crushing the emperor, when Rabbi Loew succeeded in making it halt with the help of another spell. And it is said that the fallen ceiling can still be seen today in that room, which is kept locked.[7]

Rabbi Judah Loew is best known for creating the Golem, a man made out of clay who protected the Jews of Prague, but there are many other tales recounting the marvels of the Maharal, as Rabbi Loew is known. Many of these concern his use of powers deriving from his knowledge of Kabbalah, the Jewish mystical tradition. Only the purest and most eminent sages were considered capable of engaging in kabbalistic studies. Therefore the emperor's demand to see the patriarchs was not only unreasonable but also inevitably exposed him to danger. This follows the pattern of many warning tales about those who lost their sanity or even their lives by undertaking mystical studies without the proper background or preparation.[8] Here the king is saved from destruction only because Rabbi Loew is able to prevent the ceiling from collapsing.

The magic of being able to invoke the vision of the patriarchs reflects the rabbinic principle that past, present, and future all exist at the same time.[9] This tradition of immortality reflects the vivid presence of the patriarchs in the lives of the people, where they were very much alive.

Two arks were said to accompany the Israelites in their desert wandering, one containing the remains of Joseph, and the other, the Ark of the Tabernacle.[10] The one represents the past and the other, the future. This accurately portrays how past and future are linked in Jewish tradition, carried side by side, at the head of the caravan. In this way past and present exist at the same time, and the past, as portrayed in these tales, is very much alive.

Four Types of Jewish Tales

The Jewish people are known as the People of the Book with good reason. They love to read books, especially the Bible. But they could also be called the People of the Stories, for as they wandered from place to place, they always took their stories with them. The stories a people tell not only serve as bearers of their tradition but also reveal a great deal about them, especially their fantasies and fears. Folktales emerge out of an anonymous folk process that reshapes the tale every time it is told. They are a crucial stage in the evolution from myth to literature. These stages include myth, legend, folklore and, finally, literature. Myth, the earliest expression of a people, focuses on the sacred stories told about gods and creation, heaven and hell, and existence before and after this world. Legends recount the exploits of heroes, some historical, some imaginary. Just as Jason and Hercules are heroes in Greek tradition, so Jewish heroes include King David and King Solomon, the legendary Rabbi Adam and the Ba'al Shem Tov. So, too, are the forces of evil portrayed in these tales, not only as evil wizards and witches, but also as every kind of demonic being, including the dybbuk, an evil spirit who takes possession of a living person.

Folktales are truly a mirror of the lives of the people, transmitted orally within a community until they are finally written down. Jewish folktales find expression in many types of tales, but the most popular are fairy tales, folktales, supernatural tales, and mystical tales. This collection focuses on these four types of tales, which represent the vast majority of Jewish folktales.[11] Readers will soon discover that each of these types of tales has its own distinctive characteristics.

There is a seamless link between the four stages of the evolution from myth to literature, and each prior phase continues to exist as a substratum of the new one. So that legend is built on myth, and folklore on myth and legend. Literature draws on all these forms and invents new ones of its own. The long era of anonymity that shaped myth, legend, and folklore comes to an end, and for the first time, creators are self-conscious about their creation and insist on taking credit for it.

Most Jewish folktales follow the recognizable models of world folklore. Fairy tales, the most popular and best known type of folktale, share all the themes and magical elements found in the classic fairytales collected by the Brothers Grimm. Magic rings and magic carpets are as common as they are in the *Arabian Nights*. In the stories gathered here, there are a multitude of kings and queens, princes and princesses, arduous quests to enchanted kingdoms, witches and wizards, magic mirrors, and magic pools, where whoever immerses himself recovers his youth. There are enchanted kingdoms and invisible beings, such as angels, spirits, and demons. A good half of the tales collected by the Israel Folktale Archives are such universal tales, without explicit Jewish elements.[12] Many of these are variants of famous tales told throughout the world, such as Rapunzel, Cinderella, Bluebeard, and Snow White. Yet, by reading closely, it is possible to recognize the Jewish elements even in these universal tales.

The telling of tales represents an important transmission of tradition. As rich as is the written tradition in Judaism, the oral tradition is just as abundant. That is because it was given legitimacy by the ancient belief in the divine origin of the Oral Torah, an oral commentary on the Torah, said to have been given by God to Moses along with the Written Torah.[13] Thus Judaism has two Torahs, one written and one oral, and the oral tradition has flourished ever since.

The major development in the study of Jewish folklore in the twentieth century was the methodical collection of orally transmitted Jewish tales. The body of folklore collected in Eastern Europe in the expeditions of S. Ansky, the first Jewish ethnologist, and other early Jewish ethnologists, and those collected in Israel by the Israel Folktale Archives, founded by Professor Dov Noy, include oral variants of stories that have been told and retold in Jewish tradition for a thousand years or more. There are even striking oral variants of biblical stories, daring in their own ways to retell the old tale. Here, for example, is an oral retelling of the binding of Isaac in Genesis 22, collected from Jews from India:[14]

> Abraham and Sarah lived in the Land of Israel and their lives were good, but they didn't have any children. One day Abraham prayed

to God and said, "If You give me a son, I'll give him to You as a sacrifice."

At the age of one hundred, Abraham had a son and he named him Isaac. The boy grew and Abraham forgot his promise to God. After several years God came to Abraham in a dream and said, "Abraham, you promised that you would give Me your son as a sacrifice."

In the morning, when Abraham awoke, he remembered the dream, and he said to Sarah, "I am going to take my son to study. Don't worry about him. He will be with me."

Abraham took Isaac and went to the forest. They were both silent. But when they arrived, Isaac said, "Father, why did you bring me here?" Abraham said, "My son, before you were born I had to make a vow that if I had a son, I would sacrifice him to God."

Isaac said, "Father, I am ready." So Abraham tied the hands of Isaac behind his back and laid him on the wood, and he took the knife in his hand and put it on Isaac's neck. At that instant Abraham heard the voice of God: "Abraham, Abraham, leave the child. I have already received the sacrifice you wanted to give Me. Look, there is a sheep. Sacrifice it to Me instead of your son." So Abraham untied his son, caught the sheep, and sacrificed it to God.

This oral retelling of the binding of Isaac resembles the biblical account, but makes some crucial changes in it. Instead of being a divine test, it is a bargain arrived at between man and God. The oral tale from India follows a folk model in which a parent desperate for a child is forced to give that child back as a sacrifice. Rather than being portrayed as a divine test, as it is in the Bible, the story is presented as a primitive agreement between God and Abraham. This version probably evolved over a long period of oral transmission, to the point that it had become a variant of the biblical tale. Nevertheless, this oral tale ends as does the biblical one, with God stopping the sacrifice at the last minute.[15] Above all, the oral tale shows how the biblical stories are still being retold in far-flung Jewish communities, such as the Bene Israel of India, where the oral tradition is still alive. And it provides an indication of the remarkable quality of these oral tales, which were transmitted orally for centuries before they were written down.

Each of the four primary types—fairy tales, folktales, supernatural tales, and mystical tales—seems to have its own purpose. Fairy tales are fantasies of enchantment. Folktales portray the lives of the folk as they imagined them, with a rich helping of magical and divine intervention. Supernatural tales portray fears about the powers of evil, such as demons and *dybbuks* and other kinds of supernatural beings, especially the ubiquitous demoness Lilith. And mystical tales serve as teaching stories of some of the greatest rabbis, such as Rabbi Akiba, Rabbi Isaac Luria, or the Ba'al Shem Tov. What follows is a brief characterization of each of these four widely represented types of tales.

JEWISH FAIRY TALES

Fairy tales are no longer regarded as belonging solely to the realm of children. As scholars such as C. G. Jung, Maria Von Franz, and Bruno Bettelheim have demonstrated, fairy tales can be understood in many ways—as fantasies or as psychic maps. Fairy tales not only reveal a great deal about human nature and psychology but they are also a magical mirror into the fantasy lives of past generations. Equally they serve as teaching stories of determination and faith, for every fairy tale includes immense obstacles that must be overcome.

A common theme in many fairy tales is that of a poor man who marries a princess, or, as in Cinderella, a poor maiden who marries a prince. Of particular interest is "The Princess in the Tower," an eighth-century version of Rapunzel, which may well be the world's earliest version of this tale.[16] According to the Talmud, God makes matches, pairing this one with that one, and, it is said, every match is as hard to make as parting the waters of the Red Sea. Here a bird reports to King Solomon what it has overheard flying through the heavens—that his daughter, the princess, is destined to marry a poor man within a year. To prevent the decree from taking place, Solomon sends the princess to live in a tower on a desert island. Naturally fate intervenes—in the form of the Ziz, a giant mythical bird that brings a sleeping young man to the balcony of the princess. By the time King Solomon arrives at the end of a year, she has a husband, a poor scribe from the city of Acco, and they have a child, a boy whose name is Solomon. Thus King Solomon learns that not even the wisest of men can outfox fate.

In Jewish folklore there is an interesting amalgam of the magical and the spiritual. For example, King Solomon has a magic ring with God's Name, known as the Tetragrammaton, engraved on it. Using the power of the ring, he can accomplish anything—fly on a magic carpet to a mysterious palace or defeat and capture Ashmodai, the king of demons. The powers of that ring are inextricably linked to the power of God's Name, which, like God, is limitless. In Jewish mysticism, a word contains the power of whatever it signifies. Thus God's Name has unlimited power for King Solomon, who knows how to pronounce it. Later this secret knowledge was said to be known only by one sage in each generation.

More than half of Jewish fairytales are quests. In "King Solomon and Ashmodai," from ancient Israel, Solomon sends his general, Benayahu, on a quest to capture the king of demons. In the sequel, "The Beggar King," King Solomon, reduced to being a beggar, goes on a quest for ten years to recover his throne. "The Golden Mountain," from Morocco, is an Aladdin-like quest for hidden treasure. And in "The Golden Tree," from India, a king sets out to find the golden tree of his dreams.

Above all, all the tales included in this section are recognizably fairy tales, following the familiar pattern, fully making use of magical devices, as well as divine intervention. As in all fairy tales, every obstacle is overcome and everyone lives happily ever after. While other types of Jewish tales may include some fairy-tale elements, such as magical spells or quests, in no others is it as certain that good will triumph over evil.

FOLKTALES

In broad terms, all one hundred tales in this collection are folktales. The term is used here in that sense, but also to identify a characteristic type of story that is not a fairy tale, not a supernatural or mystical tale, but still a recognizable Jewish tale. These stories are identified here simply as folktales. They often involve divine intervention, as in "The Sabbath Lion," when the Sabbath Queen sends a lion to protect a boy who has been abandoned by his caravan because he refuses to travel on the Sabbath. So too do they often involve dreams or visions. In "The Cave of Mattathias," a Hasid trapped in a snowstorm dreams of meeting Mattathias, the father of the Maccabees, who lived long ago, in a cave in the Holy Land. Mattathias gives him an important message to deliver to Rabbi Menachem Mendel of Riminov, and then miraculously transports him to the rabbi's home, saving the Hasid's life.

Such miracles appear in almost every tale in this section, but not in the context of an enchanted world, as with fairy tales, or in the Kingdom of Demons, as in many supernatural tales. Instead, miracles are brought about by great sages who demonstrate almost unlimited powers. In "A Flock of Angels," Rabbi Asenath Barzani pronounces a holy name, and angels appear out of nowhere to beat out a synagogue fire with their wings. Or in "The Magic Wine Cup," the wine cup at Rabbi Hayim Pinto's seder grows large enough to magically bring forth a treasure chest that was lost at sea.

The Talmud, codified in the fifth century, is the source for many kinds of Jewish folktales. Many of these stories serve as models for later variants, so that a great many types of Jewish tales find their source in the Talmud. Some retell stories about biblical figures, such as Abraham and Moses, and recount tales of great rabbis, such as Akiba, Meir, and Shimon bar Yohai. Some of the earliest tales about King Solomon are found in the Talmud, such as "An Appointment with Death," about the mythical city of Luz, where no one dies:

> One morning, as King Solomon awoke, he heard a chirping outside his window. He sat up in bed and listened carefully, for he knew the language of the birds, and he overheard them say that the Angel of Death had been sent to take the lives of two of his closest advisers. King Solomon was startled by this unexpected news, and he summoned the two men and revealed what he had learned of their fate.
>
> The two were terrified and begged King Solomon to help them. Solomon told them their only hope was to find their way to the city of Luz, for the Angel of Death was forbidden to enter there. Therefore the inhabitants of Luz were immortal—as long as they stayed within the walls of the charmed city. The location of that city was a well-kept secret, since it would otherwise be deluged by those seeking immortality, but it was well known to King Solomon. He revealed it to the two frightened men, and they departed at once. They whipped their camels across the hot desert all day, and just before nightfall they finally

saw the walls of that fabled city. Immortality was within reach and they rode as fast as they could to the city gates.

But when they arrived, they saw, to their horror, the Angel of Death waiting for them. "How did you know to look for us here?" they asked. The angel replied: "This is where I was told to meet you."[17]

The name of this city comes from Genesis 28:19: *He named that site Bethel, but previously the name of the city had been Luz.* Since the location of that city was such a holy place, the Talmud asserts that anyone who lived there was safe from the Angel of Death. In this brief tale, King Solomon, the wisest of men, tries to deceive the Angel of Death by sending the two doomed men there, to escape him, but in the end he discovers that he cannot outfox fate. This is the same moral of several stories about King Solomon, as the point is made that no one can escape the dictates of fate.[18]

Even more elementary, we can read into this tale how powerful is the fear of death and the Angel of Death. Out of this fear grows the fantasy of a city of immortals. Many cultures have such a myth, and it is still a popular theme in modern works of fiction, including John O'Hara's *Appointment in Samarra* and James Hilton's *Lost Horizon.* The version in the Talmud appears to be the earliest expression of this motif.

SUPERNATURAL TALES

Fairy tales give expression to fantasy. But there are also other kinds of fantasies, including sexual ones, and those inspired by fear—dark tales of the unknown. These manifest themselves in supernatural stories about demons, dybbuks, witches or wizards, and various kinds of invisible beings. The battle against the forces of evil was a pitched one, with demonic dangers waiting at every turn. These tales, such as those from *Sefer Hasidim,* are darker, and they generally do not have a happy ending.

These supernatural tales are a direct mirror into the world of Jewish superstition and fantasy. Since ancient times, Jewish storytellers have described a world with invisible creatures—angels, spirits, and demons. Angels serve as messengers of God. Spirits of the dead haunt this world as ghosts. And demons are forces of evil, capable of stealing a person's soul.

Belief in these mysterious, invisible creatures has lasted for thousands of years; even today, in some Jewish circles, people still believe in them. This supernatural world is balanced with the forces of God, such as the angels, opposed to the forces of evil, a multitude of demons. In addition to angels and demons, the other world includes spirits—souls of the dead who are still present among us. Sometimes one of these wandering spirits, while seeking to evade avenging angels, enters the body of a woman, taking possession of her as a dybbuk. That is what happens in the Italian folktale "The Dybbuk in the Well." Such possession by dybbuk requires an exorcism, an elaborate rite requiring ten rabbis.[19]

As for demons, they are ruled over by Satan, who also appears in the Bible. In the pseudepigraphal literature, Satan was said to be a fallen angel, also known as Samael, Lucifer, or simply as the Devil. Jewish folklore, on the other hand, holds that demons are ruled over by Ashmodai, the king of demons, and Lilith, his queen. They make their home in the Kingdom of Demons, but their primary role is to try to lead people astray. A bride who is not careful may end up marrying a demon instead of her intended groom, while the charm sewn into a dress may drive a pious woman to lascivious behavior.

Belief in such things as marriage with demons and the existence of ghosts gave birth to many remarkable tales. In these tales, anything is possible. A young woman can be married to a river demon without even knowing it; a man can encounter the ghost of the fiancée he abandoned; a bridegroom who vanished on the day of his wedding can return 130 years later. These stories explain the role of the supernatural creatures in people's lives, and serve as miracle stories as well as warning tales. This is the lore of the supernatural that so intrigued Isaac Bashevis Singer, whose stories often draw on supernatural themes.

Some of the best known of these supernatural tales concern a young man or woman who is tricked into marrying a demonic double, as happens in the story "The Other Side," from Eastern Europe.[20] Others concern Lilith, who appears both as the incarnation of lust and as a dangerous witch. These dual characteristics made the presence of Lilith in the lives of the people inescapable, especially for women, for whom Lilith threatened not only the lives of their infants, but also their husbands' affection. The kind of temptation Lilith posed, even to the most righteous, is found in "The Woman in the Forest," a Hasidic tale about Rabbi Elimelekh of Lizensk:[21]

> The holy rabbi, Reb Elimelekh of Lizensk, was once a young man. He spent all day studying in the house of study, and at night he walked home through the forest, always taking the same path. One night, as he was walking through the forest, he saw a light in the distance. Curious about it, he left the path and followed the light. It was coming from a cottage deep in the forest. As he came closer, he peered into the window, and there he saw a young woman with long, dark hair, wearing a thin nightgown.
>
> As soon as he saw her, Reb Elimelekh knew he did not belong there, and he turned to go. Just then the door to the cottage opened, and the woman called out: "Reb Melekh, wait! Please, come in." So, being a polite young man, Reb Elimelekh went in. As soon as he came in, the woman closed the door and stood before him and said: "Reb Melekh, I have seen you pass through the forest many times, and I have often hoped you would visit me. You know, I bathed in the spring today and I am clean. Surely the sin would be slight, but the pleasure would be abundant." And she dropped her gown.
>
> Reb Elimelekh wrestled with himself, as did Jacob with the angel. And at last he wrenched out, "No!" At that instant the woman

vanished, and the cottage disappeared, and Reb Elimelekh found himself standing alone in the forest, and there were glowworms at his feet.

The woman in this tale is not identified, but everyone among the Hasidim who heard it knew exactly who she was—Lilith, or one of the daughters of Lilith. So vivid was the presence of Lilith in their lives that she became the primary focus of their sexual fantasies and fears. Lilith is brazen from the first, calling Rabbi Elimelekh not by his full name, Elimelekh, meaning "my God is King," but by his familiar name, Melekh. This conveniently lets her avoid pronouncing God's name, which, as a demoness, she is forbidden to do. The fact that her hair is long indicates that she is unmarried, while having bathed in the spring informs him that she has purified herself in a *mikveh*, a ritual bath. Since a *mikveh* requires running water, many springs served as ritual baths. By telling him that about the spring, she is stating that she has purified herself for sex.

Finally, she appeals to his knowledge of the law when she tells him that the sin will be slight but the pleasure abundant. According to Deuteronomy 22:22, *If a man be found lying with a married woman, then they shall both die.* However, the expected parallel about a married man lying with an unmarried woman is missing, and according to rabbinic principles of interpretation, what is not stated is not a law. Therefore, what Lilith says to him is valid, not only demonstrating her mastery of the law but also tempting him with the knowledge that Jewish law does not identify what she proposes as adultery, a mortal sin.

Thus Lilith comes equipped with many weapons. She not only uses the power of lust, her greatest weapon, but she also appeals to his intelligence. Rabbi Elimelekh escapes, but only after a considerable struggle. The glowworms at the end indicate that Lilith has lost her power over him and has been revealed in her true form, that of a worm. Or the story can be read as a Hasidic sexual fantasy that has reached its conclusion. The fact that the tale is attributed to Rabbi Elimelekh of Lizhensk indicates that Lilith was brazen enough to approach even the holiest of men. Indeed, this was her intention, for if she could corrupt the best ones, the others would be sure to follow. Rabbi Elimelekh resists, but barely.

In discussing Lilith, it is important to keep in mind that the stories about Lilith found in traditional sources are all examples of tales told by men. Since these stories were told and preserved by men, they should be viewed as men's stories. Until the twentieth century, there were no sources of explicitly women's tales. However, beginning with the expeditions of S. Ansky and the Yiddish folktale collections of Y. L. Cahan, women's voices have begun to be heard. Approximately half of the oral tales collected by the Israel Folktale Archives, which to date has collected more than twenty-three thousand tales from sixty-nine countries, are from female tellers.[22]

These women's tales are often strikingly different from those told by men. For example, in virtually all of the men's tales about Lilith, there are strong elements of fear and lust—fear that Lilith will strangle their infants, and lust for Lilith, who is the personification of lust. Jewish women, on the other hand, have a very different attitude toward Lilith. She threatened the lives of their children and their husband's affection. Therefore, in an orally collected story such as "The Hair in the Milk," from Yemen, the midwife, who knows all of Lilith's tricks, traps her in a bottle, and prevents her from harming the newborn infant. She shows no fear of Lilith whatsoever, and forces the demoness to do her will. In these women's tales, the heroine is often the old midwife, who knows secrets not only of healing but also of how to protect against the forces of evil. The midwife also plays a heroic role in "The Underwater Palace," p. 318, from Eastern Europe.

It seems clear that any modern study of Jewish tales should include these orally collected tales, especially those told by women, and that the boundaries of the canon of Jewish folklore should include the stories collected by early Jewish folklorists such as S. Y. Ansky and Y. L. Cahan, and preserved by the YIVO Archives in New York and the Israel Folktale Archives in Haifa. Such oral tales are well represented in this collection, where a third of the stories included are from oral sources.

MYSTICAL TALES

Wondrous stories about the powers of the rabbis are a staple of Jewish literature. Such stories are told about the talmudic sages, the kabbalistic rabbis, and the Hasidic masters. A body of stories inevitably grew up around the key figures, such as Rabbi Akiba, Rabbi Isaac Luria, or the Ba'al Shem Tov. These stories are inevitably hagiographic, and many of them attribute unlimited powers to these sages. In "The Cave of Shimon bar Yohai," the prophet Elijah visits Rabbi Shimon bar Yohai every day in the cave where he is hiding from the Romans, and brings him teachings from on high, and that is the origin of the *Zohar*, the central text of Kabbalah. In "The Angel of Forgetfulness," the Ari knows where to find water from Miriam's well, the well that was said to have followed the Israelites in the wilderness, so that they always had fresh water. In "The Tree of Life," the Ba'al Shem Tov brings his Hasidim into a mysterious garden, which turns out to be the Garden of Eden. There are cycles of stories about each of these rabbis and many others, recounting miracles and showing them to be mystical masters.

Virtually all of the mystical tales included here serve dual purposes as teaching stories and hagiographic tales. They often draw on talmudic models, drawing intentional parallels with the great sages. The Ari modeled himself on Rabbi Shimon bar Yohai, as he is portrayed in the *Zohar*. The Ba'al Shem Tov modeled himself on the Ari. And all subsequent Hasidic masters modeled themselves on the Ba'al Shem Tov. Take, for example, the theme of heavenly ascent. The Talmud tells of four sages who entered Paradise.[23] They include Rabbi Akiba, who "ascended and descended in peace," and, many centuries later, the Kotzker Rebbe, who is reported to have journeyed through the palaces of heaven.[24] In the eyes of his Hasidim, the account of such a heavenly journey reveals the Kotzker Rebbe to be as great as those sages, perhaps as great as Rabbi Akiba. For this reason, intentional parallels were drawn between earlier rabbis and later ones.

The talmudic legend of the *Lamed-vav Tzaddikim* tells of thirty-six righteous ones who live in each generation. God permits the world to exist because of these hidden saints. Each of the great sages seeks in his own way to achieve righteousness. In doing so, they serve as a model of the tzaddik for their followers, who view them as holy masters. During his expeditions in eastern Europe, S. Ansky, the first Jewish ethnologist, collected folktales, songs, and religious objects. Among the tales he collected was one about Reb Shmelke of Nicolsburg (1726–1788). Ansky later included this brief tale about Reb Shmelke's whip in act I of his famous drama *The Dybbuk* (1926):

> Two men, one poor, the other wealthy and influential, came before Reb Shmelke as litigants. As Reb Shmelke listened carefully, each presented his side of the case. Then he rendered his judgment in favor of the poor man. The rich man became livid and declared that he would not abide by the verdict. Reb Shmelke remained calm and said: "You will obey. When a rabbi renders his decision, it must be obeyed."
>
> At this the rich man became furious and said, "I abhor you and all your rabbis!" Then Reb Shmelke stood up, looked the man in the eyes, and said, "If you do not obey my order this instant, I'll take out my whip." Hearing this, the rich man began to heap abuse on the rabbi, who stood up and pulled open a drawer of his desk. At that instant the Primal Serpent sprang forth and wrapped itself around the rich man's neck. He fell to his knees, filled with terror, and begged for forgiveness. Reb Shmelke said: "Warn your children, and let them warn their children, to follow the way of the rebbe or fear his whip!" And then he removed the snake.

Reb Shmelke of Nicolsburg is a pithy character, but he is not usually portrayed as being this fierce. However, his loyalty to the poor rather than the rich is well known, and the rich man in this tale rejects the authority of the rabbi, as well as that of the Torah. The whip that Reb Shmelke uses is the Primal Serpent, known as the *Nahash ha-Kadmoni*, a kabbalistic concept that represents a kind of archetypal serpent, over which Reb Shmelke has sufficient control to call upon as he wishes.

This concept evolved in kabbalistic thought from the speaking serpent of Genesis into a more archetypal being, much as Lilith came to represent a principle of evil in kabbalistic cosmology. This suggests that the great Hasidic masters understood not only how to align their lives with the side of good but also how to control the elements of evil. It is interesting to note that in Ansky's play, four Hasidim discuss this tale after telling it, creating a kind of commentary about it. One of them argues that it couldn't have been the Primal Serpent that Reb Shmelke called forth, since that serpent was Satan, the Evil One. Another replies that there were many witnesses to this event, and therefore it should not be questioned. The first wonders if there are any names that can call forth the Evil One, and a third replies that he can be called forth only with God's Name, the Tetragrammaton. This, then, is what Reb Shmelke must have done.

Even this little tale serves many purposes. It demonstrates Reb Shmelke's powers, invoking the serpent of Eden in its manifestation as the Primal Serpent—which, nevertheless, is under Reb Shmelke's control. Finally, it is a powerful warning tales about the necessity of obeying the rulings of rabbis and the authority of the Torah.

Other sages and rabbis take decisive action when it is needed, as in this Hasidic tale about Reb Elimelekh of Lizensk, where a single motion from the rebbe has monumental consequences:

> One Friday afternoon, not long before the Sabbath, it became known that the king was planning to sign an evil decree against the Jews. There was dismay everywhere, but Reb Elimelech of Lizensk insisted on celebrating the Sabbath as always, for, he said, "You must never turn away from the Sabbath Queen."
>
> After saying the Sabbath blessings, they sat down to the meal. Among the guests was Reb Menachem Mendel, who later became the rabbi of Riminov. A bowl of soup was set before Reb Elimelech. The others waited for him to begin eating, but he did not. He waited, saying nothing, with a distant look on his face. All at once he knocked over the bowl of soup, spilling it all over the table.
>
> Later it was learned that just as the king was about to sign the evil decree, he accidentally knocked over the inkwell. Ink spilled all over the parchment. When he saw this, the king tore up the decree and commanded that none like it ever be drawn up again.[25]

This famous tale about Rabbi Elimelekh demonstrates his role as a wonder worker. Lilith may have tempted him as a young man, but here he is portrayed as a powerful sorcerer, making use of sympathetic magic to cause the king's inkwell to spill at the instant he knocks over a bowl of soup, blotting out the evil decree against the Jews.

In almost all such stories where these mystical powers are drawn on, the rabbi is responding to a dire situation, often the danger of a pogrom. The people lived in great fear of these evil decrees, and the fantasy of magically reversing them is a common theme in many Jewish folktales. The most prominent of these is "The Golem," where Rabbi Judah Loew uses Kabbalistic magic to protect the Jews of Prague, creating a man out of clay and bringing him to life. Thus the stories about the Golem should be seen as a Jewish fantasy that grew up when the reality was that their lives were in great danger, and there was nothing they could do to stop the plague of pogroms. This tells us quite a bit about how a folktale can assuage fear with fantasy, and gives us considerable insight into the working of the Jewish imagination.

All four types of tales included here—fairy tales, folktales, supernatural tales, and mystical tales—are found in every stage of postbiblical Jewish literature, from the Talmud to the tales of the Hasidim. Examples of all four types of tales are also found in the collections of YIVO and the Israel Folktale Archives. They are the most popular tales because they have the most compelling narratives, especially quests. All of Jewish history has been a great quest—to return to the Garden of Eden, to escape from Egyptian bondage, to return to the Land of Israel, to hasten the coming of the Messiah. The upheaval in Jewish life, which has often led to the edge of the abyss, is subjected to the powers of God at every turn in these tales. And even though this world includes witches and demons, and other figures of good and evil, ultimately God makes the final judgments, and gives an underlying order and meaning to everything. And the covenant between God and Israel assures the eventual victory of the Jews over all the forces of evil, even if that time will have to wait until the coming of the Messiah.

The Jewish Mythical Imagination

Mythology plays a central role in Jewish folklore. Mythic motifs can be found in virtually every tale, and there are often multiple motifs interwoven in the same story.[26] These sometimes shape the central narrative, but more often their presence underlies the tale, serving as a mythic foundation. In order to fully comprehend a folktale, it is necessary to recognize its component myths, and then to examine how they impact the tale. Often, the myth finds its origin in the Torah, in a central episode or simply in a verse. Some element of the original story becomes embellished, so that a new story is created, and this new tale inspires countless others. This process of reimagining is characteristic of all postbiblical Jewish literature.[27]

Although there are a vast number of myths in Jewish tradition, they can be classified in ten primary categories: (1) Myths of God, (2) Myths of Creation, (3) Myths of Heaven, (4) Myths of Hell, (5) Myths of the Holy Word, (6) Myths of the Holy Time, (7) Myths of the Holy People, (8) Myths of the Holy Land, (9) Myths of Exile, and (10) Myths of the Messiah.[28] Each of these categories includes hundreds of myths, and these myths have been woven into the narrative threads of Jewish folklore. Whenever any allusion to them is found, we encounter the mythological strata of the story.

Consider, for example, the ram that Abraham sacrificed on Mount Moriah in place of Isaac.[29] We know nothing about it except that its horns were entangled in a bush, where Abraham found it. Yet in the rabbinic elaborations of the story, the ram came to be regarded as a kind of holy being. It is said to be one of the ten things created on the eve of the first Sabbath.[30] From this perspective, the ram had been waiting since the time of creation to fulfill its purpose at Mount Moriah. Furthermore, nothing of the ram was wasted. Its skin became Elijah's mantle, its gut was used in David's harp, one of its horns was sounded by Moses at Mount Sinai, and the other will be blown by Elijah at the End of Days.[31] Even in this brief elaboration of the biblical tale, the binding of Isaac has become linked to Moses, King David, and Elijah. This indicates that the biblical story of the binding of Isaac was considered so seminal it was tied to the revelation at Sinai and to the redemption at the End of Days. In this way one mythic theme is linked to another, and all of Jewish history becomes a single narrative unfolding of God's plan for His people, the Jews.

To illustrate how these extensively mythic motifs are woven into Jewish folk narratives, let us examine one story, "A Vision at the Wailing Wall."[32] It appears in the first collection of stories about Rabbi Isaac Luria, known as the Ari, who lived in Safed in the sixteenth century.[33] Just before Rosh ha-Shanah, the Ari reveals to his disciple, Rabbi Abraham Berukhim, that he is fated to die that year—unless he undertakes a pilgrimage to the Wailing Wall and has a vision of God's Bride, the *Shekhinah*. Rabbi Abraham makes the journey and does indeed have such a vision, and thereby survives for another cycle of life.[34] This story takes place entirely within a Jewish framework. It takes place during the Days of Awe, the holiest time of the year. It involves the Ari, whom many regard as the greatest Jewish mystic. In all respects, it is a thoroughly Jewish tale.

At the same time, the foundation of this story is drawn from Jewish mythology. Let us consider each of the ten mythic categories for any evidence of them in the story.

Myths of God. God is said to record everyone's fate on Rosh ha-Shanah, the Day of Judgment, by inscribing that person's name in the Book of Life or in the "other book," the Book of Death. This gives God an active role in the story, since it is He who determines Rabbi Abraham's fate. Furthermore, since the *Shekhinah* represents not only God's Bride but also the feminine aspect of God, the vision of the *Shekhinah* at the core of the story must be recognized as a mystical vision of God.[35] Thus this story incorporates myths about the masculine and feminine aspects of God in one tale. Like Rabbi Abraham's vision, this indicates that the story reflects a very inclusive view of the nature of God, thoroughly incorporating the feminine into the divine, as is the case in kabbalistic theology.

Myths of Creation. The allusion to myths of creation is indirect in this story. It derives from the Ari's role as the creator of the myth of the Shattering of the Vessels and the Gathering of the Sparks.[36] This is one of the major creation myths in Judaism, along with the creation myth of Genesis and the kabbalistic myth of the ten *sefirot*. This myth is the basis of the key concept of *tikkun olam*, repair of the world, which very much reflects the views of the modern environmental movement.

Myths of Heaven. The myth of the heavenly ledgers, in which the Ari reads of Rabbi Abraham's fate, is one of the myths of heaven. God alone has access to these heavenly books, so that the Ari's ability to read in them is truly extraordinary.[37] The Torah itself had its origin in heaven, where it is said to be written on the arm of God, with black fire on white fire.[38]

Myths of Hell. The allusion to Gehenna, Jewish hell, in this story is indirect, in that the Ari instructs Rabbi Abraham to fast and repent for three days and nights. Rabbi Abraham puts on sackcloth and ashes and repents so that his soul will be purified when he stands before God at the Wall. This is the same ritual used by the people of Ninveh in the book of Jonah (3:5–6) to repent. It is the same ritual used for mourning, when the Kaddish, the prayer for the dead, is said. The Kaddish is believed to have theurgic effects on the souls of the dead, for whom it is said. This is based on the belief that most of those who die have enough sins to require punishment in Gehenna, Jewish hell, for up to a year. When their punishments end, the purified souls are set free to ascend into Paradise. The torments of Gehenna are quite terrible, similar to those found in Dante's *Inferno*, but those fortunate enough to have someone say Kaddish for them are spared these punishments.

Myths of the Holy Word. God gave Moses tablets of the Law that were written by the finger of God. God also dictated the Torah to Moses, who served as God's scribe. Thus the origin of the Torah was in heaven. The Books of Life and Death in which God inscribes the names of those who will live or die the next year are other examples of heavenly books, and there are other books of divine origin, such as the Book of Raziel. The angel Raziel is said to have given this book to Adam to reveal the future to him. Thus in reading from the heavenly ledgers, the Ari touches on the myths about such heavenly books.

Myths of the Holy Time. The story takes place at Rosh ha-Shanah, when God decides whether a person will live or die the next year. Ten days later, on Yom Kippur, God seals that fate. During this period, a person's fate can be changed.

Myths of the Holy People. The Ari is widely regarded as the greatest Jewish mystic. He is certainly one of the towering giants of Jewish tradition. He created the myth of Shattering of the Vessels and the Gathering of the Sparks that is the basis of the concept of *tikkun olam*, repair of the world. He also created (or recreated) the ritual of *Kabbalat Shabbat*, of greeting the Sabbath Queen, which has become an integral part of Sabbath services worldwide. The Ari's teachings, known as Lurianic Kabbalah, constitute a major school in the teachings of Kabbalah. In addition, an extensive hagiographic tradition has arisen about him in which he is portrayed as possessing great mystical powers. "A Vision at the Wailing Wall" is an example of one of these legendary tales.

Myths of the Holy Land. The entire tale takes place in the Holy Land. It starts in Safed, the second holiest Jewish city, and involves a quest—a pilgrimage—to Jerusalem, the holiest Jewish city, to the holiest Jewish site there, the Wailing Wall. The sacred dimension of the Holy Land is underscored throughout the tale.

Myths of Exile. When Rabbi Abraham reaches the Wailing Wall, he encounters two personifications of the *Shekhinah*: as an old woman in mourning and as a beautiful bride. Both allude to the exile of the *Shekhinah*, the key kabbalistic myth found in the *Zohar* that describes how the *Shekhinah* exiled herself from heaven after the destruction of the Temple.[39] The old woman is mourning over the Temple and over the exile of her children, the children of Israel. The bride offers a prophecy that the exile will come to an end.

Myths of the Messiah. In Rabbi Abraham's second vision, that of the *Shekhinah* as a beautiful bride, she tells him, "Know that My exile will come to an end, and My inheritance will not go to waste. *Your children shall return to their country and there is hope for your future*" (Jer. 31:17). According to Kabbalah, the exile of the *Shekhinah* will not end until the coming of the Messiah. One of the three requirements of the Messiah is to rebuild the Temple in Jerusalem, and when this takes place, the exile of the *Shekhinah* will come to an end. Thus Rabbi Abraham's vision includes a prophecy about the coming messianic era.

It is somewhat astonishing to find that one tale includes allusions to all the major myths of Judaism. Yet this should not be seen as an unusual case, for the interweaving of mythic elements in Jewish folklore is ubiquitous. These mythic threads reinforce the Jewish framework in which these tales exist, and work as a whole to create a unique body of literature, including scripture, rabbinic legends, biblical commentaries, medieval Jewish folklore, kabbalistic texts, and hasidic tales, that exists as part of an extensive mythic tradition.

What Makes a Jewish Folktale Jewish?

From the tales discussed so far, it should be apparent that Jewish tradition has found a way to reimagine the Bible and incorporate biblical figures into postbiblical legends and folktales. What we have is a living tradition where the Bible is not a closed book, but an open invitation to the Jewish folk imagination. This creative license grows out of the tradition of the Oral Torah, which Moses is said to have received at Mount Sinai along with the Written Torah. As one midrash puts it, "God dictated the Torah to Moses during the day, and at night He explained it to him."[40] The Oral Torah was used to justify all kinds of additions and changes to the tradition, and provided a license to reimagine the Bible. It seems self-evident that such tales, which model themselves after and build upon existing Jewish tradition, should be acknowledged as an integral part of it. But this also raises the question of how to identify a Jewish tale.

Professor Dov Noy of Hebrew University, the preeminent Jewish folklorist of our time, has proposed four main factors in determining whether a tale can be considered Jewish: the time, the place, the characters, and the message. The *time* refers to a story that takes place during Jewish sacred time, such as the Sabbath or one of the holidays, such as Rosh ha-Shanah, Yom Kippur, or Passover. The story "A Flock of Angels," for example, takes place at Rosh Hodesh, the monthly celebration of the new moon. The *place* refers to a story that takes place in the land of Israel, or in a synagogue, a sukkah, or some other Jewish context. The encounter with a ghost in "The Lost Melody" takes place in a synagogue. The *character* can be one of the patriarchs or prophets, a king or a great rabbi, or even a simple Jew. The unlikely hero of "The Wooden Sword" is a poor Jewish woodcutter, who outfoxes a king. The *message* is usually a moral or lesson. As Professor Noy notes, "There is an ubiquitous instructional element in literally all Jewish folktales."[41]

Many of these tales grow out of biblical verses. For example, the talmudic tale of "The Golden Dove," about a miraculous golden dove found in the desert, is directly linked to the verse, *The wings of the dove are covered with silver, and her pinions with the shimmer of gold* (Ps. 68:14).

Sometimes the Jewish content of a folktale can be elusive, but once it is recognized, it seems self-evident. All that is necessary is to delve into the tale and seek its roots. Consider, for example, "The Cottage of Candles," a tale collected orally in Israel from a Jew from Afghanistan.[42] Here a man sets out on a lifelong quest to find justice, searching for it everywhere, like Diogenes going through the streets of Athens looking for truth. But at the end of his life, the man who searched for justice is tested to see if he himself is just.

Remarkably, this story combines two powerful types of tales, the quest and the divine test. The quest is one of the most popular types of Jewish folktales; more than half of all Jewish fairy tales are quests.[43] But here the quest is not a conventional one for a lost princess, the sword of Moses, or a golden bird, but for an abstraction—justice, a subject central to Jewish teachings.

It is important to note the futility of the man's quest for justice—"never did he find it." The story presents a bleak view of the state of justice in the world. At the same time, the conclusion of the tale, where the man fails the divine test, is equally bleak. Even though the story is a quest, there is no happy ending. Here the fact that it comes from Afghanistan seems entirely appropriate; even today Afghanistan is a harsh land where justice is hard to find. So the country of origin of a tale should be considered, for a story is somehow connected to the place it came from.

On the surface, there seem to be only two specific Jewish elements in the tale. One appears at the beginning: "There once was a Jew who set out into the world to find justice." The other is the famous biblical injunction *Justice, justice shall you pursue* (Deut. 16:20). These two elements in themselves might not make a convincing case that the story was Jewish, but a closer examination makes its Jewish roots apparent.

While the role of the verse from Deuteronomy is central in setting up the quest that is the focus of the first episode, there is another crucial verse hidden in the story: *The soul of man is the candle of God* (Prov. 20:27). This verse almost certainly inspired the second key episode, that of the cottage of candles, where the man who seeks justice is tested to see if he himself is truly just. Together these two verses serve as the foundation of the story, and testify to its Jewish origins.

That is how Jewish folklore works—like an archeological dig. In the case of "The Cottage of Candles," the two biblical verses are the foundation of the story. *Justice, justice shall you pursue* sets in motion the quest that propels the story, and *The soul of man is the candle of God* is the focus of the climactic episode about the cottage of candles. It seems likely that meditation on these biblical verses gave birth to this story over a long period of time. This makes the story itself a kind of commentary on these verses. Thus we discover that one unexpected purpose of folktales is to serve as a biblical commentary, much as do the midrashim. By putting the two biblical verses together in the same story, the folk process that brought this story into being brings together the powerful motifs of the quest and the divine test. This suggests that verses in themselves can provide narrative inspiration.

The quest sets up the narrative framework, but it is the divine test that is the real focus of the tale. As described here, it is comparable to the divine tests given to Adam and Eve (Gen. 3), Abraham (Gen. 22), and Job (Job 1:12). Adam and Eve fail the test when they eat the forbidden fruit, but Abraham demonstrates his willingness to sacrifice Isaac, and Job retains his faith in God despite a series of tragedies. Thus Abraham and Job pass the test. In "The Cottage of Candles," then, we find another example of a divine test, this one created by Jewish folk tradition.[44] And, like Adam and Eve, the one who is tested fails the test.

So too can the old man who tends the soul-candles and conducts the test be linked to a variety of Jewish traditions. As the Keeper of the Soul-Candles, he might be Elijah, for Elijah the Prophet often appears in such roles. Or he might be one of the *Lamed-vav Tzaddikim*, the Thirty-Six Hidden Saints, who are said to be the pillars of the world and are often described as living in forests.[45] It is also possible to view the old man as the Angel of Death, who has come to take the man's soul. Or he might even be identified as God, who has descended to this world to administer the test Himself. Whoever he is, the old man in the cottage oversees the divine test, and each of these interpretations places the story firmly in Jewish tradition.

There is also an implicit parallel between the soul-candles, which burn as long as a person lives, and the Jewish custom of lighting *yahrzeit* candles on the anniversary of a person's death. These memorial candles, known as *nerot neshamah* or soul-candles, are intended to last for twenty-four hours, and remain lit until they burn out. The lighting of the *yahrzeit* candle is a ritual based the same verse that inspired the episode of the cottage of candles, *the soul of man is the candle of God*. Just as the candles are lit to commemorate the person who has died, the act of reading or telling a folktale makes it possible to commemorate the generations that created those tales, creating a bridge of tradition from the past to the present.

The man in this story, who is never named, is clearly attempting to fulfill the biblical injunction about pursuing justice. He has taken the biblical verse *Justice, justice shall you pursue* literally—he has devoted his life to pursuing justice. Thus the story grows out of a literal reading of a biblical verse. One way of reading the tale is to see that in arriving at this cottage of candles, the man is on the verge of completing his lifelong quest, but he is first tested to see if he himself is truly just. Instead of proving worthy, he attempts to lengthen his life by stealing years from someone else. But he is caught and made to face the consequences of his action. In this sense he finds justice, for justice is exactly meted out. His error was to continually seek justice out in the world, but never within himself.

For all of these reasons, "The Cottage of Candles" is a richly Jewish tale, with many links to the tradition, even if this is not apparent at first. The example of this story should indicate that many other Jewish tales that may not appear to have a Jewish character do in fact draw on existing Jewish models, like the divine test, or respond to biblical verses, as in this tale, or have characters that can be linked to those found in traditional Jewish sources.

But what about more universal types of tales, such as fairy tales? Stories such as "The Golden Mountain" or "The Wonderful Healing Leaves" are set in enchanted kingdoms, without any apparent Jewish time, place, or character. In what way can they be identified as Jewish tales? True, tales about well-known Jewish figures such as Elijah or King Solomon, or about Lilith, the queen of demons, abound in Jewish folklore, but there are also a great many classic fairy tales, especially among the tales collected orally in the modern era that do not feature obvious Jewish elements. Indeed, approximately half of the tales collected by the Israel Folktale Archives in Israel lack explicit Jewish content, although they were collected from Jews, and served for hundreds of years—or longer—as an integral part of Jewish oral tradition. Here Professor Noy's fourth factor, that of the Jewish meaning, saves the day. For these stories inevitably have meanings that are harmonious with Jewish teachings. That is one of the main reasons why they were preserved in the first place.

Sometimes there is a melding of Jewish and the universal elements, as in "The Exiled Princess," an Eastern European version of Cinderella.[46] Here, however, the roles are reversed. This Yiddish variant of Cinderella is characterized by its Jewish elements. This Cinderella is a princess who is condemned for disobeying her father, the king, and escapes with her life. She becomes lost in a forest and is taken in as a servant by the wife of a rabbi. Like Cinderella, who attended the royal ball, the exiled princess attends Jewish weddings, wearing one of her royal gowns, so that no one recognizes her. The rabbi's son falls in love with her, unaware that she is the servant girl. But that the entire tale is a fantasy becomes apparent in the willingness of the parents to let the gentile servant marry their son after she has saved them from the fire, without concern for the need for her to convert, which would be a major factor in real life.[47]

The Stories of Reb Nachman

Then there are special Jewish stories that have been included in this book—those told by Rabbi Nachman of Bratslav. Reb Nachman is widely acknowledged as the greatest Jewish storyteller. He is very much a Jewish Hans Christian Andersen, drawing inspiration from folklore but creating original tales. His stories appear to be complex fairy tales, but they are actually allegories about kabbalistic mysteries. Despite the low status of folklore,[48] and its universal as opposed to specifically Jewish character, Reb Nachman felt drawn to this mode of expression in a powerful way. Certainly, the enchanted world of fairy tales, with its solutions that inevitably draw on the magical and the ability of the good to prevail despite the odds, had enormous appeal to Reb Nachman and reflect his own world vision, in which the power of faith can surmount any obstacle.[49]

One clue for this attraction can be found in the dreams of Reb Nachman that have been preserved. The most striking quality is their similarity to his tales, such as "The Master of Prayer" or "The Seven Beggars," as the following dream, recorded in its entirety, demonstrates:[50]

> In my dream I woke up in a forest. The forest was boundless; I wanted to return. Someone came to me and said: "This forest is so long it is infinite. All the instruments and the vessels of this world are made from this forest." He showed me a way out of the forest, which brought me to a river. I wanted to reach the end of the river. A man came to me and said: "This river is endless. All the people of this world drink from this river." Then he showed me a mill that stood at the side of the river, and someone came to me and said: "All the food for all the people in the world is ground in this mill." Then I reentered the forest, and there I saw a smith working, and they told me: "This smith makes the vessels for the whole world."[51]

Such dreams raise the possibility that Reb Nachman based his tales on his dreams, elaborating on them in the retelling. Certainly, it is clear that sacred quests consumed his imagination. Even Reb Nachman's teachings to his Hasidim were highly imaginative, as in this teaching about the angel of losses:

> There is an angel who watches over people, even in the dark. This is Yode'a, the angel of losses. He watches lives unfold, recording every detail before it fades. This angel has servants, and his servants have servants. Some of these servants are angels, and some are not. Each of the angels carries a shovel, and they spend all their time digging, searching for losses. For a great deal is lost in our lives. Every tzaddik is a servant of the angel Yode'a, for even a tzaddik who searches after lost things is himself sometimes lost. Then it is necessary to search in the dark, in the realm of the unknown. And with what do you search in the darkness? With the light of the soul. For the soul is a light planted in the tzaddik to seek after whatever has been lost. What kind of light is it? Not a torch, but a small candle. Yet even so, with it you can search inside deep wells, where darkness is unbroken, peering into every corner and crevice. It is necessary to be guided by that light, small though it may be.[52]

In this teaching Reb Nachman appears to have invented this angel, Yode'a, the angel of losses. "Yode'a" means "to know" in Hebrew. Thus the angel's name reflects its purpose, which is to recall all that has been lost. This angel recognizes how much is lost in a person's life, and searches to recover it, following the concept of *tikkun olam*, repair of the world. Indeed, the existence of this angel is another expression of the pattern of the Ari's myth of the Shattering of the Vessels and the Gathering of the Sparks.[53]

Much like Reb Pinhas of Koretz, Reb Nachman was highly aware of surrounding spirits.[54] For Reb Pinhas these were often angels. See, for example, "The Angel of Friendship," which tells of an angel that comes into being whenever two friends meet. In describing the angel of losses, Reb Nachman identifies a previously unknown angel who, along with his servants, searches for what has been lost. The efforts of this angel are clearly linked to the pattern of restoration that is the essential purpose of the myth of the Ari. This is made explicit in the second phase of the Ari's myth, about gathering the scattered sparks. These scattered sparks are not unlike the losses that Yode'a collects, for the sparks too have been lost and must be found in order to be redeemed.

Among the Bratslav Hasidim, it is believed that Reb Nachman made a vow to his Hasidim as he lay dying that he would always be their rebbe. For this reason, his Hasidim have never appointed a successor, for they believe that Reb Nachman's wandering spirit remains in this world as their guardian and guide. There are many tales about the wandering spirit of Rabbi Nachman told in Bratslaver circles. One of the most famous is about a letter from the beyond. It tells how, as a young man, Reb Yisrael Ber Odesser once ate by mistake on the seventeenth of Tammuz, a fast day, and became so downcast he even contemplated suicide. But before doing so, he decided to open a book at random to see if he could find any reason to live. He closed his eyes and took down a book from the shelf. When he looked at it, he found it was one of Reb Nachman's. And when he opened it, a letter fell out—a letter from Reb Nachman himself that spoke to him directly and transformed his life. In the letter Reb Nachman said: "It was very hard for me to descend to you. My precious student, be strong and courageous. My fire will burn until the Messiah will come. As a sign that this letter is true, on the seventeenth of Tammuz they will say that you are not fasting." This letter transformed Reb Yisrael's life, and he always maintained that Reb Nachman had sent it to him from heaven.[55]

To demonstrate how Reb Nachman fused fairy tales and kabbalistic allegories, consider his first tale, "The Lost Princess."[56] This story appears in all respects to be a characteristic fairy tale, with a king, a lost princess, a quest, three giants, and an enchanted palace. In brief, the king becomes angry with his daughter, saying "Go to the Devil!" and the next day she is gone. He sends his most trusted minister to search for her, and the search lasts many generations, until the minister learns that she is living in a palace of pearls on a golden mountain, and he undertakes a quest to find that mysterious palace.

Some readers might be tempted to dismiss "The Lost Princess" as a simple fairy tale, but they would be missing its rich allegorical meaning. For Reb Nachman based this tale on the model of the rabbinic *mashal* or parable, in which the king always represents God.[57] There are hundreds of rabbinic parables that inevitably begin, "There once was a king. . . ." This identification of the king with God signals that this tale can be read as an allegory, and all of Reb Nachman's tales—and there are ten of them collected here—function in a similar fashion.[58]

Even though "The Lost Princess" uses the universal language of the fairy tale, Bratslaver commentary explicitly interprets it as an allegory about the central kabbalistic myth of the exile of God's Bride, the *Shekhinah.* This myth is found in the *Zohar,* the central text of Jewish mysticism, dating from the thirteenth century:

> When the Temple was still standing, Israel would perform their rites, and bring offerings and sacrifices. And the *Shekhinah* rested upon them in the Temple, like a mother hovering over her children, and all faces were resplendent with light, so that there was blessing both above and below.
>
> When the Temple was destroyed, the *Shekhinah* came and went up to all those places where she used to dwell, and she would weep for Her home and for Israel, who had gone into exile, and for all the righteous and the pious ones who had perished. At that time the Holy One, blessed be He, questioned the *Shekhinah,* and said to her, "What ails you?" And she replied, weeping, "My children are in exile, and the Sanctuary has been burnt, so why should I remain here?" Now the Temple is destroyed and the *Shekhinah* is with Israel in exile and there is no joy to be found, above or below.[59]

Reb Nachman's followers view "The Lost Princess" as an allegorical retelling of this kabbalistic myth. In the Introduction to *Sippure Ma'asiyot,* the primary collection of Reb Nachman's tales, Rabbi Nathan of Nemirov, Reb Nachman's scribe, offers the following interpretation:

> "This story is about every man in every time, for the entire story occurs to every man individually, for everyone of Israel must occupy himself with this *tikkun,* namely to raise up the Shekhinah from her exile, to raise her up from the dust, and to liberate the Holy Kingdom from among the idolaters and the Other Side among whom she has been caught. . . . Thus one finds that everyone in Israel is occupied with the search for the king's daughter, to take her back to her father, for Israel as a whole has the character of the minister who searches for her."[60]

"The Lost Princess" and all of Reb Nachman's tales were read by his Hasidim with the kind of intense scrutiny reserved for sacred texts. It was an article of faith with them that his stories could best be understood allegorically, and indeed "The Lost Princess" lends itself to such an interpretation. As noted, the king is easily recognizable as God, and the six sons and one daughter can be readily identified as the six days of the week and the Sabbath. And the identification of the Sabbath with a princess naturally evokes the Sabbath Queen, which is one of the primary identities of the *Shekhinah.*

It is also possible to discern many allegorical links to biblical episodes and Jewish symbolism in this tale. Indeed, in a symbolic fashion, "The Lost Princess" retells the key stories of the Torah, from the Creation to the giving of the Torah to the messianic era. In addition to the allusion to the six days of creation and the Sabbath, the minister's eating of the apple recalls the eating of the forbidden fruit. By eating it on the final fast day, the minister repeats the sin of the Fall and must wait for another generation, symbolized by the seventy years he sleeps. The episode of the water turning into wine can be linked with the story of the Flood and the sin of Noah in becoming drunk. Also, the three giants that the minister encounters in the desert can be identified as the three towering patriarchs, Abraham, Isaac, and Jacob, while the trees they carry as staffs can be identified with the Torah, as in the passage *It* (the Torah) *is a Tree of Life to those who cling to it.*[61] The wandering of the minister in the desert suggests the wandering of the Israelites during the Egyptian exodus. So too does the minister's search for the palace of pearls repeat the Israelites' search for the Holy Land. As for the scarf with the words written by the tears of the lost princess, it represents the sacred writings of the Torah.

These symbolic parallels to the biblical chronology demonstrate that "The Lost Princess" can also be understood as reflecting the collective Jewish experience, reliving the archetypal experiences represented in these key biblical episodes. That such a collective interpretation of the text was intended is confirmed by the Haggadah for Passover, where it is stated that "we were slaves unto Pharaoh in Egypt," meaning that "in every generation each person must regard himself as if he himself went forth out of Egypt."

So too can this seminal story be understood on the level of personal inner experience. Once the link has been perceived between the lost princess and the *Shekhinah,* the allegorical meaning of Rabbi Nachman's tale reveals itself as a fairy-tale retelling of the myth of the exile of the *Shekhinah.* The king's angry words, which result in the disappearance of the princess, are equivalent to the destruction of the Temple in Jerusalem and the subsequent exile of both the *Shekhinah* and the Children of Israel. At the same time, they are equivalent to the expulsion from the Garden of Eden, the wandering in the wilderness, and other variations on the myth of exile, which is another of the primary Jewish myths.[62]

From a psychological perspective, the figure of the lost princess in Reb Nachman's tale might be identified as an anima figure, Jung's concept for the feminine aspect of a man, just as an animus is the masculine aspect of a woman. As such, the lost princess represents a crucial missing element in the psychic equation, which the minister seeks to restore in his quest.

There are three strong possibilities for the identity of the loyal minister: he might be identified as being a tzaddik, a righteous one, who must search and find the lost princess and bring her back to the king or, symbolically, to God; or the minister could be identified with the nation of Israel whose task it is to search for the lost princess, or the *Shekhinah,* in her exile; or the minister could be identified with the Messiah, and here the linkage seems quite natural, for kabbalistic myth holds that the exile of the *Shekhinah* will not end until the Temple is rebuilt, which is not destined to take place until the advent of the Messiah.

All three of these interpretations of the role of the minister seem quite accurate, and each permits the tale to be seen from another important perspective. When the minister is seen as the nation of Israel, the responsibility for finding the lost princess rests on every Jew, and the importance of this doctrine to each individual is emphasized. When the minister is viewed as a tzaddik, the key role of the tzaddik in bringing about the reunion of *Shekhinah* and Messiah is underscored. And by identifying the minister with the Messiah we can recognize that Reb Nachman has combined two primary Jewish myths, that of the exile of the *Shekhinah* and that of coming of the Messiah, into one fairy tale, thus demonstrating their interdependence. Nor is it necessary to narrow these interpretations to one. In that sense, "The Lost Princess" should be seen as a kind of commentary, revealing an important connection between two guiding mythic principles, and therefore serving, above all, as a teaching story. One of the beautiful things about the process of commentary in Jewish texts is that multiple readings are not only permitted but also encouraged. Therefore we can easily accept the legitimacy of all three interpretations. That Reb Nachman was able to include such a comprehensive range of meanings within the framework of a traditional fairy tale indicates the kind of genius he brought to the Jewish folk tradition, infusing it with kabbalistic secrets and messianic longings.

So important are the stories of Reb Nachman that ten of them have been included here. The stories themselves are almost always cast as fairy tales, but they are open to many interpretations. Sometimes they serve as biblical commentaries, as in the case of "The Prince and the Slave." That story tells of a prince and a slave born on the same day who were switched by a midwife. In fact, it is a fairy tale retelling of the story of Jacob and Esau, and serves as a kind of midrash to defend Jacob's receiving the birthright and the blessing of the firstborn. Just as "The Lost Princess" includes allusions to many biblical episodes, so does "The Prince and the Slave" refer directly to the biblical source.

Since Reb Nachman's followers, the Bratslav Hasidim, consider his stories to be sacred teachings, they have created a rich body of commentary about them. Each of Reb Nachman's tales is interpreted as being as rich and complex in its meaning as "The Lost Princess." Nor do these commentaries go beyond the purpose of the tales, for Reb Nachman intended them, above all, to serve as teaching stories. But the truth is that all Jewish folktales are teaching stories, and efforts to interpret them as such are often richly rewarded.

NOTES

1. *Ma'aseh me-ha-Hayyat.* See "The Spice of the Sabbath" in Schwartz, *Tree of Souls*, pp. 316–317.

2. Sarah's death is reported in Gen. 23:1–2, Abraham's in Gen. 25:7–8.

3. From Kafka, *Parables and Paradoxes*, pp. 61–65. See Schwartz, *Tree of Souls*, pp. 445–446.

4. See "The Metamorphosis and Enthronement of Enoch," pp. 156–158, "Abraham Never Died," p. 348, and "Jacob Never Died," p. 370, in Schwartz, *Tree of Souls.*

5. In *Folklore in the Old Testament,* James Frazer suggests it was God's intention that Adam be immortal. Therefore God warned Adam not to eat the fruit of the Tree of Knowledge, for the Tree of Knowledge was originally the Tree of Death. Thus Frazer sees this divine test as a myth about the origin of death: "We may suppose that in the original story there were two trees, a tree of life and a tree of death; that it was open to man to eat of the one and live forever, or to eat of the other and die; that God, out of good will to his creature, advised man to eat of the tree of life and warned him not to eat of the tree of death; and that man, misled by the serpent, ate of the wrong tree and so forfeited the immortality that his benevolent Creator had designed for him." (See Theodor H. Gaster's *Myth, Legend, and Custom in the Old Testament,* p. 33, which updates Frazer's *Folklore in the Old Testament.*)

6. As proof that God intended Adam to be immortal, *Genesis Rabbah* 21:5 states that "Adam was not meant to experience death." In *Avodat ha-Kodesh* 27 Rabbi Meir ibn Gabbai states that "God intended for Adam to live forever."

7. From *Sippurim: Prager Sammlung jüdischer Legenden in neuer Auswahl and Bearbeitung.* Version of L. Weisel. First published in Prague, 1847.

8. See "The Four Who Entered Paradise" in Schwartz, *Tree of Souls,* pp. 173–174.

9. See "Past and Present in Midrashic Literature," by Marc Bregman.

10. This brief legend embellishes the biblical observation *And Moses took with him the bones of Joseph* (Exod. 13:19), which confirms that Moses took the coffin of Joseph with him, as Joseph had required. The sources of this and other traditions about the coffin of Joseph are found in *Targum Pseudo-Yonathan* on Gen. 50:26, Ex. 13:19; *B. Sota* 13a–b; *Mekhilta de-Rabbi Ishmael, be-Shalah* 1:86–110; *Pesikta de-Rav Kahana* 11:12. See "The Coffin of Joseph" in Schwartz, *Tree of Souls,* pp. 379–380.

11. Not included are some specialized types of tales, such as fables, parables, animal tales, nursery tales, and humorous tales. Life stories, known as *memorat,* are also not included. There have been many attempts to classify folktales, and Jewish folktales in particular. The best known of these is the Aarne-Thompson system found in *The Types of the Folktale,* which classifies folktales in more than two thousand categories. See Appendix E, p. 466. Professor Dov Noy devoted his dissertation to linking these Aarne-Thompson categories with Jewish sources. See his "Motif Index of Talmudic-Midrashic Literature." Others, such as Heda Jason, expanded the Aarne-Thompson system by adding Jewish tale types.

12. To date, the Israel Folktale Archives has collected more than 23,000 stories.

13. "God dictated the Torah to Moses during the day, and explained it to him at night." Friedlander, *Pirke de Rabbi Eliezer,* p. 46.

14. IFA 9586, collected by Haya ben-Avraham from Daniel Sigauker of India.

15. This version of the story demonstrates how the underlying models of human sacrifice are transformed in the biblical tale, which recasts a sacrifice narrative into one that sets the precedent for no more human sacrifice. It is possible that the biblical account of the binding of Isaac intentionally changed the pattern of the pagan myth of human sacrifice into a myth of

animal sacrifice instead. This represents a major step in civilizing human society.

16. Preface to *Midrash Tanhuma.*

17. *B. Suk.* 53b. See "The Cave of King David," p. 210, and "The City of Luz," p. 105, for other tales about a quest to the city of Luz.

18. See "The Princess in the Tower," p. 50, and "The Maiden in the Tree," p. 160.

19. See the final act of S. Ansky's drama *The Dybbuk* for an accurate reenactment of an exorcism ceremony. For another example of a tale of dybbuk possession, see "The Widow of Safed" in Schwartz, *Tree of Souls,* pp. 228–230.

20. See "The Other Side," p. 283. For other tales about marriage with demons, see "Yona and the River Demon, p. 287, "The Cellar," p. 260, and "The Queen of Sheba," p. 230.

21. *Ohel Elimelekh; Sefer Or Yesharim* story no. 199; *Zikaron Tov.*

22. For examples of orally collected stories gathered from women, see Barbara Rush, *The Book of Jewish Women's Tales.*

23. *B. Hag.* 14b. See "The Four Who Entered Paradise" in Schwartz, *Tree of Souls,* pp. 173–174.

24. "The Ocean of Tears," p. 374.

25. From *Em la-Binah,* edited by Yekutiel Aryeh Kamelhar (Lemberg, 1909).

26. To assist in identifying the underlying myths in many of these stories, the commentaries on the stories, beginning on page 381, often include references to these myths in Schwartz, *Tree of Souls: The Mythology of Judaism.*

27. See the editor's *Reimagining the Bible: The Storytelling of the Rabbis.*

28. For further elaboration of these mythic categories, see Schwartz, *Tree of Souls: The Mythology of Judaism,* pp. xlv–lxii.

29. Genesis 22.

30. *B. RH* 16a.

31. Friedlander, *Pirke de Rabbi Eliezer* 31.

32. This story can be found on p. 333.

33. *Shivhei ha-Ari.*

34. The twenty-two years the Ari prophesizes for him represent the twenty-two letters of the Hebrew alphabet, therefore a new cycle of life.

35. See Schwartz, *Tree of Souls,* xlvii–xlix. For myths of the *Shekhinah,* see pp. 47–63.

36. See "The Shattering of the Vessels and the Gathering of the Sparks" in Schwartz, *Tree of Souls,* pp. 122–124.

37. See "The Book of Life and the Book of Death" in Schwartz, *Tree of Souls,* pp. 289–291.

38. *Aseret ha-Dibrot* in *Beit ha-Midrash* 1:62; *Merkavah Rabbah.* See "The Torah Written on the Arm of God" in Schwartz, *Tree of Souls,* p. 252.

39. See "The Exile of the *Shekhinah*" in Schwartz, *Tree of Souls,* pp. 57–58.

40. Friedlander, *Pirke de Rabbi Eliezer,* 46. See Schwartz, *Reimagining the Bible,* pp. 3–40.

41. See Dov Noy, "What Is Jewish about the Jewish Folktale?"

42. IFA 7830, collected by Zevulon Kort from Ben Zion Asherov. The story can be found on p. 325.

43. Indeed, virtually half of the stories collected here are quests. The list of quest stories can be found in Appendix D, p. 464.

44. It is interesting to note that his quest in this tale is in many ways parallel to that of the man from the country in Kafka's famous parable

"Before the Law" from *The Trial*, who comes to the gates of the Law seeking justice. Readers have long noted that Kafka's parable is relevant to both human and divine justice. Therefore it too can be regarded as an example of a divine test. Kafka's friend and biographer, Max Brod, comments on Kafka's story: "Kafka's deeply ironic legend 'Before the Law' is not the reminiscence or retelling of this ancient lore, as it would seem at first glance, but an original creation drawn deeply from his archaic soul. It is yet another proof of his profound roots in Judaism, whose potency and creative images rose to new activities in his unconscious"; *Johannes Reuchlin und sein Kampf* (Stuttgart: W. Kohlhammer, 1965), pp. 274–275. Moshe Idel identifies the quest in Kafka's tale as the remnant of a mystical one. See *Kabbalah: New Perspectives*, p. 271.

45. See "The Thirty-Six Just Men," in Schwartz, *Tree of Souls*, p. 397. For a list of stories about the *Lamed-vav Tzaddikim* included here, see Appendix D, p. 465.

46. From *Yiddishe Folkmayses* (Yiddish), edited by Yehuda L. Cahan. Cahan was an important early Jewish folklorist and one of the founders of the YIVO archives.

47. Such a conversion takes place in "The Flight of the Eagle" in Schwartz, *Elijah's Violin*, pp. 82–88, where a young man marries a princess, who converts to Judaism and takes on the name of Sarah.

48. In the eyes of the rabbis, folklore lacks the status of the sacred books of Jewish tradition, such as those of the Bible, the Talmud, the Midrash, and the Kabbalah. Traditionally, the folktales that were preserved in these texts were explicitly linked to Jewish tradition. Therefore, the work of modern folklorists such as S. Ansky, Y. L. Cahan, and Dov Noy has been a revelation, as half the tales collected are universal, without explicit Jewish content, and women's tales have been collected for the first time.

49. Nor is Reb Nachman's following limited to his Hasidim. Modern scholars deeply immersed in his teachings and tales include Martin Buber, Adin Steinsaltz, Aryeh Kaplan, Arthur Green, Eli Wiesel, Gedaliah Fleer, Y. David Shulman, Ora Wiskind-Elper, and Shaul Magid.

50. From *Fragments of a Future Scroll* by Rabbi Zalman Schachter-Shalomi, p. 99. This book contains an extensive translation of Nachman's dreams, pp. 95–100. Additional dreams are reported in Arthur Green's *Tormented Master*, pp. 165–166. See also "The Dream-Tales of Nahman of Bratslav," in *Rabbinic Fantasies: Imaginative Narratives from Classical Hebrew Literature*, edited by David Stern and Mark Jay Mirsky, pp. 333–347.

51. See Schachter-Shalomi, *Fragments of a Future Scroll*, pp. 95–100.

52. *Be'er ha-Hasidut*, edited by Eliezer Steinman, 1:189.

53. See "The Shattering of the Vessels and the Gathering of the Sparks" in Schwartz, *Tree of Souls*, pp. 122–124.

54. See "A Vision of Light" in Schwartz, *Gabriel's Palace*, pp. 231–232, and "The Souls of Trees," included here, p. 223.

55. *Michtav Mi-Rebbe Nachman* by Rabbi Yisrael Ber Odesser. Other accounts of the letter assert that Rabbi Nachman directed Rabbi Odesser to try to have Rabbi Nachman's remains moved from the city of Uman in the Ukraine to Israel, because of Reb Nachman's intense love of the Holy Land. Acting at the request of Rabbi Odesser, Haim Herzog, the president of Israel, received permission from the local authorities to move Rabbi Nachman's burial place, but this move was opposed by other leading Bratslaver rabbis and the plan was canceled. See the January 15, 1993, issue of the

Forward. For another example of a Bratslav tale about Reb Nachman, see "Reb Nachman's Chair," p. 364.

56. From *Sippure Ma'asiyot.* See "The Lost Princess," p. 119.

57. See *Parables in Midrash: Narrative and Exegesis in Rabbinic Literature* by David Stern.

58. The ten stories here told by Reb Nachman are "The Lost Princess," p. 119, "The Prince and the Slave," p. 125, "The Prince Who Was Made of Precious Gems," p. 130, "The Water Palace," p. 135, "The Pirate Princess," p. 141, "A Garment for the Moon," p. 147, "The Wooden Sword," p. 171, "The Prince Who Thought He Was a Rooster," p. 219, "The Treasure," p. 221, and "The Perfect Saint," p. 304. There are also two stories about Reb Nachman, "The Souls of Trees," p. 223, and "Reb Nachman's Chair," p. 364. Note that "The Treasure" and "The Wooden Sword" were likely existing folktales when Reb Nachman told them. The other eight stories are all his original creations.

59. *Zohar* 1:203a. See "The Exile of the *Shekhinah*" in Schwartz, *Tree of Souls,* pp. 57–58.

60. *Sippurei Ma'asiyot,* Introduction and *Likutei Moharan,* p. 94.

61. Proverbs 3:18.

62. See Schwartz, *Tree of Souls,* pp. lix–lx.

Fairy Tales

1. An Apple from the Tree of Life

he daughter of the sultan of Turkey had fallen ill. Not even the finest doctors in all of Istanbul could heal her. The sultan brought them together and asked them when she would recover. One after another, the doctors hung their heads and said, "I don't know." But the very last doctor said, "Nothing can help her now except for an apple from the Tree of Life."

"What apple is that?" the sultan demanded to know. "And where can it be found?"

The last doctor said, "I have only heard of such an apple. But surely it can be found in the Garden of Eden. Two trees are said to grow in the center of the garden. The Tree of Life is one of them, and the Tree of Knowledge is the other. It is said that whoever tastes an apple from the Tree of Life, no matter how ill he may be, will recover his health."

The eyes of the sultan grew wide. "I must obtain one of these enchanted apples," the sultan said. "Who knows where this garden can be found?"

"Those who know best about the garden," the doctor replied, "are the Jews. What we know about the garden is told in the Bible. That is the holiest book of the Jews."

The face of the sultan grew red. "Bring in the leaders of the Jews at once!" he shouted.

Before an hour had passed, three of the best known rabbis of the city stood before the sultan, wondering why they had been summoned on such short notice.

"As you know," the sultan said, looking very grim, "my daughter is deathly ill. Her only hope is something that is in your power to supply, and supply it you must. For if you fail, my wrath will fall upon you." "Your Majesty," one of the rabbis said, "you know that we will gladly do whatever we can. But what do you want us to do?"

"Know then," said the sultan, "that I need an apple from the Tree of Life. And I need it soon—within three days. If I don't have it by then, you and all of your people will be banished!" And the sultan dismissed the three rabbis with a wave of his hand.

The three rabbis discussed the matter among themselves, and they all agreed that what the sultan was asking for was simply impossible. No one knew where the Garden of Eden could be found. And even if they did, how could anyone go there and come back within three days?

So the leaders gathered all the people in the synagogues, and they went from one synagogue to another, telling them the terrible news. All the people despaired, for no one believed it would be possible to obtain an enchanted apple from the Tree of Life in such a short time.

Now one of the three rabbis who had met with the sultan had a daughter named Leah. How she wished that such a wondrous apple could be found, so that the sultan's daughter could recover, and the danger to all the Jews would disappear.

Leah saw that her father was deeply worried by the sultan's demands, so she said, "Surely, Father, we must not give up hope. Miracles have happened before. Let us pray for one to happen to us. Tell me, is there anyone who knows the way to the Garden of Eden?"

"Only one of the thirty-six hidden saints," her father replied. "It is said that there are thirty-six righteous ones who are the pillar of existence. But no one knows where they can be found."

"But, Father," Leah said, "I have heard of an old Jew who lives alone in the forest. It is whispered that he might be one of the thirty-six."

Now the rabbi remembered that he, too, had heard such things said about this old man. So he and his daughter set out at once to look for him.

It was not easy to find their way through that dark forest, but everyone did their best to assist the rabbi and his daughter, and finally they reached the old man's house. They knocked on his door, and when he opened it, Leah was astonished to see a light surrounding his face.

The old man listened carefully as the rabbi explained what the sultan had demanded of them. Then he went to a shelf, took down an ancient book, and opened it. There, pressed in its pages, was a green leaf, perfectly preserved.

The old man took the leaf in his hand. "This leaf has been pressed between the pages of this book for many centuries. It is said to have been picked from one of the trees in the Garden of Eden. Let your daughter place this leaf on her pillow and she will dream of that glorious garden."

"My daughter?" asked the astonished rabbi.

"Yes," said the old man. "For she is the one destined to journey there."

Neither Leah nor her father could believe their good fortune, yet they were mystified that the old man had given the precious leaf to Leah instead of to her father. Still, they both thanked the old man and set out to return to their home.

On their way, Leah and her father stopped at an inn, and before she went to sleep, Leah gently placed the ancient leaf on her pillow. Even though it was so very old, it looked as fresh as if it had been picked that very day. It also gave off a most wonderful scent that filled the room.

Bathed in that beautiful scent, Leah closed her eyes, and soon she was sound asleep.

In her dream, Leah found herself in the most splendid garden she had ever seen. Every kind of fruit tree grew there, and the whole garden was filled with a beautiful, unforgettable scent. Leah suddenly realized that she had indeed traveled to the Garden of Eden. She knew that she must hurry, she must find the Tree of Life before it was too late. Tomorrow was the last day the sultan had given them to bring back the enchanted apple.

Leah looked up and saw that there was an angel sleeping in every tree. She called out to one, and when the angel opened its eyes, she asked for its help in finding the Tree of Life. The angel agreed to serve as her guide, but told her that it could take her only to the center of the garden. She would have to figure out for herself which of the two trees that grew there was the Tree of Life.

With the angel's help, Leah soon found herself in the center of that wonderful garden. There two trees grew, each a mirror image of the other. Apples hung from the branches of both trees. She looked from one tree to the other for a clue as to which was the Tree of Life. But which one should she choose?

Then Leah happened to notice a serpent hidden in the branches of one of the trees, and she was certain that must be the Tree of Knowledge.

Without further hesitation, she plucked a ripe apple from the other tree, and in the same instant, she woke up.

Leah opened her eyes, surprised to find herself back in the inn. Then she saw it—a ripe and shining apple resting on her pillow right where the fragrant leaf had been. An apple from the Tree of Life! Somehow she had brought it back in her dream. Leah could barely believe her eyes. She realized that a miracle had truly taken place, and she jumped up, grabbed the apple, and showed it to her father, who had not slept a wink. His eyes opened wide when he saw it, and even wider when she told him her dream. He shed tears of joy, for now he knew that they could still be saved.

Wasting not a moment, they set out for the sultan's palace, and when they arrived, the rabbi presented the sultan with the apple. When the sultan saw the rabbi's joy, he, too, was overjoyed. He himself brought the fragrant apple to his ailing daughter, and held it beneath her nose. All at once she opened her eyes. Then he asked her to take a bite of it, and as soon as she did, the color returned to her face, and she sat up. Within the hour she had made a miraculous recovery.

The sultan hugged his daughter and declared that day to be a holiday for all. Then the sultan publicly thanked the Jews for saving her, and never again did he threaten them.

As for Leah and her father, the sultan invited them to live in the palace, and Leah and the sultan's daughter became the best of friends. Leah never tired of telling her about her astonishing dream, and about the enchanted apple she had brought back. And the sultan's daughter never tired of hearing this tale, for she, better than anyone else, knew that every word was true.

—Eastern Europe: nineteenth century

2. Elijah's Violin

Once upon a time there was a king who had three daughters. Now he loved them dearly, but one day he had to leave them to go off to war. Before he left he spoke to his daughters and said, "If I am victorious in this war, I will bring each of you a gift. Tell me, what would you like?" The eldest spoke up and said, "I would like a diamond in the shape of a star." And the second daughter said, "I would like a gown woven from pure gold." But the youngest said, "I only want you to come home safely from the war." The king was pleased to hear this, and he said, "Thank you, daughter, for your good wish. But you must ask me to bring you something, as your sisters did. Think it over for three days, then tell me before I depart what it is that you want."

Now the youngest daughter was sitting alone on a rock next to the lake outside the palace, when there appeared before her an old woman, who asked her, "What is wrong, child?" And she replied: "I do not know what gift to ask of my father, the king." The old woman said: "You must ask your father for Elijah's violin." So the princess agreed that this would be her request.

At the end of three days the king said to his daughter: "What gift have you decided upon?" And the princess replied: "I would like you to bring me Elijah's violin." The king agreed and set out to war.

Now the king led his troops to victory in every battle, and after his triumph he sought and found the gifts for his two eldest daughters, the star-shaped diamond and the golden gown, but he was unable to find Elijah's violin anywhere. The king asked his generals if they knew where it could be found, but none of them had heard of it. And he asked his wise men, but none of them had read of it in any book. And he asked his soothsayers, but none of them could find it in the stars. So the ship of the king departed, and sailed until it came to land. The king ordered his crew to cast anchor there, to see if Elijah's violin was to be found in that place. And in this way he embarked on a long quest, which took him to the four corners of the world. After many trials and tribulations, he was led to an old man who lived in a cave, and the old man said: "Elijah's violin is in the possession of the king of this country." He also said that the king had a daughter imprisoned in stone and whoever freed his daughter from the stone would be richly rewarded. Then the old man gave the king three long hairs and he said: "These three strands are from the bow of Elijah's violin. Burn these when you are in the presence of the princess."

The king thanked the old man, and took the three hairs from the bow of Elijah's violin, and put them safely away. Then he asked the old man what he might give him in return. And the old man said: "There will come a day when you will repay me in full, for your daughter will set free the imprisoned melodies." And the king wondered at this, and he said: "Tell me, old man, what is your name?" The old man replied: "My name is Elijah." And then the old man returned to the shadows of the cave, and the king set off to rescue the princess who was imprisoned in stone.

When the king approached the palace in which the stone princess lived, he advised his generals and wise men and soothsayers that he preferred to proceed on his own, and that they should camp there and wait for him. And when he came to the gates of the palace and announced that his purpose was to set free the imprisoned princess, he was given an audience with the king and queen at once. For they had left orders that no one who offered to free her was to be refused, but that anyone who failed was to be put to death. That same day the visiting king was taken into the presence of the princess.

Now it was a great shock for him to see the princess, for she seemed to be alive and dead at the same time, as if she were a living sculpture. But much greater was his surprise when she began to speak—for the enchantment under which she had fallen permitted her the power of speech but no other. While the princess was speaking, it seemed as if she were alive. But when she fell silent, it was as if she had turned completely to stone. He could not bear her silence, so he asked her: "Tell me, how did it happen that you were turned to stone?"

The princess replied: "One day I was wandering through the palace, and I came upon a stairway I had never known about, and I followed it until I came to a room where there was a mirror with a golden frame. As I stood before it, my mirror image stole out of the glass and forced me to take its place within. And from that moment I found myself turned to stone, with only my power of speech remaining. No one has known how to set me free. Since then there have been reports that someone who looks exactly like me, and claims to be me, has been seen in the kingdom, but slips away like a shadow if anyone comes too close." And then the princess was silent, and it was the silence of stone.

The king remembered the strands from the bow of Elijah's violin that the old man had given him, and took them out and threw them into the fire that until then had done little to keep the room warm. Then the chill of the room seemed to melt, and at the same time the stone princess turned to flesh and blood again. And the king who had set her free said to her: "Now that you have been freed from this spell, your mirror image surely has been returned to its place in the mirror. To keep it there you must blindfold yourself and take a stone and shatter the glass. That way your mirror image will remain in its world of reflections, and will not take your place in this world again." The princess promised she would do this, and she did so before the end of the day. Her father, the king, was so grateful that he told the king who had broken the spell that he could have any gift of his choice. Nor did he refuse him Elijah's violin, for that is what he requested as his reward.

Now that the king had gathered the gifts for all three of his daughters, he sailed with his soldiers directly home. And because the winds were with them, it took them only seven days, and when the king arrived he gave the gifts to his daughters. The first two took their gifts and hurried off to try them on, but the youngest hugged her father first, and then took the violin to her room. And that is how the princess who was the youngest daughter of the king came to possess Elijah's violin.

Now when the princess first opened the case of the violin, what did she find? A small, perfectly carved violin that had been preserved for many centuries, and next to it a bow. And when she put the bow to the strings, a clear melody sailed forth, effortlessly. And while she played the violin, it seemed that the violin was playing itself, as if it had many melodies stored up, which sought to emerge from within. And even before she finished playing there appeared before her a handsome young man, who asked her: "Why have you brought me to this place?"

The princess was amazed to see him, and she said: "But how did you enter this room?" He showed her the window through which he had entered. Then the princess asked: "But where do you come from?" To which the young man replied: "From far away." And the princess asked: "Then how did you come to be here?" The young man answered: "The music of the violin brought me." Nor did the princess question him more than that, for she understood at once that the violin she had played was enchanted, and that she and the prince, for he was a prince, had been brought together through its magic.

After that, the princess would take out Elijah's violin whenever she missed the prince, and each time she would play it, the prince would arrive soon after the melodies floated outside her window. Before long the prince and the princess exchanged rings and vowed that one day they would be wed.

Then it happened, after some time had passed, that the eldest sister of the princess heard her speaking to the prince in her room. She hurried to the second sister, and said: "Someone has been visiting our sister in her room." They decided to search her room to see what they could learn, and so they persuaded the youngest princess to join them in the baths. When they arrived there the eldest said she had forgotten her soap, and left to fetch it. But instead she went to her sister's room and began to search through it. When she found the ring of the prince, she threw it and broke the window through which the prince entered the room. And when she saw the case of the violin, she opened it and began to play, but the melody that emerged was a dark one, filled with brooding. And as the music filled the air, the prince was compelled to appear. He sought to enter by the broken window, but was wounded by the sharp glass and was forced to turn back.

When the youngest princess returned from the baths, she could feel that something had happened in her room, but she did not know what it was. So she took out Elijah's violin and began to play, but this time the prince did not appear. Then she saw that the window was broken, and that three drops of blood were on the curtain. When she realized that her sisters must have discovered her secret, and brought harm to the prince, the princess became very sad and left the palace to sit on the rock by the lake. While she was sitting there the old woman appeared, and asked her what had happened. The princess told her all that had taken place, and the old woman said: "Pretend that you are ill, so that the doctor will order that no one be admitted to your room until you are well. Meanwhile, you must set out and find the prince who has been wounded, for only you can heal him. To do so you must pluck three strands from the bow of Elijah's violin, and take them with you. Then you must burn those strands when you are in the presence of the prince."

The princess did as the old woman had said, and the doctor ordered that no one be admitted to her room. She then set out on a quest to find the wounded prince, so that she might heal him.

So it was that the princess walked and walked through all of that kingdom and the forest surrounding it, until she grew tired and sat down to rest beneath an elder tree. She was so tired that she lay down to sleep. But no sooner did she close her eyes than she discovered she understood the speech of the doves that perched on the branches above her. When she opened her eyes, their speech sounded only like chirping, but when she closed her eyes once more, the language of the doves was clear to her, and she heard them say: "The prince has been wounded, and the way to his palace is impossible to find without a map. And where can a map be found? Only in the leaves of this tree."

Then the princess arose at once, and plucked one of the leaves from the tree. And when she looked at it, she found she was able to read it like a map. She saw where she stood in the forest, and the way she must take to emerge from there, and how she could reach the palace where the wounded prince waited to be healed. After this she followed the map directly to that kingdom. There she disguised herself as a man, and presented herself as a doctor before the king. The king warned her that thirty-nine doctors had already tried to heal the prince, and all had failed and been put to death. The fate of this doctor would be the same as that of the others if he did not succeed.

The disguised princess agreed to these terms, but requested that she be left alone with the prince. As soon as she entered the prince's room and saw him asleep on the bed, she was overcome with emotion and wanted to embrace him. But, remembering her purpose, she cast the strands from the bow of Elijah's violin into the flames of the fireplace, and as soon as they started to burn, the wounds of the prince healed, and he opened his eyes and saw the princess, who had cast off her disguise. Then she called in the king and queen, who were overjoyed to find that the prince had recovered, and they agreed at once that the prince and princess should be wed. So it was that they came to be married and that they lived together in great wealth, peace, and virtue for all the days of their lives, and many were the times when the melodies of Elijah's violin were heard drifting over that land.

—Egypt: oral tradition

3. The Witches of Ashkelon

ong ago, in the city of Ashkelon, the people were plagued by a coven of eighty witches who lived in a cave at the outskirts of the city. Those witches were sworn enemies of the people of Ashkelon, and saw to it that spells were cast that brought harm to them in ways large and small. Not only did they play nasty tricks, such as turning wine into vinegar, or causing the fire to go out, but they also brought about grave dangers, casting spells that kept the rain from falling, and causing the cows to go dry. And sometimes the vengeance of the witches was directed at one person, as when they caused a rabbi to become a bird, and his wife a butterfly.

Now it happened that there were three witnesses to this foul deed, the three children of the unfortunate couple. They had seen the witches approach their parents and strike them with their magic wands, transforming their father into a bird and their mother into a butterfly, both of which had flown away and not been seen again. And after this event became known, the people of Ashkelon were outraged, and turned to Rabbi Shimon ben Shetah to rid the city of its curse. At first Rabbi Shimon seemed hesitant to move against the witches. But then it happened that one of his disciples dreamed that he was strolling in an orchard through which a river ran. In the dream this disciple saw Rabbi Shimon trying to reach the water but unable to do so, and he also saw Miriam, the sister of Moses, and she had an object in her hand. He asked her what it was, and she showed him an iron key, and said that she had been sent to deliver it to Rabbi Shimon. And when the disciple asked what key it was, she said it was the key to Gehenna, where the souls of the wicked are punished, the very gates of Hell, and that it would shortly be delivered to Rabbi Shimon unless he fulfilled his vow to rid the city of the curse of the witches.

Now when the disciple awoke, he wasted no time, but hurried to Rabbi Shimon and told him his dream. And Rabbi Shimon said: "I do not doubt that what you say is true. Surely this is a message from heaven that has been delivered to me, for I have told no one of my vow to eliminate the witches."

So it was that Rabbi Shimon thought up a plan. Then he waited for the rainy season to begin, and when it did, he gathered together eighty men. He told each of them to bring a large clay pot and a fresh garment, and when they had assembled, he told them to put their dry robes into the pots, and to place the pots upside down upon their heads. In this way he led them to the cave of the eighty witches. When they were almost there, he took them to a nearby cave and said: "When I whistle once, put on your robes, and when I whistle a second time, come together and enter their cave. Then each of you should take hold of one of the witches and start to dance with her. And while you are all dancing, lift the witches off the ground, as if this were part of the dance. But once you have raised them up, do not allow their feet to touch the ground again. For it is well known that when a witch's feet are not touching the earth, she is powerless."

So Rabbi Shimon went to the cave of the witches and knocked at the door. They called out: "Who is there, and what do you want?" He replied, "Open up! It is one of your own!" And the witches said, "Who are you?" And Rabbi Shimon said, "I am a sorcerer. I want to show you my powers, and for you to show me yours." "What can you show us?" they asked. "I can make eighty men appear, with dry robes, who will dance with you." And when the witches heard this, they said: "Come in, come in, for we would like to see you perform such a feat!"

Then the witches opened the door of the cave, and Rabbi Shimon entered. And when he was inside they saw that his robe was dry, and they could not understand this, since the rain was pouring outside. They said: "How is it that your clothes are dry?" And he replied: "I made myself small and walked between the raindrops." And they said: "Ah, you have great powers!"

Then the witches began to show him their powers: One of them made a table move to the center of the room without touching it, and another conjured up a tablecloth that descended from the ceiling onto the table, and it was covered with all the signs and symbols of the witches. Still a third pronounced a spell, and the table was covered with the finest food and drink. Then they said: "Now it is your turn to show us what you can do."

Then Rabbi Shimon said: "Yes, now I will show you the wonders I promised. For when I have whistled twice, eighty men as dry as I am will appear and will dance with you." Then he whistled once, and the men, hearing this, put on the dry robes, and when he whistled a second time, they all rushed into the cave. The witches shrieked with delight when the men appeared, their robes dry, exactly as he had promised. And each man chose a witch for a partner and began to dance with her, whirling wildly, and in a flash the men had lifted all the witches off the ground. At first the witches thought it was a part of the dance, but when the men did not put them down and began to carry them out the door, they began to shriek in fear, for witches are terrified of the rain. And just as soon as the witches were struck by the rain, all of them were transformed.

Those who had caused the wine to turn into vinegar were changed into grapes which were ripe on the vines, waiting to be plucked and crushed in the winepress.

Those who had caused the fire to go out burst into flames, and burned until they were ashes, which were scattered by the winds to the four corners of the world.

Those who had stopped the rain from falling were turned into puddles, which formed into a stream, which flowed to a river, which flowed into the sea. And later these waters rose up into the sky and formed into clouds, and in time, when the clouds grew full, they fell down to earth as rain.

Those who had caused the cows to go dry became grass in the pasture, which the cows grazed upon, and from which they produced an excellent milk.

And those who had turned the man into a bird and his wife into a butterfly were turned into worms that scurried along the ground until they were swallowed by hungry birds which swooped down and picked them up.

And when all the witches were transformed, the spells they had cast were broken, and the bird and the butterfly again became the rabbi and his wife.

Thus were the witches punished for their evil doings, and the city of Ashkelon was rid of its curse for all time.

—Babylon: c. fifth century

4. The Bird of Happiness

here once was a young boy named Aaron, who had spent his entire life wandering in the desert. His parents had been slaves, but they had run away to find a place where they could be free. Every day they searched for food and water, while the sun beat down on their backs, and sand blew in their faces. Still, Aaron never lost hope, for his mother would say, "One day the Bird of Happiness will guide us to Jerusalem." For that was their dream—to reach the city of Jerusalem. But how could they find their way there?

Every night, when they stopped to rest, Aaron's father would teach him what it meant to be a Jew. They had no books, but his father remembered the Bible stories he had learned as a boy, and he remembered the Ten Commandments, and these he taught to his son. Aaron took them to heart and let them be his guide.

So it was that they wandered for many years, and still the desert stretched endlessly before them. Then one night, Aaron had a strange and vivid dream. In the dream he was traveling with his parents when the world suddenly grew dark. Aaron's parents said, "Quickly, Aaron, crouch down and cover yourself with a blanket. A sandstorm is coming!" And as soon as he did, sand started swirling around him and beating down on the blanket, and the sandstorm lasted a long time. At last it subsided, and Aaron and his parents threw off the blankets. But when they did, they found that their food had been scattered and their water spilt, and, even worse, their footprints had been covered by sand, and they could no longer tell where they had come from or where they should go.

Just when everything looked hopeless, Aaron saw something on the horizon. At first it was only a speck, but soon he saw that it was a beautiful white bird. That bird came closer and closer, and just as it flew over Aaron, it dropped something from its beak, and in the dream, Aaron caught it! At that moment Aaron woke up and discovered that he was clutching something in his right hand—a glowing stone. Aaron jumped up and showed it to his parents, and when his they saw it and heard his dream, they were amazed, and his mother said, "This means that the Bird of Happiness is coming that much closer."

After that Aaron hung the glowing stone from a leather thong around his neck, and it proved to be a wonderful guide. For when they were traveling in the right direction, the stone would glow, but when they were going in the wrong direction, it remained dark. In this way the glowing stone guided them to every oasis, where pools of fresh water were surrounded by trees bearing sweet fruit. And each time they came to such an oasis, they said a prayer of thanks.

So it was that after years of wandering through shifting sands and blazing sun, Aaron and his parents finally came to the walls of a great city—the first city that Aaron had ever seen. As they passed through the gates, they were surprised to see a huge crowd had gathered in the streets. Aaron wondered about this, because his father had told him that in cities people live in houses. Aaron's father went up to a man and said, "Excuse me, sir, but could you tell us what city this is?" The man said: "Why, don't you know where you are? This is Jerusalem." "It is?" said Aaron's father, and they were astonished, for that meant they had finally reached the city of their dreams.

Then Aaron's father asked why everyone was standing the streets. The man said, "Three days ago our king died. And it is the custom in our city to let the will of heaven decide who will be our next king. So on the third day after the king's death, the rare Bird of Happiness is released and circles above the city, and whoever the bird lands on is chosen to be the next king of Jerusalem. The bird is about to be released. That is why everyone is standing in the street."

Just then there was a great shout from the crowd, and Aaron looked up and saw a white bird soaring on high and circling above the city, and there was something strangely familiar about that bird. It spiraled lower and lower, while Aaron's glowing jewel glowed more brightly than ever before. And suddenly the bird swooped down and landed on Aaron's head! There was a great shout from the crowd, and all at once Aaron was picked up and carried off, while his parents ran after them, crying, "That's our son. Where are you taking him?"

The crowd brought Aaron to the king's palace, where he was placed on the king's throne, with the Bird of Happiness still perched on his head. Everyone bowed low before him, and they declared that he, Aaron, the poor boy wandering in the desert, the son of slaves, was their king. At first Aaron thought it must all be a dream, but then he felt the tugging of the bird's talons in his hair, and he knew that it must be real.

Three days later there was a great coronation, and Aaron was officially crowned king of Jerusalem. After that Aaron and his parents lived in the palace. No longer did they wonder what they would eat or drink or where they would sleep at night. As king of Jerusalem, every important question was brought before Aaron to decide. Now while Aaron had never gone to school or even seen a book, he let the Ten Commandments be his guide in deciding what was right and what was wrong, and he found that they served him very well. Plus, he had the secret assistance of the glowing stone. For whenever the answer to a question was yes, the stone would glow brightly. But if the answer was no, it would remain dark.

At first the nobles of Jerusalem were worried that the fate of the city was being entrusted to such a young boy. But as they listened to his decisions, they came to realize that he was very wise. There was only one thing they wondered about. The young king had asked that a simple shack be built out of branches next to the palace. There he spent an hour each day—but no one knew what he did.

Finally, the king's minister could not contain his curiosity, and he asked the young king about his strange actions. Aaron said, "When I go into that shack, I put on the rags I was wearing when I came here, and I stand before the mirror so that I can remember where I came from. For only then can I know where I must go."

When the minister heard this, he knew that heaven had truly blessed them with a wise young king. After that he served Aaron faithfully for many years, and in this way Aaron became one of the great kings of Jerusalem, as great as King David, as great as King Solomon. And every day Aaron and his parents thanked God for all their blessings—and especially for the Bird of Happiness.

—Iraq: oral tradition

5. THE GOLDEN MOUNTAIN

any years ago there was a king who ruled over a vast kingdom, and was believed by many to be the wealthiest man in the world. This king had a daughter who was curious to know about everything—why the sun rises and sets, why spring follows winter, why the moon is full at some times and is only a sliver at others. So it was that when the princess learned there was a wise old man in their kingdom, a soothsayer who knew how to read the stars, she begged her father to bring him to the palace to teach her what he knew.

Now the king's daughter was very precious to him, and he was especially proud that she so loved to learn. Therefore he sent a messenger in a golden carriage to bring the old man to the palace. When the messenger arrived he said to the old man: "You need not be afraid, for the king will do you no harm." So the old man accompanied the messenger to the palace.

When the old man arrived, he was given an audience with the king at once. The king said to him: "It is known that you possess the knowledge of how to read the stars. I would like you to reveal this secret to my daughter, the princess, who has a great thirst for knowledge. As your reward, I shall build you the finest observatory in the world, from which you may gaze at the stars."

Then the old man said: "I agree to teach the princess on these terms, but there must be one more condition—that no one else be present while I instruct her." The king agreed to this condition, and the old man began to teach the princess how to read the stars. The princess listened carefully to everything he had to say, and proved to be a fine student. At the end of one year the old soothsayer had taught her all he knew about the stars, and when he returned to his home he found the observatory had already been built, as the king had promised.

Now the princess quickly put all that she had learned to good use. For she read in the stars that an evil king in a bordering kingdom was planning a secret invasion. The princess warned her father about this, and he set a trap for the invading army, which was easily defeated. After this, the princess became the king's primary adviser, and he came to depend on her in many ways.

Some time passed, and one night the princess read in the stars of a mountain that had a vast treasure of gold hidden within it, and that only one person in the world knew how to enter it. And she also learned that this was none other than the old man who had taught her how to read the stars.

Then the princess reported what she had learned to her father, the king, and begged him to send for the old man again, so that he could reveal the secret of where the golden mountain could be found, and how it could be entered. The king agreed to his daughter's request, and sent a messenger in a golden carriage to bring the soothsayer back to the palace. And when the old man arrived, the king told him what his daughter had discovered in the stars, and asked him to reveal the secret of the golden mountain to her. As a reward, the king promised to have a telescope made for him that would bring the stars a thousand times closer to his eyes.

Now at first the old man hesitated, for he knew there were dangers associated with the golden mountain. But when the king insisted, he agreed to reveal the secret to the princess, but on the condition, as before, that no one else be present.

When the soothsayer met with the princess, she begged him to take her to the golden mountain that very night. "In that case," the old man told her, "We must hurry, for we have to be there exactly at midnight." So it was that the two of them made their way in complete darkness, and reached the mountain at the appointed time. There the soothsayer uttered a spell, which caused a large stone of the mountain to move with much rumbling, so that they could enter the cavern. But as they did, the old man, "Be warned, princess, that the mountain will remain open for only half an hour, and we must return before half past midnight, for then the stone will close, and if we have not departed from the cavern, we will be trapped there."

Inside the golden mountain the princess beheld treasures unmatched in all the world, even in the treasuries of her father, the king. She saw golden apples, silver raindrops, and a multitude of diamonds in the shape of snowflakes. She was dazzled by the unimaginable splendor she saw there, and would not have remembered to take her leave had the old man not reminded her. And shortly after they left the cavern, the stone entrance closed. Then they returned to the palace, and the soothsayer received the telescope the king had promised him, and returned to his home. But before he said, "Take care, princess, if you ever decide to return to the mountain. Most of all, never forget to leave on time."

The following night the princess decided she wanted to return to the golden mountain, for just as they were leaving the night before she had glimpsed a golden seashell so exquisite that she had dreamed about it all night, and now she wanted to make it her own. She traveled there by herself, and when she reached the mountain it was almost midnight, and she repeated the spell that the old man had uttered, for she had listened very carefully while he had spoken. Once again there was a great rumbling, and the stone moved, and she was able to enter the mountain. But in the darkness her gown caught on a thorn bush as she entered, and a single golden thread became unraveled, although the princess did not notice this.

Inside the mountain, the eyes of the princess were again so dazzled by the golden treasury that she became dizzy. But she had not forgotten the golden seashell she had come there to seek out, and soon she held it in her hand. It was truly a miracle to behold, for it resembled an actual seashell of the most beautiful kind in every respect, except it was made entirely of gold. Knowing that real seashells echo the sea, the princess held the golden shell up to her ear, and to her amazement she heard voices speaking there. That is how she discovered it was a magic seashell in which she could hear anything being said anywhere in the world. If she held it in one position, she would hear one conversation, and if she moved it ever so slightly, another would take its place. Now the princess was fascinated by this magic shell and did not notice the swift passage of time. Suddenly she realized it was time for her to leave the cavern, and she rushed to the entrance, but it was too late—the entrance to the cavern was closed, and she was trapped inside the golden mountain.

The next morning cries for help were heard from inside the mountain, and when it was discovered that the princess was missing, the king understood it must be the voice of his daughter they heard. Then he commanded his soldiers to take pickaxes and other tools and to dig into the mountain to pull her out. But it was all in vain, for every pickaxe broke against the mountain, and before long even the king conceded they would never save the princess that way. Then the king announced that anyone who could free the princess would be wed to her and would also receive half his kingdom. Many journeyed to the mountain and sought to free the princess with one spell or another, but none of them succeeded in making the mountain open, and the princess remained trapped inside.

Now in that kingdom there was a clever lad whose name was Yousef, and although his family was poor, he always managed to find something so that they never went hungry. One day Yousef was walking in the marketplace when he heard an old woman cry out that she had an oud to sell. But everyone who looked at the oud only laughed in her face, for it was very old and battered, and besides, it was missing all of its strings. Now Yousef had only three copper coins in his pocket, but he said to himself: "The oud is old and worn, but I could polish it, and someday, when I have more money, I will buy strings and play it."

So Yousef approached the old woman, and offered three copper coins for the old oud. The old woman accepted the offer at once. Then she motioned for him to come closer, and she whispered in his ear: "This is a fine oud you have bought, my lad, for it is a magic oud. But for it to perform its magic, it requires golden strings, for no others will do." Then the old woman turned to go, and disappeared in the crowded marketplace. And even though Yousef ran after her, he could not find her, and he was sorry she had left before he could ask her what kind of magic the oud could do, and now it was too late.

It was at that time that the princess had become trapped in the golden mountain, and the king sought help in setting her free. Like many others, Yousef liked to imagine how wonderful it would be if he was the one who freed her. And even though he had no idea how to do this, Yousef decided to go to the golden mountain to see for himself. So he took leave of his parents, took his only possession, the stringless oud, and set out on his journey.

Meanwhile the princess had begun to despair of ever escaping from the cavern. At first she had hoped that those trying to get her out would succeed, for she was able to listen to all their comments with the aid of her magic seashell. In this way she soon discovered that they had failed, and learned that the king, in his desperation, had offered her hand to whoever succeeded in releasing her. Then it occurred to the princess that she might be able to open the mountain from within by pronouncing the spell, but this too failed, for the spell was effective only from the outside. Soon after she had become trapped there, she searched through the cavern of treasures to see if there was anything to eat or drink, and she found a spring deep in the cavern, which had its source inside the mountain. So, too, did she find growing next to it a carob tree, which sustained her. And to pass the time she put the golden seashell to her ear, and heard in it all that her parents and others in the kingdom said about her, and learned how much they grieved over what had happened. So too did she listen to the lectures of wise men all over the world, for she had not lost her love for learning. And in this way several months passed, with the princess no nearer to freedom than she was in the first place.

Then one day the boy Yousef arrived at the golden mountain. He saw the crowds that gathered there during the day, because what had happened to the princess had made it a famous place. But when it grew dark, they all left and returned to town, leaving Yousef alone there, for he had nowhere else to go. He found a place for himself on the ground, and was about to go to sleep when he suddenly saw something glint in the moonlight. And when he arose and went over to see what it was, he was amazed to find a long, golden thread—the very one that had become caught in the thorn bush as the princess had entered the cavern. Yousef carefully pulled the golden thread from the bush without pricking his fingers on the thorns, and when he had it in his hand it occurred to him that he might try to string his oud with it. For, after all, the old woman had told him its magic would work only with golden strings. And when he had strung the oud, he found that the golden thread was just long enough to serve for all its strings.

So it was that as midnight arrived Yousef plucked the strings of the magic oud for the first time. And all at once it sang out with a melodious voice, almost human, and each time he plucked a string, it sang out another word, of something that sounded to Yousef like a spell. Suddenly he heard a loud rumbling. Then the princess, who had heard every word pronounced by the magic oud with the aid of the golden shell, hurried outside, and ran straight to the boy who had released her, and embraced him, and thanked him again and again for setting her free.

Then Yousef and the princess returned to the palace, he with his magic oud, and she with her magic seashell, and when the king saw that his beloved daughter had been freed, he was overjoyed. So too did he keep his promise, and soon there was a lavish wedding at which Yousef and the princess were wed. And the princess soon found out that the clever Yousef loved to learn as much as she did, and she taught him all that she knew, so that one day he became the wise ruler of that kingdom, where he was admired and respected by all.

—Morocco: oral tradition

6. The Princess in the Tower

ing Solomon had a lovely and charming daughter, whose name was Keziah. This daughter was the apple of his eye, and he often thought that he would let her marry only a great ruler, for no one else, he felt, would be worthy of her. Then it happened, during a war, when King Solomon's soldiers were crossing a river on a very hot day, that Solomon called upon the birds to protect them from the heat. In a moment the wings of thousands of birds beat above their heads, shielding them from the sun. And while this was taking place, an eagle, whose wings were sheltering King Solomon himself, whispered to Solomon, who understood the language of the birds, that it had overheard a voice from heaven announce that King Solomon's beloved daughter Keziah was destined to marry a poor man. And this wedding would take place before a year had passed.

Now King Solomon was very upset to hear this, for he only wanted Keziah to marry a prince or king. The words of the eagle consumed him day and night, until at last he decided to try to outfox fate, by having a high tower built in the sea, where Keziah would stay until the year had passed. That way, he believed, he could prevent the undesirable union from taking place.

Therefore Solomon commanded that the building of a lofty tower be undertaken by his most trusted servants, on the farthest and most remote island of his empire. And he ordered the tower be built without entrances or doors of any kind, except for an entrance on the roof, and with only a single window in his daughter's chamber, from which she could look out to the sea. So too was the tower to be furnished with the finest furniture and many treasures, and seventy servants, all women, were to be sent to satisfy the princess's every wish and command, with abundant food to last a year.

Now with the great resources available to King Solomon, the tower was soon completed. Then Solomon called in Keziah and said to her: "Keziah, I am sending you on a long voyage, to a beautiful island. I ask that you make your home there for one year. When you return I shall explain why I am sending you there. Meanwhile, while you are there, you will lack for nothing." And Keziah replied: "Your wisdom, father, is well known throughout the world. I know you love me, as I do you, and that you are sending me on this journey for a good reason. Therefore I will willingly go, and I do not doubt it will be for the best."

King Solomon thanked the Lord for having blessed him with such a wise and loving daughter. And a few days later the princess Keziah took her leave of the king and set sail. The ship sailed for forty days and nights, and at last arrived at the distant island where the tower had been built. To gain entrance a rope was put around the princess, and she was pulled up to the roof, where the only entrance to the tower was to be found. Once inside, the princess was met by the seventy serving women who had been sent there before her, and she made her home at the top of the tower in a room that overlooked the sea.

Meanwhile, far away, in the city of Acco, there lived a young man whose name was Reuven, a scholar and a scribe, who was poor in possessions, but rich in knowledge and learning. In order to support his family, Reuven gathered wood in the forest, and brought it into town to sell. So it was that once he was wandering in the wilderness when night fell, and he had to sleep beneath the stars. However, as the night passed, it grew colder and colder, until he could no longer bear the chill, and he began to wander about, searching for somewhere to keep warm. In the dark he stumbled upon the carcass of an ox that had been slain by a lion that very day. The carcass was torn open, and the ox was still warm, and Reuven was so cold that he lay down inside it, where it was warm, and fell into a deep sleep. Then, during the night, a giant eagle known as a Ziz swooped down and picked up the ox in its claws, and bore it away, with Reuven still sleeping inside it. As fate would have it, the Ziz carried the ox to the balcony of the tower where the princess was living. There the Ziz ate its fill of the ox and flew off back into the wilderness, with the young man still asleep inside it.

Now it was the custom of the princess to awaken very early and to go out on the balcony to watch the sun rise over the sea. And when she went out that day, she found the youth asleep in the carcass of the ox, and her surprise was great. She gently woke him and said: "Who are you, and how did you come to be here?" And when Reuven opened his eyes and found himself in that place, with a girl of peerless beauty standing before him, he assumed he was still dreaming. He rubbed his eyes, but nothing changed, and he realized that some kind of miracle had taken place. Then he said: "My name is Reuven. I am a scribe from the city of Acco. Last night I was sleeping in the wilderness when it became very cold, and I found the carcass of this ox, and slept inside it to keep warm. But I do not know how I came to be here."

Then the princess noticed three very large feathers lying beside the ox. She picked them up and showed them to Reuven and said: "These are the feathers of a giant bird, perhaps an eagle, which must have carried the ox here to devour, and brought you along with it." And when he saw the feathers, Reuven realized the princess must be correct, and then he was even more amazed that such a thing had happened. Nor did he regret the turn of events, for from the first instant he had seen the beauty of the princess, he had bound his heart to her. So too was the princess taken with the youth who had appeared so unexpectedly.

Now after sleeping inside the ox, Reuven badly needed a bath, so the princess invited him into her chamber, where she let him bathe and gave him a new robe to wear. And when he emerged from the bath, she was greatly struck by how handsome he was. Then she shared her breakfast with him, and after they had eaten she told him who she was, and how she had come to be there. Then she said: "This tower has been built so that it is impossible to leave it, for there are no doors of any kind except for the one on the roof where we entered. And even if you succeeded in descending from the tower, nothing would be gained, for no ship ever passes this secluded island. Perhaps it was fated that you come here; therefore, stay until the day my father, King Solomon, comes to fetch me at the end of a year."

Thus Reuven remained in the tower with the princess Keziah, and every day their love for each other deepened. Before long Reuven asked the princess to marry him, and when she agreed, he wrote out a marriage contract which they signed, and then they exchanged vows and called upon God and the angels Michael and Gabriel to be their witnesses. And thus they became man and wife.

So it was that by the end of the year Reuven and Keziah had become the happy parents of a beautiful child, a boy, whom they named Solomon. And when the ship arrived to take the princess back to the palace in Jerusalem, King Solomon disembarked from it, for he had come to bring her back himself. Imagine his astonishment when he discovered that his daughter was married, and the mother of a fine son, his namesake! Solomon was overwhelmed, and he understood for the first time how vain it was to try to prevent the decrees of Providence from taking place. And Solomon also recognized Reuven's fine qualities, and that he was a scholar and a scribe, and he did not oppose him, but welcomed him as if he were his own son.

Thereupon King Solomon accompanied his daughter and her husband and their child to Jerusalem, where a lavish wedding was held for the princess and her beloved to share their joy with all of the inhabitants of the kingdom. And afterward they lived together in joy and peace for all the days of their lives.

—Palestine: c. eighth to tenth centuries

7. King Solomon and Ashmodai

ow King David had had a long and full life, and the time had come when he saw that he would soon take leave of this world, and that his son, Solomon, would take his place as king. So King David called in Solomon and said to him: "Solomon, my son, now that I am growing old there is a secret I wish to share with you, a secret I have been saving for many years. It concerns a dream that came to me on the night you were born. In the dream I was following a path at night, when I came upon a ladder that reached from earth into heaven. I knew at once that I must ascend that ladder, for I longed to know where it would lead me. And as soon as I stepped on the first rung, I heard a melody like a distant harp, more beautiful than any I had ever heard. And with each rung I climbed, the melody grew clearer and drew me closer.

"When at last I reached the top rung of the ladder, I found myself in a city that resembled Jerusalem in every respect, except that the stones of the houses and the streets were made of gold. I wandered through those streets in a daze, marveling at this mirror image of Jerusalem in the heavens, until I reached a Temple of great splendor in the center of that golden city. Just then an old man in a white robe approached me, and said: 'Welcome, King David. We have been expecting your arrival.' I asked the old man who he was, and he told me that he was Abraham, our first Father. He took me and led me to the entrance of the Temple, and there we were met by two other men, also robed in white, our Fathers Isaac and Jacob. They took me through the Temple, and showed me each and every aspect of it, and when the splendor of the Temple had been revealed to me in all its glory, Abraham said: 'The heavenly Jerusalem is like the earthly Jerusalem in every respect, except that the Temple that has existed here since the creation of the world has yet to be built on earth. It is for you, King David, to bring the vision of this Temple back to the world of men and, when the time comes, to share it with your son, Solomon, who is about to be born. For it is destined that Solomon shall bring the Temple on earth into being.' "

Solomon was amazed when he heard these words, and he understood that his destiny had been revealed to him. From that moment on he thought only of the Temple he would construct in the center of the city, which would resemble the celestial Temple in every way, exactly as King David had described it, so that the heavenly city would finally find its mirror image on earth.

Not long after, King David left this world and rejoined the Fathers in Paradise. And when Solomon became king and set out to build the Temple, he soon realized that he must find a way to fashion the stones that would be used in building the altar, *so that no hammer or ax or any iron tool was heard in the Temple while it was being built* (1 Kings 6:7). Solomon called in his wise men and asked for their advice. One of them recalled the legend of a creature no larger than a grain of barley, known as the Shamir, which could cut through mountains the way a knife cuts through butter, but the man did not know if it really existed or not. Solomon then used his powers to conjure up two demons, one male and one female, to see if they knew where it might be found. When the demons had been brought forth and questioned, they told Solomon that the Shamir did exist, but that they did not know where it might be found. Their king, Ashmodai, however, surely would know this secret, and might even have the Shamir in his possession. Solomon then asked them where Ashmodai could be found, and they told him that his palace had been built on the highest peak of the Mountains of Darkness. There Ashmodai had an underground cistern, from which he alone drew his drinking water. Every day he sealed that cistern and covered it with a huge boulder. Then he left to rule the Kingdom of Demons. When he returned he would check the seal to be certain no one had tampered with it, and when he was thus assured, he removed the rock and satisfied his thirst.

Now that Solomon knew where Ashmodai could be found, he summoned Benayahu, his most trusted minister, and sent him with six men to the palace of Ashmodai, in order to capture the king of demons and to bring him back. To assist them in their quest, Solomon first whispered a secret to Benayahu, and then gave him four things: a chain with God's Name engraved on every link; his magic ring, on which God's Name was also inscribed; a large skin of wine; and a bundle of wool. Then Benayahu journeyed until he reached the Mountains of Darkness, and he and his men climbed the highest peak, where they discovered the cistern of Ashmodai. There they hid themselves in trees until Ashmodai left his palace and came to the cistern. But when they saw him, Benayahu and his men were terrified, for Ashmodai was very terrible in appearance—he was a winged giant with the feet of a cock, with the beard of a he-goat, and with fire shooting forth from his nostrils. Yet they put their trust in the power of the Name, and they did not lose heart.

When Ashmodai had finished drinking from the cistern, he sealed and covered it as usual and left. As soon as he was gone, Benayahu and his men climbed down from the trees and bore a hole in the cistern, letting all the water run out. Then they closed the hole with the wool they had brought with them. After that they bore a second hole, higher up, and let the wine flow in through there. Finally they covered both holes with dirt, so as not to make Ashmodai suspicious. Then they concealed themselves in the trees, waiting for him to return.

When Ashmodai finally appeared many hours later, he lifted the stone off the top of the cistern, checked the seal and saw it was unbroken, and lowered the bucket to drink. But when he drew up the bucket he was astonished to find that the water had turned to wine. At first he was reluctant to drink it, but since he saw no sign of tampering and his thirst was very great, he finally drank a bucketful of the wine, and then another and yet another. In this way he became drunk and fell to the ground in a stupor, and soon was deep asleep. Benayahu and his men then came down from the branches and wrapped the chain around Ashmodai's hands, and around his neck.

On waking, Ashmodai discovered that he had been chained, and roared with anger. But when he tried to break the chain, he found that he could not. Just then Benayahu and the others came out of hiding, and as Benayahu held up Solomon's magic ring they shouted: "The Name of your Master is upon you!" And when Ashmodai saw that he was under the power of the Name, he ceased to resist, for his power flourished only in the absence of everything holy. And so he let himself be led away.

Nor did Ashmodai try to escape his captors during all of the journey to Jerusalem, but he did act in peculiar ways, of which Benayahu took note. When they passed a wedding, Ashmodai wept, and when they came upon a man who asked a shoemaker to make him shoes that would last for seven years, he laughed. Later, when they met a blind man who had lost his way, Ashmodai directed him to the proper path, and when they came upon a magician who bragged of his great skill, Ashmodai had nothing but contempt.

After they reached the palace, Benayahu told King Solomon of Ashmodai's strange behavior, and Solomon decided to wait three days before receiving him. On the first day the king instructed his guard to tell Ashmodai he could not see him because he was drunk. When Ashmodai heard this he said nothing, but took two bricks and placed them one on top of the other. When the guard reported this to Solomon, the king laughed and said: "By this he means to say that you should give me more to drink." The second day the guard was instructed to say Solomon could not see him because he had eaten too much and felt sleepy. When Ashmodai heard this he again said nothing, but took one brick down from the other. "By this," Solomon explained, "he means to say that you should give me less to eat." Then on the third day Ashmodai was brought before Solomon. As soon as he stood before him, Ashmodai marked off four ells on the floor and said: "Tell me, King Solomon, why do you seek to conquer the world? Is not the kingdom you rule enough for you? Do you seek to rule over the Kingdom of Demons as well? Do you not know that before long all you will need will be the four ells of a single grave?"

But Solomon ignored these questions and said: "Tell me first, Ashmodai, what was the meaning of your strange behavior on the way to my kingdom?" To this Ashmodai replied: "When I saw the wedding, I wept, because I knew that the bridegroom had less than a week to live. I laughed at him who wanted his shoes to last for seven years, since he would not own them for seven days. I set the blind man on the right path because he was one of the hidden saints, whom even demons must respect. And I had only contempt for the magician who boasted of his powers, since he did not even know that a buried treasure lay at his feet. Now, King Solomon, if you please, let me know why you have gone to all the trouble of having me captured."

Then King Solomon said: "It is my fate and destiny to build a great Temple in this holy city to honor the King of the Universe, who rules over us all, even kings such as you and I, Ashmodai. But I cannot fashion the stones for the altar without the aid of the Shamir, and you, I have learned, have possession of it."

"No, I do not possess the Shamir," said Ashmodai. "But I know it was created at twilight on the eve of the first Sabbath, and left in the care of Rahab, Prince of the Sea, who has entrusted it to the White Eagle." Then Solomon asked: "But what does the White Eagle do with the Shamir?" Ashmodai replied: "It places the Shamir on the high mountains and the Shamir splits and forms canyons, where wild fruit trees grow, and from the fruit of these trees the White Eagle is able to feed its brood." Then Solomon said: "And where can the White Eagle be found?"

Ashmodai answered: "It makes its nest on the peak of the mountain where I make my home." When Solomon heard this, he directed Benayahu to return to the Mountains of Darkness, in order to recover the Shamir.

This time Benayahu went alone, taking only a plate of glass with him. And when he reached the nest of the White Eagle on the highest peak of the Mountains of Darkness, he covered it with the plate of glass. Then he hid himself behind a huge rock and waited. When the eagle returned to feed its brood and found it could see them, but could not reach them because of the glass, it flew off and soon returned with a small object in its beak. This was the Shamir, which it then set down on the plate of glass. At that moment Benayahu came out shouting and making a great clamor, and so frightened the White Eagle that it flew off. Then Benayahu took the Shamir, lifted the plate of glass off the nest, and returned triumphantly to his king. That is how King Solomon was able to fashion the stones of the altar, and thus complete the House of the Lord in the Holy Land that was the mirror image of the Temple in the celestial city on high.

—Babylon: c. fifth century

8. The Beggar King

During the construction of the Temple in Jerusalem, King Solomon kept Ashmodai, the king of demons, as his prisoner, to prevent any of the forces of evil, which Ashmodai commanded, from interfering with the building of the Temple. When the Temple was completed, King Solomon called in Ashmodai, and told him that he was prepared to set him free if Ashmodai would first reveal a single secret to him. Ashmodai said: "Tell me first, O king, what secret it is that you want to know." Solomon said: "Of a great many mysteries am I master, Ashmodai, of the language of the birds, of the secrets of the wind, and of the mysteries of God's Name. But there is one secret that has eluded me so far—that is the secret of illusion. And it is of great importance that I learn this secret, for as king I often am called upon to distinguish truth from illusion."

Ashmodai nodded when he heard these words from King Solomon, and he said: "I agree, King Solomon, to reveal this secret to you. But I cannot do so while I stand here in these chains, nor unless you surrender the ring you wear, inscribed with God's Name. For in the presence of the Name my lips are sealed." When Solomon heard this, he found the words of Ashmodai plausible, and for the sake of learning the secret, he had Ashmodai released from his chains and surrendered his ring to him. But no sooner was Ashmodai free and in possession of the ring than he flung it a great distance, so that it was soon lost on the horizon, and sank into the sea. Then the king of demons approached King Solomon, who stood before him unprotected. He picked up King Solomon from his throne, and hurled him through the window hundreds of miles.

Now Solomon flew through the air like an arrow, and at last fell down in a field in a foreign country. When he stood up he was like a drunken man who has lost his way, who does not know where he is going or what he is doing. He wandered this way for a long time, until he became thirsty, and at last he came to a pool. But when he bent down to drink and saw his reflection in the water, it was not the reflection of a great king he saw, but that of a miserable beggar. For the light that had lit up his face had vanished, and there was no longer a crown upon his head.

Overwhelmed with the vastness of his loss, Solomon lay down in sorrow and slept. And while he slept he dreamed that the evening star, the first to be seen, the very ruler of the heavens at night, fell from its place and sank like a meteor into the sea. When Solomon awoke from this dream he trembled, for he recognized its meaning. And in the morning he set off on his wanderings, which lasted for many years.

So it was that, deprived of his kingdom, King Solomon made his way begging for his daily bread. At first, it is true, he insisted he was a king everywhere he went. But those who saw him in his rags paid no attention, and believed him to be merely another beggar gone mad. Then, after three years of wandering, Solomon reached the kingdom ruled by King Ammon. One day, while he stood in the streets of the capital city, the royal cook passed by him, bearing baskets laden with food of all kinds. The beggar king offered to help carry these baskets, and in this way he found favor with the royal cook. For many weeks after that Solomon worked as a laborer in the king's kitchen, until one day he pleaded with the cook, who had become his friend, to let him prepare the royal meal. The royal cook granted his wish, and Solomon prepared a sumptuous feast. When King Ammon tasted this food, he summoned the royal cook and said: "Who was it who cooked this food? For never before have you brought me food so exquisite." Then the cook admitted that the meal had been prepared by Solomon, and thereupon the king ordered that Solomon alone should prepare his meals.

As the head royal cook, Solomon soon came to the attention of Naamah, the daughter of the king. And before long Naamah recognized that she loved Solomon, and wanted him for her husband. Solomon, too, fell in love with the princess, and at last a day came when she announced to her father that she wished them to be wed. But when King Ammon heard this he was consumed with anger that his daughter, the princess, should choose a cook for her husband, when princes from all over the world were at her feet. And in his anger he commanded that the couple should be taken to a desert, and left there to die.

So it happened that Solomon and Naamah found themselves alone in a vast wilderness. They had no supplies of food or water, and the sun overhead was like a fire burning on their bodies. All they possessed were the clothes on their backs and the walking stick that Solomon carried with him. But it occurred to Solomon that this staff might serve as a divining rod, and by using it in this way he found an underground stream, which flowed beneath the sand. There he dug a well, which the clear waters of the stream filled with fresh water, and it was there that Solomon and Naamah made their home. With the fruit they found, they sustained themselves, and with the stones they gathered Solomon built a stone hut in that place, and digging furrows into the earth he used the waters of the stream to fertilize the land. There Solomon planted every species of fruit which was to be found scattered throughout the wilderness, including every variety of cactus that bore fruit.

So it was that over a period of years, Solomon and his wife established a home in that desert, and turned it into an oasis. Together they were the parents of three children, two boys and a girl, whom they brought up there. In time Solomon forgot about his life as a king, and came to think of himself as one who made his home in the desert. Nor did he miss his former life, for his days were full, and his nights were peaceful, while as king he had passed many sleepless nights trying to reach just decisions. In this way many years passed, twelve in all.

Then one day it happened that from out of nowhere a dark cloud covered the desert as far as they could see in every direction, and the rains poured down in great sheets. In a short time a great wave was rolling through the desert, and when this wave struck Solomon's hut it tore it to pieces, and carried off Solomon's wife at the same time. Solomon fought off the waves, with one child held in his left arm, and the other two in his right. A moment later another wave struck them, and at that moment the child in his left arm was torn away from his grasp. Solomon reached for that child, and in this way he lost his grip on the other two, so that all three children were lost at the same time. Then the world went dark around him, and he was carried a great distance by the currents.

When Solomon awoke he found that his arms were chained. Looking up, he discovered that he had been captured by thieves, who had found him unconscious after the flood. The thieves took Solomon with them, to sell as a slave, but Solomon did not care that this was his fate. He was filled with grief at the loss of his family. So it was that Solomon was sold as a slave to a caravan, which brought him across the burning desert, and finally sold him as a slave to a blacksmith in a foreign kingdom.

As the slave of a blacksmith, it was the duty of Solomon to work the bellows, so that the fire would continue to burn, and since Solomon was a steady worker, the blacksmith soon came to trust and respect him. Now this blacksmith had a son who wished to become a goldsmith, and who was already quite accomplished at this craft. It happened that among Solomon's many skills he was a highly accomplished goldsmith, and in his free time he taught the son of the blacksmith, whose skills grew so considerable he was able to take a position in the court of the king.

Once, when the young goldsmith was visiting his father, he spoke to Solomon, who begged him to let him fashion a treasure for the king. The son agreed, and in this way Solomon came to fashion a golden dove, set with rubies, moonstones, emeralds, turquoise, mother-of-pearl, and diamonds. In the beak of the dove he placed a golden twig, and from the twig he hung three golden bells like buds. Now when the goldsmith presented this treasure to the king, he was overwhelmed with its magnificence and the great skill of its creator. He asked the goldsmith how it happened that this treasure was so superior to anything he had previously created. Then the goldsmith confessed that it had been created by a slave who worked for his father, the blacksmith. So it was that the king ordered Solomon to be purchased from the blacksmith, and made chief goldsmith in his palace.

In this way Solomon came to the attention of the king, who recognized that he possessed great wisdom. Little by little, the king came to Solomon to discuss the affairs of his kingdom, and to seek his advice in matters great and small. Now it happened at that time that the king's daughter was possessed by a dream that haunted her night after night. In this dream she saw a man climbing into a cave high in a cliff that faced a cove shaped like a half moon. She never saw the face of the climber but, as often happens in dreams, her eyes were able to see him as he entered the cave, and she watched him take out of a crevice in the wall a jewel of immense beauty, illumined from within, as if by a flame.

Now the princess became possessed by the idea that she must somehow make that jewel her own, and while she pined away over it, her health declined, and she refused to leave her chamber in the palace. At last there came a night when she was able to glimpse the face of the man who climbed up the cliff in the recurring dream, and the face she saw was that of Solomon.

When the princess reported this dream to her father, the king, he understood at once that he must ask his wise goldsmith, Solomon, to set off on a quest to find that cave, and to bring back the jewel his daughter craved so terribly. Nor did Solomon hesitate to undertake this task, but set out at once. And how did he proceed? He remembered that the cove in the dream of the princess had been shaped like a half moon. It was there that she had envisioned the cliff, with the cave in its side, which he must seek out.

So it was that Solomon journeyed for many years, and at each place he came to he asked if there was a cove shaped like a half moon, but nowhere had anyone heard of such a place. Then one day Solomon heard a child call out to another in the street: "Let us go to the cove of the half moon." Now when Solomon heard these words he could hardly believe his luck, and he went to the child and asked him if he knew the way to such a cove. The boy told him that he did, and he led Solomon there.

When they reached the crescent-shaped cove, and Solomon saw the cliff and the cave in its side, he was delighted, and he gave the child a piece of silver and then set off to climb the cliff. It took him over an hour to reach the cave, high up the cliff, and when he crawled inside he was worn out. Still, he searched through every crevice in the cave, but he could not find anything resembling the jewel in the princess's dream. All he found was a rough rock in one crevice, and there was nothing to distinguish that rock from any other. But since there was no other clue, Solomon struck the rock against the wall of the cave, and it broke in two. At that instant a beautiful, glowing jewel fell from inside it, and Solomon was thrilled when he saw its great beauty, how it glowed from within. Then he knew that his quest was complete. Putting the jewel in a pouch strapped to his body, he lay down in the cave and fell asleep.

So tired was Solomon from his efforts that he slept for several hours. When he woke up he found that the cave was no longer lit from the light outside, for the sky had grown dark. Then Solomon went to the entrance of the cave, and when he looked down he saw that the tide had come in, and that the waters had risen, and lapped near the entrance of the cave. Just then another wave came in and started to flood the cave, and Solomon realized he was in great danger of drowning. He clung to a rock as the next wave washed in, and as it started to recede he threw himself from the entrance of the cave into the waters, and in this way he was carried a great distance.

When the wave at last set Solomon down, he saw that it had returned him to the kingdom from which he had set out on the quest for the glowing jewel. With great joy and relief, Solomon hurried to the palace of the king, and presented the jewel and reported all that had happened on his quest. And when the princess saw the jewel of her dreams her sadness turned to joy, and her recovery was swift and complete.

Now the king of that kingdom was so grateful to Solomon for making possible the recovery of the princess that he told him he could have whatever he wanted. Solomon then told him, for the first time, his true history, and the fact that he himself was once a great king. So it was that Solomon asked only for his freedom, in order to recover his kingdom. The king granted his wish at once, and ordered a ship to be made ready and well stocked for the voyage.

That night there was a great feast and many happy toasts were offered. Solomon's ship was launched the next day, and he left to search for his lost kingdom. To occupy himself on the long voyage, Solomon decided that he would take up fishing. And the first time he cast his rod into the water, he found at the end of the line a magnificent golden fish, unlike any he had ever seen. Solomon was so delighted with this fish that he decided he would not entrust it to the ship's cook; rather, he would prepare it himself. But when Solomon cut the fish open, he was astonished to find in its belly his own magic ring, engraved with God's Name, which Ashmodai had cast into the sea. Solomon rejoiced to recover the ring, and placed it on his finger, and at that instant he found himself seated on his throne in Jerusalem, with the demon Ashmodai standing before him. And Ashmodai said: "We have been waiting for you for almost an hour, O king. Tell me, now, have you learned something of the secret of Illusion?"

Solomon was staggered to learn that he had been absent only such a short time. It had seemed like many years to him. But when he asked his ministers, they all confirmed that barely an hour had passed. Then Solomon commanded from his throne that Ashmodai be set free, since he had fulfilled Solomon's request. And no sooner did Solomon say this than Ashmodai flew away, and he was not seen again in that kingdom during the rest of King Solomon's reign, in which Solomon demonstrated a wisdom unmatched among men, and an evenhanded mercy that was remarked upon by all.

—Babylon: c. fifth century

9. The Wonder Child

ong ago, there lived a rabbi and his wife who had no children. They prayed every day for a child of their own, but their prayers were never answered.

Now it is said that the sky opens at midnight on the night of Shavuot, and any prayers or wishes made at that time come true. So one Shavuot the rabbi and his wife decided to stay awake, so that their prayers would be certain to reach God's ears.

To their amazement, at midnight the sky parted like the waters of the Red Sea, and for one instant the world was filled with the glory of heaven. And in that instant both the rabbi and his wife wished for a child. That night the rabbi's wife dreamed of a wonder child, a girl who would be born to them clutching a precious jewel. In the dream the rabbi's wife was told that the child must keep the jewel with her at all times, for her soul was inside it. And if she ever lost that jewel, she would fall into a deep sleep from which she would not awaken until the jewel was returned.

The next morning, the rabbi's wife told her husband the dream, and he was much amazed. And, indeed, things occurred exactly as foretold, and nine months later a beautiful baby girl was born to them. In her right hand she clutched a precious jewel, which seemed to glow with a light of its own. The rabbi and his wife named their daughter Kohava, which means "star," and the rabbi set the jewel in a necklace for her to wear around her neck.

One day, when Kohava was only three years old, she picked up her mother's flute. She had never played a flute before, but the moment she put it to her lips, beautiful melodies poured forth. Not only could she play any musical instrument, but at a very early age, she taught herself to paint lovely pictures, to write the letters of the alphabet, and to read books. Her favorites were the books on her father's shelves that told stories of the ancient days when Abraham and Moses walked in the world.

As the years passed, Kohava grew into a beautiful girl. Her lustrous black hair shone in the sunlight. Her dark eyes sparkled like the dazzling jewel she wore around her neck. Her skin was as smooth as the outside of a peach, and her smile brought happiness to everyone who met her.

Now the rabbi and his wife realized that their daughter was truly a wonder child, as the dream had promised, and they gave thanks to God. But in their hearts was the fear that someday she might be separated from her necklace and lose her soul. That is why the rabbi and his wife watched carefully over Kohava and rarely let her leave home.

One day the rabbi and his wife learned that the queen was going to visit the bathhouse that very day and that she had invited all the women of the village to come there. Kohava asked her mother if she, too, could go, for she had never seen the queen. At first her mother was afraid, but at last she agreed to let her go.

When the two arrived at the bathhouse, the women looked at Kohava in amazement. "Where did she come from? Why, she is more beautiful than the queen!" they exclaimed.

When the queen heard this, she grew angry. "Who is this girl?" she asked her servants. They replied that Kohava was a Jewish girl of great beauty and that it was said that she could play any musical instrument set before her.

The queen demanded to see Kohava for herself. And when she realized that the girl's beauty did indeed outshine her own, she was filled with jealousy, and with the sudden fear that her son, the prince, might see Kohava and fall in love with her. And that would be a terrible thing, for she wanted the prince to marry a princess, not a poor Jewish girl.

The queen had one of her servants bring forth a flute and commanded the girl to play it. At once Kohava played a melody so beautiful it brought tears to everyone's eyes. Everyone's, that is, except the queen's. Then the queen commanded that the girl play a violin, and after that a harp. And from every instrument that Kohava touched, beautiful melodies poured forth. When the queen saw that Kohava truly had a great talent, she ordered: "This girl must return with me at once to my palace to serve as one of my royal musicians."

The rabbi's wife was heartsick at the thought of Kohava's going off to live in the palace, yet she knew they must obey the queen. But before Kohava left, her mother took her aside and whispered that she should never, ever take off her necklace, nor should she tell anyone that it held her soul. Then the mother and daughter kissed good-bye, and Kohava rode off in the royal carriage with the queen.

Now the queen had no intention of letting Kohava be a musician, for in that way her son, the prince, might see her. Alas, as soon as they reached the palace, she shut Kohava in the dungeon and ordered that she be left to starve.

So it was that the confused girl found herself imprisoned and frightened for her very life. She would have died of hunger had not the prison guard, overwhelmed by her beauty and gentleness, brought her food in secret. In her dark cell, Kohava wept for her mother and father, and prayed to be saved from the evil queen.

One day the queen went down to the dungeon to see for herself if Kohava was still alive. As she walked into the dark cell, she was surprised to see a glowing light. When she looked closer, she realized that the light was coming from the jewel Kohava wore around her neck, and that the girl was, indeed, still alive.

"Give me that necklace!" the queen demanded. "I want it for myself." Kohava was terrified, for she remembered her mother's warning. But the queen, not waiting for Kohava to obey, pulled it off herself. And the moment she did, Kohava sank into a deep sleep.

The queen was delighted. "Ah, I'm rid of her for good," she cried. Then she ordered the prison guard to bury Kohava far away from the palace where no one could ever find her. But when the guard reached the wood far from the palace, he saw that Kohava was still breathing, and he realized that she was only asleep. So he brought her to a hut he knew of in that forest, and left her there. Day after day, Kohava slept a long, dreamless sleep, and no one except the guard knew she was there.

One afternoon, when the prince was out riding in the woods, he saw that very hut and decided to stop there and rest. When the prince entered, he was astonished to find a sleeping girl, and he lost his heart to her the moment he saw her. The prince wanted to tell her of his love, but when he realized that she would not wake up, he was very sad. So the prince put a guard outside the hut to protect the sleeping beauty. Every day he came to visit her, and every day he shed tears because she could not be awakened.

As the days passed, the queen noticed the sadness of her son, and one day she asked him what was wrong. He told his mother that he was in love with a beautiful young girl.

"Is she a princess?" asked the queen.

"Surely," said the prince, "she is a princess."

"In that case," said the queen, "would you like to give her a gift to show your love?"

"Oh, yes," said the prince, "I would like that very much."

"Then I know just the gift for a beautiful princess," replied the queen. "It is something very special." And she brought forth the jewel that she had taken from Kohava. The prince took the necklace to the sleeping girl at once, and the moment he put it around her neck, she woke up.

"Who are you?" asked Kohava as she looked around the small hut. "And where am I?"

The prince told Kohava how he had found her and how she had awakened at the very instant he had placed the necklace around her neck.

Kohava looked at the jewel and remembered how the queen had snatched it from her. "Where did you get this?" she asked.

That is how Kohava learned that the one who had saved her was none other than the queen's son. And when the prince learned of his mother's evil deed, he realized that Kohava's life was in danger. He decided to leave the girl in the hut while he hurried back to the palace.

When he arrived, he went straight to the queen. "Mother, I have great news," he said. "I'd like to get married."

"I can see how much you love this princess," said the queen. "I will give orders for the wedding preparations to begin at once!"

Every servant worked night and day. The cooks prepared a magnificent feast, the gardeners cut huge bouquets of roses, and the maids polished the silver goblets until they shone. By the seventh day everything was ready. All the people of the kingdom were invited to the wedding. They gathered at the palace and whispered to one another, "Who is the bride?" For not even the queen had seen her. But when the bride arrived, she was wearing seven veils, and no one could tell who she was.

Among the guests at the wedding were the rabbi and his wife, who had come hoping they might see their daughter, Kohava, from whom they had not heard since the day the queen had taken her to the palace.

At last the wedding vows were spoken, and the guests waited breathlessly as the prince lifted the veils, one by one. And as he lifted the seventh veil, everyone gasped at Kohava's great beauty. Everyone, that is, except the rabbi and his wife, who could not believe their eyes, and the queen, who thought she was seeing a ghost. Screaming with terror, she ran from the palace as fast as she could and never was seen again.

So it was that the prince and his new bride became the rulers of the kingdom, and Kohava was reunited with her father and mother. At the palace Kohava continued to play music and make people happy with her songs. And the love that Kohava and the prince had for each other grew deeper over the years, and they lived happily ever after.

—Egypt: oral tradition

10. The Princess and the Slave

n a faraway land lived a mighty ruler, whose name was King Nazim. Now this king had an exceptionally beautiful daughter, who was his only child, and the king loved her more than life itself. Her eyes were blue, her lips red, and her smile was like the sun at midday. Kings came from a great distance to meet her, and many wealthy princes requested her hand in marriage. But one and all, King Nazim turned them down, finding every suitor flawed and unworthy of his daughter. Still, those who wanted her were like bees buzzing around the hive, and for each prince he turned away two others arrived who sought her hand.

And it is true that the princess was worthy of all this attention, for she was not only beautiful and charming but also very pious and pure. She loved to study so much that she had to have one tutor after another, for she soon learned everything they knew. So her father was understandably proud and protective of her, and demanded the highest standards of those who sought her hand.

Now despite all his efforts to see that the princess found a perfect match, King Nazim was haunted by a recurrent nightmare. In these dreams he was told that the one destined to marry his daughter was none other than his Hebrew slave, whose name was Samuel. Now of course this was preposterous, for not only was Samuel a slave but he was also an old man, more than ninety years old. It is true that he was of a great size, and he was still strong as an ox, but as a suitor he simply could not even be considered.

At first the king did not pay any attention to these dreams, but when they kept recurring, he became anxious. At last he called his wise men together and told them the dream and asked for their advice. They discussed many solutions, but at last they told the king to command the slave Samuel to go into the wilderness in search of his prophet Moses, since he was a Hebrew. And to send him on this quest with a riddle to which he must have the answer before he could return. The riddle was "It is possible to contain a garden in the world. But how can the world be contained in a garden?" The advisers laughed heartily when they concocted this riddle, for they were quite certain it could not be answered. And the king agreed that this was a fine way to get rid of the worrisome fellow, for he would dare not return until he had completed the quest.

So it was that the slave Samuel was sent on his way. And although he had food and water to last for many months, for he could carry a great load, still he wept the whole way. For he understood that he was being sent into exile, but he could not imagine why, since he had been a faithful and dependable slave all of his life. And even though he felt that it was surely impossible to find Moses the Redeemer in this world, still he set out in search of him, since that is what he had been commanded to do.

Samuel traveled for many months on his quest, even though he knew it was hopeless. One day when he was very tired, and began to feel like an old man for the first time, he sat down to rest under a large tree in the wilderness. He was about to fall asleep when he heard a voice whispering to him, saying: "Where are you going?" Samuel quickly sat up and looked around, but there was no one to be seen. Then he became frightened, for perhaps he had been found by an enemy, and the most dangerous enemy is one who cannot be seen. Then the voice spoke again and repeated the question. This time Samuel found his voice and said: "Who is speaking to me?" And the voice replied: "It is I, the tree you are sitting beneath." Samuel could hardly believe his ears, but since there was no one to be seen in the wilderness, and no one was hiding in the tree, there did not seem to be any other explanation.

Just then the tree asked its question for the third time, and Samuel said: "I am searching for Moses, so that I may ask him a question." "If that is so," said the tree, "then I have one request to make—when you find Moses, please ask him why a giant tree such as I am does not bear any fruit. For if there were ripe and juicy fruit on my branches, a hungry man like yourself would have been able to break his fast and delight in it." "Yes," said Samuel, "I will certainly fulfill your request if I succeed in finding Moses."

After a good long rest, Samuel got up and continued on his endless way. He reached a hill overlooking a steep valley, and saw that there was something at the base of it, although he could not quite make out what it was. So he traveled down to the bottom of the valley, and there he found two marble pools, one next to the other. One pool had been built out of black marble and was filled with dark water, while the other was made of white marble, and was filled with clear water, but gave forth a repugnant odor, so that no traveler would risk tasting it, and if he did, he would discover it was bitter indeed.

Now when Samuel saw the two pools filled with water, his soul was filled with longing to rest there and satisfy his thirst. And when he realized that neither pool contained water that was any good for drinking, he was very disappointed. Then, as he was sitting there, he suddenly heard a voice speaking to him as if from far away. It was a muddled and murky voice, but Samuel could make out its words. The voice asked him where he was going. Again Samuel looked around and saw that no one else was there, and he was still trying to figure out who had spoken when the voice repeated its question. "Who is it that is speaking?" asked Samuel. "It is I, the voice of the two pools," came the reply. Then Samuel answered the voice's question and told it of his quest. "If that is the case," said the voice, "when you reach Moses will you please ask him why it is that we pools, made of the finest marble, have waters that are muddy and bitter? For if they had been clear and sweet a sad and exhausted traveler like yourself would have been able to quench his thirst." And Samuel said that he would gladly ask Moses this question, should he ever succeed in finding him.

After he had rested by the side of the two pools, Samuel got up and went on his way. He walked on for days and weeks and months, his tired body swinging from side to side, his hands rising and falling, his eyes blurry, his feet worn and aching. Tears washed over his cheeks, and his sadness ate away at his patience and strength. After all, who knew where Moses the Redeemer might be found? For since he had ascended Mount Nevo he had never been seen again, and now the poor slave Samuel had been commanded to seek him out!

Then it happened after many years had passed that Samuel reached a mountain in the wilderness. Since he did not have a map to guide him, he did not know where he was, but he was very pleased to find at the base of that mountain a fine fig tree, filled with ripe figs. He plucked one of them and tasted it, and it seemed to him as sweet as the very fruit of Paradise. Then Samuel ate his fill of those delicious figs, and lay down to sleep. He slept for a long time, and when he woke up he saw that he was sleeping in a shadow, where before he had been sleeping in the sun, and he assumed that the day had passed and the night fallen. He did not realize that he had slept through a day and a night, and that it was already the next day. And why did he not see the sun? Because someone was standing above him, who cast a long shadow. And whose shadow was it? It belonged to Moses, who had come down from the peak of that mountain where he made his home, because he knew that the slave Samuel had finally found him. And where was it that Samuel had come? To Mount Nevo in the wilderness of the Sinai, for that is where Moses makes his home.

So it was that when Samuel sat up and saw the man standing over him, whose face shone with a beautiful glow and whose long beard was pure white, Samuel suddenly knew that he had succeeded in his quest, for the dignified presence who stood there could be none other than Moses the Redeemer himself. Then Samuel lowered his eyes and said in a whisper: "Tell me, good sir, what is your name?" "Surely you know who I am," answered the old man. "I am the one you have been searching for all these years. And although you have doubted so many times that you would ever find me, you should know that it was destined before you were born that we should meet today. Now, tell me, are there any questions you want me to answer?"

For a moment Samuel was dizzy, since his long search had come to so sudden a conclusion, and for a moment the three questions that had been on his tongue day and night were lost to him, as if they had flown away. Then his memory was restored, and he said to Moses: "It is possible to contain a garden in the world. But how can the world be contained in a garden?" "That should be obvious to a man of the Hebrew faith, such as yourself," said Moses, "for is it not true that this world is God's garden?" And Samuel smiled when he heard this, for the riddle had tormented him all those years, and now that he knew the solution, it seemed so simple that he was amazed it had never occurred to him.

After this Samuel remembered the question he had brought from the giant tree, and asked Moses why it was that such a magnificent tree did not bear fruit. And Moses said: "It is true that the Holy One, blessed be He, did not bless this tree with abundant fruit, but that is because God gave it a very special virtue among all the other trees in the world. And what is that virtue? It is to be found in the leaves of that tree, for whoever takes a handful of those green leaves from its branches and cooks them in water and drinks the potion will be cured of any sickness or disease, and become a healthy man in his body and soul."

Then Samuel asked the third question he had promised to bring to Moses, that of the two pools. And Moses said: "It is true that the water of these pools is not intended for drinking. But that is because they have another purpose, unique among the waters of the world. And what is that? It happens that any man who immerses himself in the black pool, and then immerses himself in the white one, will in an instant become a young man of eighteen, and the same holds true for a woman, who will also become young again. But anyone who dips himself in the white pool first and then in the black will lose his youth and become a very old man full of days, very bent and worn."

Then Samuel kissed the hands of Moses and thanked Moses from the bottom of his heart for seeing fit to meet him there at the foot of Mount Nevo. Samuel then made his way back to the two pools. There he told the voice of the pools all that Moses had said, and then took off his clothes, and immersed himself in the black pool. After this he entered the white pool, and when he emerged from it he was a young handsome lad of eighteen, feeling stronger than he had ever felt in his life. So it was that Samuel left those pools singing and giving thanks to the Lord and to Moses for having revealed this secret to him, and making it possible for that miracle to take place. And every time he reached a body of water, he leaned over it to study his reflection, and at last he came to the happy conclusion that the wonderful transformation had indeed taken place.

Now Samuel felt light, and he ran like a deer. Before long he covered a vast distance and arrived at the great tree. When he stood beneath it, he told the tree the secret of its healing leaves, as Moses had told him, and then he climbed up the trunk of the tree and filled his bag with those green leaves, for he knew that such a wonderful cure would be invaluable. After this Samuel continued on his way, and his singing echoed in the empty fields, and there was no end to his happiness. For as much as he walked his feet retained their spring, and the way seemed shortened, and only a few days passed before he reached the gates of the city from which he had departed so long ago.

Now as soon as he had entered the city, Samuel saw that everyone was wearing black, and that their eyes were downcast and full of tears. He wondered what could have happened, and thought that perhaps the king had died. Then he asked one of the men he saw in the street, and he learned that not long after he had left on his quest the king's beloved daughter had fallen into a deep sleep, from which she could not be wakened. She had slept this way ever since, and it was as if a dark cloud had covered that city, for since then the lives of the people had grown sad and bitter, for they dearly loved the princess. As for the king, his despair was so great that he had retreated to his chamber and was neither seen nor heard from. Of course doctors had come from all over the world, but none had been able to cure her. In his desperation the king had it announced that whoever cured the princess would be married to her, and would also receive half of the kingdom.

When Samuel heard this, he decided at once to bring about her cure. He quickly built a house near the palace, and on the door he hung a sign that identified him as a doctor. And when the messengers of the king passed the house and saw the sign, they came to the young doctor, whom no one, of course, recognized, and asked him if he was wise enough to cure the princess. Samuel told them that this indeed was the case, and he assured them that he could put a quick end to her long coma.

So it was that the next day Samuel went to the palace and when he arrived he was brought to the king at once. The king was surprised to see such a young doctor, but he was not about to turn down any possible cure. Then Samuel was taken into the presence of the princess, who slept on her bed with all the signs of life, although she was very pale. She was just as beautiful as ever, as if she had not aged, but she could not be awakened. So Samuel went about his work and took out a handful of the leaves of the giant tree and boiled them in water. And when the steam of the boiling water had filled the room, the princess breathed it in and began to stir. All of a sudden her eyes opened, and she smiled. And all who were present let out a cry of delight, for the princess had been brought out of her endless sleep. Then Samuel offered her a long wooden spoon full of the cool boiled water, and put it near her lips. And after she had swallowed it the princess regained her color and was no longer as pale as death. Then she sat up and looked at the handsome doctor, and in that moment she lost her heart to him.

So it was that soon the wedding between the young doctor and the princess took place, attended by everyone in the city. Never had there been a wedding such as that, and the people spoke of it for years to come. And after the wedding Samuel revealed his true identity to the king and his bride. At first they refused to believe what he said, but after he described every detail of his quest, and of the long years he had spent in the wilderness, they realized that what he said must be true. Then the king asked if Moses had solved the riddle, since the king and his advisers had considered it to have no solution. Samuel then told them what Moses had said: that the garden which could contain the world was this world, since this world is God's garden. And the king was so moved by the wisdom of the reply that he decided then and there to become a Jew, and the princess also chose to make this her faith.

So it was that the king and his son-in-law Samuel began to study the Torah together every day. And from its holy words the king drew the wisdom to guide him in his judgments, so that his rulings were just and merciful. And when the king's life came to an end, Samuel and the princess ascended to the throne and ruled the kingdom together. Their love for each other was legendary, and they were the wisest rulers since the days of Joseph in Egypt, and the finest leaders since the days of Moses the Redeemer himself.

—Morocco: oral tradition

11. The Golden Tree

ne of the emperors of India had five wives. Four of them each bore him a son, but the fifth, the youngest and most beautiful of all, was childless. The other wives took every opportunity to insult her because of this, and to incite the emperor against her, so that she might be banished. For a long time they did not succeed, because the emperor greatly loved this wife. But in the end they harped on it so often that his resistance broke down, and he agreed to their demands. So he banished his youngest wife, and sent her from the palace alone, without providing her with any silver or gold or the least amount of food or water.

In great shame the queen left the capital of that kingdom, and walked wherever her legs carried her. In this way she came at last to a dense forest. She roamed there a whole day without food to eat or a drop of water to drink, and in the evening she began to be afraid. With the last of her strength she climbed a tall tree in order to protect herself from beasts of prey, but because of her hunger and fear she could not fall asleep. When at last the dawn appeared, she was exhausted and barely managed to climb down from the tree. She tried to walk, but after an hour she felt ill and sat down to rest. Suddenly she heard a rustling in the trees and there appeared before her an aged wanderer. The queen panicked and started to flee, but the old man said: "Why are you afraid? I will not harm you." Then the queen, who had no strength left, stopped and burst into tears.

"Don't cry, my daughter," said the old man. "My home is not far from here. There you can rest undisturbed and eat as much as you like. I am poor, but the forest has always supplied me with all I need."

The young queen looked at the old man, and she saw that his eyes were clear and honest, and that his face had a light of its own, and she agreed to follow him. Less than an hour later they arrived at a hut that looked miserable from the outside, but inside it was neat and clean. The old man quickly gave the queen water to drink and to bathe in, and then bread to eat and wine to drink. The queen ate, drank, and fell asleep. And while she slept she dreamed she was walking in a beautiful garden, where there was a lovely pool surrounding a golden tree. She gazed at the golden tree with wonder, for she had never seen anything like it in her life. The leaves were of the thinnest gold, resembling the leaves of no other tree, and the blossoms on it were clusters of diamonds that lit up the surroundings with a strong and beautiful light. While the queen gazed at the tree she noticed an old man approaching her, who wore white robes, and it was the same old man who had helped her in the forest. When he stood before her, the old man handed her a golden amulet on a chain, and that amulet was in the shape of a golden tree. Without their exchanging any words, the queen understood that the amulet was meant for her, and she took it and placed it around her neck. Then she awoke.

The queen did not know how long she had slept, but when she opened her eyes she was astounded to find she was still wearing the amulet of the golden tree—she had received it in her dream. Then she understood that the old man, who sat in the next room praying, had been sent to guide and protect her, and she was no longer afraid. "Good morning, dear father!" she said to the old man.

"Good morning," he replied. "Come, let us eat."

The queen came to the table, which she found set with all kinds of foods of the forest. Then she ate a meal of tender greens and various nuts and berries, and she was surprised to find that each of them was as tasty as the delicacies that had been prepared in the palace, while the water of the stream had a rich taste almost like that of wine. After they had eaten, the old man asked the queen to tell him about herself. She then told him about how the other wives of the emperor had conspired against her because she was childless, and how the king had banished her because of this. She added that it was all the more unjust because, according to the signs, she was pregnant.

"Stay here until the king realizes his error and his recklessness," said the old man. And the queen agreed to stay.

So it was that she spent her days living in that hut, gathering nuts and berries with the old man, and assisting him in his work—for this old man was a masterful craftsman, who created beautiful objects out of gold and other precious metals, which he himself mined from a rich lode in a cave he knew of in that forest. So too did he purify the metals himself, and cast them into treasures of many sizes and shapes. But the most beautiful of all were those he fashioned in the shape of a golden tree, like the amulet of the queen. The queen watched the old man work with fascination, and greatly admired his creations. But she wondered how the old man sold his treasures, for she never saw him leave the forest, and why, since he was such a great craftsman, he remained so poor. At last she asked him about this, and he said: "I do not create these objects to be sold. Rather, when I have finished one, I beat it down and begin again. For it is the creating that matters to me, and nothing else."

At last, when the time came, the queen gave birth to a healthy and handsome son. Her joy and that of the old man, whom she called "Grandfather," was great indeed. And it was on the night the child was born that the emperor had for the first time a vivid dream in which he found himself standing beside a golden tree. And the leaves of that tree looked like beaten gold, its blossoms were clusters of diamonds, and its trunk was the purest gold he had ever seen. The emperor caught his breath and came closer to the tree, and there in the golden trunk he saw the reflection of the queen whom he had banished from his sight. Then he was filled with remorse at having sent her away, for he understood that she had been precious to him, and he tried to take hold of the trunk. But as soon as he touched it, it disappeared, and he awoke.

Now when the emperor awoke from this dream he was filled with grief—for the loss of both his queen and the golden tree. The dream continued to haunt him all day, and that night the dream recurred. Once again he saw the reflection of the banished queen in the trunk of the golden tree, but the instant he tried to grasp it, it was gone. After that the dream came back every night, haunting the emperor. At last he called in his vizier, and ordered him to bring all of the dream interpreters in the kingdom to the palace, so that he might know what this dream meant. But when the emperor met with the dream interpreters, he found they were divided as to the meaning of the dream.

Some of them thought the dream revealed how much the emperor longed for his banished wife. They suggested he send messengers throughout the kingdom to search for her and to bring her back, for if he did, the dream would surely stop haunting him.

But other dream interpreters felt that the king need only command his goldsmith to recreate the golden tree, that he might make it his own, and in this way he would be freed from the recurring dream.

Finally, there were those among the dream interpreters who insisted that no such simple solution would suffice and that the emperor must set out alone in search of that golden tree and find it for himself.

Now the emperor hoped that he might succeed in finding his banished queen, for he greatly longed for her, and was deeply ashamed of what he had done. Therefore he sent messengers throughout the kingdom to announce that he was seeking her, and that she was welcome to return. But these messengers failed to find the queen, and returned empty-handed, and the king began to fear that the queen might have starved or otherwise met her death, and he was filled with grief. Meanwhile the dream of the golden tree in which he saw the reflection of the queen continued to torment him every night, so that he woke up shaking and covered with sweat. For every time he reached out for that golden tree it vanished and always continued to elude him.

Then the king ordered the gold to be brought from his treasury, and the golden bracelets of his wives to be collected as well—for he was angry with his wives for having convinced him to expel the youngest queen. He had all of this gold melted down, and had his goldsmith attempt to create a golden sculpture like that of the golden tree. And even though this goldsmith was known to be the greatest in all the kingdom, the tree he created failed to resemble that of the emperor's dream, and he ordered that it be melted down, and that the goldsmith create it again. When this was repeated three times, without success, the emperor concluded that the goldsmith could not duplicate the golden tree of his dreams. Nor did his creations cause the nightmare—for that is how he had come to think of it—to end.

At last, out of desperation, the emperor announced that he would give half of his kingdom to whoever could help him find that golden tree. Many days passed, and no one was able to help him, for none knew of such a golden tree. Then the emperor fell ill because of his bitterness, and he finally concluded that he must undertake the quest to find the golden tree himself, as the last group of dream interpreters had advised him. His sons, the princes, offered to undertake the search for him, but he insisted that he alone would undertake the quest. And that is what the emperor did—leaving the eldest prince in charge of the kingdom until he returned, and disguising himself as a beggar, so as not to attract robbers, he set off on the long journey by himself. For he knew he would have no peace until he had found the golden tree for himself, and held it in his grasp.

So it was that the emperor traveled throughout the kingdom, and everywhere he went he asked if anyone knew of such a tree. But no one had ever even heard of it, and all his efforts were in vain. After many months had passed, he despaired of ever finding the golden tree, and thought of returning home, resigned to being cursed with the recurring dream until the end of his days. Then, as he traveled through the forest, he saw an aged wayfarer, and decided to ask him if perhaps he had ever heard of the golden tree. The old man nodded in reply, and said: "First come home with me, to rest from your journey. Then shall we speak of the blessed golden tree."

Now in the hut of the old man the emperor saw a woman, whose face was hidden behind a veil, and with her was a young child, but he did not recognize them as the queen and his son. Of course, the queen recognized her husband, even though he was disguised as a beggar, but she did not reveal herself, nor their son. The emperor joined them for a meal, and afterward the old man said: "The golden tree you are seeking can only be found in this vast forest. To reach it you must continue to walk in the forest until you come to a large river, deep and wide. Follow that stream until it becomes a river and its waters grow warm. Keep following it until you reach its source. There you will find the golden tree. But take heed—as you come closer to the source, the waters of that river will grow turbulent and boiling hot, for they emerge from a great fountain that has its source deep within the earth. And the golden tree grows within that fountain, surrounded by it on all sides. Many have tried to reach it, but all have failed and drowned in the boiling waters. But if you take my shoes, and wear them when you enter the waters, the heat of the waters will have no effect. Then you may succeed where others have failed, but if you make use of my shoes, be certain to return them to me, for if you do not the golden tree will be lost to you once more." Then the old man took off his shoes and gave them to the emperor, who thanked the old man many times, and promised to return the shoes as soon as his mission was complete. Then he tied the shoes to his waist, to wear only when he reached the source of the river, and he set out to continue his quest.

Before he had traveled very far, the emperor came upon the stream the old man had described, and followed it until it turned into a river, and he followed that river as its waters grew warmer and more wild. And at the same time the forest grew more dense, and the ground became warm beneath his feet as he made his way through the thicket that covered the banks of the river. But even though he had to struggle to make his way, he did not think of turning back.

At last the emperor reached the river's source, where the waters rose up as high as a house, and gave off great clouds of steam, which covered the entire area in a thick fog. And when he saw how wild the waters were, he lost heart, for he was certain they could never be crossed. Still, he held out hope that the sandals the old man had given him might make it possible to reach the golden tree, which could faintly be seen through the heavy fog as a bright light glowing from within the fountain.

Then the emperor put on the old man's sandals and stepped into the waters. Then, instead of being hot, the waters were cool to his touch, and the fog disappeared. Now, too, he saw the golden tree revealed before him, in the very center of the fountain, even more beautiful than it had appeared in his dreams. And when he slipped into the waters, he found that he could not sink in them below his waist, and in this way he floated to the fountain, carried by the currents, until at last he was swept into the fountain itself, where he found a circular rock on which to stand, surrounded by a wall of gushing water.

There, in that sacred circle, the emperor saw the golden tree face to face, as had happened so often in his dreams. But now he was astounded to discover that the golden tree was not a motionless object created out of gold, but was itself a golden fountain that sprang up in that place, with molten gold that formed the shape of a golden tree. And with a strange certainty, an intuition that came to him from nowhere, the emperor reached out and grasped the molten trunk of the golden fountain, and it did not burn his hands, nor did it disappear. Instead, a portion of it solidified at his touch, as long as his outstretched arm. Then, with the golden tree firmly in his grasp, the emperor stepped out of the fountain, and slipped back into the currents, where he found the gold to be weightless, so that it floated like a log. Then, as he floated away, he looked back and saw for the last time the golden glow formed from the light of the molten tree, and he understood that the golden fountain never stopped flowing, but that it formed another golden tree every instant. And all of those trees were different, but at the same time they all had the same essential form, and he marveled at the infinite shapes that a golden tree could take. Then he returned his gaze to the golden tree that carried him through those waters, and he saw that it too had retained the essential form of the molten tree, even though the gold had hardened, and he knew that he had finally resolved the dream that had haunted him for so long.

At last, when the emperor emerged from the fog with the golden tree in his hand, it took on its proper weight. Exhausted, he sat down on the bank of the river and examined his treasure. Then it happened, to his amazement, that he saw in it the reflection of the banished queen, and once again he was grieved at her loss. Finally he arose and used all of his strength to carry the golden tree back downstream, until he reached the hut of the old man. For he did not doubt that if he failed to return the shoes of the old man, the golden tree would be lost to him again, this time for good. And when he entered the hut, bearing the wondrous treasure in his hands, the old man and the boy marveled at it, and even the queen examined it through her veil. Then the emperor thanked the old man for all he had done for him, and out of his remaining grief over what he had done to his queen, he confessed to the old man about how he had banished her, and how he rued the day he had given in to his wicked wives. It was then that the queen lifted her veil, and the emperor found himself face to face with his youngest wife again at last, and he also saw the amulet of the golden tree that she wore. Then he prostrated himself at her feet, and begged for her forgiveness, and for her to return with him to the palace. And when the queen saw how bitterly he regretted banishing her, she accepted his apologies. Then she introduced him to the child, their son, about whom he had never known. The king was overwhelmed at his good fortune, for all that he had sought after had been given to him at the same time.

The next morning the emperor and the queen and their son took their leave of the old man with many fond farewells and set off to return to the palace. And when the emperor went to pick up the golden tree, he discovered that it had become almost weightless and that he could carry it without effort. When they had returned, the emperor wasted no time, but quickly divorced his other wives, and treated the queen with the greatest love and respect. As for the golden tree, he planted it in the royal garden outside their window, where their son often played.

—India: oral tradition

12. The Mute Princess

n a certain kingdom there was a beautiful princess who never spoke to anyone. She was so silent that many people assumed she was mute. But her father, the king, was certain that she could speak, but that she had chosen, for reasons of her own, to remain silent. Thus when suitors came to ask for her hand in marriage, the king permitted them to meet her on the following condition: "You have one evening to spend with my daughter. If in that time you succeed in getting her to speak, even if it is only one word, then she shall be your bride. But if you fail—you will be hanged on the gallows at dawn." Still, there had been many young men who boasted that they could win the heart of the princess and open her lips, but she kept silent in their presence, as verified by a witness who remained with them, and in the end they lost their lives.

Now in another country there lived a prince who was both handsome and wise. One day this prince said to his father: "I wish to set out to wander in the land, to learn the ways of man and to amass wisdom and knowledge." The king replied: "You may set out, if you wish to, my son. For surely you shall be a better ruler once you have become more familiar with the ways of the world. But you must return before the end of a year."

So the prince set out on his travels with his father's blessings. And in his wanderings he learned many things, and became skilled in many tasks. But never did he stay in any one place too long, for he wanted to see as much of the world as he could before it was time to return from his travels. In this way he arrived at the kingdom of the mute princess, and when he heard of the king's challenge to make the princess speak, he desired to seek her hand for himself.

Therefore the prince came before the king, who admired the young man, and tried to warn him against the danger. But the prince accepted the condition, even though his life was at stake. That evening he joined the princess in her chamber, in the company of a faithful witness. The prince, the princess, and the witness all sat in the room and were silent, for the prince did not even attempt to strike up a conversation with the princess, and this astonished her, for all the previous suitors had kept trying to make her speak.

After an hour's silence, the prince turned to the witness and said: "Let us speak, in order to pass the time, for tomorrow I will be hanged."

The witness replied: "I am not permitted to speak to you or to say anything. I am only a witness whose job it is to listen."

Then the prince said: "And if I were to ask you something, would you reply?"

"Perhaps I would and perhaps I wouldn't," said the witness.

"Well, in that case," said the prince, "listen carefully. Three men—a carpenter, a tailor, and a *maggid*—were traveling together and came to a desolate wilderness, and when night fell they made a campfire and prepared to sleep. But for safety's sake they decided that each one of them would stand guard for a third of the night. The carpenter would take the first shift, the tailor the second, and the *maggid* the third.

"So it was that the carpenter stood watch while his companions slept. In order to pass the time, he took a piece of wood from a nearby tree, and carved a statue of a girl. By the time he finished the carving, his shift was over, and he woke the tailor to take over while he slept."

"The tailor awoke and rubbed his eyes, and when he had wiped the sleep away he saw the lovely statue the carpenter had made. And because he liked it very much, he decided to dress it in suitable garb. So he did. He took out his work tools and some pieces of cloth, made a dress, and put it on the statue, and the clothes gave the statue the appearance of life. When he had finished his work he saw that it was time to wake the *maggid*. He woke him and went back to sleep. The *maggid* arose and saw the statue of the girl and was startled, for it had been carved so well, it seemed to be alive. But after he touched it he understood it was the workmanship of his two companions. He said to himself: 'The statue is so perfect, it would be fit for God to breathe the breath of life into it.'"

"Then the *maggid* stood and prayed, and call upon the Creator of all to bless the girl with the breath of life. And the Creator of the universe heard his prayer, and turned the statue into a living, life-size human being."

"When the carpenter and the tailor awoke the next morning, and saw that the statue had become a living girl, each man said: 'She belongs to me.'"

"The carpenter said: 'I made her and molded her and gave her shape, therefore I have the greatest right to her.'"

"The tailor said: 'I dressed her, and my contribution to her human appearance is greater than yours.'"

"The *maggid* said: 'I prayed and asked for life to be breathed into her, and that is the main thing; therefore, she belongs to me.'"

Then the prince who had told this story to the witness said: "So, the question is, who do you think has the greatest right to the girl?"

"It is a difficult question, and I can't decide it now," said the witness. "Tomorrow I will put it before our men of judgment, and they will decide."

"You forget," said the prince, "that tomorrow I will no longer be alive. For I will be hanged before I hear the verdict."

Then the princess, who had listened to the tale with great interest, could no longer remain indifferent to this matter of justice. She spoke up and said: "The right of the *maggid* is the greatest, and therefore the girl should go with him, for it is he who caused her to be given life, and that was decisive in her creation."

"Thank you, princess," said the prince, bowing to her. "I am persuaded that your verdict is the just one."

The next morning the executioner came at dawn and started to drag the prince to the gallows despite his protests, for the executioner assumed that the princess had remained silent, as she always did. It was only when the witness intervened and confirmed that the princess had indeed spoken that the execution was put off, and the young man brought before the king.

"I find it difficult to believe that my daughter has broken her silence after all this time," said the king. "But we'll give you the benefit of the doubt, and allow you to spend another night with her, in the presence of two reliable witnesses, and we'll see what happens."

The second evening, when the four of them sat together, the prince and the princess and the two witnesses, the prince said to the witnesses: "Tell us a tale to while away the time, for tomorrow I shall die."

The witnesses said: "We will not speak, for we are only witnesses, and our job is to listen and remain silent."

"In that case," said the prince, "will you reply if I ask you something?"

"Perhaps . . ." they replied.

Then the prince said: "Three companions climbed together to the top of a mountain. One of them had a magic jewel through which he could see to the ends of the earth. Another had a flying carpet, and the third had a potion with which to revive the dead.

"The one with the magic jewel looked through it and saw in a faraway land a great crowd following a coffin to a grave site. And when he told his companions what he saw, the one with the flying carpet said: 'Get on the carpet quickly and we will attend the funeral, for it must have been a great man who has died.'

"The three friends sat down on the magic carpet, and in the wink of an eye it carried them where they wanted to go. And after they joined the procession, they asked the mourners who had died and why there was such sorrow. The mourners told them that the king's fair and lovely daughter had died while still very young. And when the three heard this, they made their way to the king and said: 'We can revive your daughter, sire.' The grieving king replied: 'Whoever can revive my daughter shall have her for a bride.'

"Then the one with the magic potion stood near the girl's body and sprinkled the potion on her, and all at once she began to breathe. But after she had been revived, and embraced her father and mother amid great rejoicing, the three men began to argue over her.

"The one with the magic jewel said: 'If it were not for me, the princess would have been buried and not have been revived, for it is I who saw the funeral procession. Since she was saved because of me, she belongs to me.'

"The owner of the flying carpet said: 'If it were not for my magic carpet, which carried us a great distance as fast as lightning, we would not have arrived in time to revive the girl. Therefore she should be my bride.'

"Then the one who had brought the magic potion said: 'If it were not for my potion, the princess would now be in her grave, so I have a greater right to her than either of you.' "

Then the prince who had told this story asked the witnesses for their decision, but they said: "It is a difficult matter which we cannot decide by ourselves. Tomorrow we will ask the judges for their verdict."

"But I am to be hanged at dawn," said the prince, "and I will go to my grave without knowing the your answer."

Here the princess intervened and said: "I will reply to your question. I believe that the man who revived the princess with his magic potion should receive her as his bride, for without his potion she could not have been revived."

Then the prince thanked the princess, and agreed that she was correct.

The next day, at dawn, the executioner again arrived and began to drag the prince away, but the witnesses stopped him and said: "The princess spoke to the young man, and he does not deserve to die."

Now when the king heard the witnesses, he did not believe his ears: "It can't be that my daughter has finally spoken after having remained silent for so long. But since I have some doubt about it, let us have a third and final test, this time in the presence of three reliable witnesses."

And on the third evening the prince asked the three witnesses to tell him a tale to pass the time, but they refused. Then he said to them: "And if I ask you something, will you be so kind as to reply?" "Perhaps . . ." they said.

So the prince began another tale: "Three people were walking together—a nobleman, his wife, and a servant. Evening drew near, and the sun went down, and the three were compelled to spend the night in a remote field. During the night they were attacked by highwaymen, who robbed them and beheaded the nobleman and the servant, and his wife alone escaped. She sat down and wept and waited for daylight.

"Meanwhile she heard two owls conversing in the branches of a tree. One said: 'Oh, my, what a terrible thing has happened to the poor nobleman and his servant, and now the nobleman's wife is very miserable.'

"'Yes,' said the second owl, but if someone were to take some leaves from this tree, pound them, squeeze out their juice, and sprinkle it on the bodies, the dead men would surely be revived.'

"Now when the woman heard this, she hastened to pick some leaves of that tree and crushed and squeezed them, as the owls had said. Then she put the decapitated heads next to the bodies and sprinkled them with the fluid, and they were revived. But when it was daylight, the woman saw that she had made a terrible mistake: she had connected the nobleman's head to the servant's body, and the servant's head to the nobleman's body, and the error could not be corrected.

"The two men began to argue over the woman. The noble man's head, connected to the servant's body, said: 'She is my wife and I am her husband, as my face reveals.' And the servant's head, connected to the nobleman's body, said: 'She is my wife, as my body clearly shows.'

"The question is this," said the prince to the three witnesses. "To whom does the woman belong, to the nobleman's head connected to the servant's body, or to the servant's head connected to the nobleman's body?"

The witnesses said: "It is too complicated a matter for us to decide. It can be solved only by men of judgment."

At this point the princess broke in, for she could not contain herself any longer, and she said: "The woman belongs to the nobleman's head connected to the servant's body, for the head is the repository of all memory and knowledge, and it can be seen by all, whereas the rest of the body is covered with clothing."

The prince said: "Thank you, your highness, for your excellent reply, which is surely correct. Now, let us sleep and await tomorrow."

The next day the three witnesses testified that the princess had indeed spoken to the prince, and no one could still doubt it. Then the king arranged a lavish wedding for the princess and prince, and she returned with the prince to his country with a royal salute. So it was that the prince and princess lived together in love all the days of their lives. And the prince often entertained his wife with tales, and the princess did not hesitate to speak the words of love she felt for him.

—Yemen: oral tradition

13. The Enchanted Journey

nce it happened that the holy sage Rabbi Adam, who had powers equal to those of the greatest sorcerer, looked into his magic mirror and saw a faraway kingdom where evil ministers were going to pressure its king to sign a wicked decree against the Jews that very day. The decree had already been written, and all that remained was to have the king sign it and affix his royal seal. Then Rabbi Adam, who had at his command many great powers, took down a bottle of ink from the shelf and poured a small amount into the palm of his hand, forming a mirror. After this he unfolded from a prayer book the paper on which he had written the Name of God. And at that moment every shadow and every echo disappeared, and everything became bright. And when he looked into the mirror, he saw the room in which the evil ministers were meeting with the king at that very moment, and with his eyes fixed on that scene, Rabbi Adam pronounced God's secret Name.

A moment later Rabbi Adam appeared before the king and his ministers, a most dignified visitor. All were greatly surprised, and could not imagine how he could have entered the palace, especially since the ministers had left strict orders that no one else was to be admitted to the king. So great was their astonishment that they were speechless, and did not think to object when Rabbi Adam said: "I must have a word with the king." Instead, they all moved aside to let him pass, and he accompanied the king outside that room into the palace garden.

Now the king was very curious to know what it was that the old man wanted to see him about, but Rabbi Adam refused to say anything until they reached the well. There he motioned for the king to look down, and when he did, the king saw on the surface of the water an image of a ship standing ready to sail. The king could not understand how such an image was possible in a well, and he raised his eyes to ask Rabbi Adam about this. But when he did, the king found himself standing on a dock before the very ship he had just seen reflected in the well. The king was dumbstruck, and whirled around to look for the palace, but it was nowhere to be found. Instead, there was a vast wilderness behind him. The king's heart sank when he saw this, and he grew very afraid. Just then he saw that the ship was about to cast off, and he ran to board it as fast as he could and reached it only a moment before it set sail.

The king sailed on that ship for several weeks, but he was unable to speak with any of the passengers, for he did not know their language. At last the ship arrived in the port of a beautiful city, and all of the passengers disembarked, and so too did the king. He wandered from street to street, observing the city with fascination, amazed by the beauty of the place. Now and then he would approach a passerby and ask him for the name of the city, but in vain, for no one understood him.

After he had walked for some time, the king reached an inn and realized that he desired to refresh himself. But when he entered the inn and tried to speak to the innkeeper, he found that no one spoke his language. Unable to make himself understood, the king left the inn hungry and disappointed, and wandered around the streets and markets. "What shall I do?" the king thought. "I must find someone to whom I can speak, or I shall die of hunger." Then he saw a boy in the street, and tried to explain his situation to him, but again they were not able to communicate.

Suddenly the king saw someone he thought he recognized. It was a Jewish musician who had once tutored his daughter, the princess, in the playing of musical instruments. "He will surely help me," the king thought, greatly relieved at having found someone he knew. And the musician did recognize the king at once, although he was amazed to find him there, especially since that country and the king's were at war. He greeted the king, and asked him how he had come to be there. And then, speaking in a rush of words, the king told the musician what had happened to him, and begged him for something to eat. The musician took the king to his home, and saw to it that he received a fine meal. After that he invited the king to stay in his home, for there was nowhere else for him to go. At first the king thought that he would set sail immediately for his own kingdom, but when he discovered that the country he was in was at war with his own, and that no ships were allowed to sail there, he was terrified. For he knew that if his true identity became known to the authorities, his life would be in extreme danger.

Now the king was not a foolish man, and when he realized that the war could last for many years, he understood that he must try to make a new home in this kingdom, and that he must also keep his identity hidden. In order not to attract attention to himself, he decided to dress as a Jew, and to learn Jewish customs and beliefs.

Days passed, and the king was surprised to discover that he greatly enjoyed his study of the Torah and the other sacred texts. He decided eventually that he wanted to become a Jew, and had himself circumcised. The family of the musician was very proud of him, and prepared a festive meal in his honor. So it was that the king continued his diligent studies until he acquired a vast knowledge of the Torah, and before long his great knowledge became recognized, and he was numbered among the finest Jewish scholars. Many important men desired him for a son-in-law, and he finally married the daughter of a wealthy man. He became the father of three sons, whom he raised in the spirit of the Torah and dearly loved.

Seven years passed, and then it happened that the princess of this kingdom became very sick, and none of the doctors in the land were able to cure her. In desperation her father, the king, commanded the Jews to find a way to save her, or else they would all lose their lives. The Jews turned to their wisest men for help, and when they met to discuss what could be done, the exiled king offered to try to heal the princess, although he did not know how.

He left for the palace, and when he arrived he was taken before the king of that kingdom, who warned him again that if he failed to cure her, he and all the rest of the Jews would be doomed. Then he was taken to the room of the princess. There he examined her and found she had an abscess that had formed in her throat, which was slowly choking her to death. And when he saw this, he grew greatly afraid, for he did not know what to do next. But as always, since he had become a Jew, he put his faith in God, and he decided to pray. So he put on his tallit and tefillin, and stood in a corner and prayed for God's help.

Now the princess had never before seen anyone dressed that way, and she thought it was very funny. She began to laugh, and she laughed so hard that the swelling in her throat broke open and her life was saved. And when her father, the king, found out that this had happened, he was overjoyed, and he told the Jew that he could name his reward. So it was that the exiled king had two requests. First, he asked that the king sign a decree promising the Jews protection during all the rest of his reign; and second, he asked for a ship for himself and his family, stocked with provisions, on which they could set sail. The princess's father gladly agreed to these requests, and signed the decree at once and had it announced in public.

Not long afterward the exiled king and his new family took leave of all their fellow Jews and set sail on a voyage for the kingdom he had left behind. For he had long ago revealed to his family his true identity, and they had agreed to accompany him on the voyage there, so that he could resume his life as king. But after they had sailed for three weeks a great storm arose, and the ship sank. Everyone was drowned except for the king, who swam toward a distant shore. He swam for hours and finally arrived exhausted at an island. There he threw himself upon the ground and began to weep over the loss of his family.

As he lay there weeping, the king suddenly heard a voice above him. Looking up, he found himself in his palace garden, beside the well. Next to him stood Rabbi Adam, who said: "It is time for you to return to the palace, O king. Your ministers have been waiting for you for more than two hours."

When he heard this and saw where he was, the king was greatly confused, for he could understand neither how he had gotten there, nor what the old man was talking about. He knew that he had not been gone two hours, but more than seven years, and just now he had lost the family that he had so loved.

Then the king stood up and hurried into the palace, where he found his ministers all together, as he had left them so long ago. He began to tell them all that had happened to him, but they stood there dumbfounded, with looks of confusion on their faces. At last one of them found the courage to speak, and said: "But just two hours ago Your Majesty left the palace with the old man, and walked into the garden. What has happened to cause you to lose all sense of time and imagine that seven years have passed?" And the king was at a loss for words, for he did not understand what had occurred.

Then the king looked up and saw that Rabbi Adam was still standing in the garden. He rushed outside and came to him and said: "If you can explain what has happened, please tell me at once, for my life has been turned upside down."

Then Rabbi Adam said: "It is true that you were away from the palace for only two hours. Everything that happened to you was a vision I showed you, so that you would understand the full implications of the wicked decree against the Jews that you were about to sign."

When the king heard this, he was seized with fear and trembling, and he understood that the vision had showed him the true ways of the Jews, which were not at all like what the evil ministers had told him. And although the experiences of the seven years were still vivid in his mind, and his love and admiration of the Jews unchanged, he found that he had forgotten all of his knowledge of the Torah.

Then the king returned to the palace and commanded that the evil ministers all be arrested. And when this was done he signed a decree promising to protect the Jews during all of his reign, and gave it to Rabbi Adam. And after that the king sought out new ministers from among the Jews, and the lives of the Jews of that kingdom flourished, and they lived in peace.

—Eastern Europe: c. nineteenth century

14. The Magic Mirror of Rabbi Adam

Now Rabbi Adam possessed a magic mirror that had once belonged to King David, which permitted him to see things that took place all over the world, and he made it his task to watch over his fellow Jews in that mirror. One day Rabbi Adam looked into this magic mirror and saw that a Jew in a certain city was in mortal danger, although he had done nothing to deserve the fate that awaited him. When he saw this, Rabbi Adam resolved to do something to help this Jew, and he mounted his horse and pronounced a spell, so that the hooves of the horse flew along the ground without touching it, and before an hour had passed Rabbi Adam had arrived in the city of the Jew who was in danger.

As soon as he arrived, Rabbi Adam walked through the city, and saw its streets and markets, and they were crowded with man and beast like sand on the seashore. Rabbi Adam spoke to a man in the marketplace and asked: "Why are so many people all crowded together here?" And the man replied: "Throughout the year the city is quiet and subdued. Only for two weeks of the year does it seethe like a boiling pot, and merchants come here from all corners of the land to sell their wares. These days are the market days, and all the townspeople live for an entire year from the earnings of these two weeks."

Rabbi Adam came to a tavern, and found there many merchants who were eating and drinking, and among them a Jewish merchant from a nearby city. Rabbi Adam sat down beside him and turned to him and said: "Pay heed, for when four hours have passed you will be killed." Now the merchant thought that the old man was mad, so he did not even reply to him. He continued to eat delicacies and drink wine, and then he got up and went over to the men with whom he had traveled to the market, and told them what the old man had said. They laughed and told him not to pay attention to the words of a madman, and not to worry, for what he said was surely nonsense.

An hour later Rabbi Adam returned to the merchant and said: "Know that the hours of life you have left are only three." The merchant laughed at these words, and again told his friends, and they also laughed.

When he left the tavern, the merchant returned to the market and arranged his merchandise, and before long the old man appeared before him again and said: "One hour ago I spoke to you and your mouth was filled with laughter. Now there are only two hours left of your life." And when the merchant heard this, he grew afraid for the first time, and he went to his friends and told them of his fear. They said to him: "Why didn't you stop him before he left you, for perhaps he is plotting to kill you." Then the merchant said to them: "When he comes back to me again I will not let him go until he tells me everything, but I am convinced he intends me no harm."

An hour passed, and Rabbi Adam came to the merchant and said: "Know that in one hour you will leave this world." Then the merchant grabbed his arms and shouted: "I will not release you until you tell me who you are, and who it is that is plotting to kill me." The rabbi replied: "You have spoken truly, for there are those who are plotting to kill you. I have discovered this plot, and I have come here to save you from descending into the grave." And this time the merchant recognized that what Rabbi Adam said must be the truth, and he grew afraid for his life. Then he said: "If this is the case, tell me what I should do." And the rabbi said: "Come with me and do everything that I command." The merchant stood there as rigid as a statue, and then he said: "I am ready to follow you."

Rabbi Adam and the merchant walked together until they came to an inn. There Rabbi Adam said to the innkeeper: "How much do you earn a day at the inn?" "Twenty silver shekels a day" was the reply. "If that is so," said Rabbi Adam, "behold I am giving you twenty silver shekels on the condition that you do not allow anyone else to enter your inn for the rest of the day, neither to eat nor to drink. Nor must you allow any wagon drivers to rest in your courtyard."

The innkeeper heeded his words and closed the inn. After this Rabbi Adam turned to the servant of the inn, and requested that a bathtub be brought to the merchant's room, and that it be filled with water. The servant did as Rabbi Adam asked, and then Rabbi Adam commanded the merchant to climb into the tub. The merchant took off his clothes, and climbed in as he was commanded to do. Then Rabbi Adam took out his magic mirror and told the merchant to look within it and to tell him all that he saw. The merchant stretched out his hand and took the mirror and gazed into it, and a great terror descended upon him, and he was silent. Then Rabbi Adam said: "Did I not tell you to reveal to me all that you have seen? Speak!" After this the merchant said: "I see my wife in the company of a man of my town who is known as a sorcerer. They are sitting together, eating and drinking and hugging and kissing, and on the table is a bow and arrow."

Then Rabbi Adam said: "Know that your wife has betrayed you with the evil sorcerer, and even now they are plotting your death. The danger is very great, for the sorcerer has the powers of evil at his command. He is about to shoot an arrow from that bow, and the powers of evil will guide it to you so that it pierces your heart. And after your death the sorcerer and your wife will marry, and will live together without fear of any man. But with the help of God this evil plan will not succeed. Now look again and tell me what you see in the mirror."

The merchant gazed into the mirror again, and said: "Your words are true and correct. Now the sorcerer is making ready to shoot it with his own wicked hands."

Rabbi Adam then said to him: "Do not be afraid or let your heart be faint, for now there is no turning back. Watch carefully what he does, and when you see that he is about to shoot the arrow, then put your head under the water at once. For you must hold your breath and remain submerged until the arrow has passed by you and gone astray. Afterward I will signal for you to lift your head out of the water and sit up." And this is what the merchant did, and a few seconds after he was submerged in the water, a sound was heard in the room like the hissing of an arrow, and when Rabbi Adam signaled him, the merchant lifted his head out of the water. Then Rabbi Adam had him look into the mirror once more, and asked him what he saw, and the merchant replied: "I see my wife and she is in a black mood, and the spirit of the sorcerer is raging within him."

Then Rabbi Adam said: "Good! Now continue to watch closely, and if he sends forth another arrow, do as you did the first time." And when the merchant saw the sorcerer readying the arrow to be shot, he immersed himself fully in the water, and again saved his life.

After this Rabbi Adam said to him: "Peer once more into the looking glass, and tell me what you see." And the merchant gazed into the mirror, and saw that his wife was unhappy and that the sorcerer's anger had become like a sea that could not be calmed. He reported this to Rabbi Adam, who said to him: "Look directly at him in the mirror, and if you see that he is going to attempt this evil deed a third time, do as I commanded you at first, but this time while you are submerged extend the little finger of your right hand out of the water."

Once more the merchant looked into the mirror of Rabbi Adam, and once more he saw the sorcerer take up the bow and arrow. Then he immersed himself in the water, but left the tip of his little finger exposed, just as Rabbi Adam had commanded. And as he was holding his breath under water he felt a sharp pain in his finger, and his hand fell back into the water. After this he lifted up his head, and the rabbi gave him the mirror to look into again. Gazing into the mirror, the merchant said: "Now I see that the sorcerer and my wife are rejoicing." And Rabbi Adam said: "That is because they have been deceived into thinking that they have succeeded in killing you, for your little finger stopped the enchanted arrow, and did not permit it to pass through the inn as it did the first two times. Now you can come out of the tub and put on your clothes. So far you have been saved, but danger still hovers over your head. Still, do not be afraid, just do as I tell you to do and your life will be saved." And the merchant left the tub and got dressed, as the rabbi had directed.

The next day the merchant intended to return to his own city, for the market days had ended. But Rabbi Adam said to him: "You may return to your city, but when you get there do not go to your own house. Go instead to that of relatives, and dwell there in secret. After three weeks have passed go forth from that house and go to the market. Remain there until the sorcerer sees you. Go up to him and greet him and reply truthfully to any questions that he may ask. Do not hesitate to tell him about me, and if he wants to know where I can be found, tell him that I am willing to stand in his presence to test whose powers are stronger. He will surely not decline this challenge, for he is confident of his powers. Then fix a place and time, and I will meet him there."

The merchant did as Rabbi Adam had commanded. He traveled to his home town, but when he arrived there he dwelt in secret in the house of a relative. When three weeks had passed he left the house and walked to the market in the center of town. Before he had been there very long he saw the sorcerer, who turned pale when he saw him, and approached the merchant and said: "It was said in town that you had gone to the grave." The merchant replied: "I was saved from an early grave." "Who saved you?" asked the sorcerer. "A fellow Jew saved me from the hands of those who sought to slay me." Then the sorcerer said: "Who is this man?" "A holy man, whose name is Rabbi Adam," said the merchant. Then the eyes of the sorcerer grew narrow, and he hissed: "If you do not bring this man before me, you are a dead man." And even though the evil sorcerer had revealed himself, the merchant remained calm and said: "Fix a time and a place, and I will send for him. You can be certain that he will meet you there." So it was that a meeting of the sorcerer and Rabbi Adam was set to take place in the sorcerer's home.

Now the evil sorcerer was so confident that he could defeat Rabbi Adam with his powers that he invited all the nobles of that province to witness the contest. And when the appointed hour had arrived, Rabbi Adam came there accompanied by the merchant, and they found many nobles in the house, who were eating and drinking at the sorcerer's table. One drunken noble said to Rabbi Adam: "Perform wonders for us, show us your powers!" And Rabbi Adam said: "I do not perform wonders, but I put my faith and trust in the Lord, whose powers have never failed me."

The nobles, who were not fond of Jews in the first place, did not like this reply. And they urged the sorcerer to begin the contest at once. The sorcerer complied by bringing out an empty bowl, into which he poured water. Then he passed his staff over it, and the water in the bowl vanished. The nobles gasped when they saw this, and the sorcerer passed the bowl around among them, so that they could confirm it was empty. Then, when they gave it back to him, the sorcerer passed his staff over it in the other direction, and the water reappeared, much to the amazement of the nobles.

Then the sorcerer, looking very smug, asked Rabbi Adam to perform the same feat. "Gladly," said Rabbi Adam. He stepped forward and passed his hand over the bowl of water, and again all the water disappeared. Then he passed the bowl around among the nobles, as the sorcerer had done, and when they saw that it was empty and returned it to him, he passed his hand over it in the other direction and it was filled again. But this time it was filled not with water, but with wine! The nobles were even more amazed at this, and the face of the sorcerer was pale with anger.

Then the sorcerer took down a cage in which he kept a dove. He opened the cage and took out the bird. Then he placed it on the table and passed his staff over it. All at once the dove collapsed, and lay there stiff and dead. Then the sorcerer passed his staff over it in the other direction, and the dove came back to life, flapping its wings. The nobles applauded when they saw this, and all were certain that Rabbi Adam could not duplicate this feat.

Then Rabbi Adam took his place before the dove, and passed his hand over it. Immediately the dove dropped to the table with a thump, its feet in the air. The nobles examined it and all agreed that it was surely dead. Then Rabbi Adam passed his hand over it in the other direction, and the wings of the dove began to flap, and it flew around the room. After this it landed on the table and, to the amazement of all, laid an egg. And only a moment later the egg broke open and a small fledgling inside it stretched its wings. And when the evil sorcerer saw this, a look of terrible hatred crossed his face. Then he said: "I am ready to perform one more wonder, which I am quite certain the Jewish magician cannot duplicate. But I must ask that he leave the room as I perform it, so that he does not overhear the spell that I pronounce."

Rabbi Adam departed from the room, and the sorcerer faced the nobles, his staff in his hand. He held his staff upright on the floor and pronounced a spell over it, and lo, the staff began to blossom and branch, and before long it produced green leaves and apples on the ends of the branches, which quickly grew ripe. The nobles were astonished at this wonder, and they applauded the sorcerer's accomplishment. Then the sorcerer bowed to the nobles and called Rabbi Adam into the room. And when he came in there, the sorcerer said: "Observe this tree and its delightful fruit. Now let us see how great is your power, and if you can cause the tree to wither, and become a staff once more." Then Rabbi Adam turned to the nobles and said: "Since the master of the house commanded me to leave the room when he performed this wonder, I request that he also depart from the room at this time." The nobles agreed that this was only proper, and they asked the sorcerer to leave the room until they called on him to return.

After the sorcerer left, Rabbi Adam walked around and around the tree, all the time remarking: "How good are these apples and how pleasant this tree!" As he was circling the tree, seven times in all, his eyes were fixed on an apple at the top of the tree which was exceptionally red, a delight to the eyes. He turned to the chief noble among them and said: "Honored sir, would you be so kind as to cut off this very red apple at the top of the tree?" The nobleman agreed to do this, took a knife, and cut off the desired apple and gave it to Rabbi Adam. And no sooner did he do this than the apples left on the tree began to wither, the leaves fell off, the branches withdrew, and the trunk withered until it was the staff that the sorcerer had begun with. All that remained was the apple in Rabbi Adam's hand, which had remained as ripe as ever.

After this Rabbi Adam commanded that the sorcerer be brought back into the room. One of the nobles went out to get him, and behold, he found the body of the sorcerer in one corner of the room, and his head in another. The nobles were greatly shocked at this turn of events, and they asked Rabbi Adam to explain. He said: "Whoever undertakes to perform magic puts his life at risk, for every wonder created contains one weakness, which can be the undoing of the person who has cast the spell. And in this case it was the apple at the top of the tree that was the one weakness."

Then the nobles sat in judgment over Rabbi Adam, to decide if he had sinned in bringing about the death of the sorcerer. They considered this matter for some time, and concluded that Rabbi Adam had only performed his part of the wonder, by returning the flourishing tree to a staff, and that it was the evil sorcerer's fault for putting himself at risk. The rabbi left the nobles with great honor, and they sent him home in peace.

And the merchant, who had witnessed all that had taken place, rejoiced greatly over the miracle, and thanked Rabbi Adam for saving him from the hands of the powerful sorcerer. But Rabbi Adam told him to give thanks to God, for all great miracles come from Him. After that the merchant went with his wife to a rabbinical court and divorced her. The wife left her husband's house, but in her heart were thoughts of repentance. She began to fast and pray, and eventually she returned to God with her whole heart. And the Lord, who does not desire the death of the wicked but only that they return to the ways of the righteous, accepted her repentance. But the evil sorcerer who sinned and led her to sin was lost and cut off from the earth for all time.

—Eastern Europe: c. nineteenth century

15. The King's Dream

here was once a king who oppressed the Jews of his kingdom with harsh decrees. And when the holy Rabbi Adam saw their plight and the cruel deeds of the king, he cast a deep slumber upon him, and caused him to dream. In the dream the king awoke and found that his palace had disappeared, along with everyone in it, and he was lying on his bed at the bottom of a pit. The pit was deep and dark, the smell was rancid, and the light of day was like a roof far above him. The king was overcome with terror, for he did not know what had happened, and he even feared that he might be dead.

Just then the bed on which the king lay began slowly to rise, hoisted up by a rope, until it reached the top of the pit. There the king saw the stern face of a soldier, who pulled the king off the bed and tied his arms and marched him away, without a word of explanation. The king did not understand what was happening to him, and he stumbled along behind the soldier until they reached a castle. There the soldier took him aside, and brought him before the lord of that castle, and told the lord that he had been found trespassing, and was suspected of being a spy. The king tried to explain that he was the ruler of a great kingdom, and that he had gone to sleep in his own bedchamber, but had somehow woken up in the deep pit where the soldier had found him.

There was laughter from all of those present. Then the face of the lord of the castle grew solemn, and he said: "It is well known that anyone who is caught trespassing in this kingdom is required to fulfill three demands of the person whose land he has trespassed upon. The penalty for failing to perform any one of these demands is death."

When he heard this, the king bowed his head and was silent. At last he found his voice, and said meekly; "What are the three demands?" "The first," said the lord of the castle, "is for you to empty all of the water out of the well in the garden by the break of day." And he handed the king a dipper, with which to empty the water. But when the king looked at that dipper, he saw that it had a hole in it, and could not hold water. Then he knew that a terrible curse had fallen upon him, and it appeared that his life was as good as lost.

"Take him to the well, to begin his work," said the lord of the castle. And the king was dragged of into the garden, and left alone beside the well. He lay there, stretched out on the ground, weeping over his fate, which he could not understand. He did not even try to draw up any of the water, for he knew it to be hopeless. Just then a figure emerged from the darkness and approached him. The king looked up and saw an old man with a long white beard standing above him. The old man said: "Why are you weeping?" And the king recognized that this man was not evil like the others he had met in that place, and he poured out his heart to him, and told him all that had happened.

After the king had finished telling his tale, the old man said: "How do you expect to empty the well if you do not begin to work?" And the king was confused, and he said: "Did I not tell you that the dipper has a hole in it?" "Is that true?" asked Rabbi Adam, for that is who it was. And he took the dipper in his hand and looked at it, and when he handed it back to the king, it was perfect once more, as if there had never been a hole in it. Then the king put the dipper into the well, and the water came rushing into it, and still it was not full. And even when the water ceased flowing, the dipper was not full, for Rabbi Adam had given it the fullness of the Lord, which is without limits. So it was that the king succeeded in emptying the well that night.

At dawn the lord of the castle arrived with many guards, certain that the king had not succeeded in performing the impossible task. Imagine his surprise when he peered down into the well and saw the muddy bottom, for it was completely empty, and even the spring, which had fed the well, had gone dry. The face of the king turned pale, and he said: "I do not know how you have accomplished this first task, but I doubt very much if you will complete the second."

"And what would that be?" asked the king. "Simply to build a palace of feathers by dawn tomorrow morning," said the lord of the castle. Then he laughed a terrible laugh, and left the desolate king alone in the garden.

Again the king slumped to the ground and cursed his fate. And as he lay there weeping, Rabbi Adam again approached him and said: "Why are you weeping?" The king told him the impossible task that the lord of the castle had given him. But Rabbi Adam told him not to lose hope, and took a whistle out of his pocket. He gave it to the king, and told him to blow on it. The king did so, and all at once there was the beating of a thousand wings all around them, and a flood of feathers began to fall at their feet. Nor did the feathers form uneven piles, but magically arranged themselves into a feather palace, with a fine foundation and many ramps and arches.

Now when dawn arrived, the evil lord of the castle came out to the garden, certain that he would put the king to death that day. But when he saw the magnificent feather palace, he could not believe his eyes. Then he looked for the king, but he could not find him. So he entered the feather palace, and there inside the bedroom chamber, sleeping on a feather bed, he found him. And when the lord of the castle saw this, he was enraged, and he said: "Wake up, my tired man. I see that you have worked hard all night. So I have decided to give you a long rest. Your task is really quite simple. In fact, anyone could do it. All that is required is that you let your fingernails grow, and cut them once in a while. And when you have filled up a snuffbox with your nail clippings, you shall have fulfilled the three tasks. But until then you must remain my prisoner!"

And the king, who had been deep asleep, sat up and listened to his terrible sentence. Then he heard a sound that made his blood run cold, and when he looked up he saw a dark metal box being dragged toward him. As he feared, it was a prison the evil lord had made for him. It had been constructed to the measurements of his body, and when he was inside it he could not move at all. There was only a small opening at the top of the box for the king to receive food and water.

So it was that the poor king was imprisoned in that metal prison, and once a day he was fed stale bread and a little water, and once a month the box was opened long enough for the nails of his hands to be cut, and the clippings were dropped into the snuffbox. In this way six terrible months passed, but even so the snuffbox was not even half full. Then one day, after the guard had departed, Rabbi Adam appeared and spoke to the king through the tiny opening in his metal prison. He said: "Would you like to get out once again into the light of day?"

"With joy and tears if only I could," said the king, who recognized Rabbi Adam's voice.

"And what would be my reward if I freed you?" asked Rabbi Adam. "I would give you half my kingdom," answered the king. "I do not ask for gold or power," said Rabbi Adam. "All I ask is that you sign a decree revoking the harsh decrees against the Jews, and affix your royal seal to it."

"Yes, yes," said the king, "I agree to sign it at once if you can only set me free." Rabbi Adam then touched the lock on the metal prison, and it sprang open, and he released the king. Then, after the king had signed the decree that Rabbi Adam had prepared, and affixed his seal to it, revoking the evil decrees against the Jews, Rabbi Adam gave him a new set of clothing, and led him to safety. Once they were far from the castle grounds, Rabbi Adam took him to an open field, and before long they reached the bed on which the king had been asleep when he had found himself in the pit.

Rabbi Adam directed the king to lie down on the bed, and when he did, Rabbi Adam lowered it into the pit. And the next thing the king knew was that he awoke and found himself in his palace chamber once more. Greatly relieved, he arose and called for his servants. But when they came in, he could not understand why they did not seem surprised to see him. Then he said: "Why don't you ask me how I am? Is there a single faithful servant left among you? Do you not wonder how I escaped after having been held captive for half a year?"

At last one of the servants found the courage to speak and said: "Surely the king must have had a dream, for the king's bodyguards stood guard at his door all night." The king could not understand how the servant could say this, and suddenly he caught sight of the snuffbox sitting on his dresser. He opened it and found that it was half full of nail clippings. This confirmed the events he had just experienced, and he chased the servants from the room. He paced back and forth, and thought of all that had happened to him. And when he remembered how Rabbi Adam had helped him so often, he cried aloud: "Of all the faithful servants in my household, is there not one who can serve me as the holy Jew did?"

Just then a horse-drawn coach approached the palace, and Rabbi Adam stepped out. The king recognized him at once and ran out to greet him. He embraced him and brought him into the palace. When they were both seated, with the servants standing around them, the king said to Rabbi Adam: "How can I explain my captivity to my servants, when they believe I spent the entire night steeping in my own bed? For you were a witness to all that took place. Indeed, without your help my life would have been lost long ago."

Then Rabbi Adam said: "You have spoken the truth, but your servants are also correct. Listen and I will explain all that has happened to you." Then, amazed and speechless, the king and the servants listened to all that Rabbi Adam said.

"When the king announced his evil decree against the Jews," Rabbi Adam began, "the heavens were in an uproar, and the king was sentenced to death. During the night, when the king fell asleep, his soul departed from his body and was handed over to the evil spirits to be punished. These appeared to him in the form of the lord of the castle and his soldiers. But I came and argued on his behalf, and so I finally saved his soul. His trials in the castle of the evil lord were the journey of his soul through the various stations, until it returned to him at dawn. The snuffbox half full of nail clippings is a sign of the truth of this experience.

"And now," Rabbi Adam continued, "the king surely remembers this decree, which he signed." And Rabbi Adam took out the decree, with the king's signature and seal affixed to it, and when the king saw it, he understood the meaning of his dream, and had it announced that the decrees against the Jews had been abolished. And when the Jews of this kingdom heard of Rabbi Adam's accomplishment, they lifted their voices in prayer, and thanked God for His infinite mercy.

—Eastern Europe: c. sixteenth century

16. The Exiled Princess

ong ago there were a king and queen who had only one child, a daughter. They were very wealthy, as befits royalty, and lived in a great palace. The king concerned himself with the details of ruling his kingdom, and the queen, who was very kindhearted, concerned herself with charity, to which she gave generously. And she impressed upon her daughter, the princess, the importance of being generous.

Time passed and the queen died. Eventually the king remarried, and the stepmother disliked the princess, and especially did not like her generosity, for the new queen was very selfish, and wanted to keep her riches for herself. But when the princess continued to be kind to poor people, the stepmother went to the king and complained that if the girl did not stop, they would end up impoverished. Now the king did not really mind that his daughter was so generous, but he could not bear the nagging of his wife. So he told the princess to give less to others. But the princess could not bear to see poverty, and she ended up giving more rather than less. The stepmother was quick to notice this, and she threatened to leave the king unless he put a halt to it. The king again warned the princess, and told her that if she disobeyed him, she would be expelled from the palace. Still, the girl insisted on giving even more to charity than before.

When the king learned this, he grew very angry and called in his servants and told them to take the princess, to blindfold her and tie her hands, and to lead her into the forest, and return without her. So it was that the reluctant servants, who loved the kind princess but were afraid to disobey the king, packed up all her dearest belongings, including her crown and the bridal gown of her mother, and led her into the forest, blindfolded and with her hands tied. But before they left her alone, they loosened the ropes that held her hands and hurried off, believing that in any case she would lose her life to the beasts that roamed there.

When the servants had gone, the princess freed her hands from her bonds, loosened her blindfold, and began to weep bitterly. She remained standing throughout the night, terrified at every noise she heard. But at dawn, when she was still weeping, she saw an old man who was walking through the forest. The old man approached her and said: "Why do you weep so bitterly, my child?"

Then the princess told him everything that had happened, and he said: "Come with me, child, and I will lead you out of this forest to a road. Take your belongings and follow this road and you will come to a town. When you arrive, ask for the way to the almshouse, and you will have a place to stay."

So it was that the old man led the princess out of that forest, to the road. There he took his leave of her and returned to the forest, where he lived, and the princess followed the road until she came to a town. When she arrived there it was already Friday evening, and the night was beginning to grow dark. Then she noticed a light in the distance, and followed its beams until she reached a small house. She was very hungry and thirsty, and sat down on the steps of that house and wept. Now in that house lived a rabbi and his wife, who had an only son. And when the wife had finished saying the prayer over the Sabbath candles, and had called out "Amen," she heard the sound of crying from outside the window. Then she went to the window and called out: "Who is there? If you are a demon, go away; if you are a human being, come in." Then she opened the door and found a girl sitting on the steps and asked her: "Why are you crying, my child?" And the girl replied that she was an orphan with no one in the world, and that she had been traveling alone when she had met an old man who had told her there was an almshouse in that town where she could find a place to stay.

When the rabbi's wife heard this, she said: "Where will you go on Friday night after the candles have already been lit? Come, spend the Sabbath with us, and I will take you to the almshouse at the end of the Sabbath." And so it was—the girl spent the Sabbath in the rabbi's house. But when it was time for her to be taken to the almshouse, she pleaded with the rabbi's wife: "Please let me stay here and let me be your servant. I ask only for food and drink." The wife replied: "I would not mind if you were here, but I have nowhere to keep you." Then the girl continued to plead: "Let me stay here. I can sleep on the floor next to the stove, it is good enough for me. Please, just not the almshouse." The rabbi's wife considered the matter, and decided that it might be worthwhile, after all, to have a servant for the mere price of food and drink, and she agreed to let the girl stay. So it was that the princess remained there, and served them well. And even though her portion was small, the girl always saved a part of it for the beggars who wandered through the town.

Now this rabbi was highly respected in that town, and when the wealthy landowners held a wedding for one of their children, or some other celebration, they invited him to attend with his family. And before long a wealthy man held a wedding for his daughter. The rabbi and his wife and son were invited and they all went, and the girl remained alone in the house. But she too wanted to attend, for she had never been to a Jewish wedding. So she took out the parcel of her belongings, which the king's servants had packed for her, and chose one of her finest gowns, put it on, and went to the wedding.

When she got there, everyone stared at her, for she was very beautiful in her royal gown. But no one knew where she came from, and if she belonged to the guests of the groom or those of the bride. She was soon asked to dance, and she danced with everyone. And the rabbi's son also noticed her, and asked her to dance with him many times, without recognizing her at all; nor did she reveal who she was. Finally she noticed that it was getting late, and she pulled herself away from him and ran home. There she quickly put away her fine gown, donned her rags, and crawled back beside the stove, just as the rabbi and his wife and son returned.

Time passed, but the rabbi's son could not stop thinking of the beautiful girl with whom he had danced, although he did not even know who she was. Then there was another wedding, and again the rabbi and his wife and son were invited. When they had all left for the wedding, the girl again decided to go, and she put on an even more beautiful dress. This time the rabbi's son saw her at once, and again asked her to dance. They danced and danced all evening, until she saw that it was getting late. Then she tore herself away from him and ran home. But this time, because of her great haste, she broke an earring, and part of it fell into the wash basin and lay there, although she did not notice it. Then she put on her rags and pretended to be sleeping by the stove.

Now when the rabbi's son returned home with his parents, he was still under the spell of the beautiful girl who had danced with him all night. And when he took the wash basin, he recognized the earring he found in it, and he wondered from where it had come. Then he first became suspicious that it might belong to the servant girl who lived in their house, for he knew that the mysterious girl with whom he had danced at the wedding must live somewhere. And he could not stop thinking of her, for he was in love with her.

Sometime later there was again a celebration held by one of the town's landowners, and again the rabbi's family was invited. But as they were about to leave the house, the rabbi's son told his parents that he did not feel well, and would join them later. Meanwhile he waited in his room, although the servant girl thought that he had left with his parents. Then she dressed in an even more beautiful gown, and left for the celebration. And when the rabbi's son came out of his room and saw that she had gone, he too went to the celebration, and spent the evening dancing with the beautiful girl. And while dancing with her he noticed that she was wearing only one earring, and he knew that the part of the earring he had found in the basin belonged to her. Then he whispered to her that he had learned her secret, and when she saw it was true, she tore herself away from him and ran back to the house. There she quickly changed her clothes and crawled back beside the stove.

So it was that the rabbi and his wife soon learned that their son wanted to marry the servant girl. But such a match did not suit them. They said: "A rabbi's son should not marry a servant. No, we will not permit it!" The son was heartbroken, and so was the girl. But he dared not disobey his parents.

Then one night, while the family slept, a fire started in the chimney of their house. The servant girl was awakened by the smoke and hurried to wake all the others. And because she was so alert, they were able to bring the fire under control, and the house was saved, as well as their lives. Then the rabbi and his wife were very grateful to the girl, and they realized that even though she was poor she was a fine, trustworthy person, and so they agreed to let their son marry her after all. A wedding was planned, and the rabbi's wife told the girl that she would sew a wedding dress for her, but the girl told her that she already had a dress of her own to wear. Then she took out her mother's bridal gown, and a crown, which the king's servants had packed for her, and she put them on, and the gown was embroidered with precious stones, which were also set in the crown, and the rabbi and his wife and son were amazed when they saw them. Then she told them the whole story of how she had been cast out by her father, the king, because she had insisted on giving charity. And it was then that the rabbi and his wife fully recognized what a pure soul she was, and they were also very proud to learn that their son was marrying a princess.

Now after the king had sent his daughter, the princess, into exile, he greatly regretted what he had done. And his terrible mistake haunted him day and night, until his remorse became so great that he decided to go off in search of her, and vowed that he would not return to the throne until she had been found. And before he departed he divorced the evil wife who had insisted he expel his daughter, and banished her from the kingdom so that she would know the fate that she had brought upon the exiled princess.

So it was that the king searched for the princess for more than a year, but he did not succeed in finding her. Meanwhile, she had married the rabbi's son, and they knew great happiness together, for their love was very strong. Before long the princess found that she was with child, much to her delight and that of her husband. And shortly before she gave birth she had a dream in which she saw the old man who had led her out of the forest. He told her that her father had set out alone to search for her throughout the world, and that he was in the vicinity of that town. Her father had put aside his royal garments and had dressed himself as a beggar in order not to draw attention to himself. So too did the old man tell her to invite all the poor people in that town to the circumcision, and in this way her father would also come. And when she saw him, she should give him all the kinds of food found at the ceremony, but it should be left unsalted. For as a king, he would be too accustomed to the taste of salt to do without it. And so it was as the old man said: the princess gave birth to a handsome son, and a circumcision was held on the eighth day, to which all of the town's poor were invited. And among them the princess recognized one of the men as her father, but he did not recognize her.

Then the princess called in a servant and told him to seat the beggar who was her father at a separate table, and to give him a fine variety of food, but all without salt. So it was that her father was served soup and fish and fine meat, which had a wonderful smell, but after he had tasted only a morsel from each dish, he did not touch them anymore.

After the dinner each of the poor guests went to congratulate the princess and received a nice gift from her of half a silver ruble. At last the old beggar also went to her to thank her, and she asked him how he had liked the food. He replied: "The food was very good, but I couldn't eat any of it." And then the princess looked into his eyes and said: "Know then that I felt an even bitterer taste when you ordered me taken to the forest and left there alone!" Now the old king could not believe his ears, and he suddenly realized that the young mother who stood before him was none other than his lost daughter, the princess. And he fell down at her feet and begged her to forgive him for the great wrong he had done her. And when she saw his tears, the princess too began to cry, and she embraced her father, and they were reunited at last.

So it was that the king was able to return to the capital and resume his life on the throne. And he brought with him not only his daughter, whom he now realized that he loved more than life itself, and her newborn son, but also her husband, the rabbi's son, and the rabbi and his wife as well. And the king appointed the rabbi and his son to be his ministers, and he came to value their advice more than any other, for they spent their time immersed in the study of the Torah, and were steeped in its wisdom. As for the princess, she saw to it that the needs of the poor of that kingdom were amply met, and that charity was the rule and not the exception. And so they all lived happily in the palace for the rest of their lives.

—Eastern Europe: oral tradition

17. The Wonderful Healing Leaves

nce upon a time there was a king and a queen who had three daughters. The king wanted his daughters to marry wealthy princes, and in the case of his first daughter and his second, they did. But the youngest princess fell in love with a poor man, and wanted to marry him. The king and queen opposed the marriage, but the princess went ahead and secretly married her beloved. And when this became known to the king, he was furious, and banished his daughter from the palace. Thereafter she lived happily but in poverty with her husband, whom she loved.

One day it happened that the king awoke and found that he had somehow become blind. He summoned doctors from all corners of the kingdom, but none of them could restore his sight. Then a doctor came from a distant city, who said he had heard that there was a special tree in the Land of No Return whose leaves could heal blindness. But, the doctor added, no one who had gone there to obtain those leaves had ever returned.

Even though the way to the tree of the healing leaves appeared to be fraught with danger, it was the king's last hope. So he called on the two princes who were married to his daughters, and asked them to set out on the journey, and promised that if they succeeded they would each receive one third of his kingdom on their return. But he warned them not to come back empty-handed, or it would cost them their lives. Of course, the princes could not refuse to undertake such a journey, so after they had equipped themselves with speedy horses and many provisions, they set out on the quest for the healing leaves.

Meanwhile, when the king's youngest daughter, who was married to the poor man, found out about her father's blindness and the quest for the healing leaves, she asked her mother, the queen, to permit her husband also to join the search, on the same conditions as those set for the two princes. The queen took pity on her, and gave the poor lad a lame horse and meager provisions, and two weeks after the two princes had already departed, he too set out on the quest.

Now after the two princes had ridden for seven days, they reached the province that bordered the Land of No Return. There the princes were told: "Many are those who have tried to reach the area where the healing leaves can be found, but none of them has ever returned. It is said that the way to the tree on which the leaves grow is guarded by a dragon and a viper, who destroy all those who come within their reach."

When the two princes heard this, they became frightened, and they did not want to continue the quest. But they knew they could not return empty-handed, or it would cost them their lives. Therefore they decided to stay at the place they had reached, and together they opened an inn there.

Two weeks later the lad who was married to the youngest princess arrived at their inn. He did not recognize them, nor did they recognize him, for they had never met. He stayed there that night, and in the morning he went about asking if anyone knew the way to the Land of No Return. So it was that he spoke to the same people who had warned the two princes. But the young man was not afraid, nor would he abandon the quest. And when the people saw that he was determined to go there, they told him that the only one who knew how to reach the tree of the healing leaves was a giant who lived in the valley below. But that giant himself was very terrible, and ate all those who came within his reach.

Still the lad was not afraid, and he mounted his horse and traveled to the valley that very day, and rode until he reached a house that was as high as a mountain. Another man would have been overcome with terror to see how high was the door of that house, but not the husband of the youngest daughter of the king. Without hesitation he approached the door and knocked on it. Then the wife of the giant opened the door, and when she saw it was a man, she told him to leave at once, for his life was in danger. But the lad insisted that he must talk to the giant, in order to find out how to reach the Land of No Return. And when she saw that he was determined to stay, she allowed him to come in and fed him and then hid him under the bed.

Before long the giant returned home, and as soon as he entered he declared: "Surely my nose does not deceive me—for I can smell the blood of a man even a mile away." The giant's wife tried to convince him that no man was foolish enough to come there, but the giant kept insisting it must be so, and at last she revealed that the lad was hidden under the bed. Then the lad came out, stood before the giant, and said: "Sir giant, you are my host and I am in your power. You can do with me whatever you like. But first let me tell you my story." And the giant was amazed at his bravery and said: "Go on and tell me the tale."

Then the lad told the giant about the blindness of the king, and how he had come in search of the healing leaves. And when the giant saw that he was willing to go to the Land of No Return, even though no one had ever come back from there, he said to him: "Since you do not tremble before me, and are not afraid to risk your life by entering the Land of No Return, I shall not kill you, for you are the first man I have met who is not a coward." Then the giant invited the lad to eat and sleep in his home, and so it was that the lad spent the night there as his guest.

In the morning the lad arose early, and the giant said to him: "When you leave here, you must ride on the road for seven days, until you come to a crossroads. On one of the roads it is written 'A happy journey,' and on the other, 'He who follows this path shall not return.' You must not ponder there, but take the road from which there is no return. Continue to follow this road until it comes to a dead end. This is the first danger. When you come there you must say: 'What a beautiful path! Had I all the horses of the king I would come and dance here!' Then the path will continue, so you can pass.

"The next danger," continued the giant, "is a valley filled with poisonous snakes, through which no man can pass. When you come to it you must say: 'What a beautiful valley filled with honey! If only someone brought some of this honey to the palace of the king, he would gladly eat it!" Then the snakes will disappear, and you will be able to pass.

"The third danger is a valley filled with blood and all kinds of beasts, through which no man can pass. When you come to it you must say: 'What tasty butter! Had I the bread of the king, I would spread this tasty butter on it!' Then the valley will dry up, and you will be able to pass.

"After this," the giant went on, "you will come to a palace, guarded by a dragon and a viper. If their eyes are open, it means they are sleeping; if their eyes are closed, they are fully awake. Wait until their eyes are open, and then you will be able to pass. From there you must enter the palace, and walk down the corridor until you come to the queen's door, which is guarded by four lions. If their eyes are open it means they are sleeping; if their eyes are closed, they are awake. Now, the door to the queen's chamber, which they guard, is made entirely of bells, and when it is opened the sound of the bells wakes the lions. I will give you two packages of cotton with which to muffle the bells. When the eyes of the lions are open, muffle the bells and open the door. There you will find the queen sleeping, for when she sleeps all the beasts sleep with their eyes open, and beside her bed grows the tree with the healing leaves. Fill one bag with the leaves, and also fill your pockets, for they are very precious. Then go to the queen and exchange rings with her. After that, when you return, you must do everything you did before, but in reverse order."

The lad listened closely to what he had to do, and when the giant had finished telling him, he gratefully thanked him and set off down the road. He acted according to the giant's instructions, so he was able to continue on the path that ended, and to cross the valley filled with snakes and the one filled with blood and beasts. And when he reached the palace he waited until the eyes of the dragon and the viper were open, which meant that they were asleep, and he entered the palace. So too did he wait for the four lions to open their eyes, meaning that they too were asleep, and he entered the chamber of the queen, who was sleeping on her bed. And beside her bed he found the tree with the wonderful healing leaves, its branches reaching to the ceiling, its roots growing beneath the floor. Then the lad filled a big sack with those leaves and his pockets as well, and exchanged his ring with that of the queen. And on the way back he did everything he had done to get there, but in reverse. So it was that two weeks later he returned with the bag full of leaves and the queen's ring on his finger, and came to the inn run by the two princes.

Now when the princes saw the sack, they asked the lad what was inside it, and he told them the whole story, although he forgot to mention that he had exchanged rings with the queen. Then the two princes pretended to be very friendly, and invited him to spend the night, and he agreed.

But while the lad slept, the two princes threw a drug into his eyes to blind him, and put him in a sack and left him in a closet in the inn. They themselves took the bag of the healing leaves and set out to return to the palace of the king. And when they arrived the king's blindness was cured by the healing leaves, and he appointed the two princes to be his ministers, and rewarded each of them with one third of his kingdom.

Meanwhile, when the lad awoke and found himself in a sack, he did not give up hope, but struggled until he had managed to free himself. But when he did, he discovered he was blind, and he was deeply grieved. Then he remembered the healing leaves he had kept in his pockets, and took some of them and rubbed them against his eyes, and his sight was restored. After that he returned to his wife, the king's youngest daughter, and said to her: "I have brought the healing leaves." But to his surprise she laughed at him and said: "The two princes brought them back long before you, and the king has regained his sight." And the lad understood that his long quest had all been in vain.

Now it happened that when the queen of the Land of No Return awoke from her sleep, she saw that her ring had disappeared, replaced by another, and that many leaves were missing from the tree. She immediately unrolled her flying carpet, and searched high and low for whoever had taken her ring and the leaves. After searching in many places, she heard of the king who had been cured of his blindness, and when she arrived at the palace she threatened to send the dragon to destroy the city if she was not told how the cure had come to pass. Then the princes came forward and showed the leaves to her in the presence of the king. She said: "Tell me where you got them from." And they replied: "We found a forest and picked the leaves off a tree." "They are lying!" hissed the queen. "Beat them!"

Just then the lad arrived at the palace and told the queen how he had obtained the leaves, and showed her the ones he still had left, which he had carried in his pockets. Then the lad showed the queen her ring, and she knew that he was telling the truth. But she wanted to know how the princes had returned with the leaves before him, and so the lad told her all that had happened, and all the trouble that they had caused him. After that the lad gave back the ring to the queen, and she got on her flying carpet and returned to her kingdom. And the king, who had heard all that the lad had said, now understood what had really taken place. He banished the two princes and invited his youngest daughter and her husband to live in the palace, where the young man soon became his most trusted minister, and they all lived happily ever after.

—Iraqi Kurdistan: oral tradition

18. The City of Luz

ong ago there was a kingdom that had been ruled by the same dynasty for more than ten centuries. And it was the custom in this kingdom, each time a new ruler was crowned, to bring forth the royal mantle—the very mantle that had been used when the first king was crowned. Now this mantle had been woven of the finest silk, and had been dyed a shade of blue that was unique, for nowhere else was that color to be found. And when it was wrapped around the shoulders of each new king, the people clapped and cheered for their new ruler.

It came to pass that the old king decided to step down from the throne to allow his son, the prince, to be crowned in his place. Preparations for the lavish ceremony were begun a year in advance, and it was then that a servant was sent to fetch the royal mantle from the golden chest where it had lain for forty years. But when the chest was unlocked, the servant discovered to his horror that the royal mantle had been devoured by moths, and that all that remained of it were rags.

When the old king heard about this, he began to tremble with fear, for the mantle was the symbol of the dynasty, and if another were used, the seal of authority of the king could be endangered. Therefore the king called in his ministers, and asked for their advice. They all agreed it was a very serious matter, and warned the king that if the people found out, his enemies might proclaim it as a sign that after ten centuries the dynasty was coming to an end. The ministers told the king that he must find a way to have another mantle made, of the same color. For the people would not accept any other.

Then the king gathered together all of the royal soothsayers, and asked for their advice. But none of them knew of a way to duplicate the shade of the color, and they were silent. Then at last the oldest soothsayer among them spoke and said: "I remember hearing as a child, O king, that the royal mantle was a gift of the Jews. If that is true, then they must know how to prepare the dye and duplicate the color."

Now when the king heard this, he wasted no time, but ordered that the leaders of the Jews be brought to the palace the very next morning. And when they stood before him, the king showed them what was left of the royal mantle, and he said: "It was your people, the Jews, who gave this mantle to the first king of this dynasty. Somehow a moth must have entered the golden chest in which it was stored, and during the past forty years the moths multiplied and destroyed the royal mantle. This is all that remains. In one year the coronation of my son is to take place. Plans have already been made, a palace is being built for the occasion, and many great kings have been invited to attend. It cannot be delayed. I want you to take one of these rags with you, and before nine months have passed, I want you to deliver the dye that produces this exact color. If you do not, all of the Jews in this kingdom will be doomed. So too must you keep this mission a secret, for if you do not, there will be a bitter end."

The Jewish leaders were terribly frightened when they heard the harsh edict of the king, for they too were familiar with the legend that the royal mantle had been a gift of the Jews. That was the same blue dye the Torah commands be used in the corner fringes of the prayer shawl worn by the men, known as the tallit. But the secret of how to produce that dye, known as *tekhelet*, had been lost for centuries, and since then a white thread had been used in its place. One of the leaders tried to explain this to the king, but he grew flushed with anger, and sent them from his presence, reminding them that the edict was still in effect.

In great fear the Jewish leaders met in the synagogue and discussed the matter. They knew that they could not reveal the edict to the rest of the community, since the king had commanded it be kept secret on penalty of death, and besides, they did not want the others to become terrified as well. Therefore they vowed to keep the matter a secret among themselves, and not to reveal it even to their wives.

After this they considered the problem of how to obtain the dye, the secret of which had been lost for so many centuries. For no one knew for certain if it were made from a shellfish or snail, and therefore it could not be produced. Long ago the rabbis had decided that it would be better to leave the corner of the prayer shawl white rather than to err in trying to fulfill the commandment, and this is what had been done. Now, though, they were forced to seek out the dye once again.

Then one old rabbi among them, whose name was Rabbi Abraham, spoke and said: "There can be no doubt that we must find a way to satisfy the demand of the king, otherwise he will carry out the threat he has made, and we will all be doomed. Let us concentrate, then, on fulfilling this task, even though it appears to be impossible."

The others recognized that what the old rabbi had said made sense. Then Rabbi Isaac, who was highly respected, spoke and said: "The question is, where can this dye be found? I recall it is said in the Talmud that the secret of how to prepare the dye was known in the city of Luz. That is the city in the Holy Land built at the place where Jacob dreamed of the ladder that reached from earth into heaven, with angels ascending and descending upon it."

"Yes, that is true," said Rabbi Abraham, "and according to the Talmud the natives of the city of Luz are spared the fate that is inescapable for all other men—the inevitability of death. For when God decreed that man must die, he left one place on earth where the Angel of Death never held sway, and that is the city of Luz. Not even the armies of Nebuchadnezzar could disturb the city."

"But, with all respect," said the youngest among them, whose name was Rabbi Jacob, "what good does it do for us to think of the city of Luz, for it is to be found in the Holy Land. The journey there could take a year in itself, as well as a year to return, and the king has commanded that we deliver the dye to him within nine months. Even if it were possible to reach the city of Luz, and even if the secret of how to prepare the dye is still known there, how could this be accomplished in the time remaining?"

After Rabbi Jacob had spoken there was silence for a long time, for what he said was all too true—the journey to the Holy Land and its return could not take place in the time remaining to them. All of their faces were fixed in a frown, but suddenly the face of the old rabbi lit up and he said: "Fear not, for all hope is not yet lost!" And all of the others turned to him with wonder in their eyes, for they could not imagine what he had to say. Then Rabbi Abraham said: "All my life I have kept the secret that I am about to reveal to you, which I learned from my father, and he from his father before him, a secret held in our family for many generations. My father made me vow never to reveal it unless a day should come when lives hang in the balance, and only this secret can save them."

All of the others held their breaths in anticipation of a secret that had been kept for so long, but was about to be revealed. Then the old rabbi said: "This, then, is the secret: When the End of Days has come and the era of the Messiah is upon us, all souls will travel to Jerusalem for the resurrection. And how will they get there? Through underground caves. And the secret that I know is the location of one of these caves, which leads directly to the Holy Land itself, to a place that is not far from the city of Luz! And the entire journey to the Holy Land through this cave will not take longer than a week!"

When the others heard this, they could not believe their ears, and for the first time a ray of hope entered their hearts.

Then Rabbi Abraham continued: "This, then, is what we should do: Let us choose two among us to undertake this mission. I would go myself, for I have always longed to enter that cave, but I know that it is too long a journey for an old man, and there must be no delay. I will take the two who are chosen to the mouth of the cave, which is hidden, and reveal it to them. I am afraid that no others may accompany us, for the location of the cave must be kept secret."

Things had developed so quickly that all of the leaders were in a state of awe, and they wondered who among them should be chosen to go. At last one of them spoke and said: "The important decision that now lies before us is who we shall send on this quest, on which all of our lives and those of our families depend. In such a case we must choose those in whose hands we can safely entrust our lives." All of the others nodded in agreement, and then Rabbi Abraham spoke again: "When I was a child, there was once a situation of life or death such as this, in which it was essential to choose the right one to represent us before the king, who had just signed an evil decree against the Jews. Then the elders gathered outside this very synagogue at midnight on the night of a full moon and the decision was made there. I know this because I concealed myself behind a tree and observed all that took place. If you will accompany me outside, we may be able to reach our decision, for it is almost midnight, and tonight there is a full moon."

Then all of the others followed Rabbi Abraham out of the synagogue. He led them to a tree nearby, where the full moon could be seen through the branches. "Let each of you stand before this tree," said Rabbi Abraham, "as did the elders in my childhood. And let us see if anyone's shadow, cast by the moon, is long enough to reach the door of the synagogue. For the elders believed that the one whose shadow reached the door was destined to represent them. That night when I was a child there was only one among them—and it was my own father—whose shadow reached the door. And it was he who went before the king, and convinced him to cancel the evil decree against us."

The others nodded, and one by one they stood by the tree, but one after another they discovered that their shadows fell short of the synagogue. Soon there were only two of them left who had not yet taken the test, Rabbi Isaac and Rabbi Jacob. But when Rabbi Isaac took his place by the tree, his shadow seemed to grow longer before their very eyes, until the edge of it touched the base of the door. The rabbis cheered, for at last one of them had been found worthy of the quest. Then it was Rabbi Jacob's turn, and when he stood before the tree, his shadow grew so long that it reached not only to the door of the synagogue, but climbed up to the very handle. All of the others gasped when they saw this, and they understood that in this way the Holy One had identified those who should undertake this essential mission.

That night Rabbi Isaac and Rabbi Jacob packed their belongings for the journey, and took leave of their wives and families, although they did not tell them where they were going. At dawn they met Rabbi Abraham at the synagogue, and he gave them a letter of introduction to take with them, and then led them to the forest that surrounded their town. They walked through the forest until the sun was high in the sky, and at last they reached a small spring. The old rabbi followed this stream until they reached a carob tree of great beauty, which was filled with fruit, behind which the stream seemed to disappear. Then Rabbi Abraham said to them: "Behind this tree lies the mouth of the cave that leads to the Holy Land. Know that not any man can enter this cave, but only those who possess pure souls will be permitted to pass. All others will be stopped by the flaming sword inside the entrance, which guards the way. If the sword stops spinning and permits you to pass, then you will know that the test of the shadows chose well. And if the sword does not stop spinning, then you must turn back, for it is not destined that you go on."

Then Rabbi Abraham pointed to the unlit torches that the two younger rabbis carried, and he said: "If you do succeed in passing the flaming sword, you should hold your torches near it, and light them with that fire. It will last all of your journey through the cave, for that is the same fire that Moses saw when he beheld the burning bush, which burned but was not consumed. You should also know that the water of the stream that runs through this cave is pure, and will sustain you. Know too that the carobs that grow on this tree will be your only food for the seven days that you journey through the cave. For while you are there only your spirit will requires sustenance, and not your body; that is why you must eat carobs, for in no other food is such a pure essence of the spirit contained. Therefore fill your pockets with them." This is what the two rabbis did, and then they stepped behind the tree and found the mouth of the cave, just as Rabbi Abraham had said.

Rabbi Isaac, who was the elder of the two, entered first, and when he had passed beyond the first turn in the cave, he was confronted with a flaming circle that whirled before him, and he knew that this was the flaming sword of which Rabbi Abraham had spoken. As Rabbi Isaac stood there, the whirling sword slowed down, so that he could see the blade, but it did not stop. A moment later Rabbi Jacob joined him, and as soon as he stood beside him, the flaming sword came to a halt. Then the two rabbis did not hesitate, but hurried past it into the cave. And no sooner had they gone beyond it than the sword started spinning again. Then the two rabbis held out their torches near the flaming sword until each torch caught fire. And the fire burned with a purity unlike anything they had ever seen, and illumined the cave for a great distance. So it was that at last they were on their way to the city of Luz, and there was no turning back.

As Rabbi Isaac and Rabbi Jacob made their way through the long cave, following the stream in its twists and turns, they saw that the walls of the cave were lined with beautiful stone that seemed precious in itself. And the farther they went, the more the air was pervaded with a perfume, like the scent of balsam, and the rabbis were intoxicated with that scent.

After they had traveled for six days they reached a large cavern that was like a room built of well-hewn stones. At the far end of that room they saw a wooden tabernacle that had been set up there in a crevice in the wall of the cavern. And before the Ark there was a stone that seemed to resemble a pulpit. Then the two rabbis did not hesitate, but approached the pulpit together, and although they did not have prayer books with them, when they opened their mouths and sang, the words rose up by themselves and were carried upward as if on wings. And the echo of their voices filled the cavern so that it sounded as if a chorus of many voices had joined them in prayer, although no one else was to be seen.

Afterward the two rabbis spent all of the seventh day in that cavern, for they knew it was the Sabbath, and they did not want to continue traveling on the day of rest. All that day their spirits were high, and they were at peace. And the next morning, when they had gone only a short distance, they saw a golden glow, and knew that they were about to reach the other end of the cave. And when they came there, they found another carob tree, even more beautiful than the first. And as they stepped from the cave they fell to the earth and kissed the ground of the Holy Land, and gave thanks for their good fortune in reaching that sacred place. Then they left their torches burning in the entrance of the cave and replenished their supply of carobs, which they had grown to love, and set off to find their way to the city of Luz.

Not far from the entrance of the cave they saw a hut in the woods, and hurried to it. There they met an old man who lived alone. They asked him about the way to the city of Luz, and he pointed out the path to them, but warned them that they would have to cross woods and swamps and heavy underbrush along the way. So it was that they walked and walked until they could hardly move their feet any longer. Their garments were torn by brambles, and their shoes were worn out by the time they reached Luz.

Once they arrived in the city, the two rabbis asked at once to be brought to the rabbi of Luz. When they met him they showed him the letter of introduction written by Rabbi Abraham, and they revealed the purpose of their quest and asked for his advice. Imagine their astonishment when the rabbi said: "My friends, you have come to the city of Luz, but this is the modern city of Luz, and the place you are seeking is the ancient city of Luz. It is to be found many miles from here, in the wilderness, but only God can say whether or not you will be permitted to enter it. In any case, when you reach the city, keep these words in mind: 'The nut has no mouth.'"

The two rabbis almost wept when they learned that they still had not reached their destination. They were so weary and the wilderness looked so terrifying that they almost fainted in despair. But then they remembered the grave danger facing their people, who had put all of their trust in them, and their courage was renewed. They returned to the wilderness, walking rapidly through the thick underbrush and black forests and on through great stretches of fields. They walked for days, and it seemed as if they had walked to the ends of the earth. At last they reached a clearing, and within it they saw a city encircled by a high wall—the ancient city of Luz. The two rabbis threw up their hands in joy that they had reached it at last. Then they ran from the forest to the clearing, despite their exhaustion, and reached the wall of the city. From where they stood they saw no entrance, so they decided to walk around the wall until they reached the gate.

The two rabbis began their walk beside a giant almond tree that stood outside the wall of the city. The wall itself, built in a circle, was several miles in diameter, and it took them three hours to circle the entire city and to return to the tree whence they had started. But when they reached it, they were appalled, for they realized that there was no gate to the city at all. Never had they heard of such a thing, and their eyes filled with tears, for they had not expected that there would be still more obstacles to overcome. Still, they were determined not to give up now that they had traveled so far.

It was then that Rabbi Isaac remembered the words of the rabbi of the modern city of Luz, and he said to Rabbi Jacob: "What could the old rabbi have meant when he said that 'The nut has no mouth'?" And Rabbi Jacob replied: "Perhaps it is a riddle in which we may discover the secret of how to enter the city." Then the two rabbis sat down beneath the almond tree, and contemplated the riddle. Suddenly an idea occurred to Rabbi Jacob, and he said: "Let us remember that the word for nut is 'luz,' and that this is also the name of the city. Perhaps this almond tree we are sitting beneath, which stands outside the city, somehow bears on the mystery."

Then the two rabbis went closer to the tree and examined it, and to their amazement they discovered that its trunk was hollow, and that the opening was large enough to admit a man. Then Rabbi Isaac said: "Perhaps by saying that 'The nut has no mouth,' the old rabbi was telling us that no man could discover how to enter the city, for perhaps it has no gate but this almond tree." "Yes," said Rabbi Jacob, "let us step into the hollow trunk and see if it leads anywhere."

This they did, and to their amazement they found that the hollow trunk led to the entrance of a cave. Then they entered the cave, which led beneath the wall of the city. "Surely we have discovered the entrance," said Rabbi Jacob, and Rabbi Isaac agreed that indeed this must be so, for no other entrance was to be seen. And behold, before they had traveled very far, they saw the faint light that signified they had reached the other end of the cave. And when they emerged from the cave, they found themselves in the city of Luz.

Now at first the rabbis thought that the city was a city like every other, and the people seemed like those seen everywhere else. Children played in the streets, and men and women went about their business. But soon they saw strange sights. They saw very, very old men walking in the streets. Some had beards so long they tripped over them. Finally, the two rabbis approached one of these old men, who seemed downcast. Rabbi Isaac said to him: "Tell us, what is the matter?" And the old man replied: "Alas, my father has punished me because I fell asleep by the bed of my grandfather, and did not hear him ask me for a glass of water." The two rabbis were amazed to hear this, and they asked the old man how old he was. "I am three hundred years old," said the old man. "And how old is your father?" they both asked at the same time. "He is five hundred years old," came the reply. "And your grandfather?" "He is eight hundred." "And is his father still living?" "Yes, he is," said the old man, "and may all Jews be saved from such a fate. He is one thousand years old, and sleeps all week in his bed and only wakes on the Sabbath."

The two rabbis were astonished to hear what the old man said, and they were especially surprised that he did not consider living to such an age a great blessing. Rabbi Jacob asked him about this, and the old man said: "It is a terrible thing to have to live forever. For God has cursed us with eternal life." Now the two rabbis had not forgotten that Rabbi Abraham had told them that the inhabitants of the city were immortal, but it was amazing to hear it firsthand.

Then Rabbi Isaac said: "And it is impossible, then, for any inhabitant of this city to depart from this life?" "Yes, unless they first depart from the city," said the old man. And Rabbi Jacob said: "But why would anyone, young or old, choose to take leave of this city?" And the old man said: "Because sometimes we grow tired of living."

The two rabbis looked at each other and realized that the old man had been talking about himself. Then Rabbi Isaac said to him: "Tell us, old man, what is it that you do for a living?" "It is my work to produce the blue dye that is used in prayer shawls," said the old man. The two rabbis were overjoyed to hear this, and Rabbi Jacob said: "Surely Providence has sent you to us as we were sent to you." Then he revealed the purpose of their mission to him, and when he had learned it, the eyes of the old man came alive, and he said to the two rabbis: "Come with me to the home of our rabbi, and repeat to him what you have told me, and then perhaps he will realize how important is my work in the eyes of the Lord."

So the two rabbis accompanied the old man to the home of the rabbi of Luz. However, when they arrived they were told that the rabbi was very ill. When they asked what was wrong, the rabbi's disciples told them that the rabbi had once tasted a carob when he was a child, eight hundred years ago, which a stranger had brought into the city. And since that had been the last stranger who had entered the city, the rabbi had never been able to taste another carob, since carob trees did not grow in that city. Lately he had been taken with a terrible longing to taste the fruit of the carob once again, but it was impossible to obtain it for him, for no inhabitant who left the city was ever able to return.

Then Rabbi Jacob smiled and put his hand in his pocket and pulled out a handful of carobs. And he said: "We are strangers who have just entered the city from the outside; here are the carobs that the rabbi has been longing for." And when the disciples saw the carobs, they hurried to bring the two rabbis into the presence of the old rabbi.

At first the old rabbi of Luz was angry to be disturbed, but when he saw that they had brought him the carobs he so longed for, tears of joy filled his eyes. And no sooner did he take the first bite of the carob than his strength returned, and his pale color became ruddy again. Then he found the strength to sit up in bed, and asked the two rabbis to tell him who they were, and why they had come to that city. So it was that they told their tale and explained the reason for their quest. And as soon as the old rabbi learned of the vital mission, he commanded the dyemaker to hurry home to get a bottle of the dye that the two rabbis needed.

While he was gone, Rabbi Jacob turned to the old rabbi and said: "Why is it that the Holy One, Blessed be He, permits the inhabitants of the city of Luz to be immortal?" And the old rabbi replied: "No one knows for certain why this is so. There are those who say that after the sin of Adam and Eve, God wanted to preserve one boundary in the world that the Angel of Death could not cross. Others say that when God decreed that man would live from dust to dust, he left one small bone that the grave does not consume. This bone is called the luz, and it will be from this bone that man will be resurrected at the End of Days. And in the same way that God left one bone in the back which is not destroyed, so he also left one place on earth where the Angel of Death cannot enter, and that is this city. Still others, those who feel that our eternal lives are a blessing, say that the Holy One made Luz immortal because it was here that Jacob dreamed of the ladder reaching from earth to heaven, since this is one of the Gates of Heaven. But those who despise our eternal lives say that this city has been cursed by God because when Jacob ran away from Esau, the people refused to let him rest here, and he had to sleep in the wilderness. Therefore, God cursed us with eternal life."

"Tell me," said Rabbi Isaac, "why would anyone choose to abandon such a city? And why can these wanderers never come back?" The old rabbi replied, "Why do they leave? Some may have grown tired of living, others are said to have been called by an angel to another place. No one knows what they found once they left the city. Perhaps they lost the way and spent their lives trying to find the road that would lead them back. Or perhaps the Angel of Death took them as they turned to go, and buried them in the fields beyond the wall."

"In any case," the old rabbi continued, "whatever the reason, the histories of this city, reaching back for centuries, do not record a single war, a single flood or fire, nor the death of a single man, for all who are born here have their name inscribed in the Book of Life, and there it remains unless they depart from the city."

Just as the old rabbi finished this explanation, the old dyemaker returned with a bottle of the unique blue dye in his hand, and gave it to Rabbi Jacob. Then Rabbi Jacob, who had carried with him the rag that had been part of the royal mantle, took it out and compared it to the dye in the bottle, and the color was identical. Then he gave the bottle to Rabbi Isaac for safekeeping, and Rabbi Isaac put it in a pouch and tied the pouch to his belt. And now that they had completed the quest, they knew they had to hurry, for they had no time to waste, but Rabbi Jacob had one last question before they departed. He said to the dyemaker: "Tell me, does this dye come from a shellfish or from a snail, for this is a question that our rabbis still debate." "It comes from a snail that is found only in this city," said the dyemaker, "and for every bottle the size of that I have given you, twelve thousand snails are required." The two rabbis were amazed when they heard this, and they realized that the bottle of dye they had obtained was even more precious than they had thought. Then they took their leave from the old rabbi and the dyemaker with many thanks, and set out on their journey home. They made their way to the cave that ran beneath the city, and returned the same way they had entered.

Somehow the distance did not seem as far this time, and the hours flew, and before long they reached the carob tree that guarded the way to the cave, where their torches were still burning, and a week later they arrived back in their own kingdom. And when they came to the synagogue, they found all of the leaders assembled together, praying for their safe return. And when they showed them the dye that perfectly matched what was left of the old mantle, there was great rejoicing, for their lives had been saved. Then they revealed all that had happened to them, and the others marveled at the tale. Now not only could they satisfy the king, but there was also enough of the dye for the fringes of every prayer shawl as well, making it possible to fulfill the commandment once more, and this is what they did. Now only three months had passed since the departure of the two rabbis, and when they showed the dye to the king, he was overjoyed to see that it was exactly that which was needed, and ordered that a new royal mantle be made up at once, identical to the first. And as a gift to the Jews who had caused the precious mantle to be restored to his dynasty, the king signed a decree freeing the Jews from all taxes and harsh decrees for as long as the dynasty should last, and had it announced everywhere. And thus began a period in which the lives of the Jews blossomed as never before, for the Holy One had seen to it that they were blessed with great abundance.

—Eastern Europe: c. nineteenth century

19. The Boy Israel and the Witch

here once was a young man, Israel ben Eliezer, who loved to spend hours alone in the forest. Others wondered why he so enjoyed being alone there, and some even accused him of being lazy, although this was certainly not the case. No, the truth was that one day, while walking in the forest, the boy had discovered a pure spring, and after he drank the water of that spring, he found that he could understand the language of the birds. Now he kept this discovery a secret, for he soon learned that the birds are acquainted with all kinds of mysteries, and he did not want these powers to fall into the wrong hands.

At that time there was a severe drought that had lasted for many months. As a result the plants did not grow, and the harvest was in danger. And although the people often prayed for rain, none was forthcoming. Then one day, while he was sitting in the forest, the boy Israel heard two birds speaking in a tree, and one of them said: "The plants are thirsty, and so are the animals, and so are the people. And all because the evil witch has cast a spell on the rain." "Yes," said the other bird, "it is all the witch's fault.

"If only someone knew that the drought was caused by the evil spell that the witch wrote out, and concealed in an amulet, which keeps the clouds from forming, so that it cannot rain. And if only someone knew that the witch hid the amulet in a metal case at the foot of this tree, and that if they found it and burned the spell written inside it until it was ashes, and scattered those ashes on the pure stream that flows in this forest, then the spell would be broken, and the clouds could form again and fill with water, and the rain could fall."

Now when the boy Israel heard this, he was astounded, for he too had wondered why the terrible drought had descended, and now he knew. And now he knew, as well, what needed to be done in order to break the spell. Then Israel did not hesitate, but stood up and began to dig at the base of that tree. And lo and behold, before he had dug for very long he struck something hard, and found a small metal case buried there, which was locked. But when Israel struck it against a rock, the case broke open, and an amulet fell out. And inside that amulet was a folded paper on which was written the terrible spell that had prevented the clouds from forming and had thus brought about the drought.

Then Israel wasted no time, but made a fire and burned the spell until it was ashes, and then carried the ashes to the pure spring he had discovered in the forest. And when he scattered the ashes on the water, they burst like bubbles as soon as they touched it. Suddenly the sky was covered by dark clouds, which soon broke open, and a fine rain fell that refreshed all the thirsty plants and animals and people, and everyone was very happy that the drought had come to an end.

Now when the first drops of rain began to fall, the witch was astonished, for she believed her spell was still in effect. And as soon as the rain stopped falling—for she did not want to get wet, since witches are afraid of water—she hurried to the tree where she had buried the amulet with the evil spell, and when she saw that it was no longer there, she was furious. Then she went back home and pronounced the words of a spell that made a demon appear, to serve as her slave. When the demon stood before her, she said: "Waste no time, demon, but find out who has discovered how to break my spell. For I am anxious to take my revenge, and then to cast another evil spell."

So the demon went out into the forest to listen to what the birds had to say. For demons all understand the language of the birds, and know too that they are privy to many secrets. Thus it did not take the demon long to learn that it was the boy Israel who had discovered the secret of how to break the spell, for all the birds were speaking in admiration of him.

Now when the witch learned that it was a boy who had broken the spell, she was furious. For she had assumed that a great wizard or sorcerer or holy man had broken it. But a mere boy! The thought of it made her tremble with fury. Then the witch went directly to the house where the boy Israel lived, and knocked on the door. But Israel was not home then, for he was learning Torah at the House of Study. Yet his mother was home, and it was she who opened the door, and when she saw who had knocked she grew afraid, for she knew that the visitor was evil. She told the witch that Israel was not there, and then the witch hissed and said: "Tell your son that I know what he has done, and that if he ever gets in my way again I will cast a spell on him. Then, if he is lucky, I will turn him into a bird, and if he is not, I will make him into a stone, and cast it to the bottom of the deepest well!" And with that the witch turned away and left, and Israel's mother shivered with fear, for she knew that the evil witch had the power to do everything that she had said.

So it was that as soon as Israel came home, his mother told him of the witch's visit and of her warning. Then she asked him what it was that he had done. So Israel told his mother how he had found the amulet buried in the forest, and how he had burned the paper on which the spell had been written, breaking it. When she had heard this, Israel's mother grew even more afraid, and she warned him to stay out of the witch's way, for if he didn't, the witch would cast a spell on him, as she had threatened. But Israel would not promise to avoid the witch no matter how much his mother pleaded, and only said: "I am not afraid of her, for I have trust in God."

Not long afterward a strange thing happened: the Ark of the Covenant in the House of Prayer, where the scroll of the Torah was kept, became locked, and despite the efforts of many men, it could not be opened, and thus the Torah could not be taken out. Now the Jews of that town were very frightened when this happened, for it was a very bad sign. They fasted and prayed and purified themselves, but nothing made any difference, and the doors of the Ark remained closed. Since this had happened during the Days of Awe, the time between Rosh ha-Shanah, the New Year, and Yom Kippur, the Day of Atonement, the people were especially frightened. But so far no one had succeeded in finding out what had caused this terrible thing to take place.

The boy Israel was also very unhappy about this, and he wondered if he might learn anything about it from the birds. So he went off alone into the forest, and drank from the pure spring, and sat down under a nearby tree. And while he was sitting there, he heard one bird say to another: "The Jews are all so sad because the door to the Ark is closed, and they are cut off from the blessings of the Torah." "Yes," said the other bird, "but if only someone knew that this was caused by the witch, to revenge herself on the boy Israel, because he is Jewish. For she has taken a foul rag that she has dipped in the blood of seven unclean animals, and has hidden it under the synagogue, right beneath the Ark. And that is why the doors to the Ark have remained closed—to protect the Torah from that terrible impurity. And all that someone has to do is to take that rag and burn it in a fire, and scatter its ashes on the pure spring, and the doors of the Ark will swing open."

Now as soon as Israel heard this, he ran back to town and crawled beneath the floor of the synagogue and there, directly beneath the place of the Ark, he found the foul rag, exactly where the bird had described it. Then he picked it up and wrapped it in some clean rags, so that he would not have to touch it again, and burned it in a fire, and carried the ashes into the forest, where he scattered them on the pure spring, and once again they burst like bubbles.

After this Israel returned to town, and when he arrived he found that the people were all dancing and singing in the streets, for the doors of the Ark had opened, and the terrible danger had passed. Israel too was very happy, although he did not reveal his role in breaking the evil spell, for he was very modest, and did not want to draw attention to himself.

But when the witch found out that the spell had been broken, and that the doors of the Ark had opened, she fell into a fury. Then she invoked the demon slave again, and sent him to find out what had happened. It did not take him very long to learn that the boy Israel was responsible, for although the people of the town did not know it, the secret was well known among the birds. And when the witch learned that it was Israel who had foiled her evil plans again, her wrath was terrible to behold, and she decided that she would punish him once and for all.

Now the boy Israel was no fool, and he knew very well that the witch might try to harm him, and that he had to be especially careful. He decided to go into the forest and to drink from the pure stream and to listen to what the birds had to say, so that he might have a warning if the witch tried to revenge herself in some way. And no sooner did he drink from the stream and sit down at the base of the tree, than he heard one bird say to another: "My, how the witch has fallen into a terrible fury. And now she has sent a demon after the boy Israel, to touch him. And when that happens he will turn into a stone, which the demon will deliver to the witch, and the witch will drop it to the bottom of the deepest well." "Yes," said the other bird, "but what a shame if this should happen—then there would be no one to struggle against the evil witch. Oh, if only Israel knew that he could protect himself against the demon by lighting a torch and carrying it with him, for demons are afraid of fire. Any demon who is touched with fire is condemned to serve as a slave in Gehenna for a thousand years, where fire burns everywhere day and night. So too could Israel protect himself with water, and especially the water of the pure spring. For if a demon is splashed with the water of the pure spring, he will become a small fish that will surely be swallowed by a larger one, and cease to exist." "Yes," said the first bird, "that is all true. And it is also true that the water of the pure spring could destroy the wicked witch as well, for if she were to be splashed with it, that would be the end of her."

Now when Israel heard what the birds had said, he made a torch and lit it in a fire. He finished lighting the torch just in time, for a moment later he heard something approaching him in the forest, and saw that it was the demon. Then Israel took the torch and hid behind a large rock, and waited until the demon had passed him. Then he jumped out, with the torch stretched out toward the demon, who found himself trapped between the fire of the torch and the pure stream. Then Israel said: "If you take one step toward me, demon, I will throw this torch at you, and you can spend the next thousand years in Gehenna. And if you do not do as I say, I will push you into the stream, and you can become a fish that will serve as food for a bigger fish, and that will be the end of you." And the demon saw that he had fallen into Israel's trap, so he agreed to do whatever Israel told him to do.

Then Israel told the demon to create a long chain that not even a demon could break, and to shackle it to his own right hand. This the demon did, and Israel took the other end in his hand. After this he told the demon to create a bucket, which he also did, and Israel filled the bucket with the water from the pure spring. Then Israel picked up a stone and tossed it to the demon, and told him to take it to the house of the witch, and to give it to her there. And he warned the demon that if he disobeyed, he would not hesitate to splash him with the water, for he would be close behind.

So it was that the demon approached the house of the witch and knocked on the door. And when the witch answered it, the demon handed her the stone, and said it was the stone that the boy Israel had become. Then the witch let out a terrible, shrill laugh, and while she was laughing, Israel ran up with the bucket of water in his hand, and threw most of the water at her. Suddenly her laugh turned to a horrible scream, and all at once she disappeared, and all that remained of her was a puddle of water. And when the demon saw the witch vanish, he panicked and started to run away, but slipped on the puddle, and suddenly there was a little fish flipping around where the demon had been.

Then Israel picked up the little fish and put it in the bucket, and carried it into the witch's house. He filled a jug he found there with the fish and water, and closed it tightly with a cork. Then he carried the jug into the forest, and hid it there in the hollow trunk of a tree.

Years later, when the boy Israel grew up and became famous as the Ba'al Shem Tov, he was traveling with his disciples through that same forest. Then he walked off alone and came to the hollow tree and looked inside and saw that the jug was still standing there, with the little fish still swimming around inside it. When he came back he was laughing, and when his disciples asked him why, he told them this story.

—Eastern Europe: nineteenth century

20. The Lost Princess

nce there was a king who had six sons and one daughter. His daughter was very dear to him, but one day he became angry with her for a moment, and an evil word escaped his lips. That night the princess went to her chamber, as usual, to sleep, but in the morning she could not be found. And when her father, the king, realized she was missing, he was filled with sorrow and remorse, and he began to search for her everywhere. Then the king's minister, seeing that the king was in sorrow, asked to be given a servant and a horse and enough silver for expenses, in order that he might undertake the search.

So it was that the minister traveled through all of the realm in search of the lost princess, across deserts and mountains, through forests and fields. He searched for her for many years. One day, as he was traveling in a desert, he glimpsed a path he had never seen, and he said to himself: "Since I have been searching for the princess in this desert such a long time, perhaps I shall follow this path and come to a city." After following the path for a great distance, he finally arrived at a splendid palace, guarded by many soldiers. Now the minister was afraid the guards would not let him enter, but still he dismounted and walked toward the palace, and to his surprise the gatekeeper opened the gate for him at once, without asking any questions. From there he passed from the courtyard into the palace, and after that he entered the chamber of the king who commanded all the troops. Nor did anyone try to stop him from entering into the presence of the king. There many musicians played their instruments, conducted by the king, and the minister stood off in a corner of the royal chamber, and waited to see what would happen. After a while the king commanded his servants to bring in the queen. They left with great rejoicing, and the musicians sang and played as she entered the room. And when they led her to the throne, the minister saw that she was the lost princess.

Before long the queen looked up and saw the minister in the corner of the chamber and recognized him at once. Then she rose from her throne and said: "Do you recognize me?" And he replied: "Yes, you are the lost princess. But how did you come to be here?" And she answered: "Because of that evil word that escaped from the mouth of my father. For this is the palace of the Evil One." Then the minister told her that her father, the king, was very sad in her absence, and that he had sent the minister to find her, and that he had been searching for many years. After this he asked her: "How can I take you away from here?" And she replied: "It is not possible to free me until you dwell in one place for a year, and throughout the year yearn to set me free. And on the last day of that year you must fast and not sleep for a full day and night."

Then the minister left that palace and did as she said. He went to a forest, and made his home there. And at the end of the year, on the last day, he fasted and did not sleep. But that day he noticed a tree on which very beautiful apples were growing. He desired them very much, and finally arose and plucked one of the apples. But as soon as he ate it, he fell down and sleep snatched him away. He slept for a very long time, and although his servant shook him, he could not wake him up.

When at last the minister woke from his sleep, he asked his servant: "Where am I?" And the servant told him: "You are in a forest, where you have been sleeping a very long time, and all the time I sustained myself with nuts and fruits." The minister despaired, but found his way back to the palace of the lost princess, and there he met her again in the chamber of the king. And when she saw him she was filled with sadness and said: "Had you come on that day, you could have taken me away from here, but because of that one day all has been lost. Still, I understand that fasting is very difficult, especially on the last day, for then the Evil Inclination becomes most powerful. Therefore return and dwell again for another year, but on the last day you are permitted to eat. However, do not sleep, and do not drink any wine lest you sleep, for it is important above all to remain awake."

Then he went and did as she said. And on the last day of the long year he saw for the first time a spring whose waters were reddish, and whose smell was that of wine. The minister pointed out the spring to his servant, then went and tasted of its waters, only to fall asleep again, and this time he slept for many years. Near the end of that time many soldiers passed by, and the servant of the minister concealed himself. And after the troops had passed, a carriage came by, in which sat the daughter of the king. As soon as she recognized the minister she left the carriage and approached him. And although she shook him very strongly, he did not wake up, and she began to lament, saying that he had made such a long effort, and suffered for so many years to free her, and because of one error on that last day, he had lost everything. She wept greatly over this, and then took the kerchief from her head and wrote a message on it with her tears. Then she returned to her carriage and drove away.

Not long afterward the minister awoke and asked his servant: "Where am I?" The servant told him all that had happened, about the troops that had passed by there and the carriage that had stopped, and how the lost princess had tried so hard to wake him up. Then the minister saw the kerchief and asked: "Where did this come from?" And the servant told him that the lost princess had written on it with her tears. So the minister took it and lifted it up toward the sun, and read the message that was written there. It said that she was no longer to be found in the first palace, but from then on would make her home in a palace of pearls upon a golden mountain, and that it was there that he would find her.

So the minister left his servant and went off alone to search for her. He searched for many years. Finally he decided that such a palace of pearls could not be found in any inhabited place, for by then he knew well the map of the world. Therefore he decided to search for her in the desert, and after searching for many years he encountered a giant, who carried a tree for a staff. Then the minister told him the whole story of the lost princess, and how he was searching for a palace of pearls upon a golden mountain. The giant said that surely such a thing did not exist. But the minister began to weep, and he insisted that it must surely exist somewhere. And at last the giant said: "Since you are so certain, I shall call all the animals which are in my charge, for they run about the whole world. Perhaps one of them will know about a palace of pearls." Then he called all the animals, from the smallest to the largest, of every kind, and asked them all what they might know, but not one of them had seen any such thing. Then the giant said: "You see, they have confirmed that your quest is hopeless. Listen to me and turn back, for surely you cannot find what does not exist." But the man insisted that it must exist. So the giant said to him: "Behold, farther in the desert lives my brother, who is in charge of all the birds. Perhaps they will know where to find it, since they fly high in the air. Go to him and tell him that I have sent you. And since you are so determined to carry on with your quest, let me assist you, so that at least you will not be hindered by a lack of gold." And he gave him a pouch, and said: "Dip your hand into this pouch whenever you need golden coins, and you will always find as many as you will ever need." And the minister thanked the giant many times for his valuable gift, and for all of his help, and left to search for the giant's brother, who was in charge of all the birds.

So it was that the man walked for many years, seeking the second giant. At last he encountered him, also carrying a great tree for a staff, and he told him about his quest. But this giant also put him off, insisting that such a thing could not be. But when the man refused to give up, the giant said: "Behold, I am in charge of all the birds. I shall call them together, and perhaps they will know." So all the birds were called, each and every one, from the smallest to the largest, and they all replied that they did not know of any such palace of pearls. Then the giant said to him: "Now you must surely see that your quest is folly. Listen to me and turn back, for surely such a palace is not to be found in this world." But the minister would not abandon his quest, and at last the giant said to him: "Still farther in the desert lives my brother, who is in charge of the winds, and they cross the world back and forth every day. Perhaps they will know. I hope so, for never have I seen anyone so determined to complete a quest, even though you are beset with difficulty after difficulty. Therefore let me give you this gift, and perhaps it will be of use to you someday." And he reached into his pocket and pulled out a golden key and gave it to him. And he said: "This key can open any lock in the world. If there is a door that you must enter, simply insert this key into the lock, and when you turn it, the door will open." The minister thanked the giant many times for this priceless gift, and for his help, and set off to search for the giant in charge of the winds.

The man walked for many years, searching for the giant. At last he encountered him carrying a tree, and told him the whole story. And although this giant also tried to put him off, the minister at last convinced him to call all the winds together for his sake, so that he could ask them what they might know. The giant called all the winds to come there, but none of them knew about a palace of pearls on a golden mountain. Then the giant turned to him and said: "You see, you have been searching for something that does not exist." And the man began to weep and said: "I am still certain it can be found in this world." Meanwhile, one last wind arrived, and the giant was angry with it and said: "Why did you come so late? Did I not command that all the winds in the world should come here? Why did you not come with the others?" And the wind answered that it had been held up, because it had to bear the daughter of a king to a palace of pearls on a golden mountain. And when he heard this the minister rejoiced. Then the giant in charge of the winds said to the minister: "You have been searching for such a long time, my poor man, and you have had so many difficulties. Therefore let me give you this gift, which may someday be of use to you." And he reached into his pocket and pulled out a whistle, which he gave to the man. The giant said: "If you are ever in danger or in need of help, just blow on this whistle, and one of the winds will come to your assistance, and will do whatever is in its power to do." The minister thanked the giant many times for such a wonderful gift, and for all of his help. Then the giant commanded the wind to bring him to that palace. And the wind carried him there, and brought him to the gates of the city at the base of the golden mountain, on top of which the palace of pearls was to be found.

Now few strangers had ever entered this city, and once they had been admitted, they were never permitted to leave again, nor could any of the other inhabitants depart. For this was the hidden and secret palace of the Evil One, from which he cast his spells, like the spell that gave him power over the lost princess. And he had kept the existence of that city and palace secret for many centuries, since none had left the city to tell the tale. So it was that when the wind set the minister down before the gates of the city, the guards refused to let him enter. But he dipped his hand into the magic pouch the first giant had given him, and bribed them with golden coins, and thus he managed to enter the city after all. Then he went to the market to buy himself food, for he had to tarry there, since it required much thought and wisdom to set the princess free.

Now when the minister came to the market, he saw a servant who bought all of the fruits of a vendor. And after the servant left with them, the minister approached the vendor and said: "Surely all of those fruits cannot be for a single family." And the vendor replied: "Of course not. They are for those who live in the palace of pearls on the top of this mountain, for the king sees to it that the finest foods are selected for those who live there. And today the king's servants judged my fruits the finest, and that is why he purchased them all."

"Tell me," said the minister, "who is it that lives in the palace of pearls? For I am a stranger here, and I do not know."

The vendor replied: "Only the king and his servants, as far as I know. Although it is rumored that a princess also makes her home there, for not long ago the king selected twelve ladies-in-waiting from among our daughters, and took them to live in the palace, where they are said to serve her."

Now when the minister heard this, he decided to disguise himself as a merchant, and to present himself at the palace of pearls. First he went and bought the clothes of a wayfaring merchant and a fur hat. After this he asked to know who was the finest seamstress in the city, and he was shown to her house. When he came there, he asked her how much it would cost to sew the finest dress of silk and lace. And when the seamstress told him, he said: "Therefore sew twelve of these dresses." And he put his hand into the magic pouch given to him by the first giant, and he paid her in full with golden coins. Then he asked her how long it would take to sew all twelve dresses, and the seamstress told him to come back in twelve days.

So it was that the minister stayed at an inn in that city until the dresses were ready. In the meantime he found out what he could about the king who ruled that kingdom and about his prisoner, the lost princess. In this way he learned that the palace of pearls was the hidden abode of the Evil One himself. So too did he learn that the princess was locked in a room that had seven locks, and that in the next chamber lived the twelve ladies-in-waiting.

When twelve days had passed, the minister returned to the seamstress, and found that the dresses were ready. Then he put the dresses in his merchant's pack, and climbed the golden mountain until he reached the palace of pearls. When he reached the gates of the palace, he showed the guard his merchandise and was admitted with ease, for new merchants were few and far between in that city, and the ladies-in-waiting were always happy to examine their wares, since they had little else to do.

So it was that the merchant was shown to the chamber of the twelve ladies-in-waiting, who were delighted to see him. He took out one dress for each of them, and when they saw how beautiful they were, they all rushed off to try the dresses on, and to study themselves in the mirror, and thus they left the merchant alone in that room. He looked around and saw that one door had seven locks on it, and he knew that must be the chamber of the lost princess. He hurried to that door and took out the golden key that the second giant had given him. With the key he quickly opened all seven locks, and went into the room. There he saw the lost princess, sitting at the window and sobbing over her fate. She was very surprised to see anyone at all, for she was kept apart even from her ladies-in-waiting. And when the minister saw that she did not recognize him in his disguise, he took out of his pocket the kerchief she had left with him, on which she had written with her tears. And when the lost princess saw this, she knew that the minister had found her at last, and she embraced him and wept tears of joy.

Then the minister said: "Come, let us hurry and depart the palace before the ladies-in-waiting return." "Alas," said the princess, "we cannot escape that way. For the Evil One has cast his spell so that it cannot be broken as long as my feet or those of my rescuer touch the ground. And it is this spell that is keeping me captive here even more than the seven locks on the door, which you have somehow opened."

At first the minister despaired over this unexpected obstacle, but then he remembered the whistle he had received from the third giant. He took it out of his pocket and blew on it, and in an instant a wind blew into the room through the open window and said: "How can I be of help to you?" Then the minister told the wind about the spell, and asked if it could carry them away from there with neither the feet of the princess nor his own touching the ground. "Of course I can do that!" said the wind. "But where is it that you want to go?" And the minister told the wind to take them back to the palace of the king who was the father of the princess, and the next thing they knew they found themselves soaring through the heavens, and before long the wind set them down in the kingdom from which they had been gone for so long. So it was that the loyal minister at last succeeded in his quest, and when the king and the princess, who was no longer lost, were reunited, their sadness changed to a joy so great it cannot be described. May everyone know such great joy at least once in a lifetime!

—Eastern Europe: nineteenth century
A tale of Reb Nachman of Bratslav

21. The Prince and the Slave

nce a queen and her slave each gave birth at the same time. And the midwife, who was actually an evil witch, switched the two infants, and gave the prince to the slave, and the son of the slave to the queen. In this way the two were raised by the wrong parents, and the prince grew up thinking he was a slave, and the slave grew up believing he was the prince.

The witch was very proud of herself, for in this way she had confused the destinies of these children and added confusion to the world. She was so proud, in fact, that she had the overwhelming desire to tell someone about her accomplishment. But of course she had to keep her evil deed a secret; if the king and queen were to find out, they would take back their child, the true prince. Yet the witch could not bear to keep this secret to herself, and one day she went over to the open window and whispered it there, certain no one would hear her. And it is true that no human being heard those words, but the wind caught them, and carried them until they reached the birds, and the birds spoke of the exchanged children among themselves.

Now in the forest there lived an old man who knew the language of the birds. He heard what they were saying, and he whispered what he heard to many another, until the rumor of the exchange was known throughout the kingdom, although no one dared to bring this rumor to the attention of the king or queen.

So it was that the true prince was raised as a slave and taught how to serve. And the true son of the slave was raised as a prince and taught how to rule. But in time the rumor that they had been exchanged reached them both. Now the false prince did not mention this rumor to the king and queen, of course, and while the true prince knew that he resembled the king as do two drops of water, he had no other proof of his origin. In due time, the slave came to inherit the throne, and was crowned king.

As king, the son of the slave immediately ordered the exile of the true prince. In truth he would have preferred to have had him killed, but he was afraid that this might somehow cause him to be overthrown. For he believed that he would remain the ruler as long as the true prince remained a slave. Thus the prince was sent into exile far from the country of his birth. This new misfortune was unexpected, and he could not understand why he was so cursed with bad luck, for not only had he been deprived of his kingdom, but he had even been exiled from it.

As for the slave who had become king, even though he wielded great power he was not happy, for the thought that he was actually the son of a slave gnawed away at him. So too did he feel guilty for sending the true prince into exile. Once it happened that the false king was hunting in the forest with the royal ministers. They were pursuing a deer but could not catch it. Hours passed, but the king would not abandon the chase. At last the royal ministers caught up with him and told him it was time to turn back, since night was falling. But the false king was by now obsessed with that deer and refused to turn back. When he saw that the others were terrified of being in the forest at night, he ordered them to return without him, and since they could not disobey his order, they did so. In this way the false king continued to chase after that deer for many days, until the days turned into weeks, and still he could not catch it. But by this time he found himself lost in a deep forest, far from the kingdom he ruled.

Now shortly after he was sent into exile, the true prince dreamed that he came to a city where a fair was taking place. In the dream he was told to go to the fair and to take the first job he was offered, whatever it was. The prince remembered this dream when he woke, but he paid it little heed. Yet when he dreamed it a second and then a third time, he realized that the dream was compelling him to go there, and he decided to go. He walked until he came to a large road, and he followed that road until he reached a city, and just as in his dream, there was a fair taking place. Shortly after he arrived he met a merchant, who asked him if he wanted to work. He needed some men to help him drive home the cattle he had purchased at the fair. And the prince agreed to work for him, as he had been told to do in the dream.

Now it happened that this merchant was a vicious, hateful man, who drove his workers as hard as he drove the cattle. And one morning, when three cattle suddenly ran off into the forest, the merchant shouted at the prince to chase after them, and not to return without all three. So the prince went dashing off into the forest, trying to catch up with the cattle. But each time he approached them, they would run off, each in another direction, and in this way they led him further and further into the forest, until he was quite lost.

By that time the sun was about to set, and the prince realized that the forest could be very dangerous at night. He looked around and saw a large tree nearby and climbed into it just as the forest grew dark. And as soon as darkness fell, a terrible laughter rang through the forest, which made the prince's blood grow cold, and he gave thanks that he had found refuge in that tree. Just then the prince heard a cough nearby and discovered another man huddled in that tree. "What are you doing here?" The prince asked. The other replied, "I can ask the same of you." Then the prince said, "I was chasing after cattle that ran away." And the man in the tree said, "I was following a deer on the hunt, and it led me to this forsaken forest." For the other man in that tree was none other than the son of the slave who had been made a king.

Meanwhile the terrible laughter would ring out from time to time, causing both men to shudder with fear. The prince told the other that to pass the time they should speak, and so the slave told of his life as king, and the prince came to realize he was in that tree with the very one who had usurped his throne. Then he decided to conceal his true identity for the time being, lest the other try to kill him, since he had already sent him into exile.

Now the false king had not eaten for several days, and he was truly famished. And it happened that the prince had been carrying some bread with him when he had run off into the forest. So the false king wasted no time in asking if the other had any food. But the prince realized that while he was lost in the forest, food was of great value, more valuable than gold. And at that moment he saw a way for him to take back what was truly his. So he said, "I have only enough bread to sustain myself until I get out of his terrible forest." The false king could not accept this, and he offered to pay any price the other would ask. The prince told him that in that forest nothing was more precious than bread, and asked what the king would offer for it. Then the false king said, "I would give everything for some of that bread. I would even give up my kingdom." "Let us agree, then," said the prince, "that this is what shall be done. I will divide the bread I have with you, and you will become my slave, and all of your property will become mine." "Yes, yes," said the son of the slave, and at that moment he became the slave it was his destiny to be, and the prince was restored to his true place as the son of a king.

At daybreak the prince looked down from the tree and saw the three cattle grazing nearby. And the slave looked up and saw the deer he had chased for so long. But the prince realized that he did not have to chase after the cattle, for he was no longer a slave. And the slave realized he was no longer hunting that deer for sport, for he was no longer king. Nor could he run after that deer without the permission of the other, since he was now his slave. And the changes that had taken place in that tree overnight amazed and overwhelmed both the prince and the slave, for their roles had truly been reversed.

The prince saw that the slave still longed to chase after that deer. So he said, "It is not in my nature to expect someone to be my slave, for I have served as a slave for too long to want that. Instead, I ask that you sign a statement that all you possess now belongs to me. And after that you shall be free to chase that deer to the ends of the earth, should you so desire." Then the slave broke off a piece of the bark of that tree, and on the smooth side of it he wrote with the pen that he had once used as king that he was giving everything to the prince. Then he climbed down from that tree and began to chase after the deer again, but it only led him still further into the woods. And he never emerged from that forest again.

As for the prince, he cared nothing for the chase any longer. He abandoned those cattle as if they had been sins left behind after repentance. Then he set off to find his way out of that forest, and by following the signs he had left when he had entered there, he found his way to a path, and that path led him to a road, and that road led him to a kingdom. He came to the gate of that kingdom and sought to be allowed in. The gatekeeper, however, refused to open the gate. When the prince asked why, the gatekeeper told him that he had come to a kingdom that had lost its name. Only those who were prepared to restore the lost name were permitted to enter those gates. And the gatekeeper asked the prince if he were willing to undertake such a task. The prince had not expected this, and he did not know how to reply. So he said, "This is a matter for deep consideration. I will come back when I am able to give you an answer." And he left and went back into the forest.

But now he was in a different part of the forest, far from the shrill and terrifying laughter. Instead, that night a wondrous music, the most beautiful the prince had ever heard, came drifting in the darkness. All night long his heart sailed on that music, filled with longing. And in the morning he understood that the music had filled him with the desire to restore the kingdom's lost name. He climbed down from the tree and all day he thought about that music, wondering what might be its unearthly source and hoping that it might return that night. And by the time three stars could be seen, the music drifted again throughout the forest.

Then the prince found that he was unafraid of the dark and climbed down from the tree to seek out the source of that music. He let the music lead him, for it grew louder as he drew closer to its source. In this way he was led to another tree, in whose branches the full moon could be seen. When the prince came closer, he saw that in the place where the full moon rested, some kind of vessel was glowing in the dark. He did not know if it was the light of the moon that shone on it, or if the light came from within. And he climbed up into that tree and stared at that glowing source all that night and fell into a deep trance.

At dawn, just as the sun rose, the prince came out of the trance. He realized it had been brought on by the unearthly music and the glowing light. And he discovered, as well, that he felt strengthened and refreshed as he had not felt in years. Then the prince looked up into the place where that light had been and from which the music had come. And there he saw a wooden vessel, which he realized must be some kind of musical instrument. So he climbed up into the branches until the vessel was within his reach, and he took it from a hollow place in the trunk.

Perched in that tree, the prince examined the instrument, turning it over and over. It had been carved from a very rich wood, and engraved with intricate designs and various signs and symbols. They were not in any language the prince had ever seen, and when he discovered that he could read them, he was most astonished. He surmised that listening to that music during the trance had somehow made it possible for him to read those symbols. And by reading them he learned the secret of that strange instrument and knew he was ready to restore the lost name of the kingdom.

Taking the precious instrument with him, the prince returned to the gate. This time, when the gatekeeper asked his question, the prince replied that he was indeed prepared to restore the kingdom's lost name, and the gate was opened to him. In that kingdom there was a garden, and it was said that whoever could enter that garden and come out of it in peace would restore the lost name. But until then, all of those who had entered there had soon come running out, terrified. For they had been greeted by a horrible screaming, which had frightened them out of their wits. The prince, too, was greeted by these cries, but they did not sound like screaming to him. Instead he understood the meaning of these sounds, for since he had fallen into the trance, he also understood this language. That is how he heard the pleas of the spirits who called out for him to restore the lost name. And from listening to these cries, he learned that everything in that garden had an order, which had been lost over time. Now everything was out of place. If only he could restore everything to its proper place, the name of the kingdom would be restored at last.

Following the guidance of the spirits, who were more than happy to help him, the prince did whatever they told him to do to restore the garden to its old order. He moved the statue of the king who had established that garden to the center, and when he did a fountain that had been dry for a long, long time sprang up around it. And when he had done everything that needed to be done, the spirits led him to the throne in that garden. There the prince discovered that it was carved out of the same wood as was the enchanted instrument. He took out the instrument and placed it on the throne. And all at once a music emerged from that instrument that carried the true name of that kingdom to every corner of the land, so that everyone knew that the lost name had been restored at last, and each and every inhabitant knew what it was. For that was the Kingdom of Music, which had been ruled by silence for so long. And now the true ruler, music, took its place. And even though music is invisible, still everyone who can hear knows of its existence. Only the deaf are deprived of its beauty. And when the inhabitants heard that unearthly, enchanting music, they realized how empty their lives had been without it, and how heavily the silence had weighed upon them.

So it was that when he emerged from that garden in peace, the prince was met by the elders of the kingdom, and each one thanked him with all his heart for restoring the music to the kingdom, and thus restoring its name. And they invited him to become their king, for they had always known that whoever could restore the lost name was the one who should serve as their king as well. The prince agreed to become their king and served for many years to come. And in the end he even found a way to unite that Kingdom of Music with his own, which he had been born to rule in the first place. And that was a joyous day indeed.

—Eastern Europe: nineteenth century
A tale of Reb Nachman of Bratslav

22. The Prince Who Was Made of Precious Gems

here once was a great king who ruled over a vast kingdom. This king possessed unlimited wealth and power, and had everything a man can have, except that he had no children, and thus had no one to inherit his throne. Now the king longed to have an heir, for the thought that his kingdom would one day fall into the hands of strangers haunted him. So it was that he spent much of his time consulting with doctors and wise men, as well as with every kind of sorcerer and soothsayer. But none of these was able to help him, and the king and queen despaired of ever having a child of their own.

Then one day, when the king was very desperate, he turned to his ministers and asked them if they could think of anything else that he might do. An evil minister among them spoke up and said: "If I may be permitted to speak, my king, I have a proposal which might possibly provide the solution to your dilemma." The king replied: "Yes, yes, speak up." And the evil minister said: "It is rumored, my lord, that there are secret sorcerers among the Jews of our kingdom who possess great powers. They are said to have learned the secrets of King Solomon. I propose, O king, that we demand of the Jews that they bring forth one of these sorcerers, and let him beg their God to provide you with an heir, or else let them pay with their lives!"

Now the truth is that the evil minister did not believe the rumors he had heard about the powers of the secret sorcerers among the Jews, but he hoped to draw disaster upon their heads, as well as to put himself into a position where he might one day inherit the throne. The king was deceived by his proposal, and ordered that the Jews bring forth such a wise man, who would intercede on his behalf. He added that if he was not blessed with a child by the end of one year, the Jews of his kingdom would pay with their lives! So it was that the frightened Jews turned to their rabbis, and begged for their help. And the rabbis met with each other, and agreed that their only hope was to search for one of the hidden saints among them, known as the *Lamed-vav Tzaddikim*, or Thirty-six Just Men, who are the pillars that support the world. For the prayers of such a man would surely be heard. But since these holy men are hidden, no one knows for certain who they are, and therefore no one knew where one might be found.

Time passed and the people grew more frightened, and still no hidden saint was identified. Then it happened that on the same night three rabbis in three different cities in that kingdom had an identical dream. In their dream they met with one of the Just Men, who lived in a cave deep in the forest, from which the sound of a nearby waterfall could be heard. And when the dream of these rabbis became known, it was recognized as a miracle, and many of the men organized search parties, and set out to find the hidden saint who lived in a cave somewhere in the forest. So too did the three rabbis who dreamed the same dream join this search, and traveled together, in hope that they would recognize some detail from their dreams. They searched for many weeks, but there was no sign of the cave they had found in their dream. Then it happened one day that they heard the sound of a waterfall, and it reminded them of the sound of falling water they had heard inside the cave of the hidden saint. Then they searched very carefully in that area, and at last they discovered his cave.

When the three rabbis entered the cave, they recognized it at once. There too was the same old man with a white beard whom they had first met in a dream. He was seated on a stone ledge, intent in his study of an ancient text, which he read in the light cast by the flames burning within. When he saw the three rabbis, the old man stood up and said: "Come in. I have been expecting you. Yes, we last met in a dream. I have spent my life alone, in the study of the sacred texts. But if my help is needed in this time of danger, there is no other choice. Therefore I will agree to come with you and to meet the king, as long as you vow never to reveal where this cave is hidden." The rabbis gladly made such a vow, and the hidden saint accompanied them to the palace of the king, where he was given an audience at once. The king was very surprised by his ragged appearance, but he accepted that the ways of the Jews might be foreign, and besides, he had no better hope. The king told the Just Man that he and his wife, the queen, greatly longed for a child. It was for this that they had sought his assistance. The Just Man assured the king and queen that they would be parents, and he promised them that before the year was out they would indeed be blessed with a child.

And within the year the queen gave birth to a beautiful daughter, who was the apple of everyone's eye. She was exceptionally beautiful, and when she was four years old she already knew how to read and write, as well as how to play the violin. She also had a great gift for languages, and had already mastered six. Kings traveled to that kingdom to see her, and from a young age the king began to receive marriage offers for her from the rulers of many kingdoms, who wanted to make a match with their sons. That is when the king realized that his daughter was destined to serve as a queen in a foreign realm, while his own kingdom might fall into the hands of strangers. Once more he began to brood. And when the evil minister saw that he still was not satisfied, he again proposed forcing the Jews to come to the king's assistance, for he still hoped to bring down disaster upon them. And the king agreed that this would be done.

So it was that the Jews were forced once more to seek out the hidden saint. Again they turned to the three rabbis who alone knew where he was hidden, for they had vowed never to reveal his location. But when they came to his cave, they found that the Just Man had taken leave of this world, to claim his portion in Paradise. At first the three rabbis despaired, for where were they to find another hidden saint? But then they said among themselves:

"Surely such a holy man must have known that one day we might need his assistance again. Come, then, let us search the cave for any clues he might have left us as to where his successor might be found." For they knew that whenever a Just Man leaves this life, there is always another who takes his place, so that the number of them remains at thirty-six at all times.

Then the rabbis carefully searched through the cave where the hidden saint had made his home. There they found that he had few possessions except for his sacred texts, which were all well worn. But then one of the rabbis noticed a crevice that they had overlooked, and inside it he found a small, finely crafted silver mirror, engraved with intricate designs and secret symbols. When he looked into that mirror, he saw reflected there a man he did not recognize, yet he knew at once who that man must be—the very hidden saint they were seeking. He showed the mirror to the others, who agreed they must seek out the man reflected there. Together they set out, wandering from village to village, and showing the mirror to whomever they met, until at last they found someone who recognized him, and directed them to the village in which he made his home. When at last they found him, they told him of the king's order and of their quest. At first the man refused to believe that he had inherited the mantle of one of the *Lamed-vav Tzaddikim*, but when the rabbis showed him the mirror that reflected his face, and told him how they had found it, he accepted all that they said, and agreed to come with them. After that the Just Man prayed for guidance, and his prayers were answered, and he learned in a dream what it was that he should do to bring about the birth of a son for the king.

So it was that this Just Man soon found himself in the presence of the king, as had the hidden saint who had served before him. This time the king was careful to specify his desire for a son, who would serve as the heir to his throne. The Just Man assured him that his wish would be fulfilled, if the king would agree to supply him with one of every kind of precious gem. Without hesitation the king said, "I would give up half of my kingdom for a son." Then the king ordered that one of every kind of precious gem be gathered, and delivered to the hidden saint. This was done, and then, in the presence of the king, the Just Man crushed each gem, ground it to dust, and mixed it with wine, for that is what he had been told to do in his dream. This wine he poured into the cups of the king and queen, half into one and half into the other. Then the king and queen each drank the potion, and before the Just Man took his leave he said: "Before a year is out you will have a son who will be made entirely of precious gems. He will have the charms and qualities of each of the gems that was mixed into your wine, for each gem has its own special charm."

Once more the prophecy proved true, and before the year was out the queen gave birth to a son, and the king was exceedingly pleased, even though the child was not made of gems, but was flesh and blood, like every other child. And just like his sister, this child was very beautiful and very wise. Before the age of four he could read and write, play many musical instruments, and speak a dozen languages. Kings came from every corner of the earth to see him, and to propose that their daughters might one day be his queen. So it was that the young prince became the center of attention, and his sister became jealous, and her love for him turned to hate. Her one consolation was that he was not made of precious gems, as the Just Man had predicted. Then one day the prince was chopping wood and cut his finger, and when the princess came over to bandage it, she saw a gem gleaming on the inside. Then she was overcome with jealousy, and decided to pretend to be ill, that she too might receive some attention. So she went into her room, and refused to come out of it, even to eat.

Now the king and queen were very concerned about their daughter, and they summoned doctors from all over the kingdom, but they were all unable to cure her mysterious illness. Then the king called in his sorcerers, and among these there was a wicked one, who had made an alliance with the evil minister. This sorcerer saw that the princess was only pretending to be ill, and when he confronted her she confessed it was true, and revealed her hatred for her brother, the prince. Then the princess asked the wicked sorcerer if there was any way to cause a person to become ill. And he said that he knew of a way to cause a person to be covered with scabs. Then she asked if another sorcerer could cure this disease, and the sorcerer replied that if the talisman that had caused the disease was concealed in water, the spell could not be broken.

So it was that the princess fell into the trap set for her by the evil minister and the wicked sorcerer. For they had long wanted to find a way to be rid of the young prince, so that the evil minister might fulfill his dream of one day becoming king. Until then they had been afraid to act on their own, but now that the princess could be blamed, they became bolder, and the wicked sorcerer cast a spell on the prince, and caused him to be covered with scabs all over his face and body. Then he gave the talisman with which he had cast the spell to the princess, who hid it under a rock in a pool outside of the palace. Of course the king sent for all of his doctors, but none of them was able to cure the prince. Then he summoned his sorcerers, but none of their spells had any effect. Finally the king decreed that the Jews must assist him once more, and find a cure for the prince, or else they would pay with their lives.

So it was that the people turned once again to the Just Man who had already interceded with the Holy One in their behalf. Now the Just Man believed, like the rest of the world, that the prince was merely flesh and blood. For this reason he began to doubt the dream in which he had learned that the prince would be made of precious gems, and was afraid that he would be unable to bring about a cure. Still, because of the danger to the Jews, he went before the king, and sought to undertake a cure. And through his prayers it was revealed to him that the disease of the prince had been caused by witchcraft. This the Just Man reported to the king, and told him that nothing could be done unless the talisman containing the spell was recovered, and the one who bewitched the prince was cast into the sea. When the king heard this he said: "I will give you all of the sorcerers in my kingdom. You can cast them all into the sea. I would do anything to save my son."

Now the young princess was present when the king said this, and she became very frightened that her role was about to be revealed. Then she hurried off to be certain that the talisman was still safely hidden. And when the Just Man saw her hurry away, he became suspicious, and told the king to have her followed. In this way a guard followed her to the pool outside the palace. But when the princess bent over to lift up the stone under which the talisman was hidden, she fell in the water and began to cry out. This caused a great commotion, and the king and the Just Man hurried outside to see what had happened. But the Just Man told the king not to worry, for the princess would surely be saved by the guard who had followed her, and now the prince would recover. And as soon as the guard pulled the princess to safety, she confessed that she had asked the wicked sorcerer to cast the spell, and revealed where the talisman was hidden. And when the king heard this, he understood that the princess was not to blame, but that she had been led astray, and he forgave her. Then the king had the wicked sorcerer brought before him, and forced him to confess, and the sorcerer also admitted that the evil minister had put him up to the plan.

So it was that the wicked sorcerer and the evil minister were cast into the sea, and the prince began to recover the same day. The scabs that had afflicted him began to fall away, and as they did it was revealed to the world that he consisted entirely of precious gems. And all those who came to know him found that he possessed the charms and qualities of those very gems.

—Eastern Europe: nineteenth century
A tale of Reb Nachman of Bratslav

23. The Water Palace

n a faraway land there was a king who had conquered many kingdoms, and whose wealth was boundless. His palace was filled with treasures of every kind—there were golden objects encrusted with precious jewels, rare rugs from every corner of the world, and mirrors made of silver so highly polished that they reflected better than any mirror of glass. Even though there was nothing this great king lacked, nevertheless he was not satisfied, and he always searched for something more precious than what he already possessed.

Then one year it happened that this king received the king of a faraway kingdom, who had embarked on the long journey to see with his own eyes the mysterious water palace found on the southern shores of that kingdom. Now this water palace was truly one of the greatest wonders of the world, for it consisted entirely of water. The floors and walls of the palace were made of water, the grounds and gardens that surrounded it were made of water, and the fruit trees that grew there—all were made of water. And this palace was surrounded by ten walls, one inside the other, all of them made of water. And because the palace and walls consisted of water, it was impossible to enter there, for whoever tried to do so would surely drown. Still, travelers came from all over the world to marvel at the wonder of that palace, which remained unchanged amidst the waves, not far from the shore.

Now it happened that when the king who ruled that kingdom met the king from the distant kingdom, he also met the visiting king's daughter, the princess, who had traveled with him, along with their guards and servants. And the extraordinary beauty of that princess struck the wealthy king with amazement. He knew at once that he would not rest until he had made her his own, for to him it was she, and not the water palace, that was the most precious treasure.

Therefore the wealthy king offered to accompany the visiting king and the princess on the journey to the water palace, and put all of his resources at their disposal. Before long their caravan departed for the journey south. The procession was led by the two kings and the princess, dressed in the silks and diamonds of a court celebration. Behind them came their countless servants, walking together in twos and threes. The caravan was watched by the subjects of the kingdom as it passed through the forests and fields; it proceeded in a stately manner, not so fast as to frighten the horses or cause the carriages to shake, while the two kings and the princess held the diamond-studded reins in their hands. During the journey the wealthy king took every opportunity to speak to the princess who rode beside him, for he felt a longing for her which was unlike anything he had ever known, so sharp was his craving that she might be his wife.

Now at first the princess paid little attention to this king, and resisted his approaches, but when the caravan arrived at the cove facing the water palace, the princess, like everyone else, was awed by it. The more she looked at its enchanted beauty, the more certain she became that she had somehow seen it before, perhaps in a dream. Nor did she want to depart from that place when the sun began to set, but insisted on staying there as night fell, for she had heard that the water palace was somehow illumined from within, so that its every ramp and arch could be seen even on the darkest night. And the wealthy king, out of his longing for the princess, chose to remain with her in that place, and when he observed how much she was drawn to the palace, an idea entered his mind of how he might convince her to become his bride. Late that night he told her that if she would marry him and become his queen, he would agree to build an ivory palace on the very shore where she stood, facing the water palace, and that he would make that palace their home. And when the princess understood that in this way she would never have to part from the pristine beauty of the water palace, she accepted, although she did not truly love him, and she agreed that she would become his queen.

The king was enthralled at the prospect of spending his life with this beautiful princess. Soon preparations were made for their wedding, which was declared a holiday for all, and at the same time construction of the ivory palace was begun. And because the king put all of his vast resources into building it, the palace was completed by the day of their wedding. At the king's command the architect had sought to model it after the water palace in every respect that could be seen—for neither he nor anyone else had entered it. And the bridal chamber of the king and the princess had been built to face directly the inaccessible palace surrounded by and constructed of water.

Then it happened on the very night the king and princess were wed, as the king slept beside his bride for the first time, that he had a vivid dream in which the princess approached the bed on which he lay, with a bow and arrow, and both arrow and bow were made of gold. And before he could speak, she took aim and shot the golden arrow into his heart. Now when the king awoke from this dream he was shaken and afraid for his life. He left the sleeping princess, and ordered a servant to stand guard outside that chamber, to prevent her from leaving it until the king had consulted with his advisers.

The next morning, when the princess awoke, the king was not there, but she simply assumed that he had returned to his duties. And since her food was brought to her, she did not question the matter, but instead hurried to the window from which the water palace could be seen, and filled her eyes with its unearthly beauty.

Meanwhile, the king had gathered all of his dream interpreters together, and he told them his dream. Then he called on his oldest interpreter, and bid him to speak. He said that the king need not fear, for the arrow that the princess had shot into the king's heart was surely the arrow of love, and the dream had come because he was so filled with love for her. Then the king called on another interpreter, and the second confirmed what the first had said, adding that the king had been "slain," so to speak, by the great beauty of his bride. But the third to speak disputed this interpretation, and insisted that the dream posed grave danger to the king, since it prophesied that the princess would bring about his death. After this every other dream interpreter agreed with this interpretation, for they saw in it a way to rid themselves of the princess, who had already caused them to lose much of their influence over the king. And when they had all spoken, the king returned to the first two interpreters and, out of fear, they too agreed that the interpretation of the others was correct, and withdrew their own.

After this the king asked them what he should do with the princess, who posed such a danger to his life. Those two who had understood the dream as a sign of his love suggested that he banish her. But the king refused this idea from the first, for the thought that she might ever belong to another tormented him, since he had made such an effort to make her his own. And those who had interpreted the dream as a warning told the king to put her to death. But the king refused this advice as well, for he was afraid that his grief at her death would be unbearable. Therefore he decided to delay his decision and meanwhile he continued to live with his bride, although he kept a guard near them at all times. And every day he had the palace searched for the golden bow and arrow, but never was any hidden weapon to be found.

Yet, even with these precautions the king could not forget his dream. He thought of it whenever he was in the presence of the princess, and it came to haunt him day and night, until his love for her became spoiled. As for the princess, she saw how her husband had become remote and sensed that he did not trust her, although she could not imagine why. Thus, little by little, her trust in him also faded. Then there was nothing that kept her in that place except for the enchanted vision of the water palace, which possessed her even when she slept, so that she dreamed of it every night. So it was that the princess spent more and more time sitting at her window, letting the watery ramps and arches of the palace beckon to her, for while she could not bear to live with the king any longer, she also knew that she could not bear to abandon the mysterious palace.

One night, in her desperation, the princess slipped away from the king while he was sleeping, and climbed out of the window that faced the water palace, and made her way from the ivory palace to the palace in the sea. But before long the king awoke and found the princess missing, and became enraged. He assumed that she had left to get the golden bow, and that she intended to kill him that very night. He shouted for his guards, and they came running, and word was quickly spread to search for the princess wherever she could be found, and it was soon reported that she had been seen running along the shore, in the direction of the water palace. Before long the princess heard the clamor of the guards behind her, and knew that they were already in pursuit. Therefore she walked directly into the water, for she preferred to drown rather than to be captured by the king. And when the king, who had accompanied his guards, saw this, he shouted to the guards to shoot their arrows at her, and to kill her, as he thought she had intended to kill him.

Now there were ten guards with the king, and each of those guards carried a bow and arrow, and each of those arrows had been dipped in a poison, and each of the poisons was more deadly than the next. The guards took aim as they saw the princess running into the sea, and shot their ten arrows at the same time. And each of those arrows pierced the princess, and she was gravely wounded and fell into the water. But the instant she touched the water a wave rose up and carried her out into the sea, through every one of the gates of the ten walls that surrounded the water palace. For there was a gate in every wall, and each of those gates opened when the wave carried her close to it, and closed again the instant she had passed through. At last the wave brought her into the innermost chamber of the water palace, and set her down on a circular bed, where she fainted and fell into a deep sleep, and not even the waves that washed against the wall of the palace caused her to waken.

Meanwhile the king and his guards had become so obsessed with capturing her that they did not stop when they reached the sea, but continued to pursue her into the water as if they were still on land. Then a great wave came and carried them far off from the shore, where they struggled and soon sank. Every one of them, including the king, was drowned.

Now when the people of this kingdom learned that the king had drowned, and that the princess had also very likely lost her life, they sent a messenger to her father, who had not yet left the kingdom, and invited him to become their king, for they had recognized that he was a wise and good man, and would not lead them astray. The father of the princess agreed to remain in their kingdom and serve as their king until another king could be found, for he still hoped that his daughter might have somehow survived and reached safety in the water palace.

After the new king had been installed, he made a proclamation that whoever succeeded in reaching the water palace and discovering the fate of the princess would receive a great reward, and if she was alive, whoever brought her back from there would become her husband, and would succeed him as king. Then brave princes and many other daring young men came from all over the world and sought to reach the water palace. Some tried to swim out to it, and some tried to travel in rafts, and others in boats. But one and all, they failed to pass through the ten walls that surrounded it, and many were drowned making the effort. And among those who survived, all insisted that the princess never could have reached the water palace, and that even if she had, she could not have passed through the ten walls, and must surely have drowned in the strong currents there. But even as the months passed and nothing was heard of the princess, the king refused to give up the hope that his daughter might still be alive.

Now in a nearby kingdom there lived a young prince whose family had ruled that realm for many generations until their army had met defeat at the hands of the wealthy king. The prince's father had died defending their kingdom, and the prince, who had barely escaped with his life, had gone into hiding. But in his heart he was determined that someday he would defeat the king who had brought about his father's death and had taken their kingdom by force. So this prince disguised himself as a wandering beggar, and traveled to the kingdom of the water palace. Like all the others who entered that land, he was told the tale of how the king had lost his life pursuing the princess, and of the reward that awaited whoever could reach the water palace and discover her fate. The prince was exhilarated when he heard this news, and he decided at once to present himself, still as a beggar, to the new king, in the hope that he could somehow win back his father's kingdom.

That night the beggar prince dreamed that birds flew to the seashore from every corner of the world. And in the dream he heard them singing melodies, ten in all. As they reached the shore each dropped a single feather, until at last the feathers formed into a swan-shaped boat. And no sooner was it complete than a wave arose and picked up the boat of feathers, and carried it on top of the waves. When the prince awoke he remembered this dream, and even recalled each of the ten melodies. And he realized that such a boat of feathers might well suit his purpose in rescuing the princess.

Later that day the beggar prince was given an audience with the king, during which he offered to seek to accomplish what so many others had already failed to do—to penetrate the ten walls of the water palace. And because a considerable time had passed since anyone else had offered to undertake the risk, the king welcomed his offer, even though it came from a beggar. Then the prince told the king that it would be necessary to gather one feather from every kind of bird in that kingdom, from the most glorious to the most common, for with those feathers he intended to build a boat of feathers with which he might confront the waves. For, he said, only a boat of feathers could pass over the ten walls, since any other would be too heavy. And the king ordered that the feathers be gathered, and the prince built a fine swan-shaped boat with them, exactly like the one he had seen in his dream.

On the morning that the beggar prince was to set off in the boat of feathers to try to make his way to the water palace, the king accompanied him to the shore, followed by a great many of his subjects. And when the beggar prince placed the boat in the water, all were amazed at how lightly it floated. Then he climbed into the boat of feathers, and the first wave that came carried it off so that it seemed to fly, so lightly did it travel on the waters. With all those who watched as witnesses, the boat sailed above the ten walls with room to spare, and in this way the beggar prince soon reached the water palace, and made his way inside. Now why he did not sink is a mystery which has remained unknown to this day. But there, in the innermost chamber, he found the princess, still deeply asleep. For she had not awakened since she had been carried into that chamber, nor could she be awakened until the ten arrows were removed, and she was cured of the ten poisons.

It was there, behind those walls of water, with the winds raising up the billows of the sea, that the beggar prince removed the ten different arrows from the princess. And with each of his ten fingers he felt one of the ten pulses, and set about to cure her, using the ten different melodies he had learned in his dream. And when he had felt the tenth pulse and sung the tenth melody, the eyes of the princess opened, and she sat up on the bed. And she knew from the first glance that the one who stood before her was her true love, as the suspicious king had never been. So the beggar prince took the princess out of the water palace, and returned with her in the boat of feathers to the shore. There she was reunited with her father, the king, who wept long and hard when he saw his beloved daughter was still alive. Then the beggar revealed his true identity as a prince, and it was announced that they would be wed. So it was that in this way the prince came to rule both his own kingdom, and that of the king who had usurped it. And it is said that once a year, on the anniversary of the day the beggar prince took the princess out of the water palace, they would return there together in that boat of feathers, and spend the day in the innermost chamber, where she had slept for so long, although what they did or spoke of in that place has never been revealed.

—Eastern Europe: nineteenth century
A tale of Reb Nachman of Bratslav

24. The Pirate Princess

nce upon a time there were two kings, each of whom was childless. And each one set out to discover a remedy that would make it possible for a child to be born to him. Now fate led both kings to the cave of an old sorcerer on the same day, and the sorcerer met with them at the same time. And after each had explained what it was that he sought, the two kings were amazed to discover that they both were on the same quest—each searching for a remedy so that he might be blessed with a child of his own.

After they had spoken, the sorcerer said to them: "I have read in the stars that each of you is destined to have a child, one a boy and one a girl. And I have also read there that these two are destined to marry. If you permit their marriage to take place, you and your descendants will share a great blessing. But if you keep them apart, for any reason, many will suffer before they are reunited." Then the sorcerer stood up, and the kings left the cave. But before they parted they each vowed that if one had a boy and the other a girl, the children would be betrothed.

It happened that before a year had passed the two kings had each become fathers, one to a beautiful boy, and the other to a lovely girl. But the demands of their kingdoms were very great and the distractions endless, and so it happened that they forgot their vows to each other. And when their children came of age, they sent them off to study in a foreign land. And fate caused them both to study under a famous scholar, who was, in fact, the sorcerer who had predicted their birth.

In this way the prince and princess met, and knew from the first that they loved each other, and wanted to be wed. Yet even though the sorcerer saw this, he did not reveal their destiny to them, for he wanted them to stay together solely by the power of their love. So it was that for several years the prince and the princess were together every day. When their studies came to an end, he returned to his kingdom and she to hers. But when they were apart each became dejected, and soon it became plain for all to see that they were unhappy, but no one knew why.

At last the king who was the father of the prince asked him why he had become so sad. Then the prince revealed his love for the foreign princess, and when the king heard this, and learned who she was, he recognized the father of the princess to be the king with whom he had made the vow to betroth their children. Therefore he wrote a letter to the other king, and reminded him of the vow, and suggested that their children should now be wed. And he gave the letter to the prince, and sent him to deliver it in person to the king.

Now when the king who was the father of the princess received the prince and read the letter, he grew afraid, for he had forgotten about the vow he had made with the prince's father. And he had since betrothed the princess to a prince whose father ruled a rich and powerful kingdom. Therefore the king decided to delay the prince for as long as possible, until the princess had been wed to another. So he invited the prince to remain in the palace, so that he might observe him, and see if he had been properly prepared to be a ruler. But the king also left orders that the prince was not to be permitted to see the princess, nor was she to be told of his presence there.

In this way the prince and princess remained apart, although they were both living in the same palace. But one day the princess overheard two of the servants whispering about the prince and learned in which chamber he was staying. Then she made a point of passing in front of that chamber as often as possible. Before long the prince caught a glimpse of her in his mirror, and soon they managed to meet in secret. Then the princess told the prince how her father had betrothed her to another, and they decided to run away together that very night.

So it was that the prince and the princess climbed out of their windows at midnight, and ran together until they reached the ship of the prince. They set sail in the middle of the night, and by the time it was discovered that they were missing, they were already far away. They continued to sail together for a long time, until they were in need of fresh food and water. Soon afterward they spied an island and sailed there, docked the ship, and walked together into the forest. There the princess climbed a fruit tree and tossed the fruit that she picked down to the prince, who filled up a sack with it. But it happened that a wealthy merchant's son was passing near that island in a ship, and he was observing the island with his telescope. In this way he happened to see the princess in the tree, and he was astonished at her beauty. He had his ship brought to shore, and he set out with several sailors, armed with weapons, to capture the lovely girl in the tree, and to make her come with him whether she wanted to or not.

Now when the princess, from the vantage point in the tree, saw the men coming in their direction, and saw the long swords they carried, she told the prince to hide and not to reveal himself, no matter what happened. Then she tossed her ring to him, which he caught, and she vowed that even if they were separated, they would one day be reunited. The prince hid himself in the dense woods, and saw the merchant's son and his men arrive at the foot of the tree, but there was nothing he could do about it, for he was unarmed.

At first the merchant's son spoke sweetly to the princess, but when she refused to reply he ordered his men to cut the tree down. And then, when she saw she could not escape, the princess descended from the tree and returned with the merchant's son to the ship. But before she boarded the ship, the princess made the merchant's son vow not to touch her until they were married in his land. And even though she was his prisoner, he agreed to this vow, for he was smitten with love for her, and hoped to win her love as well.

Nor would the princess tell him who she was, but she promised that once they were wed she would reveal the secret, but until then he must not ask to know. And the merchant's son also agreed to honor this condition.

When the ship reached the land of the merchant's son, filled with much valuable merchandise, the princess asked the merchant to inform his family that he had brought his future bride with him. The merchant agreed to this, and also to her request that all of sailors on the ship should be given wine to share in their celebration.

So the merchant's son left the ship to inform his family, and the sailors began to celebrate. Before long they were all drunken, and they decided to leave the ship to look around the town. And when she had the ship to herself, the princess untied it from its moorings and unfurled the sails and set sail by herself.

Meanwhile the family of the merchant's son all came down to the harbor to greet his bride-to-be. But when they found the ship missing, including all its merchandise, the merchant was furious with his son. All the merchant's son could say was "Ask the sailors," and when they searched for the sailors they found them sprawled drunken around town, and neither then, nor later, when they were sober again, did they have any idea at all of what had happened to the ship. Then, in a great rage, the merchant drove his son out of his house, to become a wanderer in the world.

Meanwhile the princess continued to sail the ship, intent on searching for her lost love. As it happened, she sailed by the kingdom of a king who had built his palace on the shore of the sea. That king liked to watch the passing ships with his telescope. So it was that he noticed a ship that seemed to be sailing without any guidance. He sent his sailors to catch up with it, and to bring it into port. This they did, and in this way the princess was captured again, and became a prisoner of the king.

But when the king met his lovely prisoner, who had been sailing the ship by herself, he was greatly struck with her beauty and royal bearing, and he desired to marry her. This she agreed to do on three conditions: that the king not touch her until after their wedding; that her ship not be unloaded until the same time, so that none would say she had come empty-handed; and, finally, that she be given eleven ladies-in-waiting, to remain with her in her palace chamber. The king agreed to these conditions, and made plans for a lavish wedding. So too did he sent the daughters of eleven lords to serve as her ladies-in-waiting. And before long they had all become good friends, and they all played musical instruments together to amuse themselves.

One day before the wedding the princess invited her ladies-in-waiting to go with her onto the deck of the ship, to see what a ship was like. They all were glad to join her there, for they had never been on a ship, and they greatly enjoyed themselves. Then the princess offered them the good wine that she had found stored there, and they drank the wine and soon became intoxicated and fell asleep. Then the princess went and untied the moorings and raised the sails and once again escaped with the ship.

Now when the king was told that the ship was no longer docked, he became afraid that the princess would be distressed to hear it was missing, for he did not know that it was she who had taken it. But when they looked for her in her chamber, they did not find her there, nor did they find her ladies-in-waiting. Finally they realized that the princess and her ladies had disappeared along with the ship, and the lords who were the fathers of the ladies were enraged, and forced the king to give up his throne, and afterward drove him from the land, so that he too became a wanderer in the world.

Now the princess and the eleven ladies were already far away at sea when the ladies awoke. And when they saw that they had sailed far beyond the shore, they were afraid and wanted to turn back, for they had never sailed in a ship. But the princess said to them: "Let us tarry here awhile." So they did, but when the ladies asked her why she had set sail, the princess said that a storm had arisen, and she had was afraid that the ship might crash into the harbor, and therefore she had set out to sea. Soon after that a storm did arise, and the ladies saw that they could not turn back, but were at the mercy of the currents. And when the storm subsided, they found themselves lost at sea, with no idea of how to get back, so they agreed to sail with the princess until they reached land.

So it was that the princess and the eleven ladies sailed until they came to an island, and landed there, hoping to find fresh food and water. But that turned out to be an island of bloodthirsty pirates, and when their sentries saw the ladies on the island, they approached them with their weapons drawn, and brought them to the leader of the pirates, proposing to kill them right then and there.

Now when they stood before the pirate chief, the princess spoke for the others and said: "We too are pirates, but while you are pirates who use force, we are pirates who use wisdom. If you were wise the twelve of you"—for there were twelve pirates in all—"would each take one of us for a wife, and make use of our wisdom, which will surely help you to become far richer. And for our part we will each contribute a twelfth of the merchandise we have captured as pirates, which you will find on our ship."

Now the chief among the pirates was taken with the great beauty of the princess, and thought to himself how nice it would be to take her for a wife. So too did he think that what she had said made sense, and when the pirates saw all the wealth in the ship, which the princess had taken from the merchant's son, they agreed that they were indeed fine pirates. Therefore the pirates agreed among themselves that they would each, according to his rank, choose a lady to take for a wife. And after the chief of the pirates had chosen the princess, and the other pirates had made their choices among the ladies, the princess invited them to share the fine wine that they had on their ship.

So the princess poured out twelve goblets of wine for them, and the pirates drank until they all became drunk and fell asleep. Then she spoke to the ladies and said: "Now let us go and each kill her man," and they went and slaughtered them all. And there, on that island, they found such great wealth as is not possessed by any king. There was such an abundance that they resolved to take only the gold and precious gems, and unloaded all the merchandise from the ship, to make room for it. In this way they filled the whole ship with treasures, and prepared to set sail. But before they did, the princess had each of them sew a uniform to wear, so that they would all look like sailors, and then they set out to sea.

Once again they sailed for a long time, until they reached a distant port. There they docked the ship and descended into the city, wearing the sailors' uniforms they had sewn. They roamed about the city, looking very much like men, and in this way reached the center of town, where they heard a great commotion and saw people all running in one direction. One of the ladies inquired as to what was the matter, and she learned that the king of that country had just died childless, and that in such a case it was the custom of the country to have the queen go up to the roof of the palace and from there to throw down the dead king's crown. And whoever caught that crown would become king and marry the queen.

Now the princess had hardly heard of this custom when she was struck with a heavy object, which landed on her head. She cried out, "Oh, my head!" But immediately she was surrounded by a great crowd, who raised her onto their shoulders and cried out: "Long live our king!" The crown had indeed fallen on her head, and since she was wearing men's clothing, no one knew that she was a woman.

After the funeral of the former king, the wedding between the new king and the old king's widow was to take place. But the viziers, seeing that the new king was very young, preferred to marry the new king to the daughter of the chief vizier. The queen agreed that this could be done, for she no longer wished to rule, and the wedding was set for the very next day.

Now the princess, disguised as a man, was afraid of what would happen when the truth came out, and she did not know what to do. Finally she called in the daughter of the vizier, and after pledging her to secrecy, she confessed that she was a woman, and told her how she had been traveling with the other ladies, and how they had just reached the center of town when the crown had landed on her head. The girl promised to help her, and together they worked out an excuse for postponing the wedding.

Meanwhile the disguised princess had the sculptors of the city brought into the palace, and ordered them to make many sculptures of their new king, and to put these up at every crossroads leading to and from the city. Soldiers were to be stationed wherever a sculpture was placed, and they were commanded to arrest anyone who stopped and showed great emotion upon seeing it.

It happened that three such people came along and were arrested. The first was the prince who was the true bridegroom of the princess. The second was the son of the merchant whose ship the princess had seized, and who had afterward been banished by his father. And the third to be arrested was the king who had been driven out of his kingdom because the princess had sailed off with the eleven daughters of the high lords. Each had recognized the features of the princess, even though the sculpture represented a man.

Then, on the day of the wedding, the princess had these three brought into her presence, and she asked them what had happened to them since she had last seen them, and they told her their stories. The prince who was her true love had journeyed all over the world in search of her. He had come to the kingdom where she had escaped with the merchant's boat, and had passed through the kingdom where the king had been driven out because the princess had escaped with the eleven ladies. And he had also found the island of the pirates, and found their bodies there, along with the clothes of the princess and the ladies. So it was that he had sailed after them and reached that kingdom, which was the closest to the island of the pirates, where he had been searching for her when he had come upon the sculpture of the king, and had recognized her face. So too had the merchant's son and the deposed king traveled around the world, seeking only their daily bread, and wondering why such disaster had befallen them.

And when the princess had heard what they had to say, she turned first to the king who had lost his kingdom and said: "You, king, were driven out because of the eleven ladies who were lost. Take back your ladies. Return to your country and your kingdom, where you will surely be welcomed." And to the merchant's son she said: "Your father drove you out because of a ship filled with merchandise that was lost. Now you can take back your ship, which is filled with much more valuable treasures, whose worth is many times that which you had in it before." Finally she turned to the prince who was her true bridegroom: "It is you to whom I was betrothed before any other. Come, let us be married to each other."

Then the princess called in all the viziers and ministers, and revealed that she was not a man, but a beautiful woman. And she showed them the ring the prince carried with him, which she had given him in the forest before she had been captured by the merchant's son, which proved that it was he to whom she was truly betrothed. And the viziers were so impressed with the character of the prince and princess that they asked them to remain among them as their king and queen, and this they agreed to do. That day the prince and princess were married in a great celebration, and afterward they ruled with an evenhanded mercy that all admired, and they lived happily ever after.

—Eastern Europe: nineteenth century
A tale of Reb Nachman of Bratslav

25. A Garment for the Moon

nce upon a time, the moon came to the sun with a complaint: the sun was able to shine during the warmth of day, especially during the summer, while the moon could shine only during the cool of night. The sun saw that the moon was unhappy with her lot, particularly in the wintertime, so he told the moon he would have a garment sewn for her, to keep her warm. Then he called upon all the great tailors to make a garment for the moon. The simple tailors also wanted to help, but they weren't invited, so they said among themselves, "We're not going to go."

After discussing the matter for some time, the great tailors came to the conclusion that it was simply impossible to sew a garment that would fit, because the moon is sometimes little and sometimes big. What measurements were they to use?

But after the great tailors gave up the task, the simple tailors decided to try. When the great tailors heard about this, they said, "If we couldn't do it, how can you?" But the simple tailors refused to give up. They met among themselves to discuss how this garment might be made. Many suggestions were given, but none of them could solve the problem of the moon's changing size.

Just when they were about to give up, one poor tailor among them stood up and said, "I have heard of a faraway kingdom where there is a fabric that has the substance of light. This fabric stretches to whatever size is required: it becomes large if the object to be fitted is large, and shrinks as much as necessary if the object is small." The other tailors all cried out at the same time: "Why that is just what we need to sew a garment for the moon!" They all agreed that they must obtain that wonderful material so that the sun could fulfill its promise and the moon could keep warm on cold winter nights. But where were they to find it? They discussed this among themselves, and decided that the poor tailor who had heard of this fabric must set out on a journey to this land, find it and bring it back. They collected a few kopeks among themselves with which to purchase the fabric, and they each wished their fellow tailor good luck.

The tailor, whose name was Yankel, packed a few clothes in a sack and took along a few loaves of bread, and set out on his journey. But how was he to begin to search for that distant land? He stopped wherever he went and asked the people if they knew where that kingdom was, but when the people heard that Yankel was searching for a cloth made out of light so that he and his fellow tailors could sew a garment for the moon, they always broke out laughing and assumed that Yankel was just a fool.

Yankel traveled for many months, sleeping under the stars, until the nights began to grow colder. As he lay on the ground at night and looked up at the moon, Yankel thought he saw the moon shiver, and he was determined to keep going so that the moon could have a garment of her own.

Then one day that Yankel arrived at a great river, and took the ferry across to the other side. Since the river was so wide, it took quite a while to get across, so Yankel decided to ask the old ferryman if he knew the location of the kingdom in which that fabric could be found. The ferryman did not laugh as had so many others, but told him he would find what he was seeking on the other side of that river. And when Yankel heard this, he could hardly believe his ears, for in his heart of hearts he too had begun to wonder if that kingdom truly existed.

Then Yankel asked the ferryman if this fabric was easy to acquire, or if it was very dear. And the ferryman told him that it was very dear indeed, for only the queen of that land possessed a gown woven of that wonderful material. When Yankel heard this his heart sank, for how was he, a poor man, to obtain this material if only a queen could afford to own it? Still, he had traveled so far, and he did not intend to abandon his quest just when he had finally reached that faraway kingdom. He consoled himself by hoping that the queen might assist him when she heard why he was seeking that fabric.

Now when he entered that city, Yankel was surprised to see everyone walking around with a sad face. He wondered about this, and at last he stopped someone and asked why this was. The man replied, "You must be a stranger here, for everyone knows the reason. We are sad because our beloved queen is sad." Now Yankel was sorry to hear this, since he had hoped the queen might help him, but what chance would there be if she were so unhappy? Then Yankel himself began to grow sad, so that his face resembled the faces of the inhabitants of that city. For how could he ask the queen for help if she were so sad?

At last Yankel asked someone, "Why is it that the queen is so sad?" The man replied, "Because her royal garment, which is woven out of light, has become unraveled. Now she has nothing to wear to the wedding of her daughter, the princess. And since she has nothing to wear, the wedding has been delayed, who knows for how long?"

When Yankel heard this, his heart leaped. For after all, was he not a tailor? And did he not make his living—a meager one, it is true—by repairing garments, as well as sewing new ones? In fact, Yankel spent most of his time restoring old garments, for his customers were the poor folk who could not afford new ones. But Yankel wondered if there were no tailors in that land who might repair the queen's gown themselves. He asked the man about this, and the man said, "Of course we have tailors here. But none of them know a thing about working with cloth woven out of light. For the royal garment was made long ago, and handed down from one generation to the next. And since the material stretched or shrank as needed, it has fit every queen to perfection. But now that the garment has become unwoven, there is no one who knows how to repair it, for this secret was lost long ago."

Now when Yankel heard this, he remained hopeful, but he was also afraid, for if none of the tailors of that kingdom knew what to do, how would he? Still, he had not given up hope when the great tailors of his own kingdom did, nor would he give up hope now.

Then Yankel told the stranger he was a tailor, and that he was willing to try his hand at repairing the garment for the queen. The stranger was delighted to hear this, and told Yankel that the queen had announced some time ago that any tailors who entered that kingdom were to be brought to the palace, to attempt to repair the royal gown, since all of the tailors of that kingdom had already tried and failed. So he led Yankel to the palace, and when the guards heard he was a tailor, they quickly gave him an audience with the queen.

Now when Yankel found himself, a poor tailor, standing in the splendor of that court, before a great and powerful queen, he was overcome with fear, for it was only then that he realized he had forgotten to ask what would happen if he failed. Now, though, it was too late, and with a quivering voice Yankel told the queen he was willing to try to repair her royal gown.

The queen nodded sadly and said, "I wish that repairing it was all that was needed. But the problem is more serious than that. You see, the fabric of the gown has begun to unravel, and because it is woven out of light, when it unravels it simply turns back to light and disappears. Therefore it is not only a matter of repair, for it is first necessary to create some new material. But the secret of how to weave cloth out of light has long been lost."

Now Yankel realized that if he could discover that secret, he would be able to produce the fabric needed to weave a garment for the moon. So he told the queen that although he did not know how such miraculous material could be made, he was willing to search for the secret, no matter how long it would take for him to find. The queen was very impressed with his determination, for the tailors of that kingdom had quickly abandoned hope. She told him she would gladly help him any way she could and certainly wished him luck, for she longed to attend the wedding of her daughter, the princess, but she could not without wearing the royal gown woven out of light, as had been the custom in that kingdom for so many centuries.

Then Yankel asked to see the garment that had become unraveled, for that seemed like a reasonable way to begin. And the queen had the garment brought at once, and gave him a room in which to examine it.

Now when Yankel sat down to study that royal gown he was amazed at its beauty, for the fabric was like moonlight, exquisitely woven and without any sign of stitches or seams. He also marveled at how supple it was—it would stretch as far as he pulled it, but when released would shrink back to its original shape. So too did the sleeve fit snugly around his arm when he placed it inside, only to grow back to its natural size when he took his arm out. And the more he studied it, the more Yankel thought that this material would make a fine garment for the moon.

Then Yankel examined the hem of the garment, where the unraveling had begun. He searched for the loose end of the thread of light, and when at last he found it, he saw that as soon as the thread unraveled it turned to light and disappeared, just as the queen had said. Meanwhile Yankel had become so absorbed in the task of studying that wonderful garment he did not notice that many hours had passed, and night had fallen. And while he worked, the full moon rose up in the sky until it was framed in the window of the chamber in which Yankel sat, and cast its light inside. And when the light of the moon struck that garment, a remarkable change took place—the gown began to glow with a wonderful, pale light. This change startled Yankel, and he jumped back, for it seemed as if the garment had come to life. It was then that a miracle took place—the hem of the garment, which had been unraveling and growing shorter, began to grow larger again in the light of the moon. Yankel was astounded, for the weaving of light that had seemed so impossible was taking place right before his eyes. And suddenly, in a moment of true inspiration, Yankel snipped off a tiny piece of the garment and held it up in the moonlight. And as he watched, the swatch began to grow, little by little, as if it were being woven in the light, until it was ten times larger than it had been at first. And Yankel knew that he had stumbled upon the secret of that precious material, woven out of moonlight.

Meanwhile, the light of the moon had continued to restore the queen's gown, and by the time the sun came up, the dress had been completely repaired. Yankel proudly showed it to the queen, who was amazed at his skill, for the garment was as good as new. Then the queen tried it on, and the garment shrank until it fit her perfectly. And when she looked into the mirror and saw how beautiful she looked in it, her sadness turned to joy, for now she could make plans for the wedding of the princess. But before she did, she asked Yankel how she might reward him, and told him he could have anything his heart desired. Then Yankel took out the tiny piece of cloth he had snipped from the hem of the garment, and asked the queen if he might keep it as a memento. The queen readily granted this request, and saw to it that Yankel received a bag of gold coins as well. Then she thanked him once more from the bottom of her heart and hurried off to make preparations for the wedding. And Yankel took his leave and made his way back to the city from which he had come.

Now since Yankel had traveled very far to reach that kingdom, it took him many months to return. During that time there were many full moons, and while the full moon shone in the sky, Yankel would take out the small piece of material and hold it up to the light of the moon. And on each night of the full moon the size of the cloth would multiply tenfold, until by the time Yankel returned home it was so immense that it was large enough to fit the moon.

When Yankel finally reached his town and all the simple tailors saw the magnificent fabric he had brought with him, their hearts leaped for joy, and they all joined together to sew a garment for the moon. So it was that the sun was finally able to keep its promise, and give the moon a wonderful garment to keep her warm on cold nights. That garment fit perfectly, expanding when the moon grew larger and shrinking when it grew small. And the moon has kept that garment to this very day, wearing it with pride and joy since, after all, it was created out of its own light.

—Eastern Europe: nineteenth century
A tale of Reb Nachman of Bratslav

Folktales

26. Leaves from the Garden of Eden

he largest stable in the city of Ludomir was owned by Shepsel. From morning until nightfall mail coaches would arrive, exchanging their tired horses for fresh ones. Shepsel was helped in his work by the boy Hayim, an orphan who made his home with Shepsel and his family. Hayim's parents had died while he was very young, and he had roamed the streets before Shepsel had taken him in. Soon, however, they all regarded him as a member of the family. And he was especially close to Shepsel's daughter, Leah. They were like brother and sister.

Now Hayim was a hard worker in the stables, just like Shepsel. They worked side by side all day long. But one day Hayim took ill, and each day he seemed to grow weaker. Leah nursed him during his illness, and she was deeply grieved at his death, as was Shepsel and the rest of the family.

When the period of mourning had ended, however, Leah did not seem to recover from her grief. She had loved the boy deeply, and she could not bear the loss. Shepsel and his wife sat at her bedside every day, praying for her recovery. One day, while Shepsel was sitting at her bedside, he fell asleep and began to dream. In the dream, Hayim the stable boy appeared before him, his face glowing with joy.

"Where did you come from?" asked Shepsel, who remembered, even in the dream, that the boy was no longer in this world. "And why are you so joyful?"

The boy replied, "Let me tell you all that has happened to me. When I left this world, I was brought before the heavenly court. I explained that I only knew a few prayers, for that is all I had been taught. But I had served you, my master, as faithfully as I could. So too did I tend the horses with care. And I always tried to be honest.

"The court ruled that I had earned a place in the Garden of Eden, and that is where I make my home. And because I had tended horses in my earthly life, I have been put in charge of the heavenly horses that pull the golden coaches of the tzaddikim."

Then the boy asked Shepsel about his family. And Shepsel broke into tears and told him how much Leah had grieved over his death, and now she too was in grave danger. And the boy said: "Don't worry. There are leaves growing in the Garden of Eden that can heal any illness. Wait, and I will fetch you some." And a moment later, the boy brought Shepsel a handful of leaves and said: "Boil these in a pot of water and give them to Leah to drink." And as Shepsel accepted the leaves, he awoke. And scattered all over the bed were leaves that had blown in from the open window. And when he picked them up, he saw that those leaves did not grow anywhere in that land. So too did they bear a wonderful fragrance, like that in his dream.

Shepsel hurried to boil some of those leaves in water, and he gave it to his daughter to drink. As he did, he told her about his dream, and about the leaves that Hayim had brought her from the Garden of Eden. And when Leah drank that water and learned of that miracle, she began to recover at once—by the third day she was out of bed and walking around.

Soon after that, Leah was betrothed and wed. And she named her first son Hayim, after the stable boy. And it is said that she loved her child as much as she had loved her adopted brother.

—Eastern Europe: nineteenth century

27. A Palace of Bird Beaks

There once was a king named Solomon, who was known throughout the world for his wisdom. He could command the winds and birds to come whenever he called them. He even knew the languages of every bird and animal on earth.

Kings and queens from all over the world came to Jerusalem to pay homage to King Solomon, and he welcomed each one as a royal guest. Once the Queen of Sheba came to visit him. She brought him many precious gifts from her kingdom, and the king asked her what gift she would like in return.

"Oh, I would like something that no other queen on earth has ever had," said the Queen of Sheba. "Build me a palace of bird beaks!"

"In that case," King Solomon said, "let such a palace be built."

Then King Solomon called forth all the birds in the world and commanded them to come to his palace, prepared to give up their beaks. Before even a day had gone by, thousands of birds filled the sky, beating their wings and swooping down to the palace. All came: the strong eagle, the tiny hummingbird, the bluebird, the mockingbird, and every bird that lived on earth. The birds were not very happy at having to give up their beaks. But what could they do? They were among the smallest creatures in the kingdom. Soon every bird had flocked to the palace except one—the hoopoe—a little bird with colorful feathers and a fine, pointed beak. As time passed and it did not arrive, the king became angry.

"Fetch the hoopoe and bring it here!" he shouted to his servants. "Let it be punished for failing to obey the king!"

At last the hoopoe was brought before the king.

"Where have you been?" King Solomon demanded. "Why have you kept me waiting?"

"Please, your Majesty, do not be angry with me," said the hoopoe. "I have come here from the ends of the earth. I have flown over gardens, forests, oceans, and deserts, and from all that I have seen, I have gained much wisdom. Punish me if you must, but first give me a chance to prove that I have not just been flying lazily about. Let me ask you three riddles. If you can answer them correctly, then do what you will with me. But if there is even one of them that you cannot answer, then spare my life."

The other birds gasped. How dare a bird bargain with the king! But King Solomon admired this bold little creature, and he accepted the challenge. "Very well," he said, "go ask your riddles. After all, how can your wisdom be compared to the that of a king?"

So the hoopoe spoke. "This is the first riddle. Tell me, your Majesty, who is it who was never born and has never died?"

The king did not even pause to think. "The Lord of the world, blessed be He, " he said at once. And as he spoke, King Solomon thought, "The Lord of the world who created all creatures to be free."

The hoopoe continued. "Here is the second riddle. Tell me, your Majesty, what water never rises from the ground and never falls from the sky?"

King Solomon smiled, for he knew the answer. "The answer is a tear," he said, "a tear that falls from an eye that cries with sadness." And as he finished answering, King Solomon looked around and saw all those birds stretched out before him, waiting sadly and helplessly for their beaks to be cut off. The king too was saddened, and a tear came to his eye.

Now a strange thing happened. Although King Solomon was certain that his wisdom was perfect, for just a moment it occurred to him that perhaps he had done a foolish thing in agreeing to build a palace of bird beaks.

Then the hoopoe spoke again, and this time it trembled, for it had only one riddle left, only one more chance to save itself.

"Your Majesty, what is it that is delicate enough to put food in a baby's mouth, yet strong enough to bore holes in the hardest wood?" It did not take King Solomon long to reply. "Why, a bird's beak, of course!" he answered. And looking around at that great gathering of birds, he realized how special those creatures were, and how very precious their beaks were to them.

Meanwhile the hoopoe bowed its head. "Punish me as you will, your Majesty, for you have answered my three riddles." And it waited in silence to hear the harsh punishment of the king.

But the king was smiling. "Dear hoopoe," he announced in a loud voice, so that all the birds could hear, "I am known throughout the world for my wisdom, yet you are the one who is truly wise. You have shown me that a king should never be too proud to admit he has made a mistake. I have decided not to build a palace of bird beaks after all!"

At this, all the birds wanted to flap their wings in joy, but they did not dare to interrupt the king. Then the brave hoopoe spoke up and said, "Your majesty, how can we ever thank you? Even though we cannot give the Queen of Sheba a palace of bird beaks, we would be glad to build a palace of feathers for her."

The Queen of Sheba was delighted by this offer, for such a palace would be just as unique as one built out of bird beaks. And as soon as she agreed, flocks of birds stirred up great winds as they swooped down to donate feathers for the palace. And when there was a mountain of feathers lying before them, the birds built a palace of great beauty out of those feathers. And when they were finished, the Queen of Sheba was speechless, for never had she received such a beautiful gift.

Then King Solomon said to the hoopoe, "For your wisdom, hoopoe, you shall be rewarded." Then the king called forth the royal jeweler and bade him make the bird a small crown, much like that of the king. And when the crown was finished, King Solomon placed it upon the head of the hoopoe. That is why the hoopoe wears a crown on its forehead to this day, to remind all the birds who see it of the wise hoopoe who saved their beaks.

—Yemen: oral tradition

28. The Maiden in the Tree

uring her stay in Jerusalem, the Queen of Sheba was the guest of King Solomon, who told her about the wonders of the Holy One, blessed be He. How God watches over everything that takes place in the world. How nothing, not even the future, is hidden from Him. Indeed, that God is a matchmaker, though every match is as difficult to make as it was to part the waters of the Red Sea. Now when the Queen of Sheba heard this, she could not restrain herself and said, "I have believed everything you have told me except for this—that your God makes matches. Let me, I beg you, put this matter to a test. Let us walk together through the streets of Jerusalem. I shall select an unmarried maiden, and you will see to it that she is sent away to a distant and remote place, far from any man who might be her destined match. There let her be imprisoned in a large tree, with no way to escape. Then we shall have a fair test of whether or not your God shall provide her match." King Solomon agreed at once to this test, and within the hour they were walking together through the streets of Jerusalem.

Along the way they saw many unmarried maidens, some walking by, some shopping in the marketplace, some selling jewels, some selling nuts and dates, some selling all kinds of beautiful cloth. The Queen of Sheba observed all these, but passed them by. Then they came to a well, where the queen saw a beautiful maiden with red hair pouring water from a bucket into a jug. The queen turned to King Solomon and said, "That is the one! Let us see what will happen if she is taken to a distant and forgotten place for five years, to make her home in a tree. Then, I wonder, how your God will complete her match!"

King Solomon approached the maiden and asked her to take them to her home. The maiden was overwhelmed to find herself in the presence of King Solomon and the Queen of Sheba, and she led them to the home of her parents. There the king declared that he wished to employ the maiden for a period of five years. The sum he offered was very great, and the maiden's parents gladly accepted it. Only when the maiden had returned with him to the palace did King Solomon reveal to her that she was to live alone on an island for five years. The maiden was heartbroken and could not imagine why she deserved such a terrible fate. Still, she did not protest, for she knew that she was powerless before the great king.

Before long the maiden found herself on a deserted island, far from the company of men. In a forest on the island a great tree had been prepared to serve as her home. The tree was over five hundred years old, and it was wide enough to contain a small chamber. It had one door, but it was locked from without. A window had been carved into its trunk, large enough to pass to the maiden all that she might need, but too small for her to escape. The room contained some furniture from the king's palace, along with some musical instruments for her to play, and even a loom on which to weave. And that, in fact, is what she did most of the time, for she was a remarkably fine weaver. As she weaved she sang all the songs that she had ever learned and many others that she made up as well. And so the maiden passed her lonely existence in that tree, her only companion a magic pheasant that King Solomon sent to guard over her, and to bring her all that she might need. For he had long entrusted that pheasant with special tasks.

In this way, several years passed, and still the maiden remained alone inside that hollow tree. Many were the days and nights when she pined for her family so far away, and wondered how she had come to know such a strange fate. And yet she did not despair, for she knew that eventually she would be freed from there. Meanwhile she tried to fill her days with weaving and singing, so that the time would pass more quickly and she would not feel so all alone.

Now one day it came to pass that a ship was sailing over the sea and the son of the captain asked his father if he might steer the ship himself. The captain let him take the wheel, and just then a sudden tempest arose, which tossed the ship to and fro. The storm became stronger and stronger until some of the passengers were tossed over the sides of the ship, into the wild currents, where they drowned. And among those who fell in the water and were thought to be lost was, alas, the captain's son.

When the storm finally subsided, the captain spent many days searching for survivors, especially his son. But not even one was sighted, and it began to appear that all had been lost. At last, when there was no hope left that any of them might be found, the captain returned to his homeland. There he continued to mourn over the loss of his son, blaming himself. For he believed that if he, and not his son, had been at the wheel when the storm struck, he might have guided the ship to safety, and his son might still be among the living.

But the truth is that his son had not drowned. Alone among all the passengers, he had clung to a plank that had floated nearby, and he clung to it for days before the currents carried him to a distant island. Night had already fallen so he lay himself down under a tree to sleep. The next morning he was very hungry when he awoke, and he began to look for something to eat. In his pocket he found that he had carried with him only three things, a little mirror, a knife and a pair of scissors. When he found fruit on a tree he climbed up, cut off the fruit and ate it. And so he was able to sustain himself.

The island was not very large, and as he was wandering through the forest, the young man came upon a great hollow tree, where he sat down to rest. While he was sitting there, a pheasant with a basket in its beak landed on one of its branches. The pheasant perched on a branch next to a small opening, which looked like a kind of window. From the basket, it took out food, which it passed through the window with its beak. Something inside the tree seemed to take the food, but the young man could not see what it was. He thought it might be some kind of animal, and he was very curious about all he had seen.

So the young man hid near the tree, and finally caught a glimpse of the maiden's red hair as she passed in front of that small window. Now the maiden had not cut her hair in all those years, and it had grown very long and trailed behind her. To the young man it seemed that the long hair belonged to an animal, although he could not imagine what it was. At last he crept closer and peered into the window, and there he saw the beautiful maiden.

The young man knocked on the trunk of the tree three times, and the maiden inside was greatly surprised. Suddenly she was filled with both fear and longing—for she did not know who had found her in that remote place. She called out, "Who is there?" And the young man replied, "I was cast alone upon this island when my ship sank. But who are you?" Then the maiden told him how she had come to be there by a whim of King Solomon and the Queen of Sheba. He was truly amazed at her tale. He talked to her through the little window for a long time, long after the sun had set. And by the time it rose the next day they were still talking. And by then they were in love.

That day the young man took out his scissors and cut away the vines around the window and took his knife and carved away the frame until it was large enough for him to climb inside. And that is how he and the maiden came to live inside that hollow tree.

When the pheasant arrived the next day, it discovered that the princess was no longer alone. The pheasant flew quickly to King Solomon's palace and told him everything. Solomon was delighted at this news, but he kept it secret from the Queen of Sheba. Instead he ordered the pheasant to take enough food for them both, including the finest delicacies from the king's table.

Now the captain's son grew to greatly love the maiden who dwelt with him in the tree. One day he showed her the mirror which he had carried with him when he had fallen from the ship. She looked in the mirror and was amazed at what she saw, for she had grown very beautiful indeed. The young man, too, recognized her great beauty, and before long he asked her to be his wife. She loved him as much as he did her, and so they agreed to marry, and invited to the wedding all the birds and beasts of the forest. The birds sang, the animals danced, and it was a beautiful wedding.

A year passed and the pheasant continued to bring food for them both, as well as clothing and shoes. So too did the pheasant teach them the language of the birds. In another year the maiden had a child, a lovely girl. The pheasant reported this happy news to King Solomon, and the king told him to be sure to bring enough food for them all. So too did he begin to think that perhaps the time had come to let the Queen of Sheba know about the maiden's fate.

Not long after that there was a grand wedding for King Solomon's son. All the emperors and queens were invited to attend, and among the guests was the Queen of Sheba. King Solomon had also directed the pheasant to invite a pair of every kind of bird and beast. So the pheasant flew to every corner of the earth and proclaimed that such pairs of every kind should come to the king's celebration. The birds flew on their own, but for the animals Solomon sent a gigantic boat, steered by the pheasant. It was the very ark of Noah that had once saved all those kinds of animals from the Flood. And the young couple emerged from the tree with their child and joined them, for they too had been invited to be guests at the wedding.

When the boat reached land, everyone jumped off and began to follow the pheasant. As they traveled to Jerusalem, the young man noticed that next to every well they passed there was the portrait of a young man, and it was always the same picture. He asked the pheasant about it, and pheasant replied, "The portrait you see is that of the son of a ship's captain who was lost at sea. His father wept greatly and lamented over his son, but people comforted him and told him not to weep, for God would have mercy on his son and save him. So the captain had the portrait of his son put next to every well, in the hope that someone would recognize him, and bring him back."

Now when the young man heard this tale, he began to cry. He told the pheasant that he was the captain's son who had once been lost at sea. And he was still sobbing when he reached King Solomon's palace. King Solomon wondered why he was weeping, and the young man told him the whole story. So Solomon had messengers sent to the captain, and before long he and his son were reunited, and that was a great day indeed.

So too did King Solomon see to it that the father and mother of the maiden who had lived in the tree were also present, and they were overjoyed to see her again. As for the Queen of Sheba, she saw with her own eyes how God had blessed that maiden and joined her with her destined one. Then the queen's doubts were all gone, and she knew well that the Holy One, blessed be He, does indeed make matches. And never again did she doubt the word of King Solomon.

—Eastern Europe: nineteenth century

29. The Sabbath Lion

ong ago, in the faraway city of Tangiers, there lived a Jewish widow and her seven children. She had to work from dawn until dark to feed her large family. The woman's eldest son, Yosef, was only ten years old, but he tried to help his mother as much as he could.

Every day, except Saturday, Yosef went to the marketplace to sweep the shopkeepers' stalls and keep their baskets full of fresh fruits and vegetables. Because he was such a good worker, the shopkeepers gave Yosef a small bag of rice, a few oranges, and, every now and then, nuts and dates to take home to his family.

Young Yosef rested only on the Sabbath. How he loved and honored this holy day! On Friday evenings, his mother lit the Sabbath candles and said a blessing. Then Yosef, holding his glass high, said the blessing over the wine. And raising the challah, he said the blessing over this special Sabbath bread. After that, Yosef and all the children turned to the door and sang a song welcoming the Sabbath Queen: "Come, O Sabbath Queen, and bring peace and blessing on thy wing!" Then they had their finest meal of the week, with candles glowing brightly around them.

On Saturday mornings, Yosef and his brothers walked to the synagogue to pray. Yosef did not travel or do any work on the Sabbath, because it was forbidden. And he knew that a peaceful Sabbath gave him the strength to work hard the rest of the week.

One day, when Yosef was working in the market, he saw a stranger speaking to one of the shopkeepers. He overheard the man ask where a certain family could be found. Yosef ran over. "That's my family!" he cried. "Let me lead you to my house." And when they arrived there, the stranger handed Yosef's mother a letter. Then he bowed and left. Yosef's mother read the letter and turned pale. "What's the matter, Mother?" the children asked. Their mother answered, "Strange news has come our way. It seems that your father had an uncle who lived in the city of Cairo, in the land of Egypt. And when he died, there was no one to leave his fortune to, so he left it to us." Hearing this, the children gasped—soon they would have money for food and maybe even a few new clothes!

Yet their mother still looked worried. "The money would be a great blessing," she said, "but I would have to travel all the way to Egypt to claim it. How can I take seven young children on such a long journey? I have no one to leave you with, and you're too young to be left alone."

"Please, Mother," said Yosef, "let me go to Cairo to get it."

"But Yosef, you are too young. The sun is very hot. Wild animals live in the desert. No, no, no, it would not be safe for you to cross the desert."

"Please, Mother," begged Yosef, "have faith in God. Has He not sent us a great blessing? We must not ignore it."

When Yosef's mother saw how strong her son's faith was, she finally agreed to let him go. But it was very expensive to travel across the desert in a caravan. Yosef's mother emptied all the hidden boxes in which she had been saving money for Passover and found just enough for the journey. Then she rushed out of the house to pay the caravan leader for Yosef's trip.

Because Yosef would not travel on the Sabbath, she asked the caravan leader if he would agree to rest on the Sabbath day. But the leader said, "It is dangerous to rest in the hot desert, where wild animals attack. If you want us to stop on your Sabbath, you will have to pay more." And the man named a large sum of money.

Yosef's mother was shocked. She had already given him all her savings. What else could she do? So the poor woman sold her golden wedding ring, the only valuable possession she had left. Then she gave the money to the leader of the caravan in exchange for his promise to rest on the Sabbath.

The caravan left Tangiers early Sunday morning. In his sack Yosef carried a letter from his mother, explaining that she had sent her son to collect the family's inheritance. He also took a pouch with candles, a small bottle of wine, a wine cup, and a little challah his mother had baked, so he could celebrate the Sabbath even when he was far from home. So too did he bring a wooden spice box and a candle with many wicks for the blessings at the end of the Sabbath.

The caravan trudged through the vast desert. Everywhere Yosef looked, he saw sand and only sand. The days passed slowly. The camels walked carefully across the burning sands, and the caravan would rest only when it was almost dark. Then Yosef would climb down from his camel and help the men set up tents for the night and gather brush for the campfire. And, at the first sight of dawn, the caravan would be once again on its way.

Six long days passed, and finally it was Friday afternoon, almost the eve of the Sabbath. Yosef went to the leader of the caravan to remind him of their agreement.

"What agreement?" the man asked, much to Yosef's dismay. "I don't know of any agreement.

"Why, my mother sold her wedding ring and paid you to stop on the Sabbath! You promised!" shouted Yosef, beginning to cry.

The leader of the caravan stared boldly into Yosef's eyes.

"We are going on," he said, "for there is still a bit of daylight left and tomorrow we will ride all day. If you want to come with us, come! If not, stay here by yourself!"

Yosef looked up and saw that before long, the sun would be setting, and he knew that he had to prepare for the Sabbath.

"Well, are you coming?" asked the caravan leader, his voice nasty and impatient.

Poor Yosef wanted to continue with the caravan, where he would be safe. But no matter what the dangers were, even if he were to be lost in the desert forever, Yosef could never break the Sabbath. And so his answer to the leader was firm: "No, I'm not coming. Go on without me. I must stay behind." And as the camels of the caravan left, he watched them disappear into the distance until he could see nothing but a cloud of dust.

The sun was setting and the Sabbath was about to begin. Yosef knew that he must light the campfire quickly before the sun had set, and that he must put enough brush on the fire to burn through the night. This he did, and then, as it grew dark, he sat down and sang his song to the Sabbath Queen: "Come, O Sabbath Queen, and bring peace and blessing on thy wing."

There Yosef sat, surrounded by the desert, without even a tree for shelter, with only the fire to keep wild animals away. He was afraid, so he closed his eyes and prayed with all his heart. But when he opened them, he saw something that made him tremble. For there in the distance was a huge lion, moving swiftly in his direction.

As the lion came closer, Yosef froze in terror, certain that his life was about to end. But when the lion was so close that Yosef could almost touch it, the huge beast quietly lay down at his feet. Yosef was afraid that the lion would pounce on him, but when it turned its head, Yosef saw that its eyes were kind.

Then he opened his pouch and took out the candles, the challah, the wine, and the wine cup. He lit the candles in the fire, and in a clear voice he recited all the blessings. As he did so, he was filled with a feeling of peace, as if he were at home, celebrating the Sabbath with his mother and his brothers and sisters. Soon afterward, he fell asleep.

Yosef awoke at dawn, and there was the lion, still watching over him. The hours of the day passed. Yosef sang Sabbath songs and recited Sabbath prayers. He felt as calm and peaceful as he had the night before. And never during all that time did the lion move from where it lay. Yosef was glad that he was not alone, and he was thankful for the company of his Sabbath friend.

At last the sun set, and Yosef took out his wooden spice box, the candle with many wicks, and a cup of wine, and he said the special prayers for the end of the Sabbath. All this time the lion seemed to listen patiently. And then, when the prayers were over, the lion's kind eyes looked into Yosef's. That is when Yosef understood what had happened: The Sabbath Queen had sent the lion as a wonderful present to protect him.

He stroked the lion's mane and put his arms around its neck. The lion brushed its tail against its back, which was the lion's way of telling Yosef to climb on its back. And no sooner did Yosef do so than the lion raced off across the desert, with the boy clinging to its mane, while the moon and the stars lit their way.

Soon they arrived at an oasis, where there were lush fig trees and a clear freshwater pool. After a long, cool drink and a meal of figs, Yosef felt much better. He said a prayer of thanks and then he and the lion set off again.

Early Sunday morning, Yosef saw a cloud of dust in the distance. It was the caravan! The lion had caught up with it in only one night.

Now when the travelers saw a great lion with someone riding on it, they were terrified. They quickly threw themselves down before Yosef, afraid the lion would devour them all.

The caravan leader watched in fear as the lion brought Yosef directly to him. In a shaky voice, he welcomed Yosef back and asked him to be the new leader. He also gave back every penny Yosef's mother had paid him, and never again did he break a promise for as long as he lived.

So it was that Yosef and the Sabbath lion led the caravan all the rest of the way to Cairo. There they rode through the narrow streets, where people screamed and scattered this way and that, running from the huge beast coming toward them.

Soon the lion, with the boy still on its back, arrived at the office where Yosef was to collect the money. From their hiding places, everyone watched in amazement as the lion stood guard and Yosef went inside. A short time later he came out, clutching two bags of silver coins, jumped on the lion's back, and rode away.

Yosef and the lion sped through the desert once more. And before long Yosef saw the walled city of Tangiers, where his mother, brothers, and sisters awaited him. Suddenly the lion stopped. Yosef knew that the lion had completed its task. The time had come to bid his friend good-bye. He petted the lion and hugged it hard. The lion nodded as it rubbed against Yosef. Then it ran off into the desert and disappeared. With one last look behind him, Yosef passed through the gates of the city and hurried down the streets of Tangiers to his home.

When Yosef's family saw that he had returned unharmed, they said prayers of thanks. And now that he had completed his task, the family could buy food and clothing and, yes, even a silver spice box for the closing of the Sabbath. And every Sabbath after that, the children begged Yosef to tell them his story, and he gladly did. For never did a Sabbath pass that he did not remember the Sabbath Queen and the wonderful lion she sent to him.

—Morocco: oral tradition

30. Katanya

nce upon a time there was a poor old woman. All her life she had wished for a child of her own. But though she wished and wished, she never had any children. Her husband died, and still she wanted a child. "Oh, how wonderful it would be if only I had a little boy or girl," she said. So she prayed to God to help her.

God saw how lonely the old woman was and sent Elijah to visit her. Sometimes Elijah disguises himself as a beggar, and sometimes he dresses like a merchant. And he often uses the powers of God to work his magic.

Now this old woman had worked hard all of her life, but she had no money left and nothing to sell for food. So each day she went to the market to ask the merchants for what they could spare: one peach, one apricot, one little olive. Sometimes they took pity on her and gave her a piece of fruit. And some days that was all she had to eat.

But one day all the merchants were in a bad mood because the king had raised their taxes. And when the old woman begged for fruit, each and every one of them shooed her away. She did not get anything—not one peach, not one apricot, not one little olive. The old woman was very sad, for it looked as if she would go hungry all day long.

Just as she was about to leave the market, she noticed a merchant she had never seen before, an old man who looked as poor as she was. As she walked over to the old man, she saw that all he had left were six brown dates, drying in the sun.

"Could you spare just one?" she asked.

"Surely," said the old man (who was really Elijah). "Take the one you want."

Now five of the dates were very little, but one was big, and that is the one she chose. "Thank you, kind sir," she said, and went on her way.

When she got home, the old woman placed the date on the windowsill, where sunlight shone on it. "You know, the old woman said to herself, this is such a beautiful date, I don't have the heart to eat it." So she left it there, even though she was hungry, and went out to see if she could find something else to eat.

The sun continued to shine on the date until it was quite warm. Soon the date began to stir, as if something were inside it. All at once it broke open and out popped a little girl. She was no bigger than a little finger, and she wore a pretty dress of many colors. The little girl stood up on the windowsill and looked around. The house was quite bare. Only a bed and a table and a chair stood in the room and it needed cleaning, for the old woman's broom had only a few straws left.

The first thing the little girl did was to climb out the window. She saw a ball of string hanging on the wall and, grabbing one end of the string, she lowered herself down to the ground. There she picked some of the short grasses, because she was very short herself, and she tied the bundle together with another piece of straw. "Oh, what a perfect broom for me!" she cried.

Back up the string and onto the windowsill she climbed, and then she started to clean the house. She swept from corner to corner, until the floor sparkled like new.

Meanwhile, the old woman was still walking on the road, searching for some food, when whom should she meet but the old man who had given her the date! The old man smiled and this time he gave her a large shiny olive. She thanked him and he continued on his way. When the old woman bit into the olive, what did she find inside but a golden coin! She hurried after the old man to give it back, but he was nowhere to be found. The golden coin was hers to keep. What a lucky day for me! she thought.

But she was even more surprised when she got home, for there was her house, all neat and clean! She couldn't believe her eyes. "Who did this?" she asked out loud.

"I did, Mother," said a tiny voice.

The old woman looked around. There on the windowsill, where the old woman had left the date, was the tiniest girl in the world, no bigger than the woman's little finger. The old woman blinked to see if she was dreaming. "Did you call me Mother?"

"Yes, Mother," said the girl. And that is when the old woman understood that the kind old man must have been Elijah the prophet. And she hugged the tiny girl very carefully, so as not to hurt her.

Then she asked the girl her name. But the girl did not answer. "No one has given me a name," she said at last.

"Then I will name you!" said the old woman. She thought and thought. "I will call you Katanya, the little one," she said. And so it was that her name became Katanya.

Katanya and the old woman lived together happily in that little hut. With the help of the golden coin they never had to go hungry. And the first thing the old woman did with the money was to pay back every merchant who had given her fruit to eat.

The old woman loved Katanya with all her heart. She made a little bed for her inside a teacup. She fashioned a fur hat for her from a bunny's tail, shoes out of tiny nutshells, and dresses made of rose petals. But of all her clothes, Katanya loved best her dress of many colors, the one she had been wearing when she first popped out of the date.

Katanya helped her mother by sweeping out the house with her tiny broom. She even cleaned between the boards of the floor, an easy task for her, since she was so small. While she did her chores, Katanya sang. She had a beautiful voice that sounded as if a full grown girl were singing. Katanya's voice filled the city with gladness, bringing joy to everyone who heard it.

One day the prince was riding down the street, when he heard a lovely song drifting from an open window. The voice was so beautiful that he fell instantly in love. When he returned to the palace, he told his father, the king: "Father, I have found a lovely bride, and I wish to be married."

"Very well, my son," said the king in surprise, "but who is the bride?"

"I wish to marry the girl whose beautiful singing I heard today," said the prince.

The king sent a servant at once to the house of the old woman and invited her to come with her daughter to the palace. The servant told the woman: "I have brought a tailor with me who will sew dresses for you both."

But when the old woman told Katanya this, the girl shook her head. "No, no, no! I love my dress of many colors, and that's what I will wear." So the tailor fitted the old woman, but when he asked to see the girl, he was told that she already had a pretty dress.

A few days later, the old woman put on her new dress and went to the palace, with Katanya hiding inside the pocket. The king welcomed her, but the prince was very sad. "Your daughter was invited to join us too," he said.

"Why has she not come?"

All at once a tiny voice came from the pocket: "Here I am!" Then Katanya's head peeked out.

"Is it you I heard singing?" asked the prince, much amazed.

"Perhaps," she answered.

"In that case," said the prince, "could you sing for us now? If you are the girl I heard, then it is you I want to marry, even though you are small."

Katanya smiled, for what the prince said was very nice indeed. And she sang a song more beautiful than any he had ever heard.

So it was that Katanya married the prince and became Princess Katanya. At her wedding she wore her favorite dress of many colors. And the old woman came to live at the palace along with her. And all of them lived happily ever after.

—Turkey: oral tradition

31. The Wooden Sword

ong ago, on a hot summer night in Afghanistan, the king decided to leave the palace and go out into the city for some fresh air. So he took off his royal garments and put on the clothes of a peasant, and went by himself to wander through the streets of his city. At first he went to the center of town, and from there he walked until he reached a poor section on the outskirts of the city. After a while the heat began to bother him, and he saw that one of the houses there had a light in the window, and a pleasant singing voice reached the king's ears. The king came closer and peered through the window of that house, and there he saw a man sitting at the table beside his wife. On the table were different kinds of fruits and salads and a small bottle of arak. The man drank a glass of the arak and tasted the fruits and sang praises to God.

The king stood at the window for a few minutes, astonished by the peace and serenity of this poor man, and he wondered what might be the source of his joy. So the king knocked on the door, and when the man inside asked who it was, he told him that he was a wanderer, and he asked if he might be accepted as a guest. Then the man immediately opened the door and invited the king inside, and offered him food and drink, and the man himself resumed his joyful ways. After a while the king asked his host what he did to earn a living, and the man replied: "I am a poor Jew. I wander in the streets during the days and fix shoes, and with whatever I earn I buy enough to sustain my wife and myself." And the king said: "But what will happen to you when you get old and won't be able to work?" And the man replied: "I don't have to worry, for there is someone who looks out for me." This reply surprised the king, and he said: "Who is this guardian? I see that you and your wife are home alone and that you don't have children." At this the man laughed and said: "It is not a man who protects me, but God, may His Name be blessed forever." The king laughed when he heard this, and he got up and said: "It is late and I must go. But if I come here again, will I be welcome?" And the man told him he would be welcome any time.

The king went back to his palace and decided to test this man, to see how he would fare in times of adversity. So he issued a command forbidding anyone to fix shoes in the streets. And the next day, when the Jew got up and came to the city, he was astonished to see an order denying him his livelihood. Then he lifted his eyes to heaven and said: "God, the door to my livelihood has been shut. But I am confident that you will open another one to take its place." And when he looked around him he saw a man carrying water from the well, and he said to himself: "From now on I will be a water carrier." So he went to the market and traded his tools for fixing shoes for a bucket, and then he went to the well and filled it and carried it into town until he found someone who needed the water, and he did this all day long. And by the time evening came he found that he had as much money as usual, which was enough to purchase food for his wife and himself.

That night the king returned to the house of the Jew to see how he was faring after the order he had given. And the king was astonished when he peered through the window and saw that the man was as happy as ever. So he went to the door and knocked, and the man invited him to join them at the table. Then the king said: "What did you do today? For surely you saw the announcement of the king." The man replied: "The Holy One, blessed be He, did not abandon me, and just because the king closed one door to me, God opened another to take its place." And the man told the king about how he had become a water carrier, and how well his work had gone.

After a while the king took his leave and returned to the palace. The next day he gave an order that made it forbidden for water to be sold to anyone, and from then on each person had to draw water for himself.

When the Jew returned to the well, he discovered that his new occupation had been outlawed by the king. And while he stood there, trying to think of what he might do, a group of woodcutters passed by him on their way to the forest to cut wood. Then he decided that he would become a woodcutter, and he went to the market and traded his bucket for an axe. Then he went out into the forest and worked hard all day long cutting wood. And in the evening, after he had sold what he had cut, he found that he had earned as much as he did when he was a shoemaker and a water carrier.

In the evening the king returned to his house, curious to know how he had done that day. And when he learned that the Jew had found a new occupation, he decided on a new plan to test the man. The next morning the king ordered the captain of his guards to come to him, and he said: "Take your soldiers to the road that leads to the forest, and stop all the woodcutters who pass and bring them to the palace. Then dress them as palace guards and give them swords, and order them to guard the palace." The captain of the guards did as the king had commanded, and among the woodcutters who were brought to the palace was the Jew. The woodcutters were made to guard all day, and in the evening the new guards were all sent home with their new uniforms and their swords. But they were not paid anything, for the guards received their wages only once a month.

So it was that the Jew returned home empty-handed, and he was very puzzled, for he did not have enough to live for another day, much less for another month. Then he saw his new sword hanging in its sheath, and he had a clever idea. First he made a sword of the same size and shape out of wood, like the kind he had when he was a child, and put it in the sheath. Then he took the sword of the king and sold it, and the money he got for it was enough to live on until the end of the month. After this he went to the market and bought food and drink for himself and his wife and returned home, a happy man.

What a surprise it was for the king that night, when he returned to the Jew's house and found him sitting as usual, singing happy songs in praise of God, as if he did not have a worry in the world. The king asked him what he had done that day, and the man told him all that had happened. Then the king said: "And what are you going to do if the king hears about the sword?" And the man replied: "I don't worry about things that haven't happened. I simply trust in God not to abandon me, and my confidence in Him is strong."

The next day, when the palace guards came to their posts, the king ordered that they report to the center of the city, for there was to be an execution that day, and it was the custom for all the citizens to go to see the sentence carried out. And when everyone was assembled and the execution was about to take place, the king ordered that the Jew be called upon to cut off the head of the condemned man, who had stolen a melon from the palace garden. Now when he heard this, the Jew became very afraid and said to the officer who had given him the order: "Do not ask me to do this, for I have never even killed a fly!" The officer said: "It is an order of the king that you must obey, and if you do not it will cost you your life!" And when the Jew saw that there was no escape, he asked to be given a few minutes to pray to God to give him courage, and then he would do what he was told.

Then the Jew stood up in front of the large crowd and prayed silently. After this he lifted his eyes to heaven and said in a loud voice: "My Lord, you know me very well, and you know that I have never killed anyone in my whole life, and now I am commanded to do. Please, Lord, if this man in front of me is guilty, let me take my sword from its sheath and cut off his head in a single blow. But if he is not guilty, let my sword turn to wood, as a sign of his innocence." And by then all eyes were on the Jew, and he reached into his sheath and pulled out his sword and held it up high. And when everyone saw that it was wooden, the crowd gasped and then clapped and cheered, for they assumed that a miracle had taken place. The king was delighted when he saw the wisdom of the Jew, and called him over and said: "Do you recognize me?" The Jew looked at the king closely and at last he said: "You are my guest! It is you who have visited my house four times!" And the king said: "That is right, and from now on you will be my guest, for I see that you are a man of wisdom, whose confidence in God is strong and unwavering. I intend to make you my right hand and to listen to your advice."

So it was that the Jew and his wife came to live in the palace, where the Jew became the trusted adviser of the king. And all this came about because of his unshakable confidence in God, may His Name be blessed forever and forever.

—Afghanistan: oral tradition

32. The Water Witch

here once were two children who went down to the sea every morning to throw bread crumbs on the water. The children were so poor that they barely had enough food for themselves. But they remembered the words in the Bible: *Cast your bread on the waters, for a time will come when you will find it again.*

The girl's name was Hava, which means Eve, and the boy's name was Shlomo, which means Solomon, and they were the children of a poor boat maker and his wife.

Every morning Shlomo and Hava would run down to the shore and watch for the same fish who came each day to eat their bread crumbs. As they watched, day after day, that fish grew bigger and bigger until it was the biggest fish they had ever seen.

Now not far from shore lived a water witch, who saw the good deed that the children did every day. And every day her heart grew blacker because she couldn't bear to see good deeds being done.

One day, after the big fish left, the witch called, "Children, children, come closer so you can hear me."

The children looked around but could see no one. The witch called again, "Here, here in the sea!" So Shlomo and Hava looked across the waves and saw an old woman rising up out of the water, smoking a pipe! They could hardly believe their eyes. How could a pipe stay lit when it was wet? They walked to the very edge of the water to see how such a thing could happen. That is exactly what the witch had been waiting for. She quickly threw a magic net around them and dragged them, kicking and screaming, deep beneath the waves. But the children didn't drown. The magic net was like a big bubble filled with air, so they could still breathe inside it. The witch dragged the net all the way down to the ocean floor, to a little cage she had built there. Then she pushed the net inside, with the children still trapped in it.

Finally she locked the cage door. "You are my prisoners," she cackled. And she disappeared, leaving the children all alone.

Shlomo and Hava were frightened. Who could find them there trapped in a cage at the bottom of the sea?

They were hungry too. Shlomo reached into his pocket and found two carobs that he had picked on his way to the shore that morning. One he gave to Hava and one he kept for himself. The two nibbled on the carobs slowly, so as not to use up their small supply of food.

When the children did not return home that day, their mother and father ran down to the shore crying, "Shlomo! Hava! Where are you?" But the children were nowhere to be seen.

The next morning the big fish came back to the shore for his daily food, but the children who fed him bread crumbs were not there. Where can they be? he wondered. The fish swam from one place to another, asking all the other fish, "Have you seen the children who give me bread every day?" That is how he soon learned what the wicked witch had done.

Then the big fish swam quickly to the palace beneath the sea where the great whale Leviathan, king of the sea, ruled the ocean.

"My lord of the sea, a terrible thing has happened," he told the king. "Two kind children have been kidnapped by the water witch and imprisoned at the bottom of the sea. Please help me set them free."

"Yes, it's time to stop the evil water witch," said Leviathan. "Here is a seashell, and inside it is a magic stone. Take it to the children and tell them that whatever the stone touches that is alive will die. But whatever the stone touches that is dead will be brought to life."

The big fish took the seashell in his mouth, and off he swam.

The children were sobbing in each other's arms when they saw their friend, the big fish, swimming their way. The fish circled the cage several times, then spit the seashell out of his mouth and into their little prison. Shlomo picked up the seashell and was just about to turn it over when, to the children's amazement, the fish spoke.

"Fear not," said their friend, "for inside that seashell is a magic stone, sent to you by Leviathan, king of the sea. Whatever that stone touches that is alive will die, but whatever the stone touches that is dead will be brought to life. Surely you can use it to save yourselves." The children were filled with joy, for now they had reason to hope again.

The fish swam away, but Shlomo and Hava remained there all day long. Another day passed, and another, and still the witch did not come back. The children were growing hungry and weak, for the carobs were all gone. But as they waited, they thought of a plan.

On the evening of the third day, the water witch returned, certain that the children had starved to death. When Shlomo and Hava saw the witch coming, they both lay down and closed their eyes, pretending to be dead.

The witch laughed to herself and took out the key. "So, my little dears, now that you are dead, I can use the net to capture other children." But the moment the witch opened the gate, Shlomo and Hava quickly sat up.

My, how the witch was surprised! "I didn't leave you even a crumb of food. How can it be that you are still alive?" she demanded.

"Oh," answered Shlomo, "we have a magic stone inside this shell. Whenever we are hungry, we only have to rub the stone, and it gives us all we need to eat."

"Give it to me!" shrieked the witch.

"It's mine!" Shlomo cried.

The witch snatched the shell from Shlomo's hands. But the moment she touched the magic stone, she fell down dead. Then the big fish, who had been hiding nearby, swam to the open door of the cage. "Drag the witch inside," the fish called out. The children didn't know why the fish wanted them to do this, but he was their friend, so they obeyed.

Next the fish said, "Pick up the key and come out. Then lock the door." And again the children did what the fish requested.

"Now reach between the bars of the cage," the fish told them, "and use the seashell to push the magic stone against the arm of the witch but be sure not to touch the stone yourself!"

Shlomo did as he was told and quickly pulled his arm back. At once the witch sat up, and when she found herself locked in the cage, oh, she was furious.

"Give me the key!" she shouted. Instead, Shlomo tossed the key to the fish, who swallowed it!

The big fish took the magic net into his mouth and pulled it to the shore of the sea. There the children climbed out, waved good-bye to the fish, and ran home as fast as they could. How happy their mother and father were to see them!

After that, Shlomo and Hava returned to the shore every day to feed bread crumbs to their friend the fish.

And never again were they bothered by the evil water witch.

—The Orient: c. ninth–eleventh centuries

33. Drawing the Wind

ong ago, on the Spanish island of Majorca, a young boy spent most of each day at the shore, sketching the ships that sailed into the harbor. Solomon was a wonderful artist, everyone agreed. His drawings seemed so real that people wondered if the waves in his pictures were as wet as they seemed—or the sun as hot.

His father was a great rabbi who really preferred Solomon to spend his time studying, but Solomon would always slip away to the shore.

A few days before Rosh ha-Shanah, a ship arrived from the city of Barcelona. Solomon overheard one of the sailors talking to a local merchant.

"There's news from Spain that will make every Jew on this island tremble."

"What is it?" asked the merchant.

"The king and queen have decreed that all the Jews in the land must give up their religion and become Christian."

"And if they refuse?"

"Then they must leave at once," said the sailor.

"But what if they want to stay?"

"Then they lose their lives."

Solomon was frightened. He didn't want to leave his beautiful island. He ran home to tell the news to his father, Rabbi Simeon ben Tsemah Duran.

"Must we leave, Father?" asked Solomon.

"I cannot leave, my son," said his father. "The other Jews look to me for guidance. I must stay until they all escape. But you should go, and I will join you later in Algiers."

"I won't leave you," said Solomon. "You are all I have since Mother died. Surely God will protect us."

Rabbi Simeon hugged his brave son. "Then let us work together and spread the word that everyone must meet in the synagogue." They hurried through the village, knocking at the doors of every Jewish home and shop.

When everyone had gathered at the house of prayer, Rabbi Simeon told them about the terrible decree.

"Save us!" they cried out in fear.

They hoped their beloved rabbi would work a miracle. For they knew his prayers had once turned back a plague of locusts. Another time, when crops were withering in the fields, his prayers had brought rain.

"You have only three choices," Rabbi Simeon told the men. "You can escape by sailing to Algiers. You can stay and pretend to convert, but secretly remain a Jew. Or you can defy the king and queen. As for me, I would rather go to my grave than say I am giving up my religion." Solomon realized how strong his father was and how he strengthened and comforted his people.

In the days that followed, most of the Jews crowded onto ships, taking very little with them. They saw to it that the women and children took the first available ships. Some Jews stayed and pretended to convert, in order to save their lives. They were known as Conversos, but in secret they continued to follow their Jewish ways.

Only a handful of Jews openly refused to convert. Among them were Solomon's father and Solomon himself. They planned to leave together, once they were certain that all those who wanted to escape had done so.

By then it was the start of Rosh ha-Shanah. Rabbi Simeon and Solomon and those few who dared enter the synagogue prayed with great intensity, in hope that their names would be written in the Book of Life. For on Rosh ha-Shanah that decision is said to be made on high. Surely God would hear their prayers and guard over them.

All went well the first day, but on the second day of Rosh ha-Shanah, just after the sounding of the shofar, soldiers rushed into the synagogue and dragged them all away. They were cast into a prison cell, where Rabbi Simeon continued to lead the prayers by heart. Solomon would have been terrified if he hadn't seen how calm his father remained.

None of them slept that night. Even though Rosh ha-Shanah had ended, they stayed awake, praying. The cell was very dark, with only one high window. But at dawn it let a little sunlight in. When Rabbi Simeon saw it, he said, "Have faith, my brothers. For just as there is a bit of light, so there is hope, and I feel that God has heard our prayers and will protect us."

The guard overheard them and laughed. "You think you have hope. You have just three days to live. Then you die. Let's see what your God does for you then."

Rabbi Simeon saw how frightened they were. So he turned to Solomon and said, "Won't you help us pass the time? Why don't you draw one of those ships you do so well?"

Solomon couldn't believe his ears. His father was asking him to draw? Solomon felt in his pocket and pulled out his last piece of chalk. When he looked up, he thought he saw a hint of a smile on his father's face.

Solomon remembered all the ships he had watched from the shore, and he began to draw the one he thought was the most beautiful on the sunlit wall. The wind he drew filled the great sails, and he added barrels of wine and bushels of wheat.

Solomon's father and the other men watched him draw until the sun set and the prison cell was enveloped in darkness. Then they began to pray to God to save them. Once again, they prayed all night.

The next day, Solomon continued to work on his drawing. Little by little he finished every detail of the ship, and then he drew the sea around it. The waves looked as if they might spill right off the wall and splash onto the floor.

The picture seemed finished, but Solomon didn't want to stop. His father suggested that he draw the two of them, there on the deck. This Solomon did, and all the men marveled at the fine resemblances. Then the second day in prison ended, and again they prayed throughout the night.

When the sun rose on the third day, one of the men asked Solomon to draw him on the ship, too. "For I would like to be with you." And one by one, the others made the same request. But when darkness fell, Solomon had not finished drawing the last man.

That night they prayed to God with all their hearts, for they knew the execution was set for sunrise the next day. All of the men shook with fear, except for Rabbi Simeon. Solomon took strength from his father, and he, too, remained unafraid.

As soon as the first light of dawn came through the window, Solomon took out his chalk and quickly finished drawing the last man.

Just as he drew the final line, he heard keys jangling. The soldiers were coming to unlock the door to their cell. Then Solomon and all the men would be taken to the courtyard for their execution.

Solomon turned to his father and saw that he was deep in prayer. And, at that very moment, he heard his father pronounce God's secret name out loud.

Suddenly Solomon could not hear the guards in the hallway, and when he looked down, he saw that he was standing on the deck of the beautiful ship he had drawn on the prison wall.

His father and all the other men in the picture were with him, safely aboard a real ship floating on a real sea. The sails strained against the wind, just as they had in Solomon's drawing, and the ship sped away from danger.

All the Jews from the prison cell rejoiced with Solomon and his father—for they knew they were aboard a ship of miracles, on their way to freedom. They would never forget that Rosh ha-Shanah when God had seen fit to save them.

—The Balkans: oral tradition

34. A Flock of Angels

ong ago, in the Kurdish town of Mosul, there lived a young woman named Asenath who was known for performing wonders. Her blessings were often sought by women who wished to have babies, or by sick people who wished to be cured. Her touch had healing powers, especially for children.

Asenath had learned everything from her father, Rabbi Samuel Barzani, who was well acquainted with the secrets of Heaven. He had taught these secrets to her until her wisdom and powers were as great as his own. It was whispered among the people that the spirit of her father rested upon her, and for this reason she was known as Rabbi Asenath.

After Rabbi Samuel died, he often came to his daughter in dreams. He would reveal dangers to her and tell her how to ward them off, saving many lives. One night Asenath dreamed that Rabbi Samuel told her to go to the Kurdish town of Amadiyah for Rosh Hodesh, the celebration of the new moon. He told her that the Jews of Amadiyah needed her protection.

When it became known that Rabbi Asenath was planning to travel to Amadiyah, the people of her town pleaded with her not to go, for things had become dangerous for the Jews living there. "All Jews have been warned to stay away from Amadiyah," they warned her. "If you go, you will surely be risking your life!" But Asenath had made up her mind. She bid farewell to the people of her town and began her journey.

When Rabbi Asenath reached the town that she had visited so often, she was given great respect as a holy woman. But the people were upset when she told them that they should celebrate Rosh Hodesh outdoors, so they could see the crescent of the new moon, as was their custom. They wanted to stay in the safety of the synagogue, for they knew they were surrounded by enemies and that their very lives were in danger. "Don't be afraid," she told them. And their faith in God and their trust in her were so great that they agreed to proceed as in the past, despite the danger.

So on the night of Rosh Hodesh, all the people came out to celebrate the new moon and the new month. At first they were cautious, yet soon they were singing and dancing in the town square with abandon. But suddenly there were shouts and they saw flames shoot up into the sky. The synagogue had been set on fire! Thank God, no one had been inside it. Yet they could not bear to see their synagogue consumed in flames. Many men had to be held back so they wouldn't run inside and be burned to death while trying to save the Torah scrolls. Everywhere people wept, falling to their knees, for they knew the flames were fast approaching the Ark where the Torahs were kept.

At that very moment, Rabbi Asenath whispered a secret name, one that she had learned from her father. All at once the people heard a loud flapping and a great wind swirled around them, and they thought that a flock of birds must be overhead. But when they looked up, they saw a flock of angels descending to the roof of the synagogue. The angels beat the flames with their wings, until every last spark had been put out. Then they rose up into the heavens like a flock of white doves and were gone.

The people were awestruck. They cried out, "Angels! Angels!" And when the smoke cleared, they saw that another miracle had taken place: the synagogue had not burned. Nor was a single letter of any of the Torahs touched by the flames.

When the enemies of the Jews learned of the miracle of the angels and saw how the synagogue had been saved from the fire, they dared not harm the hair of even a single Jew.

As for the Jews of that town, they wept and prayed and thanked God for saving this day for them and their beloved synagogue. And they were so grateful to Rabbi Asenath that they renamed the synagogue after her, and it is still standing to this day.

And all this came to pass because of Rabbi Asenath's courage and loyalty in honoring her father's wish, conveyed in a dream, that she go to that town for the celebration of the new moon.

—Kurdistan: oral tradition

35. Milk and Honey

here once was a shepherd boy named Joshua who lived in a forest near a little Polish village. Each day he herded his family's goats through the forest to a clearing where they grazed. And while they did, Joshua sat beneath a tree and studied the page of Talmud his father had taught him the night before. So too did he play Sabbath songs on his wooden flute. And at sunset Joshua led the goats back home, where his little sister Leah was waiting. She helped him milk the goats and feed the chickens, so that Joshua would have more time to teach her how to read.

At night, after dinner, their father told them stories he had heard from his parents and grandparents. There were tales of sages and heroes, of angels and demons, of witches and wizards, all of which Joshua loved. But most of all, he loved to hear tales about the holy city of Jerusalem, so far away. He especially liked stories about the Wailing Wall, where people left messages for God in the cracks of the wall. It was Joshua's dream to go there.

One morning, Joshua's mother handed him a cup of goat's milk. He thought it was unusually sweet, as if it had honey in it. The rest of the family agreed that it was the best milk they had ever tasted, and Joshua's father said, "Joshua, do you know which of the goats this milk came from?" Joshua said, "Of course I do. It came from the youngest one."

"Tell me Joshua," said his father, "do you know where that goat has been grazing? For if you do, you could take the other goats there, and they too might give such delicious milk."

"I'll try to find out," said was Joshua, "but that goat wanders off every day and doesn't come back until sunset."

"In that case, follow it," his father said.

The next day Joshua led the goats out to the forest and sat down under his favorite tree, determined to keep his eye on the youngest goat. Before long Joshua took out his wooden recorder and started to play it, and the melody was so beautiful he closed his eyes for just an instant. But when he opened them, the goat was gone. Nor did it come back until it was time to return home. This happened the next day and the next, and meanwhile the goat continued to give that delicious milk. Joshua's father saved some of it for the family and sold the rest in the village nearby.

At breakfast the next day Joshua's father said, "Something strange happened yesterday. I delivered milk to this old woman who's been sick. She's been too weak to come out to meet me, so I've brought the milk to her. Well, yesterday she came out of her house looking much better and smiling and she said, 'That milk, that milk you gave me, I think it cured me. I want more of that milk!'"

Then Joshua's father turned to him and said, "So, Joshua, did you ever find out where that goat was grazing?"

"No, no . . . I tried . . . it's a very tricky goat," Joshua said.

"Now Joshua," his father said, "if that milk has special healing abilities, we really need to find out where the goat is grazing."

Joshua said, "I'll tell you what. I'll put a bell around the goat. Then even if it runs away, I'll hear the bell and I'll be able to follow it."

His father said "Good idea!"

So Joshua found a little bell and tied it around the neck of the goat. And that day when he led the goats out to the forest, he heard the bell tinkling, and he smiled to himself, thinking, "He's not going to get away this time!"

When they got out to the forest, Joshua kept an eye on the goat, which grazed nearby, as he began to play his flute. Then he closed his eyes for just a instant, carried away by the melody. And when he opened them, the goat was gone. But Joshua still could hear the tinkling of the bell, so he jumped up and raced off in that direction. He caught sight of the goat just before it ran behind a bush. So Joshua crept up to the bush and pushed it aside—but when he did, the goat wasn't there. Instead, there was the entrance to a cave, a cave he had never seen before. And from inside the cave he heard the faint jingling of the bell.

Joshua didn't know what to do. Should he follow the goat into that cave? What if there were spiders or snakes in there? But then he remembered how badly his father wanted to know where the goat had been grazing, and all at once he felt very brave and he dashed inside.

At first the cave was large enough that Joshua could stand up in it, but before long it grew narrow, and he had to bend low, and sometimes crawl, and he wondered where the goat was leading him. He continued to hear the goat's bell in the distance and little by little the darkness in the cave began to lift, and Joshua knew he must be approaching the other end of the cave. Then Joshua came to a turn in the passage and he saw the goat running out of the cave. He hurried to catch up with it, but when he stepped outside, Joshua was astonished to find that he was no longer in the forest. Where did it go? Instead, he was standing in a beautiful orchard, where he saw trees he had never seen before—date trees and fig trees and olive trees. There were no trees like that in Poland. Where was he? Then Joshua looked up, and there, beneath a nearby date tree, calmly grazed the young goat.

Joshua walked over to the goat and petted it, and he tied it to the tree with the rope he used for a belt. Where he stood, the scent of dates was so enticing that Joshua reached up and picked one. He bit into it, and it was the sweetest date he had ever tasted, as sweet as honey. Joshua understood that the goat must have been grazing there, but he could not figure out where he was, for he seemed to have come to another land.

Then Joshua looked up and saw a synagogue nearby. Just then the service ended and ten men came out. One was walking in his direction, and when he passed Joshua he said, "Hello young man. I see you are wearing the clothes of the old country."

Joshua said, "Yes, we are new here. Tell me, what is this beautiful place?"

"Why, this is the Holy Land," said the man. "Don't you know you are in the city of Jerusalem?"

"I am?" Joshua said, and his heart skipped a beat. But how could that be possible? He had traveled only a short distance through the cave, and the Holy Land was so far away. It must have been a miracle. But Joshua wanted to be sure. So he asked the man if the *Kotel*, the Wailing Wall, was nearby.

The man said. "That is what most strangers want to know. Yes, the Wall is very close. Just follow this path past the synagogue, and soon you will reach the marketplace. From there, anyone can guide you there." Joshua gratefully thanked the man and hurried off in that direction.

That path led Joshua to a teeming marketplace. Joshua felt at home there, for he had often accompanied his father to the market in his village. Everyone was buying and selling and bargaining, and every kind of food could be found, from raisins and dates to sweet-smelling oranges. But Joshua wasn't hungry—he was filled with thoughts about the Wall. As he walked through the marketplace, Joshua found himself walking next to an old man, wearing a white robe, carrying a staff. The old man greeted him, "Shalom aleichem." Then he asked, "Where are you going?"

"Aleichem shalom," Joshua said. "I am going to the Kotel."

The old man replied, "I am going there too. Let us go together."

So the old man led Joshua through the streets of Jerusalem. As they walked along, Joshua heard prayers coming from every direction, for there were many synagogues in that part of the city. Joshua recognized the prayers, but the melodies were different from those in his village. Still, the words were the same. And knowing those words made him feel at home in that distant place.

At last they came to the Wailing Wall. Joshua's heart leaped at the sight of it. Joshua and the old man hastened to the Wall, where dozens of men and women had gathered, all pouring out their hearts and leaving messages for God in the cracks in the Wall. With their tears, they implored God's help, and they mourned the destruction of the Temple and the scattering of the Jewish people all over the world.

Joshua stood close to the Wall and kissed it, with tears rolling down his cheeks. He had been waiting all his life for that moment: to stand before that wall in the city of Jerusalem in the land that God had promised to Abraham so long ago. Looking up, Joshua thought he saw some kind of holy presence hovering above the wall, and he knew that he was in a very sacred place.

Joshua began to recite the prayers he knew so well, praying with a passion he had never known, certain that God was listening to every word.

When he finished, he looked up and saw that the old man was writing a message, which he rolled up and left in a crack in the Wall. He turned to Joshua and said, "Would you like to leave a message?" Joshua smiled and held out his hand and the old man handed him a pen and a slip of paper. Joshua thanked him and wrote a message in which he said: "God, how can I ever thank you for bringing me to this holy place? I am so grateful to be here. But God, I miss my parents. Isn't there some way that they could join me?" and he signed it "Joshua." Then he rolled up the message and put it in a crack in the Wall.

Now at the very instant that message touched the Wall, the goat in the orchard reared up and broke its rope. It ran through the cave back to the forest, and from there directly to Joshua's house. And when Joshua's parents saw that the young goat had come back without him, they were very worried. So when the goat suddenly turned around and ran back to the forest, they all ran after it, calling out for Joshua. Even the family's animals ran after them. They saw the goat go behind the bush, and that is when they discovered the entrance to the cave. Joshua's father said, "The goat must be trying to lead us to Joshua. Perhaps he has been hurt. Quickly, let's see where this cave leads us." So they all went into the cave.

Meanwhile, Joshua thanked the old man and said good-bye to him. Now he was hungry, but he didn't have a single coin. Then Joshua remembered the goat. He could milk the goat and sell the milk in the market. Then he would have enough money to buy some food. So he hurried back to the orchard, where he had tied the goat. But when he got there the rope was broken, and the goat was missing. Joshua was heartbroken. That goat was his best friend in the Holy Land. Where could it have gone? Just then Joshua heard sounds coming from the cave, and all at once the goat came running out of it. He was so happy to see it. Joshua embraced the goat, and as he did, he heard familiar voices. He ran toward the cave just as his father, his mother, and his sister Leah came running out. Joshua was overjoyed. He rushed into their arms and they all shed tears of joy, for they had been reunited. And their faithful animals were with them as well, for they were still following them.

Then Joshua said, "Do you know where we are?"

"No," said his father, "what place is this? It can't be Poland."

And Joshua said, "No, it is not Poland. You have reached the land of Israel, the city of Jerusalem."

"How can that be?" said his father. "It takes months to travel to the Holy Land."

And Joshua said, "It's a miracle. I just prayed at the Wall for you to join me here. And God has answered my prayer."

And when they saw the orchards of Jerusalem instead of the forests of Poland, his family realized that a miracle truly had taken place. And since God had brought them there, they decided to stay and make their home there. And their lives in the land of Israel were blessed, and they are still living there to this day.

—Eastern Europe: oral tradition

36. The Goat Whose Horns Reached to Heaven

here once was a goat with horns so long they reached all the way to heaven. With his feet on the earth and his horns cradling the stars, it was possible for him to be in two worlds at the same time. This goat walked among men for many centuries, seeking to help those in need.

If a child was lost at night, the goat would let it take hold of one of its horns and lead it home.

Or if a couple were childless and their prayers unanswered, the goat would lift their prayers all the way to Paradise. And with the help of the goat, the man and woman were at last blessed with a child.

Or sometimes the goat would whisper in a man's ear some secret it had overheard among the angels, and heavenly ideas would enter this world.

One night, as the goat was wandering through the streets of a Polish town, it passed a very sad man. The goat, which could speak, said, "Why, young man, are you so downcast?"

The man replied: "I am a poor man, of few possessions. And now I have lost the finest thing I owed, a snuffbox made of horn. I will never be able to afford another like it."

The goat wanted to help the man, so he said: "My horns are very long. Why don't you cut off a bit of one of them and make yourself another snuffbox?"

The man was very grateful for such a generous offer, and the goat lowered its horns so that the man could cut off what he needed. From that horn he carved a beautiful snuffbox and filled it with tobacco. And the very next day he discovered that the tobacco left in the snuffbox had acquired the most wonderful fragrance, for the horn from which the snuffbox was made had reached all the way to heaven.

Now the man shared a bit of that tobacco with everyone in his minyan and none of them ever forgot its fragrance. They all wanted to know where he had gotten that snuffbox. So he told them about the kind goat he had encountered, and everyone sought out the goat and requested just a small piece of his horns, enough to make a snuffbox. And the goat always lowered its horns and let them cut off a little bit.

In time the wonder of these snuffboxes became known in many cities, and many were those who sought out the sacred goat. Nor did the goat ever refuse anyone who asked for some of its horn. Eventually its horns became so short they barely reached the clouds, and before long they barely reached the top of the trees, and finally, they could not be seen at all.

Now those who seek out the goat can no longer find it. It looks like every other goat, and without its horns there is no way of knowing. Nor can we be sure if it is still wandering among us, or if it has gone off until its horns grow back. And how long will that take? It could be a very long time. And some say that the footsteps of the Messiah will not be heard until the horns of the goat again reach all the way to heaven.

—Eastern Europe: nineteenth century

37. The Golden Dove

abbah bar bar Hanna was once traveling in a caravan with several other sages. After riding for many hours, they came to an oasis and stopped to eat and rest. Later, after they had resumed their journey, Rabbah suddenly realized that he had forgotten to say the blessing after meals. He did not think it was permitted to say those prayers at a distance from where he had eaten, so he decided to return to the previous site.

Now Rabbah was a master of the law, but so were the other sages in the caravan. They might not agree with him, and by the time the matter was decided, they would be even farther away than they were. Instead Rabbah told his companions he was returning to the oasis to recover a golden dove he had left behind. They all agreed that such a great treasure could not be abandoned, and they wished him luck in finding it.

So Rabbah turned back on his own until he reached that place. There he uttered the blessing, and just as he finished, he looked down and saw something glittering in the sand. Rabbah dug it out and saw that it was a golden dove. As he held it, the heat of his hands warmed its wings, and the dove began to throb as if it were alive. This so surprised Rabbah that he opened his hands and the dove took flight, ascending all the way to Paradise. There it built its nest in the branches of the tree outside the palace of the Messiah, where its song fills the heavens. That is why the palace of the Messiah is known as the "Bird's Nest."

And every year, on Rosh ha-Shanah, the Messiah sends forth the dove to see if the world is ready to hear his footsteps, just as Noah did to see if the waters had receded. And if the time is right, the returning dove will perch on the gates of the palace to signal that it is time for them to be opened. But if the world is not yet ready, the dove returns to its nest and is silent for three days, for the time of the coming of the Messiah has been delayed once more.

—Babylon: c. fifth century

38. The Twelve Golden Calves

n the city of Kaifeng, there lived a Jew whose name was Shi Ziyu, who was known by his Hebrew name of Yehuda. Yehuda worked in his small workshop, where he wove silk, satin, and brocade. All that he created was so beautiful that he sold every piece, and he wanted to expand his workshop, so that he could produce more. Next to his workshop there was an abandoned yard. Yehuda would have liked to purchase it, but even though it wasn't expensive, he still could not afford it.

One night Yehuda had a vivid dream. He saw twelve golden calves dancing outside his workshop. In the dream he was puzzled about why they were there. When he went outside, they all nodded to him, and ran away. He followed after them and they led him to the abandoned yard nearby. There they played happily and even did somersaults. Then they all ran to one corner of that yard and disappeared. That is when Yehuda awoke. He wondered about this strange dream, but didn't pay much attention to it.

Then it happened that the dream repeated itself the next night, and the next. After it recurred the third time, Yehuda started to wonder what it meant. He told his wife about it, but she dismissed it, saying "A dream is just a dream." But Yehuda decided to seek the advice of a wise man who lived in Kaifeng, who was known for interpreting dreams. The wise man said: "The place where the calves led you must be a good place. If you buy it, it might bring you good fortune."

Yehuda was struck by this interpretation, and he felt it was a sign that he should risk all his savings and purchase that yard. He did so, but even after he owned the land, he was too poor to build a silk mill.

One rainy day Yehuda walked through the yard, thinking about his dream of the golden calves. In every dream they had run into one corner of the yard and disappeared. He went to that corner and noticed one place where the land seemed a little lower. Rainwater was flowing into it. Yehuda decided to fill it in, so that it didn't get bigger. He took a shovel and began to dig, and when he did, he discovered a cavern. Yehuda reached in and touched something hard. He quickly uncovered it, and pulled out a beautiful gold-plated treasure box. When he opened it, he couldn't believe his eyes—inside were twelve gold ingots.

Yehuda picked up the box and showed it to his wife, and the two of them thanked God and celebrated their good fortune. Now Yehuda was able to build the silk mill he so desired. When the mill was completed, it produced some of the most beautiful satin tapestry in all of China. Even the emperor purchased twelve bolts of the finest brocade. He was so pleased with it, that he wrote a testimonial, saying it was the number one silk mill in the world. After that the brocade made in Yehuda's silk mill became more precious than gold, and the mill itself become one of the city's main sources of revenue. And Yehuda gave thanks to God every day for his abundant blessings.

—China: oral tradition

39. The Sword of Moses

In the last words spoken by Moses, he spoke of a sword that could protect and shield his people. In the Talmud it is said that this sword was given to Moses when he received the Torah. In days of trial for the Jewish people in every generation, the thought of this sword stirs them with longing, for they are sorely in need of a shield against their troubles. But where is the sword of Moses to be found? No one knew, but there was a tradition among the Jews of Iraq that the sword could be found in the mountains of Kurdistan.

Now there were three young Jews who longed to find the sword of Moses so that they could end the oppression of their people. They set out on a quest to the mountains of the north to see if the legend about the sword was true. It took them many months just to cross a vast desert and reach those high mountains. But they believed they were on a divine mission, and would not stop until they had succeeded in finding the sword.

Now what was it they expected from that sword? Sometimes the three friends talked about this. The eldest among them, who was the leader, said that he believed the sword would permit them to conquer armies. The second lad said he believed the sword would only serve to protect, and not to conquer. And the third of the friends thought that finding the sword might somehow bring with it the coming of the Messiah and the redemption of the End of Days. They often debated these matters among themselves, but the one thing they all agreed on was that the sword had to be found, for the people were sorely in need of its protection.

Once they had reached the mountains, the three friends sought information about the sword, but no one seemed to know anything about it. Word of their quest reached the head of a nearby village, a blind old man, embittered by his affliction, who still held on tightly to the reins of power. Now this old man had heard the legend of the enchanted sword of Moses buried in those mountains, although he did not believe it. But he did believe that the Jews must intend to conquer their neighbors if they were searching for such a sword, and he decided to teach the three young men a lesson.

So this old man called in one of his servants and ordered him to go secretly to the camp of the three Jews and to bury an old, rusty sword nearby. After that, the servant should lead them to it, and when they dug it out, he was to have them arrested, for the place it was to be buried was part of that village's land.

This servant, himself a conniving and evil man, buried the rusty sword exactly as he was ordered, quite close to the camp of the three friends. Then he disguised himself as a wood gatherer and passed the camp with a load of wood slung over his back. The three friends saw him and invited him to join them in their meal. This he did, and while they were eating the three friends asked the man if he had ever heard of the sword of Moses. He acted surprised and told them that he had indeed heard of it and that it was supposed to be buried nearby. He pointed in the direction of the place where he had hidden the rusty sword. The three friends became very excited, and decided to start searching there first thing in the morning. The evil servant took his leave and reported all that had happened to the head of the village. Then he took several men with him and waited behind the rocks for the three young men. When the three friends succeeded in finding the rusty sword, the men jumped out and arrested them.

When the evil servant laughed at their capture, the three friends realized they had been tricked. They became very downcast, for they knew that the sword they had found must not be the sword of Moses after all. And they wondered how they could ever continue on their quest if they were prisoners of these villagers.

Not long afterward, the three friends were brought before the blind head of the village. He accused them of plotting to overthrow their neighbors, but the young men said that all they had found was a rusty sword that could hurt no one. Then the old man asked them directly, "And are you not searching for the sword of Moses?" The eldest of the three, who was also the cleverest, did not deny that this was true, since they had asked the evil servant about finding it. But he added, "You are not mistaken about the object of our search, but you are wrong about our purpose. It is not true that we want to use the sword for rebellion. No, we are searching for it because it will make us rich. And if you set us free to search for it, we will divide the money with you when we have found it."

Now this was the best thing that could have been said to that greedy old man, for although he doubted they would succeed in finding the sword, he liked the idea of sharing in the riches if they did. So he agreed to let them go free, in exchange for a vow that they would give him half the price they received for the sword. The young men gladly made this vow, since they knew well that if they did find the sword they would never sell it for all the riches in the world.

Thus the three young men were able to continue their quest, with the desire to find the sword of Moses still burning within them. But which way were they to turn? It would be foolish to start digging anywhere in the mountains, for they could spend the rest of their lives there and not find anything. No, they needed a clue; but they had none, except for the words of Moses in the Torah, which they carried in their hearts. So they called upon those words yet one more time, and raked through them as if through coals, hoping to find a clue that would direct them. Moses had said: *O happy Israel! Who is like you, a people delivered by the Lord, your protecting shield, your sword triumphant! Your enemies shall dwindle away before you, and you shall tread on their high places* (Deut. 33:29).

The three each meditated on these words, as they had so many times before. Then the first of them spoke and said, "It seems as if the words of Moses are a prophecy. For is it not true that our enemies have dwindled away, and that we have escaped their clutches? And are we not now treading upon their high places?" The others realized that what he said was true—and their hope was renewed that they could succeed in fulfilling the other part of the prophecy as well, the one concerning the sword of Moses.

Then the second lad, who had also been meditating on the words of Moses, said, "Perhaps there are still other clues to be found in the words of Moses. It occurs to me that perhaps we should be seeking not only the sword of Moses, but the shield of which he also spoke. For surely that shield will be found in the same place as the sword, and a shield is much larger than a sword and should be easier to find."

His companions considered his words with great seriousness, and realized how wise they were, and they wondered why they had not thought more of the shield of Moses. But still they did not know where to start looking. Then the third lad spoke and said, "Surely we must begin by ascending one of these mountains. True, we do not know which one, but I suggest that we ascend the very tallest, which lies at the center of them. For Moses towered above all other men, and it seems to me that his sword would be hidden on the highest mountain." The other two friends marveled at the wise words of their companion, and they began the ascent.

Now by the end of the first day of climbing, the three friends had reached a small ledge on that high mountain, and to their surprise they found there the entrance to a cave. They were amazed to see a cave up that high, and they agreed that the cave must be searched. But first they made a fire and rested and ate a warm meal. Afterward they put their fire out, lit a torch, and then entered the cave. Now the cave was quite narrow. They were able to proceed only one step at a time, and even then they had to squeeze their way between the walls of the cave. And so they continued for what seemed a great distance, as the cave descended inside the mountain. In fact, they traveled so far downward that they wondered if they had descended as far as they had ascended in the first place, or perhaps even further. And as they descended in that cave, a sound began to reach their ears, like the sound of running water.

At last those narrow passages opened into a large cavern. No sooner had they entered than they saw the glittering waters of the stream that flowed from there. The three lads hurried to that stream, and when they stood above the waters they saw something glittering in its currents. "Why, it's a fish!" cried one of the lads. The others saw that not only was it a fish, but a golden fish, with golden scales, swimming in the currents of the stream. Then the eldest realized that such a golden fish must be a very important sign, and he cried out to the others, "Hurry, let us follow that fish!"

So they ran along the side of that stream, and followed the golden fish as it glided slowly through the waters. But soon they reached a place where the passage was so narrow they could not follow. And when the eldest realized that they were about to lose the fish, he suddenly reached out and caught it—so quickly that even he was surprised.

His companions hurried over to examine the fish in the light of the torch, and when they did they saw an amazing thing: there on one side of the golden fish was inscribed the shape of a sword! And on the blade of that sword were four Hebrew letters! How could such a thing be possible? The three friends were stunned, and they realized at once that it was a sign sent to them to guide them further on their quest.

Now of course those young men knew Hebrew, for they had studied the holy tongue from the time they had learned to read. And so they each read that word, but they did not know what it meant, for it was a word they had never seen before. It was the eldest of the young men who realized that the golden fish had served its purpose by bringing them this word. He said to the others, "Now let us set the fish free, for surely it was a messenger of God, and has brought us this word, which must be a great clue in our quest." The others agreed, so he set the fish free in the waters, and it quickly swam out of their sight. And they wondered what secret that mysterious word held for them.

So far, none of them had tried to pronounce the word. Now one of them spoke it as he imagined it must be said, for there seemed to be many ways it could be pronounced. In fact, the second lad had imagined it another way, which he too spoke aloud. But the third, the eldest, had thought of a different way, and as soon as he pronounced it, the three friends suddenly found themselves standing outside again, at the foot of the mountain, at the very spot where they had begun their climb! The startled young men could not understand how they had come to be there, for an instant earlier they had been in the cave, deep inside the mountain. They wondered if it was because of the word, but they could not imagine how that could be. All three friends agreed, however, not to pronounce the word again, since they did not understand its power, and did not know what would happen if they did. And they decided that until they learned more about that word, they must continue their search for the sword of Moses.

Now the three friends did not know it, but from the time they had left the village, they had been followed by the servant of the blind man and several of his henchmen. For the blind man was not satisfied with only half the sword of Moses; he wanted the whole thing. So he had the three young Jews followed, intending to steal the sword from them when they found it, and then take their lives.

Now when the three lads had ascended the mountain, the henchmen waited at the base of the mountain, not far from where the friends had made camp. So when they saw the three of them suddenly appear at the base of the mountain, without having seen them descend, the henchmen could not believe their eyes. The evil servant did not know what to do, so he sent a messenger back to the village. When the blind man heard what had happened, he guessed that the three had found the sword, and somehow used its magic to descend from the mountain. His lust to have such power in his own hands grew very great, and he ordered the servant to have the three killed at once, and to bring all their possessions back to him, without opening them. For the blind man secretly feared that the evil servant would try to take the power of the magical sword for himself. And he was right, the servant was planning to do exactly that: to steal the sword for himself.

So it was that the three friends were surrounded by enemies on all sides, and knew nothing about it. They were absorbed in trying to decipher the secret of the golden fish and to continue their quest for the magic sword. Then all at once, they heard the cries of their pursuers, and ran for their lives. They ascended that tall mountain again as fast as they could, but the villagers had climbed mountains all their lives and drew closer with every step. The three lads climbed faster and faster, until they finally reached the peak of the mountain, and there was no place left for them to go.

What were they to do? As they stood upon that high peak and looked down, they saw that the other side of the mountain was too steep to climb down. There was nowhere for them to go, and when they heard the villagers getting ever closer the eldest lad decided to pronounce the word as he had pronounced it in the cave. And he spoke the holy Name out loud—for that is what it was—and in an instant the peak of the nearest mountain, although several miles away, moved from its place, so that it was but a single step away for them. The three companions took that step, until they stood together on the second peak. And just before the evil villagers reached the top of the other mountain, the lad pronounced the Name again, and the second mountain returned to where it had been before.

And there, on that high peak, they watched the spears and arrows of the amazed villagers fall harmlessly into the valley below. The three companions then realized they were just beginning to understand how great was the power of that holy Name, for such power could only come from the most powerful of the seventy-two Names of God, since the Holy One is the source of all power and being. And little by little they began to understand that the sword of which Moses had spoken might not have been an actual sword at all, but that magical word itself, which served as both a sword and shield for the Jewish people. At that moment, high on that mountain peak, they realized that they had indeed succeeded in their quest. For the word that they had read in that cave from the side of the golden fish, was itself the very sword of Moses for which they had searched.

Up so high, they felt much closer to the heavens than they had ever felt before. And they knew that they would use that "sword" in their generation as Moses had used it in his—to liberate their people, the Children of Israel, so that they might end their long exile and return to the Holy Land of their forefathers. For Moses had said: *You shall come in to the land that the Lord your God has given you for an inheritance, and possess it and dwell therein* (Jer. 10:15). And they were certain that just as the words of Moses about the sword had been fulfilled, so too would the prophecy about the return to the Holy Land come true as well as that of the coming of the Messiah at the End of Days.

—Iraqi Kurdistan: oral tradition

40. The Groom Who Was Destined to Die on His Wedding Day

t is well known that babies cry from the moment they are born. Why? Because the angel in charge of birth tells them when they are destined to die. For a person's fate is sealed from the time of his birth, and the circumstances of his death are already known.

Now one night, just as a baby was born, the angel told him, "You will die from a snake bite on the day of your wedding." As soon as the baby heard this, he broke into loud cries. And while most babies quickly forget what the angel told them, this baby remembered. And from the time he began to speak, he told his parents what the angel had said. After that, his parents were afraid to let him marry, out of fear that he would die on the day of his wedding.

Years passed, the child grew, and his older brothers had all been married, and the young man also wanted to marry. But every time he brought this up, his parents discouraged him, reminding him of what the angel had said. But when his parents saw that he would not give up the idea of marriage, they approached a wise sage and asked for his advice. He told them: "Your son can marry on condition that you wrap him from head to foot in five sheep skins on the day of his wedding. And as you travel to the wedding be sure that his feet don't touch the ground. Have his brothers carry him on a chair to his bride."

So it was that on the day of the wedding his parents wrapped the groom in five sheep skins, and his brothers carried him in a chair, so that his feet didn't touch the ground. Then, as they traveled to the house of the bride, a huge poisonous snake, hidden in a tree, suddenly dropped down and bit the foot of the groom, but it couldn't bite through the thick sheep skins that covered him. His brothers quickly killed the snake and buried it under a large stone. After that they took the groom down from the chair, unwrapped the sheep skins, and he continued to the house of the bride by foot. The wedding ceremony took place in peace, and the bride and groom returned to his village, and everyone was greatly relieved that he had survived.

Many years passed. The groom's brothers aged and died, his own children grew old and died, and even his grandchildren died of old age, but he kept on living. By now he was so old he couldn't speak, and he could barely stand. His descendants saw that he was suffering, but they didn't know what they could do for him. So they went to one of the wise men of that generation and told him the story of how he had escaped death on his wedding day.

The sage said to them: "I heard this story from my father. Because he escaped death when he was fated to die, he cannot die at all."

His descendants said, "What are we going to do? He is so old and is suffering so much."

The sage told them: "You must find the place where the snake was buried, and take the dust from there and mix it with water and let the old man drink it. Only then will he be able to die."

The groom's descendants went back to the big stone where the snake was buried, and they took dust from beneath it and mixed it with water and let the old man drink it. And right after that, he died.

—Ethiopia: oral tradition

41. The Three Tasks of Elijah

t has often been told how the prophet Elijah, wearing a disguise, has brought salvation to a Jew in distress. There was one time, however, when Elijah did not disguise himself, but presented himself to a poor man whose family was starving and said, "I know about the suffering of your family, and I wish to assist you in some way. Since I have no money to give you, all I can offer is myself. Therefore I want you to take me to town and sell me to the highest bidder."

The poor man was greatly startled at these words, for he could not imagine that anyone, not even Elijah, would be willing to make such a sacrifice. He blessed Elijah for his kindness, but refused to accept his offer, for no Jew should have to serve as a slave. But Elijah insisted, and reminded the man about the pangs of hunger his children were feeling at that very moment. At last the man agreed to sell Elijah, if that was what he wanted. They went to the marketplace, and the man announced that an auction was to be held for this slave.

Now among those at that auction was a servant of the king, who observed the knowing look on Elijah's face, and purchased him for the king for a sum of seventy dinars. And the poor man bought food with that money, and after that his family never went hungry again, for his business flourished and his fortune grew. And when he grew rich, he gave charity to every poor person he met, for he never forgot the sacrifice of Elijah, who had permitted himself to be sold.

As for Elijah, he was brought before the king, who at first was astonished that his servant had purchased such an old slave. "And what is it that you think this slave can do?" asked the king. "Can he carry bricks? If not, I do not need him, for the construction of my palace is shortly to take place." Then the king turned toward Elijah and said, "Tell me, old man, can you at least read?" And Elijah said, "Yes, that I can certainly do." "Well, then," said the king, "perhaps we will find something useful for you to do."

As Elijah was being led away, he heard the king say to his servant, "Go into the city and locate the finest architect and bring him to me, for I must have someone draw up the plans for my palace." When Elijah heard this, he spoke up and said, "May it please your majesty, but I too am an architect, and I do not doubt that I could design exactly the palace that you dream of." The king was pleased to hear this, for he had very particular plans of his own for his new palace and had feared an architect would have his own ideas. So he agreed to let Elijah be the first to draw up the plans.

In the days that followed, the king described the palace he wanted to Elijah, who listened intently. And when the king had finished describing it down to the last detail, Elijah set about to drawing it. The king was astonished when Elijah presented the plans to the king the very next day, and when the king looked at them, he saw that the slave had found a place for every single thing the king had wanted. Then the king grew excited and said, "It is true, old man, that you have succeeded in putting my every wish into your plans. I doubt if any other architect could have done as well. But it is one thing to draw up plans, and another to bring them into being. Are you prepared to oversee the building of the palace as well?"

Elijah replied at once: "This too, my lord king, I can do. But if I am to serve as your builder, how can I remain a slave? For what free men will want to take orders from a slave?" The king agreed, but now that he had discovered the great skills of this slave, he was reluctant to set him free. So he said, "Freedom is the most precious thing in the world; its value cannot be calculated. If you want your freedom, building a palace will not suffice to attain it. Let us count it as one of three things you will do at my command. And if you fulfill all three commands in full, then I will give you your freedom."

Now the truth is that Elijah had the powers to free himself at any time, simply by disappearing. But he did not, because he had been sold as a slave, and as a slave he would serve until he was set free. So Elijah agreed to perform three things for the king, as he commanded—so long as they did not involve anything evil. And the king issued a proclamation, that if the slave Elijah completed the building of the palace and two other tasks as well, that he was to be set free. But he did not write down what those two other tasks were, nor did he tell Elijah at the time.

That night Elijah offered a prayer to the Holy One, blessed be He, that the palace might be built at once, for the sooner Elijah was freed from slavery, the sooner he could return to the task of assisting Jews in need. And the next morning the king and all the people of that city were astounded to see that the palace had been built, complete in every respect, exactly as the king had described it. The king was overwhelmed with joy at the splendor of his palace, and at the same time he began to realize that his slave Elijah had wondrous powers, far greater than he had imagined. He was loath to let him go, for the slave was too precious to him. So he had Elijah called in and said to him, "What you have done is a miracle, without a doubt. I am very grateful to you, and I will think of you always as I wander the halls of my new palace. But now it is time for you to undertake your second task." Elijah nodded his head in agreement, for he was ready to do so at once.

Then the king said, "I have heard it said the Jews believe that when the Messiah comes, there will be precious stones that will take the place of the sun. For your second task, I would like to see these stones with my own eyes."

The king had thought long and hard about this task, for he felt sure that it was impossible to fulfill. And it was very difficult, even for Elijah—but for a reason unknown to the king. For it was written in the Book of Life that when Elijah entered the cave where the precious gems were hidden, the era of the Messiah was to begin. Yet the destined time had not arrived, and Elijah did not dare hasten the End of Days. Therefore he was silent for a long time, but at last he replied and said, "I will see to it, my lord king, that this desire of yours is fulfilled. But only if you will first agree to three conditions. The first is that you must agree to follow whoever comes to lead you to these stones; the second is that you must permit yourself to be blindfolded when you are taken there and when you return, for the location is a great secret; and the third is that you will not take any of those precious stones with you when you leave." The king was still doubtful that such precious stones even existed, so he readily agreed to these conditions. Then Elijah told the king that he would hear from whoever would serve as his guide within three days, and he bowed low and took his leave.

Now at the same time, far out at sea, there was a ship that was foundering in a terrible storm, about to sink. Among all the passengers, there was a Jewish lad. Suddenly Elijah appeared before him, although he was invisible to everyone else. Elijah told the lad that if he would agree to approach the king of the land toward which they had been sailing, he would save the ship. The boy was to lead the king to a cave, which Elijah would reveal. The boy protested that a king would not heed one so young as he, but still he agreed to do as Elijah said, for the ship had started to sink. And as soon as the boy agreed, the storm subsided and the passengers were saved. Elijah then told the boy how to find his way to the secret cave, and when he was certain that the boy understood, he vanished.

As soon as the ship arrived in port, the boy went to the palace of the king, and announced that he had come to lead the king to the precious stones. The boy was soon taken to the king, who had left orders that anyone making such a claim was to be given an audience at once. Now the king was astonished to see that his guide was a boy, but he had agreed to go with whomever Elijah sent to lead him. So too was he reluctant to be blindfolded, but because he had given his word he permitted it. But both to protect himself and to discover the secret of the location, should it prove to exist, the king ordered that the head of the palace guards should secretly follow behind them.

Now Elijah had foreseen that the king might send someone to follow them, and he saw to it that the head of the palace guards was deceived by an illusion, in which it appeared to him that the boy led the king in one direction, when they actually went in another. By following Elijah's instructions, the boy led the blindfolded king to a cave some three miles from the palace. When they were inside the cave, the boy told the king to take off the blindfold, and when he did, the king was almost blinded by the bright light that shone from the precious stones gathered there. He could not believe his eyes at first, but when his eyes grew more accustomed to the great light, he realized that any one of those precious stones would be worth more than any diamond in the world. The king was so seized with the desire to possess those diamonds that he reached out to seize one of them, but at the instant he touched it all of the precious stones vanished, and the cave became pitch black. Then the king realized that such sacred stones could not be possessed, and in the face of such power he was glad he had not lost his life. Then he meekly put on his blindfold and followed the boy back to the palace and bade him good-bye. He was certain that his guard would have learned the way to that sacred cave. But when he returned, the king discovered that his trusted guard had been following them when they had suddenly disappeared from his sight, and at last he had given up searching for them and returned to the palace. Then, more than ever, the king did not want to lose the great powers possessed by his slave. But in order to prevent him from becoming free, he had to think of a third task simply impossible to perform. The king gave this matter a great deal of thought, and at the end of three days he called for Elijah and told him that now that the second task had been fulfilled, he was ready to assign the third one. Elijah told him that he was ready.

Then the king smiled and took out a silken scarf and handed it to Elijah and said, "Here, my good man, is a gift. This scarf is now yours. But tell me how much would it be worth if you purchased it in the market?" Elijah looked at the scarf, which had a rainbow of colors, and said: "Since it has come from far away, and is beautiful as well, it might be worth as much as one golden coin. And considering, as well, that it belonged to the king, its value might be increased to two gold coins." The king nodded at this assessment and said: "As always, you are a very shrewd man. For I perceive that the scarf's value is exactly as you put it. Yet, as you know, it is the task of the merchant to sell something for more than he paid for it. This, then, is your last and final task, if you can fulfill it: you are to take this scarf to the market and offer it for sale. And if you are able to sell it for ten thousand gold coins, then you will have completed the final task and you will be a free man. But if you sell it for even a dinar less than ten thousand, you will have failed to fulfill the final task, and you will remain my slave for the rest of your life." The king broke out in cruel laughter, for he believed that he had finally outwitted the wise Elijah. The king knew well that he was the only one in that kingdom who possessed such great wealth. Yet Elijah showed no sign of worry. He bowed courteously, and told the king that the sale would take place in three days, and then took his leave.

Now where was it that Elijah went? Directly to the Garden of Eden, with the scarf in his hand. There he went to the base of the Tree of Life, and gathered up one hundred leaves that had fallen there, and wrapped them in that scarf. Then he returned to the city where he was a slave, and each time he met a poor Jew on the street he gave him one of the leaves and told him that by boiling the leaf in water and drinking the potion, he could cure any illness. So it was that some of the Jews were able to cure those in their families who had been afflicted all their lives with illness, and others were able to sell their leaves for a great sum, enough to sustain them for the rest of their lives.

By the time Elijah had reached the palace, he had given away every one of the leaves. But the scarf in which he had carried them had absorbed forever the fragrance of Paradise, and all who caught a scent of it knew for a moment a peace unknown in this world. When Elijah returned he went directly to the marketplace and called a crowd together in order to sell the scarf, just as the king had commanded. Now the king had come to the market that day in disguise, for he wanted to see for himself if Elijah would succeed in selling the scarf for ten thousand gold coins. At last a crowd had gathered, and one by one Elijah called them up to examine the scarf, which he spread on a table. As they did, each of them caught a scent of that otherworldly fragrance unknown outside of Paradise. And as soon as they did, each and every one of them knew that the scarf was priceless. Every man, woman and child in that crowd bid for that scarf, but none of them could offer ten thousand gold coins, for not one of them was that rich.

As for the king, he too had caught the scent of that fragrance, and he became possessed by a great longing to possess that scarf, which he had foolishly given to Elijah without realizing its value. So the king too joined in the bidding, but Elijah rejected every bid until the king shouted "Ten thousand gold coins! I must have that scarf!" "Sold!" said Elijah, and everyone turned and wondered who could be so wealthy as to buy a scarf for ten thousand gold coins.

The king then took Elijah aside and revealed his true identity. Yet Elijah did not seem surprised. When the king asked him why, Elijah said, "I knew that there was no one else in this land who was so wealthy, therefore the bidder had to be you. Yet you need not feel that the price is too high, for know that this scarf you have purchased will give you a priceless blessing. All you need do is to spread it out on your bed and sleep upon it, and when you fall asleep you will be transported to Paradise and permitted to share in its glory all night. Therefore peace shall be with you for the rest of your life, and what more precious gift is there than peace?"

When the king heard this, he finally came to realize how wise Elijah was, and how great his power. He felt humble in the face of such a blessing, for as he held the scarf in his hand, he already began to feel its blessing of peace. Then the king set down in writing and sealed with his seal that Elijah was no longer a slave, but a free man. He also gave Elijah those ten thousand golden coins, even though it was almost half his treasure. And he sent Elijah on his way in peace.

Elijah was happy to be a free man again, free to bestow blessings on his people. It is said that he gave one of those ten thousand gold coins to each and every Jew he met, in that city and throughout the land, until every gold coin had been given out. In this way he brought on a blessed year for his people, which they never forgot as long as they lived.

—Tunisia: c. eleventh century

42. The Staff of Elijah

ong ago there was an old man who had once been very wealthy and had given charity willingly, but in his old age found himself impoverished. His neighbors remembered how generous he had been when he had been rich, so they often invited him to their homes and saw to it that his needs were met.

Once, when the Sabbath was over, the old man returned home, lit a candle, and was startled to find a Jew sitting on his bed. The old man was taken aback and said, "Who are you?" The stranger did not answer directly, but instead asked a question of his own, "Tell me, may I remain in your home for a few days? I have been traveling far and wide, and I need a place to rest." The old man replied, "Certainly you may stay, but what shall you eat, for I myself am dependent on the kindness of others?" The stranger said, "No matter," and remained as the guest of the old man. The two shared the old man's food, meager as it was, and the stranger accompanied the old man to the synagogue.

After three days the stranger prepared to depart, but before he set out, he said to the old man, "You have been so kind to me, and I wish to repay you, but all I have is this staff. Take it. It will help you. But someday you will have to return it to its place." Now these were strange words, which the old man did not understand. "Where is its place?" he asked. The stranger replied, "On Mount Carmel." This confused the old man even more, for Mount Carmel is in the Holy Land, far away from where the old man made his home. "Who are you?" he asked. And the stranger revealed that he was none other than Elijah the Prophet. Then the old man was afraid, overcome and thrilled all at once. He accepted the staff from Elijah with many thanks, and accompanied him to the door and saw him off. But when Elijah had taken but a few steps, he disappeared from the old man's sight, and the old man realized that this had truly been the prophet of old.

The old man soon discovered the powers of the staff. Once, when he had walked a long distance and was feeling faint, he sat down at the edge of the road and placed his staff so that only his feet touched it. At once he felt his strength renewed, as though he had become much younger. He was able to stand up easily and returned home full of life. After that he used the staff to revive himself whenever he began to feel the burden of his age, and his spirits always lifted at the very instant his feet touched the wondrous staff.

The next day the old man took the staff with him when he went to the market. While he was walking, the staff suddenly became stuck in a crack between the stones. The old man bent down to pull it out, and when he did he found several silver pieces in the shadow of the staff. What a blessing, he thought, for now he would be able to support himself again, and even have enough to give charity.

One night the old man was awakened by the sound of screams and cries. He ran outside with the staff in his hand to see what was happening, and discovered that the Jewish quarter had been invaded by a mob who were trying to set it afire. Suddenly the old man felt filled with a great strength, and he ran directly into the mob, swinging the staff. The other Jews marveled at the old man's courage and took heart, and they too joined the fight. In this way the rioters were quickly defeated, and never again did they dare to attack the Jewish quarter.

After this, the old man became a hero among the Jews of the town, and they decided to collect enough money for him to fulfill his lifelong wish of going to the Holy Land. So it was that he was able to make the journey after all, despite his age. After many months his ship arrived in Jaffa and the old man disembarked. His wish was to travel to the Wailing Wall in Jerusalem, but somehow he ended up in a wagon bound for Safed.

When the wagon was crossing Mount Carmel, one of its wheels broke off. There was nothing that could be done until the wheel was repaired, which would take some time. To pass the time the old man took a walk on the mountain, and along the way he spotted a tree from which a branch had been cut off. He came closer, and marveled that the wood of the tree was so similar to that of his staff. He raised up the staff against that place in the tree to compare it, and at the instant it touched the tree it fused to it and turned into one of its branches. While the old man watched in complete amazement, the branch began to bud and bear leaves, so that it soon resembled every other branch of that tree.

It was then that the old man recalled the words of Elijah, and understood that his mission was complete: the staff of Elijah had been returned to its place of origin. With a wonderful feeling the old man returned to the wagon just as the wheel was ready for travel, and he continued on his journey. After visiting the holy city of Safed, he traveled to Jerusalem, as he had first intended, and before long reached the Wailing Wall. As he stood and prayed before the Wall, a gust of wind carried a leaf to his feet. And when the old man bent down and picked it up, he somehow knew for certain it was a leaf from the tree from which his staff had been taken. The old man kept that leaf, and it remained green all the years of his life. And he lived many more years in the Holy Land, the happiest he had ever known.

—Romania: oral tradition

43. Miriam's Tambourine

ong ago, in the land of Babylon, there lived a rabbi and his son who made their home in a small hut deep in the forest, where they spent their days in the study of the mysteries of the Torah. During the day they read from the sacred texts, and at night they peered into the stars and read in them as clearly as in any book. And they were the purest souls to be found in that land.

In those days the Jews of Babylon led lives of peace, for since the days of Daniel there had always been a Jewish adviser to the king, who had protected the interests of his people. There was a remarkable tradition connected to the appointment of this minister. For since the time of Daniel, each king had kept a golden chest beside the throne, and in that chest was a precious book. And that book could be opened only by the one man in each generation who was destined to serve as the king's minister. In the past, this one man had always been found among the Jews of Babylon, and now, it was time once again to seek out the one who would advise the king.

But this time, none of those who journeyed to the palace from every city in Babylon was able to open the book. The Jews of Babylon began to worry, for the longer they went without a Jewish minister, the more dangerous it was, since there was no one to look out for them. So they sent messengers to every city where Jews could be found, to invite them to the palace. Perhaps one of them would be able to open the book. Many came, but none succeeded.

The messengers were sent out again, this time to the most remote villages and forests. One messenger learned of a rabbi and his son living alone deep in the woods, and he sought them out. Now the rabbi and his son were happy to welcome the messenger, for few visitors ever came to their door. And when they learned of his mission, they agreed at once to journey to the palace and attempt to open the king's book. Then the messenger rode off to search for any others who might have been missed, and the rabbi and his son set out on foot to reach the capital.

While they walked, the rabbi and his son spoke of that mysterious book, which only one man in each generation could open. It was said to have been delivered to Daniel by an angel while he was inside the lion's den. There he learned that he was the first mortal to open that book, and that after him, only one man in each generation would be able to do so. So secret were the mysteries of that book that not even the angels were permitted to read it. Both the rabbi and his son longed to read in that book and share in those mysteries.

So involved did the rabbi and his son become in their contemplation of this mysterious book, that they did not even notice if it was day or night. And when at last they stopped walking and looked around, they found themselves in a strange place, which they did not recognize. For they had paid no attention to the path on which they were walking, and had become totally lost. Yet they did not become frightened; they had complete faith that God would not lead them astray.

They walked on, and in the distance they saw a beautiful palace, which shone as if it were made of pearl. Around it was a high wall, and when they reached the wall they found the gate locked. They peered through the gate, and marveled at the beauty of the palace. Their hearts were drawn to it, and they longed to enter there. Yet how could they pass through the gate? It was then that the first miracle occurred, for that gate opened only once every hundred years, and then only for an instant. Fate had seen to it that the rabbi and his son had arrived there at exactly the moment it was set to fly open. And when it did open, they did not hesitate. Without a word, they both hurried through the gate before it slammed shut.

Now when the rabbi and his son found themselves standing inside that garden, before that splendid palace, they were filled with joy. They hurried to the door of the palace, and in it they found a golden key. They turned the key and entered. Inside the palace they found an old woman with beautiful wise eyes. She was taking leaves out of a silver basket and crushing them between her fingers, into fine powder which she let fall into a golden basket at her side. When the rabbi and his son entered, she looked up; she did not seem surprised to see them. They approached her and the rabbi said, "Peace be with you." "Peace be with you," she said. Then the rabbi asked her what she was doing. "I have children everywhere who suffer from one Sabbath to the next," she said. "But on the eve of the Sabbath, I take the powder made from these leaves and cast it into the wind. And the wind carries it to the four corners of the earth, so that all those who breathe in even the smallest speck have a taste of Paradise, and the Sabbath is filled with joy for them."

The rabbi and his son marveled at this, for they had known the peace and joy of Sabbath many times, and now they knew why. By then they were both very curious to know who the old woman was, and the rabbi asked her name. She said, "My name is Sarah." "And what is your husband's name?" asked the rabbi. "His name is Abraham," she said. And when he heard this, the rabbi wondered if they might not be the same Sarah and Abraham who are the mother and father of every Jew. And Sarah nodded that it was true. And the rabbi asked, "Where is Abraham?" And Sarah said, "He has gone into the Garden of Eden to fetch freshly fallen leaves."

It was then that the rabbi's son (who had not yet reached his Bar Mitzvah) recognized the hand of fate in their coming to that place. He told Sarah of the journey they had set out on, to attempt to open the book that had once belonged to Daniel. She nodded as the young boy spoke, and then she said, "That book can only be opened by one who has the purest soul. And while both of your souls are very pure, still they are not pure enough to open the book." The rabbi and his son were very sorry to hear this, for they had hoped that at least one of them might be able to succeed. The rabbi said,

"But tell us, Sarah, is there any way that we can purify our souls enough to open the book?" And Sarah replied, "Yes, there is one way. You must descend into Miriam's Well, and purify yourselves in those sacred waters."

Now both the rabbi and his son had heard of Miriam's Well. That was the well that had followed the children of Israel in their desert wanderings, the well God had given them in honor of the righteousness of Miriam, sister of Moses and Aaron. But that well had not been seen since the days of the wandering in the wilderness. Yet, if it were possible for them to find Sarah, perhaps it was also possible to find Miriam's Well. The rabbi asked Sarah where the well could be found, and she said, "You would come to it if you followed the path outside the palace. But it would be futile to go there, for the Evil One has placed serpents all around the entrance to the well. No one can enter there and purify themselves." This bad news greatly saddened the rabbi and his son, for they had felt so near their goal, and now again it seemed impossible to reach. With a sad voice, the rabbi's son asked, "Is there any way to get past the serpents?" Sarah smiled and said, "Yes, but only with the help of Miriam's tambourine."

Once again, hope burned in their hearts, and they wondered where they might find Miriam's tambourine, and if it were the same one that she had played after the Israelites had crossed the Red Sea. So they asked Sarah about this, and she told them that it was indeed the very same tambourine the maidens of Israel had played as they danced at the Red Sea. They asked her where they might find it, and she said simply, "Why, with Miriam." And when they asked where Miriam could be found, Sarah said, "If you go through that palace, into the garden, and pass through a hollow tree, you will reach the entrance to a cave. And if you travel through that cave, you will reach the shore of the Red Sea. And there, at the shore of the Red Sea, you will find Miriam, for that is where she makes her home."

Then the rabbi and his son thanked Sarah and set off at once to find that cave. Before long, after passing through the most beautiful garden they had ever seen, they reached a magnificent tree that turned out to be hollow, just as Sarah had said. And when they stepped into the hollow trunk, they found the entrance to a cave. They crawled through that long cave, mysteriously illumined with a pale light, until they reached the shore of the sea. There they found a beautiful young woman, sitting on a rock beside the shore and playing a tambourine, with schools of fish crowded around her, and dolphins doing turns in the air. And as soon as they heard the wonderful rhythm of that tambourine, both the rabbi and his son were spellbound, and began to dance. They danced with the greatest joy they had ever known, for they were feeling the same joy the Israelites had felt after they had escaped the clutches of the Egyptians by passing through the parted waters of the Red Sea.

Now they might have danced there forever had the young woman not put down the tambourine. When she did, their feet came to rest, and they knew they had indeed found Miriam the Prophetess, and that the tambourine she played must be the very one they were seeking. The rabbi and his son introduced themselves to Miriam, and told her of their quest. Then, without a moment's hesitation, Miriam gave them the tambourine, and said, "Go, and, God willing, you will expel the serpents nesting there. For know that none of us who inhabit this place can accomplish that, only mortals such as yourselves, who have found your way here. Meanwhile I will wait here for you to return, for this is my home, beside the sea. Know that the sound of this tambourine has great power; it causes those with pure souls to be filled with joy, and evil creatures to cringe and flee as fast as they can. Now please hurry, for if I go as long as a day without hearing the music of my tambourine, my eternal life will come to an end."

The rabbi and his son knew that if Miriam were willing to entrust them with her miraculous tambourine, their quest must be very precious in her eyes. They gratefully accepted the tambourine, took their leave, and hurried back to the cave. They passed through the cave, and then the hollow tree, until they made their way back to the garden and onto the path before the palace. At last they came to the well they had been seeking. It was set deep within the earth, surrounded by stones that had long ago fused together. Somehow that miraculous well, with its living waters, had followed the Israelites as they wandered from place to place, and had given them fresh water to drink. But now, the rabbi and his son both saw, a multitude of serpents were nesting at its entrance, depriving the world of its wonderful powers.

Then they approached the well, and knew that they had reached the most solemn moment of their lives. When they stood there all the serpents raised their heads, as if to strike, but they paid them no heed. The rabbi handed the tambourine to his son and told him to start to play. Then the boy struck the tambourine for the first time, and as soon as he did, a wonderful, spell-binding music emerged from it, with a strong, insistent rhythm. This time the rabbi and his son were not compelled to dance, for Miriam was not playing; instead the sounds made all of the serpents writhe in agony, and they began at once to slither and crawl away as fast as they could go. They headed directly for the garden gate, and slipped beneath it, never to return, and the purity of the well and the garden was restored at last.

Then, while his son continued to play that tambourine, the rabbi found that the wonderful music gave him the strength to climb down the stones on the inside of the well. When he reached the water, he immersed himself, and felt his soul purified to its very kernel. So it was that when the rabbi climbed out of the well, he took the tambourine from his son, and played its wondrous music once again as his son descended into those life-giving waters, and likewise purified his soul. And when they departed from that place, they found that their eyes had been opened, and that all manner of angels and spirits who flocked around that garden became apparent to them. Then they hurried back to the hollow tree and passed through the cave, for they wanted to bring the tambourine back to Miriam as soon as possible. It was not long before they stood before her shining beauty, and when they returned the tambourine she blessed them both and told them that their wonderful deed would always be remembered.

After that the rabbi and his son hurried back to the gate of the garden, and took their leave, and followed the path they found there. And lo and behold, by morning they found themselves standing before the palace of the king. There they were given an audience, and like so many others who had come before them, they approached the book that had been sealed so long. The rabbi had only to touch the cover of the book lightly, and it opened to him, and all who surrounded him cheered, for the new minister of the king had finally been found.

Thus it came to pass that the rabbi became the king's trusted adviser and served him for many years, referring to the book for every important decision, and making certain that his fellow Jews were spared any persecution. And when the rabbi took his leave of this world, they did not have to look far to find the one who would take his place. For his son, who had also immersed himself in Miriam's Well and had been cleansed as fully as his father, had no difficulty in opening the book and understanding its wisdom. He too served as the king's minister for many years, and that was a time of abundance for the Jews of that land.

—Eastern Europe: nineteenth century

44. The Cave of King David

ne night the Turkish sultan disguised himself and walked about his city. When he entered the Jewish quarter, he heard singing, and when he went closer, he saw that the people were dancing in a great circle. He asked about the song and was told that the words were "David, King of Israel, is alive and still exists."

When the sultan heard this, it confirmed all his suspicions about the Jews. The Jews were not loyal to him, but to their own king.

The next day the sultan called in the kabbalist Rabbi Rafael Recanti, who was the leader of the Jewish community, and made these accusations. The rabbi insisted that King David had died long ago, but the sultan would hear none of it. He demanded that the rabbi bring him a gift that could come only from King David, and if he did not, he would destroy all the Jews of that land.

Rabbi Recanti was very frightened. And he knew that he must turn to heaven for guidance, for only a miracle could make it possible for him to fulfill the king's command. So he fasted for several days and immersed himself in the *mikveh,* and at last he heard a heavenly voice announce that he must go to the city of Luz in the Holy Land. There he would find King David, who, in truth, was still alive. So too did the heavenly voice reveal the holy name that would make it possible for him to go there.

Now the way to the city of Luz is one of the most closely guarded secrets. The histories of the city, reaching back for centuries, are filled with every detail of learning and life. Yet these same histories, though complete, do not record a single death, nor a single flood or fire, for all who live inside its walls are immortal, and even the Angel of Death can do them no harm.

Now that heaven had opened a path for him, Rabbi Recanti rushed down it, as did the Children of Israel when the waters of the Red Sea parted. He pronounced the holy name that had been revealed to him, and in a single breath he found himself inside the walls of that city. There he saw an old, old man, far older than any he had ever seen before. He asked the old man if King David could be found there. And the old man said: "No. King David lives in a cave out in the desert, near a spring. Once a year a flock of birds fly in that direction, and today is the day they will arrive here. Follow the birds to the spring, and immerse yourself in the waters before you enter the cave."

Rabbi Recanti thanked the old man and left the city. Just as he stepped beyond its gates, he heard a flapping of wings and saw a flock of birds that filled the sky. Once more he pronounced the holy name that had brought him to that place, and he found himself flying as fast as that flock to the spring the old man had spoken of, with the cave nearby.

Rabbi Recanti immersed himself in that spring and then entered the cave. There he saw King David reclining on a couch. Above him hung his sword and the crown of the kingdom. King David welcomed him, for he too had heard the heavenly voice announcing the rabbi's visit, and he knew of the danger facing the Turkish Jews.

King David brought forth two pitchers of water and gave them to Rabbi Recanti. He told him to wash his hands in the waters of the first pitcher. And the instant the waters touched the rabbi's hands, his skin grew white as snow, as happens with leprosy. The rabbi was very frightened, but King David told him not to worry, just to pour the water of the other pitcher over his hands. And as soon as he did this, Rabbi Recanti's skin was restored to its healthy state. Then King David said: "Now that you know the power of the waters in these pitchers, take them to the sultan. He will understand that this gift could come from no one but me. For the waters of the first pitcher are from Gehenna, and those of the second are from the Garden of Eden."

When Rabbi Recanti took his leave of King David, he pronounced the holy name for the third and final time. And in an instant he found himself back in the land of Turkey, before the palace of the sultan. There he was granted an audience, and he gave the sultan the two pitchers that he had received from King David.

The sultan wanted to know what was so precious about the water in those pitchers. Rabbi Recanti suggested that the sultan pour the water from the first over his hands. When the sultan did, his skin turned leprous and the sultan was horrified. He knew that if anyone found out, his reign would be over, for the disease would be seen as a sign that he was no longer fit to rule. The sultan pleaded with Rabbi Recanti to cure him, and the rabbi assured him that he would if he promised not to harm the Jews of Turkey in any way. The sultan quickly vowed to do so, and the rabbi told him to wash his hands in the water of the second pitcher. And as soon as the sultan did, he recovered. Then the sultan knew that none could have sent him those enchanted waters but King David himself, and never again did he threaten the Jews of his kingdom.

—Eastern Europe: nineteenth century

45. The Magic Wine Cup

n the days before Passover, a stranger was seen wandering through the streets of Mogador in the land of Morocco. Even though he was dressed in rags, he did not look like a beggar, and from the fringes on the garment he was wearing it was clear that he was a Jew.

Some of Rabbi Hayim Pinto's students wondered about this man when they saw him in the city market. And when they returned to the yeshivah, they told the rabbi about him. Rabbi Pinto had them describe the man in great detail. Then he asked them if the man had looked happy or sad. They told the rabbi that he had looked terribly sad. Indeed, just looking at his face made them sad as well.

Now, Passover is a time to remember the poor, and it was Rabbi Pinto's custom to invite the poor Jews of the city to his seder. So on the eve of Passover he sent his students into the city to bring back all the poor Jews they could find. He told them to search especially for the stranger they had told him about, and to be sure that the came back with them.

So the rabbi's students searched every corner of the city for the poor, who were delighted to learn that they would have a place to celebrate the first night of Passover. But when the students finally found the stranger, he was sitting alone under a barren tree, and he refused to accompany them to the rabbi's seder. "For you it is the holiday of Passover," he said, "but for me it is a time of mourning." The students did their best to persuade him, but in the end they returned empty-handed.

Now, when they told Rabbi Pinto that the man had refused their invitation, the rabbi said, "If you can't convince him to come here, whisper this word in his ear," and he whispered it to each of his students. So the students returned to the stranger, still sitting under the tree, and they tried once more to invite him to join the rabbi's seder. Again he refused, but this time one of the students whispered the rabbi's word into the man's ear. And as soon as he heard it, the man's eyes opened wide. He stood up and agreed to accompany them at once.

When that Jew arrived at the rabbi's house, he was greeted warmly by Rabbi Pinto. The man returned the rabbi's greetings, and then he asked, "How is it, Rabbi, that you knew the name of the ship that brought about my misfortune?"

"Join our seder," Rabbi Pinto replied, "and you will understand how it became known to me. For now, please make yourself at home. I will have a bath prepared for you, and my students will give you fresh clothing."

The man thanked the rabbi, but he was still curious about how he had known his secret.

That night, when everyone was seated at the seder, Rabbi Pinto introduced the guest and asked him to tell the others his story. This he did. "I was born in the city of Marrakesh," he said, "and I traveled to Spain and worked there until I had become quite wealthy. After several years, I began to miss my native land of Morocco, and I thought about returning there to raise a family. With all that I had saved, I bought precious jewels.

"There was a widow I had befriended. When she learned I was planning to return to Morocco, where her daughter lives, she asked me to bring her daughter her rightful inheritance, jewels that had belonged to her father. I agreed to do so, and I carried everything in a wooden case. But when a storm sank the ship in which I was traveling, the case was lost at sea. Somehow I managed to grab a plank and reached the shores of this city a few weeks ago. I know that I am fortunate to be alive, but after all these years, I have nothing. Even so, that is not what grieves me the most. Above all, I am heartbroken that I cannot fulfill my mission for the widow."

Now, when all those seated at the seder heard this story, their hearts went out to the poor man who had suffered such a misfortune. Among them, there was one beautiful young woman who had tears flowing down her face. And when the man saw her grief, he, too, broke down and wept.

Rabbi Pinto said, "Do not grieve as we celebrate the seder, but watch closely." He pointed to the kiddush cup, which was filled with wine, and pronounced a spell over it. That spell called forth Rahab, the Angel of the Sea.

Just then everyone at the table heard a deep voice say, "Yes, Rabbi Pinto, what is your command?" They trembled with fear, for they could not see where the voice was coming from.

Then the rabbi said, "I call upon you, Rahab, Prince of the Sea, for help in finding what has been lost."

Suddenly, to everyone's amazement, the kiddush cup began to grow larger and larger, and the wine in it was transformed into the waves of the sea. One after another the waves rose and fell, and eventually they cast up a small wooden case, which floated on the surface. The guest could hardly contain himself. "Master, that is my case!" he cried.

"Take it out!" said Rabbi Pinto. So the man reached into the enormous cup, took out the wooden case and set it on the table. At that instant the cup returned to its original size, and the waters in it became wine once more.

As everyone watched in awe, the man opened the case and saw that nothing was missing. He shed tears of joy. Then Rabbi Pinto said to him, "Now, let me introduce you to the widow's daughter to whom you were delivering the jewels." At that, the young woman who had wept at hearing the man's tale stood up with a radiant smile, and the man almost fainted with surprise. When he had regained his composure, he picked up the wooden case and placed it in her hands, much to the delight of everyone present. Then Rabbi Pinto smiled and said, "Know that nothing happens by accident. All is foretold by the Holy One, blessed be He, as is your meeting here today, for now I can tell you that I heard a heavenly voice announce that you two are destined to be wed."

So it was that everyone celebrated that seder with great happiness, and not long after, the blessed couple was wed. From then on, every Passover, when they filled the kiddush cup, they told the story of Rabbi Pinto and the magic wine cup that had changed their lives.

—Syria: oral tradition

46. The Hair in the Milk

here once was a woman who was about to give birth. They called the old midwife, who had learned the secrets of her trade from her mother and grandmother before her. Not long after she arrived, one of the servants served the expectant mother a glass of milk. Just as she was about to drink it, the woman looked into the cup, put it down with shaky hands, and suddenly fainted.

The midwife picked up the cup and saw that there was a long black hair in the milk. She looked around, but none of the other women had hair that was so long or so black. Then she knew what to do. She quickly poured the milk into a jug, the hair along with it. Then she corked the jug and shook it with all her might, using both hands. All at once there was a scream from inside the jug. Another might have dropped and broken it then, but not the midwife. Instead, she listened. And from inside the bottle she heard a distant voice crying, "Stop! Please let me go! I beg for forgiveness!"

The first impulse of the midwife was to carry the jug to the sea and throw it as far as she could. Instead, she took it outside and when all the doors and windows of the house were locked, she lifted the cork, set it down, and peered inside the bottle. Then all at once the head of a woman popped out. And the first thing the midwife noticed was that her hair was very black and so long that it fell back into the bottle. "Lilith!" the midwife hissed, and she started to pick up the cork to replace it in the bottle. But she found that it had become so heavy that she could not raise it even one inch. And then, for the first time, the midwife became afraid.

"What are you doing here!" the midwife shouted.

"Set me free from this bottle and I will do you no harm," Lilith replied, for that is who it was.

"First tell me why you have come to this house," said the woman. "I have come for the mother or the child, of course," said Lilith. "You know that. But now I will forswear doing any harm to them if you will only let me go."

"That is not enough," said the midwife.

"What more do you want?" asked Lilith.

"First, how did you know that a woman was here who was about to give birth?" demanded the midwife. And Lilith replied, "As I was flying past, I smelled the odor of mother's milk. I wanted to steal the afterbirth—we feed it to our children."

"And what happens then?" asked the wise midwife.

"Then the woman dies," Lilith whispered.

In a sudden motion the midwife grabbed Lilith by the hair, pulling her out of the bottle at the same time. The demoness struggled to get free of her, but the woman held on with all her might, for she knew that a demoness is helpless when held by her hair. When Lilith stopped struggling, the woman said, "Know that you will not leave here until you tell us how to save this woman from you once and for all!"

And Lilith, seeing that she had no choice, said, "Take saliva from the woman's mouth and put it in a bucket filled with water." They did this. Then Lilith blew on the foam of the water, and at that instant the woman awoke from her faint.

The midwife then said, "How is it that you did not fear to approach this house?"

Lilith replied, "The mezuzah of the house is defective, and the people do not have an amulet against me hung on the infant's bed. Now, will you set me free?"

"Not yet!" said the midwife, holding Lilith's hair just as tightly. "There is more that I want of you."

"What is it?" Lilith asked.

"That you serve this family in every way, especially the mother and child, and protect them from every danger for three years."

"And what if I do not agree?" asked Lilith.

"Then I will throw you and the bottle into an old trunk, lock it, and cast it to the bottom of the sea, with you still in it!" cried the midwife, ready to carry out the threat.

Lilith saw that the midwife was a formidable opponent. Her voice grew calm and reassuring. "I vow to do as you say, and to serve this family for three years. Nor will any demons dare to approach while I am here, for I am their queen."

Then the midwife demanded, "Swear in the names of the angels Senoy, Sansenoy, and Semangelof," and Lilith saw that there was no escape. For those were the three angels who had commanded her to return to Adam when she had left him and flown to a cave by the Red Sea. And she had vowed that whenever she saw or heard their names, she would do no harm. So Lilith swore in the names of the three angels, and after that she did indeed remain captive there and serve as a faithful servant. For the words of a vow are sacred not only among men and the angels, but among the demons as well. She pumped water from the well, cut wood, and guarded the woman and her child at all times so that no harm came to them.

Long before Lilith left, the text of the mezuzah was repaired. And when she took her leave, she promised that she would never come back. Nor did Lilith or her daughters attempt to return to that house, and the family lived a life of peace.

—Turkish Kurdistan: oral tradition

47. The Cave of Mattathias

In a village near the city of Riminov there was a Hasid whose custom it was to bring newly made oil to Reb Menachem Mendel of Riminov, and the rabbi would light the first candle of Hanukah in his presence.

One year the winter was hard, the land covered with snow, and everyone was locked in his home. But when the eve of Hanukah arrived, the Hasid was still planning to deliver the oil. His family pleaded with him not to go, but he was determined, and in the end he set out across the deep snow.

That morning he entered the forest that separated his village from Riminov, and the moment he did, it began to snow. The snow fell so fast that it covered every landmark, and when at last it stopped, the Hasid found that he was lost. The whole world was covered with snow.

Now the Hasid began to regret not listening to his family. Surely the rabbi would have forgiven his absence. Meanwhile, it had become so cold that he began to fear he might freeze. He realized that if he were to die there in the forest, he might not even be taken to a Jewish grave. That is when he remembered the oil he was carrying. In order to save his life, he would have to use it. There was no other choice.

As quickly as his numb fingers could move, he tore some of the lining out of his coat and fashioned it into a wick, and he put that wick into the snow. Then he poured oil on it and prayed with great intensity. Finally, he lit the first candle of Hanukah, and the flame seemed to light up the whole forest. And all the wolves moving through the forest saw that light and ran back to their hiding places.

After this the exhausted Hasid lay down on the snow and fell asleep. He dreamed he was walking in a warm land, and before him he saw a great mountain, and next to that mountain stood a palm tree. At the foot of the mountain was the opening of a cave. In the dream, the Hasid entered the cave and found a candle burning there. He picked up that candle, and it lit the way for him until he came to a large cavern, where an old man with a very long beard was seated. There was a sword on his thigh, and his hands were busy making wicks. All of that cavern was piled high with bales of wicks. The old man looked up when the Hasid entered and said: "Blessed be you in the Name of God."

The Hasid returned the old man's blessing and asked him who he was. He answered: "I am Mattathias, father of the Maccabees. During my lifetime I lit a big torch. I hoped that all of Israel would join me, but only a few obeyed my call. Now heaven has sent me to watch for the little candles in the houses of Israel to come together to form a very big flame. And that flame will announce the Redemption and the End of Days.

"Meanwhile, I prepare the wicks for the day when everyone will contribute his candle to this great flame. And now, there is something that you must do for me. When you reach the Rabbi of Riminov, tell him that the wicks are ready, and he should do whatever he can to light the flame that we have awaited so long."

Amazed at all he had heard, the Hasid promised to give the message to the rabbi. As he turned to leave the cave, he awoke and found himself standing in front of the rabbi's house. Just then the rabbi himself opened the door, and his face was glowing. He said: "The power of lighting the Hanukah candles is very great. Whoever dedicates his soul to this deed brings the time of Redemption that much closer."

—Eastern Europe: oral tradition

48. The Prince Who Thought He Was a Rooster

here once was a prince who thought he was a rooster. While other princes spent their days slaying dragons, courting princesses, or learning how to rule a kingdom, this prince cast off his royal robes and spent his days crouching beneath a table, refusing to eat any food except kernels of corn.

His father, the king, was very upset at this behavior. "Send for the best doctors in all the land, " he proclaimed. "A great reward will be given to anyone who can cure my son."

Doctors came from all corners of the kingdom. Each tried to cure the prince, but none of them succeeded. The prince still thought he was a rooster. He ate corn, preened his feathers, and strutted about, crying, "Cock-a-doodle-do! Cock-a-doodle-do!"

When the king had almost given up hope, a wise man, passing through the kingdom, appeared before him. "Let me stay alone with the prince for one week, and I will cure him," he said to the king.

"Everyone else has failed," the king moaned, "but you are welcome to try."

Thus the wise man entered the prince's chamber. There he took off his clothes, crawled under the table, and began to eat kernels of corn, just like the prince.

The prince looked at the man with suspicion. "Who are you?" he asked.

"I am a rooster," said the wise man, and he continued to munch on the corn. After a short while he asked the prince, "Who are you?"

"I too am a rooster," said the prince.

And after that the prince treated the wise man as an equal. The two strutted about, preening their feathers and crying, "Cock-a-doodle-do!"

When they had made their home under the table for a while and had become good friends, the wise man suddenly crawled out into the prince's chamber and dressed himself.

The prince was shocked.

"A rooster doesn't wear clothes!" he said.

The wise man remained calm. "I am a rooster and I am wearing clothes!"

The prince considered this for a day or two. Then he decided to imitate his friend, and he, too, put on clothes.

A few days later, the wise man took some of the food that was being delivered to them every day, food that they had refused to eat. He carried it beneath the table and ate it.

The prince was astonished. "Roosters don't eat that kind of food!"

But the wise man calmly said, "A rooster can eat any food he wants and still be a good rooster." And he continued to eat the tasty food.

The prince watched this for a while. Then he decided to imitate his friend, and he, too, ate the food.

The next day the wise man stopped crouching beneath the table. He stood up proudly on his two feet and started to walk like a man.

"What are you doing?" asked the prince. "A rooster can't get up and walk around like that!"

But the wise man said firmly, "I am a rooster, and if I want to walk like this—I will!" And he continued to walk upright.

The prince peered at him from beneath the table. Then he decided to imitate his friend and he, too, stood up and walked on his two feet.

So, in this way, the prince began to eat, dress, and walk like a man. The week's time was up and no longer did he act like a rooster. The king was overjoyed, of course, and welcomed his son back with open arms.

As for the wise man, why, he collected his reward and went happily on his way.

—Eastern Europe: nineteenth century
A tale of Reb Nachman of Bratslav

49. The Treasure

nce there was a poor woodcutter who lived with his family at the outskirts of the forest and sold firewood to the other poor people who lived there. This man worked very hard and his rewards were few. One night he had a dream in which he traveled down a path until he came to a bridge. A soldier was stationed there, who crossed the bridge back and forth. Led by a strange certainty, the man went beneath the bridge and began to dig in a certain place. Before long he struck something, and when he had uncovered it he found it was a chest. And when he opened the chest, he found a treasure inside it. The treasure was so precious that he gasped when he saw it. Just then the man awoke and realized he had been dreaming. He sighed, for in the dream he had been overjoyed at having discovered that treasure, and now it had all vanished into thin air.

During the day, though, as he worked cutting wood in the forest, the man daydreamed a bit about that treasure, and it crossed his mind that he could search for it. But he dismissed this thought as foolish—after all, it was only a dream. So he went about his work and forgot all about it.

That night, however, the man again dreamed about the bridge, and the treasure buried beneath it. And this time the dream was even more vivid, for now the man could see the face of the guard who paced back and forth on the bridge. When he awoke he found his desire for that treasure was even stronger, and he was unable to fall back to sleep, for now that he had dreamed the same dream twice, he began to wonder if it was a sign that he really should seek out the treasure. But in the morning he laughed at himself for taking the dream so seriously. For how would he ever know where to begin to search? After all, there were a great many bridges in the world and he could not dig beneath every one of them.

But when the dream recurred for the third time, the man realized that his destiny was calling to him, and he vowed to find that treasure no matter how difficult it might be. His wife tried to dissuade him, but when she saw he was determined to go, she wished him well and prayed that his dream might come true. And so the man set out into the world to search for a bridge he had only seen in a dream.

But where does one find such a bridge? The woodcutter decided to walk into town, to see if someone knew where it might be found. When he got there, he asked people about it, but since he was unable to say which bridge it was or what river it crossed, they just shrugged and walked on. If he could just recall some detail about it. He thought for a long time, and then he remembered that the guard on the bridge had worn a helmet with a feather in it. So the next time he asked someone, he mentioned that helmet, and soon he learned that the guards of the king wore helmets like that in the capital of that country.

Now the capital was a great distance from there, but when this detail of his dream turned out to be real, the woodcutter decided he must go there at once. For he had become confident that his dream might be true after all.

After many months and many hardships, the woodcutter reached the capital. Before he had walked very far from the gates of the city he saw a river. He decided to follow that river, hoping it might lead him to the bridge he was searching for. And sure enough, before he had walked a mile he a bridge exactly like the one he had seen in his dream. Not only that, but the guard pacing up and down on it was the very guard he had glimpsed in his dream! A chill went down the woodcutter's spine as he approached the bridge. He greeted the soldier, and asked him if he might dig beneath the bridge. When the soldier heard this, he seemed startled, and he asked the man why he would want to do such a thing. With no other choice, the woodcutter told the guard about his dream. When he heard it, the man laughed heartily and said, "If you have come all this way just because of a dream, you are indeed foolish. And your dream is merely a common one. Why, I have just dreamed three nights in a row of a treasure beneath an old oak tree at the entrance of a forest." And the soldier went on to describe the tree and the place he had found the treasure. And as he did, the man suddenly realized that the guard was describing the woodcutter's own home in a distant province of that land. It suddenly dawned on the woodcutter that the dream had led him to that bridge not to dig beneath it, but to hear the dream of that guard. And as if to confirm this, the guard suddenly became stern and said, "As to your request to dig here, why that is out of the question. This bridge belongs to the king, and if I permitted the ground beneath it to be dug up, I would soon be deprived of my head. Go now, and if I see you here again I will not hesitate to arrest you!" And he angrily chased the woodcutter from there, and frightened him out of his wits.

So it was that the woodcutter traveled back to where he had come from, to his family and home. And when his wife saw that he had returned empty-handed, she was not even sorry, so happy was she to have him back. But no sooner had he kissed his wife and children than he hurried out to the giant oak tree at the entrance to the forest, and dug beneath it. And before he had dug very far, he struck something, which turned out to be the very treasure he had seen in his dream, buried behind his very own house.

—Eastern Europe: nineteenth century
A tale of Reb Nachman of Bratslav

50. The Souls of Trees

One day Reb Nachman of Bratslav told his Hasidim to tell Reb Lepke the coachman to prepare for a journey. When the Hasidim asked where he was going, all Reb Nachman would say was, "Someone needs our help."

Soon the coachman arrived, and Reb Nachman invited three of his Hasidim to join him. Then, just as they were about to depart, Reb Lepke asked Reb Nachman where he wanted to go. Reb Nachman replied, "Hold the reins lightly, Reb Lepke, and let the horses go wherever they please." The coachman was surprised, but he did as the rabbi asked.

The Hasidim rode for many hours, while the horses took one road after another, proceeding as if they knew exactly where they were going. When the sun began to set, the Hasidim wondered where they would spend the night. At last one of them asked Reb Nachman, and all he would say was "God will provide."

Then, just as darkness was falling, the carriage reached an inn. Reb Nachman called out for the coachman to stop, and everyone got out. The Hasidim had never been to this inn before, so they were delighted to find that it was run by a Jew and his wife. Now the innkeeper had heard of Reb Nachman and he was honored that the great-grandson of the Ba'al Shem Tov was a guest at his inn, and he treated him with great respect.

Reb Nachman and his Hasidim joined the other guests for evening prayers. All together there were ten men, just enough to make a minyan. After that the innkeeper's wife served a fine meal, and the guests stayed up for many hours discussing the Torah. It was late when the innkeeper showed the Hasidim to their rooms. But before he left Reb Nachman, he said, "Rabbi, could I speak to you in private?"

"Surely," said Reb Nachman, and he offered the innkeeper a chair. When the man was seated, he told Reb Nachman his story: "My wife and I have been married for ten years, and we love each other. But there is one sadness that fills our lives and overshadows everything else." And Reb Nachman looked more closely at the man and saw that he did, indeed, seem to be sad. And Reb Nachman said, "Yes, what is it?" And the man replied, "There is nothing in the world that we long for more than a child of our own. But so far God has not blessed us with a son or daughter. Rabbi, is there anything you can do to help us?"

Reb Nachman said, "It is late and I am tired. Let me think about this overnight, and in the morning I'll let you know if there is anything I can do." The innkeeper was pleased with this reply and took his leave of Reb

Nachman. Soon Reb Nachman and all the Hasidism were all sound asleep, but in the middle of the night, Reb Nachman began to cry out, waking everyone in the inn. They came running to see what had happened.

When they came in, they found Reb Nachman sitting up in bed, with a dazed look. He ignored all those who had gathered there. Instead, he took a book out of his bag, closed his eyes, and opened it, pointing to a passage. Then he opened his eyes, read what was written there, nodded, closed the book, and put it away. Then he turned to everyone gathered there and said, "Everyone can go back to sleep. I will be all right. Goodnight." Then everyone went back to sleep, except for the innkeeper and his wife, who didn't get a wink of sleep, for they were very curious to know what the rabbi would tell them.

The next day, after morning prayers, Reb Nachman signaled for the innkeeper and his wife to join him. When they were alone he said, "Tell me, were the walls of this inn built out of saplings that were cut down before their time?" The innkeeper and his wife looked at each other, and the innkeeper said, "Yes, rabbi, it is true. But how did you know?"

Reb Nachman said, "All night I dreamed I was surrounded by the bodies of the dead. I was very frightened. When I awoke and opened that book, the words I read there were 'Cutting down a tree before its time is the same as killing a soul.' That is how I learned that it was the souls of the trees crying out to me. So too did I learn why you and your wife can't have children."

"Rabbi," cried the innkeeper, "What possible connection could there be?"

Reb Nachman said, "There is an angel named Lailah, who is the angel of conception. It is Lailah who delivers the soul of the unborn child. But each time Lailah approaches your inn to bring you the blessing of a child, she is driven back by the sighs and moans and cries of the souls of the trees that were cut down too soon."

"Oh, Rabbi, that is terrible," said the innkeeper. "Is there anything we can do about it?"

"Yes," said Reb Nachman. "You must plant trees. Plant twice as many trees as you cut down. Take good care of them and see that none are cut down. If you do this for three years, you will be blessed with a child."

The couple was overjoyed to hear this and the innkeeper thanked Reb Nachman for revealing this mystery to them. And that very day, even before Reb Nachman and his Hasidim took their leave, they began planting trees.

All the trees that the couple planted grew tall and strong. And after three years, Lailah returned to their home. Then the lullaby of the living trees soothed the cries of the trees that had been cut down, so that Lailah was able to reach the couple's house, tap on their window three times, and bless them with a child. And every year after that the innkeeper's wife gave birth to another child, until they had seven children, and all of them were as tall and straight and strong as a fine tree.

—Eastern Europe: nineteenth century

Supernatural Tales

51. The Finger

ne night long ago, in the city of Safed, three young men went out for a walk. Reuven, the eldest, was to be married the next day to a beautiful and wealthy maiden, and his companions laughed and joked and teased their friend. The moon was full that night, and the young men decided to leave the beaten path and walk in the thick forest that surrounded the city.

The moonlight illumined even the darkest parts of the forest, and they passed through it fearlessly. At last they reached the riverbank and rested on large rocks near the shore, while they watched the river below. Here they continued to make merry, for they felt as if they were intoxicated.

It was during this time that one of them noticed something strange nearby. It was an object the size of a finger that stuck out of the earth. They got up to examine it, assuming it was a root. But when they came closer, they saw to their amazement that is was indeed a finger that emerged there.

Now on a different night the young men might have felt pity for one buried so near the surface. But filled with high spirits, they jested about it instead. One of them said, "Who among us will put a wedding ring on this finger?" And Reuven, the groom-to-be, quickly replied that it must be he, because he was to be the first one to marry. Then, as his friends looked on in amusement, Reuven took off his ring and slipped it on that finger, pronouncing as he did the words *Harai at m'kudeshet li*—"You are betrothed to me"—three times, as the law requires. But no sooner did he finish speaking than the finger began to twitch, much to the horror of the young men, who jumped back at the sight.

Suddenly the whole hand reached out from the earth, twitching and grasping. And as they stared at it in horror, frozen in place, the ground began to rumble, as if the earth were about to open. Suddenly the body of a woman, wearing a tattered shroud, rose out of the earth, her dead eyes staring directly into those of Reuven, her arms open as she cried out, "My husband!" in a terrible and terrifying voice. Hearing this, the three friends screamed in horror and took to their heels, running through the forest as fast they could go. But this time the way was dark, for the moon had slipped behind a cloud, and as they ran they tore their clothes on thorns and branches, but never did they stop running or even dare to look back until they had reached their homes in the city. For all the time they ran they heard the unearthly wail of the dead woman close behind. Only when they were safely in their own homes, with the doors locked and the windows barred, did they dare breathe a sigh of relief and tend to the many cuts they had acquired in their wild dash through the forest.

The next morning the three friends met together, still pale and shaken. And they agreed to keep the horrible events of the night a secret, for they were deeply ashamed of their jest and its terrible consequences. Then Reuven went to the ritual bath to prepare for the wedding and left his friends alone with their confused thoughts.

Now a great many people had gathered, for Reuven and his bride belonged to two of the most distinguished families in Safed. But just as the ceremony was about to begin, a bloodcurdling shriek came from the back of the crowd, followed by the screams of many others, provoking a panic. For there stood the corpse of a woman wearing only a worm-eaten shroud. Most of the crowd—including the bride and the families of the bride and groom—ran away when they saw her, until none were left there except for Reuven and the rabbi, who had been about to pronounce the wedding vows.

The rabbi, alone among all of those present, retained his composure. He addressed himself to the corpse and said, "Why is it, woman, that you have left your final resting place and returned to the living?" And the corpse replied, in her unearthly voice, "What blemish does the bridegroom find in me, that he should want to wed another? For cannot all the world see that he is wed to me?" And she held up her hand, on which the ring of the bridegroom could be seen, with his initials engraved on it. Then the rabbi turned to the bridegroom, who was crouched in terror behind him, and asked if what the woman said was true. In a trembling voice the young man told of his walk through the forest with his friends and of the jest they had played when they had found the finger sticking out of the earth. And the rabbi asked, "Did you pronounce the sacred vow three times?" The young man meekly nodded. And the rabbi asked, "Was it done in the presence of two witnesses?" Again Reuven nodded. Then the rabbi looked very grave and said that the rabbinic court would have to be convened to discuss the matter, for in the eyes of the law it appeared that the young man had indeed bound himself to that corpse in matrimony. When the bridegroom heard these terrible words, he fainted dead away and had to be carried off to his home.

In the days that followed, the city of Safed was in an uproar, for who had ever heard of a living man marrying a corpse? And the parents of Reuven begged the rabbi to find a way to free their son from the terrible curse. As for the rabbi, he immersed himself in meditation and in the study of responsa, searching for a precedent. But there was none; instead one would have to be set. On the day the court was convened, the rabbi called upon the corpse to appear, and she did so, still wearing the worm-eaten shroud in which she had been buried. Under oath she told what young Reuven had done in the forest. Then the rabbi called upon the two friends, who reluctantly confirmed what she said. At last the rabbi called upon the bridegroom, who also confessed that the vow had been made, but pleaded with the court to annul the marriage, for he had never intended for it to happen.

Then the court addressed the dead woman and asked her if she would relinquish her claim, but the corpse was adamant that the marriage must be consummated. For while she had lived she had never married and had thus been denied her hour of joy. And she was determined to receive after death what she had been denied in life.

Then the rabbi called upon the parents of the bridegroom, who testified that the betrothal of their son to the daughter of the wealthy man had been made even before the birth of the children. The two couples had vowed that if one had a boy child and one a girl, then they were to be wed. And the parents of the bride confirmed this vow.

Finally, when all the testimony had been taken, the court gathered together to discuss the case, while young Reuven trembled, his eyes avoiding the terrible corpse that also stood waiting among them. At last the court reached a decision, which the rabbi announced. He said, "It is true that in the presence of two witnesses, Reuven unwittingly made a vow of marriage that appears to be valid." Here the rabbi paused, and the young man and his parents were filled with terror. Then the rabbi continued, "There are, however, other factors that must be considered. First, the wedding vow would deny the betrothal, and it is widely known that one vow may not be permitted to negate an earlier one. Second, the vow of the bridegroom was not made with intention. Finally, there is no precedent for a claim on the living by the dead. Therefore the vows cannot be accepted as valid, because the bride is not from among the living. The marriage is thus declared null and void!"

Now when the rabbi uttered these words, young Reuven fainted again, this time from relief. But the corpse, having lost her chance to wed either in life or in death, let forth an ear-shattering shriek, which pierced the souls of all those assembled there and filled their hearts with horror. Then she collapsed upon the ground and became again as one of the dead.

When those assembled had at last calmed down, the rabbi gave orders to have the corpse reburied, with proper ritual and at a greater depth, so that such a tragedy would never happen again. And after her burial, the rabbi called upon the parents of the true bride to fulfill the vow they had made before their daughter had been born and to complete the wedding ceremony, which had been so terribly interrupted. This was done and at last the wedding of Reuven and his true bride took place.

—Palestine: sixteenth century

52. The Queen of Sheba

In the city of Worms there was an innkeeper who was very poor. His inn, known as the Devil's Head, was on the outskirts of the town. Few travelers stayed there, and those who did could barely pay for lodging. Wealthy travelers stayed at the other inn, The House with the Sign of the Sun. The poor innkeeper was very jealous of it and wished that his inn would flourish instead.

One day the poor innkeeper was in his storeroom, bemoaning his fate, when a lovely voice said, "Your riches are but an arm's reach away." Startled, the man looked around and saw a beautiful woman standing there, with long black hair—the most beautiful woman he had ever seen. Her dress clung to her body, revealing a ripeness that astonished the man. And her demeanor was worthy of a queen.

"Who are you?" the man stammered. "I am the Queen of Sheba," she replied. "I have been sent to fulfill your dreams. If you will come to me at this time every day and give yourself to me, I will make you a wealthy man." The man could hardly believe what he heard. His head began to spin. His blood became hot and he was filled with desire for the woman who stood there, the very incarnation of lust. He did not consider how she had gotten there or how she could be the Queen of Sheba. And before he knew it, he found himself in her embrace. Afterward, the Queen of Sheba handed him a bag filled with silver coins, and when he opened it, the innkeeper was overjoyed, for now he would be able to pay all his debts and live as a wealthy man at last.

The next day at the same time, the innkeeper came back to his storeroom, to which he alone held the key. There he found the Queen of Sheba bathing in a golden basin. When he entered she stepped out of the bath, naked, and he was once again overwhelmed by her beauty. As soon as she was dry she lay down on a bed. The man did not ask himself where the basin and bed had come from, but gave himself up to the delights she offered, and it was midafternoon before he emerged, bearing another bag of silver coins.

That day the man hurried off to purchase a beautiful dress and a golden ring for his wife to wear on the Sabbath. His wife was astonished by these gifts, but she did not ask to know where their wealth had come from. Instead she celebrated with her husband, relieved that a little good fortune had come their way at last.

All that night the innkeeper dreamed he was back in the arms of the Queen of Sheba, and his body trembled with sensual delight. In the morning he could barely wait for the time to go into the storeroom. At last he did, and there he found his demon mistress waiting for him. They embraced as lovers, and afterward, as the man lay back exhausted, the Queen of Sheba said, "By now you know how much abundance I have to offer you. Stay with me and you will be a wealthy man. But if you speak about me to anyone at all, it will be on penalty of death."

The man was startled to learn this, but he insisted he would never tell anyone, for his wife would surely demand a divorce, his children would never forgive him, and no one would frequent his inn. So she said no more about it, and gave him another bag of silver coins, from a store that seemed to be inexhaustible.

In the days that followed, the way of life of the innkeeper and his wife was completely transformed, as was the inn itself, which he had remodeled until it became far more luxurious than The House with the Sign of the Sun. The wife of the innkeeper purchased an entirely new wardrobe, and it became her custom to wear beautiful dresses not only on the Sabbath and holidays, but on every day of the week. They acquired many servants to maintain the inn, and the innkeeper found that all of his tasks were taken care of by someone else. The only problem was that his wife began to wonder where the riches came from. But the innkeeper refused to discuss it, much to her frustration. And in the days of luxury that followed, she had very little to do but to muse about this matter and harp on it every chance she got.

Meanwhile, the man returned to the storeroom every day to do the bidding of the Queen of Sheba. And she, in turn, saw to it that his riches continued to grow. By this time the man had become a slave to the desires of the Queen of Sheba. He served her in any way that she saw fit, for by then his dependence on her was complete.

Because the innkeeper refused to divulge the secret of their wealth, his wife began to spy on him to see what she could discover by herself. Before long she noticed that he disappeared late in the morning and was not seen again until the middle of the afternoon. Soon she found out that he was in the storeroom during that time, and she wondered what he was doing in there. One day she casually asked him about it, and he replied that he had gotten into the habit of napping on sacks of grain.

This reply did not satisfy the wife, however, and early one morning she took the storeroom key and had a copy of it made for herself. Then she returned her husband's key, undetected. One afternoon, when her curiosity could not be restrained any longer, she quietly opened the door to the storeroom while he was in it. So it was that she saw her husband asleep in the arms of the Queen of Sheba. Overcome by the sight, she quietly shut the door, so that no one would know that she had been there. But the Queen of Sheba observed all that had taken place. And she woke the man and said, "You must have told your wife our secret, and now you must die!" The man pleaded with her, saying that he had never told anyone, especially not his wife. But the Queen of Sheba insisted that his wife had just opened the door and seen them together. The man was terrified to learn this and saw that his luck had run out. He so begged for his life that at last the Queen of Sheba agreed to spare him. "But you will never see me again," she said, "for

I will never come back to you. So too will your wealth disappear. I am taking back everything. And I intend to strangle the two children that I have had with you—you did not even know about them, did you? I will wring their necks. In three days' time, go to the bridge over the Rhine River, and there you will see a coffin floating on the water, and inside will lie the children you fathered with me." And then, all at once, the Queen of Sheba disappeared, and the golden basin in which she bathed disappeared as well, as did the bed they had been sleeping on, and the bag of coins she had brought to give him. It was then that he realized that she must have been a demoness, maybe even Lilith herself.

The innkeeper staggered out of the storeroom and ran to the place where he had hidden all of the silver coins he had received from her. He found the bags there, but when he reached inside, all the coins had dissolved into foul water, which soiled his hands. From there he rushed to his wife's closet, where all her new dresses had vanished, along with everything else they had bought with those coins. So too did all the repairs done on the inn vanish, for they had been an illusion to start with, and the servants, merely cohorts of the Queen of Sheba. And the man and his wife were just as poor as they had been before he had met the Queen of Sheba, but it was much more terrible this time.

—Germany: sixteenth century

53. The Bride of Demons

n the city of Frankfurt a girl was about to be married, and on the eve of the Sabbath before the marriage she and her mother had a dispute over what she was going to wear. The girl refused to wear the wedding dress of her mother; she wanted one of her own. In particular, there was a dress she had seen in the market that she could not get out of her mind. She wanted to buy it, even though it would take all of her savings. But her mother wanted her to save the money. At last her mother became so angry with her that she said, "Go to the Devil!" And she walked out of the girl's room and slammed the door.

Shortly after that the girl left the house. She walked into town and went directly to the merchant who had the wedding dress. For she was prepared to purchase it, even over the objections of her mother. Just as she arrived she saw a splendidly dressed woman of great beauty shopping there with a servant. This woman had selected many dresses for herself, and among them was the very dress the girl longed to have for her own.

Trembling, the girl went up to the woman and said, "Please, madam, do not be angry with me, but I was hoping to purchase that one dress for my wedding." The girl pointed to a dress in the pile, and the woman pulled it out and put it on top. She said, "What a beautiful girl you are. I am certain that you would indeed look magnificent in the dress. Perhaps I can give it to you as a wedding present." Now the girl was quite surprised to hear this, but at the same time she saw that the woman possessed great wealth, and might even regard the gift as only a small act of charity. Still, she said, "No, I would not ask for that. Only that you permit me to purchase the dress myself." "No, my dear," said the woman, "I would love to make this dress a wedding present for you, and I will do so. I only ask that you come with me to my house, so that I may see how fine you look in it."

Now the girl was overjoyed, for she longed to have that dress. And she thought to herself how happy her mother would be when she learned that no savings had been spent to get it. So she thanked the woman for her kind offer and said that she would be happy to go with her to her home.

After that the woman completed the purchase, buying all of the dresses, including the one that the girl so wanted. Then she led her to her waiting carriage, and they set out together. All this time the girl was in a daze, and she could not wait to try on that dress.

In a very short time they arrived at a great mansion, which to the girl looked more like a palace. The girl had not even dreamed that such wealth could exist in the world. She walked into the house, staring at everything, and not believing her eyes. Once inside, the woman quickly took out the dress and handed it to the girl, directing her to a room where she might try it on. The girl entered that room and saw that it was filled with many mirrors, in which she could see herself from every angle. She closed the door and quickly took off her old dress and put on the new one.

The dress was truly magnificent, woven with gold and silver threads, with many ornaments forming a beautiful pattern. And when the girl put it on she recognized for the first time just how beautiful she was, and at that moment she made a wish: that she could always be like she was at that moment, dressed as a bride in that room of mirrors, in which her image was reflected everywhere. Then the happy girl went to the door to show the woman how well the dress fit her. But the door was locked.

The girl did not return home that afternoon, nor did she come back in time for dinner. After dinner her parents went out to look for her, but they could not find her, and the next day was the Sabbath. So they hurried to Rabbi Naphtali Cohen, who told them to observe the Sabbath as usual, as if she were there, and continue all the preparations for the wedding. And that is what they did.

That night, before going to sleep, the rabbi asked a dream question, in which he sought to learn why the girl had disappeared and what had happened to her. And in a dream he learned the truth.

Now when the family of the bridegroom arrived and saw that the bride was not there, the rabbi asked the bridegroom if he were willing to risk his soul for her. And when the bridegroom said yes, the rabbi ordered his carriage to be made ready, and he and the bridegroom set out together and rode until they were out of the city.

At last they arrived at a field, and the rabbi took the young man to the center of the field and told him to stay there. After that the rabbi made a great circle with his staff around the bridegroom, and he said to him, "Know that your bride has been kidnapped by Lilith, queen of demons. She has taken her away to be a bride for her son, who is also the son of Ashmodai, king of demons. You are your intended's only hope, for only one who would be willing to risk his soul for her could save her in this hour of danger.

"Now I must leave. Soon you will be surrounded by a swarm of demons. They will curse and humiliate you and attempt to harm you. But as long as you stay inside this circle, you need not fear them. Nor should you reply to them in any way. Before long many carriages will arrive, which will ignore you, and you should also ignore them. Then a golden carriage will arrive, whose driver will be blind in one eye. And next to him will sit the king of demons. And you must look him in the eyes and say, 'Why did you take my bride?' And you must not turn away from his gaze, no matter what."

And so it happened, exactly as Rabbi Naphtali had said. Swarms of demons appeared out of nowhere and stood outside the circle and taunted him in every possible way and threatened his life, but the bridegroom said nothing. After this, many carriages arrived, and the last was a golden carriage, driven by a man with one eye. And next to the driver sat a most imposing man, whom the bridegroom knew at once must be the king of demons.

The trembling bridegroom refused to succumb to his terror, and he looked into the eyes of the king of demons and said, "Why have you taken my bride?" And Ashmodai stared back at the bridegroom and replied, "Because her mother gave her as a present to me, and because she herself made a wish to remain in my palace forever." The bridegroom answered, "Her mother cannot do that, because she was already betrothed to me, nor do I believe that my bride truly intended to remain a prisoner in your kingdom." Just then the bridegroom heard a cry, followed by weeping and sobbing. And he knew that it must be his bride, held prisoner in that very place. And he longed to look at her, for he had never in his life met her, but he remembered the words of the rabbi and did not turn his gaze away from that of the king of demons. If he had, he would have seen his bride buried in the earth up to her neck, for she was almost lost to the Devil. But just the knowledge that she was there gave the young man renewed strength. A great anger came over him and he stared into the eyes of Ashmodai and said, "She is mine, not yours. She will come with me." And while the two continued to stare at each other, neither turning aside, the rabbi and his people suddenly arrived, and they dug her out of the earth while the other demons looked on but did not harm them. She was still wearing the dress that Lilith had given her, but it was no longer beautiful—it was covered with worms and maggots. They took her away and tore off the wormy shroud, replacing it with a clean garment. And at that moment the demons disappeared, including Ashmodai.

When the rabbi was certain that the demons were gone, he led the bridegroom out of the charmed circle to his carriage, where his bride wept great tears of relief. And as they rode back to town the rabbi said to him, "You have done well indeed, for had you turned your eyes away from those of Ashmodai for even an instant, your bride would have been lost for good. But because you did not, she was set free."

When they returned to Frankfurt they celebrated the wedding with great joy. The girl wore the wedding dress that had belonged to her mother, and everyone said that they had never seen a more beautiful bride.

—Germany: eighteenth century

54. Helen of Troy

ne day in a small town in the south of France, a disheveled man arrived and purchased an old house. This man's body was hunched over, as if with defeat, his eyes focused on the ground. But when he lifted his head, it was seen that his eyes had a ferocious look, like that of one obsessed. This man's name was Joseph della Reina, but that is all he revealed about himself. He refused to say where he had come from, or in what kind of work he had been engaged. Rarely was he seen to depart from the house, not even to go to the market, and his absence made him the subject of rumors among the people of that town. Some said that he was a sorcerer, others that he was the Devil himself. He was sometimes heard speaking to someone in his house, although he lived alone and no one was ever seen entering or leaving there. His presence in that town was unsettling.

Now, if the truth be known, this old man was indeed a wizard. Once, long ago, he had been a sage and had even been regarded as a holy man. But fate had dragged him to the other side, and now he was wedded to Lilith, the queen of demons. For it was none other than Lilith herself to whom he spoke, for she instructed him in the ways of black magic. It was through the use of this magic that he sustained himself by transporting exotic fruits from around the world: carobs from the Holy Land, olives from Greece, mountain apples from the lands of the south. In his youth he had spent many a day fasting for some holy purpose. Now he loved to savor succulent fruits and partake of delicious dishes, and with the help of Lilith he was able to indulge himself as much as he wished.

But he was driven by other desires besides that for food. Most of all he wished to possess the most desirable woman in the world. Nor was Lilith jealous of this; on the contrary, she encouraged him to fulfill his every lust. Now in all of Europe it was known that Queen Dolphina of France was the most beautiful woman alive. And Joseph della Reina was determined that she would be his, on his own terms, in his own house. And with the help of Lilith, he was able to snatch her for himself.

First, using the spells that he had learned, many of them involving holy names that he had once used for holy purposes, Joseph della Reina created the illusion that the modest house in which he lived was a palace. From outside it seemed exactly as it had been, old and dilapidated, but on the inside it appeared vast and without end, with many floors, each with an infinity of rooms. For with the help of Lilith, he had cast a spell that had transported the palace of Ashmodai, king of demons, inside his very house. And because that palace was itself an illusion, it was no problem to make it fit in such a small place. In fact, this was a much larger home than was usual for the palace, which normally was hidden in a secret cavern in the Mountains of Darkness.

Once he had created the impression of vast wealth, Joseph della Reina pronounced the names that enabled him to snatch Queen Dolphina just as she fell asleep, so that her body vanished from the royal bed and suddenly appeared on the bed of Joseph della Reina. The queen was awakened from her sleep by the touch of hands undressing her, and when she opened her eyes and saw the terrifying visage of Joseph della Reina hovering above her, she almost fainted. To comfort herself she kept repeating that it must be a dream. But it was not.

In fact, the horror was only beginning, for the look in Joseph della Reina's eyes was so terrible that the queen sorely feared for her life. Thus she did not resist when he plucked the flower of her beauty, for she saw that it would be futile.

Afterward Joseph della Reina spoke for the first time. "You were wise, Your Majesty, not to try to withhold your favors from me, for you are fully within my power, and your very life rests in my hands. Know that you will return to the palace of the king by morning, but that you must remain here all night. Indeed, the night belongs to us, and we will meet on many occasions, as you shall see." And the queen trembled when she heard these words, knowing that she had fallen into the hands of a mad wizard. She looked around the room and saw that it was filled with precious objects, more than in her own palace. And she knew that such wealth, combined with the power that had transported her there, was a formidable menace indeed.

The thought that she must remain all night with a madman terrified the queen, and in desperation she sought to establish a conversation with him, that she might be spared his renewed lust. She said, "I did not know that such a master made his home in our kingdom. If you had come to the palace and revealed your great powers, surely you would have been made my husband's viceroy. Even now it is not too late. Return me to my chamber, and I shall put all that has happened out of my mind and see to it that you receive an audience with my husband, the king."

Joseph della Reina laughed hideously when he heard this. "Why should I serve the king, who is but a king among men? My King rules all the forces of the Other Side, all the legions of demons, all the gates of Hell!" And poor Queen Dolphina realized that she was the victim of one who had made himself a slave to the powers of evil. Still, she tried to remain calm. "Who, then, are you?" she asked. "And how did you come to be here?"

Now when Queen Dolphina asked this question, a terrible pang of remorse passed through Joseph della Reina, and for a moment he recalled the promise he had thrown away when Redemption had been almost at hand. Since that day, so many years ago, he had not spoken to another human being. His only companion had been Lilith, who had infected him with her evil ways, so that not a spark of holiness remained within him. No one alive knew what had happened to him, for the disciples of his folly had all lost their lives. And a great longing to reveal his history came over him, and, as if in a trance, Joseph della Reina began to speak.

"My name is Joseph della Reina. I dare to disclose my name because there is no mortal power greater than my own. When you return try, if you wish, to seek me out. Send the palace guard, send an entire legion of your army; it will do you no good. No one can find me. So safe am I from any revenge on the part of your paramour that I will reveal to you all that you have asked, even more: I will tell you my history, as terrible as it is. Know that in the world there are only a handful of sages to whom the prophet Elijah comes to reveal the hidden truths of the Torah. Once, long ago, I was one of these. Elijah was my constant companion; from his lips I drew down the fire of Sinai as if for the first time. From him I heard the very same truths that were revealed to Moses on high, and whose echo has been lost in this world since that time. And from all the secrets and mysteries that became transparent to me, I came to realize that my greatest desire was not an impossible wish, but one that could be accomplished. What was this, you wonder? I longed, more than anything else, to bring to this world the Age of Redemption; I longed to hasten the coming of the only one who can bring the End of Days any closer; I sought to beckon the Messiah himself from the palace known as the Bird's Nest, where he makes his home on high.

"These thoughts haunted me for many days, until I could not restrain myself any longer, and one day I begged Elijah to reveal this secret to me. At that, Elijah grew silent and departed. Nor did he return. When I realized he had abandoned me, I fell into a great sorrow. I recalled how Adam had stood in the river Gihon after his sin, until his skin began to sag, and I too stood in the river and wept and prayed and fasted for many days. At last Elijah sought me out and asked why I had prayed so insistently for his return. I told him that my only desire was to restore the Shekhinah, the Bride of God, to her rightful abode and bring her exile to an end. Elijah told me that what I sought to do was very dangerous and not likely to succeed, and he asked me to abandon the quest. But when he saw that I was willing to give up my life to accomplish this deed, he imparted many secrets and revealed many mysteries. Elijah told me all that I would have to do in order to bring an end to the reign of evil. And this was to capture none other than the rulers of the Dark Kingdom, Ashmodai, the king, and Lilith, the queen. The same Lilith who now is my wife!" The searing memory of his great fall suddenly struck Joseph della Reina anew, and for a long time he was silent. And Queen Dolphina began to recognize for the first time a kernel of humanity in him that was still capable of regret.

Now Joseph della Reina's silent brooding lasted for a very long time, and finally the sky began to grow light. When he realized that dawn was imminent he jumped up, turned his back on the queen, and whispered in reverse the holy names that had made it possible for him to snatch her in the first place. An instant later the queen found herself back in her own royal chamber, next to her husband, the king, who was sound asleep. The queen was greatly relieved when she realized that she had escaped from the clutches of that madman, but she was still haunted by the horror of that night. Worst of all was the memory of his promise to snatch her away again. Did he mean the very next night? She could not even bear to consider the thought. And even though she remembered well his warning that they could not find him, she did not intend to be his victim without a struggle. And without any further hesitation, she woke the king and told him her terrible tale.

Now, as might be expected, the king had a hard time believing the story of the queen. After all, guards had been posted at the door all night, the windows had been locked, and he himself had been sleeping beside her. He thought that it must have been a terrible and very vivid dream that had afflicted her. Still, even such a dream would be a bad sign, and that day he called upon his soothsayers to reveal its meaning. But when the soothsayers, who were far more familiar with the ways of black magic, heard all that the queen had to say, they quickly confirmed her account to the king, who finally came to accept it as true. And then a great fury possessed him, a veritable darkness and lust for revenge. For his wife had been ravished and his honor had been sullied in the most terrible way. Nor had the danger passed, for the queen remained in very grave jeopardy indeed.

That evening the king saw to it that guards were posted not only outside their chamber but also within. He himself remained awake, for he intended to see with his own eyes if the queen did, in fact, disappear, for he still hoped against hope that it was only a dream. The soothsayers had warned them that the most dangerous time was at midnight, and as it approached the king became even more vigilant, holding his wife tightly in his arms. Then, just at the stroke of twelve, the queen suddenly vanished. No one had entered, but she was snatched from his arms before their eyes. And when the king saw this, his terror was so great he fainted.

Far away, in the south, the queen suddenly found herself once more in Joseph della Reina's palace of illusion. As before, his intention was to possess her at once, and she felt even more helpless than before, for all the efforts of the king to save her had failed. Afterward, without being asked, Joseph della Reina continued his story, and that is when the queen realized how eager he was to tell it. He said:

"From the prophet Elijah I had learned that the secret of how to capture Ashmodai and Lilith, the very rulers of the forces of darkness, could be imparted only by Metatron, prince of the angels. And in order to invoke Metatron and call down his fiery chariot, it was required that my disciples and I subsist on as little as possible for twenty-one days, until our bodies were purified. Furthermore, we were to immerse ourselves twenty-one times every day. We were to strengthen ourselves as necessary only by smelling spices, especially pure frankincense. And after the twenty-one days, we were to fast three days and nights, and on the third day, at the time of the afternoon prayers, we were to put on our tefillin and cover our faces with our prayer shawls, and then, and only then, were we to pronounce a series of holy names. And he revealed those names to me.

"We did exactly as Elijah had directed, until, by the end of the third day of fasting, it felt as if our souls were about to take flight. We each put on our *tallit* and tefillin, and at last I spoke the holy names that Elijah had revealed. Thunder and lightning roared over us, and the sky split open, and we fell on our faces in terror. The whole earth shook as if it were about to split asunder.

A great whirlwind swirled around us, and out of the whirlwind spoke a terrible voice: 'Speak, you who are flesh and blood, dust and worms! Why have you called me here? Is this how you honor your Maker?' I replied, 'Forgive me. I am like a lifeless stone in your presence. Without your help I have not even the strength to speak.'

"Then the angel Metatron—for that is who it was—touched me, and a shock passed through my body, as if I had been struck with lightning. I found that my strength had not only been restored, but was much increased. I revealed my intention to the prince of the angels, and when he saw that I sought to restore the world to its once perfect state, at last he revealed the great mystery that I so longed to learn: how the capture of the evil rulers might be accomplished. And Metatron warned us to be very careful not to forget any detail of what he had told us. Then the angel departed in his fiery chariot, leaving us in a state of shock and awe, for all that we had sought was now within our grasp."

Here again, as Joseph della Reina recalled how close he had come to completing his quest, he fell into a morose silence, while Queen Dolphina continued to pray for the night to end. And yet, if the truth be known, she also found herself curious to know how this madman had sought to capture the rulers of Darkness and how he had failed. And she wondered if this tale might contain a hint of how she might be set free from his grasp.

At the first light of dawn Joseph della Reina arose as before, spoke the spell with his back turned, and an instant later the queen found herself back in her bedroom, where the king and his guards had spent a miserable night. The king was so happy to see his wife that he shed tears and embraced her, and he vowed that he would find a way to save her from the monster who had snatched her out of his arms. That day the king called in all of his soothsayers and told them that their lives would be in danger if they did not protect the queen from this terrible magic. The soothsayers tried to explain that the level of sorcery was far greater than they had ever encountered, but the king refused to listen. At last one of the soothsayers came forward and said, "I have read, Your Majesty, that the only way to gain power over such a sorcerer is to obtain an object that belongs to him. It does not seem likely that we can prevent him from taking her again tonight, if that is indeed his wish, but perhaps the queen can find a way to bring back one of his possessions. Then we can make use of our own magic." And when the queen was informed of this, she promised to bring back something, whatever was possible, for she, more than anyone else, wanted that nightmare to end.

That night at midnight it happened again—the queen vanished in sight of all of those attempting to guard her. Again she found herself in the arms of a madman, who ravished her without hesitation. As he did, the queen tried to turn her thoughts away from him and concentrated on finding something that she might take back with her that night, something that might serve to reveal to the wizards the precise location of that palace. It was then that her eyes lit upon a golden wine goblet next to the bed. She reached for it unseen by Joseph della Reina and slipped it beneath the pillow. And this single act helped her to endure the long hours remaining before dawn.

As before, Joseph della Reina had barely satisfied his lust when he began to speak, continuing to tell the tale as if in a trance. "No sooner had Metatron departed in the fiery chariot than we set out to complete the quest. As he had directed us, we traveled to Mount Seir and ascended it. And there we performed many matters of holiness and we ate little and immersed ourselves in the prayers of unification.

"After that we began to search everywhere on the mountain, for the angel had made it known that in a certain ruin the wicked Ashmodai and his wife, Lilith, would be found in the form of two black dogs, male and female. Before long we did indeed discover that ruin, and by peering through the holes in the wall we saw the two terrible dogs, just as the angel had described them. So too did the dogs see us, and they began to growl, low at first and then louder and louder, until they were howling. That terrible noise raised the hair on the back of my neck and caused me great pain, but we did not turn back. No, we entered the ruin, in our hands two chains, the links of which were engraved with God's Name. We held these chains out before us and went forward toward the dogs, who did not attempt to flee, but seemed frozen in place. At last we threw the chains around their necks, and all at once the dogs vanished, and in their place stood the two demons, on whose faces were inscribed the agony of defeat.

"Then a great thrill passed through all of us, for we had accomplished what none other had even dared to attempt, and the rulers of evil were our own prisoners, to do with as we pleased. Now the angel had warned us to take care not to give them any kind of sustenance. And soon enough the two of them began to beg to eat and drink, but we gave them nothing at all. Instead we led them down the mountain, for that is what the angel had directed us to do. All along the way they pleaded with us for at least a drop of water, for their throats were parched. These requests moved me, but I still managed to deny them, for I reminded myself of the angel's warning.

"Just as we were about to reach the base of the mountain—that mountain on which the power of the demons was most abundant—Lilith and Ashmodai made the most heartrending pleas, claiming that they could not go on, for they were without strength. They begged that at least they should be permitted to sniff some incense, to regain enough strength to complete the descent. And I found it hard to refuse, for I could not imagine that such a minor gesture could be dangerous. Therefore I did permit them one such sniff of our incense, and that is all it took for both to break free of their chains. A moment later I saw Ashmodai pick up one of my disciples and cast him a great distance. One after another, each of my disciples was cast from the mountain in that way, and all of them, I am certain, met their death.

"In less than a minute I was the only one left. Ashmodai looked at me fiercely and my heart almost stopped heating. Then he picked me up and cast me as he had the others, so that I found myself flying through the air as if I had wings. That flight seemed to last so long that I felt that I must have passed over half the Earth. Suddenly I found myself crashing downward, into a green area, and then, all at once, I found myself landing in arms that broke my fall and embraced me. And when I looked up, I saw that it was none other than Lilith herself who had caught me. Of course I was much amazed, and when she saw this, she said, 'You may wonder why I have saved your life, when it was your intention to destroy me. The answer is that I have recognized in you an ember of evil, and now that you are mine I shall fan that ember until it bursts into flame!'"

With these words Joseph della Reina stopped speaking and glared at Queen Dolphina. The look in his eyes was so terrifying that she was afraid that he might kill her then and there. But that moment of hatred passed, followed by one of great grief, and as before he fell into a morose state and was silent. Queen Dolphina remained completely still, barely breathing, for she was so afraid of what he might do next. But at the same time she marveled at all he had told her, and she understood at last how he had become so evil. For he was completely in the power of the demoness Lilith, who had enabled him to transport her, the queen, to his chamber, to do with as he wished.

It seemed years before dawn at last arrived. And as it did, Joseph della Reina pulled himself up and mumbled the words that released the queen from his spell. But just as he turned his back, she reached under the pillow and clutched the golden goblet, and when, an instant later, she found herself back in the royal chamber, the goblet was still in her hand! The king was the first to see it. He grabbed it and gave it to the soothsayers and demanded that they discover where it came from. Then they hurried off to do their magic, hoping that the secret might be revealed. And lo and behold, before even an hour had passed they returned smiling, for their spells had worked, and now they knew the very town in which the evil sorcerer resided; even more, they knew the very house in which he could be found. Upon learning this the king did not hesitate, but ordered that all of his palace guards set out at once, in order to reach that town before midnight. And within minutes the guards were urging their stallions to gallop in that direction.

Now it was normally a two-day journey to that town from the capital, but this time the soldiers did not stop to eat or drink or rest, even for a moment. They pushed themselves and their horses relentlessly, so that they might arrive before midnight and thus spare the queen another night of torture. And at the very stroke of twelve they arrived at the sorcerer's door. True, the house did not resemble the palace the queen had described, but the soothsayers had warned them that that might be the case. And without a moment's hesitation they broke down the door, just as Joseph della Reina was about to pronounce the spell to transport the queen to his bed. He could not believe he had been found. For a terrible moment they stared at one another, then he pronounced a spell—not the spell to snatch the queen, but one to make himself invisible—and suddenly he vanished from before their eyes. The soldiers could not believe they had lost him so suddenly, and they searched the palace from top to bottom, but not a sign of the sorcerer was to be found. For he had walked among them, invisible, and slipped out the door.

Now the spell of invisibility lasted for only a few hours, and then it could not be renewed until a full day had passed. Joseph della Reina knew that he had to find a safe place to hide by the time the spell wore off. For the soldiers had seen him, and now there would be guards searching everywhere. Joseph della Reina remembered that there was a cave near the sea, on the side of a cliff. Lilith had first taken him there when he had been cast from the Holy Land to France by Ashmodai. And beneath the light of the full moon he set out for the sea. He reached it shortly before the spell wore off and quickly hid himself inside the dark cave, where he could not be seen even when he was visible. And only when he was finally safe did he realize how frightened he had been. How had they found him in the first place? He could not imagine, unless the queen had taken some object of his back to her palace. Now he would have to give the queen up. He could not dare risk trying to capture her again.

For the first few days after this near catastrophe, Joseph della Reina slept in the dark of the cave. Each time that he awoke and recalled his humiliation, he forced himself to fall back to sleep. At last his hunger kept him awake, and he knew that he would have to sustain himself. Once again he invoked the spells that Lilith had taught him, transporting the palace of Ashmodai, with all of its furnishings, into that very cave. So too did he make use of the spells that provided him with whatever he wanted to eat. And in that place he slowly recovered from his shock. For it was not the first great shock of his life, yet somehow it was almost as hard for him to bear. To have failed as a holy man was one thing, but to have failed as a wizard was another. Thoughts of revenge obsessed him, but he knew the king had his own sorcerers waiting to combat his magic and that it was too dangerous to challenge them again.

At last Joseph della Reina's lust was restored to him. And one day a thought occurred to him that gave him something for which to live. Perhaps it was true that Queen Dolphina was the most beautiful woman in the world, but that was true only of that time. In the past there had been many others far more beautiful, and above them all was one whose beauty had provoked the Trojan War—Helen of Troy. The thought of possessing such a legendary beauty for himself slowly took possession of Joseph della Reina, blotting out the memory of Queen Dolphina and the humiliation he had known at her hands. And before long he became consumed with the thought that he must make Helen of Troy his own.

Now between the secrets the angels had revealed to Joseph della Reina and those that Lilith had supplied, his powers were very great, and at last he found a way not only to transport a human being across a great space, but across the centuries as well. The first time he cast the spell he shivered in anticipation. For a moment the illusory palace in which he lived seemed to flicker, as if the illusion were about to end, then all at once the cries of an infant shocked Joseph della Reina, and he found, to his amazement, an infant loudly crying on his bed. The shock soon passed, though, when he realized that he had succeeded in his basic attempt, but that he had called Helen from out of the past too young for his purposes.

Quickly, impatiently, Joseph della Reina pronounced a spell that sent the infant back, and then he spoke again, to summon an older Helen. Again the palace flickered, this time more than before, then a figure suddenly appeared on the bed, that of Helen of Troy. But it was not Helen as Joseph della Reina had expected to find her. No, this Helen wore a worm-eaten shroud and consisted solely of bones. But what was far more horrible was that the skeleton was alive—in invoking it from the past Joseph della Reina had brought it back to life. And as he watched in horror, the arms of the skeleton opened and reached out to embrace him.

A wave of pure horror washed over Joseph della Reina, and he dashed from that room, but there too the bones of the once-lovely Helen awaited him, seeking an embrace, and the terrified sorcerer ran from the house. In his terror he forgot that the palace was but an illusion, and that his true home was in a cave on the side of a cliff overlooking the sea. No sooner did he step out of the door than he found himself falling. And a second before his body shattered on the rocks below, he saw the bones of Helen awaiting him, her arms open.

—Palestine: sixteenth century

55. The Homunculus of Maimonides

oses ben Maimon, known as Maimonides, was a student of the prophet Elijah, who not only revealed all the mysteries of the Torah to him but also gave him two secret books—*The Book of Creation* and *The Book of Healing*. With the aid of these two wondrous texts Maimonides was able to understand the greatest secrets of nature and to heal all diseases. His fame spread over all of Europe, and in the most distant lands people spoke of the great wisdom of the famous Jewish doctor in Cordova.

Now it happened that the only son of a rich businessman in London, whose lust for learning could not be satisfied by the teachers in his own country, secretly left his parents' home and traveled to Cordova. It would not be enough, this young man thought, to be the student of this doctor; he wanted to observe the greatly esteemed man in his own home and enter into the secrets and mysteries that the teacher reserved for himself alone. Therefore the young man employed a cunning device to achieve his goal. He appeared before the rabbi, dressed in a poor and humble manner, and presented himself as completely dumb. By means of piteous expressions and beseeching gestures, he made the rabbi understand that he wanted to serve him.

Maimonides was moved by the fate of the young man and accepted him as his servant. And by virtue of his attentiveness and punctuality, the speechless servant so earned the favor of his master that his help was soon requested at each experiment. During this time the student increased his theoretical knowledge as well. For in his master's absence he studied his master's books and writings with great industry, so that after only a few years he was almost his equal.

Now it so happened that a distinguished man of the court fell ill of a strange disease. Although there was no sign of injury on any portion of his body, from time to time he would fall into a kind of frenzy and twirl about, as if driven by unseen forces, until he fell to the ground exhausted.

All the Spanish doctors tested their skill in vain; the disease grew worse and worse, and the courtier's life was in great danger. As a last resort they sent for the Jewish doctor Maimonides. He immediately recognized the problem. "The sick man has a worm in his brain. There is only one way to save him: bore through the skull and remove the worm." For a long time the courtier could not persuade himself to undergo the operation. But as the disease got increasingly worse, he finally agreed.

Maimonides and his speechless servant came into the sick man's house with all the necessary instruments and found that a large number of doctors had assembled there to observe the procedure. With a sure and skilled hand Maimonides performed the dangerous operation. A portion of the skull was removed, and they could see the worm lying motionless on the delicate brain. Everyone present was astonished at the wisdom and skill of the Jewish doctor. Now Maimonides reached for some small pincers to remove the worm. Just then a strange voice from behind him cried out, "Stop, master! You'll kill the man!" Startled, Maimonides dropped the pincers and turned in amazement to the speaker. It was his servant. "What is this? Have you deceived me?" asked Maimonides in anger. "Forgive me, master. I will explain the reason for my deception later. But now let us save the sick man. Look, the worm has been sucking powerfully on the brain, and if you pull it away with force, you will injure the organ and the man's life will be lost." "What can we do to remove the worm?" asked Maimonides. "Sir," replied the student, "you explained it yourself in your writings. Lay a plant on the place and the worm will willingly leave its position to bore into it." So Maimonides sent for a plant, the courtier was cured, and Maimonides became the king's official physician.

After this operation Maimonides forgave his pupil for his deception and treated him as an equal. In time the two became inseparable. Their researches were pursued largely in common, and when one of them was at a loss, the other came to his assistance. Thus together they studied almost all branches of knowledge.

One day as they were sitting together in the study, the master said, "I see that you have almost surpassed me in learning. For you have absorbed what took me years of struggle to understand. And your powerful free spirit can go much further than mine, for it is more in tune with earthly matters than my own. Let us therefore follow a path together that past generations have never pursued. We want to observe the secrets of creation and destruction in nature, and then solve the great riddle of creation." "My lord and master," answered the young man, "I am still young, and I am not certain how to distinguish what is true from what is false. I do not yet understand how far it is permitted for the human spirit to enter into the secrets of nature, but such daring seems to me sinful for a son of man and can only incite the wrath of the Creator."

"All of this," the master replied with a sweep of his arm, "belongs to the human spirit, which can observe and employ it as it wishes. The human spirit can search until it finds the truth, until it can even create a world."

"Sir, your words frighten me. I am, however, ready to follow you wherever this may lead. By your side I cannot stumble."

"Now I recognize once more my worthy pupil," said Maimonides, as he turned to the bookshelf and removed a large folio of *The Book of Creation* from a hidden drawer.

"Have you read any of this book?" he asked. "Often have I read with amazement, and not without terror, the wonders it contains," the pupil replied. "What do you think of the secrets found here?" Maimonides asked. "I doubt that they are true," said the pupil. "But it seems that your powerful spirit wishes to be convinced."

"We shall make experiments," Maimonides said. He opened the folio and pointed to a particular passage. "Here it says, 'Kill a healthy man, cut his body into pieces, and place the pieces in an airless glass container. Sprinkle upon them an essence gathered from the sap of the Tree of Life and the balsam of immortality, and after nine months the pieces of this body will be living again. It will be unharmable and immortal.' "

"Master, whom shall we get for this dangerous experiment?" the young man asked anxiously. "You or me," responded Maimonides, "the lot shall decide. But first let us swear, in the Name of the Eternal One, that the living one will permit the dead pieces to ripen, and will not, for whatever reason, hypocritically destroy the apparatus prematurely, in order to destroy the embryo life." Both men laid their hands on the Holy Scroll and swore to the Almighty. The lot was cast and fell to the pupil. Maimonides conjured up the Angel of Death, and the young man fell lifeless to the ground. Maimonides cut the body into pieces, placed it in a glass container, sprinkled it with the wondrous essence, and left the room, which he carefully locked and did not reenter for four months.

Finally, tortured by doubt and curiosity, Maimonides returned to the room and looked at the mass of dead flesh. And behold, there were no longer severed pieces but structured limbs, as if crystallized in the glass container. Happy about the restoration of his student, he left the room and waited a month. In the fifth month the form of the human body could already be recognized. In the sixth the arteries and nerves were visible, and in the seventh movement and life in the organs could be perceived. The researcher, however, became worried. Maimonides was now convinced of the veracity of *The Book of Creation*. And he was terrified about the future. "What horror threatens the human race if I let this being come into being? If this immortal man, with all his power, wanders among his brothers, will not people deify him and pray to him, and will not that holy revelation, the Laws of Moses, be denied and finally entirely forgotten?" Thus thought Maimonides as he left the room. At the end of the eighth month, uncertain and deeply troubled, he approached the growing being and was staggered as the almost completely developed face smiled at him. Unable to bear the demonic grin, he ran out of the room. "Oh, Lord, what have I done! It is true that man should not investigate too deeply; what is beyond this sphere leads to Hell."

A few days later Maimonides appeared before the Great Council and explained the case. After lengthy reflection the learned rabbis agreed: to protect against a horror for mankind, and to preserve God's honor, that vow might be broken and such a man killed. This decision they based on a verse in Psalms: *Disregard the law; the time has come to act for God* (Ps. 119:126).

At the beginning of the ninth month, Maimonides stepped into the room, intending to destroy his creation. He brought a dog and a cat with him, and he released them and let them fly at each other. In the midst of this fighting, the glass container crashed to the floor and broke into a thousand pieces. The dead man lay at Maimonides' feet. After he recovered himself, Maimonides buried the body and took the pernicious volume and threw it into the flames of the fireplace. But nothing was the same again. Maimonides was attacked by the learned men of the court, accused of magical practices, and escaped judgment only by a timely flight to Egypt. But even there he was pursued and treated as an enemy both by his fellow Jews and by unbelievers, and from then on his life was filled with sorrow.

—Eastern Europe: nineteenth century

56. The Beast

There once was a wealthy man and wife who longed, more than anything else, to have a child of their own. Over the years they had tried every known remedy in order to conceive, including potions of every kind, but still the couple was without children. Now the man, who was a merchant, heard from others that there was a wise old man among the Jews, whose name was Elijah, who could help them have a child. And when they had exhausted every other means, the merchant and his wife went to the Jewish Quarter of Cairo and sought out the old man.

They found that Elijah lived in an almost empty hut in the poorest part of the quarter. He possessed nothing except for the robe he wore and a prayer book. The merchant and his wife wondered to themselves how such a poor man could be of help to them. Still, they were desperate, so they told the old man how much they longed to have a child, and they offered to pay him whatever he asked if he could help them. Elijah said, "What do you want, a son or a daughter?" The merchant replied, "More than anything else in the world, I want to have a son of my own." Then Elijah told them to bring him pen and paper, and when they did, he wrote out an amulet, using holy names. He told them to place that amulet in a cup of wine and for both of them to drink from that cup, and in nine months' time they would have a son of their own.

Somehow the quiet confidence of Elijah soothed the pair and gave them hope. Then the merchant said, "We will always be grateful if what you have said comes true. Tell me, how can I repay you?" Elijah replied, "Do nothing for now. But when the child is born, make a donation in the charity box of the synagogue on the corner of this street, which serves the poorest Jews. That will suffice." Then the merchant and his wife thanked him many times, and turned to go. But before they left, the old man said, "Wait. There is one more thing that I must tell you." The merchant and his wife turned back, wondering what it was. And Elijah said, "The son that will be born to you is not destined to be wed. He must remain unmarried all his life. For it is written that on the night he weds, he will be devoured by a beast!"

As they heard this prophecy, the high hopes of the couple were suddenly shaken. They stood silent, but at last the merchant said, "Is there nothing we can do to spare our child this terrible fate?" And the old man answered, "No, I am sorry to say. All that you can do is avoid making any match for him, and when he is old enough to understand, explain that it is his destiny to remain unwed." And the merchant and his wife assured Elijah that they would heed his warning, and that if indeed they were blessed with a son, they would see to it that he was never betrothed. Then they took their leave, but this time they were much more solemn.

When they returned home the merchant placed the amulet that Elijah had written into a silver goblet and filled it with his finest wine, a bottle that had been saved since he had been born. The merchant and his wife drank from the goblet, one sip at a time, until it was empty. That is when they discovered that the amulet had dissolved into the wine; not a trace of it was to be found. And when the couple saw this, they sensed that the prophecy of the old man would indeed come true, and they would become parents. But they did not think about his admonition.

To their mutual delight the merchant's wife soon found that she was with child, and at the end of nine months she gave birth to a beautiful boy, and the merchant and his wife felt they had been greatly blessed. The merchant did not forget his promise to Elijah to give money to the synagogue for the poor. He gave them a great donation, enough to sustain them for a full year. But he did not dwell on the warning of the old man, for the time his son would think of marriage was far off.

In the years that followed, the man and his wife raised their son with loving care, for he was more precious to them than anything in the world. From time to time a marriage was proposed for him, for such early betrothals were the custom. The boy's parents always turned down these offers, giving one excuse or another, but never, of course, the true reason. The day came, however, when the young man himself informed his parents that he wished to be wed. The parents argued long into the night about whether to tell him the prophecy of the old man. In the end they decided not to, and instead made up their minds to see to it that the boy was indeed wed, but under circumstances that would protect him from every danger. Now in his travels the merchant had once come into possession of a small island in a distant sea. That island was uninhabited by man or beast, and the merchant thought it would be the perfect place to have the wedding. Therefore, once the match had been made, the merchant saw to it that a fine mansion was built on that island, surrounded with a large stone wall that would protect his son from every kind of danger. So too did he have guards posted to guard the mansion day and night.

One year later, when the time for the wedding had arrived, the merchant was informed that the mansion was ready. Then the merchant had his finest sailing ship outfitted and brought both families on board, along with the bride and groom and many guests. (Of course the bride and groom were never permitted to glimpse each other, as was the custom.) The voyage was a time of great rejoicing, and the merchant and his wife never dwelt on the prophecy of the old man. For they felt that they had done everything possible to protect their son from danger.

When the ship docked at last on that lovely island, all expressed wonder and delight. The sand of the beaches was pure white, and there were fruit trees of every kind, as well as wild grapes and berries. So too were all the guests astonished at the extravagant mansion. It was constructed of marble, like a palace, and the chamber of the bride and groom was set at the top of a spiral tower. There, the merchant felt sure, his son would be safe.

The wedding festivities continued for three days and nights before the vows were finally said. It was then that the merchant's son saw his bride for the first time. She was astonishingly beautiful, with raven hair that reached to her waist, and the young man felt himself to be the most fortunate groom in the world. At last he and his bride climbed the stairs to the tower together and stood on the threshold of the bridal chamber. The young man led his bride inside and closed the door. As he gazed at her he was filled with awe at her beauty. He admired especially her hands, with their fine, slender fingers and long nails. He smiled shyly at her, but she seemed afraid to lift her eyes from the floor. When at last she did, the young man was astonished to see a look of wild desire in them unlike anything he had ever seen. When he stepped forward to embrace her, he suddenly heard a low growl. The young man looked around in confusion, wondering where it could have come from. He turned back just in time to see the fangs of the beast as it leaped at him from the very place his bride had been.

—Egypt: oral tradition

57. The Haunted Violin

here was a carpenter in the city of Worms who was called upon to make a coffin. When the coffin was finished, there was one board left over. The carpenter decided to use it to carve a violin. That night, however, he had a dream in which the dead man for whom he had made the coffin came to him and warned him not to do so. The carpenter recalled this dream when he awoke, but dismissed it, as he did all dreams.

That day he started to carve the violin. He proceeded very slowly, perfecting it over a period of weeks. When he was finished he saw that the violin was very well made indeed, and he was proud of himself. He polished the wood and strung the violin and looked forward to the time that he might play it, once he had made a bow. That night the dead man came back to him in a dream and again warned him not to play the violin. But upon waking, the carpenter again dismissed the dream.

That day he carved the bow and polished its wood until it shone like that of the violin. It was late at night when the bow was finished, so he decided not to try it out until the next day. That night the dead man came back to him once again, and said he was warning him for the last time not to play the violin. But when the carpenter awoke, the first thing he did was to pick up the violin and run the bow across its strings. A haunting melody rose up, as if on its own, and no sooner had he played but a single refrain than the room grew dark, as if the sun had been blotted out. The carpenter ran to the window, opened it in confusion, and peered outside, but the darkness was so deep he could not see anything.

Suddenly a great force from behind, like invisible hands, shoved him out the window. Before he knew it, the carpenter found himself tumbling down, and an instant later he plunged into something soft and treacherous, like mud. With horror he realized it was quicksand, relentlessly sucking him under the earth. It had already reached his arms when he understood how imminent was his danger, and he thrashed about wildly, but it was too late. The quicksand dragged him under as he drew his last breath.

The son of the carpenter found his father's body lying on the floor of his workshop, a violin in his hands. That night the same dead man who had warned his father came to the son in a dream and revealed all that had happened. The very next day the son burned the violin. And as it went up in flames he heard the voice of the carpenter crying out as if from a great distance. Then he knew that somewhere his soul was still being tortured.

—Germany: twelfth century

58. The Knife

here was a man in the city of Worms whose widowed mother died without leaving a will. Now he knew very well that she had been wealthy, and he searched everywhere in the house but he could not find where her fortune was hidden. The matter became an obsession to him. He searched through everything again and again. He looked between the pages of each and every book she owned. Nothing. Then he dug up the yard to a depth of three feet. Still nothing. After that he began to tear out the floors, in case the money was hidden there. It was not. At last he realized that he simply could not find it on his own. So he decided to go to a witch for help.

Now this witch was famous for the power of her spells. She said, "Yes, yes, I can find it, if you are willing to pay the price—one half of the inheritance."

The desperate man said, "One half is better than nothing."

Then the witch said, "Good. Now you must leave, for no one can be present when I work my magic." And when he was gone she took out a knife and said a spell over it. Then she hid the knife beneath her pillow and went to sleep.

That night the witch dreamed that a demon came to her who had a knife in his heart. The demon cried out to the witch, "Take the knife out of my heart!"

And the witch said, "No! Not until you bring me this man's mother, and she reveals where she hid the inheritance. Until then the knife will stay exactly where it is!" At that she woke up, and she felt beneath the pillow—and the knife was gone. And she smiled to herself.

The next night the witch dreamed that the same demon came back to her, the knife still in his heart. He was accompanied by a younger demon and the man's mother. The young demon said, "Take the knife out of my father's heart!"

"No," the witch replied, "not until she reveals where she hid her fortune."

"That I will never do!" the woman said.

"Why not?" asked the witch. "After all, you are dead; what good will it do you now?" And the woman replied, "If I had wanted him to know where the money was, I would have told him. I don't want him to know." With that the dream came to end and the witch awoke. And the knife was still gone.

The third night the demon came back, in the same company, the knife still in his heart. He looked feeble and unable to speak. His son spoke for him and begged the witch to remove the knife. The witch insisted she would not take it out until the woman revealed the secret. Then the demon's son begged the woman to take heed of the suffering of his father and to speak, and at last she relented, saying, "To spare you any more suffering I will reveal this much, and this much only: the money is hidden in a box." At that the dream ended.

When the witch awoke the first thing she did was to pronounce another spell. Then she put her hand beneath the pillow and found that the knife was there. So she knew that the demon no longer had the knife in his heart. Then she hurried off to the home of the man and told him the hint she had wrenched out of his mother. This clue astonished him, because he had looked in all the boxes first, and several times thereafter, and he had found nothing. That is what he told the witch, and the witch replied, "Look in the boxes. And when you find the inheritance, remember that half of it belongs to me." And she turned and left.

Now the minute the witch went away, the man tore each and every box apart, and in this way he found one with a false bottom, with the fortune hidden beneath it.

Now that the reluctant inheritance was his, the man decided to leave town at once, for he had no intention of sharing the money with the witch. This he did, and on the third day the witch came back to his house and discovered that he was gone. But she was not worried. And that night she placed the knife under her pillow again.

—Germany: twelfth century

59. The Charm in the Dress

n the city of Worms there was a beautiful woman, God-fearing and kindhearted, who devoted herself to good and charitable works. She was beloved by rich and poor alike, all of whom praised her and spoke well of her. One day her husband was shopping in the marketplace when he saw beautiful material for sale, and he thought that it would make a fine garment for his wife. So he purchased it and took it to a tailor to make a dress from it. This the tailor agreed to do, and the man left the material with him and departed.

Now the tailor soon cut and sewed that dress, and when it was almost finished a Gentile wizard happened to enter the tailor's shop. This man saw the lovely dress and said to himself, "The garment becomes the wearer, and the wearer is surely beautiful." And he craved her.

What did the wizard do? He went home and wrote out a magic charm on a slip of paper, came back, gave it to the tailor, and told him to sew it into the dress, and to hide it well so that it would be neither felt nor seen. The tailor was reluctant to do it, but the wizard offered him a considerable sum, and he let himself be bribed.

The next day the woman's husband picked up the dress from the tailor and brought it home as a gift for his wife. She found it to be exceptionally beautiful and decided to save it to wear on the eve of Yom Kippur, which was soon approaching. And because this tailor had made many other dresses for her and knew her size very well, she did not even try it on, but put it away for that time.

On the eve of Yom Kippur, after the meal before the fast, the woman donned the dress for the first time to wear to the synagogue. But the moment she put it on an impure spirit took possession of her, and she was filled with desire for a man she had never met, but that she somehow knew how to find. When her husband asked her to accompany him to the synagogue, she replied that she was not feeling well and would follow a little later. So he went to the synagogue by himself, and after he had gone the woman stepped outside, but instead of following after him, her legs carried her toward the villain's house, as the charm commanded.

The dazed woman walked until she found herself before a strange door and knocked on it. And no sooner did the wizard open the door than this woman, who had never seen him before, fell into his arms and kissed and hugged him as if they had always been lovers. So too did she transgress by eating and drinking everything he offered her, without a thought that it was the eve of Yom Kippur, and that the food, in any case, was unacceptable. And after the meal the wizard led her to his bedroom to lie down.

The woman followed after him unquestioningly, as if in a trance, and when he began to undress, she did as well. But as soon as she removed the dress, the unclean spirit immediately left her and she came to her senses, and her remorse was terrible to behold. She decided to leave at once and reached for her dress, but the instant she put it on her desire for him returned, twofold. She forgot her determination to go and was ready to give herself to him again.

Once again she undressed, in order to consummate their lust, but again, the moment the dress was off, waves of remorse washed over her. It was then she realized that the dress must be exerting some kind of power over her, and she decided then and there to leave without it, before she committed an even greater sin. Thus, dressed only in her chemise, she hurried out of the house arid through the streets of the Jewish quarter, terrified that someone would see her. But, of course, everyone was in the synagogue for Yom Kippur, and so no one saw her before she reached home.

Once there she wept bitterly over what had occurred and also gave thanks to God that her sin had not been greater. She was terrified that her husband might find out what had happened and decided to keep it secret, lest he cast her out. So it was that when her husband returned from the synagogue and asked why she hadn't come, she told him that she felt too ill to go and decided to stay at home. And her husband, who trusted her completely, did not question her explanation at all.

A few days later the wizard decided to sell the dress in the marketplace, in hope of finding another beautiful victim for his lust. And it happened that the woman's husband was shopping there, and he saw the dress and recognized it at once, for there was none other like it. Naturally he was stunned by the sight and could not understand how it came to be there. Still, he did not reveal his feelings, but bartered for the dress and purchased it for a second time. And the wizard sold it to him, ignorant of the fact that he was the husband of his first victim, for the wizard was hoping another victim would soon be knocking at his door.

When the husband came home that day he said to his wife, "Where is the dress that you wore on Yom Kippur?" She pretended to go and look for it, and after a while she came back empty-handed and said that she could not find it, and he saw that she was afraid. Then he took out the dress that he had purchased in the market and showed it to her and said, "How is it that this dress came into a stranger's hand in the marketplace, where I purchased it for the second time today?" And when the woman saw the dress, she fell down in a faint, and when she recovered she confessed to her husband all that had happened to her, fantastic as it was.

The man immediately took the dress to the rabbinic court and asked them to examine it. They ripped apart all of the seams and studied it thoroughly, and in this way they discovered the hidden charm. And when they read it, they understood why the woman had lost her will when she was wearing the dress. Then the rabbis accompanied the husband to the tailor who had sewed the dress and confronted him with the charm. And when he saw it, he grew very afraid and confessed that he had been bribed by the man to sew it into the dress.

After that the rabbis went to the authorities and accused the man of witchcraft and offered as evidence the dress, the charm, and the testimony of the tailor and the righteous woman who had been the victim of the spell.

So it was that a few days later the wizard heard a knock on his door, and assuming it was his next victim, he opened the door with a smile, only to find himself confronted with guards, who dragged him off to court, where he was shortly condemned to death. And within a week the sentence was carried out, and justice was done. As for the tailor, he was punished by being forbidden to practice his livelihood, because he could not be trusted, and was forced to become a water carrier, bearing the heavy yoke of the buckets all day long. And with every step he took, he repented his sin and gave thanks that it had not cost him his life.

—Germany: sixteenth century

60. Lilith's Cave

here was a house in Tunis said to be haunted by demons. Once it had belonged to a wealthy family, but demons had invaded the house to hold a wedding, and when the wealthy owner had resisted, neither he nor his wife had ever been seen again. After that the house was boarded up, and no one entered it.

At last the house was sold for next to nothing to a man who planned to tear it down and build another in its place. But before he did, his wife convinced him to take out any valuables that might remain there. When the old people heard of their plan, they warned them not to go inside it, but they refused to heed them.

The man struggled with the key to unlock the door, and after he opened it, they found that the expensive furnishings inside had molded; nothing of value had survived. But before they left, the wife insisted on opening the door to the cellar as well, and at last the husband kicked the door in, despite the fact that the demons were rumored to make their home there. Much to their surprise they found the cellar furnishings in perfect condition; none seemed to have aged at all. They were worthy of a place in a palace, and especially valuable was a mirror with an ornate gold frame, which in itself was worth far more than they had paid for the house.

The wife brought the mirror and all of the fine furnishings in the cellar to her own home and proudly displayed it. She hung the mirror in the room of their daughter, a dark-haired coquette. The girl glanced at herself in the mirror all the time, and in this way she was drawn into Lilith's web. For a daughter of Lilith made her home in that mirror. And when it was taken from the haunted house, the demoness came with it. For every mirror is a gateway to the Other World and leads directly to Lilith's cave. That is the cave on the shore of the Red Sea where Lilith went after she abandoned Adam for all time, where she sported with her demon lovers. From these unions multitudes of demons were born who flocked from that cave and infiltrated the world. And when they want to return, they simply enter the nearest mirror. That is why it is said that Lilith makes her home in every mirror.

Nine months after the wife brought those furnishings into the house, she was found dead one morning, having choked on a feather she breathed in from one of the silken pillows she had taken from the cellar. After her death her husband sold all of the furniture and gave the proceeds to charity. He only wanted to get rid of it. All he kept was the gold-framed mirror, for his daughter refused to part with it.

In the days that followed, things went from bad to worse. During the day the girl avoided her household duties, nor did she give her widowed father any assistance. Instead she spent her time before the mirror, admiring herself.

Now the daughter of Lilith who made her home in that mirror watched every movement of the girl who posed before it. And one day she slipped out of the mirror and took possession of the girl, entering through her eyes. In this way she took control of her, stirring her desire at will.

So it happened that this young girl, driven by the evil wishes of Lilith's daughter, ran around with young men who lived in the same neighborhood. She started coming home later and later, and a time came when she sometimes did not come home at night at all. Her father suffered greatly over this, filled with shame. For he knew that once her reputation had been ruined, no worthy young man would marry her.

And in this he was right, for the daughter of Lilith that possessed the girl never let her come close enough to any one young man to feel love for him. For if this had happened, the power of the demoness over the girl would have been broken. Instead, she drove her on, commanding her roving eye to seek out yet another.

Once, when she had not returned home for two nights and her bed had not been slept in all that time, her father was possessed by a great fury and uttered a curse against her. The curse was so severe that even he was surprised to hear it spoken: "May the Lord turn my unworthy daughter into a bat, flitting around from place to place, from one man to the next, without ever becoming attached to any one! Because she has chosen to abandon herself to the night, may she be doomed to live in darkness! And may she be fated to bear this curse as long as the shame lives in my heart!"

At that moment the young woman, in the arms of a young man, suddenly screamed and vanished from the room. And all that he saw in that instant was a bat that flew out the window uttering a terrible cry.

—Tunisia: oral tradition

61. The Cellar

here once was a goldsmith in the city of Posen who was secretly married to the demoness Lilith. The demoness lived in the cellar, where the goldsmith had his workshop. He spent time with his demon lover every day, while keeping her existence secret from his family. His family assumed that he was working hard at his craft, but, if the truth be known, the goldsmith had completely abandoned his trade. Instead, Lilith conjured gold jewelry, finely crafted and even embedded with diamonds, and left it on his workbench. So too did she transform the dark cellar into a palatial chamber, where the goldsmith spent his time in her arms. Little by little he yielded everything to Lilith, lusting after her day and night.

Now there was only one key to the cellar, which the goldsmith kept with him at all times. In this way he was able to conceal Lilith's presence for many years. Meanwhile, their fortune increased. And the wife of the goldsmith felt that her lot was a good one. She used to say to her friends, whose husbands were merchants: "Your husbands go who knows where, and meet who knows who, and do who knows what? But my husband, I always know where he is—in the cellar."

Then it happened one Passover, at the seder, as they read the Haggadah, when they reached the passage *And he went down into Egypt,* that the goldsmith was suddenly overcome with lust for his demon wife. At first he tried to repress it, but it was the most powerful desire he had ever known. At last, without explanation, he got up and walked away from the table and descended the stairs to the cellar. His family was alarmed, for they knew he would never work at such a time. And for the first time his wife got up and followed after him. From the top of the stairs she saw him take out the key and unlock the door and go inside. Seized by a curiosity, she descended the stairs to the cellar and knelt down and peered through the keyhole. And what she saw astounded her, for there was no sign of the dark cellar she recalled. Instead, she saw a palatial chamber. And there, on a round bed, was her husband in the embrace of a beautiful, naked woman. Suddenly feeling faint, the goldsmith's wife crept back up the stairs and returned to the seder table, pale and trembling. When her family asked her what was wrong, she said that their father was not been feeling well and that he wanted them to continue the seder without him. And so they did.

Later that night, after the seder had ended, the goldsmith returned to his bedroom. He offered no explanation for leaving the seder, and his wife said nothing. But the next day she went to Rabbi Sheftel and told him all that she had seen. And the rabbi made it known that he wanted to see the goldsmith at once.

When the goldsmith came to the rabbi's study, the rabbi said, "Have you ever heard of someone getting up in the middle of the seder and leaving the table?"

The goldsmith was silent for a long time. Then he said, "It would be unusual."

"That is true," said the rabbi. "So could you explain why you left the seder?"

The goldsmith said, "I was remembering my parents and seders past, and I was overcome with grief."

"Liar!" shouted the rabbi. "I know where you went and I know what you did." And the goldsmith began to tremble, for he realized that he had been caught. He pleaded with the rabbi, saying, "Please, Rabbi, I know my sin is unforgivable, but I have lost my will to Lilith and there is nothing I can do about it. I am at her mercy." And Rabbi Sheftel said, "About this you are wrong."

Then Rabbi Sheftel went to a drawer and took out a very old silver amulet, one that had been handed down for many generations. It was an amulet against the demoness Lilith and her daughters and the text inside it contained the words "Out, Lilith!" The rabbi gave the amulet to the goldsmith and said, "You must keep this amulet in your possession at all times, day and night. Keep it in your pocket during the day, and put it under your pillow at night. As long as you keep that amulet nearby, Lilith will have no power over you." The goldsmith wept and gratefully thanked the rabbi and placed the amulet in his pocket, vowing never to be parted from it. When he got home his wife made him tell her everything, and she put her hope in that amulet to save them from that evil creature.

The next day the goldsmith discovered, to his amazement, that his desire for Lilith had vanished, and he did not feel tempted to lose himself in her embrace. For two more days he restrained himself from temptation, but on the third night he forgot to put the amulet under his pillow. And that night Lilith came to him in a dream and embraced him. And when he awoke in the middle of the night, he was filled with lust for his demon lover. Then he crept out of bed and went down to the cellar. But when he returned at dawn, he found his wife sitting up in bed and the lamp was lit and there was a terrible look on her face.

"I know where you've been," she said.

"It's your fault," the goldsmith retorted. "You forgot to remind me to put the amulet under my pillow."

"Don't worry," she said, "I'll never forget again. Meanwhile you must see Rabbi Sheftel today."

"Is that really necessary?" the goldsmith asked.

"Yes!" his wife insisted.

So the goldsmith went to see Rabbi Sheftel. And when the rabbi heard what had happened, he shouted, "Fool! Do you realize that your soul hangs by a thread? Have you forgotten the punishments of Gehenna?"

And the goldsmith cried out, "No, Rabbi, no! Please help me."

And Rabbi Sheftel said, "You must take the greatest care to see to it that you never forget the amulet again. Without it, your soul is lost!"

After that the goldsmith took much greater care with the amulet. So too did his wife check his pocket several times a day, and at night she slid her hand under his pillow to make sure it was there. In this way a month passed, two months, three months, and much to his amazement, the amulet worked. He lost his desire for Lilith. Indeed, she was repugnant to him.

After three months, even his wife began to be reassured. She told him that she was proud of him, and that he should go to Rabbi Sheftel and tell him how well things were going. And the goldsmith, who was proud of himself, agreed to go. And when Rabbi Sheftel heard the news, he smiled and said, "Good. I'm glad things are going so well. Now it's time for the next step."

"What next step?" asked the goldsmith.

"Do you intend to keep Lilith in your cellar?" the rabbi asked. "Get rid of her!"

"No, no, Rabbi, you don't understand. She's much too powerful. I'm terrified of her," the goldsmith pleaded.

"Listen to me carefully," Rabbi Sheftel said. "Hold the amulet before you as you open the cellar door. Then command her to get out of your house!"

When the goldsmith got home, his wife insisted he tell her everything. And when he did, she shouted, "Yes, yes! Get rid of her! I'm tired of having a demoness living in my house!"

The goldsmith said, "All right. I'll do it. But not today."

The next day his wife said, "Get rid of her."

"Not today," the goldsmith said, "tomorrow."

The next day his wife said firmly, "Get rid of her now!"

So the goldsmith took out the amulet, and, with trembling legs, descended the stairs to the cellar. He fumbled with the key and finally managed to unlock the door and push it open. And even though he held the amulet before him, he still glimpsed Lilith, lying naked on the bed.

She said, "Yes, what is it? Is there something you want to tell me?"

The goldsmith said, "You . . . you must leave."

Lilith replied: "What? Are you asking me to leave my home and the home of our children?"

"What children?" the goldsmith cried.

And Lilith answered, "Oh, did I forget to tell you about them? Boys, come here."

And three young demons, each one the spitting image of the goldsmith, came forth. And Lilith said, "Now, do you really want to expel your own sons? Where will they go? Humans will reject them because they are half demon, and the demons will reject them because they are half human. I'll tell you what. I'll make a deal with you. You want me to go away, is that right?"

The goldsmith meekly nodded.

"You want me out of your life for all time, is that right?" Lilith said.

Again the goldsmith nodded.

"In that case," Lilith said, "I will leave you alone. I will not come to you awake or asleep, you poor man. Your life will be dry as a bone! But I will only go if you bequeath this cellar to your demon sons, for all time."

And the goldsmith realized that this was the best he could hope for, and he also felt sympathy for his demon sons, for even though they were demons, they were still his own. So he made the vow as Lilith demanded and backed out of the cellar and slammed the door. Then he quickly ran up the stairs and took seven locks and seven seals and sealed up the door. After that he gathered his family together and said, with a terrible look on his face, "No one in this family will ever go near the cellar again, or even mention it!" And no one ever did.

The next day the goldsmith reported the agreement to Rabbi Sheftel, and the rabbi agreed that the goldsmith had no other choice. And Rabbi Sheftel recorded the entire account in his diary, for it was an exceptional case, but he never spoke of it to anyone, even his wife.

Now Lilith proved to be true to her word. She never tempted the goldsmith again. At last the goldsmith, now grown old, took leave of this world, and his soul ascended on high, for he had truly repented. But the demons were still living in the cellar.

Not long after the goldsmith's death, his wife decided to sell the house. A young couple purchased it, who had just been married. The new owners needed to store things in the cellar, and they sent a workman to unlock the door. He removed the seven locks and broke the seven seals, and pushed the door open. But the moment he did, a terrible scream was heard, and when the couple ran down to see what had happened, they found the workman lying dead outside the cellar door.

The incident so frightened the new owners that they ran out of the house and never came back and put it up for sale. But all of Posen had heard of the workman's strange death, and nobody wanted to live there. At last the house was abandoned and boarded up, with the cellar door still unlocked, for no one was willing to go down there.

After that the house became known as haunted. People whispered about it and children were warned to keep away from it, and everyone who had to pass by walked on the other side of the street. Then, in the months that followed, strange events began to take place. Candles in nearby homes would blow out, even though no windows were open. The finest food would burn, and the best wine turn to vinegar. Then more terrible things happened—infant boys would die for no reason on the night before their circumcision.

Reports of these disasters, large and small, all centered on the area of the haunted house, and it did not take long for the people to conclude that the demons had escaped from the cellar. This rumor put the city in an uproar, and the rabbinic council met to decide what to do. Rabbi Sheftel was no longer living, so they sent a messenger to summon Rabbi Yoel ben Isaac, the Ba'al Shem of Zamosc, who was known as a great wonder worker. Rabbi Yoel came to Posen and went into the abandoned house. He went down to the cellar and stood before the open door and called upon the demons to come forth.

Soon three demons appeared, and Rabbi Yoel said, "By what right are you living in this human habitation?"

The eldest demon son replied: "Our father, the goldsmith, bequeathed this cellar to us."

Rabbi Yoel replied: "This is a matter to be decided by the rabbinic court. You are hereby commanded, in the name of the rabbis, to appear in court in three days time." And he turned and left.

Three days later the Beit Din met to hear the case. The humans sat on one side of the partition, while the demons sat on the other side. The wife of the goldsmith was called upon to confirm that she had sold the house to the couple. They, in turn, were called upon to confirm their ownership, which they did. So too did they testify about the workman who had lost his life. Then other witnesses were called to describe the plague of demons that had infested that part of the city. After that the court called upon the demons to testify, from behind the partition, and they told their side of the story: "Our father, the goldsmith, made a vow, and bequeathed the cellar to us for all time. He reported this vow to Rabbi Sheftel. Rabbi Sheftel recorded this vow in his diary. You will find it entered on such-and-such a date."

When the court heard this, they sent a messenger to Rabbi Sheftel's widow. She provided the diary, and there they read the tragic story of the goldsmith and the she-demon, and about the agreement the goldsmith had made to save his soul. After that the rabbis consulted among themselves for many hours, and the demons, assembled behind the partition, were heard to rustle as they waited for the verdict.

At last Rabbi Yoel announced it: "It is true that the goldsmith left the cellar of his house to his demon offspring. But he gave them the cellar, and the cellar only. Their area of habitation was restricted to there, and did not include the rest of the house, and certainly not the other houses in the neighborhood. By transgressing beyond the boundary set for them, the demons lost the right to remain in the cellar. This, then, is the court's decision: every demon living in that cellar is hereby commanded to abandon it and to depart from our midst at once! From now on you may only dwell in the wilderness, for that shall be your home!"

When this verdict was announced, a roar like thunder rose up from behind the partition, and the synagogue began to shake. Everyone was afraid that the roof would collapse. The rabbis shouted, "Open the doors!" And when the doors were opened, a swarm of demons was seen to depart. They passed over the city like a dark cloud and were gone. And that was the last anyone heard of those demons in the city of Posen.

—Eastern Europe: seventeenth century

62. The Dead Fiancée

here once was a Hasid of the holy rabbi of Koznitz who was without children. Every few months he called upon the *Maggid* of Koznitz to pray on his behalf that God bless him with children. But the rabbi was always silent when the Hasid made this request, and never indicated if he would assist him. As the years passed and the couple remained childless, the Hasid's wife grew bitter over her lot. And when she could not bear it any longer, she cried out to her husband, "Go, now, to the holy rabbi. And don't leave his doorstep until he replies to you, for my life is empty without children." The man asked, "What if the rabbi tells me to divorce you?" And the wife answered, "We shall do whatever the rabbi tells us to do."

The man went to the rabbi once again and threw himself on his mercy. The rabbi listened, then said, "If you are willing to make a great sacrifice, to go on a long journey that will leave you impoverished, you may yet succeed in having a child." The Hasid saw that the prospect was a difficult one, but he was willing to undertake it. He told the rabbi, however, that he must first consult with his wife. And when his wife heard the rabbi's words, she said, "Wealth means nothing if there is no one to remember me. Therefore do as the rabbi says, and perhaps God will have mercy on us after all."

The man returned to the rabbi and was told, "Go home, sell all of your possessions, and take the gold with you. Do not keep anything, or your journey will be in vain. Your wife will have to find a way to sustain herself while you are gone. Then go to the Seer of Lublin, and tell him that I have sent you. Tell him what you are seeking, and then do exactly what he tells you to do, nothing more or less."

So the man journeyed from Koznitz to Lublin and sought an audience with the Seer of Lublin. But the rabbi was unable to see him for the first week, nor did he call him in for an audience during the second long week of waiting. Meanwhile, the cost to the man was considerable, for he had to pay an inn for his room and board. Still, he dared not repeat his request, for fear of provoking the rabbi's wrath. So he continued to wait even though other petitioners were often called in soon after their arrival. And at the end of the third week, just as the man was beginning to give up hope, the audience took place.

When the man came into the presence of the rabbi, he saw that the holy man was immersed in study. Naturally the man did not interrupt, but waited for a signal to speak. The rabbi continued to read, however, and did not lift his eyes from the page. At last, after a very long silence, the rabbi said, "In your youth you were betrothed for four years to a young woman,

Miriam Shifra, but when you came of age you broke this engagement on your own, without even informing her or her parents. She continued to wait for you until the news finally reached her that you had already been wed to another. This caused her great grief, and her father did not find another for her to wed. Now her hour of joy has passed, and you are to blame. Go to her and seek her forgiveness. For only if she forgives you will a soul from on high be set free to become your child."

The Hasid was staggered, for he had not even said why he had come, and yet the rabbi knew things about him that the man had never spoken of to anyone. And he realized that this must indeed be the reason he had remained childless, and he said, "Rabbi, I cannot imagine how you know this, but it is true, although I have put it out of my mind for many years. I had even forgotten the name of the woman. But now I will do exactly as you say." And the Seer said, "In two months' time there will be a bazaar in the town of Balta, where she can be found. Go there, and don't leave until you have spoken with her."

So the man set out for Balta, and along the way he sought information about her everywhere he went, in hope that he might find her before he reached that town. But all his effort came to naught, as no one had ever heard of her. So he continued his journey until he reached Balta, where he took up residence in an inn. Each day he walked through the streets asking about her, but to no avail. And in the evening he returned to the room and spent the night praying to fulfill his quest. That is how the days passed until the time arrived for the great bazaar. Crowds of people jammed the streets, and the man went everywhere among them, asking if they had heard of Miriam Shifra. But no one knew anything at all. The Hasid's frustration was very great, and many times he thought of leaving that town and returning home in defeat. And he stayed only because the Seer had told him not to leave until he had found her.

When the bazaar was about to end, and the merchants were all packing their goods, the Hasid realized that if he did not learn anything that day, there would be no point in remaining any longer. So he stood by the gate of the town, speaking to everyone who came or went, but to no avail. In the evening a cold rain began to fall, and the few remaining merchants quickly packed up and set out to find shelter. Soon the streets were almost completely empty, and the Hasid had a sense of despair far greater than anything he had ever known.

The cold rain had begun to chill him, and he sought refuge under the eaves of a store. But the owner told him to leave, and once more he found himself out in the rain. Looking around he saw two women taking shelter near a house, and he went there. When he reached the house he saw that one of the women was very beautiful, exceptionally so. She was dressed in embroidered silk and wore many jewels. He was astonished to see such a wealthy woman standing outside in the rain, but he assumed that she had been caught there when it had started. In any case, the Hasid stepped away from her, to keep his proper distance.

When the woman saw this, an ironic smile crossed her lips. She turned to her servant and said, "Do you see that man standing there? He betrayed me when I was young, and now he's trying to escape from me again." When the Hasid overheard these words, he was staggered. Was it possible? Meekly he approached the woman and said, "What do you mean? Is it true that I was once engaged to you?" The woman replied, "Are you still pretending that it is not so? That is how you have acted all these years, leaving me forgotten like one of the dead. Tell me, do you at least recall my name?" And the Hasid spoke in a whisper, "Are you Miriam Shifra?" And when the woman nodded, the Hasid broke into sobs. When he found his voice, he said, "I have come here to seek you out. You have every right to despise me, and it is too late for me to right the matter, but I hope it is not too late for you to forgive me. For I have come seeking your forgiveness, so that my wife and I may have children of our own. The Seer of Lublin told me that until you do, we will never know the blessing of a child. Now I beg you to forgive my sin, if you can, and I would do anything to repay you."

The woman stared hard at him and saw that his repentance was true. And she said, "There is nothing I need that you could give me. But I have a very poor brother, a scholar of the Torah, who lives in the town of Sublack. His daughter is of the age to be wed, but my brother does not have enough to pay for the dowry and the wedding. Therefore go to him and give him three hundred silver coins. And tell him that you are giving it in my honor and at my request. When the deed is done, I will forgive you with all my heart. Then, I am certain, God will bless you with children and grandchildren, all of whom will have a love of the Torah."

As the Hasid heard these words, a great weight was lifted from him. Then the woman said that she had to go, stepped out into the street, and went around the corner. But when the Hasid hurried after her, she had disappeared. Then, in a state of shock and relief, he made his way back to the inn where he was staying, and in the morning he set out for the town of Sublack.

When the Hasid located her brother, he found him very distracted. The Hasid asked him what was wrong, and the man said, "My daughter was engaged to the son of a master here in Sublack, and I promised a dowry of three hundred silver pieces, but I have not been able to save that much. Now I have received a letter saying that they will cancel the wedding if they do not receive the money in three days. So my daughter is sitting and crying and can't be comforted, and my soul is bitter because there is nothing I can do." And when the Hasid heard this, his heart leaped, because he had exactly three hundred silver pieces left of all that he had brought with him. He did not hesitate, but took out his money pouch, handed it to the man, and said, "Here, take this, and may the wedding be a great joy to everyone." And when the man saw that it was exactly the amount he needed, he was overwhelmed.

"Why are you helping me like this? I have never heard of such generosity."

Then the Hasid said, "I am a messenger from your sister, Miriam Shifra. She directed me to give these coins to you for your daughter's dowry." A very strange look came over the man's face, and he said, "Where did you see my sister? When did she tell you that?" The Hasid replied, "I saw her in the marketplace in Balta about three weeks ago." Then the man shouted, "My sister has been dead for ten years! Come with me and I will show you her grave!" And when the Hasid heard this, a chill ran down his spine, for he realized that the woman he had met in Balta was not one of the living. When he stopped trembling he related everything that had happened and how the sister had promised to forgive him if he paid the dowry. And when the man heard this, he realized that his sister must indeed have come back from the beyond to help him, and he too turned pale. The two of them sat in silence for a long time, contemplating the miracle that had taken place. At last the man said, "Please, describe the woman you met, so I'll know if she resembled my sister." Then the Hasid described her great beauty and the way she was dressed. When the man heard this description, he broke into tears and left the room. And when he returned, he carried with him the very same dress that the woman had worn. He said, "This was my sister's favorite dress. After her death it came into the possession of my wife, but she has never worn it, in honor of my sister, whom she loved very much." The Hasid stood up and took the dress in his hands, and when he did, he felt that it was still slightly damp, as if it had been exposed to the rain. And in that moment he heard a distant voice whisper, "All is forgiven," but when he looked to see who had spoken, there was no one there. The Hasid felt the tears well up within him, and he began to cry like an infant, shamelessly and without restraint. And the man also broke into tears, for he too had heard the whispered words, and he had recognized the voice that had spoken—that of his sister.

After that the Hasid remained as the man's honored guest and was present at the daughter's wedding and shared in its joy. When he left that town, he first returned to Lublin, to tell the Seer all that had happened. But when he arrived he found that the Seer already knew. And the Seer said, "The gates of repentance are open to all. Nor must the gates of forgiveness be closed to those who would truly repent." The Hasid asked for a blessing, so that he and his wife might be fruitful and multiply. The Seer gave him a great blessing, that his lineage might live through many generations and that all of his children would have a great love of the Torah. And that is exactly what came to pass.

—Eastern Europe: nineteenth century

63. The Demon Princess

ong ago there was a wealthy merchant who had only one son, and he saw to it that his son was well instructed in the Torah. Years passed and his son grew older and married, and when the merchant lay on his deathbed he called his son to him and said: "Know that I possess great riches, and I am leaving all of it to you—on one condition, that you swear never to sail across the sea. For I have made my fortune through sea voyages, and I know all too well the dangers lurking at sea. Therefore, if you should break the vow, then I bequeath everything to heaven." Then the son solemnly swore that he would never undertake a sea voyage, and shortly after that his father passed away from the world.

A year or two later a ship reached the harbor of that town, loaded with gold, silver, and many precious gems. When the men of that ship had disembarked, they tried to seek out the rich merchant, and when they discovered he had died, they came to his son instead. They told him of the ship's arrival and that all of its treasures had belonged to his father, who had entrusted it to them. And now that he had died, it belonged to his son. So it was that the happy man went with them to the ship, and carried back many loads of riches to his home. And afterward he had a great feast for the sailors, and thanked them many times for their honesty, for less scrupulous men might have kept the treasures for themselves. And while they feasted, one of the men asked him, "What did your father tell you about his properties beyond the sea?" And the man replied that his father had said nothing about them, and furthermore had made him vow never to set foot in a ship.

Then the man said, "Know that your father's holding over the sea are immense, ten times as much as the cargo we brought with us. If your father had forgotten about them when he had you take that vow, it would be null and void. In that case, you could accompany us across the sea to recover the properties that are rightfully yours."

Now at first the merchant's son resisted their entreaties, but eventually he decided it made no sense to abandon such riches, and in the end he accompanied the sailors, and set sail on a voyage across the sea. And the Holy One, angered at the breaking of an oath, raised a great storm, causing the ship to founder and sink. All the sailors who had convinced the merchant's son to accompany them were drowned. As for the young man who had broken the vow, he was cast up upon a desert island at the end of the world. There he found himself naked and barely alive, and he knew that he had roused the wrath of the Lord.

In his great exhaustion the man fell into a deep sleep, and when he finally woke up he realized that he was very hungry and thirsty, so he set out to explore the island on which he had been exiled. After wandering for a day he reached an immense tree, whose boughs hung over the sea, and he wondered who might have planted it. He climbed into the boughs of that tree and kept warm by wrapping himself in its leaves.

Around midnight the man was suddenly awakened by a great roaring, and he discovered, to his horror, a lion prowling at the bottom of the tree. And when the lion roared again, the man began to panic and climbed higher into the branches of the tree, until he was out of reach of the lion. But there he suddenly found himself confronted with a mighty bird, resembling a giant hawk. When the bird saw him, it opened its mouth and tried to swallow him, and the man saved himself by quickly mounting on its back, and clinging to the feathers around its neck. Then the bird, startled to have this strange being on its back, immediately flapped its wings and took flight, hoping to shake the rider off into the sea.

Thus the terrified man found himself flying on the back of a giant bird, with nothing but the sea beneath him. And as he clung to that bird's crown of feathers, he prayed to God to deliver him in his hour of peril. The bird continued to fly all day, and toward evening they reached land, and passed over a kingdom. Looking down, the man could see that houses had been built there. And as the bird flew low over the land, the man threw himself from its back and went tumbling to the ground. There he lay hurt and bruised by the fall, and he shivered with cold all night. And by dawn he was very faint, since he had not eaten for more than two days. Still he raised himself and began to walk until he reached a town, and there he found a synagogue, and when he saw it, he wept with joy, for he knew that he had found Jews, who might take pity on him and help him to return to his home.

Entering the synagogue he found only the *shammash*, and told him his tale. And the man was very shocked when the *shammash* said: "I am sorry to tell you that all the trials you have suffered so far will be as nothing compared to those which await you in this land." Now the man could not understand this at all, for Jews are commanded by the Torah to be merciful, and he asked the *shammash* to explain what he meant. Then the *shammash* said: "The country you have reached is not a land of men, but the kingdom of demons, which is ruled by Ashmodai, king of demons. And when it is discovered that a man of flesh and blood has come here, your life will be as good as lost. For humans are not permitted to set foot in this kingdom." And when the man heard that he had reached the land of demons, he began to tremble and almost fainted. Then he fell at the feet of the *shammash*, and pleaded with him to help him escape. And the *shammash*, who was a pious demon, took pity on him, and placed him under his protection.

Soon afterward other demons began to arrive for the morning services, and before long one of them suddenly cried out, "I smell the smell of a human!" and all the others agreed, and they soon discovered the man among them. But then the *shammash* spoke up and said, "You must not harm this man, for he is under my protection." And because of their respect for the *shammash,* they agreed not to harm him, but they wanted to know how he had reached their kingdom, so remote from all human habitation.

Then the merchant's son told them his sad tale, without omitting anything that had happened. And when the demons learned that he had broken the vow he had made to his dying father, they were filled with wrath and said: "How can we permit one who has broken a holy oath to remain among us? For the penalty for this transgression is death!" But the *shammash* replied: "He cannot be killed until he has been brought before our king to decide his fate." And the others said: "Well spoken." So it was agreed to leave his fate in the hands of their king, Ashmodai.

Now it had been a long time since any other human being had been in that kingdom, and Ashmodai invited him to spend the night in his palace until he had reached a decision. There Ashmodai spoke with the man and asked him if he had studied Torah, and when he discovered that he was well versed in all the sacred texts, Ashmodai said, "Because you are a scholar, you have found grace in my eyes, and I will spare your life. For the Holy One has already seen to it that you have been well punished for the sin of breaking the vow. And if you will swear to me that you will teach my son all you know, you may remain in the safety of my palace." Now the man was very grateful and relieved to hear this, and he swore to that effect. So it was that Ashmodai took him into his palace, presented him to his son, and treated him with the reverence due to a teacher.

Three years passed, during which the man diligently taught Torah to the son of the king of demons. Then it happened that Ashmodai had to go off to war, and before he left he put the man in charge of the palace, for he had grown to trust and respect him. Ashmodai gave him the keys to all of his treasuries, and ordered the servants to obey him. Then Ashmodai said: "Now you have the keys to every room in this palace except one, and you are permitted to enter every room except that one." And after that Ashmodai went off to war.

In the days that followed the man took charge of the palace. One day he happened to pass the room Ashmodai had forbidden him to enter, and he wondered what might be in there. So he went to the door and peered through the keyhole, and there he saw the Ashmodai's daughter seated on a golden throne, with servant girls dancing and playing around her. And when the man saw her great beauty, he could not tear his eyes away from her, and at last he decided to enter there. So he tried to open the door, and discovered that it was unlocked. But no sooner did he enter than the daughter of Ashmodai pointed to him and said: "O foolish man, why have you disobeyed the command of my father? For no man is permitted to see my unveiled face. My father is already aware of your transgression, for he sees everything that takes place in his magic mirror, and he will soon arrive to punish you!" And when the man heard this, he threw himself at the feet of the demon princess and implored her to save him from her father's anger. And the princess took pity on him and said: "When my father arrives, tell him that you entered here because of your love for me, and say that you want us to be married. I know that this will please him, because he has often mentioned that you and I should be wed, since you are such a learned man." And the man thanked her with all his heart for this advice.

Before long the enraged king of demons returned to the palace and demanded to know why the man had disobeyed him and entered his daughter's chamber. Then the man said what the princess had told him to say. And when Ashmodai heard this reason, his anger vanished, and he said, "I shall gladly give you my daughter for your wife." Then he commanded that a festive wedding be prepared, and he invited all the demons who inhabited that kingdom. So too was a marriage contract written, and the man received as the dowry innumerable treasures, which made his wealth second only to that of Ashmodai himself. And after the wedding, when the man was alone with his bride, he promised her that he would love her always and never forsake her. The demon princess had him swear to this, and write down the oath, which he did, and give it to her for safekeeping.

Before a year was out the demon princess gave birth to their child, a boy they circumcised on the eighth day and named Solomon. One day, as the man sat playing with his child, he suddenly sighed deeply. "Why do you sigh?" she asked. He replied: "For the wife and children I left so far behind in my native land." Now the demon princess was deeply hurt when she heard this, and she said: "Is there anything you want for? Am I not beautiful in your eyes? Are there any riches or honors you long for? Tell me, and I will fulfill your wish." Then the man said: "There is nothing that I lack. It is just that when I hold my son Solomon, I am reminded of my other children."

So it was that more and more often the daughter of Ashmodai found her husband sighing for the family he had lost. At last she decided to let him return to them for a while, for otherwise he would never be satisfied. So she said to him, "I will grant you one year to spend with your family. All I ask is that you take an oath to return to me at that time, and put it in writing." The man was exceedingly grateful for this opportunity, and he made the vow and set it down in writing. Then the demon princess commanded one of her servants to fly the man to his country, for demons have wings, and they can travel great distances in the wink of an eye. So too did she command the demon to accompany him while he was there. And the servant demon swept up the man in his arms, and in a flash they stood before the door of his home in his long-lost country. There the man had a joyous reunion with his family, who had given him up for dead.

Now as soon as the servant demon had arrived in that country, he took on human form, and appeared to be as normal as any man. When the man saw that this change had taken place, he decided not to inform his family of the demon's true identity, for fear that it might frighten them. So too did he decide not to reveal the fact that he had married the daughter of Ashmodai, king of demons. He preferred to regard his trials and tribulations as a bad nightmare, which at last had finally come to an end.

But the servant of the demon princess took up residence in the Jewish section of that town in order to keep an eye on him, and to ensure his return at the end of the year. And each time the merchant's son encountered him, in the marketplace or in the synagogue, he would be reminded of his vows. One day when the man could not bear it any longer, he went up to the demon and said, "You are wasting your time here. I will never return with you to the land of demons." The demon said: "And what of the marriage vows you have made, and the oath that you would return to your wife at the end of the year?" "Those vows were forced on me, and I only made them to save my life. Therefore they are null and void, according to the law." When the demon realized that the man was not about to change his mind, he departed from that town and returned to the kingdom of demons. There he informed the demon princess of her husband's intentions. But the daughter of Ashmodai grew angry with the servant demon and insisted this could not be true, as the man had signed an oath. And she told the demon that they would wait until the end of the year to see if the man would keep his vow.

At the end of the year the demon princess sent for the same servant demon, and told him to go to the man and to remind him it was time to return to her. This the demon did, but when he approached the man as he was leaving the House of Study, the man shouted for him to depart at once, for he had already made it clear that he would never return with him. So the servant demon came back to the princess, and reported what the man had said. Still, the princess could not believe he would dare to break a written oath. And she went to her father, Ashmodai, and asked him what she should do. Ashmodai thought the matter over and said: "Take your son with you and go to this man, and I will send my army with you to his city. First send his son, Solomon, to ask him to return to you, and if he refuses, go to the synagogue and make your case known before the congregation. Tell them that if they do not force him to accompany you, an army of demons will demolish their town, and their lives will be lost. And when he who has betrayed you has returned, I will see to it that he is properly punished for his crime!"

So it was that the demon princess did as her father said, and traveled to the man's city with her son and an army of demons. First she waited outside the city gates and sent the boy to approach his father. The boy came to his house while the man was sleeping, and gently woke him. The man was astonished to see his demon son and embraced him and asked what he was doing there. Solomon told him that he had come there accompanied by his mother and an army of demons, so that the man would accompany them to their kingdom. When the man heard this, he grew terrified, but he still insisted he would never return. And despite all of the boy's pleading, the man could not be moved. So the sad boy took his leave and returned to his mother and told her what his father had said. After this the demon princess bid the army to wait there until she saw if she would receive justice from the town. If she did, she would spare the inhabitants, but if she did not, they would all to be killed. Then she went directly to the synagogue, and she arrived there just as services were about to begin. She walked up to the pulpit, and stood before the congregation, and told them who she was and why she had come there. She showed them her wedding contract and the written vow the man had made that he would return to her at the end of a year. And she bid that a Beit Din, a rabbinic court, be called together, to determine if the man should be forced to return with her or not.

Now when the documents were examined and found to be valid, it was realized that a Beit Din must be convened to settle the matter. This was done, and the demon princess entered first, and when she faced the court she said: "This man came to be in our land because he broke the oath he made to his father. My father, the king, showed him great favor and saved him from those who were determined to take his life. I have also saved him from certain death, at the hands of my father, whose command this man disobeyed. And after this my father gave me to him as a wife, and made him a prince and commander over his armies. So it was that this man married me according to the laws of Moses, and this boy, Solomon, is our child. And when he wished to return to his family for a visit, I permitted him to go, and he vowed never to forsake me. Here are all the documents that prove what I have said to be true. And now this man wants to repay good with evil, and prefers to abandon his wife and son."

Then the judges examined the documents, and when they proved to be authentic, they turned to the man and said: "Why do you not return to her, after she has done so much for you? And how can you justify breaking a vow that you yourself have signed?"

Then the man said: "I have sworn and acted under constraint, for I feared for my life. Therefore the vows I signed are null and void. Furthermore, it is unnatural for a man to be married to a demon, and I prefer to remain with the wife of my youth."

Now after the man had said this, and it was apparent to all that he would not voluntarily accompany the demon princess to her kingdom, she spoke up and said: "All will agree that if a man wishes to divorce his wife, he must first give her a bill of divorce and return her all dowry." And the judges replied: "Yes, that is the case." Then the princess showed them that it was written in the marriage contract that in the event of divorce the man must pay her an immense amount of money, more than was possessed by any king. And when the judges saw this, they said to the man: "According to the law, you must either pay her in full or go with her."

Then the princess said: "I see that you are honest judges, who act according to the law. But since it is apparent to all that this man refuses to accompany me, I hereby renounce the right of compelling him to return by force. Instead, if you will ask him to give me one last kiss, I will depart from him and return to my home."

Then the judges said to him: "Do as she asks, and give her one last kiss, and then you will be free from all obligations toward her." So the man went and kissed her, hoping to be free of her at last, but instead she kissed him with the kiss of death, and snatched away all of his breath, so that his lifeless body slumped to the floor. Then the demon princess turned to the judges and said: "This is the reward of one who transgressed the will of his father and broke an oath. Now if you all do not wish to die, take my son Solomon and raise him in the laws of God and when he is grown, marry him to the daughter of the greatest among you, and make him chief among you. For I do not wish to remain with the son of such a husband, who will always remind me of him. I shall leave him riches enough that nothing will be wanting, and you shall also give him half of his father's property."

Then the congregation vowed to do as she told them, and they promised that when the boy Solomon had grown they would proclaim him their chief. After this the demon princess departed and returned to her kingdom, taking her father's army with her. And never again did she return to the land of men, but remained in the kingdom of demons ruled by her father, Ashmodai, where she lives to this very day.

—North Africa: thirteenth century

64. The Speaking Head

n the city of Prague there once was a wealthy merchant whose young son possessed knowledge and wisdom far in advance of his years. When the merchant discovered his son's remarkable gifts, he hired the finest teacher in Prague to serve as his exclusive tutor. And in the hands of this rabbi the natural gifts of the boy, whose name was Mordecai, flourished, so that by the time he was twelve he was permitted to partake in discussions with some of the most learned rabbis in Prague.

Now young Mordecai's father intended that his son be wed to a maiden from one of the finest families. Therefore he announced that no offers would be considered unless they included a dowry so large that only a few of the wealthiest men in Prague could afford to pay it, and of these none had a daughter of marriageable age.

When Mordecai was in his twelfth year his father began to do business with a rich merchant from another country, who always purchased vast amounts of goods from him. While in Prague this merchant stayed at the home of Mordecai's father, and they enjoyed each other's company. At last a day came when the merchant sought to make a match between his only daughter and young Mordecai. And that was the first time that anyone had agreed to provide the huge dowry Mordecai's father had required.

This situation created a dilemma for Mordecai's father. After all, the merchant was one of the richest men in the world, and anyone marrying his daughter would one day inherit immense wealth. But on the other hand, the father was very reluctant to have his son depart from Prague, especially to such a distant land. Therefore he went to the rabbi who served as his son's tutor and discussed the matter with him. The rabbi agreed that such a match would surely be for the boy's benefit, although he would be very sad to see him depart from Prague, for he had never known such a fine student.

At last Mordecai's father told his son of the plans that were being made for him. Now Mordecai knew that his father would take great care in making a match, and even though he was reluctant to leave home, he agreed to accept his father's decision. Shortly afterward, however, Mordecai began to have a disturbing dream in which an old man, whose hair and beard were white, gave him dire warnings. But when he awoke he could not remember what the old man had said. At first Mordecai did not pay much attention to the dream, but when it kept recurring, he finally told his father about it. But his father did not consider dreams to be very important and thought that they merely revealed that his son was afraid to take leave of his family.

So it was that the match was made and the engagement contract written. And when the time came for the wealthy merchant to leave Prague and return to his land, he entreated Mordecai's father to permit him to take Mordecai along with him, to be introduced to the bride and the rest of the family. This Mordecai's father was very reluctant to do. But when the merchant continued to implore him, Mordecai's father finally gave his consent, with the understanding that Mordecai would return to Prague in time for his Bar Mitzvah.

Soon the day came for Mordecai to set out on the long journey with the wealthy merchant. During the trip the merchant continued to treat Mordecai with great deference and respect. At last they reached the foreign land where the merchant lived. He brought Mordecai to a magnificent castle, with a high tower, which he said was his home. The merchant showed Mordecai around the castle, where every room seemed to be more splendid than the last. But Mordecai was very surprised not to see anyone else, not even a single servant. Nor did he meet the merchant's wife or his intended bride.

For the first few weeks Mordecai said nothing about this, for he was a very respectful young man. He had looked forward to studying Torah with the scholars of that town, but the doors of that the castle were locked, so that no one could enter or leave. So too did he explore every room of the castle, all of which were open, except for one room at the very top of the tower, which was locked. Mordecai wondered about this, but did not ask the merchant about it. Often he wished he had but a single text to study, so the passing of time would not be so oppressive. But, as far as he had seen, the castle was entirely barren of books. And each day he was alone except at meals, when he was joined by the merchant. Once Mordecai asked him who prepared the elaborate meals, and the merchant replied that he did so himself.

At last, however, when several months had passed, and Mordecai had not seen a single soul except for his host, he finally could not restrain himself and asked to know why he had not yet met anyone else. The merchant told him that his wife and daughter had left on a journey of their own, with all of their servants, and would be back before too long. This pacified the young man for a few weeks, but when he continued to spend day after day in the prison of that castle, he became worried. To relieve himself he wrote letters to his father, in which he confessed his confusion at the strange turn of events. He sealed these letters and gave them to the host, who promised they would be delivered. Meanwhile, he continued to await the first letter from his family, for in all that time he had not received a single one.

Meanwhile, back in Prague, months had also passed without the arrival of a single letter from Mordecai, and his family's anxiety grew until it became distress, and the distress grew until it became grief. At last Mordecai's father came to the conclusion that he had made a terrible error, and the heartbroken father became so distraught he was unable to work. He went to Mordecai's teacher, and in his grief he accused him of having misled him into agreeing to the match. So too did the father recall, now that it was too late, Mordecai's terrible dreams, and he berated himself every hour of every day for not paying more attention to them.

At last Mordecai's father sent a caravan to seek out Mordecai in the city where the wealthy merchant had said he made his home. But imagine the father's horror when the caravan returned with the news that no merchant of that name lived in that city or had ever been heard of there! As the planned time for Mordecai's Bar Mitzvah grew near, his father's grief grew even greater, and he cried out to Heaven ceaselessly to redeem him from his error, fasting and weeping from Sabbath to Sabbath. And still there was no word from Mordecai.

Now when the evil merchant saw how Mordecai was becoming restless, he began to worry the boy might try to escape. For Mordecai was well aware that the time of his Bar Mitzvah was at hand, and he knew as well that they should have set out to return more than a month before.

That very day the merchant joined the boy for a walk through the castle, which was immense. There were doorways everywhere and a multitude of passages. Just to be on the safe side, the merchant had seen to it that every room in the palace was locked, except for one, where he planned to trap the boy. Mordecai noticed that all of the doors, which were usually open, had been shut. He sensed danger, but he feared that if he let the merchant know of his suspicions, the danger would become imminent. Instead he remained alert at all times and watched for a way to escape.

The merchant led Mordecai up the tower stairs, acting unusually kind and friendly, and telling the boy that he wanted to show him the library, which was the one room that Mordecai had never entered, for it had always been locked. Now Mordecai was hungry for study and learning, and he let himself be swayed by the thought of reading once again. If only he were back in Prague, in the home of his beloved father, studying Talmud with his teacher!

When Mordecai entered that tower, he was astonished at how many dark bound books had been crowded together in one place. So many books! Not even in the great libraries of Prague had he seen such a collection. And as Mordecai peered in amazement at the books assembled there, he had the strange feeling that he had been in that dark, high-ceilinged room before, even though he knew that to be impossible. Surrounded by that sea of books, Mordecai did not notice the evil merchant slip out of the room and lock the door behind him. By the time Mordecai realized he had been trapped there, it was too late. All that he had feared most had come to pass, or so he thought.

In despair, Mordecai drifted back to the bookcase, and randomly took down a book, which he saw was a kabbalistic text. Mordecai opened it and began to read, and a moment later he was horrified to see that in the place where God's Name had been written, the Name had been blotted out. A sense of terror descended upon him. He quickly looked through all the pages and saw that this abomination had been performed on each and every holy name in that book. Swiftly Mordecai returned that book to the shelf and grabbed another one, this time a prayer book. He turned to the Shema, the prayer that he said so often to himself, to give him strength. And there too the Holy Name had been obliterated. In great confusion Mordecai began to feel his knees grow weak. He put that book back and looked around for a place to sit down.

That was when he saw the head. It was the head of an old man, his hair pure white, a look of great pain on his face. That was all there was, only a head. It rested in the center of a round table, on black velvet. When Mordecai realized that the head was missing a body, he nearly fainted. And that is when the head spoke, saying, "I see you have fallen into the same trap that I did. May God have mercy on you!"

These words, coming from the detached head, left Mordecai terrified. He cried out, "Who are you?" And the head replied, "I too was once a bright youth like yourself, with great promise. For I know who you are, Mordecai, and how proud all who have observed your learning must be. Yet know that the merchant who brought you to this place is not a man at all, but a demon, and this castle is, in fact, an illusion. And this realm is not that of men, but the kingdom in which the demons make their home. It is the Sitre Ahre you have reached, the dark side, from which it is dreadful to escape. But escape you must, for if you don't by tomorrow morning, the day of your Bar Mitzvah, your head will be severed from your body, just as mine was."

Hearing this, Mordecai began to understand that his fate was far more terrible than anything he could have imagined. And in his anguish he cried out to the speaking head, "Why have they done this terrible thing to you, and what do they want from me?" And the head replied, "These demons seek to know the ways of the future. By placing holy names beneath my tongue, they subject my soul to unbearable anguish, for these names compel me to pry into the future and reveal what I learn to them, to serve their evil cause. But I can be used thus for only eighty years, and now that the time has come to pass, the demons have sought you out to take my place!"

Mordecai shuddered. Not only would his life be lost, but his soul soiled in the worst possible way. The sin was of such magnitude he could not even bear the thought of it. But suddenly Mordecai discovered unexpected strength, a determination to outwit those malignant demons. And he begged the head to tell him if there was any way to escape. The head said, "Yes, but you must leave now. Not an instant must be lost. But the only way you will escape them and all the snares built into this palace of illusion is if you take me with you. For if you do not, they will compel me to tell them where you can be found. And my will, as you know, is not my own. No, take me with you, and I will guide you as best I can. If you succeed, all I ask is that you will bury me properly and say Kaddish, so that my soiled soul may be restored."

Mordecai vowed at once, with all his heart, that if only they escaped he would say Kaddish for him, for as long as he lived. Then the head restrained a sob and said, "But we must hurry! There is a secret compartment in this room. Quickly, go to the last bookcase in the room, and take out the center book on the top shelf."

Mordecai hurried to the bookshelf and tried to reach the book, but found that he could not. So he grabbed a chair and stood on it, and by standing on his toes he was able to pull down the center book. All at once there was a creaking, and that very instant the bookcase began to move, revealing a hidden passage. Then, for the first time since he had been locked in that room, Mordecai felt a glimmer of hope. He ran back and picked up the head, putting it under his arm, and he hurried into the passageway.

Soon after he had entered that dark place, Mordecai heard the bookcase close loudly behind him. For an instant he feared that the head had not told him the truth, but was itself an illusion of the evil demons and had lured him to that place, where he would meet a terrible end. But at that very moment the head began to speak again, in a calm, reassuring voice. The head said, "This is the top flight of a long spiral staircase. There are ten flights in all. We must reach the last flight and escape this castle before the demons find out; if not, we will become ensnared in one of their traps. So hurry!"

When Mordecai heard the voice of the speaking head, his suspicions vanished, and he reminded himself that the head offered his only hope of escape. Yet it was so dark there that Mordecai was forced to cling to the wall of the staircase, so as not to tumble down those many flights. He cried out to the head, "How do the demons find their way in this dark place?" And the head replied, "They flourish in darkness. That is why we will be much safer once we have reached the light."

These words spurred on Mordecai to hurry even more, and now that he had become familiar with the turning of the spiral staircase, he was not afraid. Each time he completed one full turn, he took note of it. They had descended seven spirals when the head suddenly cried out, "The demon has just discovered that you are missing and that you have taken me along! He is rushing off to sound the alarm."

At that instant Mordecai suddenly lost his footing and cried out. He plunged into a dark abyss and also very nearly dropped the head he held under his arm. The demons had found out in time to dissolve the remaining stairs! Mordecai realized that as long as they were falling, his fate was no longer in his own hands. And he clung to the head and began to recite the words of Shema, and the head recited the Shema with him.

While Mordecai and the speaking head were plunging through that abyss, the whole city of Prague was convulsed by grief at his absence. For the day of Mordecai's Bar Mitzvah had almost arrived, and he still had not returned; nor had any word of him been received in all that time. Of course the demon had consigned all of the boy's letters to the flames. Never before had Mordecai's father been torn by such grief, and above all he blamed himself for agreeing to let his son go.

Then, on the night before the Bar Mitzvah, Rabbi Judah Loew of Prague, known as the Maharal, had three dreams that deeply haunted him. In the first dream the Maharal found a letter nailed to his front door, like a proclamation, that stated that the life of the boy Mordecai, whose soul could bring great blessing to the Jewish people, hung in the balance, and that only the Maharal could save him. In the second dream, the Maharal heard the voice of an old man speaking, but he could not see him, nor did he know from where he spoke. The voice urged him to do all in his power to save young Mordecai, who was in mortal danger.

Then, in the third dream, the Maharal stood face to face with an old man, who said that he had returned from beyond the grave to help save his grandson, Mordecai. The old man revealed how Mordecai had fallen into the clutches of evil and was desperately trying to escape. And he told the

Maharal that somehow the Gates of Heaven had become locked, preventing prayers for the boy's well-being from reaching on high. If only the Maharal could find the way to open those gates!

It was then that the Maharal awoke, filled with apprehension. He realized that Mordecai's grandfather had come from the other world to deliver this message, and that he must do everything in his power to save the boy. Without delay the Maharal hurried to the home of Mordecai's father and revealed the miraculous dreams to him. Then Mordecai's father had his first glimmer of hope and quickly sent out messengers to all the Jews in Prague, telling them to gather in the Old Synagogue of the Maharal the next day, that of Mordecai's Bar Mitzvah, for their help was sorely needed.

The Jews of Prague turned out in great numbers, filling every seat of the Old Synagogue, and standing in the aisles as well, so that it seemed as if every Jew in the city had crowded in there. Now there were ten times as many Jews in Prague as there were seats in that great synagogue, yet there are those who insist that somehow the synagogue miraculously absorbed everyone. Then the Maharal stood before the people and told them that only if their prayers unlocked the Gates of Heaven could Mordecai's life be saved. And when they heard this, the people joined in the prayers with one voice, and they recited in full the first book of the Psalms. Among them spread the hope, still unspoken, that a miracle might occur. Yet when they had completed the first book of the Psalms, nothing happened, and somehow they knew that the Gates of Heaven were still tightly shut.

Then the Maharal asked them to recite the second book of Psalms in unison, and this they did. Somehow the Maharal perceived that the gates had begun to shudder, but were still locked. Then he directed the congregation to read with one voice the third and final book of Psalms. And this they began to do.

Meanwhile, Mordecai and the speaking head were still falling through that abyss. Mordecai asked the head why they were falling for so long, and the head replied, "Because the fate of our souls still hangs in the balance." Mordecai begged to know if there was anything they could do, and the head replied, "Don't lose faith, even for an instant. If we despair, the Other Side will devour us."

Back in the Old Synagogue, the Jews of Prague poured out their hearts and souls in the recitation of the third book of Psalms. Tears shined in every eye, and they prayed with all their might. For one and all were gripped by an intense desire to save their long-lost Mordecai, and all of them felt the grief of Mordecai's parents as if he were their very own son. As they prayed, a miracle took place—their prayers fused and ascended as one, breaking open the resistant gates. And at the instant they swung open, they heard a sudden knocking at the doors of the synagogue. The Maharal cried out, "Quickly, throw open the doors!" And when they did, they found the boy Mordecai standing there, with a strange object under his arm. For at the very instant that their prayers unlocked the gates, the endless falling came to an end, and Mordecai was miraculously restored to the place where he belonged, at the doors of that revered synagogue. It is hard to say who was more amazed to find him there, the boy or those who had prayed so hard to save him, and a thrill passed through them, one and all. Mordecai had no idea how he had gotten there, but the relief he felt was monumental, and he knew that his fate, which had hung in the balance, had somehow been redeemed.

That Bar Mitzvah was the greatest ever held in the city of Prague, and the only one where every single resident later claimed to have been present. Then Mordecai revealed all that the speaking head had done to save him from the dangers of the Other Side, and Mordecai's father saw to it that the head was buried with great honor. So too did Mordecai remember to say Kaddish as he had promised, and he never forgot how the head had helped him in his hour of direst need.

As for Mordecai himself, he had a wonderful reunion with his father and mother, who had feared for so long that they would never see him alive again. Soon afterward he became first the pupil and later the disciple of the Maharal. In time he became betrothed to the Maharal's daughter. And when Mordecai's father saw how happy they were, he knew that this had been his son's destined match from the first.

—Eastern Europe: nineteenth century

65. The Other Side

he kingdom of Satan is measure for measure like the kingdom of man. Every male child, when born, already has a double in the kingdom of demons. So too does every female, when she is born, have her shadow born there as well, in her precise shape and image, not unlike that in a mirror. For in the same hour that a heavenly voice goes forth to announce that this one will be married to that one, a partner is also prepared in the Other Side as well. There she waits for the right time, a few days before a man is to be married. And the man who is fortunate marries his partner from the family of man, but less fortunate is he who marries her demonic double. So does danger await anyone who goes down to the river alone on the fourth night of the week or on the night of the Sabbath. For he would be in danger of being kidnapped by the sons of Satan, and led to a place no man's feet should ever enter.

In one city in the Diaspora lived a pious man of great wealth who was respectful of everyone. He knew the Torah and taught it to his sons. Now two of his sons were married, but his youngest was not. This young man was a model of virtue and was very clever as well. In the entire congregation there wasn't a lad smarter than he. The rich man betrothed his son to a fine maiden, and the happiness in both houses was very great.

One day not long after his engagement, the young man went alone to the river to wash, and he was very happy, for the time of his marriage was near. It was the fourth night of the week, and no one else was to be seen on the shore or in the water. The young man did not wonder about this, but got undressed and jumped into the river to swim. Later, as he returned to shore, he saw another young man also emerging from the water. They greeted each other and as they got dressed, they conversed. The young man didn't recognize the other, but he seemed likeable enough. As they were walking back in the same direction, they discussed matters of the Torah, and the young man failed to notice that they took an unfamiliar path. All of a sudden he found himself standing before an immense mansion. A great many lights shone from within. The young man was astonished, for he had never seen it before. Just then the door of the mansion opened, and an old man of great bearing came forth, who greeted both of them and said, "Come in and rest a little before you continue on your way." They agreed to come in, and he led them to a palatial chamber, where the walls and the chairs were made of ivory.

The old man spoke with gentleness and charm, and welcomed the young men to his home. And while they were speaking, they heard the lovely voice of a girl singing from another room. Never in his life had the young man heard a voice so enchanting. After half an hour the door opened, and the maiden who had been singing came to serve them wine and pastries. She carried these on a golden tray, which she placed on the table before them. The girl was as charming as she was beautiful, and the young man could not turn his eyes away from her.

So it was that the hours passed in delightful conversation until midnight, when the young man got up to leave. The old man rose and said, "I'm sorry. I didn't realize it had gotten this late. Why don't you stay here tonight? Tomorrow I'll have my servants accompany you to your father's house. And if he is angry with you, he can come to me and I will explain." The young man promptly agreed to stay, for, if the truth be known, he was having a hard time leaving that house.

The room he gave him had walls of pure marble, and the pillows and the sheets were white as snow. All night the young man dreamed he was in the embrace of the maiden with the beautiful voice. When the sun shone into the room, pleasant feelings came into his heart, unlike any he had ever known. He got up, washed, dressed, and went into the chamber of his host. The old man welcomed him with affection and they said the morning prayers together. And afterward the old man said, "Sit down, my son," and a servant came and brought them each a drink. That morning they spoke of wisdom and Torah, and the young man thought to himself that the old man was wise indeed.

The young man stayed in that beautiful house a whole day. He ate and drank and enjoyed the company of the old man and the young man he had met at the river. The old man showed them his beautiful mansion and possessions. They went from one room to another, from one hall to another, and there was no end to the treasures the young man saw there. Time flew by, and he forgot about the house of his father.

When evening came the three of them joined together, and once again they heard the delightful voice of the girl singing. This time the young man was even more fascinated with her beautiful voice. And once again, after she had finished singing, the girl entered the hall. She brought them rare and exotic fruits and she seemed even more beautiful than the day before. The heart of the young man beat strongly, for she stood close to him, her face shining, and his spirit belonged to her.

By the third day the young man felt as if he had become a member of the family. The friend he had met at the river spoke to him when they were alone. He said, "I see that you are taken with the lovely daughter of the old man."

"Yes," said the young man, "she must be the most beautiful maiden in the world."

His friend said, "You know, the old man told me that he admired you. He said that you would make a fine husband for any young woman."

And the young man said, "Did he say that?"

"Yes," said the other. "If you'd like, I am willing to suggest that you would make a fine groom for his daughter."

And the young man said, "Why, the old man is so rich, he could marry his daughter to anyone. Why would he want her to marry me? Still, if you want to say something, go ahead." For he was deeply smitten with her.

Later that very day his newfound friend brought him the news that the maiden's father had agreed to the match. Indeed, her father had proposed that the marriage be consummated at once. The young man readily agreed to this, even though there would not be time to invite his parents. But he did not consider this; all he could think about was that he would soon be wed to that beautiful maiden. Before long servants brought him princely garments, dressed him as a bridegroom, and led him to a large hall, which stood on seventy posts. Its walls were covered with golden tiles, as in the palace of a king. Never had the young man seen anything like it. Through every doorway came guests dressed in silk and jewels. The hall was completely full, and they all stood crowded together, waiting. And soon the bride appeared with a golden crown on her head. She was wearing the jeweled gown of a princess, and the radiant splendor of her beauty illuminated the entire hall.

The bride was led to the place of the groom, and as she approached him, the young man felt as if he were about to faint. First they gave him a silver ring, with distinctive markings, and he placed the ring upon her finger. After that they told him to say, "With this ring you are consecrated to me," and he repeated the vow three times. Following that he repeated word for word whatever they asked him to say, for by now he no longer knew his own soul. As soon as the marriage was final, he heard the cheers of those assembled rising up, mixed with mocking laughter, but when he looked around all that he saw were pale shadows. He turned back to his bride, but she was no longer there. He grew dizzy, and it seemed that the doors of the room were circling around him, and suddenly he fainted.

And when he opened his eyes, he found himself lying in the mud at the edge of the river, greatly confused. Standing up, he saw that it was already very late, past midnight, and he went back home in a daze. Only with great effort did he get there. He barely managed to open the door, then collapsed in the entrance. There were screams when they found him, and the neighbors came running to see what was wrong. They poured water on him, tore off his robe, and carried him to bed, where he fell into a deep sleep.

A few hours later, when the young man opened his eyes, he found, to his horror, that he had lost the power of speech. In the days that followed, many doctors came with many remedies, but none could cure him. And in every home there was mourning over the disaster that had struck that family. And everyone was mystified, for no one knew what had happened to him.

Now there was one rabbi in that city who suspected that the forces of evil had something to do with the misfortune that had befallen that young man. Therefore every day for seven days, in the morning and in the evening, he immersed himself eighteen times, and on the seventh day, before he went to sleep, he offered up a dream question, in which he prayed to learn the truth about what had happened. And in the dream he received that night, the terrible truth was revealed to him from on high. Alarmed by what he had learned, this rabbi vowed to try to set free the young man who had become imprisoned by the sons of Satan.

So he went to the rabbinic court and revealed the secret that had been conveyed from on high, and the rabbis of the court agreed that the young man had an account to settle with the kingdom of demons. Therefore they made preparations for a trial to take place in the synagogue, and blew the shofar to announce it to the demons and commanded them to attend.

When the time set for the trial arrived, the demons sat on one side of the partition, and the humans on the other. The first witness to step forward was the rabbi who had asked the dream question. He repeated to the court all that he had learned. And he argued that the demons of the Other Side didn't have the right to deceive the young man into marrying one of their own, because he had already been betrothed. For in the eyes of the law, a betrothal is the same as a marriage.

Then the rabbis of the court asked the father of the young man to bring forth the engagement contract for his son. It clearly stated that the engagement could not be broken without the approval of both parties, and it listed as well the names of the witnesses who had been present when it was signed.

Then the rabbis called upon the demons to testify, but all they heard from the other side of the partition was a terrible din. Those assembled there found this very frightening, but the judges of the court refused to be intimidated.

At last the rabbinic court announced the verdict: the boy was freed from his vows and the false marriage was canceled. The shofar was sounded three times, and each time all the people there repeated, "You have been freed." When they had repeated this for the third time, the roof of the synagogue began to shake, and a woman's voice was heard to cry out, "Let her have him!" The rabbis called for the doors of the synagogue to be opened, and when they were, the demons took flight.

That evening the young man's father bought a fish from a passing fisherman, and when his wife cut it open she found a silver ring in its belly. When the young man was shown that ring, with its distinctive markings, he recoiled in horror. That was the very ring he had placed on the finger of his demon bride. He grabbed the ring and threw it into the fireplace, where it burst into flames and disappeared. After that the young man found he was able to speak again, and he began to recover from the terrible ordeal.

—Eastern Europe: nineteenth century

66. Yona and the River Demon

here once was a poor girl named Yona who was engaged to be married. But for years the marriage had been delayed, because the groom's family expected to receive a dowry from the bride's family. Yona's father was so poor that he could not afford to pay it. So Yona herself worked hard to save enough for the dowry, washing head coverings for the women of the village.

Now, Yona washed those kerchiefs day and night. One evening, when Yona went down to the Bosporus River, the moon was shining brightly above the waters, and the image of the moon that floated on the water seemed as real as the moon itself. Suddenly a handsome young man appeared before her. Yona wondered who he was, but she was not afraid of him, for he seemed gentle and charming.

"Why are you working so late at night?" he asked.

"I am earning money for my dowry," Yona replied.

The young man smiled. "I would like to contribute to it," he said. And he took two gold coins out of his pocket and gave them to her. Yona was very surprised by this gift. But before she could say anything, the young man turned away and disappeared into the night.

Yona put the two gold coins in the chest where she kept her dowry, and she decided to keep her meeting with the young man a secret.

The next evening, when she went back down to the river, the young man appeared again. He was more handsome than ever. He asked Yona to lift her hand, and when she did, he put a golden bracelet on her arm, saying, "You are mine and I am yours." These words astonished Yona, but before she could say anything, the young man disappeared.

Nor did he come back after that night. Days and weeks passed, but Yona never saw him again. But each night, after she returned home from the river, she found that a new gold coin had appeared in the chest of her dowry, coins identical to the ones given to her by the young man on the night they had first met. With the help of the young man, Yona succeeded in filling the chest. And the very night she completed the dowry; the handsome young man suddenly appeared at her door when Yona was alone in the house. He brought her a sack of flour and asked her to prepare a cake for him.

Yona did not know why he wanted her to do this, but she was grateful for all his gifts. So she went to work immediately, and soon the cake was ready The young man asked her to share it with him. So Yona poured glasses of wine, and they ate cake and drank together. Then the young man said goodbye and took his leave.

The next day Yona and her family carried the chest to the home of her fiancé, as was the custom at that time. It was opened as part of an elaborate ceremony led by the village rabbi. But when they opened the chest, it was completely empty. Yona screamed and fainted.

When Yona finally recovered, the village rabbi, who had known her since she was born, tried to find out what had happened. At first Yona was reluctant to say anything about the young man, but at last she revealed how she had met him at the river, and how his gifts had continued to accumulate in the chest. She also showed them the golden bracelet that he had given her on the second night, and she told them about the cake she had baked for him, which they had shared together.

When the rabbi heard this story and saw the bracelet, he sighed. "Yona, that was no human you met. It was a river demon! For they approach anyone foolish enough to go down to the river at night, and they love, above all, to trick a young girl like yourself into marrying a demon. So when the demon put that bracelet on your wrist and spoke the words "You are mine and I am yours," that was a wedding vow. And when you shared that wine and cake with him, you were celebrating your own wedding, even though you did not know it."

Yona was horrified. Was it possible that she had been wed to a demon? She began to cry, and no one could console her. As for the family of the groom, they were not sure that a wedding with their son could still take place, because it seemed as if Yona had already been wed, even if she didn't know anything about it. Besides, the dowry chest was empty.

Everyone agreed that this was clearly a matter to be decided by a court of rabbis. So the village rabbi went down to the river that night and called upon the river demon who had married the maiden Yona. Much to his amazement, the handsome young man appeared out of nowhere. The rabbi said, "Why have you deceived poor Yona in this terrible way?"

The river demon answered, "All that matters is that she is mine."

"If that is what you believe," said the rabbi, "then you must come to a court of rabbis in three days. The court will decide if your marriage is valid and binding." And the demon agreed to appear before the court, for demons are bound by the laws of God as much as any man.

On the third day, the hearing was held by the court of rabbis. Yona's father testified that she had been engaged for many years to her fiancé, long before she had ever met the demon. And the father of the groom also testified that this was true.

Then it was Yona's turn to testify. She wept the whole time as she told how she had met the young man at the river, and what had happened since. She showed the court the empty chest and described how it had been filled with gold coins. And she also took a vow that she had had no idea she was marrying a demon, for never, ever, would she do such a thing.

Then it was the turn of the river demon. He came forth, and all agreed that his presence was powerful, and that he was exceptionally handsome. And the river demon said: "Remember that Yona came to me in the first place by coming down to the river at night, for at that time the river belongs to the demons. So too did she freely accept the gifts with which we were betrothed, the gold coins and the bracelet I gave her at the time I spoke the words of the marriage vow. And that is not all. As you know, she also shared the wedding cake with me. Therefore she is my wife, and I insist on taking her back with me to the Kingdom of Demons."

Then the court of rabbis went off to decide the matter. It took them three hours to reach a decision. At last they said, "It is true that the trappings of a wedding did take place, but it is also true that it is forbidden for humans and demons to wed. Further, Yona was already engaged to someone else, and in the eyes of the law, an engagement is the same as a marriage. Finally, a person must enter into a marriage fully aware of their actions, but Yona had no idea that she was taking part in a wedding ceremony. Therefore the marriage to the demon is hereby revoked, and her marriage to her fiancé must take place by tomorrow. As for you, demon, as punishment, you must replace all the gold that disappeared from the chest of her dowry with real gold. If you do not, we will expel you to the driest desert on the face of the earth, where you will never see a river again!" When this judgment was announced, the river demon let out a shriek and vanished from their sight. But when they opened the chest, they saw it that it overflowing with gold coins—real ones that were worth a fortune.

Yona returned home with her parents that night, and as soon as she walked through the door, she took off the bracelet the demon had given her and flung it into the fireplace, where it went up in smoke. And the next day, the wedding that Yona had so longed for took place, and she and her groom had a long and happy life together, freed at last from the shadow of the river demon.

After the trial, the story of Yona was widely told, and all who heard it were forewarned not to go down to the river at night, when the river demons hold sway.

—The Balkans: oral tradition

67. The Dybbuk in the Well

ne night, after dipping in the *mikveh* outside her house, a young woman went to the well with a candle in her hand. She wanted to prepare a soup for her husband. She left the candle in a crevice near the opening of the well and lowered the bucket into the water. As she was pulling it up, the candle blew out and she was suddenly gripped by a powerful force and dragged halfway into the well. She pulled back with all her might and then she was lifted up into the air, screaming, and in that moment of terror, she fainted. Hearing her cries, her husband ran outside and found her lying in a faint next to the well. He picked her up and carried her inside and sent his brother to bring the doctor at once.

When the doctor arrived he found the woman lying in bed with her eyes closed and her mouth open, like a body without a soul. When at last she opened her eyes and tried to speak, a strange voice came forth from her. This was not her voice, but that of a man, and they realized, to their horror, that she had been possessed by a dybbuk. The doctor told her husband there was nothing more he could do for her—she needed the help of a rabbi. And the doctor himself went to alert the rabbi about this terrible turn of events.

When the rabbi arrived, he saw at once that the woman had indeed been possessed by a dybbuk. She lay on her bed helpless, with a dazed look in her eyes, while a man's voice spoke through her. The voice that came forth spoke in Italian, as did all of those present. The rabbi commanded the dybbuk to respond to his questions and asked to know his name. The dybbuk said, "My name was Yoseph ben Samuel, from Sicily."

"What were your crimes?" the rabbi asked.

And the dybbuk replied, "I was a great sinner, who was hung for my crimes."

"And did you repent before you died?"

"No, I refused to repent," the dybbuk confessed, "and I died with a curse on my lips. That is why my punishment is so terrible." Then the dybbuk began to sob, and the rabbi consoled him until he was calm enough to reply to the rabbi's questions.

The rabbi asked, "What has happened to you since your death?"

The voice of the dybbuk replied, "As soon as my spirit rose from my grave, I was confronted with avenging angels, with fiery whips, who chased after me. To escape them, I fled like the wind, and tried to hide wherever I could—in flowers, trees, and even in a stone. But whenever I emerged from my hiding place, the avenging angels were waiting. So too did I enter the body of many animals—a sheep, a goat, and, finally, a dog. But in each case the animal went mad the instant I entered it, and ran wildly until it dropped dead."

The rabbi asked, "How did you take possession of this woman?"

The dybbuk replied, "I was hiding at the bottom of the well when the woman came to draw water. I could tell she was full of lustful thoughts about her husband, and that made her vulnerable to me. I slipped into the bucket she lowered, and when she pulled it up, I entered her."

The rabbi asked the dybbuk how he had entered the woman, and the dybbuk replied, "From that place." Everyone who had gathered there was horrified to hear this, and they sobbed at her fate. Then the rabbi asked the dybbuk where he was situated in the body of the woman, and voice replied, "Between the ribs and the hips on the left side."

Then the rabbi ordered the spirit to leave the woman, and the dybbuk said, "I can't!"

"Why not?" the rabbi demanded to know.

The dybbuk replied: "Because this room is filled with avenging angels! The instant I leave her, they will punish me without mercy." The rabbi and the woman's family looked around and saw nothing, but they understood that those implacable angels must indeed be present in that place.

Then the rabbi said, "Know, dybbuk, that I call upon the avenging angels to make your punishment a thousand times worse if you remain in this woman any longer! But if you do as I command, in the name of God, I call upon the angels to show mercy toward you. Now depart from her at once!" At that instant the body of the woman shook uncontrollably, and her hips rose as if she were giving birth, and a wrenching scream came forth in her own voice, and the dybbuk was gone. An instant later everyone heard the cries of the dybbuk as the avenging angels chased after him with their fiery whips. And that is how a dybbuk was expelled in the city of Ferrara.

—Italy: sixteenth century

68. The Golem

During the reign of the Emperor Rudolf, a wonder-working rabbi lived in Prague whose name was Rabbi Judah Loew. He had been tutored in these mysteries by Rabbi Adam, whose mastery was unsurpassed. Nor did Rabbi Adam withhold anything from his disciple, and thus Rabbi Loew served as the tzaddik of his generation, as Rabbi Adam had in the generation before him.

One year it happened in the spring that Rabbi Loew had a long and vivid dream, in which he found himself in the Christian quarter of Prague, outside the Jewish ghetto. There he witnessed a terrible crime, in which a child was murdered and thrown in a sack, then carried to the Jewish section of the city, and left inside one of the houses there. In the dream Rabbi Loew saw the face of the murderer; it was the face of the evil sorcerer Thaddeus, a great enemy of the Jews who spent his days plotting ways to harm them. And Rabbi Loew understood that Thaddeus was plotting to accuse the Jews of a blood libel. This terrible accusation, the claim that Jews use blood in order to make matzah for Passover, was a terrible lie. Never had such a thing been done. But the libel had been made in almost every generation, and now the evil priest was planning to accuse the Jews of this falsehood again.

In the dream Rabbi Loew found himself helpless to do anything when he suddenly heard the sound of beating wings and looked up and saw a flock of birds flying in formation, spelling a word that he read clearly in the heavens. It was God's most sacred Name, which holds the power at the source of all being. And in the dream Rabbi Loew wrote that Name down on a piece of paper, and slipped it into the pages of the Bible he was carrying in his hand. No sooner had he done this, than he looked down at his feet, and suddenly saw the outline of a large body in the earth. Before his eyes the features of the body began to take form, and the word *Emet*, which means Truth, appeared on its forehead. Just as the eyes of the man of clay opened, Rabbi Loew awoke, the dream still vivid in his memory.

Now the rabbi recognized from the first that he must decipher this dream. For the Name of God was the most sacred word of all, and its appearance in a dream must portend matters of grave importance. He realized that it could have no other meaning than to warn him that Thaddeus was about to accuse the Jews of Prague of the blood libel, which would doubtless unleash a terrible pogrom against them. Thus the dream had come as an urgent warning, but surely it also contained the method by which the plot of the evil Thaddeus could be foiled. But what way was this? Rabbi Loew was uncertain.

Rabbi Loew decided to consult the Torah. He opened the Torah, and when he did, the first thing he saw was a slip of paper with God's Name on it—the very one he had written in his dream! He picked it up in his hand and marveled that it had come to him from the world of dreams. Rabbi Loew thought again of his dream, and of the outline of a man he had seen just before he woke up. Suddenly he had understood that his task was to bring that man into this world. But how could this be done? Surely God would guide him, and make it possible for him to bring that man into being.

There was no time to be lost. Rabbi Loew decided to undertake this mission that very night. Rabbi Loew hurried and awoke his son-in-law, Isaac ben Samson Ha-Cohen, and his foremost pupil, Jacob ben Hayim-Sassoon Ha-Levi, and told them to get dressed and to come with him at once. They wondered greatly what urgent matter had arisen, but dared not ask, knowing that the rabbi would tell them when he was ready. And in fact he said nothing at all, but led them through the darkness to the banks of the river Moldau. There Rabbi Loew told his helpers to dig out enough clay to equal the weight of the three of them. This they did, and Rabbi Loew began at once to shape that formless mass into a clay man of immense size. The others watched, astonished, as Rabbi Loew created its features, then added the word *Emet*—Truth—to its forehead, just as he had seen in the dream. Then Rabbi Loew took the slip of paper on which he had written God's Name in his dream, and he put it inside the mouth of the man of clay. He then stood up and walked around the man of clay seven times in one direction, and seven times in the other. As he did, the body of the clay man began to glow, and Isaac and Jacob could barely believe their eyes. After Rabbi Loew completed the seventh circle, he pronounced God's Name, which he, alone in his generation, knew. At that instant the clay man opened his eyes and sat up and nodded to Rabbi Loew. That is when Rabbi Loew realized that he was mute.

Then Rabbi Loew told Isaac and Jacob that the man they had created was a Golem, who would protect them from the evil sorcerer Thaddeus. They were to call him Joseph. Then Rabbi Loew took out the clothes he had brought with him, and a large pair of shoes and gave them to the Golem. The Golem dressed himself, and then joined them as they walked back to town. And Isaac and Jacob marveled that three of them had set out that night, and now four of them were returning!

Rabbi Loew presented the Golem to everyone as a new servant who would be living with them. When they were alone, Rabbi Loew told the Golem that they must set out at once to find where the evil Thaddeus had hidden the body of the child he had murdered. So Rabbi Loew and the Golem walked together through the Jewish Quarter of Prague. The Golem strode swiftly past each house, and Rabbi Loew hurried to keep up with him. At last the Golem stopped in front of a house near the gate of the ghetto, and pointed to the front door. Rabbi Loew went with him to the door and knocked. The door was opened by an old man, a pious Jew, who was very surprised to see Rabbi Loew at his door so early in the morning—and surprised, as well, at his strange companion.

Rabbi Loew hurried inside and asked the old man if there was a cellar in that house. The man said that there was, although it had not been used for many years. He showed Rabbi Loew and the Golem how to get there, and descended the steep stairway with them. At the bottom of the stairs they found the sack Rabbi Loew had seen in his dream, containing the child's body. Just then there was a loud knocking at the door, and when the old man climbed the stairs to answer it, the police demanded to be let inside. In the cellar, Rabbi Loew heard what was happening upstairs, and realized they were in terrible danger, for Thaddeus had no doubt reported the murder to the police and told them where to go. They must know as well, the Rabbi thought, to look for the body in the cellar.

Rabbi Loew turned to the Golem, who seemed to fully understand the danger. Without being told, the Golem picked up the sack with the body in it and led Rabbi Loew to a doorway in the floor of that cellar, hidden beneath a rug. They descended the stairway, closing the door behind them. It led to a dark tunnel, through which they walked for several miles. At last they arrived at another stairway, similar to the first. They climbed it, and found it led to another hidden door in another cellar. Quietly they entered, and heard loud laughter coming from above them. Rabbi Loew instantly recognized the voice of Thaddeus, who was boasting that he had fixed the Jews this time, and that their blood would begin to flow that very day. Then Rabbi Loew motioned to the Golem to leave the body there, and they returned to the dark tunnel.

By the time they had returned to the house of the pious Jew, in which Thaddeus had hidden the body, the police had already searched the whole house, including the cellar. When they found nothing, they departed. Then Rabbi Loew went to the captain of the police and reported a rumor he had heard: a child's body could be found in the cellar of the priest Thaddeus. The captain did not want to take this accusation seriously, but when he saw the Golem towering over him, he decided he had better go there and investigate. He insisted, however, that Rabbi Loew accompany him, for he intended to jail him if his accusation proved to be false.

So it was that the police arrived at the mansion of the wealthy sorcerer. Thaddeus was astounded to see Rabbi Loew and the powerful servant in the company of the police. And when the sorcerer saw the word *Emet* inscribed on the Golem's forehead, he began to tremble with fear, for he knew that Rabbi Loew had used his great powers to bring him into being. The captain informed Thaddeus of Rabbi Loew's accusation, and Thaddeus scornfully replied that they were free to search his entire house, not only the cellar. But the police said they only wanted to see the cellar, and Thaddeus took them there. Imagine his consternation when he found the body of the child that he himself had murdered, right there in his own home! He sank to the floor in a faint, and when he recovered enough to stand, the police took him into custody and thanked Rabbi Loew for having uncovered this terrible crime. Thus was the evil Thaddeus punished for his sin, and the Jews of Prague were spared the terrible pogrom that would have raged had the body been found in the Jewish Quarter.

After that the Golem remained in Rabbi Loew's home for many years, and every day and night he could be seen strolling through the streets of the ghetto, looking for anyone acting in a suspicious manner who might be trying to bring harm to the Jews. And when the enemies of Jews saw what a powerful protector they had, they ceased to plot against them, for they saw that the Jews could not be defeated. That is how Rabbi Loew and the Golem brought many years of peace to the Jews of Prague, for which they were deeply grateful. And the people gave thanks as well to the Holy One, blessed be He, for protecting them from the enemies of Israel.

—Eastern Europe: nineteenth century

69. The Werewolf

In his youth the boy Israel ben Eliezer, who would one day become known as the Ba'al Shem Tov, spent a great deal of time in the forest. It seemed impossible for the elders of the town of Okopy to convince the orphan to remain in the House of Study. So they decided to put his love of the forest to good use and assigned him the task of bringing the children through the forest each day to school. This work transformed the boy Israel from a solitary young man to one who joyously led the children, singing with them as they went. And the songs they sang were so sweet that the melodies drifted into the highest heavens and reached the Throne of Glory.

Then Satan, the Evil One, grew afraid that the innocent and pure singing of the boy Israel and the schoolchildren might free the Messiah from the chains that hold him back. And Satan knew that he must bring the singing to an end.

So Satan decided to take possession of a woodcutter who made his home in the forest. Now this man had called upon Satan to witness his sins many times, for he was not even ashamed of his sinning. And of course Satan had come to him, for he, more than any other, comes as soon as he is called. So Satan called down the evil soul of a sorcerer and had it take possession of the soul of the sinful woodcutter. And into the mind of this evil being Satan put a single thought: to bring to an end the pure song of the children who accompanied the boy Israel into the forest.

This sorcerer, who now possessed the woodcutter's body, knew a spell that turned a man into a werewolf. So three days before the rising of the full moon, the sorcerer pronounced the words of that spell, knowing that on the night the moon was full he would turn into a beast.

Now the boy Israel led the children to school shortly after sunrise, and they returned home in the late afternoon. But it had already grown dark by then, for this was the heart of winter. So it was that on the night of the full moon the boy Israel led the children through the snowy forest to their homes. And suddenly, out of nowhere, the most terrible beast imaginable leapt out at them, howling in an unearthly voice, and frightening all the children. Then, as quickly as it had appeared, the werewolf dashed off into the dark woods, and the children, one and all, started sobbing. Even the boy Israel was shaken, but still he gave thanks to God for having saved them from that terrible wolf. So too did he calm the children and lead them home.

Now many of the children were so upset that they were afraid to go to school the next day, or the next, just as Satan had hoped. In fact, a few of them started having nightmares of the worst kind. They cried out in their sleep and shed many tears. And their parents decided that they themselves must lead the children through the forest, for they thought the task too dangerous for young Israel.

Israel was very sad about this, for he knew that the singing of the children was the purest form of prayer. And he grew angry that such a beast should lurk in that forest, driving out those who would enter there. He decided to see if he could find this wolf's den, so that hunters might be able to rid them of this curse. When Israel returned to the place where they had encountered the beast, he found the huge wolf tracks and followed them through the forest. But all of a sudden, the wolf tracks disappeared, and in their place Israel saw the tracks of a man.

Israel was much amazed by this. He realized that the wolf must be supernatural—a werewolf—and he grew even more angry that something so evil should exist. Then Israel followed the tracks of the man until they led him to the hut of the woodcutter. Israel knew that woodcutter was not a pious man, but he had never imagined that he was a werewolf.

Thus Israel hid himself in the woods, day after day, and observed the woodcutter. Occasionally the man departed from his hut, but Israel never saw him cutting wood. Yet smoke was always to be seen rising up from the roof. And Israel wondered how this was possible, for the hut itself was too small to store much firewood. Then one day as Israel watched, a flock of birds happened to fly above the hut, and those passing through that smoke fell dead to the ground, one after another. This incident much amazed Israel, so he crept up and touched one of the fallen birds. Then he pulled his fingers back in horror, for the bird had been burned to a cinder in a single instant. That was when Israel realized that the fire, too, was supernatural. And he shuddered at the thought of the evil source of those flames.

Now three weeks had passed since the attack of the werewolf, and during that time Israel had not been seen at the House of Study even once. The rabbis again began to worry about him, and they asked the parents of the children to give Israel another chance. Israel was delighted when he learned that the parents were again willing to entrust him with their children.

Once Israel knew that the wolf was actually a werewolf, he knew that the beast posed a danger to them only on the night of the full moon. And he vowed that he would rid the forest of this recurring evil. Then, three days before the full moon rose, on the same night that the sorcerer pronounced the spell to make himself into a werewolf, the boy Israel had a dream he would never forget. In the dream an old man came to him who said his name was Elijah. He revealed secrets of how the evil beast could be defeated once and for all. And when Israel awoke, he recalled every detail of this dream and he was filled with certainty that he would prevail, for that is what God wanted.

So it was that on the day of the full moon, Israel led the children to school as usual, shortly after sunrise. That day he sang with more fervor than the children had ever heard, and when they joined in, their song reached to the highest heavens, sailing above even the prayers offered up that day. The angel Sandalphon gathered those songs together and wove them into a garland for the Holy One to wear as he sat on his Throne of Glory. And the Holy One, blessed be He, sent the angel Gabriel to Earth to guard over the boy Israel and shield him from all danger.

After Israel had brought the children to school, he himself returned to the forest. He went to the very place where the wolf had attacked them, and there he built a fire. He waited until the fire had burned down, and when all that remained of it were embers, he banked them with ashes, leaving little holes for air. Then he returned to the House of Study in time to lead the children home. Once again they sang in the sweetest voices ever heard. Satan shuddered at their purity and vowed to silence their song forever.

Now Israel and the children arrived at that place in the forest just before dark, and Israel quickly uncovered the embers and fanned them into a great blaze, warming them on that cold night and casting a great light. Then Israel told the children to stand by the fire, and he used his walking stick to draw a circle around them in the snow. And as he did, he whispered some words that the bewildered children could barely make out. Then Israel turned to the children and told them that no matter what happened, they were not to run outside that circle, for within it no harm would come to them. After that he began to sing, and the children, despite their fear, sang with him.

By then it had grown dark, and the full moon was seen rising in the sky. And as soon as it shone upon them, the children heard the most terrible howling from the forest. One and all they began to cry out in fear, for they recognized the howling of the werewolf. But Israel told them not to be afraid, for God would protect them as long as they remained within that circle. And when the children saw how calm Israel was, they stopped crying, though they still shivered with fear.

Then Israel took his walking stick and put the end of it into the fire. Now Israel was very fond of that staff, and the children were perplexed, for they could not imagine him burning it. But the staff did not burst into flame. Its end just glowed brightly when Israel lifted it up. And at that very moment they heard the sound of branches breaking nearby, accompanied by another terrible howl, this time so close that the children started to scream. That is when Israel suddenly swung his walking stick around and around, so that it seemed as if a burning circle hovered there. And when the terrible werewolf leaped toward them, he was surrounded by that glowing circle. It grew smaller as the wolf passed through it, and those who dared to open their eyes saw a great miracle take place: for as the wolf passed in one side and out the other, he turned into the woodcutter. And although this happened quickly, several students later insisted that they had seen a half-man, half-wolf, suspended in that flaming circle, before the body of the woodcutter crashed to the ground and began to smoke. Before long it burned to ashes, and then even the ashes disappeared. And Israel knew that somewhere that evil soul was being punished for what it had done and that it was burning in the fires of brimstone.

So Israel gathered the children together and led them back home beneath the light of the full moon, which seemed to cast a path before them. Satan knew the bitterness of defeat, and in the palaces of heaven there was great celebration, for they knew that the era of the Ba'al Shem Tov had begun at last.

—Eastern Europe: nineteenth century

70. A Combat in Magic

ne night the Ba'al Shem Tov dreamed that a strange star could be seen glowing darkly above a small town in Poland that was a day's journey from where he lived. And when he awoke, the Ba'al Shem Tov had a dread feeling that the presence of evil was to be found there. Then he woke three of his Hasidim, and they set out at once, even before dawn. Nor did they ask him where they were going, but they followed their master faithfully, for they trusted him completely.

The Ba'al Shem Tov and his Hasidim rode all day, and it was growing dark when they arrived at an inn in the small town. The Ba'al Shem Tov indicated that they would stop there, so they dismounted and led the horses to the stables. Then they followed the Ba'al Shem Tov to the door of the inn, but he hesitated before entering, and he peered up at the sky. And there, directly above that inn, shone a dark star whose presence was invisible to others, but which the Ba'al Shem Tov, with his pure vision, was able to perceive. The other Hasidim also looked up into the night sky, but they saw nothing unusual in the heavens, nor did they dare ask. Then the Ba'al Shem Tov opened the door of the inn and stepped inside, followed by the three Hasidim.

Inside they found the innkeeper sitting dejectedly by the fire. The Ba'al Shem Tov approached him and said, "May we lodge here for the night?"

And without looking up, the innkeeper said, "No."

"Is that because all the rooms are taken?" asked the Ba'al Shem.

"All of the rooms are empty," said the innkeeper.

"In that case," said the Ba'al Shem, "surely there is a place for us?"

At last the innkeeper raised his head, and when he looked into the eyes of the Ba'al Shem, which held great power, he suddenly felt less dejected, for he recognized that he was in the presence of a holy man. Then he said, "Yes, you may stay."

The Ba'al Shem signaled the Hasidim to bring in the bags, and after they left he turned to the innkeeper and said, "Tell me, why are you so sad? Perhaps I can help you."

"Tonight is Watch Night," the man replied. "Tomorrow my infant son is to be circumcised, but I have little hope for him."

"Why is that?" asked the Ba'al Shem Tov.

"Because this is my seventh son, and all of the others died at midnight of the eighth day after they were born, although there was no sign that anything was wrong with them. No, I am afraid that some evil force, some demon, must hate me for some reason, although I do not know why. It has robbed me of my sons, every one, although my wife and I are honest, God-fearing people. And I believe that tonight it will try to take its vengeance again."

"My students and I will be glad to help you during the Watch Night," said the Ba'al Shem Tov. Then turned to his Hasidim and said, "Stand next to the cradle, where the child is sleeping, and for the rest of the night, study the law without ceasing.

"Above all," he warned them, "Do not close your eyes, for if you do all will be lost."

Then he asked the innkeeper to bring them a sack, and when he did he gave it to his Hasidim and said, "If you see anything suspicious, hold this sack open above the child—and if anything falls into the sack, tie it securely and call me at once."

Then, after warning them one last time about not falling asleep, the Ba'al Shem Tov went into his room.

Now the three Hasidim did not doubt that the life of the child was in their hands. And during the night they kept each other awake by chanting prayers out loud, and whenever they heard eerie noises in the night, they shivered, for they did not know what awaited them.

At midnight the candles in the room began to flicker as if blown by a powerful wind, and suddenly they went out, despite the best efforts of the Hasidim to keep them lit. Then a strange gloom filled the room, and the only light that remained was that from the fire, which was tossed to and fro as if by a mysterious wind, causing the shadows of the Hasidim to dance grotesquely on the walls. Suddenly the fire in the fireplace went out, and the room was pitch black. The Hasidim were terrified, but they stood around the cradle and kept the sack open. All at once they saw two large green eyes glowing before them in the dark, and their blood ran cold. The creature made a hissing sound and suddenly sprang at the cradle, but the disciples held the sack open, and suddenly something fell inside it and began to thrash around. Then the Hasidim wasted no time, but tightly secured the sack with a rope, and hurried to tell the Ba'al Shem Tov.

When the Ba'al Shem Tov arrived, he was carrying his staff, and without any hesitation he began to beat the creature in the bag mercilessly, as it hissed and howled. The Hasidim watched in amazement, for they had never seen the Ba'al Shem Tov so angry, nor did they understand what the creature had done, although it had certainly given them a terrible fright. After giving it a sound beating, the Ba'al Shem Tov told his Hasidim to carry the sack out into the street and set the creature free. And when they did, a huge black cat leaped out of the sack and limped away as quickly as it could.

The next day the child was still healthy, unlike the six brothers who had preceded him, and the circumcision could take place. The innkeeper was deeply grateful to the Hasidim, and he made the Ba'al Shem Tov the *sendak*, who has the honor of holding the child during the ceremony.

Following the circumcision there was a joyous celebration, with many happy toasts. Afterward the innkeeper said, "It is strange that the duke has not joined us. For he came each previous *b'rit,* only to learn, in every case, that it had been canceled. And now, ironically, he is absent."

The Ba'al Shem Tov, however, did not consider this ironic, but deadly serious. He kept his thoughts to himself, however, and said to the innkeeper, "Perhaps the duke is not feeling well, and that is why he was unable to attend. Let me take some wine from the ceremony to him, so that he knows you have not forgotten him." The innkeeper agreed at once, and so the Ba'al Shem Tov set off to visit the duke.

Now when the Ba'al Shem Tov arrived at the home of the duke and announced his purpose, he was taken at once to his chamber. There he saw the duke covered with bandages that could not conceal his bruises. He stared at the Ba'al Shem Tov with hatred in his eyes and said, "Do not imagine for even an instant that I do not know who was responsible for what happened last night."

And the Ba'al Shem Tov replied, "I too know exactly what happened."

Then the duke said, "The only reason you succeeded was because you caught me unaware. But that will never happen again. When you face the wrath of my power, yours will seem like nothing."

"If that is a challenge," said the Ba'al Shem Tov, "then let us meet in a magical combat and see whose power will hold sway." And the duke, who was really an evil wizard, was astonished that the Ba'al Shem Tov did not shrink from his challenge and wondered just how great his powers were.

Then the two of them set a date and time for the duel. And when the day arrived, every man, woman, and child in that province had heard about it, and a great crowd had gathered in the open square where it was to take place. But not a single Jew was to be found there, for they had gathered in the synagogue to pray that the Ba'al Shem Tov might not be defeated. And among them was the innkeeper, who owed his child's life to the Ba'al Shem Tov, and he prayed more intensely than anyone else.

Now the wizard had delved deeply into the realms of evil, using the powers for his own satanic purposes, such as killing the infant sons of the innkeeper. He saw his combat with the Ba'al Shem Tov as a way to demonstrate his powers. And the first thing the evil wizard intended to do upon his victory was to destroy the Jews of that city, who had brought about his severe beating at the hands of the Ba'al Shem Tov. Yes, the wizard was delirious with the thoughts of power and revenge. But the Ba'al Shem Tov was ready for him.

The combat began at dawn. The evil wizard jumped up and pronounced a spell, and a furnace appeared behind him, of great size, with huge swirls of smoke billowing from it. All who were watching stood in awe, except for the Ba'al Shem Tov, who seemed to pay it no heed. Instead he used his staff to draw seven circles in the dust, one inside the other, and then he stood in the innermost circle. All at once the wizard threw open the furnace door and a great flame leaped out that took the shape of a fiery lion. It gave off a terrible roar that shook the earth and ran straight for the Ba'al Shem Tov.

Everyone expected the Ba'al Shem Tov to take flight, but instead he stood calmly in the center of those seven circles, words of prayer on his lips. And the moment the lion passed through the first circle, its flames burned out, as if they had been doused with water, and the lion vanished. The people were amazed to see this, and the wizard was furious, for that lion had possessed a great deal of his power. Then, once more, he opened the door of the furnace, and this time a fiery tiger sprang forth, which charged toward the Ba'al Shem Tov. But it broke through only the second circle before it disappeared.

After that the sorcerer called upon his powers yet again, and this time a great wolf leaped out, with its teeth bared, and charged toward the Ba'al Shem Tov. But just as it entered the third circle, the Ba'al Shem Tov lifted his staff off the ground, and all at once the flaming wolf turned to smoke and vanished as had all the rest. The wizard could not believe it, and at last he drew upon the most terrible spell he knew, which even he was afraid to pronounce, and when he opened the door whole herds of wild beasts came running out, not only lions, tigers, and wolves, but leopards, griffins, and wild boars. And among them were some creatures that looked like they had crept right out of Hell, and that indeed was where they had come from. For the powers the evil wizard drew upon were those of the Evil One himself, who had hoped to use the wizard to defeat the Ba'al Shem Tov.

But the Evil One could exercise his power only in the face of evil. And the Ba'al Shem Tov's soul had a kernel so pure it did not even share the blame for the Fall of Adam and Eve. It was one of the Innocent Souls that had fled before the Fall had taken place. Thus all the powers of the evil wizard and of the Evil One himself were futile against him. When the beasts charged toward him, the Ba'al Shem Tov faced them calmly. Some disappeared when they crossed the fourth circle, others when they passed through the fifth and sixth, but none breeched the seventh and innermost circle where the Ba'al Shem Tov stood. In the end the evil wizard had drained himself of all his strength and power, and when he opened the furnace door one last time, the fire that leaped out suddenly consumed him, so that nothing more than ashes remained, which were shortly scattered in the wind.

That was the end of that evil wizard and a great defeat for the Evil One in his struggle to gain power over our souls. And it was all because of the Ba'al Shem Tov and his faith in the Holy One, blessed be He, who had never abandoned him for a single second.

—Eastern Europe: eighteenth century

71. The Perfect Saint

here once was a righteous man who wished to perfect himself. He regarded sexual desire as the primary temptation to sin, and he vowed to rid himself of it. First he withdrew from his wife and became celibate. Soon, however, he found that this was not enough. Lustful thoughts still haunted him, for even though they slept apart, his desire for his wife remained. Therefore he made a vow to fast one day for each lustful thought. This, however, turned out to be impractical. After a week of fasting, he decided that he must try something else.

The only solution, it was clear, was to move out of the house. So he moved outside to the sukkah, and it was there that his wife brought his meals. He entered the house only for important reasons, such as finding a book in his library. Otherwise he was alone, away from temptation. And yet, even in the sukkah impure thoughts pursued him like demons swarming around him, polluting the sacred presence of his shelter.

At last it became clear to the man that he couldn't be anywhere near his wife at all. He would have to go far away. Yet he knew that if he left his home to wander in the world, he might glimpse other women, who might also awaken his lust. And that would be an even greater sin than desiring his own wife. No, the only answer was to become a hermit, and that was what he decided to do.

Other men might think such thoughts but never carry them out. But this man desired to be a perfect saint. So it was that he set out, alone, taking the remote byways and little-used paths and made his way into the forest. Yet even there he could find no peace. The animals were too noisy and too full of lust for life. So he kept on his way, until he finally reached the desert. And he realized that this was the place he had been searching to find.

The first days in the peace and quiet of the desert, the man was free of the desires that had clung to him for so long, but soon he began to dream. And the dreams were dreams of desire. Even there in the desert Lilith had not abandoned him! The man was overcome with grief. Was there nowhere, nowhere at all, that a man could be free of lust?

Out of his great disappointment the man began to fast. Not on purpose, but simply because he had lost his desire to live. He fasted for so long that his body grew light, and one day he simply ascended. He rose above the trees, above the clouds, and even above the stars. He ascended to the highest heavens. There he saw a pot filled with flesh and bones. It was a terrible sight to see. "What is this?" he asked. And he was told that the flesh and bones in that pot had once been an extremely beautiful woman. But she was a sinner who had warmed up her body to sin. Therefore, as a punishment, she was being warmed in that pot.

This explanation was most astonishing, and the new saint was very curious to know what that woman had looked like. When he asked about her, he was given a Divine Name with which it was possible to reassemble her as she was during her life. He pronounced this name and suddenly she stood before him, naked, and he saw that she was indeed a very great beauty. His lust for her grew until it was overpowering, and all at once he reached out to embrace her. And as he did, he fell from that high place. Some say he is still falling.

—Eastern Europe: nineteenth century
A tale of Reb Nachman of Bratslav

72. The Bridegroom Who Vanished

n the town of Shargorod there were two yeshivah lads who were loyal friends. They spent all of their days in the House of Study and immersed themselves in the Torah and Talmud with great devotion. They even spent their spare time together and were seldom separated. For they were as close as brothers.

Then it happened that one of the lads took ill and died. This unexpected event grieved his friend greatly. Still, he remained as devoted to the Torah as before.

In time his grieving subsided, and when he thought of his friend he was able to smile at the memories of how close they had been. After a few years this lad became known throughout the region for his great knowledge of the Torah. Men of wealth and distinction began to visit his poor dwelling, hoping to bring him home as a groom for one of their daughters.

Eventually a match was made. The wedding day arrived and the entire household was occupied with preparations for the wedding feast. As for the bridegroom, he was isolated in a room, waiting for the ceremony to begin. After a few hours he became restless, and he decided to step outside for a moment. Empty fields stretched before him, and on the horizon he saw a figure walking his way.

When the young man first observed him, he was barely curious to know who it was. But as the figure drew closer, it looked strangely familiar. All at once the young man recognized who it was—his friend, who had left this world. A long chill ran down his spine, but at the same time he felt a terrible longing. All the affection he held for his friend returned twofold, and he stood rooted, waiting for the other to arrive. When he did, the two friends embraced, and the young groom saw that his friend looked exactly as he used to, as if he had never aged.

It was then that his long-lost friend spoke for the first time, his voice exactly as it had been. "Tell me," he said, "do you remember what was the last point of the law we were discussing?" It had been ten years, and the young man had completely forgotten. But his friend reminded him, and suddenly the whole discussion came back to him. He had not thought of it since then, but now it mattered to him as much as before. And they launched into a long debate, like those they had had in the yeshivah, sitting at the same table, studying the pages of the Talmud together.

As they spoke, lost in their words, the two friends wandered from the field to the nearby forest. The young groom, only hours before standing beneath the bridal canopy, forgot all about his wedding. Indeed, he forgot about everything, except for the fact that he was immersed in the Torah once more with his friend. How such a thing was possible did not occur to him at that time, so natural did it seem.

As they were walking, they came upon a little hut deep in the forest. They went inside and there the Talmud lay open to the very passage that they were discussing. The young man and his friend read it out loud together, as they had done so often in the yeshivah. And almost at once they were lost in the *pilpul*, the small points of the law, where one idea led to another, and yet another, and still others beckoned.

Time flew past. The young man forgot whether it was day or night. The law, after all, was infinite, and he was lost in its complexity, as he had been in the happiest days of his life, sharing insights with his friend. Their rambling discussion led them, by one route or another, to the laws concerning the obligations of the bridegroom to the bride. At that moment the young man remembered that it was his wedding day. He looked outside and saw that it had grown dark, and the time of the wedding was at hand. Then he embraced his friend and hurried off as fast as he could, hoping that he would not provoke the fury of his new father-in-law or the disdain of his bride.

When he reached the town, he found himself confused, for it seemed changed from what he remembered. Nor could he find his father-in-law's house, and he began to grow fearful that he would be late to his own wedding. At last he asked an old woman he met about where the house could be found, and she said, "I have lived here all my life, and there is no family by that name who lives here."

The young groom pleaded with her, saying, "Please understand that this is the day of my wedding. I just left the house of my father-in-law a few hours ago. I took a little walk and lost track of time. Please tell me where their house can be found."

And she replied, "When I was a girl I heard a story about a groom who left the house a few hours before the wedding and was never seen again."

"And how long ago was that?" he asked.

And she said, "That was a hundred and thirty years ago."

And he said, "And what was the name of the groom?"

And she thought long and hard, and at last she remembered it, and she told him. And the name she recalled was his own.

—Eastern Europe: oral tradition

73. The Lost Melody

abbi Abraham was a wandering musician. He went from village to village playing his violin at the weddings of the poor. His music made others happy, and he asked for nothing more than a meal and a place to sleep.

Now Rabbi Abraham especially loved playing at orphans' weddings and at the end of every Sabbath. His favorite songs were Hasidic *niggun*s, haunting melodies without words. During the summer, when the windows were wide open, the sound of his violin was heard up and down the street. Old people as well as young listened to his wonderful playing, which brought joy to a neighborhood that was sad and poor.

On holidays, too, Rabbi Abraham could be heard playing his violin, which had been in his family for many generations. He played on the eve of Hanukah after lighting the candles. And he played on the eve of Purim.

Each year it was his custom, right after the Purim meal in his house, to take his violin and go to entertain sick and poor people. When he played for poor families, the children would hum along and the women would clap. And before he left, Rabbi Abraham would taste some wine and continue on his way to the next house.

Now one year, the holiday of Purim took place during an exceptionally cold winter. Deep snow covered the ground, and a strong wind shook roofs and shutters. Rabbi Abraham was more than sixty years old, and his wife, Bilabasha, asked him not to go out that year. But he was determined to lighten the hearts of the sick and poor on Purim, as he had done since his youth.

So Rabbi Abraham left home and went from house to house playing for the people. Nor did he refuse any food or drink that the poor gave him in thanks.

When Rabbi Abraham had not come home by midnight, Bilabasha began to worry. By one o'clock, she started to worry even more. And when the old clock showed two, Rabbi Abraham's wife woke Rabbi Levi, the driver, from a deep sleep.

Rabbi Levi hitched a horse to the sleigh and went with Bilabasha to the house of the village rabbi. They woke the rabbi. With the rabbi's assistant, the *shammash*, they lit several lamps and went to search for Rabbi Abraham. Every place they went, they were told yes, he had been there. He had played his violin, drunk a glass of wine, and gone on his way.

At last they returned home without having found Rabbi Abraham. The *shammash* was weary, but he did not return to bed, for it was time to open the ancient synagogue. But what did he see when he went inside? There was Rabbi Abraham, sitting up in the hallway of the synagogue, his ancient violin in his hand. He was playing a beautiful melody, which the *shammash* had never heard before.

"Rabbi Abraham!" cried the *shammash*. "Are you all right? Where have you been?"

"Don't bother me," said Rabbi Abraham. "I must not forget the melody that I just learned from Rabbi Menashe, the cantor."

"But Rabbi Menashe died many years ago," the *shammash* said.

"I know," said Rabbi Abraham. And he played the song over and over until he knew it by heart. Then he turned to the *shammash*. "Let me tell you what happened:

"I went from house to house, playing my violin, as I do every Purim. Everyone was very generous, and perhaps I drank a little too much wine.

"On my way home, I decided to take a shortcut through the yard of the synagogue even though I have heard that the dead pray in the synagogue every night. While passing in front of the gate, I heard a voice from inside the synagogue say, 'Will Rabbi Abraham, the son of Jacob the Cohen, come forth and pray?' At that instant I was filled with terror. Who was calling me? I wanted to escape, but I knew that I had no choice but to go inside. For when you are called to pray before the Torah, you must do it.

"As I approached the door of the synagogue, my legs were trembling. All at once, the door opened as if by itself, and I peered inside. There I saw that the Torah had been taken out of the Ark and lay open. And standing before it I saw ghostly figures as transparent as spider webs.

"Shivering with fear, I took my place before the Torah, made the blessing. and was ready to run away. But all at once I saw Rabbi Menashe, the cantor, hurrying toward me. I was very surprised to see him, for I knew that he was no longer among the living.

" 'Rabbi Abraham,' he said, 'please, have mercy. There is something that I must tell you.' I tried to remain calm, although I could hear my heart beating. I nodded for him to go on.

"The ghostly figure said, 'There is a melody I composed just before I died, which I took with me to the grave. But it is a great burden for me, for the song has never been heard by anyone else. Let me share it with you, so that you can play it for others. And as soon as you do, my melody will be set free, and you, Rabbi Abraham, will be rewarded with a long life.'

"When I heard this, I realized that I had not come there by chance. And even though I was speaking to a spirit, my fear vanished, and I listened carefully as Rabbi Menashe began to sing that *niggun*. And as soon as he finished, he and all the other ghostly figures vanished, and I took out my violin and played, so as not to forget it. Now I must play it again and again, till my fingers know it by heart." And so he did, while the *shammash* listened in amazement.

The next day Rabbi Abraham sang that magnificent melody for the first time in front of the congregation of the old synagogue. And all who were present agreed that it was truly a haunting melody, the likes of which had never been heard.

—Germany: oral tradition

74. The Demon of the Waters

In a village in the district of Radziwillow there lived a Jew whose name was Azriel Brisker. For many years he had rented the mill near the river and from this business he made a respectable livelihood. He was generous, his house was open to everyone, and he was very careful to fulfill the commandments in all ways. All the Jews who lived in the area came to pray on the Sabbath in the house of Azriel, who had set aside one room for use by the minyan. He had also arranged a hut near the river for the *mikveh,* the ritual bath.

In the next village, in another part of that district, there was a Jew whose name was Yakov Reiff. He was the owner of a tavern, and his livelihood was also quite secure. For years he and Azriel had lived in friendship and peace. Then, however, it happened that the friendship between the two was destroyed because of a dispute over a match. Yakov proposed a match between his eldest daughter and Azriel's eldest son, but Azriel refused because he felt that Yakov was not fully observant according to his standards. And from this matter they became angry at each other, and the anger festered until they became enemies, and Yakov decided to take revenge.

So Yakov went to the district office, and he convinced the official to rent him the mill in which Azriel worked and lived. The man was unwilling at first, for Azriel had made his home there for many years and had the right to remain. But by slandering Azriel and offering to pay a rent twice as high, Yakov eventually convinced the official, who finally wrote a contract, transferring the rights to the mill to Yakov. Then the official sent an announcement to Azriel that he had to move from the mill at the end of the year because the mill was going to be rented to someone else. When the announcement was received in the house of Azriel, everyone was in tears, for if they were expelled from the mill, their livelihood was lost.

Azriel sought the district official, but he refused to meet with him, and he was told to go to the district manager. Azriel went to this man, who told him that because the contract had been written, there was nothing that could be done. He suggested, however, that Azriel go to Yakov and ask him to change his mind about renting the mill. And even though Azriel knew that Yakov was stubborn, still he and his wife went to Yakov and begged him not to take their livelihood. But Yakov and his wife, Feige, hardened their hearts, turned their faces away, and shut the door behind them. And Azriel told his wife that because Yakov and his wife had closed their ears, they must turn to God for help.

Now the rabbi most admired by the Jews who lived in that part of Russia was the Saba Kadisha Mishipoli, the holy grandfather of Shipoli. Azriel and his wife arrived in Shipoli shortly before Shavuot and remained there for the holiday to meet with the rabbi.

On the first day of Shavuot they sat at the rabbi's table. When Azriel's wine glass was filled, he opened his mouth to say *L'hayim*, but his eyes filled with tears and his voice was choked. The rabbi was disturbed because Azriel was dampening his spirits on the blessed day of Shavuot. And when Azriel saw the look on his face, he grew afraid. The rabbi saw this, and he said, "Do you remember that a poor man knocked on the door of your house on a cold winter night about six years ago? And you opened the door to him and let him come in. Then you prepared something hot for him to drink and gave him a place to sleep."

"Yes, I remember this well," said Azriel. "I asked the poor man what he did, and he said that he was a scribe. And I asked him if he would examine the mezzuzah on my door, for the wind had been howling loudly outside, as if some evil forces sought to enter there. He checked it for me and he showed me how the parchment was blank in two places, and he said it was probably the work of demons. Then he wrote a new parchment for my mezzuzah. And after that we did not hear the wind howling at our door." Then the rabbi said, "I am that poor man you helped. Therefore, have no fear, for God, blessed be He, will turn the curse into a blessing, and no man will be able to move you from the place of your livelihood."

After this Azriel became like a different man, and he ate and drank with a happy heart. At the end of Shavuot Azriel and his wife went to depart from the rabbi. Then the rabbi took a letter he had written and handed it to Azriel to read. It was addressed to Yakov and said, "I have heard that you, Yakov Reiff, desire to encroach on the boundary of your neighbor Azriel Brisker. Let it be known that I am giving you warning that you will not be permitted to do so, whether you learn this earlier or later. If you have a claim to bring against Azriel, call him before a rabbinic court, according to the ways of our people. You don't punish first; first you warn. If you listen to my words, you will be blessed. But if you don't listen to my words, you will live to regret it." And he signed it.

The rabbi gave the letter to Azriel and told him to give the letter to Yakov. And the Saba Kadisha said, "It will be better if Yakov will listen. But if he won't, rent a house for yourself in a nearby village, and until he himself comes to you and begs you to take back the mill. For that is what will happen." And Azriel and his wife took their leave of the rabbi with many thanks.

Azriel and his wife did as the rabbi had instructed them, but Yakov ignored the warning. He threw the letter in Azriel's face and said, "The rabbi you went to has no power here; in our village we have our own rabbi." So Azriel left and got a house in the next village, as the rabbi had told him, and when it was time to leave the mill, he moved. And Yakov moved into the house of Azriel.

It wasn't long before Feige, the wife of Yakov, went to the hut near the mill to dip in the waters of the river, for that served as a *mikveh*. Feige took her eldest daughter to guard her clothes. And the daughter sat at the entrance of the hut, looking outside, while her mother went inside to wash and dip. But this time something terrifying happened to Feige. As she went down the stairs, the stairway collapsed and she fell into the waters and was carried away by the currents.

So it was that one of the daughters of the demons who exist in rivers, and especially in the rivers near mills, who resembled Feige in her height and in her face, came out of the water. And when Feige's daughter looked inside to see if her mother had finished dressing, she saw the demon of the waters getting dressed. Soon the demon emerged with a scarf covering her face, but the girl didn't pay attention to it, for she thought it was only to protect her from the wind. Nor did the girl ask her anything, and they didn't speak all the way home. Then the daughter went outside to play. That left only the little children in the house, for Yakov was at work in the mill. The children thought the demon was their mother, and when they asked for something she drove them away. Then she went to the kitchen and took all the food that had been cooked for the whole family and ate directly from the pots with her hands. And when the children saw that their mother was eating, they asked to be fed as well. But instead of feeding them, she kicked and shoved them until they started screaming.

When the eldest daughter heard the cries of her brothers and sisters, she rushed in to see what had happened. And how frightened she was when she saw the strange behavior of her mother, who was standing in the kitchen, her face covered with a scarf, wrapped in the same robe she had worn to the *mikveh,* eating from the pots with her hands. She cried, "Mother, Mother, that food is for the whole family!" and when she didn't get any answer, the daughter tried to pull the scarf from her face, but the demon pushed the girl away with great force, so that she fell on the floor and hit her head, which began to bleed. When the little ones saw their sister crying, they started crying as well, until one of them went and called their father from the mill. And Yakov greatly wondered what had happened, for the boy was so terrified he could not speak.

When Yakov came to the house, he saw that everyone was crying and that his wife was wearing the robe of *mikveh,* and in her hand was a pot that she had emptied. He started yelling, "Feige, Feige, what did you do?" But when he saw his daughter crying, "My head, my head," he lifted her from the floor and wrapped her head with a handkerchief. And he spoke to his wife and tried to lift the scarf in order to look in her face. But she pushed him with such great force that he fell on the floor. When he got up he begged her to tell him what was wrong, and she made a growling sound, like that of a beast, which left him terrified. Then she went up the stairs to the attic and lay down on the straw mattress there.

When Yakov recovered from the shock, he decided to try to talk to his wife again. It was already night, so Yakov took a lamp to light his way to the attic, where she was still resting. But when he reached out to lift the scarf from her face, she knocked the lamp from his hand and ran into a corner, and he was afraid to go after her. He left her alone that night, and early in the morning Yakov returned to the attic and found her deep asleep.

Nor did he wake her, for he hoped that if she got enough rest her mind would come back to her. He went downstairs quietly and went to the hut, and the first thing he noticed was that the stairway had broken. And Yakov said to himself, "Now I understand. When she went down to dip, the stairs broke under her, the floor collapsed, she fell into the depths of the waters, and she lost her mind." Yakov returned and told his daughter what he had learned. And they comforted themselves that the doctors would find a cure, now that they knew the reason for her illness.

Then, before the family even sat down at the table, the woman came downstairs and took all the food that had been prepared and ate everything and threw the pots in the hall. Then she went back to the attic and they were too frightened to follow her. And this happened again at lunch and at dinner. She came, ate everything she saw, and went back upstairs.

Three days passed in this way, and they had to cook every meal twice, for she took everything they made and didn't leave them anything. Soon it became known in the whole village that Feige, the wife of Yakov, had lost her mind. And on the fourth day of this, the daughter said to her father, "Maybe this is a punishment for us for taking the livelihood of Azriel. Perhaps we should give the mill back to him, and because of this my mother will recover."

She cried loudly when she said these things, but her father had a hard heart. He said to her, "Nonsense. We know she is sick because the stairs of the bath collapsed under her. What does the business of the mill have to do with it? People go crazy for different reasons. Tomorrow I will fetch a doctor from town, and we will listen to what he says."

So the next day Yakov went to town and came back with a doctor, along with four strong men to hold his wife so he could examine her. They waited until she came down for lunch. Then one of the men jumped out and tried to hold her, but she took the boiling pot and poured it all over the man. His face and hands were badly burned, and he let go, crying out in pain. Soon enough the other three grabbed her, but she started spinning with the pot in her hands, striking them until they ran from the house, screaming. There they waited until she took the bread and the other pot and went upstairs to eat.

Then they returned to the house to try to find a solution to this terrible problem. Yakov told the doctor what had happened in the *mikveh*, and the doctor agreed that this terrifying experience had caused her illness. And he said, "Usually for the first few weeks crazy people go wild, demonstrate great strength, and eat in an unnatural way. So the only thing to do is to give her less food until she becomes weaker. Then we'll be able to hold her in order to examine her."

And Yakov said to his daughter, "See, I was right. This happened to her because she was frightened. It is not as you thought."

Then the doctor said, "Make her some thin soup from bones and a few potatoes. For yourselves, don't cook in this house, but cook at your neighbors and eat there, so she won't take your food." Yakov thanked the doctor for his advice, and he gave him a good fee for his work. And the next day they did as he suggested, and they made only watery soup for her. And when she saw how little there was, she smashed all the dishes and took a knife and cut the pillows and threw all the feathers out the window. Many people came by to watch, but they were afraid to approach her. When she finally went upstairs again, Yakov and his daughter returned to the house and saw all the destruction. Then they realized that the doctor's advice had not worked, and they decided to prepare the next meal as usual, so that she would not cause even greater harm. And at noon she took the food with her and returned to the attic without doing any more damage. But they were afraid to go near her.

Meanwhile Feige, Yakov's real wife, had fainted when she fell into the river, and she floated on the waters until she reached the river Dnieper. Many merchant ships passed there, and there were many villages along its banks, but there were also many fields and forests. Feige was carried a great distance, until she was cast onto shore, near a forest. There she sustained herself on nuts and cherries and wove garments for herself out of grass. So too did she weave little baskets, into which she placed notes written on leaves, giving her name and that of her husband, saying that she was lost there. She cast the baskets into the river, and in time some of these notes were retrieved, and her plight became known, and the case became spoken of in many circles.

Now when one man who lived in the village of Yakov Reiff heard about the woman lost on the river, he remembered that a man of that name ran the water mill, although he didn't know the name of his wife. Still, he decided to call on him. And when he did so, Yakov told him that although his wife's name was also Feige, she was living in that house, and he told of how she had lost her mind. The man was very surprised at the strange story and asked to return the next day to see her with his own eyes.

Now in that village there was a shepherd who was said to be a sorcerer. The man told the shepherd about the madwoman and asked him to accompany him to the home of Yakov Reiff.

The next day they came to the house and hid. And at noon, when the demon went to the kitchen, the shepherd jumped from his hiding place and lifted her scarf. But when he did, he saw that she had a very strange smile, which struck terror in his heart, and he backed away. Then the woman turned away from him and ignored him as if he were not there. She took the pots and pans and the bread and went back upstairs. And after she left, the shepherd said to her husband, "This woman is not your wife. She is a demon of the waters. If she were an earth demon, I could control her and expel her. But because she is a river demon, I have no power over her."

And Yakov said, "This must be the work of Azriel. He must have gone to a sorcerer and brought down this curse upon us."

Then the shepherd said, "This is not the work of a sorcerer. There is no earthly sorcerer powerful enough to invoke the demons of the water—or to send them away. For they are among the most powerful and dangerous demons of all. Whoever is responsible for this demon is much more powerful than any sorcerer." The shepherd also warned Yakov to prepare the food on time as she desired, for she had the power to destroy the house and wreck the water mill. Yakov asked how long this would last. And the shepherd replied, "Only the one who sent her here can send her away."

Yakov said, "This must be the doing of the tzaddik who warned me not to trespass the border of Azriel." "In that case," said the shepherd, "then you have no other choice but to go to this Azriel and to beg him to accompany you to this tzaddik. For he alone can release you from this curse." And the shepherd warned him to go as soon as possible, for he knew what might happen with such a demon living in the house.

That same day Yakov went to Azriel and surrendered to him. He cried tears and confessed that he had sinned against Azriel and his family by taking away Azriel's livelihood. He came in complete repentance and told him to take the mill back. Azriel accepted his confession and agreed to forgive him, for he saw that he was suffering greatly. And they went together to Shipoli.

After Yakov greeted the tzaddik, he begged him to banish the demon from his house and restore his true wife to him. The rabbi told him, "I want you to know that the woman in your house is known as the demon of the mill. And because you took the mill from this man, the demons took your wife." Yakov said, "I accept all that I have been charged with, and I am prepared to accept the punishment." And the rabbi said, "It is true that repentance is very powerful, and everything can be repaired with God's help."

Then the rabbi had the verdict written down: "Yakov Reiff will give the contract to Azriel Brisker and will repay all the damages that he has caused. He will also give a written contract, signed by himself, which states that the rights to the mill belong to Azriel and that he renounces any claim of his own over it." And he added, "When you return, each of you should load all your possessions in wagons at night, and early in the morning Azriel will return to his original home, and Yakov will go to the house where Azriel now lives. When you meet halfway, you will descend and make peace and each will ask for forgiveness from the other. And from then on you will be friends, loyal as before. In addition, your children will marry one another, because it is destined from heaven that this should take place.

"If you listen to all the things that I have said, you will find your livelihoods restored, and God will help you. So too will Yakov's wife return safely and the trouble in the house will disappear."

Then both Yakov and Azriel took their leave of this holy man and returned home. When they reached the village of the mill, they went to the shepherd and told him the rabbi's verdict and of his assurance that the demon could now be expelled. And the shepherd said, "I hope that this will happen. Still, Yakov should remain at the mill in the morning until I arrive, so that I can be present at the time the demoness is supposed to depart." And Yakov agreed that he would wait for him.

That night both Yakov and Azriel loaded all their possessions, as the rabbi had told them to do, and early in the morning the shepherd came to Yakov at the agreed-upon hour. Then Yakov ordered the wagon to depart, and at the very moment the wagon began to move, the demoness left the house and followed after them. And when they saw this, Yakov and the shepherd both became terrified. The shepherd said, "How cruel is your fate that she is walking after you! What good did the rabbi do if this is the case!" And as he watched her following the wagon, Yakov shivered. But when the wagons passed near the hut of the ritual bath, the demoness entered the hut and disappeared within it. Yakov was afraid to go inside, but the shepherd went in after her. He opened the door slowly and cautiously, peered in, and saw to his surprise that she wasn't there. Only her clothes were to be seen, on the floor. And the shepherd ran back to Yakov and told him that she had returned to the place from which she had come. Yakov was overjoyed, and he became a true believer in the powers of the Saba Kadisha.

Then the shepherd told Yakov that the best thing to do would be to burn the hut, since surely no woman would want to immerse herself in the waters of that *mikveh* again. So Yakov burned the hut, as well as the clothes, and took his leave of the shepherd, greatly thanking him for his help.

After that Yakov returned to his own wagon and departed from the mill, which had brought such disaster upon him. On the way he lifted his eyes to heaven and thanked God for removing the evil demon from his life. He begged with tears that his wife be returned safely to him and that God forgive him for all his sins. While these thoughts filled him, Yakov met Azriel, driving the wagon of his possessions toward the mill. They both got down and wept, and they forgave each other. And so they dissolved the knot of hatred and anger that they had known. And they vowed to wed their children to each other with God's help, once the wife of Yakov had safely returned. Then they said good-bye, and each went on his way.

Meanwhile, Yakov's wife was still lost in the forest. For even though some of her baskets had been found, no one knew where to find her, for the river ran a great distance. Then it happened that three nobles went out to hunt in that part of the forest, and, as fate would have it, Feige fell into their trap.

The dogs of the hunters were chasing after two foxes, and when Feige heard the barking, she climbed a tall tree. Now when those dogs reached the tree, they started howling, and the hunters looked up and saw a woman dressed in woven grasses. They didn't know if she was human or a demon, for demons were said to dress that way. They questioned her and she told them her tale. And after that they helped her down and gave her shelter, and the next day the three men accompanied her to the village where she lived. When she got there, the whole village came out to see her, for she had been missing for three months. And there she learned that her husband and her children were no longer living in the mill and that Azriel was.

It is not difficult to imagine everyone's happiness when she was reunited with her family, and they told the whole tale from beginning to end, and none of those gathered there that day ever forgot it all the days of their lives. And they told it to their children, and it is still repeated to this day.

The next day Yakov's eldest daughter was wed to the eldest son of Azriel, and the happiness was great in their homes. After this the two families, including the bride and groom, traveled to the rabbi of Shipoli, and they told him all that had taken place. The tzaddik shared their joy and blessed them, and they were very happy when they returned to their homes. After that both Yakov and Azriel succeeded in all that they undertook and became wealthy. And from then on the heart of Yakov became like that of a different man, filled with kindness for one and all, and he was counted among the righteous of his time. And all who met him saw how he believed in the power of the Tzaddik of Shipoli and in that of the Holy One, blessed be He.

—Eastern Europe: oral tradition

75. The Underwater Palace

Long ago, in the city of Prague, not far from the river Moldau, there lived a wealthy merchant whose name was Kalman. He had but a single child, a daughter, whose name was Haminah. So beautiful was she that many thought she resembled a princess. Her adoring father had betrothed her to a young man who was a fine match, except that she could not bear the thought of marrying him. For if she did, she would lose forever her true love, the one who came to her from across the river every night. But no one knew of this, for she had kept it secret.

Every evening at twilight the maiden Haminah would go down to the bank of the river Moldau in Prague, unobserved by anyone. There she would wait in a ramshackle hut until it grew dark. Then she would go outside to the old dock and peer out over the river. At last the boat she was waiting for would come into view, and a young man of striking appearance would step out onto the shore. They would embrace for a long time, and before parting he would always say, "Let us leave together tonight." And as hard as it was for her to say, she would always reply, "Not yet."

Now as the time of the wedding approached, the secret lovers began to grow desperate. When only a few days remained, and Haminah had replied "Not yet" still another time, the young man rowed away in silence, and beneath the light of the full moon Haminah saw his boat stop, as if he had dropped anchor. Then the young man stood up in the boat and cried out, "If you truly love me, follow me!" and he dived into the waters and disappeared.

When Haminah did not return home that evening at the usual time, her father and her fiancé went out looking for her. They found her standing on the muddy riverbank, staring out over the waters, as if in a trance. They called out her name, and at that moment she made her decision. They saw her run into the river, where she soon vanished, carried off by the currents. Her father ran into the waters after her, but it was too late. Nothing was to be seen on the surface of the water except for the reflection of the moon.

In the days that followed, fishermen searched for the body of the young girl, but in vain. And every day the broken-hearted Kalman sat at home, waiting for the news that she had been found. But the river refused to surrender her body. Only when the time of mourning came to an end did Kalman resign himself to the fact that he would never see his daughter again, dead or alive. And after that he became a different man, losing all interest in his possessions. He became known for his generosity to the poor, but it gave him no pleasure, for he was walking toward the grave without offspring.

Now Kalman had a sister, whose name was Shifra. She lived in a narrow lane of Prague with her husband. Although she had no children of her own, she had brought many into the world in her role as midwife. She would often visit her brother Kalman, who seldom left home, preferring to remain in isolation with his grief.

One day when she was visiting him, her brother stood at the window and stared out at the river. He was thinking of Haminah, and he relived for the hundred thousandth time how his beloved daughter had run out into the water and had been carried off by the currents. So too did he know again the bitterness of his loss. Then he turned to his sister and said, "How long has Haminah been gone?" And she replied, "Soon it will be a year."

Just then Frau Shifra became aware of a black cat sitting on the wall outside the window. It stared at her with green eyes full of sadness and wisdom and looked as if it were trying to speak to her, to beg her for something. "Look at that cat," she said to Kalman, hoping to distract him from his grief. He looked down at the wall and at the same time the cat looked up at him, and for a long time they stared at each other. And it seemed to him that he recognized the cat from somewhere, but he couldn't remember where. Then the cat suddenly jumped down from the wall and disappeared.

During the night a sharp wind blew from the direction of the Moldau, and all the weather vanes and merchants' signs were creaking. Frau Shifra was unable to sleep. The wind howled through the narrow lane, and the raindrops clattered as they fell in the chimney. Once she raised her head and peered out the window, and she saw that same black cat sitting outside, looking as if it wanted to come in. When Frau Shifra finally fell asleep she dreamed that she opened the window, called to the cat, and it was about to enter. Just then Shifra was awakened by the sound of knocking at the door. It was the middle of the night, but such things were not unusual for her, because she was a midwife.

Already exhausted from her lack of sleep, she got out of bed, walked to the door, and looked out the peephole. "Who is there?" she asked. "Someone who needs your help," came the reply. So she opened the door.

There stood a servant, elegantly dressed. Frau Shifra was very surprised, for she assumed that he served a nobleman, and those who came to her were all Jews. She tried to elicit some information, but he was in a great hurry, so she dressed quickly and left with him. He led her through the rain to the Moldau, where he had fastened a boat to the dock. As soon as Frau Shifra realized that she was expected to cross the river on such a stormy night, she wanted to turn back. The servant turned to her and said, "What are you afraid of?" And she replied, "The wind and the waves." But no sooner had she spoken than the wind calmed down and the water became smooth. Much amazed, Frau Shifra sighed and entered the boat, and the servant began rowing. Soon the bank receded into the distance, and Frau Shifra again became fearful. She closed her eyes and decided not to open them until she reached land once more.

When the boat finally bumped another dock, she opened her eyes. To her great astonishment she saw a palace more splendid than that of the emperor. Its spires and curving walls were green and blue and glistened like a waterfall. All things around her glowed with a soft light, that of neither night nor day, and she did not know whence it came. Strange plants grew in the palace garden, and it appeared that a faint breeze was constantly fanning them.

Frau Shifra finally took heart and climbed out of the boat. That was when she discovered that she did not walk in that place, but floated, as if lifted by an invisible power at every step. In her confusion she looked up, and above her she saw schools of fish swimming about, and she realized, with great amazement, that she must be beneath the river. She was breathing, but how was that possible? She did not have long for such musings, however, because the servant hurried off, and she followed as quickly as she could.

The servant knocked on the palace door, and a splendidly dressed young man opened it, who Frau Shifra knew at once must be a prince or king. He was dressed in a green coat and green pants, and his buttons, rings, and buckles were all made of gold. The young man smiled at her and said, "We have been expecting you, good woman. Please follow me." Then he turned to go and she hastened after him, floating through the halls, which were illuminated by a mysterious light the color of pearls.

At last they arrived at a glowing green door, and when the prince opened it, Frau Shifra had the shock of her life. For there, lying on the bed inside, was none other than Haminah, holding out her hand to greet her aunt. The room glittered with gold, pearls, and diamonds, and the curtains that floated behind the bed had been embroidered with the colors of the rainbow. When Frau Shifra saw the miracle of Haminah, who was not only alive, but ready to give birth, she began to feel faint. But she pulled herself together, for she knew that she must not fail her niece. Haminah said, "Will you stay and help me?" And Frau Shifra said, "Of course."

Frau Shifra wished to ask questions but there was no time, for Haminah was well advanced in her labor. And before long a healthy infant was born, a son. Frau Shifra gave the news to the young man, who was filled with joy, and happiness radiated from all corners of the palace.

Before long, lovely singing and harp playing were heard, although the musicians kept themselves hidden. Frau Shifra listened with pleasure to this supernatural music, then turned to Haminah. "Tell me, my child, how did you come to be here? For your father thought you had drowned on that terrible night, and he has never stopped mourning."

Haminah held her baby close and said, "I had a secret love no one knew about. We met at night on the bank of the Moldau. When I refused to elope with him he dived into the waters and I thought that his life was lost. At the time my father reached the river I decided to follow my love into the grave. I descended farther and farther into the depths, certain that I was descending into a watery grave, when I saw a green light glowing from the river bottom. Suddenly I was embraced, and I knew that I had been reunited with my loved one at last. He brought me to this water palace, for it is from here that he rules the river. And it was here that we celebrated our wedding."

Frau Shifra heard this explanation, but if she had not been in that very palace, she would never have believed it. And for the first time in her life, Frau Shifra found herself speechless. Haminah continued: "You must know that my husband is not a human being. He is the ruler of the river Moldau, but the king of all waters cursed him and condemned him to live on the land. He had to wander throughout the world until he found someone who loved him so much that she would be willing to sacrifice her life. Only then would the spell be broken. Throughout the ages he was engaged to many maidens, but none were willing to follow him into the realm of the deep. Only I did and thus redeemed him from that terrible curse. Now he reigns once more over the river, and our love for each other is very strong.

"Yet," Haminah continued, "there is pain in my heart for causing grief to my father, and I long for him and the rest of my family, including you, my dear aunt. And when this longing begins to overwhelm me, my husband permits me to take the shape of a black cat and to visit the world above." And suddenly Frau Shifra realized that Haminah had been the black cat she had seen outside her brother's house and the one she had been dreaming about when the knock had come on her door. And she said, "Your father felt there was something familiar about that cat, and so did I. Wait till I tell him!" But Haminah grew pale. "No, my aunt, you must not, for if those in the world above should learn of this kingdom, our existence would be endangered. As much as I would like to let my father know, I cannot."

Frau Shifra understood, and she vowed to keep all that she had learned secret. But she also became afraid that she would not be trusted to remain silent. "Will your husband let me go back?" she asked. And the girl replied, "As long as you do not eat or drink anything here, or accept any of the rewards that are offered to you, you will be free to leave. But if you do accept anything, you will be forced to remain here for the rest of your life. All that you may safely accept are some pieces of coal you will find lying outside the door of the palace. Take a handful of these with you, and be careful not to lose them."

At that very moment the ruler of that kingdom entered the room and beckoned for Frau Shifra to follow him. She said a fond farewell to Haminah, knowing that she might never see her again, at least not in human form.

As they floated down the hall, the ruler told her that she was welcome to dine with them, but she replied that it was still the middle of the night for her, and she was not hungry. Then he led her into the treasure room, where she saw great heaps of gold, silver, pearls, and jewels. "Take whatever you like," he said. But Frau Shifra replied, "No, thank you, what my husband and I possess is sufficient for us. And I have been rewarded enough to learn that Haminah lives and that her life here is a happy one. My only desire now is to return home."

Then the ruler thanked her for all her help, and he called the servant who had brought her there. As she left the palace, Frau Shifra noticed pieces of coal sprinkled on the ground, and she bent down and picked up a handful, wrapping them in her apron. Then she climbed into the boat and closed her eyes once more, in order to forget just how far beneath the surface she really was.

Some time later the servant informed her that they had arrived at the riverbank. Frau Shifra opened her eyes and gave thanks when she saw the familiar shoreline of Prague before her. She climbed out of the boat and took leave of the servant. And when she turned around to watch him go, she saw that the boat had already disappeared, and there was nothing to be seen except circles on the surface of the water, as if someone had thrown a stone into it.

As she walked along, yawning, Frau Shifra began to realize just how exhausted she was. And she held her apron carelessly, not even thinking about the pieces of coal she carried in it. When she reached her home, she crawled into bed and was soon sound asleep.

In the morning she was awakened suddenly. Her husband was holding a large lump of gold in his hand, and he was jumping for joy. "Look at what I found at the foot of the bed!" he shouted. Frau Shifra rubbed her eyes. Was the visit to the underwater palace not a dream after all?

A moment later a great commotion was heard outside the house. Frau Shifra and her husband ran to the window, and they saw that people were streaming from all directions along the path to their house. Some of them were running around, scuffling and chasing each other, and others were hiding something in clenched fists. "They must have found gold too," her husband said. "Let's go outside and search with them. Perhaps gold has rained from the heavens instead of manna."

"We shall do no such thing," said Frau Shifra. But suddenly she thought of the apron, with the pieces of coal, and when she untied the knot she found a heap of gold glittering there. Her husband danced around the room and gave thanks, for never again would he have to worry about making a living.

Frau Shifra smiled but she remained silent. She knew that the gold on the path had fallen from her apron as she had returned from the river. And she thought of her niece Haminah with gratitude, and she recalled her promise not to reveal what had happened. So too did she keep that promise until the day she stood by the deathbed of Kalman, Haminah's father, and then she whispered the truth to him about his beloved daughter, so that he departed from this world with a smile on his face.

In the days that followed, the narrow lane outside Frau Shifra's house became known as Gold Lane, because of all the gold that had been found there. And from time to time a black cat would walk down that lane and sit outside the midwife's window. It was said that Frau Shifra always let it in so that it could hear all that was said inside. And the eyes of that cat were always melancholy, as if there were something it wanted to say. And there are those who insist that same cat can still be seen wandering the streets of Prague.

—Eastern Europe: nineteenth century

Mystical Tales

76. The Cottage of Candles

here once was a Jew who went out into the world to seek justice, as it is written *Justice, justice, shall you pursue* (Deut. 16:20). Somewhere, he was certain, true justice must exist, but he had never found it. So he set out on a quest that lasted for many years. He went from town to town and village to village, and everywhere he went, he searched for justice. But never did he find it.

In this way many years passed, until the man had explored all of the known world except for one last, great forest. He entered that forest without hesitation, for by now he was fearless, and he went everywhere in it. He went into the caves of thieves, but they mocked him and said, "Do you expect to find justice here?" And he went into the huts of witches, where they were stirring their brews, but they laughed at him and said, "Do you expect to find justice here?"

He went deeper and deeper into that forest, until at last he arrived at a little clay hut. Through the window he saw many flickering flames, and he was curious about them. So he went to the door and knocked. No answer. He knocked again. Nothing. At last he pushed the door open and stepped inside.

Now, as soon as he stepped inside that cottage, he realized that it was much larger on the inside than it had seemed to be from the outside, and it was filled with hundreds of shelves, and on every shelf there were dozens of oil candles. Some of those candles were in precious holders of gold or silver or marble, and some were in cheap holders of clay or tin. And some of the holders were filled with oil and the flames burned brightly, while others had very little oil left.

All at once an old man, with a long, white beard, wearing a white robe, appeared before him. "*Shalom aleikhem*, my son," the old man said. "How can I help you?"

The man replied, "*Aleikhem shalom*. I have gone everywhere searching for justice, but never have I seen anything like this. Tell me, what are all these candles?"

The old man said, "Each of these candles is the candle of a person's soul. As long as the candle continues to burn, that person remains alive. But when the candle burns out, that person's soul takes leave of this world."

The man asked, "Can you show me the candle of my soul?"

The old man said, "Follow me," and he led him through that long labyrinth of a cottage, which the man now saw must be endless. At last they reached a low shelf, and the old man pointed to a candle in a holder of clay and said, "That is the candle of your soul."

Now the man took one look at that candle, and he began to tremble—for the wick was very short, and there was very little oil left, and it looked as if the wick would slide into the oil and sputter out. He wondered, could the end could be so close without his knowing it? Then he noticed the candle next to his own, also in a clay holder, but that one was full of oil, and its wick was long and straight and its flame burned brightly. "And whose candle is that?" the man asked.

"I can only reveal each man's candle to himself alone," the old man said, and he turned and left.

The man stood there, quaking. All at once he was startled to hear a sputtering sound, and when he looked up, he saw smoke rising from another shelf, and he knew that somewhere, a soul had just taken leave of the world. He turned back to his own candle and saw there were only a few drops of oil left. Then he looked again at the candle next to his own, so full of oil, and a terrible idea entered his mind.

He looked for the old man in every corner of the cottage, but he didn't see him anywhere. Then he picked up the candle next to his own and lifted it up above his own. At that instant the old man appeared out of nowhere, and gripped his arm with a grip like iron. And the old man said: "Is *this* the kind of justice you are seeking?"

The man closed his eyes because it hurt so much. And when he opened his eyes, he saw that the old man was gone, and the cottage and the candles had all disappeared. He found himself standing alone in the forest, and he heard the trees whispering his fate. And he wondered, had his candle burned out? Was he, too, no longer among the living?

—Afghanistan: oral tradition

77. The Cave of Shimon bar Yohai

ear the village of Peki'in in the Galilee there is a cave known as the cave of Shimon bar Yohai. That is where Rabbi Shimon bar Yohai and his son, Eleazar, hid from the Romans after they decreed his execution. Shimon bar Yohai and his son remained in that cave for thirteen years, devoting themselves to the study of the Torah.

Many miracles took place while they lived in that cave. During the first night they spent there, a well of living water formed inside the entrance, and a large carob tree grew beside it, filled with ripe carobs, which completely hid the entrance. When Shimon bar Yohai and his son discovered the spring and the tree that had appeared overnight, they drank from the water and tasted the fruit. The water was pure and delicious and the fruit was ripe, and they knew that their faith had been rewarded and that the Holy One, blessed be He, was guarding them. And they gave thanks.

After that, Rabbi Shimon and his son cast off their clothes and spent each day buried in the sand, studying the Torah. Only when it was time to pray did they put on their white garments, and in this way they preserved them through the long years of their exile.

Then a day came when Elijah the Prophet arrived at the cave to study with Rabbi Shimon and his son. Elijah revealed great mysteries that had never been spoken of outside of heaven. And in the days that followed Elijah often returned, and Shimon bar Yohai wrote down those mysteries on parchment that Elijah brought them, which came from the ram that Abraham had sacrificed on Mount Moriah. Now that was an enchanted parchment, for it expanded to receive his words as Shimon bar Yohai wrote. And every letter he inscribed there burned in black fire on white. And the name of the book that he wrote down there, filled with the celestial mysteries, was the *Zohar*.

One day, when Eleazar went to drink from the spring, he saw a bird repeatedly escape from a hunter, and he recognized this as a sign that they were free to leave the cave. And, indeed, the emperor had died and the decree had been annulled. But they hid the book of the *Zohar* in that cave, for they knew that the world was not yet ready for its secrets to be revealed.

There the book of the *Zohar* remained for many generations, until an Ishmaelite happened to find it in the cave, and sold it to peddlers. Some of its pages came into the possession of a rabbi, who recognized their value at once. He went to all the peddlers in that area and found that they had used the pages of the book to wrap their spices. In this way he was able to collect all of the missing pages, and that is how the *Zohar* was saved and came to be handed down.

—Babylon: c. fifth century

78. A Kiss from the Master

uring the days when the tomb of Rabbi Shimon bar Yohai was still open, the wise men of Safed would enter it on Lag ba-Omer. Once, a rich man who was visiting in Safed on the eve of Lag ba-Omer was invited by his host to visit Rabbi Shimon's tomb in Meron. When they arrived, he saw that the sages were seated in a circle around Rabbi Shimon's grave. They invited the rich man to join them, and they gave him an honorable place among them.

Then, one at a time, they read passages from the *Zohar,* as was their custom. But when the guest received the book, he could not read the Aramaic in which it was written, and he was deeply ashamed.

After they finished reading, the wise men returned to their tents. But the rich man remained in the tomb, weeping bitterly, until he fell asleep. And no sooner did he sleep than he dreamed that Rabbi Shimon bar Yohai appeared to him and said, "Be comforted, for my knowledge of the Torah shall be yours." And before he departed, Rabbi Shimon kissed him on the mouth. And that is when the rich man woke up.

From the moment he opened his eyes, the rich man felt as if a new spirit were within him. He picked up the *Zohar* and opened it to the first page. There he found, much to his amazement, that he could now read the letters. Not only that, but the true meaning of every letter rose up in his vision, for the spirit of Rabbi Shimon had fused with his soul. In this way his eyes were opened to the hidden meanings of the Torah, and its mysteries were revealed to him.

Later, when the others returned to the tomb, they began to discuss one difficult passage in the *Zohar,* which none of them could comprehend. Then the rich man timidly asked if he could comment, and when they said yes, he explained that passage to them as if it were elementary, and their eyes were opened to its true meaning. The rabbis were amazed at his wisdom, for they knew he could not even read the language, and yet what he said could only come from a master of the Torah.

Then the sages demanded that the rich man explain how this transformation had taken place. So the rich man revealed his dream about Shimon bar Yohai. And when the sages heard this dream, they understood that a miracle had occurred, and that the rich man had been possessed by an *ibbur,* the spirit of a great sage who joins his soul to the soul of another, and in this way brings strength and wisdom.

After that, the rich man found that all he had to do to call forth the soul of Rabbi Shimon was to open the book of the *Zohar*. Then he would be able to understand the mysteries of the *Zohar* as if they were the aleph bet. And in the days that followed, the sages invited him to remain in Safed and to bring his family to join him. This he did, and before long they made him the head of the kabbalists of Safed, for they knew he spoke with the wisdom of Shimon bar Yohai.

—Israel: oral tradition

79. The Angel of Forgetfulness

hile Rabbi Isaac Luria, who came to be known as the Ari, was still living in Egypt, the prophet Elijah came to visit him. Elijah revealed that Isaac's days were numbered, and that the time had come for him to journey to the Holy Land, to the city of Safed. There he must seek out Rabbi Hayim Vital and make him his disciple. For it was he who would transmit his teachings to the world.

The Ari set out for the Holy Land the next day. On the night he arrived in Safed, he had a dream in which he saw a flock of birds flying backward and followed them. As they traveled, they merged into one another, until at last there was only one bird left. That bird flew directly to the tree that stood beside the Ari and addressed him: "Do you know why the flock flew backward?"

"No," said the Ari, "but I want very much to know."

"Every bird is the spark of a soul," the bird replied.

"And who, then, are you, who contains every spark?" asked the Ari.

"I am the soul of Shimon bar Yohai, and among those who bear the sparks of my soul are you, Isaac. For in this generation, half of my soul belongs to you and the other half to another, whom you must seek out."

"And who is it who bears the other half of your soul?" asked the Ari.

"Hasn't Elijah already told you that?" asked the soul of Shimon bar Yohai, and at that instant the bird took flight, and the Ari awoke. He realized at once that the bird must have meant Hayim Vital, of whom Elijah had spoken. And the Ari realized how important it was to find him.

The next day the Ari made inquiries and learned that Hayim Vital lived in the city of Damascus, where he was the head of a kabbalistic school. However, the Ari did not go to Damascus. Instead, his soul left his body every night and approached the soul of Hayim Vital to draw it closer. At first Hayim Vital resisted this approach, although he was well aware of it. For he was already recognized as a master, and he did not want to become a disciple. Thus he refused to travel to Safed.

Therefore the Ari called upon the Angel of Forgetfulness and commanded the angel to deprive Hayim Vital of his memory. This the angel did when Hayim Vital was engaged in an explanation of a difficult passage of the *Zohar*. All at once his understanding of that passage vanished. He could remember nothing of his interpretation. So he turned to another passage and the same thing happened, once, twice, and three times. He understood this as a sign that he must approach the Ari, and soon after that he left Damascus and traveled to Safed.

Even before Hayim Vital arrived, the Ari told his students that a great rabbi from Damascus would soon arrive and that they must treat him with respect, for his soul was very holy.

When Hayim Vital arrived in Safed and came to the yeshivah of the Ari, everyone treated him with honor and respect. He took a seat near the Ari, and the Ari turned to him and said: "Why did it take you so long to come here?" And Hayim Vital confessed that he had resisted the pull of the Ari's soul, but now something terrible had happened, for he had lost his memory and he was in need of the Ari's help.

And the Ari said: "Fear not, for your memory will soon be restored." Then the Ari led Hayim Vital to the shore of the Kinneret. There they found a boat, with a jug in it, and when they got in, the Ari said: "When I tell you, fill that jug with water."

Then the Ari rowed in the direction of the tomb of Rabbi Meir Ba'al ha-Ness, until they reached the place in the Kinneret that is the final resting place of Miriam's well, which had followed the Israelites so faithfully in their forty years of wandering. And when they reached the sacred waters of the well, the Ari told Hayim Vital to fill the jug. Then the Ari told him to drink of that water, and the moment he did, Hayim Vital's memory was restored.

And that is how Hayim Vital and the Ari came to be together. Nor were they ever separated again until the day of the Ari's death.

—Israel: oral tradition

80. A Vision at the Wailing Wall

he Ari had great mystical powers. By looking at a man's forehead he could read the history of his soul. He could overhear the angels. He could point out a stone in a wall and reveal whose soul was trapped inside it. And from the first of Rosh ha-Shanah he always knew who among his disciples would live and who would die, for was able to peer into the heavenly ledgers and see whose name was written in the Book of Life, and whose name was written in the Book of Death.

Now the Ari rarely disclosed this knowledge, but once, when he learned there was a way to avert the decree, he made an exception. Summoning Rabbi Abraham Berukhim, he said: "Know, Rabbi Abraham, that I have learned that this may be your last year among us—unless you do what I tell you to do."

Rabbi Abraham was staggered to learn this, and he said, "Rabbi, whatever you want me to do, I'll do."

"Good," said the Ari. "Go home, then, and fast and repent for three days and nights. Then set out for Jerusalem and go to the *kotel*, the Wailing Wall, and there pray with all your heart. If you are so blessed as to have a vision of the *Shekhinah*, you will live for another twenty-two years. But if you do not, then I am sorry to say that this will be your last year among us."

Rabbi Abraham gratefully thanked the Ari for all he had revealed. And he returned home at once and put on sackcloth and ashes and fasted for three days and nights. Then, although he could have gone by donkey or by wagon, he walked to Jerusalem. And with every step he took, he prayed to God that he might be blessed with such a vision.

When Rabbi Abraham reached the Wall, he saw that it was very crowded, for that was during the Days of Awe. But he managed to find a place by the Wall and leaned his forehead against it, and wept and prayed with all his heart and soul that he might be worthy of having such a vision of the *Shekhinah*. And all at once, he did: Out of the wall came an old woman, dressed in black, deep in mourning. And when he looked into her eyes, he became possessed of the greatest grief he had ever known. It was the grief of a mother who has lost a child; the grief of Hannah, after losing her seven sons; the grief of the *Shekhinah* over the suffering of Her children, the children of Israel, when they were sent into exile.

At that moment Rabbi Abraham fell to the ground in a faint, and he had another vision of the *Shekhinah*. But this time she appeared as a beautiful bride, wearing a bridal gown of light. She embraced him and whispered in his ear, saying, "Don't worry, my son Abraham. Know that My exile will come to an end, and My inheritance will not go to waste. *Your children shall return to their country and there is hope for your future*" (Jer. 31:17). Just then Rabbi Abraham awoke. And he felt as if the greatest weight had been lifted from his shoulders.

And when Rabbi Abraham returned to Safed, he went directly to see the Ari. And the Ari took one look at him and said, "I can see from the aura surrounding your face that you had a vision of the *Shekhinah,* and now surely you will live for another twenty-two years." And he did.

—Palestine: sixteenth century

81. Gathering Sparks

ne Rosh Hodesh, the Ari led his disciples outside at night and told them to follow him. He led them without a torch, so that only the stars lighted their way. Yet it seemed to them that there was another light that guided them, an aura that emanated from the Ari.

At last they reached their destination, the tomb of Rabbi Shimon bar Yohai in Meron. There the Ari began to pray with great intensity, and all the others joined him, swaying back and forth, until it seemed as if they were being rocked in a cradle of stars. At last they completed the prayers, and there was silence. This lasted long into the night, and for all of them it was as if they had discovered the world on the first day of creation.

Then, at midnight, the Ari began to speak. And every word seemed to them like one of the words with which the world was created. For there he revealed the mystery of the Shattering of the Vessels and the Gathering of the Sparks. How, long before the sun cast a shadow, before the Word was spoken that brought the heavens and the earth into being, a flame emerged from an unseen point. And how sparks of light sprang forth from the center of that flame, concealed in shells that set sail everywhere, above and below, like a fleet of ships, each carrying its cargo of light.

How the frail vessels broke open, split asunder, and all the sparks were scattered, like sand, like seeds, like stars.

That is when they learned why they had been created—to search for the sparks, no matter where they were hidden, and as each one was revealed, to raise it up and redeem it. For when all the scattered sparks had been gathered, the vessels would be restored, and the footsteps of the Messiah would be heard at last.

Just as the Ari finished speaking, a comet streaked across the sky. And when they saw this, all of them were filled with wonder, for they understood that they were not the only ones who had listened to the Ari that night. The words had also been heard in heaven.

—Palestine: sixteenth century

82. The Tzaddik of the Forest

n the days of the Ari there was a student named Shimon Pilam in the city of Safed who was said to know the Torah, the Talmud, and the *Zohar* by heart. And in the same city there lived a man who was educated and wealthy, who had a large orchard and many fields, as well as two ancient forests. Now this wealthy man had one daughter, who was of marriageable age. He had great difficulty in finding a worthy groom for her. No one was a fine enough scholar. Then it happened that he heard of Shimon Pilam, and he was determined that such a scholar would be his son-in-law. And, with the help of a marriage broker, the betrothal was made.

So it was that Shimon Pilam met both his bride and his father-in-law for the first time on the day he was wed. And the love between Shimon Pilam and his bride was a deep one, which had been ordained in heaven. But it was also hidden. After the morning prayers, Shimon Pilam rode a horse into one of the forests, and he was not seen again until the sun was about to set and it was time for the afternoon prayers.

What he did in that forest was a mystery, but he could not be accused of shirking his studies, for he carried the sacred books in his memory, and that way he could study them at any time. And the rich man saw that Shimon Pilam was honorable and treated his daughter well. So he never questioned his ways and went back to his life of luxury.

Now the rich man had hired two Jews to serve as the guards of the two ancient forests he owned. Each had a hut at the entrance of one of the forests, and there they watched for those who sought to cut down the trees. Once in a while they would leave their huts and walk through the forests. And it happened that one of the guards saw a horse tied to a tree. When he went closer, he saw his employer's son-in-law lowering himself into the dark, insect-infested waters. What kind of *mikveh* was this?

The man spent a long time in those waters. And when he emerged, he dressed, untied the horse, and rode out of the forest. Then the guard came out of hiding and saw, to his amazement, that those waters had turned completely pure. He bent down and drank from them, and the waters were clear and sweet. And he realized that he had witnessed a miracle of one of the hidden saints.

So it was that the guard secretly observed Shimon Pilam as he made his way through the forest, and he saw many other kinds of miracles take place. Whatever barren tree he sat beneath soon had blossoms appear on it, and whatever path he walked on had flowers spring up overnight. All of nature welcomed his presence as if he were an angel. And he secretly went on his way, healing whatever needed to be healed with a power that seemed to emanate from his very being. And indeed he was searching for the scattered sparks in that holy forest, so that he could gather them and in this way repair the world.

Now that guard was childless, and when he told his wife about the miracles he had witnessed in the forest, she begged him to go to the hidden tzaddik and ask for his blessing in having a child of their own. And one day, when he could not hold himself back any longer, the guard approached Shimon Pilam and said, "I know that you are a great tzaddik, who hides his ways from the world. There is only one thing I would ask of you, and if you help me, I promise never to reveal your secret. All I ask is that you pray for my wife and me to have a son." The tzaddik saw that his secret had been discovered, and he promised the man that within a year he and his wife would be blessed with a baby boy. And so it was that the guard's wife gave birth at the end of the year to a healthy son.

Now the guard kept his word and never revealed the secret of the tzaddik. Then one day his companion guard, who watched over the other forest, came to visit him. This guard's life had been tragic, for each of his sons had died before reaching the eighth day. And he said: "I see that God has blessed you and you have had a son. May there be many more. Tell me, was there anything you did to make this possible? Perhaps you can help me so that I can be blessed as well."

Now the guard had no intention of betraying his vow, but at the same time he wanted to help the other guard. So he said: "I will help you on one condition—that you not ask any questions but do whatever I tell you to do." The other guard quickly agreed to these terms, and the first one said: "What we have to do is to switch places, so that you will guard my forest, and I will guard yours. Then everything will be all right."

So it was that the guards switched places. And after a while the second guard observed the ways of the hidden tzaddik, who brought miracles to pass wherever he went. When he saw these miracles, the guard understood why the other had advised him to switch places. And at last he approached the tzaddik of the forest and told him of the disaster that had haunted the birth of every son. And he asked for his blessing, so that his future sons would live.

The tzaddik was silent for a long time, and at last he said: "Do you remember that when you were young you went with some friends to swim in the river and to wash in its waters? There was a large tree near the shore of that river, and at the bottom of the trunk, near the roots, there was engraved the image of a hand. And you had the urge to laugh and be merry. So you took a ring and placed it on the finger of the hand and said the wedding vows."

The guard grew pale when he heard this, for he himself had forgotten about that incident. He lowered his eyes and admitted that it was true. And the tzaddik said: "At that moment an evil spirit that lived in that place was wed to you. And since you married someone else, this evil spirit comes and kills your sons because you betrayed her and didn't fulfill the wedding vow."

The guard was staggered by these words. And he said: "I remember that day as if it were yesterday. Afterward I was ashamed of what I had done, and I put it out of my mind until now. Please, tell me, what must I do in order to free myself of that evil spirit?"

The tzaddik said: "I will write the *get*, the bill of divorce, for you, and you must take it to the same place, and put the *get* into the hand engraved there. And you must say: 'Shimon Pilam commands you to divorce me.'"

And the guard went there, and he found the place where the hand was engraved, and he did as the tzaddik told him to do, and at last he was freed of that spirit. And the sons who were born to him after that all thrived.

—Palestine: sixteenth century

83. The Angel of the Mishnah

abbi Joseph Karo was deeply devoted to the study of the Mishnah. One day when he opened the Mishnah, an angelic spirit known as a *maggid* came to him and whispered secrets of the Torah. That was the angel of the Mishnah, who brought him secrets from on high.

After that the angel appeared whenever Joseph Karo recited the Mishnah to himself. For the words of the Mishnah invoked the presence of the *maggid*, and once it had appeared it revealed great mysteries to him, and Joseph Karo recorded these revelations in his book, *Maggid Mesharim*.

Once Solomon Alkabetz, author of the hymn "Lecha Dodi," stayed up all night with Joseph Karo and several others on Shavuot, and they never stopped studying the Torah for even a moment. They sang every word with a beautiful melody, from the creation to Moses to the Song of Songs and the Book of Ruth. And then they began to read the Mishnah, and as soon as they did, the voice of the *maggid* began to speak out of the mouth of Joseph Karo. All of them heard it, but they could not understand what it was saying, for so profound were those words that they fell on them like rain, and when they tried to comprehend them, the words simply vanished from their memory.

Then all of those present were filled with awe and fell on their faces. And at that instant they found that they could understand everything the spirit said: "I am the Mishnah, and I have come to converse with you. Had there been ten of you, you would have ascended even higher. But look down now and see where you are."

At that instant, all of them looked down and saw that they had ascended high above the city of Safed, and the city seemed to be no larger than a glowing spark. And all of them, except for Joseph Karo, were afraid to find themselves at that height. Then the angel said: "Remember Rabbi Akiba, who ascended and descended in peace." And no sooner did the angel say this than they were filled with the spirit of Rabbi Akiba, and they were no longer afraid.

When the angel of the Mishnah saw this, he said: "Know that I can remain here only as long as you study the Mishnah. For I have come into being because of Rabbi Joseph Karo's love of the Mishnah." After that they all focused on the words of the *maggid*, and they suddenly understood the Mishnah as never before, and the words of the Mishnah shone before them like a pillar of fire.

Just before dawn the angel of the Mishnah informed them that he must go, and once more told them to look down. And when they did, they saw that they were lying on the floor in Joseph Karo's house, and that Joseph Karo was now speaking to them in his own voice. And there was no trace of the *maggid*'s presence. But the mysteries of the Mishnah that had been revealed to them were inscribed in their memory, as if they were black fire on white. Nor was that the last time the angel revealed itself in their presence. Over the years this took place many times, and in this way great mysteries of the Mishnah were revealed.

—Palestine: sixteenth century

84. Gabriel's Palace

n the city of Worms there is an ancient Torah inscribed on parchment of deerskin. It is said that this scroll was written by Rabbi Meir of Rothenburg, known as the Maharam, while he was imprisoned. No possession of the Jews who live there is more precious, for its origin was miraculous. Rabbi Meir had been libeled and cast into jail, and a huge ransom of twenty thousand gold coins had been placed on his head. Nevertheless, the Jews of that generation decided to raise the sum. They sent a delegation to Rabbi Meir, but he rejected their offer, saying: "I regret to deprive you of the mitzvah of redeeming a captive. Still, I prefer to remain in prison rather than to encourage this kind of extortion. All I ask is that you bring me the tools of a scribe so that I may write down my thoughts about the Torah. For, as you know, I have been forbidden to have any books." With no other choice, the delegation respected his wishes and saw to it that he received a scribe's quill, ink, and a journal.

So Rabbi Meir remained imprisoned, much to the disappointment of those who had expected to receive the ransom. And even though he had been deprived of every book, he had long since memorized not only the Torah but both Talmuds and many other holy texts as well, so he lacked for nothing. Indeed, all that he truly needed was a scroll of the Torah to read on the Sabbath.

One Friday night Rabbi Meir fell asleep, and while he slept his soul took wing and ascended on high. When he opened his eyes, a bright light blinded him. But when his eyes grew accustomed to it, he found himself in a palace chamber, in the presence of an angel, who said: "Welcome, Rabbi Meir. I am the angel Gabriel, and you have ascended to my palace. The heavenly hosts are aware of your distress, because you lack a scroll of the Torah. You have been brought here to receive one. This is one of the thirteen scrolls that Moses himself wrote before his death. One scroll was given to each of the twelve tribes, and the thirteenth was taken into heaven. This is that Torah. Now it is to remain with you. All that we ask is that you read loud enough that it can be heard here. For the sages on high will be listening to every word, since it is their Torah that you will be reading." And with awe and wonder Rabbi Meir received that celestial Torah from the arms of the angel Gabriel, and then he awoke.

When Rabbi Meir opened his eyes, it was the first crack of dawn. He looked around, still in a daze, and that is when he saw the scroll of the Torah lying upon the table and he knew that the dream had been true. Rabbi Meir washed and dressed, staring with amazement at the Torah that had been brought to him from on high. For a long time he did not dare to touch it, lest it all be a dream.

Then he began to recite the Sabbath prayers, and when the time came to read the weekly portion, the scroll of the Torah rolled open to the right place. And as Rabbi Meir began to read, the room filled with a holy light, and he felt the presence of all of the tzaddikim on high. He read slowly and clearly, taking his time with every word. And he read loud enough that not even a single word would be lost. And when he finished reading, the scroll of the Torah rolled closed on its own, and the light vanished from the room.

So it was that Rabbi Meir lived in the presence of that holy scroll, reading the Sabbath portion from it every week and studying it night and day. And during that time he discovered many truths that could only be discerned by one who read in that celestial scroll.

One day it occurred to Rabbi Meir to copy that scroll of the Torah for the generations to come, for all of the other scrolls that Moses had written had been lost over the ages. Rabbi Meir prayed that he might accomplish this, and the next morning he found a page of deer parchment in his cell. He sat at the table all day, transcribing one page from the celestial Torah. And whenever he completed a page, a new parchment would appear. In this way, Rabbi Meir wrote down every word, counting out each letter as if it were a golden coin. He worked on that scroll for twelve months, and at last he completed transcribing it without a single error. And when he reread what he had written, he discovered that heaven had assisted him in creating a perfect replica of the celestial Torah.

When Rabbi Meir awoke the next morning, he discovered that the scroll of Moses was gone, and he knew that Gabriel must have descended during the night to take it back. And Rabbi Meir knew that this meant that heaven had found the Torah he had written to be perfect and that it would now serve as a model for future generations.

Now Rabbi Meir remained imprisoned for six more years. During that time, he fashioned a wooden ark to hold the scroll of the Torah and covered it with pitch to make it waterproof. When he felt the end of his life drawing near, he sealed the ark with the scroll inside it, lowered it from his window into the Rhine River, and consigned it to its fate.

In the days that followed, the ark floated down the river until at last it approached the city of Worms. Some Gentile fishermen tried to catch it in their nets, but it always eluded them. Soon word spread about this elusive floating ark. It became the talk of the city, and many tried their luck at capturing it, but no one succeeded.

Among the Jews of the city there was an intense debate about the box. Some said that it had a demon inside, while others insisted that it was being guided by the Holy Spirit, which is why it eluded all the Gentiles who had tried to ensnare it. At last the Jews decided to see if they had any better luck. They rented a boat and set out near the last place where the box had been sighted. And sure enough, a current soon carried the box in their direction, and they were quickly able to pull it into the boat.

When they returned to shore, however, the owner of the boat, who was not Jewish, claimed the box as his own, since it was caught with his boat.

The Jews were forced to give it up, but when the Gentiles tried to lift it, they could not. Even when a dozen men tried to pick it up, they could not budge it an inch. At this they became frightened and ran away. But the Jews had no difficulty in lifting and carrying it into the synagogue. There they opened the box with trepidation. Inside they found the scroll of the Torah, inscribed on deerskin. And along with it was a message from Rabbi Meir, giving it as a gift to the community of Worms.

When the Jews of the city learned of this miracle, they celebrated and gave thanks to God. And that Torah has remained there for many generations, guarding them from danger and serving as a great blessing in their lives.

As for Rabbi Meir, he died in jail soon after he lowered the ark into the river, and his soul ascended directly to Gabriel's Palace. There he makes his home in the World to Come, serving every Sabbath as the reader of the celestial Torah kept in the Ark on high.

—Germany: oral tradition

85. Rabbi Naftali's Trance

Now Rabbi Naftali Katz of Posen had many followers, among them a rich man. One day the rich man came to the rabbi's study with his daughter. He said, "Rabbi, you've known my daughter since she was born, and now the time has come for her to be betrothed. And who, more than you, Rabbi, would know best who she should wed? So I am leaving the matter entirely in your hands. All I ask is that he be the smartest student in your yeshivah."

Rabbi Naftali said, "I have many smart students in my yeshivah."

"Yes," said the rich man, "but isn't there one smarter than all the rest?"

"Well," the rabbi said, "there is this one student who has memorized the Talmud."

"Is that possible?" asked the rich man.

Rabbi Naftali said, "Would you like a demonstration?"

"Yes," said the rich man.

So Rabbi Naftali sent for that yeshivah student, and when he came, the rabbi said, "Close the door. We're going to have a little test. Be alert."

Then the rabbi turned to the rich man and said, "Go to the bookcase and take down a tractate of the Talmud. Any one." The rich man did this.

Then Rabbi Naftali said, "Open it." The rich man opened it.

Then Rabbi Naftali handed him a pin and said, "Point to any word." The rich man did this.

"Now take the pin and put it through any letter." The rich man did.

"Now tell us," said Rabbi Naftali, "what tractate is it, what page, what word, and what letter is the pin going through." And the rich man told him.

Then Rabbi Naftali turned to the yeshivah student, and without hesitation he named the word on the other side of the page—and even the letter the pin was going through. When the astounded father saw this, he said, "I'll take him."

Soon a betrothal was made and a wedding took place, and that was the greatest wedding in the history of Posen. The beggars were still talking about it ten years later. And for a few months everything went well with the rich man's daughter and her groom. Then it happened one night that the rich man's daughter turned to put her arm around her groom—and he wasn't there. And she sat up and lit the lamp and saw that not only was he missing, but all his clothes were missing as well. And she realized, to her horror, that he had abandoned her. That meant that she was an *agunah*, an abandoned wife, for he had left without giving her a *get*, a bill of divorce.

And she could not remarry without it, unless two witnesses confirmed that he was dead.

The rich man's daughter ran screaming to her father in the middle of the night, and when he heard the news, he almost had a heart attack. Together they ran to Rabbi Naftali and banged on his door. When the rabbi opened the door he was still wearing his night clothes, and he said, "What is it? What's wrong? Has someone died?"

The rich man said: "Worse—the *mumser* has abandoned my daughter!"

Rabbi Naftali said: "No, that's terrible. I can't believe it. I would never have expected this. But, please, can we discuss it in the morning?"

So they all went back to bed, but no one got a wink of sleep. In the morning Rabbi Naftali met with them and said, "You know, I couldn't sleep at all. I never expected this. But then it occurred to me that this student has been in the yeshivah his entire life. What did he know of the ways of the world? What did he know of the ways of a wife?' "

And the rich man, who wasn't rich by accident, said, "Rabbi, are you asking us to be patient?"

Rabbi Naftali said: "You've read my mind. Give him some time. Perhaps he'll come back to his senses and return."

And the rich man said: "Rabbi, you know how much I trust you. If you want us to wait, we'll wait."

So they did. But every day they came to the rabbi to see if there was any news. But there wasn't. In this way a year passed. Thirteen years passed, and still no news of the wayward groom.

Finally one day the rich man dragged his daughter to see Rabbi Naftali. Although he was a proud man, he stood before the rabbi and wept, saying, "Rabbi, Rabbi, my daughter is growing old. Soon she will be too old to wed. Soon she will be too old to bear a child. And Rabbi, I too am getting old. I really want to have a grandson and to be there for his Bar Mitzvah, and when the time comes I want him to say Kaddish for me."

And Rabbi Naftali said: "Oh, I feel terrible. How could I have waited so long? I'll tell you what—come back tomorrow morning and I'll let you know where you can find him."

The rich man said: "What?"

The rabbi said: "Just come back in the morning and I'll tell you where he is." So the rich man and his daughter left, and as soon as they did, Rabbi Naftali called upon his three best yeshivah students. He said, "Lock the door and bring your chairs closer to mine. I am going into a trance."

One of the students said, "Rabbi, a trance? What is a trance?"

And Rabbi Naftali said, "Don't you know what a trance is? My soul is going to leave my body and look for that *mumser* until I find him."

"But Rabbi," the student asked, "is that dangerous?

"Of course it is!" Rabbi Naftali said. "Why do you think I waited thirteen years?"

The students pleaded, "Rabbi, please, don't do this. We can't get along without you."

But he insisted, saying, "I gave my word."

Then Rabbi Naftali lay back in his chair and said: "It may look to you like I'm asleep. It may look worse than that. But don't worry, I'm just in a trance. I want you to wait here and watch me like hawks until my head slumps. That will mean my soul has returned. And at that instant you must jump up and shake me until my eyes open. Or else, shalom."

And the students cried out, "Rabbi!"

And Rabbi Naftali went into a trace.

The students stood there nervously, then they started walking around him. They noticed his skin had a strange grey tinge, and his body seemed rigid. And they noticed that they were starting to be drenched in sweat. Time was moving very slowly—an hour seemed like a year; two hours seemed like ten years. All at once his head slumped and they shook him and shook him. At last he opened his eyes, gasping for breath, and said, "I couldn't find him."

The students said, "Rabbi, thank God you're back."

And Rabbi Naftali said: "No. I must go back and look again."

The students pleaded with him, but Rabbi Naftali insisted, and he went into another trance. This time his body was rigid as a board, and there was no sign at all that he was breathing. After an hour one of the students said, "Why don't we get a mirror and put it under his nose, to see if he's breathing." So they found a little mirror and held it beneath his nose, but—nothing. They didn't know what to do. They were terrified they would have to say Kaddish for their beloved rabbi. Then, after three hours, his head suddenly slumped. Then they shook him and shook him, but he didn't open his eyes. And they kept shaking him, until, finally, he opened his eyes and said, "I found him!"

The next morning, early, the rich man and his daughter came to see Rabbi Naftali. The rich man said, "Rabbi, you have something to tell us?"

"Yes," said Rabbi Naftali. "Sit down and listen carefully. I have something important to tell you—I've found him. He's in the city of Vienna."

And the rich man jumped up and cried out, "What's he doing in Vienna?"

And Rabbi Naftali said, "Please, sit down and listen. He's staying in an inn outside the city. You and you daughter must go there at once, as quickly as possible. Take two witnesses with you. You must arrive there before midnight. Go inside and look for three soldiers, and when you find them, he will be the one in the middle."

The rich man couldn't believe his ears. "But Rabbi, how could you possibly know this?" he cried out.

"Don't ask! Just do as I say." Rabbi Naftali said.

So the rich man and his daughter got up, but before they left Rabbi Naftali said, "Wait! There's one more thing."

"What is it?" the rich man asked?

"I've located him for you," Rabbi Naftali said, "but I can't guarantee he'll give your daughter a *get*."

"Rabbi, about this you don't need to worry," said the rich man. "When I get my hands on him, he'll give her a *get*!"

Then they dashed off and they grabbed the coachman and two witnesses and the father started screaming, "Faster! Faster! Faster!" They rode all day and reached the inn one minute before midnight. They leapt out of the coach and went inside. They were amazed to see that the inn was very crowded, despite the hour, but they didn't see three soldiers anywhere. Then one of the witnesses noticed a back room, and there, in a dark corner, he saw three soldiers. He ran to tell the rich man, who grabbed his daughter by the arm and pushed his way through the crowd into the back room. And when she saw the groom, she screamed and almost fainted, while the rich man rush forward and pulled the groom up by his collar, and shouted, "You *mumser!* How could you do this to my daughter? How could you do this to me?"

And the groom, who when he was living with the rich man's daughter never once raised his eyes to his father-in-law, now stared brazenly into his eyes and said, "What do you want?"

"I want a *get* for my daughter!" shouted the rich man.

The groom said, "If I had wanted to give her a *get*, I would have given her a *get*. I'm not going to give it to her."

"Yes you will!" the rich man shouted.

"No I won't!" the groom said.

They went back and forth, back and forth, shouting at each other, and it suddenly occurred to the rich man that he really wasn't going to give her a *get*. He turned to the soldiers and pleaded with them, "Please, please, help us. You have no idea how important this is. Everything depends on this."

And the soldier said, "Are you asking for our help?"

"Yes!" said the father.

Then one of the soldiers stood up, took out his sword, and cut off the head of the groom. And the head and the body fell to the floor.

The father was unbelievably shocked. "He's dead," he said.

"Yes," the soldiers said, "He's dead."

"Could we take the body with us as proof that he's dead?" the rich man asked.

The soldier said, "Didn't you bring witnesses with you?" And he pointed to the two witnesses. And they both shook their heads and said, "Yes, yes, we'll testify. He's dead!"

So the rich man and his daughter and the two witnesses left the inn and got into the coach and rode all night. They reached Posen at dawn and went straight to see Rabbi Naftali. This time he was dressed, for he had been expecting them. He invited them in and said, "Tell me everything."

So they him the whole story, and after they did, the rich man said, "Rabbi, my daughter and I, and all our descendants will be eternally grateful to you. We will never forget you. But Rabbi, please tell us, how did you know he would be there?"

Rabbi Naftali said: "After I promised to locate him for you, I went into a trance. I searched every face on earth, but I didn't find him. Then I realized he must no longer be among the living. He was either up there—in Paradise—or down there—in Gehenna. After what he did to your daughter, I knew he must be in Gehenna. So I went into another trance and went all the way down to Gehenna, and it's a long way. When I got there, I saw a giant angel, named Samriel, who is five hundred feet tall, guarding the gates. I said, "Open the gates. I'm Rabbi Naftali. I'm on a mission."

Samriel said, "No one enters here whose name is not in this book." And he had a giant book that was almost as tall as he was. And he asked me for the names of my father and mother and the city of my birth and many other questions, and he searched through the book. Then he said, "Your name does not appear in this book. That means you may not enter Gehenna."

I said, "I'm Rabbi Naftali. I'm on a mission. Open the gates."

He said no.

I said, "If you don't open the gates this instant, I'll take a vow in God's Name to pester you for eternity until you open the gates!" He decided to let me in.

When I came into Gehenna, I found two avenging angels and I told them who I was looking for. They said, "Yes, we recognize him." And they led me to where the groom was being punished with fiery whips. I asked the angels if they knew what had happened to him after he ran away. They said, "After he abandoned his bride, he was captured by thieves. They said, 'We've had our eye on you. We understand that you're a smart one. We have an offer for you. You can join us and become a thief, and we'll share everything equally with you. But if you refuse, we'll have to kill you. It's entirely up to you.' Under the circumstances, he became a thief. He robbed many people. He killed many people. But after twelve years he had a falling out with his fellow thieves, and they slew him, and his soul descended to Gehenna, where it was being punished. Then I had to convince the avenging angels to disguise themselves as soldiers and to bring him to that inn outside of Vienna, where you found him—so that you would know that he was dead. And I want you to know it was a lot of trouble!"

Then the rich man cried out, "Rabbi, Rabbi, how can we ever thank you?"

Not long after that the rich man's daughter was betrothed again, and another great wedding took place in Posen. And before the year was out she gave birth to a beautiful baby boy. And the rich man was indeed present at his Bar Mitzvah. And when the rich man's soul took leave of this world, his grandson said Kaddish for him.

—Eastern Europe: seventeenth century

86. The Spirit of Hagigah

here once was a pious man who devoted his life to only one book—tractate *Hagigah* of the Talmud. He read it over and over until he knew it by heart. And he meditated on the many mysteries contained therein, any one of which, he believed, was itself worthy of a lifetime of study. So it was that with every breath this man recalled the sacred passages of *Hagigah* and meditated on them night and day. Even in his dreams he pursued these mysteries, his soul ascending on high.

And one night his soul ascended all the way to the Palace of Hagigah in the highest heavens. When his soul entered there, his quest was complete, and at that moment this pious man took leave of this world.

But because he lived alone, no one knew what had happened to him. So a figure of a woman, dressed in white, came and stood by him and raised her voice in mourning, and her cries alerted others that he had died.

When they came there, they saw that she was not of this world, and they were stricken with awe and fear. She said: "All of his life this man studied nothing but the book of *Hagigah*. Now his soul has taken its place on high and he deserves your mourning. Therefore bury him with honor and respect his grave, and you too will be blessed in the world to come."

Then all the women gathered and sat with her, and they mourned over him, and the men were busy with the arrangements of his burial. She remained among them until after the funeral. And before she left, they asked her who she was, and she told them her name was Hagigah, and then she disappeared. For she was the spirit of that very book. And that is how they learned that the good deeds a person performs in this world plead for them in the world to come.

—Italy: sixteenth century

87. The Ladder of Prayers

he Ba'al Shem Tov once was praying with his Hasidim, but that day he was praying very slowly, with great *kavvanah*, great intensity. Not word by word, but letter by letter. At first his Hasidim waited for him, but before long they lost patience, and one by one they left.

Later the Ba'al Shem Tov came to them and said: "While I was praying, I ascended the ladder of your prayers. As I did, I heard a song of indescribable beauty, sorrowful, but full of hope. I had no idea where it came from. At last I found myself outside the palace of the Messiah, in the highest heaven. There I saw the Messiah himself standing by his window, and I saw the light that radiated from his face. He was peering at something behind me, but I could not see what it was. So I turned around and there I saw an enormous tree, whose branches reached into every corner of heaven. And in the top of that tree there was a nest, and in that nest there was a golden dove. It was the song of that dove I had heard as I ascended on high. Then I understood that the Messiah could not bear to be without that dove and its song for as much as a minute. And it occurred to me that if I could capture that dove, and bring it back to this world, the Messiah would be sure to follow.

"So I ascended higher, until I was within arm's reach of the golden dove. But just as I was about to reach for it, the ladder of your prayers collapsed."

—Eastern Europe: eighteenth century

88. The Tree of Life

t was the practice of the Ba'al Shem Tov to go out into the forest alone. What he did there was a mystery that greatly intrigued his Hasidim. So one morning, when the Ba'al Shem Tov asked three of his Hasidim if they would like to accompany him into the forest, all of them readily agreed to go. These three were Reb Sendril, Reb Yehiel Mikhal, and the Ba'al Shem Tov's brother-in-law, Reb Gershon.

Everyone climbed onto the wagon, and the Ba'al Shem Tov himself served as the driver. And although he never cracked the whip, the horses responded to his presence by racing forward, and it seemed to the Hasidim that the hooves of the horses and the wheels of the wagon flew above the ground.

Soon they arrived at the entrance to a pristine forest that none of the Hasidim recognized. Without saying a word, the Ba'al Shem Tov dismounted, unhitched the horses from the wagon, and motioned for the others to follow. Now they wondered why he did not tie the horses to a tree, and Reb Sendril asked the Ba'al Shem Tov if he wanted him to do this, and the Ba'al Shem Tov replied: "It is not necessary to tie up the horses here, but if you are worried about them wandering off, Sendril, you could stay here with them until we return." But Reb Sendril had no intention of being left behind.

Never had the Hasidim seen a forest like this. The trees were so ancient that some of them were as wide as a house and so high that they seemed to reach into heaven. When Reb Yehiel tried to peer into the top branches of an especially tall and magnificent tree, he glimpsed a nest high in its branches and saw, at the same time, a golden bird of such great beauty flying into the nest that he remained rooted in that place, trying to get another glimpse of it. Meanwhile the others continued into the forest, leaving their companion behind.

A little further on they came to a beautiful pond, and when the Hasidim saw the Ba'al Shem Tov lean over and peer into the pond, they followed his lead. But that was no ordinary pond, and what they saw was not an image of themselves, but an angelic presence that seemed to peer back at them from beneath the waters. Now the Hasidim greatly wondered about this and raised their eyes to ask the Ba'al Shem Tov, but when they did, they saw that he had already left the pond, and Reb Sendril hurried off to catch up with him. But Reb Gershon remained staring at that angel, for he understood that it was his own guardian angel he was seeing, and he could not tear himself away from the remarkable sight.

Further in the forest they came to trees that seemed to be shimmering as if they were on fire, yet they were not consumed. Reb Sendril wanted to stop to explore this strange sight, but the Ba'al Shem Tov barely paused to glance at the trees and continued on his way. But Sendril, remembering well the vision of Moses at the burning bush, remained behind, trying to discern the mystery of that fire, and he did not notice that the Ba'al Shem Tov had left him behind.

In this way hours or days passed, and the three Hasidim were lost in the mysteries of that forest. Then, all at once, they found themselves back at the House of Study, where they had started their journey. They could not understand how they had gotten there, and when they looked to the Ba'al Shem Tov for an explanation, he said: "When Moses left Egypt he knew that some of the Children of Israel would never reach the Promised Land. And, indeed, some of them crossed the Red Sea but were no longer present at the giving of the Torah, and some who were present both when the sea was crossed and the Torah was received did not reach the Promised Land. So it is that I brought you with me into Paradise. And the further we went, the fewer were those who followed. And when I came to the Tree of Life, I found that all of you had lagged behind."

—Eastern Europe: eighteenth century

89. The Enchanted Island

ne of the earliest disciples of the Ba'al Shem Tov was Rabbi Wolf Kitzes, who was famous for his ability to blow the shofar. So resonant were the sounds he drew forth that the Ba'al Shem Tov called upon him to blow the shofar during the Days of Awe, so that its voice would ascend on high all the way to the Throne of Glory.

Now it was the dream of Wolf Kitzes to travel to the Holy Land, and at last he was about to set out on his journey. Just before he left, he went to see the Ba'al Shem Tov, who embraced him and said: "God willing, you will blow the shofar in Jerusalem this year. But remember this: when anyone asks you a question, take care to consider your reply."

So Wolf Kitzes set out for the Holy Land, and when he reached the Black Sea he took a ship to Istanbul. Now for the first few weeks everything went well, but one day, during a terrible storm, the ship was struck by lightning and it split apart. All the passengers lost their lives except for Wolf Kitzes, who somehow managed to grab a long plank that floated nearby. He clung to that plank for three days and nights, until at last the current carried him to an island.

There the exhausted man crawled onto the shore and collapsed. Later, when he regained a little strength, he got up to explore the island, for he was famished from the three days he had spent at sea. Now the island seemed to be deserted, and he didn't find any fruit or anything else to eat, although he did find a freshwater brook that satisfied his thirst. Following it to its source, he discovered a spring, and there beside it was a magnificent mansion, a palace far greater than that of any king.

Wolf made his way to the door of that mansion and used the last of his strength to knock on the door. To his surprise, the door opened by itself. At first he stood in the doorway and called out, but no one replied, so he decided to see if anyone lived there. He walked through the halls, opening every door. Every room was magnificent, but still no one was to be seen. At last he opened the door to a large dining room, and there he saw the longest table he had ever seen in his life. It was so long that he could not see the other end, which seemed to be enclosed in some kind of fog. At another time he might have wondered at this, but at that moment all he noticed was that there was one place setting at the table, although there was no food to be seen.

When he came closer to the table, Wolf saw that two precious objects had been placed there. One was the largest and most beautiful shofar he had ever seen, and the other was a golden horn whose value he could not begin to guess. He stood before those precious objects and wondered which he should examine first. Just then a single grape rolled out of the golden horn, and that decided the matter for him. He picked up the horn, and as he did, an immense amount of the finest food fell out of it, rolling across the table.

Wolf was overwhelmed at this unexpected abundance and quickly sat down so that he might partake of that delicious food. He pronounced the blessings before eating, and just as he was about to take his first mouthful, he heard a deep voice that seemed to come from the far side of the table: "So, how are my children faring?" Now all that Wolf could think of was that delicious food, and he quickly replied: "So, how should they be faring?" and he took the first bite. Then the voice replied: "So be it." At that instant the fog lifted. Wolf was able to see to the other end of the table, but no one was there. That is when he noticed that the shofar was missing, although the golden horn still remained. He decided to look for the shofar once he had finished eating, and he turned back to his plate. But each time he lifted his head, it seemed that the table had grown smaller. When he had eaten his fill, he looked down and saw that the table was no bigger than a plank. At that moment a deep exhaustion came over him, his head sank down, and he fell asleep.

All at once Wolf was awakened by cold water washing over him, and when he opened his eyes, he found himself back in the sea, still clinging to the plank. And he could not decide if his visit to that mysterious mansion had been a dream or if it had really taken place. But when he realized he was no longer famished, he knew that some kind of miracle had occurred.

Not long afterward, a fishing boat found him floating in the sea and brought him back to shore. Then he knew that he must not attempt to continue his journey to the Holy Land but must return to the Ba'al Shem Tov, to tell him all that had taken place.

When Wolf Kitzes reached the small hut of the Ba'al Shem Tov, the Ba'al Shem Tov greeted him sadly and said: "What a shame, Wolf, that you did not pick up that shofar and blow on it, as you and only you can do so well. For if you did, the footsteps of the Messiah would have been heard everywhere. For that is the shofar made from the horn of the ram that Abraham offered on Mount Moriah in place of Isaac. It is said that Elijah will blow that shofar at the End of Days. And it was within your grasp to do so, so that all our waiting would come to an end.

"Or at least if you had held on to that golden horn, hunger would have been banished from the world. For that is the Horn of Plenty, and if you had brought it back, no one would ever know hunger again.

"Or if you had replied otherwise to the question that was asked of you and told the Holy One, blessed be He, about our suffering in this world, surely everything would be different.

"But at least you were wise enough to say the blessings before you ate. For if you had not, you would have been lost at sea, as were all of the others who set out in that unfortunate ship."

—Eastern Europe: eighteenth century

90. Lighting a Fire

he Ba'al Shem Tov always knew if his prayers had ascended on high, as most of them did. But once in a while, a prayer would somehow be lost and never reach the angel Sandalphon, who weaves the prayers of Israel into garlands of prayer for the Holy One to wear on His Throne of Glory. Now the Ba'al Shem Tov perceived that not only his prayers but those of Israel as well had somehow been refused and that a time of great danger had come upon them.

Late that night, the Ba'al Shem Tov came to Rabbi Dov Baer and asked him to accompany him into the forest. There was a full moon that night, and the Ba'al Shem Tov hurried along a path to a place that only he knew about. There, as Dov Baer watched, the Ba'al Shem Tov lit a fire merely by touching the branches, so that they resembled a burning bush. Nor were the branches consumed by the flames. The Ba'al Shem Tov said nothing about this, and Dov Baer dared not ask. Then, seated by the fire, the Ba'al Shem Tov closed his eyes in deep meditation. For a long time there was only the sound of the wind in the trees. Then the Ba'al Shem Tov opened his eyes, stood up, and began to pray with great intensity. Dov Baer heard the words of that prayer for the first and only time that day. Yet they remained imprinted in his memory all the days of his life.

At last the Ba'al Shem Tov stopped praying, and there was a great smile on his face. He said: "The prayers of Israel will no longer be refused."

Years later, when Dov Baer was known as the Maggid of Mezhirich, another grave danger faced Israel, concerning the blood libel. The maggid knew what he must do. He went to his Hasid, Reb Moshe Leib of Sassov, and led him into the forest to the secret place of the Ba'al Shem Tov. But he did not light a fire, for he knew that a soul such as that of the Ba'al Shem Tov existed only once in a hundred generations. Instead, he told the story to Reb Moshe Leib, and he said: "Perhaps we can no longer light the fire, but let us meditate and pray, for I still remember the prayer of the Besht." And he repeated the words of the prayer out loud for the first time since he had heard them so many years before, and not a single word was missing. Reb Moshe Leib listened with complete concentration, but he was not able to recall any of the words. And when they returned to the city, they learned that the danger had passed.

A generation later, Reb Moshe Leib of Sassov was himself called upon to fulfill a great task concerning the redemption of many captives. But because there was no one to accompany him, he went into the forest alone. He knew that he could not light the fire, nor did he know the prayer, but at least he knew the place. And that proved to be enough.

But when the time came in the next generation for Reb Israel of Rizhin to perform the task, he said to his Hasidim: "We cannot light the fire, we cannot speak the words of the prayer, we do not even know the place. But we can tell the story of what happened." And he did. And that was enough.

—Eastern Europe: nineteenth century

91. The Tefillin of the Or ha-Hayim

hen the time came for Rabbi Hayim ben Attar, known as the Or ha-Hayim, to take leave of this world, he called his wife closer. She saw how weak he was and bent nearer, and he said: "After my death a wealthy man will come from Kushta and offer you three hundred gold pieces for my tefillin. Don't refuse his offer. But be sure to tell him to be careful with the tefillin. He should never let himself become distracted for even an instant while wearing them." The wife of the Or ha-Hayim vowed to do as he had asked, and he closed his eyes and breathed his last.

All of Israel was saddened by his death. Many mourned over him for thirty days. And after the thirty days had ended, a wealthy man from Kushta came to the wife of the Or ha-Hayim and asked to purchase the rabbi's tefillin, exactly as he had foreseen. She informed the man of the rabbi's request that he take care not to be distracted while wearing the tefillin. And he, in turn, vowed to receive the tefillin on those terms. In this way did the rabbi's wife fulfill her vow to her husband, and the gold she received saved her from a life of poverty for the rest of her days.

The morning after returning home, the wealthy man put on the tefillin for the first time. As he did, he felt a transformation, as if he had received an extra soul. That day the man prayed with a fervor he had never known, nor even imagined he could attain. And he came to understand that whenever he put on those tefillin, the soul of the Or ha-Hayim would fuse with his own, and he would see the world through the eyes of the Or ha-Hayim.

After praying he took the tefillin off in the prescribed manner, and when he did, he felt the extra soul depart, exactly as happens at the end of the Sabbath. And he was filled with wonder at the miracle of those tefillin.

From that day on, the wealthy man guarded the tefillin as his most prized possession. Each time he put them on, he took care that his concentration was complete. And each time he finished binding the tefillin, the spirit of the Or ha-Hayim returned to him, and his prayers soared to the palaces on high. During this time his thoughts were much clearer, his soul much calmer, and he saw as never before the harmony of the Creator and His creation.

But once, while the man was wrapped in his tallit and tefillin, a servant distracted him with a matter concerning his store. He responded to the servant, but when he returned to his prayers, the holy spirit was gone. Nor did the soul of the Or ha-Hayim return.

At last, in desperation, the man took the tefillin to a *sofer*. And when the *sofer* opened the boxes of the tefillin and took out the parchments, he was amazed to find that they were blank, with not a single letter written on them. For the instant the man had turned away, every letter had taken flight, along with the spirit of the Or ha-Hayim.

—Palestine: nineteenth century

92. The Angel of Friendship

Among the Hasidim of Reb Pinhas of Koretz were Ze'ev Wolf of Zhitomir and Aaron Samuel ben Naftali Hertz, who had been study partners for many years and were the closest friends. For more than a year, they had been separated from Reb Pinhas and from each other. Aaron Samuel had traveled to the Holy Land, to the Holy City of Jerusalem, and had just returned to Koretz that day. Ze'ev Wolf, as it happened, returned on that same day from more than a year spent in the yeshivah of the Maggid of Mezhirich, where Reb Pinhas had sent him to study.

As each Hasid entered the House of Study, they greeted their rebbe with the traditional blessing recited when seeing a great scholar of Torah: "Blessed art thou, Oh Lord Our God, King of the Universe, Who has given of His wisdom to those who fear Him." But when the two friends laid eyes on each other after such a long time, they each instinctively cried out the traditional blessing recited when seeing a friend again after more than a year has passed: "Blessed art thou Oh Lord our God, King of the Universe, who raises the dead."

The rebbe and his students all rejoiced at this fortunate and coincidental reunion. Then one of the younger students asked the rebbe: "Why is it that when we see a friend we have not seen for a year, we are commanded to bless God for reviving the dead? Surely this is a strange commandment, since no one has died."

Reb Pinhas replied: "We learn in the *Zohar* that everyone has a light burning for them in the world above, and everyone's light is unique. When two friends meet, their lights above are united, and out of that union of two lights an angel is born. That angel has the strength to survive for only one year, unless its life is renewed when the friends meet again. But if they are separated for more than a year, the angel begins to languish and eventually wastes away. That is why we bless the dead upon meeting a friend we have not seen for more than a year, to revive the angel."

Just as the rebbe finished speaking they heard a sound like the rustling of wings, and a sudden wind swirled around the room, brushing against them, and they knew that the angel had been reborn.

—Eastern Europe: nineteenth century

93. The Underground Forest

n the eve of the third anniversary of his father's death, the student Reuven dreamed that his father came to him and told him to go to the town of Koretz. When Reuven awoke, he marveled at this dream, and at how real his father had seemed to him. And he wondered about the strange message: to go to a place where he didn't know anyone. But to whom and for what purpose? And how could he leave the yeshivah? Surely they would forbid him to go on the basis of a dream.

All day Reuven strongly felt his father's presence, and the next night the dream was repeated. But this time his father told him to go to the town of Koretz for Rosh Hodesh, the Feast of the New Moon. Reuven realized a decision must be made—whether to act on the dream or not.

The dilemma resolved itself the third night, when the dream recurred, except that this time Reuven's father told him to go to Koretz for Rosh Hodesh and seek out Reb Pinhas.

After that, Reuven decided that he must go to Koretz, no matter what. His father had compelled him. He understood that. And he wrote a letter to the head of the yeshivah explaining that he had left on business, to claim an inheritance in Koretz. This, he reasoned, would be more acceptable to him than his father's command in a dream.

Reuven took a carriage to Koretz. In the carriage were two Hasidim of that town. As Reuven listened, they spoke about Reb Pinhas. "It is said," said one Hasid, "that Reb Pinhas can read the thoughts of men." "That is true," said the other, "for I myself have heard of a man who came to Reb Pinhas when he was full of doubts that God could read his thoughts. When he knocked on the door, Reb Pinhas opened it and said: 'Young man, I myself know what you are thinking. And if I know, should not God know?' " And Reuven wondered what kind of man he had been sent to, who could read the thoughts of men.

Reuven arrived only a few hours before the eve of Rosh Hodesh, the Feast of the New Moon. Reb Pinhas greeted him and welcomed him to use the *mikveh* before Rosh Hodesh. A servant showed him where the *mikveh* could be found, in a hut behind the rebbe's house. The young man walked to the little hut and stepped inside. He saw a stairway, but from the top of the stairs he could not see the water below. Instead, he heard a deep warbling sound, like the call of an exotic bird. How strange, he thought to himself, that this calling should come from within the *mikveh*.

Curious to see for himself, the student descended the stairs. Much to his amazement, the stairway was very long, much longer than that of any other *mikveh* he had ever seen. And he soon found that he could see neither the top of the stairs nor the bottom from where he stood. He feared that something strange was taking place, as if he were descending from one world into another. Surely, he thought, no stairway could be this long!

Each step of the way, the noise from below grew louder. Soon he could make out a cacophony of forest sounds—birds whistling, wolves howling, the wind shaking the trees. He wanted to turn back, but he controlled himself and continued on. Surely, he thought, I am almost there.

At last the student reached the bottom of the abyss, but he found no sign of a *mikveh*. Instead, he found himself standing on the floor of a dense forest. Had he entered the wrong hut? The young man decided to turn back. But when he turned around, the stairs were gone. There was no sign of them at all. How would he ever return to the world above?

With no other choice, the student peered around him and saw that it was growing dark. He knew it was unsafe to stay where he was, so he looked for a tree in which to spend the night. He found one in a nearby clearing and pulled himself up into the branches. He was comfortable, but he knew he must not fall asleep or he might tumble to the ground.

When it was completely dark, a band of robbers came into that clearing and made a campfire not far from the very tree into which the student had climbed. He was well hidden in the branches, but he was terrified that the robbers would find him and strip him of everything, perhaps even his life. And it was true that they were a vicious band, for they bragged about their exploits, how many men they had killed, and who among them was the most ruthless. They bragged half the night, until they fell into a drunken sleep. And all the while the poor student trembled in the tree, holding his breath for as long as possible and then breathing very quietly. When they were asleep at last, the student was exhausted. He would have loved to sleep himself, but he knew that his life depended on remaining awake.

So it was that the student in the tree saw a serpent slither toward the branch on which the robbers' wineskin had been hung, still open. The snake slid inside the wineskin and stayed there a long time, until it was so engorged it spit up the wine, mixed with its own poison. Then the snake crawled out and disappeared into the forest.

When the robbers awoke in the morning, the student watched them take swigs of the wine. Then, one after another, they began to choke from the poison, and soon they all lay dead.

Now the student carefully lowered himself from the tree and made sure that every one of the robbers was dead. Then he looked for something to eat. In one of the robbers' bags he found a loaf of bread, but the others were crammed with stolen riches of every kind. Reuven emptied bag after bag onto the ground and was amazed at all they had carried away. But when he shook out the last bag, he found it had a false bottom. He took a knife and cut it open, and a shining object came tumbling out—a round, glowing jewel. He held it up and turned it around, but try as he might, Reuven could not see the source of the light inside it. Surely, he thought, that was a priceless treasure. And he recognized that such a precious object could only be owned by a king.

Now this student cared little for material goods. His concerns were those of the spirit. He would not have minded leaving all the gold and silver behind, but he could not abandon that glowing jewel, so he put it into his own bag. Then he buried the robbers and said a prayer over their souls, for surely they had found terrible punishments for their evil deeds. And then he went on his way, going in the direction the robbers had come from, in the hope that he would find a city or town of some kind. And he gave thanks to God for letting him survive that dangerous night.

Little by little, the faint path he followed become well worn, and that, in turn, led him to a road wide enough for the king's horse and carriage. Soon he reached the gates of that underground city.

There the student saw that the people of the city were dressed for mourning, and he asked a young man passing by what had happened. "Two tragedies have struck our kingdom at the same time. First, our king died without leaving any heir except for his daughter, the princess. And second, the king's enchanted jewel was stolen by thieves. Now this glowing jewel has always revealed who will succeed the king. But now no one knows where it is. Even so, the princess has declared that she will marry whoever brings that glowing jewel to her, for the jewel has always succeeded in reaching the one who was destined to be king. For it is guided by the hand of fate."

Now the student shivered when he heard this, for he was carrying the glowing jewel in his pack. He took his leave of the young man and set off for the palace. And when he reached it, he asked for an audience with the princess, saying that he had news of the glowing jewel.

When the guards heard this, they took him to the princess at once, and he was overwhelmed by her great beauty and by the wisdom and radiance of her eyes. "Tell me," she said, "what you know about the jewel?" The student was speechless, but he pulled the jewel out of his pack and gave it to her. The princess looked at him with amazement and said, "Then it is you who is destined to be my husband, and you who are destined to rule. But how did you come into possession of the jewel?"

So the young man told her of his night in the forest and all that he had witnessed. He offered to lead guards to that very place, to confirm his account and to recover the other items the robbers had stolen. This was done, and the guards confirmed everything he had said. So it was that the wedding soon took place, and the young man, who had been a poor student, now found himself a great king in that underground country.

Now the young man ruled using the principles of the rabbis, as he had learned in his studies of the Talmud, and the kingdom flourished. So too did the young man fall in love with the princess, now his queen. Together they had three children, two boys and a girl, and he loved all of them as much as life itself.

Then one day there was a sudden downpour that grew into a great torrent. A great wave washed through the palace and carried the king out an open window and away from that world forever. The current carried him further and further downstream, and suddenly thrust him into a great whirlpool. As he was pulled down, the young man was certain that his life had come to an end. Then, all at once, he found himself standing in a *mikveh*. Then he recalled having descended the stairs in search of the *mikveh* just before reaching the underground forest. Now he looked up and saw a short stairway nearby, with no more than ten steps. He climbed out, greatly confused, and stumbled back to the home of Reb Pinhas. The moment the rabbi opened the door, the student burst into tears and asked the rabbi how long he had been gone. "Why, no more than an hour," Reb Pinhas said. Then the student told the rabbi of all the years that he had lived through since he had gone into the *mikveh*, and he poured out his heart and begged the rabbi to explain how such things had happened to him. For it seemed to him that the world had been turned upside down.

Reb Pinhas said, "Let me first introduce you to my daughter, and then I will explain." He called forth his daughter, and when the student saw her, he almost fainted. For she was the very princess he had wed in the underground city! The rabbi saw that the young man was overwhelmed, and he quickly said: "Listen carefully to what I tell you. I learned from a heavenly voice that it was you who were destined to marry my daughter. And when you arrived here, I recognized you at once. That is why I sent you to the *mikveh*, for in this way you traveled the path of your own destiny, and now you can understand that you are indeed destined for my daughter."

So it was that the young man married the daughter of Reb Pinhas, and they loved each other as if they had already been married in another life. And they had three children, two boys and a girl, who were identical to the children he had when he was king. And Reuven loved all of them with all his heart and thanked God for restoring his family to him. And at the same time he held them dear to him at all times, for he remembered well how quickly they had been lost.

—Eastern Europe: nineteenth century

94. Reb Nachman's Chair

efore he died, Reb Nachman of Bratslav said to his Hasidim: "After my death it will not be necessary to appoint a successor, for I will always be your rebbe." Nor did anyone ever take his place. And Reb Nachman's spirit did indeed guard and guide his followers. Many tales are told of how Reb Nachman's spirit came to their assistance. One of these tales concerns Reb Nachman's chair.

Shortly before Rosh ha-Shanah in 1808, the *shohet* of Teplik brought Reb Nachman a beautiful chair that he had made for him. He had carved the chair for many months, and Reb Nachman was delighted with it. From the first everyone realized it was a very special chair, as beautiful and intricate as any throne.

That night Reb Nachman dreamed that someone brought him a throne, surrounded by fire. Everyone, men, women, and children, came to see it. Engraved on that throne were all the world's creatures, along with their mates. And as the people turned to go, bonds were formed between them and marriages were arranged at once, for each had been able to find his mate. And in the dream Reb Nachman sat down on the chair, and all at once he found himself flying through the heavens, and before him he saw Jerusalem, glowing like a jewel in the distance. It was indescribably beautiful, and as he approached it, he woke up.

Reb Nachman shared this dream with his Hasidim, and it became part of the lore of the chair. Reb Nachman used that chair every day. And when he died, his Hasidim put the empty chair next to the Ark, for they never forgot the last words of their rebbe: that he would always be with them.

The chair remained with the Bratslavers until the Second World War. Then, after the Nazis invaded, the Hasidim realized they must escape as soon as possible. But what were they to do with the chair? They decided to cut it into small pieces and to give one piece to every Hasid. Then they made a vow among themselves to meet in Jerusalem and to reassemble the chair there. And they took leave of each other and set out, each in his own way, to reach the Holy Land.

Now that was a very dangerous time, and few were those who escaped unharmed. But every Bratslaver who carried a piece of that chair arrived safely in Jerusalem. There it was reassembled. The name of the carpenter who worked on that chair was Reb Katriel, and he took as much care in restoring that chair as in repairing a broken vessel. And when it was finished, the chair looked exactly as it did when Reb Nachman first received it. Even today it can be found in the Bratslaver synagogue in Jerusalem, next to the Ark.

Israel: oral tradition

95. The Soul of the Ari

ne winter morning Reb Zevi Hirsch of Zhidachov rose very early, when it was still dark outside. Although no candles were lit, a light pervaded the rooms of his house. Reb Zevi found that the light was coming from a cupboard. There he found a precious stone with a light that glowed from within. Reb Zevi realized that the value of that stone could not be calculated, and he hid it away.

Then he fasted from the end of one Sabbath to the beginning of the next so that he might know what it was. And in a dream it was revealed that this stone had been a gift to him from heaven. If he chose to keep it, he and all of his descendants would be very wealthy. But if he preferred, he could receive the soul of the holy Ari, which would become fused with his own.

Now Reb Zevi did not desire wealth, and the choice was not difficult for him to make. He asked to know how he should return the precious stone, and in a dream he was told to fling it up toward heaven. This he did, and the stone soared on high, with fiery sparks flying from it from until nothing more could be seen.

Later one of Reb Zevi's students, who slept in the room next to his, heard a voice speaking to his master during the night. He could not imagine who this could be, so he rose and washed his hands and stood beside the wall and listened. The voice that spoke was interpreting a passage of the *Zohar,* casting great light on its mysteries. And the student was filled with wonder, but he dared not ask the rabbi about it.

During the next Sabbath, Reb Zevi began to expound on a passage from the Zohar, and the student recognized the teachings of the mysterious voice he had heard. And when Reb Zevi finished, he said: "This is what I learned from the very mouth of the Ari." Then the student knew whose voice he had heard that night.

—Eastern Europe: nineteenth century

96. The Blind Angel

Among the Hasidim of Reb Mordecai of Chernobyl was Rabbi Eliakim, a merchant of great wealth and a collector of rare and precious religious objects. So wealthy was Reb Eliakim that he even owned his own scroll of the Torah, which was prominently displayed in an Ark that had been built into a wall of his living room.

Once Reb Mordecai came to pay him a visit, and Reb Eliakim was beside himself with joy, proudly showing off his precious objects to his rabbi. And each time Reb Mordecai seemed pleased by a particular object, Reb Eliakim had it wrapped and placed in a crate for the rabbi to take back with him.

Before long the crate was almost filled with silver goblets, embroidered matzah and challah covers, and other precious treasures of Reb Eliakim, and at last the rabbi rose to take his leave, thanking Reb Eliakim for his generosity. At that moment the rabbi's eye fell on a beautiful antique silver menorah, one of Reb Eliakim's most prized possessions. For a long time the rabbi stared at that menorah, and Reb Eliakim and everyone else clearly saw that he desired it, yet Reb Eliakim could not bring himself to offer it, for it was a priceless heirloom.

Finally the Rabbi of Chernobyl broke the silence, asking, as a special favor, for the silver menorah. Everyone watched Reb Eliakim closely, for they knew how much he prized that menorah, and they saw that he was struggling with himself. At last Reb Eliakim ordered his servant to wrap the menorah, place it with the other gifts, and carry the crate to the rabbi's carriage.

When they returned home, the rabbi had the crate opened, and displayed all of the gifts he had received from Reb Eliakim except for the silver menorah, which was kept in storage. His Hasidim did not understand why he had asked for it or why he did not display it, but they dared not question the rabbi.

Time passed, and Reb Eliakim took his leave of this world, and eventually the episode of the silver menorah was forgotten. Ten years later, on the eve of Hanukah, Reb Mordecai had the menorah brought out of storage and prepared for lighting. As the flames burned brightly, reflected in the polished silver of the menorah, Reb Mordecai told his Hasidim a tale.

"This menorah once belonged to Reb Yosef David, who was a rich man for most of his life but then fell upon hard times. Reb Eliakim had desired this menorah for many years and often tried to purchase it, but no matter how much he offered, Reb Yosef David refused to sell it, for this menorah had been in his family for many generations. However, when his situation grew desperate, Reb Yosef David went to Reb Eliakim for a loan. Reb Eliakim agreed to give him a generous loan, with the silver menorah to serve as security. But when the loan was due, Reb Yosef David could not repay it, and thus he had to relinquish the menorah to Reb Eliakim.

"Now, as we know, every good deed creates an angel. But if a deed is imperfect, it produces an imperfect angel. In giving Reb Yosef David a loan, Reb Eliakim did a good deed, and therefore an angel came into being. However, because his intentions were not completely pure, Reb Eliakim's angel was blind.

"After his death, Reb Eliakim was brought before the heavenly court. His good deeds and bad deeds were weighed, and they balanced exactly. All at once the blind angel took its place on the right side of the scale, and it tipped in Reb Eliakim's favor. Seeing this, the heavenly court ruled that Reb Eliakim might be permitted to enter Paradise, but since his margin was so narrow, he would have to be led there by the blind angel.

"Ever since, Reb Eliakim and the blind angel have wandered, and his soul has found no rest. For the blind angel could not find the way to Paradise. And without some special merit, his soul would have continued to wander for many years to come. But tonight the light of this menorah reached all the way to the upper world, restoring the angel's sight, and making it possible for the angel to lead Reb Eliakim's soul to its resting place in Paradise.

"Now you know why, long ago, I asked Reb Eliakim for his menorah. For it was the merit of this gift that he needed in order to repair the eyesight of the angel. I never used it until now, as I was waiting for the right moment. Last night, I saw Reb Eliakim, led by the blind angel, in a dream. From this I knew that they were close, and tonight, as the flames ascended, that they were passing over. And now Reb Eliakim is basking in the sacred light of Paradise."

—Eastern Europe: nineteenth century

97. A New Soul

Hannah Rochel, the Maid of Ludomir, had a very lonely childhood. She lost her mother when she was very young, and she rarely saw her wealthy father. She spent her days praying at the grave of her mother and learning the Torah, and in time she came to be as knowledgeable as any young man.

One day, when Hannah Rochel went to the grave of her mother, she fell asleep. And when she awoke, she found herself alone in the graveyard. It was midnight, and it seemed as if spirits were swarming everywhere. She was terrified. She started running and fell into an open grave.

That is where they found her, barely alive. For a long time her soul fluttered between this world and the next. At last her soul ascended on high, and she found herself in a heavenly court. There she was told that she was to receive a new soul. And this, indeed, is what happened.

When Hannah Rochel opened her eyes, the first thing she said to her father was, "I have just returned from the Heavenly Court, where I have received a new soul." After that, Hannah Rochel wrapped herself in a tallit and put on tefillin. At her father's funeral she recited Kaddish for him. And she spent her days in the study of the Torah, delving into the mystical texts.

In time her wisdom was recognized, and she was regarded as a rabbi among some of the Hasidim. A synagogue was built in her honor, with her room attached to the House of Study. Rabbis and scholars assembled there, and the Maid of Ludomir, as she was now known, discoursed from behind a curtain, and all were held spellbound by her teachings.

A time came when the Maid of Ludomir decided to ascend to the Holy Land. There in Jerusalem she met an old kabbalist, who was a descendant of the great Yemenite kabbalist Rabbi Shalom Shabazi. The old kabbalist recognized the depth of her knowledge and how great was her longing for the Messiah. He, too, as he neared the end of his life, had grown impatient for the Messiah to come. They decided to meet in a cave at twilight on a certain day to pronounce the prayers that would make the footsteps of the Messiah heard in this world.

The Maid of Ludomir came to the cave on that day, but the old kabbalist did not, for an old man came to his house just as he was about to go, and delayed his departure. And that old man was Elijah, who had been sent by heaven to stop the two from offering their prayers at the same time and forcing the End of Days. When the old kabbalist did not arrive, the Maid of Ludomir went ahead without him, so great was her longing. She prayed the prayers of unification and pronounced the secret name of the Prince of the Torah. And at that instant her soul took flight and returned to its place on high. Nor could the old kabbalist ever find the entrance to that cave again when he searched for her, and no one knows where her bones are to be found.

—Eastern Europe: nineteenth century

98. The Tale of the Kugel

Hasid who was a wealthy merchant once came to Reb Menachem Mendel of Lubavitch, the Zemach Tzaddik, for permission to divorce his wife. The Hasid was worried, for he knew the rabbi regarded marriage as one of the pillars of existence and rarely gave his blessing for divorce. Nor would the man do anything without his rebbe's permission, for the rebbe was the pillar of his life. So he was quite tense when he came to the rebbe's house and requested an audience.

The Hasid arrived just before breakfast. Indeed, the first thing that struck him as he walked inside was the delicious smell of food. He had left before dawn in order to reach the rebbe's house, for he hoped to return to work before the end of the day. The rebbe's wife seated him in the living room, but she did not invite the man to join them for breakfast.

From where he sat, the man saw the rebbe enter his study to put on his tefillin and heard him chanting prayers. Even though the rabbi twice passed by the door of the living room, but he did not seem to notice the Hasid waiting there.

The morning passed. The rabbi did not emerge from his study, nor did any others come to the house. The man wondered why no other petitioners came that day and why the rebbe did not call him into his study.

Before long it was time for lunch. The man, who had not eaten that day, was tormented by the tantalizing scents of the cooking food. But still he was left to sit alone. Again the rebbe passed the doorway twice without any indication that he had seen him.

By evening the man was exhausted with hunger and waiting, but still there was no sign of the rabbi. Now the delicate smells of dinner reached him, tormenting him, in particular the smell of kugel, which he loved. If only they would take notice of him and invite him to join them for dinner! But they did not.

By the time the dinner ended, the man was deeply worried about the meaning of the rabbi's actions. So he was greatly relieved when the rabbi's wife came to him shortly thereafter and led him to the rabbi's study.

When the man walked into the study, he was struck again with the smell of kugel, even more potent than it had been in the living room. At the same moment he saw the rabbi with a plate of kugel before him. Reb Menachem Mendel looked up at him and asked him why he had come. Then the Hasid poured out his heart about his wife, who in almost ten years of marriage had failed to give him a child, leaving him without a son to say Kaddish for him. And since it is permitted to divorce a childless woman after ten years, he had come to seek the rebbe's permission.

The rebbe stood up, taking the plate of kugel in his hand, and offered it to the Hasid. "Here," he said, "first, eat some kugel; then we will talk." At that moment the man remembered that he was famished, and he gladly took the plate of kugel, picked up a piece, and took a bite of it. It was the most delicious food he had ever tasted. And yet, strange to say, he had taken no more than a single bite when his hunger vanished.

At that moment the rabbi spoke: "Go now and know that I have approved your request. There shall be a *get*, a bill of divorce, on your tenth anniversary. Be here with your wife on that day, and bring your wedding contract."

Amazed at how the rebbe had agreed without any objections, the man left, and he came back there on his tenth anniversary to divorce his wife. Not long afterward he remarried, and before a year was out he was the father of a beautiful girl. Indeed, every year after that he became the father of another daughter, until he had six girls but no boy who could say his Kaddish. And in despair he went back to the rebbe.

This time he was given an audience as soon as he entered the door. Back in the rebbe's chamber, the smell of kugel again struck him, and soon the rebbe was standing, offering him to taste some. Remembering the good luck it had brought him last time in obtaining the rebbe's approval, the man took a single bite, and at that very moment the rebbe again gave him permission to divorce his wife.

By the time he had left his wife and six daughters, the merchant was a much poorer man in wealth and in spirit, but at least he was free to seek out his Kaddish. And in less than a year he married again. This time his wish came true, and his wife's first child was a son. The man knew that he had been right all along to persevere, even at the price he had paid, and he lavished love and gifts on his son. And by the time the boy was three years old, he was recognized as a prodigy, and all who saw him predicted that he would be a great scholar in Torah.

It happened that the Hasid had to travel by ship on business. He could not bear the thought of leaving his son behind, so he hired a tutor and brought the boy with him on the voyage. Then one day there was a storm at sea, and the boat started to sink. It all happened so fast that the man was not able to save his son. He watched in horror as a great wave carried the boy off, and that was the last he ever saw of him. So great was his grief that he almost welcomed death so that he could be with his son again. But just then the mast of the ship floated by, and the man's instinct to save himself took over. He grabbed it just as a giant wave picked it up and carried it for many hours, until the man found himself washed up on a distant shore. Eventually the heartbroken father made his way back to his home town, but he could hardly bear to break the terrible news to his wife, so he went to see the rebbe first.

This time the rebbe himself opened the door, and he recognized the man's grief at once. He gently led him into his study and gave him a seat. Then the rebbe brought over a plate of food. "Would you like some kugel?" the rabbi asked. And the man, remembering all the misery that his divorces had brought on, whispered "No" and began to weep. And he wept with all his heart. When at last he looked up, he heard the rebbe say, "No, you may not have a *get*."

This greatly confused the man, and he said: "What do you mean, rebbe? I have not come to you for a *get*. Far from it. I have had enough of divorces. After two divorces I finally got the son of my dreams, and I lost him, due to my own foolishness in taking him with me on a dangerous voyage. If only it had been me, and not him, who had died!"

"Let me assure you," said the rebbe, "that you have not been divorced even once. It is only now that you have requested your first divorce. Nor do you have any children."

"What do you mean?" the man shouted. "My first divorce was many years ago. Oh, if only I had not been divorced, my life would not have been ruined."

"Here," said the rebbe, picking up a copy of a newspaper and showing it to the man. And he saw that it was the same day that he had come asking for his first divorce. And then he realized that only a short time had passed, while for him it had seemed like half a lifetime. And he realized that a strange miracle had taken place, for he had seen the futility of divorcing his wife, whose only flaw was a failure to bear him a son. The man was awed by what had happened to him, and he took leave of the rebbe.

So too did he remain married, and before the twelfth year of marriage had passed, he became the father of a fine son, much to his amazement. And he loved that son with all his heart, and from the day the boy was old enough to understand, he made him take a vow that he would never set foot in a ship. So too did the boy keep this vow, and his life flourished. And when the merchant died, his son said Kaddish for him and always kept his memory alive.

—Eastern Europe: oral tradition

99. The Ocean of Tears

Reb Yitzhak of Vorki and his son, Mendele, were inseparable. Every day Reb Yitzhak shared his wisdom with his son and taught him loving-kindness. Then it happened that Reb Yitzhak died. Mendele's grief was boundless, but he held out hope that his father might contact him from world to come. But a month passed, and no message came from Reb Yitzhak, not even a dream.

Now Mendele had been named after the Kotzker Rebbe, Reb Menachem Mendel of Kotzk, his father's closest friend. So Mendele decided to go to Kotzk, to find out why he had not heard from his father. Now the Kotzker Rebbe rarely received visitors, but when he was told that Reb Yitzhak's son was there, he received him at once.

When they were together, Mendele said, "Rebbe, my father never went on a journey without writing to me every day. You know how close we were. I was certain he would find a way to contact me from *Gan Eden*. But a month has passed and I have not heard from him."

The Kotzker said: "Mendele, I share your grief. Your father and I were like brothers. I too expected him to contact me from the world to come. But when he did not come to me, I decided to go to him.

"Now all the great sages have their own palaces in the world to come, where they continue to teach the Torah. I ascended on high until I came to the palace of Rashi. There I saw that a myriad of angels and the souls of the righteous had gathered to hear him. I took a seat in the last row, and listened with great joy to Rashi's teachings. Then I went to him and said, 'Beloved teacher Rashi, I have always treasured your teachings. But I have come here to find Reb Yitzhak of Vorki. Have you seen him?'

"And Rashi said, 'Ah, Reb Yitzhak. He brought many mysteries of the Torah to share with us. Yes, he was here, but he left.' So I thanked Rashi and ascended higher, to the palace of Maimonides. Again, a multitude of angels and righteous souls were gathered there, and I listened as the Rambam illuminated the Torah with his teachings. After he had spoken, I went to the Rambam and embraced him and thanked him for his teachings. And I told him of my mission to find your father. And he said, 'Reb Yitzhak—what a teacher! He taught us wonderful secrets of the Torah. Yes, he was here, but he left.'

"Then I took my leave and ascended to the palace of Moshe Rabbenu, our teacher Moses. There, in the presence of angels and righteous souls, I heard the Torah taught from the very lips of Moses. I wanted to remain there for all time, but then I remembered my mission. So when Moses finished,

I went to him, weeping, and I thanked him for the eternal blessings of the Torah.

"And Moses pointed to an empty place and said to me, 'Look, rebbe, we have been saving a place for you. Have you come to join us?'

"'No,' I answered with regret, 'not yet. I am on a mission to find Reb Yitzhak of Vorki. Have you seen him?'

"Moses replied: 'Ah, Reb Yitzhak. You know, I thought I had learned everything there was to know about the Torah at Mount Sinai, but Reb Yitzhak showed me how much more there is to learn. Yes, he was here, but he left.'

"So I reluctantly took leave of Moses and ascended even higher, into the highest heaven, *Aravot*. There I found myself before the palace of Avraham Aveinu, our father Abraham. I joined the fortunate angels and souls who had gathered there to hear the Torah from the lips of Abraham. I marveled at how clear Abraham's voice was, and how brightly his eyes shone. All my life I had longed to be in the presence of Abraham, and now that I was, how could I tear myself away? But then I remembered your father, and I knew I could not rest until I had found him.

"So when Abraham finished speaking, I went to him, kissed his hands, and thanked him for the abundant blessings he had brought his people. And Abraham embraced me and said, 'You, too, rebbe, have brought great honor upon us. How can I help you?' Then I poured out my heart to Abraham, and told him how much I missed Reb Yitzhak since he had taken leave of the world. And I asked Abraham if Reb Yitzhak had been there.

"'Of course he was here!" Abraham said. "He is a wonderful teacher. He taught us how to read the white letters hidden between the black letters of the Torah. We will never forget all that he taught us. But, I am sorry to say, he left.'

"And I said, 'Please, Avraham Aveinu, tell me where I can find him.'

"And Abraham said, 'If you are so determined to find him, here is what you must do: go back to the world you came from and travel to the ends of the earth. There you will find a dark forest that seems endless. If you can make your way through that forest, you will find Reb Yitzhak.'

"I wept when Abraham revealed where your father could be found. I embraced him and reluctantly took my leave. I returned to this world and traveled to the very ends of the earth. And I finally found that forest, but it was much darker than I had imagined. It seemed to take twenty years to make my way through it. But at last it came to an end, and there I saw a great ocean. But it was not like any ocean I had ever seen. Its waters rose up all the way to heaven, and fell back with a sound of sighing and moaning. And then I saw your father, Reb Yitzhak, standing by the shore of that ocean, leaning on a staff.

"'Yitzhak! Yitzhak!' I called out.

"'Mendel!' he cried. 'Mendel, how did you ever find me? Come here!'

"So I joined him, and, at last, we were together, and we embraced and wept. Then Reb Yitzhak said, 'Mendel, do you know what ocean this is?'

"And I turned to that strange ocean once again, and saw how its waves rose up and fell back and heard its sighs and moans. And I said, 'No, what ocean is this?'

"And Reb Yitzhak said, 'This is the Ocean of Tears, of all the tears shed by the Jews. And I swore, by God, that I would not move from here until God dries all the tears!' "

—Eastern Europe: oral tradition

100. The Dream Assembly

ne day, when Reb Hayim Elya entered the Beit Midrash, he overheard a heated argument among Reb Zalman's Hasidim. The question was: what was the true purpose of prayer?

Reb Shmuel Leib said: "The purpose of prayer is to recognize our Oneness with God."

Reb Feivel the Light said: "The purpose of prayer is to attune body and soul."

Reb Feivel the Dark said: "The purpose of prayer is to open up the heart and let the heart sing its praises to God."

Reb Sholem said: "It seems to me that you have overlooked the most basic purpose of prayer, which is to become a servant to God. And if you can't be a servant first, you don't have the right to be a teacher or a lover or anything else."

Then Reb Hayim Elya spoke up and said: "The whole purpose of prayer is to bring down blessings. For without these blessings, prayer serves no purpose."

Then Reb Aharon joined the discussion and said: "The purpose of prayer is to perform repentance, for without repentance, what is the point of prayer?"

All at once the Hasidim grew silent, for each one had spoken, but Reb Zalman had said nothing, and all of them knew that he understood prayer better than anyone else. Therefore they waited for him to select the one who had best recognized its purpose, as if he were the judge in a rabbinic court. But Reb Zalman did not address himself to the issue at all; instead he said: "I would like all of you to join me in a dream tonight." And at that he signaled for the evening prayers to begin and said no more about it.

Now the Hasidim were quite confused, for how is it possible to join another in a dream? Then Reb Shmuel Leib turned to the others and whispered: "I have read reports of such a thing when the rabbis joined together in a dream assembly. But that was long ago, and no such assembly has been called in our time." And the others asked Shmuel Leib if he could recall any other details he had heard, such as how they could meet together. And he thought a long time and at last he said: "I recall that when we say the prayer upon retiring, and we come to the words 'Grant that we lie down in peace, O Lord,' we must lie down; and when we come to the words 'And assist me with Thy good counsel,' we must put our heads on the pillow and listen; and when we come to the words 'Guard our going out and our coming in,' we must close our eyes. And if each of these is done at the proper time, those who joined in prayer together will be joined together in a dream."

The Hasidim listened to these words, and just then Reb Zalman began to chant the first prayer. And that night each and every one of Reb Zalman's Hasidim said the prayer before retiring, and did as Shmuel Leib had told them, and that night they met each other in a dream.

In the dream they found themselves in an orchard, where none of them had ever been before. The Hasidim were very confused to find themselves there, but then Reb Shmuel Leib remembered that Reb Zalman had told them to assemble together in a dream, and he realized that they must be dreaming. But he did not tell the others, for he was afraid that if they knew they were dreaming, they might wake up. Instead he merely said: "Have you forgotten? Reb Zalman asked us to meet him here." And then the others did recall that Reb Zalman had told them to assemble, but they did not remember that the place of the meeting was a dream. And since they knew they were supposed to be there, their fears subsided, and they looked around, to see if Reb Zalman was there.

That is when they saw him. He was sitting beneath a tree in a corner of the orchard, and all of the Hasidim hurried to him and silently assembled in a circle around him. When they had all been seated, Reb Zalman looked up. And the Hasidim all noticed that although there was no doubt that it was Reb Zalman, still he seemed different. He seemed younger and less burdened by the weight of the world. And there was a wonderful smile on his face.

Then Reb Zalman said: "To bring us here together was not a simple matter, far more difficult than ascending a ladder from earth to heaven. But now that we are here, there is something of great importance for us to accomplish. Know that there is a great mystery concerning how prayers ascend to heaven. The prayers themselves do not have wings. They have to be carried into the heights. And how are they carried? On the wings of a dove, as it is written, *And he sent forth a dove* (Gen. 8:8). But what is not known is that each generation requires its own dove that can carry its prayers to the angel Sandalphon, who weaves those prayers into garlands of prayer for the Holy One to wear on His Throne of Glory.

"Know that in every age this dove must be created anew. The first dove was created by Abraham, single-handed. But except for Moses none has been able to create the dove by himself until the time of the Ba'al Shem Tov. Even the Ari required the assistance of Hayim Vital in order to bring the dove into being. In our own age there is no one who can bring this dove into being by himself. And therefore the creation of the dove is much more difficult. Great harmony is required, and an effort that is perfectly shared. This, then, is why I have called upon us to assemble here: to bring the prayer dove into being, so that our prayers may ascend in our generation."

And then Reb Zalman stood up, and the Hasidim saw a look in his eyes that they had never seen before, a determination so complete that merely to gaze upon him was to be caught up in that power and to have no desire other than to share in undertaking that difficult, nay, impossible task.

Then Reb Zalman looked at Feivel the Dark and said: "You, Feivel, must create the feet, so that the bird can perch securely on any branch." And he turned to Feivel the Light and said: "And you, Feivel, must create its wings, so that it can soar into the heights of *Aravot*, the highest heaven." Then Reb Zalman turned to Reb Sholem and said: "You, Sholem, must create the body, and it must be perfect in every respect so that it can travel in the worlds above and below." Then Reb Zalman looked at Reb Hayim Elya and said: "You, Hayim Elya, must create its beak. This is the smallest part, but it is the most important. For the dove must transmit our prayers with its beak, and if the beak is imperfect in any way, the prayers will slip from its grasp and be lost." At last Reb Zalman turned to Reb Shmuel Leib and said: "And you, Shmuel Leib, must create its heart. For it is the heart that provides the *kavvanah* without which the prayer has no more meaning than a body without breath."

Then, after speaking, Reb Zalman sat down beneath the tree and closed his eyes. And just before waking, the last thing each of them recalled was hearing the song of a dove, and that song was so full and so ripe and so sacred that the memory of it haunted every one of them for the rest of their lives. For each time they would open the *siddur* to pray they would hear the echo of that dove. And with its song echoing in their ears they knew, without doubt, that their prayers were destined to ascend on high.

—United States: oral tradition

Sources and Commentaries

Fairy Tales

1. An Apple from the Tree of Life (Eastern Europe)

From *Dos Bukh fun Nisyoynes*, edited by Israel Osman (Los Angeles: Hotsa'at "Mashalnu," 1926).

Many Jewish tales involve quests to mythical destinations. These include the city of Luz, where all the inhabitants are safe from the Angel of Death; the River Sambatyon, which rages six days a week and rests on the Sabbath; the Mountains of Darkness, where King Solomon sends Benayahu to capture Ashmodai, the king of demons; and journeys to heaven, to which sages such as Rabbi Akiba ascend seeking mystical knowledge.

Foremost among these mythical destinations is the Garden of Eden. Many tales describe journeys to the Garden, which still exists in Jewish folklore. Alexander the Great found his way there, although he was not permitted to enter. Some patriarchs and sages, such as Abraham and Rabbi Abbahu, are reported to have entered the Garden; others, such as Lilith, are said to have been kept out. "An Apple from the Tree of Life" involves such a quest to the Garden of Eden, but here it takes place in a dream. Other quests to the Garden include "Miriam's Tambourine," p. 205, and "The Gates of Eden" in Schwartz, *Gabriel's Palace*, p. 62.

All such journeys to the Garden of Eden can be viewed as folk commentaries on the biblical account of Adam and Eve. Note that the identification of the apple as the fruit of the Tree of Knowledge is relatively late. In the Talmud (*B. Sanh.* 97b), the apple is not listed when the rabbis try to identify the forbidden fruit, but by the Middle Ages it was known as such among both Jews and Christians.

This story also draws on the tradition of the *Lamed-vav Tzaddikim*, the thirty-six righteous ones who are said to be hidden in the world. See "The Thirty-six Just Men" in Schwartz, *Tree of Souls*, p. 397.

2. Elijah's Violin (Egypt)

From *Hodesh Hodesh ve-Sippuro: 1968–1969*, edited by Edna Cheichel (Haifa: Israel Folktale Archives, 1969). IFA 8133, collected by Ilana Zohar from her mother, Flora Cohen of Egypt.

The biblical account of Elijah being taken into Paradise alive in a chariot of fire (2 Kings 2:11) gave birth to a multitude of tales in which he returns to earth to assist those in need. There are more tales about Elijah than about any other figure in Jewish folklore, but very few of these could be considered fairy tales. This makes "Elijah's Violin," which has all the characteristics of the traditional fairy tale, a rare exception.

3. **The Witches of Ashkelon (Babylon)**

From the Jerusalem Talmud, *Y. Sanh.* 6:3 and 6:6; *Y. Hag.* 2:2.

On the surface, "The Witches of Ashkelon" resembles many fairy tales about witches who are defeated by clever heroes. In this case, the hero is Rabbi Shimon ben Shetah, who captures the witches by convincing them to dance with his men who then lift them off the ground, causing them to lose their power.

Unlike many fairy tales, however, there appears to be a historical kernel to this tale, in that the Talmud reports that Rabbi Shimon ben Shetah ordered the execution of the eighty witches. The justification for the hangings of the witches in Ashkelon is found in the biblical injunction *Suffer not a witch to live* (Exod. 22:18). The historic consequences of this event are documented in the Jerusalem Talmud (Y. Sanh. 6:3, 6:6, and Y. Hag. 2:2). According to Rashi, one of the pupils of Rabbi Shimon ben Shetah dreamed that a severe punishment was in store for the rabbi because he tolerated eighty women guilty of sorcery to live in Ashkelon. Learning of this dream, Shimon ben Shetah had the women executed. Angered by the hangings, several enemies of Rabbi Shimon ben Shetah, including relatives of the witches, conspired to accuse his son of murder, and testified against him, causing him to be condemned to death. The Talmud notes that even though some witnesses recanted, the execution took place anyway, because of the dictum that once a witness has testified he cannot testify again: "It is impossible to reverse the decision, since the sentence has been promulgated. He must therefore be executed" (*B. Sanh.* 44b).

Most likely, the fairy tale associated with this event came later, attributing the capture of the witches to robbing them of their supernatural powers. This gives us insight into how a historical event can be subject to the folk process, which erases the brutal dimensions of the story and replaces them with a tale of enchantment.

4. **The Bird of Happiness (Iraq)**

IFA 280, collected by Zvi Moshe Haimovitch from Josef Shmuli of Basra, Iraq.

In this fairy tale, which has strong echoes of the Exodus from Egypt, a glowing jewel guides Aaron and his parents through the desert as they try to make their way to Jerusalem. It follows the pattern found in many fairy tales where a poor boy is elevated to a prince or king. Here Aaron is the son of slaves who ran away to find freedom, and the story emphasizes that even the son of slaves can have a glorious destiny.

The miraculous glowing jewel that Aaron receives in a dream has a long history in Jewish folklore, where it is known as the *Tzohar*. See "The *Tzohar*" in Schwartz, *Tree of Souls*, pp. 85–88. The light that glows inside it is the light of the first day of creation, when God said, *Let there be light* (Gen. 1:3). This is said to have been a sacred light, unlike the earthly light of the fourth day of creation, which came from the sun, the moon, and the stars. God removed this light from the world when Adam and Eve ate the forbidden fruit of the Tree of Knowledge, but saved a little bit of this light inside a glowing stone, and gave it to Adam and Eve when they were expelled from the Garden of Eden, as a reminder of all they had left behind. Adam and Eve, in turn, passed it down to their children, and there are rabbinic accounts of it reaching Noah and Abraham, among others. The *Tzohar* is said to have disappeared after the Temple in Jerusalem was destroyed, but it still reappears in many stories in Jewish folklore. For another such story see "The Soul of the Ari," p. 366.

In the context of this story, the glowing jewel might be seen to represent the Torah, whose sacred teachings are the primary guide of the Jewish people. And the Bird of Happiness represents freedom, which everyone searches for, especially anyone who has been a slave. Read this way, the story demonstrates how the Torah can serve as a guide to freedom.

5. **The Golden Mountain (Morocco)**

From *Shiv'im Sippurim ve-Sippur*, edited by Dov Noy (Jerusalem: Israel Folktale Archives, 1964). IFA 3911, collected by Jacob Avitsuk from Shlomo Alozh.

The central motif here, that of the mountain opened by a magic spell, obviously recalls the tale of Aladdin and the magic lamp from *The Arabian Nights*. The theme of a girl who seeks knowledge is an unusual one, especially for a Middle Eastern culture that did not consider education for women necessary. Although this is a universal type of fairy tale, without specific Jewish elements, the motif of the imprisoned princess is one of the primary themes of Jewish folklore, and the old man in the tale fits the model of one of the *Lamed-vav Tzaddikim*, the Thirty-six Just Men. See for comparison "The Princess in the Tower," pp. 47–52, "The Lost Princess," pp. 210–218, and "The Imprisoned Princess" in Schwartz, *Elijah's Violin*, pp. 254–262.

6. **The Princess in the Tower (Palestine)**

From the Preface to *Midrash Tanhuma*, edited by Solomon Buber (Vilna, 1885). A variant of "Rapunzel" from *Grimm's Fairy Tales*.

This is very likely the earliest version of "Rapunzel." Dating from the eighth century, it is also the earliest version of a tale that has many variants in Jewish folklore. Both the primary motifs of the imprisoned princess and the role of the giant bird who fulfills the dictates of fate is repeated in many tales. See "The Flight of the Eagle" in Schwartz, *Elijah's Violin*, pp. 82–88, for one such variant. A clear variant of this tale is "The Maiden in the Tree," p. 160, where King Solomon once again has a maiden imprisoned as a way of circumventing fate. The poet Hayim Nachman Bialik expanded the tale of the princess in the tower into a long romance entitled "The Princess of Aram," found in *Vay'hi Hayom* (Tel Aviv, 1934).

7. King Solomon and Ashmodai (Babylon)

From *B. Git. 68b.* An oral variant is found in *Hodesh Hodesh ve-Sippuro* 1961, edited by Dov Noy (Haifa: Israel Folktale Archives, 1962). Collected by Yakov Avitsuk from Sasson Yosef of Iraqi Kurdistan.

It is this tale, more than any other, that establishes the folk characterizations of both King Solomon and Ashmodai, king of demons. Solomon makes good use not only of his wisdom but also of the magical powers he derives from the use of God's Name. The odd characterization of Ashmodai as a pious demon is retained in almost all subsequent tales about him, and likely gave birth to the concept of a kingdom of demons, whose demonic inhabitants led a devotional life identical to that of devout Jews. For a portrait of this kingdom, see "The Demon Princess," p. 269, about a man who marries the daughter of Ashmodai.

The earliest recorded confrontation between King Solomon and Ashmodai is found in *The Testament of Solomon* 5, dated between the first and third centuries. Here, too, Ashmodai is brought bound before Solomon and behaves in a surly manner, prophesying that Solomon's kingdom will one day be divided. When questioned by Solomon, Ashmodai describes himself solely in evil terms, taking credit for causing the wickedness of men to spread throughout the world. This is in contrast to the more subtle portrait of Ashmodai found in the talmudic and successive versions. Ashmodai also reveals that his father was an angel and his mother human, suggesting that he is one of the offspring of the Sons of God and daughters of men recounted in Genesis 6. This explanation identifies Ashmodai as one of the fallen angels. See Schwartz, *Tree of Souls*, pp. 454–460.

An alternative account of the capture of Ashmodai is found in an oral variant of this tale, collected by David Hartmann from his father, Henry Hartmann of Chicago. Here Solomon lures Ashmodai from the netherworld by torturing innocent victims in the lowest cellar of his palace. With all the evil committed there, Solomon is able to create an opening to the netherworld, and as soon as Ashmodai, seeing the opening, steps through it, huge chains, with the Holy Name on them, are thrown over him, and that is how he is captured. Then, to close the hole immediately, servants release the young victims, treat their wounds, and give them many rewards.

The talmudic account of the capture of the Shamir became very famous, so much so that Sabine Baring-Gould includes it in *Curious Myths of the Middle Ages* (Mineola, N.Y.: Dover, 2005), along with famous myths such as that of the Wandering Jew and the Knights of the Holy Grail.

8. The Beggar King (Babylon)

From the *B. Git.* 68b. Episodes have also been culled from *Midrash Mishlei*, edited by Solomon Buber (Vilna, 1893); *Yalkut Shimoni*, compiled by Shimon Ashkenazi (Frankfurt, 1687); and *Emek ha-Melech*, by Naphtali Hirsh ben Elhanan (Amsterdam, 1653). An oral variant is found in *Hadre Teman*, edited by Nissim Binyamin Gamlieli (Tel Aviv, 1978).

The brief outline of this tale found in the Talmud is subjected to a great variety of embellishments in subsequent retellings, primarily focused on Solomon's adventures during his wanderings. The version presented here is an amalgam of these variants. One version, not utilized, supplies a reason for the success of Ashmodai in overthrowing Solomon: a heavenly punishment for Solomon's having disobeyed the commandment against having more than one wife (he was reputed to have had 300 wives and 700 concubines). This is found in *Belt ha-Midrash*, edited by Adolf Jellinek (Jerusalem, 1938). In the oral version recorded by Gamlieli, Solomon becomes a *darshan*, a wandering preacher, who discovers that people pay no heed to his wisdom, but reward him for trite and superficial maxims. Thus he returns to Jerusalem a wealthy and acclaimed man.

This story about King Solomon inspired the book *The Beggar King and the Secret of Happiness* by Joel ben Izzy (Chapel Hill, N.C.: Algonquin, 2005), who relates the king's quest to recover his kingdom to his own quest to recover his voice, which he lost for several years.

9. **The Wonder Child (Egypt)**

IFA 6405, collected by Ilana Zohar from her mother, Flora Cohen of Egypt. A variant is IFA 4859, told by Esther Mikhael of Iraqi Kurdistan to her granddaughter, Esther.

The fact that the wonder child is born with her soul in a jewel indicates the miraculous nature of her birth. The theme of a magical glowing jewel is a popular one in Jewish folklore. Noah was said to have hung such a glowing jewel in the ark, illuminating it for the forty days and nights of the Flood. So too was Abraham said to have worn such a jewel, which healed anyone who peered into it. See "The *Tzohar*" in Schwartz, *Tree of Souls*, pp. 85–88.

"The Wonder Child" is a Jewish-Egyptian variant of Grimms' "Snow White," with elements of Perrault's "Sleeping Beauty." Note that Ilana Zohar is also the teller of "Elijah's Violin," pp. 19–24. Together these two stories demonstrate a flourishing world of fairy tales among the generation of Jews who immigrated to Israel from Egypt.

10. **The Princess and the Slave (Morocco)**

IFA 6414, collected by Yakov Laseri from his father, Machlouf Laseri. Previously unpublished. A variant is found in *Otsar ha-Ma'asiyot*, vol. 1, edited by Reuven ben Yakov Na'ana (Jerusalem, 1960). A Turkish variant is found in IFA 2607, collected by Reuven Na'ana from an unknown Sephardic Israeli from Turkey, and a variant from Afghanistan is IFA 3145, collected by Zevulon Kort from Eliyahu Yarkone of Afghanistan. For an Arab variant of this tale, see "What Is Inscribed on the Brow the Eyes Will See," from *Arab Folktales*, edited by Inea Bushnaq (New York: Pantheon Books, 1986), pp. 172–174.

Because the body of Moses was never found, the legend grew up that he had entered Paradise alive. This, in turn, gave birth to tales such as this one, where Moses is met alive many generations later, much in the way Elijah is said to reappear in every generation. In many respects the narrative of this tale parallels and evokes that of Exodus. Samuel, the central figure, is a Hebrew slave, as were the Israelites, and the quest to find Moses certainly evokes Exodus. In the wilderness he finds a speaking tree, just as Moses found the burning bush. He reaches the very mountain, Mount Nevo, where Moses took his leave of the Israelites. After meeting with Moses, he has all of the riddles he brings with him solved, not only for himself, but for the others as well, just as the Torah of Moses resolves all questions and contains all truth. As a result, he achieves eternal youth in the waters of the enchanted pools, just as the Torah provides eternal truth for the Jewish people. This tale, then, offers a good example of how Jewish folklore is able to reimagine the biblical narrative and transform it into a fairy tale, set in another generation. This reliving of the past in a later generation is, in fact, the goal of the seder service, which recounts the Exodus narrative, emphasizing that "We were slaves unto Pharaoh in Egypt."

11. The Golden Tree (India)

From *Shomrim Ne'emanim,* edited and annotated by Dov Noy (Haifa: Israel Folktale Archives, 1976). IFA 8161, collected by Zvi Haimovitz from Yitzhak Sasson of India.

Although this is a universal type of fairy tale, it is possible to associate the golden tree in it with the Tree of Life, in that both trees seem to symbolize the origin and perpetuation of life. In this case the king's quest can be seen as an attempt to restore the damage of the Fall: the king, having exiled the only wife he loves, experiences the devastation of the Fall. He then undertakes the quest for the golden tree in order to achieve restoration of the original state. Such a quest is parallel to the role of the Messiah in Jewish myth, whose purpose it is to restore the world to its prelapsarian condition. Messianic myth insists that great suffering must precede the accomplishment of this great task, and the grueling effort of the king and his suffering over his error in expelling the queen certainly fulfill this requirement. This suggests that the entire tale may be viewed as a reworking of the Genesis myth of the Fall, in conjunction with the effort at restoration represented in the later messianic myths of Jewish mysticism. That such a profound commentary on the biblical story of the Fall was collected orally in India speaks volumes about the treasures to be found among the stories told by the Jews living there.

12. The Mute Princess (Yemen)

From *Hadre Teman,* edited by Nissim Binyamin Gamlieli (Tel Aviv, 1978). Collected by Nissim Binyamin Gamlieli from Ovadia Zandani. An Arab variant of this tale, "Four Men and One Miracle," can be found in *Arab Folktales,* edited by Inea Bushnaq (New York: Pantheon Books, 1986), pp. 305–306.

Just as the story of Scheherazade serves as the frame tale to *The Arabian Nights,* the story of the mute princess in this Yemenite tale serves as a frame around three popular tale types of Middle Eastern origin. Such tales-within-tales are themselves a common feature in much orally collected Jewish folklore. Here, in a twist on the story of Scheherazade, a young man must tell riddles to a princess to keep from being killed. These tales encouraged the participation of the listeners in deciding the outcome of the tale and in judging if the decision reached matched their own sense of justice.

13. The Enchanted Journey (Eastern Europe)

From *Eretz ha-Hayim*, collected by Hayim Liebersohn (Przemysl, Poland, 1926). Also includes episodes from *Rosinkess mit Mandlen: Aus der Volksliterature der Ostjuden*, edited by Immanuel Olsvanger (Basel: Schweizerische Kommission fur Judischen Volkskunde, 1931).

Like "The Beggar King," this tale appears to take place over a period of many years, but actually occurs in a very brief span of time. This motif of illusory time is characteristic of a number of Jewish folktales, including a similar tale about a sorcerer found in *Meshal ha-Kadmoni* by Isaac Ibn Sahula, edited by Yisrael Zemora (Tel Aviv, 1952), dating from Spain in the thirteenth century. See "The Enchanted Well" in Schwartz, *Miriam's Tambourine*, pp. 150–155. This motif is also found in the Hindu myths of *maya*, the Hindu term for illusion or mirage, and the possibility exists that this motif was transmitted by such Hindu tales. A conversation between the prophet Arjuna and the god Krishna about the meaning of *maya* is found in the *Bhagavad Gita*. See Heinreich Zimmer, *Myths and Symbols in Indian Art and Civilization* (New York: Pantheon, 1946), pp. 32–33.

14. The Magic Mirror of Rabbi Adam (Eastern Europe)

From *Sefer Sippure Kedushim*, edited by Gedalyah Nigal (Jerusalem, 1977), first published in Warsaw in 1866. Also found in *Likkute Ma'asiyot*, compiled by Yisrael ben Sasson (Jerusalem, 1909). Reprinted in *Sefer ha-Ma'asiyot*, edited by Mordecai Ben Yehezkel (Tel Aviv, 1929).

This is the best-known tale about Rabbi Adam outside of those found in Hasidic sources, especially *Shivhei ha-Besht*, concerning Rabbi Adam and the Ba'al Shem Tov. It establishes Rabbi Adam's primary role in protecting Jews suffering from religious persecution and in confronting the enemies of the Jews, who are usually identified as cruel kings and evil ministers who are often also sorcerers. Thus Rabbi Adam's magic, which derives from the power of God, is pitted against that of the black magic of the evil sorcerers, and inevitably defeats it. Rabbi Adam thus serves as the archetypal model of such medieval Jewish sorcerers, and likely inspired the legends concerning Rabbi Judah Loew, to whom the creation of the Golem is attributed.

15. The King's Dream (Eastern Europe)

From *Eretz ha-Hayim*, collected by Hayim Liebersohn (Przemysl, Poland, 1926). Also includes episodes from *Shivhei ha-Ari* (Jerusalem, 1905).

This fairy tale is a fantasy of role reversal, in which the role of the king is played by a Jew, Rabbi Adam, and the role of victim is given to a cruel king, who has signed a harsh decree against the Jews. Such tales suggest the inability of the Jews to effect change in reality, and creating such fantasies out of deep frustration in which they achieved both a sense of revenge and imaginary relief from the harsh realities of their existence. Another good example of such fantasy tales is that of the Golem. See "The Golem," p. 292. This version of "The King's Dream" combines episodes from two such tales, one deriving from Eastern Europe, the other from Safed in the sixteenth century. The similarities of the tales suggests that the plight of the Jews was considerable in both places, and that the fantasy mechanisms were also similar. For a psychological analysis of this tale, see "Dreams and Fairy Tales" by Dr. Rudolf Ekstein in the Spring 1985 issue of *Dreamworks*, pp. 130–136.

16. **The Exiled Princess (Eastern Europe)**

From *Yiddishe Folkmayses* (Yiddish), edited by Yehuda L. Cahan (Vilna, 1931). Includes an episode from *Rosinkess mit Mandlen: Aus der Volksliterature der Ostjuden* (Yiddish), edited by Immanuel Olsvanger (Basel: Schweizerische Kommission fur Judischen Volkskunde, 1931). A variant of Cinderella from *Grimm's Fairy Tales.*

See the Introduction, p. 20, for a discussion of this story.

17. **The Wonderful Healing Leaves (Iraqi Kurdistan)**

From *Hodesh Hodesh ve-Sippuro:* 1974–1975, edited by Dov Noy (Haifa: Israel Folktale Archives, 1975). IFA 10125, collected by Ofra Elias from her mother Rachel Elias.

This is a good example of the universal fairy tales of Middle Eastern origin found in abundance in the Israel Folktale Archives. Such tales were rarely preserved in writing because of the absence of specifically Jewish elements. Nevertheless, the tale functions as a teaching story in many respects, emphasizing the honesty and ingenuity of the lad, who wins back all that he is deprived of by the ruthless princes. The tale also manages to include almost every supernatural element found in fairy tales, including a giant, magical potions, spells, flying carpets, a dragon, and the Queen of the Land of No Return. The motif of healing leaves is exceptionally popular in Jewish folk tradition. See "The Spice of the Sabbath" in Schwartz, *Tree of Souls,* pp. 116–117, and, especially, "Leaves from the Garden of Eden," p. 155, and the accompanying note, p. 392.

18. **The City of Luz (Eastern Europe)**

From *Dos Bukh fun Nisyoynes* (Yiddish), edited by Israel Osman (Los Angeles, 1926).

The earliest references to the city of Luz appear in Genesis 28:19, where Luz is identified as the original name of the place where Jacob had his vision: *He named that site Bethel; but previously the name of the city had been Luz.* The nature of the city is embellished in the *B. Sota* 46b and further embellishment is found in *Genesis Rabbah* 69:8. See "The City of Luz" in Schwartz, *Tree of Souls,* pp. 476–477. The requirement for the use of the blue dye (*tekhelet*) derives from the verse Numbers 15:38: *let them attach a cord of blue to the fringe at each corner* (Num. 15:38).

This legend of a city of immortals is unique in Jewish lore, although the notion of a boundary that the Angel of Death cannot cross appears in the *Zohar* (4:151a), referring to the Land of Israel as a whole rather than to the city of Luz: "It is the Destroying Angel who brings death to all people, except those who die in the Holy Land, to whom death comes by the Angel of Mercy, who holds sway there." Here, however, the inhabitants are not spared death, only death by the Angel of Death. Instead, an angel of mercy will be sent to lead them into Paradise.

The various strata of legend concerning the city of Luz can all be found in this tale, which offers an opportunity to study the evolution of a myth. Here each detail of the earlier strata becomes exceptionally significant. Since the literal meaning of *luz*, for example, is nut tree, this tree is postulated in the Midrash as the symbol of the city and said to be found at the entrance. Then the development is taken a step further, embellishing the role of the nut tree: "This tree was hollow, and through it one entered the cave and through the cave the city" (Gen. Rab. 69:8).

The origin of the immortal nature of the city of Luz is also linked to the bone at the bottom of the spine known as the *luz* bone, which is said to survive longer than any other part of the body.

19. **The Boy Israel and the Witch (Eastern Europe)**

From *Shivhei ha-Besht* by Rabbi Dov Baer Ben Samuel, edited by Samuel A. Horodezky (Berlin, 1922).

Fairy tales are rarely found in Hasidic literature, perhaps because the primary focus of these writings is on the rebbe, the Hasidic master, and thus they are less likely to be formulated in the universal language of the fairy tale. The great exception, of course, are the complex fairy tales told by Reb Nachman of Bratslav. Especially rare are fairy tales about the childhood of the Ba'al Shem Tov, founder of Hasidim. Besides the tale included here there is perhaps only one other, found in the same source, of the boy Israel defeating a werewolf that was actually an evil sorcerer. See "The Werewolf," p. 296. The present tale of the boy Israel's defeat of the witch has been preserved in fragmentary form and required some reconstruction. But enough of it remains to indicate conclusively that it was a fairy tale in origin, probably of the universal type, which was retold casting the Ba'al Shem Tov as the young hero. This same approach is found in many Hasidic tales, which substitute a Hasidic figure for a biblical hero or talmudic sage, attempting, in this way, to draw a parallel between the Hasidic masters and revered heroes and sages.

20. **The Lost Princess (Eastern Europe)**

From *Sippure Ma'asiyot* by Reb Nachman of Bratslav, edited by Rabbi Nathan Sternhartz of Nemirov (Ostrog, Russia, 1816).

For a discussion of this story, see the Introduction, pp. 22–25.

21. **The Prince and the Slave (Eastern Europe)**

From *Sippurei Ma'asiyot*, by Reb Nachman of Bratslav, edited by Rabbi Nathan Sternhartz of Nemirov (Ostrog, Russia, 1816).

This is a tale not only about exchanged children, but, from a kabbalistic perspective, about exchanged souls. The biblical model for it is clearly the story of Jacob and Esau, which is strongly echoed in many places. From a rabbinic perspective, Jacob was justified in taking the blessing of the firstborn since he had purchased his brother's birthright (Gen. 25:33). But even so, the story leaves a nagging feeling, since Esau was indeed firstborn. The idea of the exchange thus suggests the resolution to the problem. Reb Nachman is quoted as having said about Napoleon, shortly before having told this story: "Who knows what sort of soul he has? It is possible that it was exchanged. There is a Chamber of

Exchanges, where souls are sometimes exchanged" (*Hayay Moharan*, Lemberg, 1874). According to Rabbi Aryeh Kaplan, good and evil are confused in the Chamber of Exchanges, which is therefore a place of evil. Reb Nachman's scribe, Rabbi Nathan of Nemirov, offers a midrash about the way in which this chamber came into existence. He links it to the Fall, saying that it came into being at the time Adam ate the fruit of the Tree of Knowledge. He also associates it with *the flaming sword which turned every way, to keep the way to the Tree of Life* (Gen. 3:24), the revolving swords of the cherubim guarding the gate of the Garden of Eden. This reinterprets the Hebrew for the revolving sword into the transforming sword, or the sword of reversals. He also links the Chamber of Exchanges with the staff of Moses, which was transformed into a serpent in Pharaoh's court, and then back into its original form. Rabbi Nathan also suggests the tale is an allegory of an inner dualism, in which the slave represents the body, and the prince, the soul. (This is a remarkably modern psychological view of the story, consistent with the theories of C. G. Jung.) This reading of the tale, which rings true, indicates the extent to which Reb Nachman's tales were interpreted in an allegorical manner, consistent with kabbalistic teachings. And there is no doubt that Reb Nachman himself encouraged and often even provided such readings of his tales, which for him were another aspect of his teachings. See, for example, his comments about his story, "The Prince Who Became a Rooster," p. 405. This theme of exchanged children is also found in a story told of Rabbi Judah Loew, about Black Beryl and Red Beryl, found in Yudl Rosenberg's *Niflaot Maharal* (Piotrkow, 1909). Since this collection is held by many scholars to be a nineteenth-century creation, it is possible that Yudl Rosenberg's version was influenced by Reb Nachman's tale.

22. **The Prince Who Was Made of Precious Gems (Eastern Europe)**

From *Sippure Ma'asiyot* by Reb Nachman of Bratslav, edited by Rabbi Nathan Sternhartz of Nemirov (Warsaw, 1881).

This tale is based on the tradition of the *Lamed-vav Tzaddikim*, the Thirty-six Just Men. According to the Talmud, there are thirty-six hidden saints in the world, and the world exists because of their merit. When one of them dies, another is born to take his place. Because of these thirty-six, God permits the world to exist, making them the pillars of existence. The earliest reference to this tradition appears in the Talmud, and is attributed to Abbaye: "There are not less than thirty-six righteous men in the world who receive the Divine Presence" (*B. Sanh.* 97b and *B. Suk.* 45b). Later stories about the *Lamed-vav Tzaddikim* became a staple of folk, kabbalistic, and Hasidic tales. Many of these tales describe them as living in remote places, such as forests, where they engage in mystical study. Since no one knew who these hidden saints were, it was said that every person should be treated with respect, in case they turned out to be one of them. See "The Thirty-Six Just Men" in Schwartz, *Tree of Souls*, p. 397.

Here Reb Nachman draws upon the tradition about the *Lamed-vav Tzaddikim* and incorporates it into a fairy tale, where the hidden saint saves the Jewish community by meeting the demands of a desperate king. This he appears to accomplish by prayer rather than by magic. But it is clear that prayer plays a role identical to that of magic in other fairy tales. He also reaffirms the belief that whenever one of the hidden saints dies, another takes his place, so that the number of hidden saints remains the same. In Reb Nachman's story, the clues left by the first hidden saint guide them to the new one.

The strange imagery of the prince consisting of precious jewels is clearly intended by Reb Nachman to be understood in a symbolic sense—as a symbol of his exceptional spiritual purity.

23. The Water Palace (Eastern Europe)

From *Sippure Ma'asiyot* by Reb Nachman of Bratslav, edited by Rabbi Nathan Sternhartz of Nemirov (Warsaw, 1881).

Like "The Lost Princess," this tale, excerpted from the epic story "The Seven Beggars," is likely an allegory of the exile of the *Shekhinah* and her rescue by the Messiah, since kabbalistic tradition holds that the exile of the *Shekhinah* will end at the time of the coming of the Messiah. In such a reading the innermost chamber where the princess sleeps in the water palace can be identified with the innermost sanctuary of the Temple, known as the Holy of Holies. The powerful attraction of the water palace to the princess parallels the strong attachment of the *Shekhinah* to the Temple in Jerusalem, which, according to Jewish tradition, was her home. Indeed, in the myth of the exile of the *Shekhinah* (*Zohar* 1:202b–203a), the anger of the *Shekhinah* at God over permitting the destruction of the Temple is so great that she not only confronts God but also leaves Him (see the Introduction, p. 23).

In "The Water Palace," as in "The Lost Princess," Reb Nachman portrays the *Shekhinah* figure as passive (unlike "The Pirate Princess," where the figure is much more active). However, this also echoes the kabbalistic portrayal of the *Shekhinah* as being held in captivity or "in the dust," from which she must be liberated or raised up. The prince who saves her in "The Water Palace" represents the Messiah, whose coming makes it possible for the Temple to be rebuilt and for the *Shekhinah* to come out of exile. See Schwartz, *Tree of Souls*, pp. 57–58.

24. The Pirate Princess (Eastern Europe)

From *Sippure Ma'asiyot* by Reb Nachman of Bratslav, edited by Rabbi Nathan Sternhartz of Nemirov (Warsaw, 1881).

The passive role of the princesses in "The Lost Princess" and "The Water Palace" is replaced here by a very active one, but the pirate princess is likely still to be identified with the *Shekhinah*, God's Bride in kabbalistic myth. Some kabbalistic legends hold that the *Shekhinah*, who chose to go into exile with the Children of Israel at the time of the destruction of the Temple in Jerusalem, actively seeks to bring the exile to an end. For further discussion about the myths associated with the *Shekhinah*, see Schwartz, *Tree of Souls*, pp. xlvii–xlix and 47–66.

25. A Garment for the Moon (Eastern Europe)

From *Sippurim Niflaim*, compiled by Samuel Horowitz (Jerusalem, 1935).

This is an attempt to complete a fragmentary tale of Reb Nachman's. In the original, the tale ends with the offer of the poor tailors to help the great tailors in sewing a garment for the moon, which the great tailors turn down.

Such fragmentary and incomplete tales were often told by Reb Nachman and were dutifully recorded by his scribe, Rabbi Nathan of Nemirov. The fact that the great tailors have the last word here is a clear indication that the tale was unfinished, as Reb Nachman's sympathies in such cases were always with the little people. In fact, a passage from *Bereshit Rabbah* (6:3) strongly suggests the identification of the poor tailors with the Jews: "Rabbi Levi said in the name of Rabbi Jose ben Lai: 'It is but natural that the great should count by the great, and the small by the small. Esau counts time by the sun, which is large, and Jacob by the moon, which is small.'" The discussion is continued by a sage whose name also happens to be Reb Nachman: "Said Reb Nachman: 'That is a happy augury. Esau counts by the sun, which is large: just as the sun rules by day but not by night, so does Esau enjoy this world, but has naught in the World to Come. Jacob counts by the moon, which is small: just as the moon rules by day and by night, so has Jacob a portion in this world and the World to Come." The present dependent condition of the moon on the sun echoes a talmudic myth (*B. Hul.* 60b) about competition between the sun and the moon, which is a commentary on the passage *And God made the two great lights* (Gen. 1:16): "The moon said to the Holy One, blessed be He, 'Master of the Universe, is it possible for two kings to wear one crown?' God replied: 'Go then and make yourself smaller.'" Thus the rebellion of the moon brought about its decrease. This talmudic legend is echoed in a dialogue, closely resembling that in Reb Nachman's tale, found in *Pirke de-Rabbi Eliezer*, chapter 6: "Rivalry ensued between the sun and the moon, and one said to the other, 'I am bigger than you are.' The other rejoined, 'I am bigger than you are.' What did the Holy One, blessed be He, do, so that there should be peace between them? He made the one larger and the other smaller, as it is written, *The greater light to rule by the day, and the lesser light to rule the night and the stars* (Gen. 1:16)." It seems certain that Reb Nachman had these rabbinic myths in mind when he told his enticing, fragmentary tale. It is also possible to read this tale as an allegory in which Israel is the moon, God is the sun, and the garment is the Torah, which protects Israel against the winters of exile. See "The Quarrel of the Sun and Moon" in Schwartz, *Tree of Souls*, pp. 112–113.

FOLKTALES

26. **Leaves from the Garden of Eden (Eastern Europe)**

From *Nifla'ot ha-Tzaddikim* (Piotrkow, 1911)

In "Leaves from the Garden of Eden" a miracle takes place in a dream. Here the soul of his stable boy brings leaves from the Garden of Eden to heal a man's sick daughter. Her mourning over the boy's death provoked her illness, and his miraculous assistance heals her and makes it possible for her to wed later. It is possible to see this tale as a benevolent version of S. Ansky's famous play *The Dybbuk*. There a yeshivah student who kills himself takes possession of Leah, whom he loved in vain, as she was betrothed to someone else. In both cases, the illness of the woman can be seen as a form of grieving over the death of the beloved. But in the case of *The Dybbuk*, a formal rabbinic exorcism is required to expel the soul of the dead student, while here a miracle makes it possible for the girl to recover her health and peace of mind. Ansky based *The*

Dybbuk on many tales that he heard as an ethnographer. A folktale that is probably one of the major sources for the play can be found in Gedalyah Nigal's *Sippure Dibuk b'Sifrut* (Jerusalem, 1983), pp. 146–160.

"Leaves from the Garden of Eden" is a Jewish adaptation of the well-known theme of healing leaves found in all world folklore. A universal version of this tale, from a Jewish oral source, is "The Wonderful Healing Leaves," p. 101. The motif of the Garden of Eden as the source of healing leaves is also found in "Miriam's Tambourine," p. 205. Here the patriarch Abraham collects these leaves from the Garden and give them to his wife, Sarah, who crushes the leaves and scatters their powder to the wind on the eve of the Sabbath, so that all who breathe in that powder will have a taste of Paradise and a Sabbath filled with joy. See "The Spice of the Sabbath" in Schwartz, *Tree of Souls*, pp. 316–317.

Reference to such magical leaves is also found in talmudic legends about the messianic era. In one, Elijah leads Rabbi Abbahu into the Garden of Eden and has him collect leaves in his cloak. The cloak absorbs the fragrance of the leaves, and he later sells it for twelve thousand dinars (BM 114a–b). According to the other legend, when the third holy Temple will be built, a magical tree will grow in Jerusalem. Some say that the leaves of that tree will cause the dumb to speak. Others say that the leaves of that tree will cause barren women to bear children (*B. Sanh.* 100a).

27. A Palace of Bird Beaks (Yemen)

IFA 11306, collected by Nissim Binyamin Gamlieli from Yehoshua ben Yoseph David of Yemen. From *Hadre Teman*, edited by Nissim Binyamin Gamlieli (Tel Aviv, 1978). A variant is the Moroccan tale "King Solomon and the Queen Kashira," where the queen agrees to marry Solomon only if he first builds her a palace made entirely of eagles' bones. IFA 1071, collected by Issachar Ben Ami from Friha Susan of Morocco. For an Arab variant of this tale, see "Suleyman and the Little Owl" in *Arab Folktales*, edited by Inea Bushnaq (New York: Pantheon Books, 1986), pp. 244–245.

This is one of many tales about King Solomon, who is portrayed in Jewish folklore as the wisest of men. Here, however, King Solomon learns that even the smallest of creatures have something of value to teach a mighty king. In other stories, the hoopoe bird is identified as King Solomon's favorite messenger and confidant. This story seems to have an environmental theme, in that Solomon comes to recognize that the sacrifice he is demanding of the birds far exceeds the value of the gift he is giving to the Queen of Sheba.

The following story, "The Maiden in the Tree," p. 160, also concerns King Solomon and the Queen of Sheba.

In 2008 Israel declared the hoopoe its national bird.

28. The Maiden in the Tree (Eastern Europe)

From *Rosinkess mit Mandlen: Aus der Volkliterature der Ostjuden* (Yiddish), edited by Emmanuel Olsvanger (Basel: Schweizerische Kommission fur Judischen Volkskunde, 1931).

This tale is clearly a disguised variant of Rapunzel. Here, instead of being imprisoned in a tower, the heroine is imprisoned in a tree trunk. In fact, this tale is a direct variant of "The Princess in the Tower," p. 50, which itself is probably the earliest version of Rapunzel. Like "The Princess in the Tower," the intention here is to foil fate by isolating the princess on a remote island. In fact, the attribution of her imprisonment to a whim of the Queen of Sheba makes the linkage to the other tale even more apparent. And, as in the earlier tale, the inevitable arrival on the island of the poor man destined to marry the princess takes place despite all efforts to the contrary. According to Ephraim E. Urbach, in "The Fable of the Three and the Four of H. N. Bialik" (*Ariel*, No. 38, 1975), this Eastern European version of the tale inspired Bialik's epic retelling, entitled "The Princess of Aram," found in his book *Vayehi ha-Yom* (Tel Aviv, 1934). It is interesting to note that this late Eastern European reworking of an eighth-century tale turns almost entirely to the earlier Jewish source of its inspiration, omitting other elements of the Rapunzel tale (beside the imprisonment of the heroine) which was no doubt well known by the time of its appearance. This is further evidence of the direct line of descent of Jewish lore and literature, which constantly turns to its own past traditions for inspiration.

29. **The Sabbath Lion (Morocco)**

IFA 6432, collected by A. Rabi from Avner Azolai of Morocco, from *Avotanu Sippru*, edited by Moshe Rabi, published in Jerusalem in 1976. Variants of this story are found in other countries in North Africa, including Algeria, as well as in Iran and Bukhara.

"The Sabbath Lion" offers an extreme example of the importance of observing the Sabbath. Among the many Sabbath laws, it is forbidden to travel more than a short distance. Yosef's devotion to the Sabbath puts him in peril when he refuses to travel with the caravan on that day of rest. While he might have been stranded in the desert, instead a miracle occurs—a lion appears that protects him during the night and later returns him to the caravan when the Sabbath is over, as a reward from the Sabbath Queen for his devotion to the Sabbath.

Of course, the Sabbath Queen is a personification of the Sabbath. The notion of a Sabbath Queen grows out of a brief passage in the Talmud: "Rabbi Haniah robed himself and stood at sunset on the eve of the Sabbath and exclaimed, 'Come, let us go forth to welcome the Sabbath Queen'" (B. Shabbat 199a). By the Middle Ages the notion of the Sabbath Queen became linked to the kabbalistic concept of the *Shekhinah*, the Bride of God, thus becoming identified as a goddess-like figure. The Ari created (or recreated) the ritual of Kabbalat Shabbat, going out into the fields outside Safed with his disciples to greet the Sabbath Queen. And Shlomo Alkabetz, of the Ari's circle, composed the poem "Lekhah Dodi," which celebrates the arrival of the Sabbath Queen on the Sabbath.

It is clear in this folktale that Yosef believes quite literally in the existence of the Sabbath Queen, and the arrival of the lion that protects him and helps him complete his mission to recover his family's inheritance confirms her power to assist those who properly observe the Sabbath. The moral of the story is clear: those who observe the Sabbath despite all obstacles will be richly rewarded.

30. **Katanya (Turkey)**

IFA 8900, collected by Moses Gad from Sarah Gad of Turkey.

There are more tales about the Prophet Elijah and about King Solomon in Jewish folklore than about any other figures. This is a typical Elijah tale, where the prophet appears in disguise to help a worthy person in need. Katanya, which is Hebrew for God's little one, is a Turkish variant of the Tom Thumb/Thumbelina tale type.

31. **The Wooden Sword (Afghanistan)**

From *Otzar ha-Ma'asiyot*, vol. 3, edited by Reuven ben Yakov Na'ana (Jerusalem, 1961). Collected by Reuven ben Yakov Na'ana; told by Shlomo Shalem. A variant of this tale, attributed to Reb Nachman of Bratslav, was printed in Jerusalem around 1905 by Rabbi Zvi Dov ben Avraham of Berditchev. Although no version of this tale is included in *Sippure Ma'asiyot*, the primary collection of Reb Nachman's tales, it is said to have been told about a month after the telling of his first story, "The Lost Princess," which was told on July 25, 1806.

Variants of this tale are found in many cultures. Here the Jewish version emphasizes the unshakeable faith and trust of the peasant in God, although there is no divine intervention, and he manages to save himself through his own cleverness. This is one of several tales attributed to Reb Nachman which can be traced to the older folk tradition. If he did, in fact, tell these tales, it simply indicates that he did not limit the tales he told to those that he created, but also retold those folktales that were of particular interest to him.

32. **The Water Witch (The Orient)**

From *Alpha Beta de-Ben Sira*, edited by M. Steinschneider (Berlin, 1858). An oral variant is IFA 7248, from *Sippurei Am Misanuk*, collected by Samuel Zanvel Pipe, edited by Dov Noy (Haifa, 1967). A distant variant of "Hansel and Gretel" from *Grimms' Fairy Tales.*

The key to this story is the biblical injunction *Cast your bread on the waters, for a time will come when you will find it again* (Eccles. 11:1), as this is a story about the reward for charity freely given. Leviathan, the ocean beast mentioned in Psalms 104:26, becomes the Ruler of the Sea in Jewish folklore. In the oral variant from the IFA, the water witch is identified as the Queen of Sheba. Although enchanted sea creatures such as mermaids and sirens are well known in world folklore, Jewish folklore includes lesser-known creatures, such as the water witch in this story, or the river demon in "Yona and the River Demon," p. 287. In general, bodies of water were seen as dangerous places, where demons congregate, especially at night. See "The Other Side," p. 283.

33. **Drawing the Wind (The Balkans)**

This story was collected during World War I by the folklorist Max Grunwald from an unknown Jewish teller from the Balkans. It was published in *Sippureiam, Romanssot, ve-Orehot-hayim shel Yehude Sefarad* by Max Grunwald, edited by Dov Noy (Jerusalem, 1982). There are many variants of this tale told among Sephardic communities. The Israel Folktale Archives has collected more than one hundred versions. In some the imprisoned rabbi is identified as Rabbi Ephraim ben Yisrael Ankawa of Tlemcen, Tunisia. Note that Rabbi Shimon ben Tsemah Duran was born after the Spanish Inquisition of 1492, and therefore his role in this story is legendary.

This is a tale of a miraculous escape, when a work of art is miraculously brought to life. Versions of this tale are found worldwide. For a remarkable modern version, see "How Wang Fo Was Saved" by Marguerite Yourcenar in *Oriental Tales* (New York: Farrar, Straus, & Giroux, 1985), pp. 3–20.

34. A Flock of Angels (Kurdistan)

From *Kehillot Yehudei Kurdistan,* edited by Abraham Ben-Jacob (Jerusalem, 1961). A variant is IFA 11165, collected by Avraham Keren from Yitzhak Isadore Feierstein of Poland.

This tale concerns a famous heroine of Kurdish lore known as Rabbi Asenath bat Samuel Barzani. She was given the title of "Rabbi" in recognition of her knowledge of the Torah. She was a poet, a kabbalist, and the head of a yeshivah in the seventeenth century who eventually became recognized as the chief teacher of the Torah in Kurdistan. Her father was Rabbi Samuel Barzani of Kurdistan, who appears as a great kabbalistic sorcerer in Kurdish lore. Rabbi Asenath was a Ba'al Shem, a Master of the Name, as well as a healer, who was especially sought out by women. When she drew on her knowledge of holy names, she often pronounced the names of angels. It is likely that the name Rabbi Asenath pronounced in "A Flock of Angels" was the name of an angel, rather than the Tetragrammaton. The miracle that occurs saves the synagogue from destruction, and demonstrates to the enemies of the Jews that God intends to protect them.

Note that the story takes place at Rosh Hodesh, the celebration of the new moon, which has long been identified as a woman's ceremony. The tale itself is an affirmation of that celebration, as by observing the tradition of holding the ritual outside at night instead of in the synagogue saves their lives when the synagogue is set on fire.

It should be noted that there are very few women in Jewish lore who are honored as rabbis or the equal of rabbis. There are prophetic traditions linked with Sarah, Rebecca, and Miriam, as well as Deborah. In the Talmud, the woman most respected for her knowledge was Bruria, the wife of Rabbi Meir. In the Hasidic period there was Hannah Rochel, the Maid of Ludomir, who had a following of male Hasidim. For a tale about Hannah Rochel, see "A New Soul," p. 369. Rabbi Asenath should be seen as a figure in this tradition.

35. Milk and Honey (Eastern Europe)

IFA 532, told by Dov Noy of Poland. This tale exists in several oral variants, including IFA 5842, collected by Rachel Seri from her mother, Yona Seri of Yemen, included in *Ha-Kamea ha-Kadosh,* no 11, edited by Aliza Shenhar (Haifa, 1968). Another variant is found in *Yiddisher Folklor,* edited by Y. L. Cahan (Vilna, 1938), no. 20, p. 147.

Jewish history has been marked by many exiles from Eretz Yisrael, the Land of Israel, also known as "the Land of Milk and Honey" (Exod. 3:8). Yet throughout the centuries, a small remnant of Jews always remained in the Land of Israel. Meanwhile, in most countries, Jews experienced some kind of oppression, and the great Jewish dream was to return to the land promised in the Bible. "Milk and Honey" reflects this longing.

In its original version, this story portrays the separation that took place between the younger generation who left the old country for the Land of Israel and the old generation that remained behind. Here the son sends a message to his family rolled up in the ear of the goat that comes back. But the goat is slaughtered before the note is found, and so the separation between generations becomes a fact. More recently, families have immigrated together to Israel. This change is mirrored by this version of the story, where the family follows the goat through the enchanted cave to the Land of Israel.

Jewish legends and tales are full of stories about enchanted caves that lead directly to the Land of Israel. In these stories, the caves are hidden, but someone either knows about one or finds one by accident and travels to the Land of Israel in a very short time. The stories about these caves reflect the people's great longing to reach the Land of Israel, so for away.

It is also said that these caves were created for the bones of the righteous to roll through at the End of Days. According to Jewish lore, this will be the end of the world as we know it, when the dead will be resurrected, and all Jews will assemble in the Holy Land. And they will get there by going through one of these enchanted caves. Then, according to Jewish tradition, the footsteps of the Messiah will be heard throughout the land, and the great Temple in Jerusalem will rise again in all its glory. S. Y. Agnon wrote a famous version of this folktale, "The Fable of the Goat." See *Twenty-One Stories* (New York: Schocken, 1970), pp. 26–29.

36. **The Goat Whose Horns Reached to Heaven (Eastern Europe)**

From *'Esser Tsahtsahot* by Y. Y. Berger (Piotrkow, 1910) and *Be'er ha-Hasidut*, edited by Eliezer Steinmann (Tel Aviv, 1960), vol. 1, p. 307.

This tale about a sacred goat whose horns reached to heaven was told by Rabbi Menachem Mendel of Kotzk. After a mysterious incident one Sabbath, the Kotzker Rebbe went into retreat for twenty years. He is said to have recounted this tale to his closest friend, Rabbi Yitzhak of Vorki, one of the few who were admitted to visit him. One way of reading the tale is that the rebbe himself is a kind of unique sacred goat. But his Hasidim have worn him down with their demands, as symbolized by the cutting away of the goat's horns. Another way of reading the tale is to see the goat as the goat of sacrifice, echoing the biblical ritual of sending a goat to Azazel on Yom Kippur. The goat willingly gives up the potent enchantment of his horns in order to assist others but in the process loses his powers—at least until the horns grow back. For another tale about the Kotzker Rebbe and Reb Yitzhak of Vorki, see "The Ocean of Tears," p. 374.

37. **The Golden Dove (Babylon)**

From *B. Ber.* 53b. Further myths about the golden dove are found in the *Zohar*, 2:8a–9a and 3:196b, and in Seder *Gan Eden* in *Beit ha-Midrash* 3:132–133 (Jerusalem, 1967). For an Arab variant of this tale, see "The Jewel in the Sand" in *Arab Folktales*, edited by Inea Bushnaq (New York: Pantheon Books, 1986), pp. 59–62.

The golden dove has many appearances in Jewish tradition. These are likely an outgrowth of the biblical verse *The wings of the dove are covered with silver, and her pinions with the shimmer of gold* (Ps. 68:14). The first appearance of the golden dove is found in the talmudic tale about the wandering sage Rabbah bar bar Hannah, who is the Sinbad of the Talmud. Rabbah miraculously discovers the golden dove when he leaves his caravan to say the *birkat ha-mazon*, the prayers after eating. It is his understanding of the law that the prayers must be said in the place where a person ate. This requires him to leave the caravan and return to the previous station, a dangerous endeavor. Since the other sages on the caravan may not agree with this strict interpretation of the law, he tells them that he is going back for a golden dove. But to spare him the dishonor of lying, heaven sees to it that he actually finds a golden dove there.

There are further elaborations of the myth of the golden dove in the *Zohar* (2:8a–9a): "Then the Holy One, blessed be He, beckons that bird, and it enters its nest, and comes to the Messiah, and it calls what it calls, and stirs up what it stirs up, until the nest and the Messiah are called three times from inside the Holy Throne, and all ascend." This passage from the *Zohar* makes a direct link between the golden dove and the Messiah, which does not exist in the talmudic tale. It also explains why the palace of the Messiah is known as the "Bird's Nest." See "The Ladder of Prayers," p. 350, which draws on this Kabbalistic tradition.

38. The Twelve Golden Calves (China)

From *Legends of the Chinese Jews of Kaifeng* by Xu Xin. Collected by Wang Yisha from Shi Yulian and Shi Zhong'en of Kaifeng. Originally published in *Spring and Autumn of the Chinese Jews* (Chinese), published in 1993 in Kaifeng. Based on the version of Xu Xin.

It is quite remarkable to discover that there were Jews in China. Two scholars, Wang Yisha and Xu Xin, have managed to collect some of the oral tales of the Jews of Kaifeng. Xi Xin notes that the surname of Shi Ziyu in this story was bestowed by the Song emperor on seven Jewish families.

"The Twelve Golden Calves" seems a perfect blend of a Chinese folktale based on a biblical model, that of the story of Joseph. Just as Pharoah had a dream of seven fat calves and seven lean ones, so Shi Ziyu, known as Yehuda, has a dream for three nights in a row about twelve golden calves. Just as Joseph interpreted Pharaoh's dreams, so Yehuda goes to a local dream interpreter. Note, as well, the parallels in the interpretation, in which the cows in Pharaoh's dream symbolize fat and lean years, and the golden calves in Yehuda's dream symbolize the twelve gold ingots he will discover on the land he purchases as a result of the dreams. Thus both have prophetic dreams, receive correct interpretations, and by acting on them, both Joseph and Yehuda achieve great success. Joseph becomes the Prince of Egypt, and Yehuda is able to build the silk mill he has longed for.

39. The Sword of Moses (Iraqi Kurdistan)

From *Sippurim mi-Pi Yehude Kurdistan,* edited by Dov Noy (Jerusalem: Israel Folktale Archives, 1966), IFA 6602, collected by Zvi Chaimovitz from Zion Sayda of Iraq. And from Codex Gaster 178, *The Sword of Moses,* in *Studies and Texts in Folklore, Magic, Medieval Romance, Hebrew Apocrypha and Samaritan Archeology,* edited by Moses Gaster (New York: Ktav, 1971).

For Jews scattered in various countries, almost always an oppressed minority, the longing for a Jewish state and the belief in the coming of the messianic age fused into a single dream, as this tale clearly demonstrates. Here the sword of Moses (*Your protecting shield, your sword triumphant*—Deut. 32:29) invokes the past—Moses serves as the model for a Messiah more than any other figure—and also the coming redemption of the future. Over the centuries the Jews gave allegiance to several false messiahs, most prominently Shabbatai Zevi, and the temptation to do so is suggested here in the trick played on the young Jews searching for the sword of Moses, who find instead the rusty sword, which in turn can be seen to symbolize such false messiahs. Unlike some of the followers of Shabbatai Zevi, however, who, when disillusioned, ended their search for the Messiah, the young men continue their quest, and come to an understanding that what they are seeking may not be an actual object but something more elusive and symbolic, though equally potent. Such a conclusion is harmonious with the objectives of kabbalah, where the transformation of the literal meaning into its symbolic counterpart is one of the primary goals.

40. **The Groom Who Was Destined to Die on His Wedding Day (Ethiopia)**

Collected by Rahamin Elad from Kes Yemano Tamayt. From *Tarat, Tarat: Sippurei Am mi-Pi Yehudei Etiopia,* edited by Tamar Alexander and Amla Einat (Tel Aviv, 1996), pp. 73–74.

This tale demonstrates the belief among Ethiopian Jews that a person's fate is sealed from the day of his birth. This is one expression of the widespread belief among Jews that the time and manner of a person's death is known to God. This story carries that belief a step further, in recounting how a man escaped his fate—to die on the day of his wedding—and therefore was unable to die.

This story should also be viewed as a warning tale. In virtually all cultures, the wedding day is regarded as a time of danger. Indeed, the three most dangerous turning points in a person's life are birth, marriage, and death. Among the dangers faced by those about to marry are demons who will try to substitute a demonic double for their intended ("The Other Side," p. 283, and "The Demonic Double" in Schwartz, *Invisible Kingdoms,* pp. 49–56), a grave danger that lurks on the wedding day ("The Beast," p. 249), or being led astray by the forces of evil, preventing the wedding from taking place ("The Bridegroom Who Vanished," p. 306). And in this Ethiopian Jewish tale, the bridegroom is destined from the time of his birth to die on the day of his wedding.

This tale, collected orally in Israel from an Ethiopian Jew, demonstrates that the folklore of the Ethiopian Jews retained much in common with other Jewish communities. The angel who tells the newborn infant the day he will die strongly echoes the talmudic myth of the angel Lailah, who teaches the unborn infant in the womb and then touches the upper lip of the child right after he or she is born, causing them to forget everything that was revealed. See "The Angel of Conception" in Schwartz, *Tree of Souls,* pp. 199–200. An even closer parallel is the tradition of the Jews of India that the First Eve is said to reveal a boy's future on the fifth day after his birth, three days before the *b'rit.* See "The First Eve" and "What Happened to the First Eve" in Schwartz, *Tree of Souls,* pp. 140–142. The fact that there are such far-flung traditions about a mythical figure communicating with newborns suggests it was a very ancient tradition among the Jews.

In addition, the primary motif of this story, that of the bridegroom destined to die on the day of his wedding, is also widely found in Jewish folklore. See

"The Hero Predestined to Die on His Wedding Day" by Haim Schwarzbaum, in *Folklore Research Center Studies* 4 (1974): 223–252.

Finally, there is the very interesting notion in this tale that because he escaped death on the day of his wedding, the man cannot die. This is strongly reminiscent of the Christian myth of the Wandering Jew, who was cursed by Jesus to wander until the second coming. See *The Legend of the Wandering Jew* by George K. Anderson (Providence, R.I.: Brown University Press, 1965) and *The Legend of the Wandering Jew* by Joseph Gaer (New York: New American Library, 1961). This theme also reflects the focus on death in the folklore of the Ethiopian Jews, where one of the dominant themes is that of the dead coming back to life.

The teller of this tale is identified as a "Kes" or one of the sages of the Jewish Ethiopian community. This indicates that this tale plays an important role as a teaching tale, affirming the belief that a person's fate is sealed from the day of their birth.

41. **The Three Tasks of Elijah (Tunisia)**

From *Hibbur Yafe min ha-Yeshu'ah,* compiled by Nissim ben Yaakov, in *Otzar Midrashim,* edited by Y. D. Eisenstein (New York, 1915). With episodes from *B. Baba Mezi'a* , and from *Pesikta de-Rav Kahana* 18:5, edited by Solomon Buber (Lyck, 1860).

The folkloristic role of Elijah the Prophet was formed as early as the talmudic era. It is characteristic of Elijah in this role that he is unsparing in his efforts to assist poor Jews in their time of trial, often making use of supernatural powers in order to accomplish this. Here Elijah goes as far as to sell himself as a slave, and having done so, remains a slave until he has fulfilled the king's requirements to set himself free. Of course Elijah could have freed himself at any time, but his character is such an honest one that any deception is unthinkable. Instead Elijah fulfills his tasks, then resumes his role as benefactor of the Jews. This tale derives from the oldest nonsacred Jewish anthology, and has no earlier source extant, although many of the tales in the collection were drawn from the Talmud. In order to expand the tale into the standard three-part fairytale narrative, two additional tasks have been drawn from the tales of Elijah found in the legends of the Talmud and Midrash. Isaac Bashevis Singer wrote a version of this tale, called "Elijah the Slave."

42. **The Staff of Elijah (Romania)**

From *Hailan Shesafag Demaot,* collected by Yaakov Avitsuk, edited by Dov Noy (Haifa: Israel Folktale Archives, 1965). IFA 2558, told by Azriel Zaid of Romania.

This story, drawn from the Israel Folktale Archives, is evidence that miraculous tales about Elijah the Prophet have continued to be told up to the present. The symbol of the staff naturally echoes the staff of Moses, which possessed supernatural powers, turning into a serpent in Pharaoh's court and releasing water from the rock that Moses struck in the wilderness. But the purposes for which this staff is used are more characteristic of those associated with Elijah—to protect against the enemies of Israel and to provide for poor Jews in need. However, the role of Moses is suggested in the final episode, in which the old man travels to the Holy Land and is led, as if by accident, but in fact by fate, to the tree from which the staff was taken, where it once again becomes a branch. This suggests that the ultimate destiny of every Jew is to return to the Holy Land, where Moses sought to lead Israel, and that returning there restores the branch that was cut off in the Diaspora from the living tree of Israel. In that sense, this is a proto-Zionist tale. That the staff was taken from a tree on Mount Carmel is natural, since that was the site of Elijah's defeat of the priests of Ba'al (1 Kings 18:19ff.).

43. **Miriam's Tambourine (Eastern Europe)**

From *Ma'aseh me-ha-Hayyat* (Yiddish) (Vilna, 1908).

This tale is an outgrowth of the midrash about Miriam's Well. This well is said to have followed the Children of Israel during their forty years of desert wanderings, supplying them with fresh water. The legend finds its origin in Numbers 21:16: *That is the well whereof the Lord said unto Moses: "Gather the people together, and I will give them water."* The subsequent list of places through which the Israelites traveled is the likely source for the legend of the well traveling with the people wherever they went. For the rabbis, one passage following another in the Torah indicates that the two are linked. Thus they assumed that the places listed were among those where Miriam's Well came to a rest, so that the people could drink from it.

According to the Talmud, the well was one of the ten things created on the eve of the Sabbath at twilight during the days of Creation (*B. Pes.* 54a). Since this means that the well existed long before the time of the Exodus, other rabbinic legends suggest that it not only followed the Israelites at that time but also that "Every place where our forefathers went, the well went before them" (*Pirke de-Rabbi Eliezer,* chap. 35). "Miriam's Tambourine" offers a final resting place of the well—in the Garden of Eden. In another version of the legend, Miriam's Well reached the Holy Land with the Israelites and is hidden in the Sea of Galilee (*B. Shab.* 35a). See "The Angel of Forgetfulness," p. 331, where the Ari restores his disciple's memory by having him drink water from Miriam's Well.

The theme of the book that can be opened by only person in each generation is a variant of the legend of the Book of Raziel, which the angel Raziel delivered to Adam to reveal the future to him. This book was passed down to the primary figure in each subsequent generation until it was destroyed along with the Temple (*Sefer Noah* 150). See "The Book of Raziel" in Schwartz, *Tree of Souls,* pp. 253–255. For more background on this myth of an enchanted well, see "Miriam's Well" in Schwartz, *Tree of Souls,* p. 387.

44. **The Cave of King David (Eastern Europe)**

From *Sippurei Yakov,* story 2, edited by Yakov Sofer (Dobromil, 1864).

In Jewish folklore there are a few key figures who either return from the dead or are described as never having died. *Derekh Eretz Zuta* 1 lists nine who were said to have entered Paradise alive. There are also traditions about key figures, including Adam, Abraham, Jacob, Moses, and King David, having never died. The famous song "David Melech Yisrael, Hai Hai Vikayom" insists that King David is alive and still exists. It derives from an incident recorded in the Talmud (*B. RH* 25a) where Rabbi Judah ha-Nasi sends Rabbi Hiyya to sanctify the moon and to report that this had been done by quoting this phrase about King David.

Later it was included in the liturgy for the sanctification of the moon (*kiddush levanah*) and became the basis of the popular song. It is this song that the Turkish sultan overhears in this tale.

Probably inspired by this passage and song about King David, there are a number of tales in which King David is found to be living in a distant place. This is usually the city of Luz, where the inhabitants are immortal, or, as in this tale, in a nearby cave.

There are a number of tales about King David's tomb on Mount Zion in Jerusalem. In one, the ghost of King David saves a young Jewish woman who is trapped inside the tomb at a time when Jews were forbidden to go there. Another well-known tale concerns two students who come on a quest to wake King David so that he can fulfill his role as Messiah (IFA 966, recorded by Nehamah Zion from Miriam Tschernobilski of Israel. See "The Sleeping Messiah" in Schwartz, *Tree of Souls*, p. 498.) In these tales, the King David of Jewish folklore is not the flesh-and-blood king of the Bible, but he is variously portrayed as an Orpheus-like archetypal poet, as a kindly spirit returning to help his beloved people, and as a messianic figure. He has a harp strung with gut from the ram sacrificed at Mount Moriah, and at midnight a wind blows through the window and plays beautiful melodies on that harp, waking King David and inspiring him to write the Psalms (*B. Ber.* 3a and *Midrash Tehillim* 22:8).

"The Cave of King David" is an example of the impossible quest, such as the one in the fairy tale "The Golden Feather," where a king demands that a lad who has found a golden feather must bring him the whole bird. See "The Golden Feather" in Schwartz, *Elijah's Violin*, pp. 137–147. Another fine example of an impossible quest is "The Princess and the Slave," p. 66, where an old Hebrew slave is sent on a quest to find Moses and have him answer a riddle. The biblical archetype of this kind of tale is found in the Book of Daniel, when Nebuchadnezzar demands that his soothsayers tell him not only the meaning of his dream but also the dream itself (Dan. 2:5–6). Ultimately it is Daniel, with the help of God, who provides the dream and its interpretation.

Note Rabbi Rafael Recanti's use of the Holy Name to take an enchanted journey to the city of Luz. This tale is one of several accounts of journeys to that mythical city of immortals. See "An Appointment with Death" (Introduction, p. 7), and "The City of Luz," p. 105.

45. **The Magic Wine Cup (Syria)**

IFA 6628, collected by Moshe Rabi from Avraham Etia, *Avotanu Sipru*, story no. 47, edited by Moshe Rabi (Jerusalem, 1976).

Here Rabbi Hayim Pinto shows himself to be a great kabbalistic conjurer, demonstrating powers similar to those of the late medieval Jewish sorcerer Rabbi Adam or the great Hasidic master Rabbi Elimelech of Lizensk. See, for example, "A Bowl of Soup" (Introduction, p. 13), where another miracle takes place at the table. See also "The Magic Mirror of Rabbi Adam," p. 86. In the present tale about Rabbi Pinto, he invokes Rahab, the Prince of the Sea, to recover the sunken case of jewels lost by his seder guest. The holy names that are used are usually the names of angels. In essence, these holy names serve as keys, either to the gates of the palaces of heaven or to the powers of the angels associated with them. Rahab is the angel of the sea, a kind of Jewish Neptune. The theme of calling upon Rehab to recover something in the sea is found in the Jerusalem

Talmud in *Sanh.* 7:25. For another tale about Rahab, see "Rabbi Joshua and the Witch" in Schwartz, *Miriam's Tambourine*, pp. 35–38, where Rabbi Joshua calls upon Rahab to send him an evil amulet sunk in the sea. And as Rabbi Joshua stands at the shore, the waves wash up a box containing it. This talmudic tale is no doubt the model for that of the magic kiddush cup.

46. The Hair in the Milk (Turkish Kurdistan)

From *Shishim Sippure Am*, edited by Zalman Baharav (Haifa, 1964). IFA 4563, collected by Zalman Baharav from Yakov Chaprak.

This tale is a virtual compendium of customs connected with Lilith's role as a child-destroying witch. Lilith is described as having long black hair in the Talmud (*B. Er.* 100b). Finding a hair in food or drink was regarded as a sign of bad luck; here it heralds the arrival of Lilith herself. Lilith has the ability to transform herself into any shape she desires. That is how she is able to be fully present in just a single hair. The midwife, knowing this, traps her in the jug and thus gains power over her.

The story is also warning tale about the importance of having a flawless mezzuzah at every door. Otherwise, the house will be unprotected against the forces of evil—demons, dybbuks, and other kinds of evil spirits. So too does the story underscore the need for an amulet against Lilith to be hung above a baby's bed. The forced confession of Lilith or other demons is a common theme in many folktales, found first in *The Testament of Solomon*, where King Solomon captures and then debriefs the demoness Ornasis about the identity of all the other demons. The theme of capturing a witch and seeing only her head echoes the tale found in the Jerusalem Talmud (*Y. Sanh.* 7:25d) about how Rabbi Hanina pulled a witch's head from flax that he had magically grown on a table. See "Rabbi Joshua and the Witch" in Schwartz, *Miriam's Tambourine*, pp. 35–38. There is also an echo of the tales of demons trapped in a bottle, including a variant about Ashmodai, king of demons (IFA 107, collected by Heda Yazon from Yeffet Shvili of Yemen), a common theme in *The Arabian Nights*.

"The Hair in the Milk" is a good example of a woman's tale. Note the wisdom, strength, and confidence of the midwife, who refuses to be intimidated by Lilith—the way men have been for so many centuries. Midwives are the heroines in many such tales. There are dozens of versions of the story of the midwife who goes to the land of the demons to deliver children, such as "The Underwater Palace," p. 318. See also "The Flight of the Midwife" in Schwartz, *A Journey to Paradise*, pp. 18–23, and "The Black Cat" in Schwartz, *The Wonder Child*, pp. 16–23.

Until the twentieth century, almost all of the stories from traditional Jewish sources came from men and reflected a male perspective. One of the great accomplishments of the Israel Folktale Archives, which has collected more than 23,000 tales, is that women are as prevalent as men among its tellers. For a good selection of these women's tales, see Barbara Rush's *The Book of Jewish Women's Tales* (Northvale, N.J.: J. Aronson, 1994). Of course there were tales that were told exclusively among women, which reinforced their strengths and self-image. See "Is There a Jewish Folk Religion?" by Dov Noy, in *Studies in Jewish Folklore*, edited by Frank Talmage (Cambridge, Mass.: Association for Jewish Studies, 1980).

47. The Cave of Mattathias (Eastern Europe)

From *Hag La'am*, edited by Eliezer Marcus (Jerusalem, 1990). Told by Shimon Toder. The original legend about Hanukah is found in *B. Shabbat* 21b.

Mattathias was the father of the Maccabees. Here the Hasid who risks everything to meet his rebbe on the day they share together is blessed with a dream of Mattathias still alive, living in a cave, preparing candles for the messianic era, and predicting its imminent arrival. This story builds on the rabbinic legends in which certain key biblical figures are portrayed as still alive, especially Moses and Elijah. At the same time, the Hasid is portrayed as a holy messenger, sent to the rebbe to inform him of the words of Mattathias. But the rebbe, Rabbi Menachem Mendel of Riminov, is aware of all that takes place, and acknowledges this when he greets the Hasid at the door. This links the powers of the Rabbi of Riminov to those of the sons of Mattathias, which serves to glorify the rebbe in the eyes of his followers. Such linking of the Hasidic masters with the great figures of the past is one of the most common motifs found in Hasidic tales. At the same time, this is a tale of messianic tremors, the kinds of rumors that would often shake Jewish communities. Indeed, the message from Mattathias is that the messianic era is almost upon them, hinting that the Rabbi of Riminov can have an important role to play in this event. But the real importance of this dream is the way it provides salvation to the Hasid trapped in the snow. By creating the conditions to save himself, using the oil for the Hanukah candles, he saves himself from freezing and is able to sleep, and thus to dream. The dream first transports him from a cold place to a warm one, and then brings him face to face with Mattathias, who has remained alive all this time, waiting for the Messiah and preparing wicks to light when the messianic age arrives. This dream meeting with Mattathias is a fateful one for the Hasid, for when he awakes he finds himself at the rabbi's door. A miracle has once more taken place, as happened to Rabbi Abraham Berukhim when he had a vision of the *Shekhinah* in "A Vision at the Wailing Wall," p. 333, and as it did to the rich man who was kissed by Rabbi Shimon bar Yohai in a dream in "A Kiss from the Master," p. 329. Above all, this tale reveals just how intense was the longing of the Hasidim for the Messiah.

48. The Prince Who Thought He Was a Rooster (Eastern Europe)

From *Ma'asiyiot U'Meshalim* in *Kokhavei Or* (Jerusalem, 1896). A tale of Reb Nachman of Bratslav.

While Reb Nachman is best known for his labyrinthine fairy tales, he also told parables, of which "The Prince Who Thought He Was a Rooster" is the most famous. It has humor in the portrait of the prince, crouching naked beneath a table, who believes that he is a rooster. The story follows the pattern of fairy tales in which a princess is deathly ill, and king desperately seeks someone to cure her. Reb Nachman's story is unusual in that it is a prince, and not a princess, who needs to be cured, and in this case the illness appears to be a kind of madness, although it might also be identified as a radical form of nonconformity. The wise man succeeds in his mission, but one question lingers at the end of the story—was the prince truly cured, or, despite behaving like a man, does he still believe he is a rooster?

Reb Nachman of Bratslav commented on this story: "In this way must the genuine teacher go down to the level of his people if he wishes to raise them up." This indicates that for Reb Nachman the story is a parable about the role of the teacher—and, above all, of the rabbi, in descending to the level of understanding of his students, in order to raise them up to new levels not only of understanding but also of spirituality.

49. The Treasure (Eastern Europe)

From *Ma'asiyot U'Meshalim* in *Kokhavei Or* (Jerusalem, 1896), edited by Rabbi Abraham ben Nachman of Tulchin.

This well-known tale has been attributed to Reb Nachman of Bratslav, and is included as one of his tales in several collections. But it is most likely a European folktale of medieval origin. Its attribution to Reb Nachman is, however, appropriate as far as the content of the tale is concerned. Its faith in dreams and destiny, and the moral drawn, which suggests it is necessary to travel outside of oneself in order to discover the treasure within, is certainly characteristic of Reb Nachman's teachings. One interpretation, for the Bratslav Hasidim, is that the Hasid must travel to his rebbe in order to discover himself.

The thirteen primary tales told by Reb Nachman, collected in *Sippurei Ma'asiyot*, are generally acknowledged as original creations, although they often echo themes and motifs common in folklore. But Reb Nachman also selected from the abundant pool of Jewish Eastern European folklore some tales to which he was particularly drawn, such as this one and "The Wooden Sword," p. 171. He no doubt told these to his Hasidim with the same fervor with which he told his own.

50. The Souls of Trees (Eastern Europe)

From *Sihot Moharan* in *Hayey Moharan* by Rabbi Nathan of Bratslav, no. 535 (Lemberg, 1874). For the biblical law about newly planted trees, see Leviticus 19:23.

In addition to the tales that Reb Nachman told, there are tales about Reb Nachman that were recorded by his loyal scribe, Rabbi Nathan of Nemirov. Here Reb Nachman is portrayed as being so sensitive to the existence of surrounding souls that while sleeping in an inn he has a nightmare about a massacre, which he interprets as meaning that he has heard the cries of the saplings that were cut down too soon to build that inn. Of great interest is how Reb Nachman discovers this meaning of his dream, which otherwise does not point to the suffering of trees. By opening a book at random and pointing to a passage, he uses a method of Jewish divination known as *she'elat sefer* in which a sacred text—usually the Bible—is opened at random and a passage is pointed to, which is understood to be the reply to the question.

But instead of using the Bible, which is the most common method, Reb Nachman opens a book he has brought with him and blindly points to this passage: "Cutting down a tree before its time is the same as killing a soul." This gives him the essential clue to link the dream with the trees. Such environmental notions are also found in *B. Sukkah* 29a, which states that cutting down good trees is one of the four things that eclipse the luminaries. As a master of allegory, Reb Nachman has no difficulty understanding the meaning of the oracle. With this method of divination, it is understood that the reply is from God and contains an answer of some kind. Note that Reb Nachman does the act of divination at once on waking, despite the presence of all those who have come because of his cries, and without any explanation. For in divination it is important that a person be entirely focused on the question, and nothing is permitted to cloud the reply.

Supernatural Tales

51. **The Finger (Palestine)**

From *Shivhei ha-Ari,* compiled by Shlomo Meinsterl (Jerusalem, 1905).
A variant is found in a sixteenth-century Yiddish manuscript in Cambridge (Trinity College) Hebrew mss. 136, no. 5, "A Story from Worms."

This tale follows the pattern of marriage-with-demon tales, where a man ends up tricked into marriage with a demoness. In this retelling of "The Finger," the demoness has been identified as a corpse, to further underscore the story as a tale of terror. For other examples, see "The Other Side," p. 283 and "The Cellar," p. 260.

"The Finger" is part of the cycle of tales about the Ari found in *Shivhei ha-Ari.* The closest variant is "The Demon in the Tree," in Schwartz, *Lilith's Cave,* pp. 98–100, a previously unpublished tale from an Eastern European manuscript also dating from the sixteenth century. Note that the two stories are current at the same time in Jewish communities in two parts of the world, Eastern Europe and the Middle East. "The Finger" blends elements of tales about Lilith-type demonic figures with the Venus-Ring motif. This motif involves a fiancé who, in a reckless moment, places his engagement ring on a statue of Venus; the statue is thereby brought to life, appearing on the wedding night as a ghostly presence who tries to supplant the real bride sleeping at her husband's side. Thus "The Finger" is a fusion of three popular folk traditions about the seductive Lilith, the theme of marriage with demons, and the Venus-Ring motif.

Tim Burton's film *The Corpse Bride* was inspired by "The Finger."

52. **The Queen of Sheba (Germany)**

From *Ma'aseh Nissim* (Yiddish), compiled by Jeptha Yozpa ben Naftali (Amsterdam, 1696). A variant of "The Fisherman and His Wife," from *Grimms' Fairy Tales.*

The Queen of Sheba plays a wide variety of roles in Jewish folklore. She is a heroine in the folklore of the Ethiopian Jews, and she is viewed as a worthy foil to King Solomon in stories such as "The Maiden in the Tree," p. 160, and "A Palace of Bird Beaks," p. 157. But more often she is viewed as a demonic witch and seductress in both Jewish and Arabic folklore, where she is identified with Lilith. This identification originates in the Targum to Job 1:15, where Lilith is said to have tortured Job in the guise of the Queen of Sheba. It is based on a Jewish and Arabic legend that the Queen of Sheba was actually a genie, half human and half demon. The riddles of the Queen of Sheba were said to be the same ones with which Lilith seduced Adam (*Livnat ha-Sappir,* edited by Joseph Angelino, Jerusalem, 1913). In one Arab legend King Solomon suspects the Queen of Sheba of being Lilith. In the present tale, the demoness plays a variant of the seductive role of Lilith, while calling herself the Queen of Sheba. And to the merchant, whose life she takes possession of, she does indeed embody an erotic fantasy. In later tradition the Queen of Sheba becomes identified with one particular demoness, who behaves, as one of the daughters of Lilith, in a seductive and destructive fashion, but establishes an identity of her own. Note that this is one of the few stories in which the Lilith-like figure demonstrates both mythic roles of the incarnation of lust and of the child-destroying witch: she strangles the children she had with the innkeeper as well as seducing him. The curiosity of the innkeeper's wife suggests the themes of both Pandora and Bluebeard. In this case, however, both man and wife are guilty of breaking the taboo: he by engaging in a secret tryst with a demoness, she by entering the locked room. A longer, more complex variant of this tale is found in "The Cellar," which dates from a century later. This tale, like "The Queen of Sheba," shows some of Lilith's disguises. For another example, see "The Other Side," p. 283. See also "Helen of Troy" for an additional tale about Lilith. For another fine example of a Lilith-type fantasy, see "The Woman in the Forest," in the Introduction, p. 9, which recounts a folktale told by the Belz Hasidim. In this tale, another sexual fantasy, a pious rabbi encounters the hut of a demoness in the middle of a forest, and she seeks to seduce him, almost succeeding before his resistance breaks the illusion. A brief Eastern European oral tale about the Queen of Sheba (IFA 7248, from *Sippurei Am Misanuk,* collected by Samuel Zanvel Pipe) describes her smoking a pipe and beckoning to children from the water. When the children approach her, curious about how the pipe can stay lit, she drags them into the depths. For a variant of this tale, see "The Water Witch," p. 174.

53. **The Bride of Demons (Germany)**

From *Sefer Ma'aseh Nissim,* edited by Pinhas David Braverman (Jerusalem, 1966).

One of the most common themes in Jewish folklore involves the angry curse "Go to the Devil!" It is always taken in some literal sense, as here, where the mother's angry words to her daughter are sufficient opening for Lilith to capture her as a bride for one of her demon sons. This superstition is the origin of the popular aphorism "Don't open your mouth to the Devil." This theme is also used by Reb Nachman of Bratslav in his first tale, "The Lost Princess," p. 119, casting light on his use of folk motifs in his tales. This theme is found as well in the tales of the monks, *Gesta Romanorum* no. 72 (Mineola, N.Y.: Dover, 1959). Note that "The Bride of Demons" is one of only a handful of tales in which Lilith and Ashmodai, who are reputed to be king and queen of demons, appear together. Another is "Helen of Troy," p. 236. The roles of Ashmodai and the Devil are blurred here. But it often happens in Jewish lore that Samael, Satan, and Ashmodai are used interchangeably to refer to the Devil. There is a Palestinian tradition that unless a woman pronounces the names of God when she puts her wedding dress away in its chest, a demoness will take it out and wear it, attempting to seduce the woman's husband (see Thompson, *Semitic Magic* [London: Luzac, 1908], pp. 71–72.) See "The Bridal Gown" in Olson and Schwartz, *Ask the Bones,* pp. 125–128. The magic circle in which the groom protects himself from a hoard of demons plays a similar role in "The Chronicle of Ephraim" in Schwartz, *Lilith's Cave*, pp. 148–160, and it protects the Ba'al Shem Tov from attacking beasts in "The Werewolf," p. 296 and "A Combat in Magic," p. 300.

54. Helen of Troy (Palestine)

From *Iggeret Sod ha-Ge'ullah* by Abraham ben Eliezer ha-Levi (Jerusalem, 1519). A later version is found in *Sippur Rabbi Yosef della Reina* by Shlomo Navarro (Warsaw, 1905). A third version is found in *Eder ha-Yekar* in *Samuel Abba Horodezky Jubilee Volume* (Tel Aviv, 1947), edited by Zalman Rubashov (Shazar) (Tel Aviv, 1946).

The seeds for this tale were planted in the Talmud. The talmudic tale of the four sages who entered Paradise (*B. Hag.* 14b) served as a warning against overarching ambition in attempting to discover the secrets of creation. Of the four rabbis who engaged in this kind of mystical contemplation, three were destroyed by it, and only Rabbi Akiba returned in peace. There is another talmudic tale (*B. BM* 85b) that establishes the pattern for the effort to hasten the coming of the Messiah by forcing the end, as follows.

> Elijah the Prophet was a regular visitor to the synagogue of Rabbi Judah ha-Nasi, but one day he was late. When they asked him why, he said, "I had to waken Abraham, wash his hands, let him pray, and return him to sleep; likewise with Isaac and with Jacob." They asked him, "Why couldn't you waken them together?" Elijah answered, "If they were to pray together, their power could bring the Messiah before his time." They asked, "Are there any like them in this world?" Elijah replied, "Only Rabbi Hiyya and his sons."
>
> That day Rabbi Judah ha-Nasi decreed a fast and let Rabbi Hiyya and his sons lead the prayers. When Rabbi Hiyya said, "He causes the wind to blow," the wind began to blow. When he said, "He causes the rain to fall," rain began to fall. As he was about to say, "He resurrects the dead," they said in heaven, "Who has disclosed this secret?" and the angels replied, "Elijah." They brought Elijah before the heavenly court and gave him sixty lashes of fire. After that Elijah appeared in Rabbi Judah's synagogue as a fiery bear, and chased everyone out.

There are two famous versions of the story of Joseph della Reina, the first from the fifteenth century and the second from the sixteenth century. In the earlier version, Joseph della Reina is portrayed as an excessively fervent and overly ambitious prophet, who will stop at nothing to accomplish his goal of bringing the Messiah. This forced coming of the Messiah is called "Forcing the End" or "Hastening the End." He fails in his mission and instead of conquering the forces of evil, manifested as Ashmodai, the king of demons, and Lilith, his queen, he is defeated by them. In this view, Joseph della Reina had good intentions, but he undertook something beyond his abilities, and he paid a great price. See "The Chains of the Messiah" in Schwartz, *Tree of Souls*, pp. 492–495.

However, in the sixteenth century there was an expanded version of the tale by Shlomo Navarro which appends an entirely new episode, where Ashmodai casts Joseph della Reina several hundred miles, to France, where he is caught by Lilith. When della Reina asks her why she saved him, she tells him that she saw a spark of evil in him, and, indeed, she cultivates it, until della Reina is transformed into a completely evil sorcerer. It must be assumed that this story reflects the disdain over his hubris in trying to force the Messiah. It is this later version that is included here.

This tale of Joseph della Reina builds on both of these models, creating the archetypal tale of the holy madman, or the holy man who becomes mad. Another key talmudic tale, that of the capture of Ashmodai, king of demons, by King Solomon (*B. Git.* 67b), is also echoed in the account of the attempted capture of Ashmodai and Lilith, who were identified at this time as king and queen of demons. See "King Solomon and Ashmodai," p. 53. So too is the escape of the two demons paralleled by the ending of that same legend, in which Ashmodai throws King Solomon a great distance, after which the king is forced to become a beggar for many years, while Ashmodai, in disguise, rules in his place (see "The Beggar King," p. 57.)

"Helen of Troy" might be compared with the later story "The Homunculus of Maimonides," p. 245. In both cases the holy men are tutored by Elijah, echoing the talmudic tale. The historic role of Maimonides is, however, intentionally distorted in the latter tale. See the note to "The Homunculus of Maimonides," p. 409. Traditionally Helen of Troy was linked with Lilith in Jewish folklore, as was the Queen of Sheba. Thus Joseph della Reina returns to the arms of Lilith—the arms of death—at the end.

According to a legend linked to the Ari, Joseph della Reina was reborn as a large black dog that frightened everyone with its barking. The Ari once confronted the dog, and it confessed its identity. The story emphasizes the punishment of Joseph della Reina for his sins. Thus Joseph della Reina becomes identified with what he once tried to subdue—the forces of evil, Lilith and Ashmodai, who likewise took the form of black dogs. For a version of this legend, see Mordecai ben Yehezkel, ed., *Sefer ha-Ma'aysiot* (Tel Aviv, 1918), vol. 6, no. 67. The Israeli writer Dan Tsalka has written an interesting adaptation of this legend, *The Story of the Unfortunate Josef de la Reina.* See Dan Tsalka, *On the Road to Aleppo* (Ra'annana, Israel: Even Hoshen Publishers, 1999), pp. 251–281. Other interesting retellings of this legend by the Israeli writers Yehoshua Bar-Yoseph ("The Fettered Messiah") and Asher Barash ("Rabbi Joseph Della Reina") can be found in Schwartz, *Gates to the New City*, pp. 415–418 and 408–414, respectively. It is possible to recognize a reference to the capture of Lilith and Ashmodai in this tale in the final stanza of Rabbi Isaac Luria's Sabbath hymn, "Askina Seudasa," dating from sixteenth-century Safed:

> Defeated and cast out,
> the powers of impurity,
> the menacing demons,
> the menacing demons,
> are now in chains.

55. The Homunculus of Maimonides (Eastern Europe)

From *Sippurim: Eine Sammlung jüdischer Sagen, Märchen und Geschichten für Völkerkunde* (Vienna, 1921). Version of L. Weisel, first published in Prague, 1847. Oral variants can be found in *Ha-Rambam be-Fi ha-Am be-Maroko* by Ya'akov Itiel in *Yeda Am* 2 (1954), pp. 198–199, and in *Edot Mesaprot*, edited by Avraham Shatal (Jerusalem, 1969), pp. 146–147.

The theme echoed here is that of the creation of the Golem by Rabbi Judah Loew, and like that tale, this one derives from Prague. But although the Golem was created out of necessity, in order to protect the Jews of the ghetto from the dangers of the blood libel, the homunculus of Maimonides is created purely in order to discover the secrets of creation. See "The Golem," p. 292.

It has been suggested on several occasions that the Golem cycle of legends may have inspired Mary Shelley's *Frankenstein*, since both concern the creation of a man—the Golem by kabbalistic magic and Frankenstein's monster by science. If there was indeed a folk source that served to inspire Mary Shelley, it may have been the present tale about Maimonides, which was first published at the same time as the earliest Golem legends, and which has a theme and mood far closer to that of *Frankenstein* than do the tales of the Golem. It would be difficult to demonstrate this conclusively, since Frankenstein was published in 1818 and *Sippurim*, the volume in which the present tale and earliest Golem legend appear, was not published until 1847. However, since all indications are that the stories in *Sippurim* are based on authentic folk sources, there is every reason to assume that an oral version of this tale about Maimonides was current at the time Mary Shelley wrote her famous novel and probably a century or two before that.

The theme that such probing into divine mysteries leads to disaster is common in tales with kabbalistic themes such as this. This theme goes all the way back to the famous talmudic story about the four sages who entered Paradise (*B. Hag.* 14b): Ben Azzai looked and died; Ben Zoma looked and lost his mind; Elisha ben Abuyah cut the shoots, that is, became an apostate; and only Rabbi Akiba ascended and descended in peace. See "The Four Who Entered Paradise" in Schwartz, *Tree of Souls*, pp. 173–174.

"The Homunculus of Maimonides" indicates that one of the dangers associated with mystical endeavors was the creation of a false Messiah, as expressed by the fear of Maimonides that once the gestation of the homunculus is complete, he will be immortal. This suggests the theme of the hastening of the Messiah by various kabbalistic means, including the use of holy names and other methods. Such attempts have always been portrayed as forbidden and doomed to failure. See "Helen of Troy" for another example of such a tale.

The present folktale is of particular interest because of its apparent antagonism toward Maimonides, one of the most revered figures in Judaism. As such, it must be considered to be a folk expression of the controversy that raged at several periods, including that from which this tale emerged, over the writings and teachings of Maimonides. For the background of this dispute, see *Maimonidean Criticism and the Maimonidean Controversy*, 1180–1240, by Daniel J. Silver (Leiden: E. J. Brill, 1965).

Folktales are not the usual mode of expression for such religious conflict. Tracts, books, and fiery speeches are more commonly used. But long before the eighteenth century, Maimonides had become a figure of folk proportions not unlike the greatest sages, such as Rabbi Akiba or the Ari, and was the hero of many folktales. (For an example of a more typical tale about Maimonides, see "The Healing Waters" in Schwartz, *Miriam's Tambourine*, pp. 209–216.) Therefore it was not enough to resist his teachings in the usual ways, but it was necessary to undermine his folk image as well. That seems to be the intention of this tale, which also fits into the pattern of many other warning tales.

The lack of knowledge of the true teachings of both Maimonides and the kabbalah is evident in the choice of the secret texts from which Maimonides is said to have learned his secrets. One of these, *The Book of Creation*, is the name of an actual kabbalistic text, *Sefer Yetzirah*, one of the earliest and most enigmatic kabbalistic works. It does not attempt to impart, however, secrets of the kind required to bring the slain assistant to life. Instead it concentrates on the mysteries of letters and numbers and is far more abstract and oblique. Nor does the quotation from *The Book of Creation* in the story appear in the actual text of *Sefer Yetzirah*.

The combination of anti-Maimonidean and anti-kabbalistic elements suggests that this tale emerged from the Jewish centers of Poland and Lithuania, where the old quarrel over Maimonides broke out again in the late Middle Ages. At the same time, the present tale is itself a variant of other, positive folktales about the great medical skill and supernatural powers of Maimonides. In one of these tales, found in *Shalshelet ha-Kabbalah*, by Gedalyah ibn Yachya (Venice, 1587), Maimonides is forced to swallow poison in a confrontation with the king's physicians, but provides the antidote to save himself. In another such tale, an even closer variant to the one at hand, the caliph has Maimonides beheaded, but before his execution, Maimonides instructs his students in how to reattach his head, and he fully recovers, much to the consternation of the caliph. It is not a giant step from the powers demonstrated in these tales to the creation of the immortal man in "The Homunculus of Maimonides."

"The Homunculus of Maimonides" might also be seen as a polemic against the story of the creation of the Golem. In any case, this tale about Maimonides has no historical kernel, nor is it characteristic of Maimonides in any way.

56. **The Beast (Egypt)**

From IFA 2675, recorded by Zvi Moshe Haimovitch from Shaul Ephraim of Egypt.

This is an Elijah tale and also an excellent example of how the folktale treats themes of horror. Tales of parents seeking unusual remedies to cure barrenness are a staple of all folklore, as is the notion that the child born out of such a cure may have an unusual destiny. In this tale of terror, collected orally in Israel from a Jewish immigrant from Egypt, a young man cannot escape his fate to be devoured by a beast on the day of his wedding. His parents do everything in their power to protect him, but, as in most the stories about trying to outfox fate, fate wins. The prophecy is fulfilled. An exception, which is also a variant, is "The Black Hand," in Schwartz, *Lilith's Cave*, pp. 183–184, where the prophecy that the boy will drown on the day he turns thirteen comes dangerously close to be being fulfilled. In this story, however, the warning is heeded, and the prophecy of doom avoided.

At the same time "The Beast" is a tale of sexual initiation, and the devouring can be understood, no doubt, as a sexual kind. The innocent bridegroom imagines his bride to be shy; when confronted with her bold desire, he is devoured with fear. See Haim Schwarzbaum, "The Hero Predestined to Die on His Wedding Day, AT 934B," *Folklore Research Center Studies* 4 (1974). For other tales about the dangers facing those about to wed, see "The Bridegroom Who Vanished," p. 306, "The Other Side," p. 283, and "The Groom Who Was Destined to Die on His Wedding Day," p. 196.

57. The Haunted Violin (Germany)

From *Sefer Hasidim,* attributed to Rabbi Judah the Pious, Parma edition, Hebrew manuscript de Rossi 33, published by Yehuda Wistynezki, no. 323 (Berlin, 1891).

The Ashkenazi Hasidim, out of whom emerged the dark book *Sefer Hasidim,* lived in a world in which demons and other evil beings surrounded them everywhere. These tales suggest a complete submergence in supernatural belief, almost to the point of obsession. "The Haunted Violin" is a both a warning tale and a tale of terror. By using a board of a coffin to make a violin, the carpenter does not show proper respect to the departed soul, who thereby seeks revenge. That the warning comes to him through dreams reflects the standard belief that spirits communicate this way. The tale reinforces the folk belief in the dead taking revenge on those who did not respect them. See "The Knife," following, for another dark tale from *Sefer Hasidim.*

58. The Knife (Germany)

From *Sefer Hasidim,* attributed to Rabbi Judah the Pious, Parma edition, Hebrew manuscript de Rossi 33, published by Yehuda Wistynezki, no. 1456 (Berlin, 1891).

This bleak and frightening tale accurately reflects the state of mind of those most possessed by fears of the demonic and supernatural, which is represented more by the tales found in *Sefer Hasidim* than those in any other Jewish text. The witch's practice of putting the knife beneath her pillow so that her spell would take effect parallels the superstitious practice of parents who slept with a brick beneath their pillow, in order to make their children homesick, so that they would come home. It is one more example of the kind of black magic carried out within Jewish folk tradition, as documented by Joshua Trachtenberg in *Jewish Magic and Superstition* (New York: Behrman's Jewish Book House, 1939).

The moral of the tale seems to be that those who turn to this sorcery to achieve their own ends will soon enough become the victims of the same sorcery. As with most of the tales found in *Sefer Hasidim,* the moral is enforced with terror.

59. The Charm in the Dress (Germany)

From *Ma'aseh Nissim* (Yiddish), compiled by Jeptha Yozpa ben Naftali of Worms (Amsterdam, 1696). The present version is based on a variant found in *Ma'aseh Tovim,* edited by Shlomo Bechor Chotzin (Baghdad, 1890), reprinted in *Sefer ha-Ma'aysiot,* edited by Mordecai Ben Yehezkel (Tel Aviv, 1929).

In an earlier version of this tale, found in *Ma'aseh Nissim,* from the sixteenth century, the garment is a coat and the charm is a root. Also, the woman is unmarried. In the present version, from nineteenth-century Iraq, the garment has become a dress, the charm a paper, the woman married, and the time of the sin the eve of Yom Kippur. These last two details make the sin much worse, of course. Otherwise the narratives of the tales are very similar, with the later a direct variant of the former.

This tale reflects a deep fear of sorcery, and fear, in particular, of the power of charms, such as the one here hidden in a dress. It mirrors a deeply superstitious society, with a wealth of supernatural dangers facing them, demons and witches and especially the demoness Lilith, who is associated with sexual desire. Here the charm in the dress compels the woman into sexual sin. But she is not blamed, for she fell under a powerful spell. At the same time, Jewish women who were pregnant wore charms of their own—amulets with a text warding off Lilith and her daughters. See "A Spell to Banish Lilith" in Schwartz, *Tree of Souls,* p. 218. These superstitions are so extensive that they constitute something of a Jewish folk religion. See "Is There a Jewish Folk Religion?" by Dov Noy in *Studies in Jewish Folklore,* edited by Frank Talmage (Cambridge, Mass.: Association for Jewish Studies, 1980). For a further discussion of charms and spells, see Trachtenberg, *Jewish Magic and Superstition,* pp. 116–118.

60. **Lilith's Cave (Tunisia)**

From *Le Bestiaire du Ghetto: Folklore Tunisian* (French), edited by J. Vehel and Ryvel (Raphael Levy) (Tunis, 1934).

The haunted house is a universal folk motif, but in most Jewish tales the haunting is done by demons rather than ghosts. See "The Cellar," p. 260, for a variant tale. Also see "The Demons' Wedding" in *Lilith's Cave,* pp. 107–109. The legend of Lilith first finds full expression in *Alpha-Beta de Ben Sira,* edited by M. Steinschneider (Berlin, 1868), also from North Africa, dating from around the eleventh century. That the mirror should serve to attract demons is not surprising, considering its appeal to vanity, the strange quality of duplication it confers, and the sense of another world. One of I. B. Singer's most famous tales is "The Mirror," in which the mirror also serves as the home of a demon. See *The Selected Short Stories of Isaac Bashevis Singer* (New York: Modern Library, 1966), pp. 57–67.

The possession of the girl by a daughter of Lilith is an example of demonic possession, for the one who does the possessing is a demon. This is different than possession by a dybbuk, in that a dybbuk is always a sinner who has died, and is trying to escape his punishment. The earliest examples of demonic possession are found in Josephus (*Antiquities* 8:2.5) and the Talmud (*B. Me.* 17b).

The theme of the power of the curse is a familiar one in Jewish folklore. See "The Bride of Demons," p. 233, and Reb Nachman's "The Lost Princess," p. 119. In the present tale the girl's transformation into a bat fits into a long line of human transformations into various animals found in Jewish folklore. (For the closest parallel in this collection, see "The Beast," p. 249) The girl's transformation into a bat is a variant on the theme of those who become birds until they are disenchanted. See "The Princess on the Glass Mountain" in Schwartz, *Elijah's Violin,* pp. 155–161, and "The Wizard's Apprentice" in Schwartz, *Lilith's Cave,* pp. 33–39. Whether the girl in the present tale will ever be restored to her human form is unclear. The story hints that she will remain a bat as long as her father lives, for that is how long the shame will live in his heart. Why does the father's curse come true? One tradition holds that at times the Gates of Heaven swing open and all words spoken at that time have the seal of truth imprinted on them, and every blessing and every curse comes true. This custom is identified with the whole day of Yom Kippur and with midnight on the holiday of Shavuot, when the sky is said to open. See "The Wonder Child," p. 62, for a tale of such a midnight wish.

61. The Cellar (Eastern Europe)

From *Kav ha-Yashar,* by Tsvi Hirsh Kaidanover (Frankfurt-am-Main, 1903), vol. 2, chap. 69. Also found in *Ma'asiyot me-Tzaddik Yesode 'Olam* by Lazar Schenkel (Podgaitsy, Russia, 1903) and *Mora'im Gedolim,* compiled by Y. S. Farhi (Warsaw, 1909).

Lilith plays a major role in Jewish lore as the incarnation of lust. She is believed to haunt men in their dreams and fantasies. Every time a man had a sexual dream or fantasy, he was believed to have had intercourse with Lilith, who would subsequently give birth to mutant demons, half human and half demon, who were spurned by humans and by demons alike.

All men are said to be susceptible to the powerful attraction of female demons. The Midrash recounts that hundreds of female demons flocked around Adam during the 150-year period in which he was separated from Eve. See "Adam and the Demons" in Schwartz, *Tree of Souls,* p. 215. According to the kabbalistic interpretation, even the patriarch Abraham had demonic offspring. The prooftext for this exegesis is found in Genesis 25:6: *To the sons of the concubines that he had taken, Abraham gave gifts. Then, while he was still alive, he sent them to the country of the East, away from his son Isaac.* The concubines in this reading are, of course, demons. (See Gershom Scholem, *On the Kabbalah and Its Symbolism* [New York: Schocken Books, 1965], pp. 153–157.)

The primary theme of this story, that of marriage to a demoness, is one of the most popular in Jewish folklore. "The Cellar" is an elaborate embellishment of this theme. The man in the story has two wives, one human, the other a demoness living in his cellar. The story recounts how the secret of the man's demon wife was revealed, and the history of the cellar where demons continued to live after his death. In most variants of this tale the issue of the rights of the demons versus the humans is resolved by a rabbinic court. The humans are inevitably victorious in these cases, but in his retelling of this tale, "The House of Demons," Martin Buber reverses the verdict of the original tale, ruling in favor of the demons. See Martin Buber, *Tales of Angels, Spirits and Demons* (New York: Hawk's Well Press, 1958), pp. 24–34.

The story recounted here is a famous seventeenth-century folktale from the ethical text *Kav ha-Yashar.* It is likely a variant of the "The Demon Princess," p. 269, where a man is forced to wed the daughter of Ashmodai, the king of demons. For other variants, see "The Queen of Sheba," p. 230, "The Other Side," p. 283, and "Yona and the River Demon," p. 287. "The Finger," p. 227, and "The Demon of the Waters," p. 310, may also be regarded as distant variants of this theme.

One of the most popular and pervasive beliefs in Jewish folk tradition is that the demoness Lilith or one of her daughters, the Lilin, seek to steal a man's seed, in order to produce offspring who are half human and half demon. These demonic sons are said to haunt their fathers all their lives. These folk traditions grow out of a belief in extreme sexual purity, where any accidental or intentional spilling of a man's seed is regarded as a sin, the sin of Onan

(Gen. 38:8–10). So, too, do they reflect the widespread belief—and fear—of succubi, in the form of Lilith and her daughters. For more on nocturnal emissions, see *B. Berakhot* 57b and *B. Yevamot* 76a.

The struggle portrayed in this and other similar tales might also be seen as a struggle between Jews and Gentiles, where the offspring of Jewish men and Gentile women are half-Jewish, half-Gentile. Indeed, this story might well serve as a disguised allegory of Jewish-Gentile relationships in which the offspring are spurned by both sides.

See "The Cellar" in Schwartz, *Tree of Souls*, pp. 220–221, for additional sources and studies.

62. **The Dead Fiancée (Eastern Europe)**

From *Kehal Hasidim*, compiled by Aharon Valden (Warsaw, no date). Also found in *'Adat Tzaddikim*, compiled by M. L. Frumkin (Lemberg, Russia, 1877). A variant, concerning the Rabbi of Belz instead of the Seer of Lublin, is found in *Petirat Rabbenu ha-Kadosh mi-Belz* (Lemberg, 1894). An oral version is IFA 708, told by Dvora Fus from the shtetl of Lewdow near Vilna, Lithuania. This story has also been linked to the Maggid of Koznitz. But in most versions it is the Seer of Lublin who plays the prophetic role.

With a remarkable demonstration of his prophetic wisdom, Rabbi Yakov Yitzhak of Lublin, known as the Seer of Lublin, perceives that a man's failure to have children stems from his broken engagement. The Ba'al Shem Tov, too, was said to have had such prophetic vision. The theme of a broken vow causing barrenness is found in the famous medieval Jewish folktale "The Weasel and the Well" (*B. Ket.* 62b, also *Ma'aseh Book* no. 73). Here a young man saves a maiden who has fallen into a well, and they fall in love and vow to be wed. They call upon a passing weasel to witness their vow. When the young man marries someone else, the weasel kills each of his children, until he discovers the cause of his misfortune and seeks forgiveness from the spurned maiden, who has refused to marry any other because of her vow to him.

"The Dead Fiancée" is one of many Jewish tales that turns on the issue of a vow. These vows fall into two categories: those that are honored, which inevitably results in great rewards, and those that are ignored, which always provokes misfortune. See, the following tale, "The Demon Princess," p. 269, for another example of a story about a broken vow.

63. **The Demon Princess (North Africa)**

From *Ma'aseh Yerushalmi*, edited by Yehuda L. Zlotnik (Jerusalem, 1946). First published in Constantinople in the sixteenth century. A variant is found in *Sippurim: Prager Sammulung Jüdischer Legenden in Neuer Auswahl und Bearbeitung* (Vienna: R. Lowit Verlag, 1921). An oral variant is IFA 8129, collected by Lili David from Rachel ha-Rambam of Persia.

This is one of the most important tales in all of Jewish folklore. Not only does it establish the nature of the Kingdom of Demons but it also serves as a model for many subsequent variants about marriage with demons, as well as many other tales about those who find their way to the Kingdom of Demons. In most of these variants there is a marriage between a human male and a female demon, a pairing likely inspired by the legends about the demon Lilith, who seeks out men who sleep alone in order to seduce them. The offspring of these matches are said to be beings half human, half demon, who are at home in neither world. In the variant found in *Sippurim,* the daughter of Ashmodai is herself one of these mixed breeds, as her mother was a human who was snatched as a child and raised by Ashmodai.

The earliest tale reporting a sexual encounter between a man and a demoness is found in *Midrash Tanhuma*:

> On Yom Kippur a demon in the shape of a woman came to a pious man and seduced him and made love to him. Afterward the man was very sorry, until Elijah the Prophet came to him and asked him why he was so upset. And he told him all the things that had happened to him. And Elijah said: "You are free from sin, for this was a demon." After that the man reported this to his rabbi, who said: "Surely this judgment is true, for Elijah would never have come to a guilty man." (*Midrash Tanhuma* 1:20, edited by Solomon Buber, Vilna, 1981)

Other tales on the theme of marriage with demons are "The Other Side," p. 283, "The Queen of Sheba," p. 230, "The Cellar," p. 260, "Yona and the River Demon," p. 287, and "The Finger," p. 227. Also see "The Demon in the Tree" in Schwartz, *Lilith's Cave,* pp. 98–100.

64. **The Speaking Head (Eastern Europe)**

From *Noraot Anshe Ma'aseh* (Warsaw, no date) and *Pe'er Mi-kedoshim* (Lemberg, Russia, 1864). A variant is found in *Der Golem: Jüdischer Märchen und Legenden aus dem alten Prag,* edited by Eduard Petiska (Wiesbaden, 1972). Another variant is found in *Hadre Temen,* edited by Nissim Binyamin Gamlieli (Tel Aviv, 1978). An oral version is IFA 779, collected by Devora Fus from her mother of the shtetl of Lewdow, near Vilna, Lithuania. In this variant, it is a rabbi, rather than a boy of Bar Mitzvah age, who is tricked.

The theme of the speaking head might, at first, appear to be a variant of that of the Golem, the man of clay brought to life by Rabbi Judah Loew. And indeed this is the legendary tale of the childhood trauma of Rabbi Loew's son-in-law. However, in "Teraphim: From Popular Belief to a Folktale" Joseph Dan identifies this theme with a midrash found in *Midrash Tanhuma* dating from around the eighth century, which explains that the reason Rachel stole the *teraphim,* the family idols, from her father, Laban (Gen. 31:19), was because the idols could be forced to speak by the use of holy names and would therefore be used to track them down. According to the midrash, the idols were made from shrunken heads—hardly a common Jewish theme—with holy names placed beneath their tongues, who were compelled to reply to every question. See "Rachel and the Stolen Idols" in Schwartz, *Tree of Souls,* pp. 354–355.

The visit from the grave of Mordecai's grandfather by Rabbi Loew is typical of the grateful dead motif in Jewish folklore, where the person who sees to it that another receives a proper burial is later saved in a supernatural fashion by the spirit of the deceased. This follows the theme of the importance of showing respect for the dead. For an example of what happens when such respect is not given, see "The Haunted Violin," p. 252.

It is interesting to note that a tale about a speaking head is found in *The Book of the Thousand Nights and a Night,* translated by Richard Burton, vol. 1, "The Tale of the Wazir and the Sage Durban" (New York: Heritage Press, 1962), p. 69:

> "Among my books I have one, the rarest of rarities, which I would present to thee as an offering: keep it as a treasure in your treasury."
>
> "And what is this book?" asked the King.
>
> The Sage answered, "Things beyond compare; and the least of secrets is that if, directly after you have cut off my head, you open three pages of this book and read three lines of the page on the left, my head shall speak and answer any question you wish to ask of it."
>
> The King said, "O physician, are you really telling me that when I cut off your head it will speak to me?"
>
> He replied, "Yes, O King!"

Since some of the tales in the *Arabian Nights* are as old or older than the seventh century, and *Midrash Tanhuma* dates from around the eighth century, it is possible that this motif of a speaking head was a widely known in the Middle East at that time. Note also the parallel themes found in "The Homunculus of Maimonides," p. 245.

The plotline of the first part of "The Speaking Head," concerning the betrothal to a wealthy stranger from a distant land, is a variant of "The Demon Bridegroom," story no. 179 from *The Ma'aseh Book,* dating from 1602. Here a father demands an excessive dowry for his daughter, as well as an equally noble lineage. The demon, disguised as a noble, persuades the father to give him the daughter as a wife. After the wedding he insists on taking her back to his kingdom at once. They are accompanied by friends of the family until they reach the gates of his city—the very gates of hell. The unfortunate bride is forced to go with him, while the others return to the father to inform him of her terrible fate. It is interesting to note that this same plot is found in the story "Schalken the Painter" by Sheridan Le Fanu, published in 1839, which is widely regarded as one of the earliest, if not the first, supernatural work of fiction. (See *Lost Souls: A Collection of English Ghost Stories,* edited by Jack Sullivan [Athens: Ohio University Press, 1983], pp. 1–3 and 14–33). As such, "The Demon Bridegroom" might be one of the missing links between folklore and fiction. It is widely recognized that anonymous folktales eventually evolved into more self-conscious works of fiction, composed by a single author, but this is the rare case where it is possible to find the folktale—or at least a variant of it—that may well have served as the inspiration for such an early and important fictional tale of the supernatural as "Schalken the Painter."

65. **The Other Side (Eastern Europe)**

From *Tzefunot ve-Aggadot,* by Micha Joseph Bin Gorion (Berditchevsky) (Tel Aviv, 1957).

The injunction to refrain from going to the *mikveh* or swimming of any kind on the fourth night or the night of the Sabbath derives from a statement in *B. Pesahim* 112B: "One should not go out alone on the fourth night of the week or on the night of the Sabbath. And if he does, his blood is on his own head, because of the danger. What is the danger? An evil spirit. This evil spirit is identified as Agrat bat Nahalat, who controls eighteen myriads (180,000) malicious spirits." Agrat, who is also described as the queen of demons, is generally identified as Lilith in her most dangerous manifestation. This injunction against going out especially applied to swimming, because demons were believed to proliferate in large bodies of water.

Of great interest in this tale is the concept of the demonic double. Although it is not stated explicitly, the tale suggests that the young man who emerges from the river at the same time as the betrothed man is his own demonic double. Likewise, the demon bride he weds is the demonic double of his intended bride. See "Demonic Doubles" in Schwartz, *Tree of Souls*, p. 130.

The mansion where the young man meets his demonic bride is in the *Yenne Velt*, the world of spirits and demons. Here the demons find a way to trick the man into marrying the demon bride, who is the demonic double of his *bashert*, his destined one. This is a late variant of *Ma'aseh Yerushalmi*, edited by Y. L. Zlotnik (Jerusalem: 1946), from the twelfth century, and follows the pattern of that tale in calling on a rabbinic court to rule on the matter.

66. **Yona and the River Demon (The Balkans)**

From *Sippurei Am, Romanssot, ve-Orehot-hayim shel Yehudei Sefarad* by Max Grunwald, tale no. 50, edited by Dov Noy (Jerusalem, 1982). Collected by Max Grunwald from an unknown teller from the Balkans.

Rivers and other bodies of water were believed to attract demons. This may go back to the association of Lilith with the Red Sea, where Lilith made her home after leaving Adam. These river demons were considered among the most dangerous. See "The Demon of the Waters," p. 310. For another tale of danger associated with water, see "The Dybbuk in the Well," p. 290. Note that this tale concerns a maiden who is inadvertently married to a demon. As such, it is far rarer than the stories about men taking demonic brides. For a variant about such a marriage between a woman and a demon, see "The Underwater Palace," p. 318.

67. **The Dybbuk in the Well (Italy)**

From *Shalshelet ha-Kabbalah* by Gedalyah ibn Yahya (Venice, 1587). Also included in *Nishmat Hayim*, edited by Menashe ben Israel (Amsterdam, 1650) and in *Sippurei Dibuk b'Sifrut Yisrael*, edited by Gedalyah Nigal (Jerusalem, 1983).

This dybbuk tale is said to have taken place in the Italian city of Ferrara in 1535. Virtually all tales of dybbuk possession were reported as actual events, and usually include the name of the possessed, the name of the dybbuk when he was alive, the city where the possession took place, the year, and the name of the rabbi who performed the exorcism. In this tale, it appears that the rabbi who performed the exorcism is Rabbi Gedalyah Yahya, who compiled *Shelshelet ha-Kabbalah*, in which this story can be found. It is possible that he was trying to include himself in the chain of tradition. However, as *Shelshelet ha-Kabbalah* incorporates many sources, it is also possible that it was an oral narrative collected by Rabbi Yahya.

In most cases of dybbuk possession, as we find here, the dybbuk is the spirit of a man who sinned during his lifetime and died without repenting, and the one possessed is a woman. Indeed, possession by dybbuk may be regarded as a socially recognized form of a madness among women in the Jewish communities of the Middle Ages.

Note the erotic dimensions of this story. The woman has just come from the *mikveh*, the ritual bath in which a woman purifies herself at the end of her period. For it is only after this purification that the husband and wife are able to engage in intercourse again, until the woman's period returns.

Although their union is sanctioned by marriage, the dybbuk is attuned to the negative, vulnerable aspects of a person's life, and would regard all sexual thoughts as lustful. The dybbuk enters her from "that place," i.e., the vagina, and takes its place inside her womb. The possession takes place right after the woman comes from the *mikveh*. See "The Demon of the Waters," p. 310, where a similar accident occurs to a woman in a *mikveh*, making these stories variants.

Rabbi Gedalyah ibn Yahya (ca. 1515–ca. 1587) studied in the yeshiva of Ferrara, where the exorcism recounted here took place in 1535. He was expelled, along with other Jews, by Pope Pius V in 1569. He led a wandering life for eight years, and in 1575 he finally settled in Alexandria. His book *Shalshelet ha-Kabbalah*, which he worked on for forty years, recounts the history and genealogy of the Jews from the time of Moses.

For other dybbuk tales, see "The Widow of Safed" in Schwartz, *Tree of Souls*, pp. 228–230, and "The Exorcism of Witches from a Boy's Body" in Schwartz, *Lilith's Cave*, pp. 200–201. The most famous account of dybbuk possession is S. Ansky's classic Yiddish play *The Dybbuk*. For more on the fate of the soul after death, see "The Transmigration of Souls" in Schwartz, *Tree of Souls*, pp. 169–170, and "When a Man Dies" in *Tree of Souls*, pp. 231–232.

68. **The Golem (Eastern Europe)**

From *Nifla'ot Maharal*, edited by Yudel Rosenberg (Piotrkow, 1909).

Almost no legend has captured the popular imagination as has that of the Golem, the creature resembling a man created from clay by Rabbi Judah Loew of Prague (known as the Maharal) and brought to life by the use of various magical incantations, including holy names. This creature, according to the legend, protected the Jews of Prague from various dangers, especially that of the blood libel accusation—that is, of using the blood of Christian children in the making of matzah (unleavened bread) for Passover—with its disastrous consequences. Here the Golem discovers the body of a murdered Christian child who has been carried into the Jewish ghetto, and carries it back through underground tunnels into the basement of the actual murderer, the priest Thaddeus, thus staving off a pogrom. Knowledge of this legend is primarily derived from *Niflaot Maharal*, a collection of tales about Rabbi Loew and the Golem, published in 1909 by Rabbi Yudel Rosenberg, who claimed that they had been compiled in the sixteenth century by a relative of Rabbi Loew. Recent scholars, including Dov Sadan, Gershom Scholem, and Eli Yassif, have insisted, however, that Rabbi Rosenberg himself was the author of the book, which he based loosely on the existing legends. Such legends certainly existed. In 1808 Jacob Grimm published a description of the legend in *Journal for Hermits*. The issue here is whether these are authentic sixteenth-century legends, deriving from the period in which Rabbi Judah Loew lived in Prague or immediately afterward, or if they were largely the creation of Rabbi Rosenberg in the nineteenth century. The earliest published legends about Rabbi Loew are those found in the *Sippurim* series, edited by Wolf Pascheles, first published in Prague in 1847.

There are a number of precedents for the creation of the Golem in earlier Jewish literature, including the description of a calf that was created magically found in the Talmud: Rabbi Hanina and Rabbi Oshaia spent every Sabbath eve in studying the laws of creation, by means of which they created a third-grown calf and ate it (*B. Sanh.* 67b). There is also a legend about Solomon Ibn Gabirol, in which he is described as having created a female Golem, for allegedly sexual purposes: They say that Rabbi Solomon Ibn Gabirol created a woman who served him. When he was denounced to the authorities, he showed them that she was not a full or complete creature. And he restored her to the pieces of wood of which she had been constructed (*Ma'aseh Ta'atulim*, edited by S. Rubin, Vienna, 1887).

Part of the popularity of the Golem legend is due to the fact that it prefigures the modern myth of Frankenstein, where the creature is brought to life not with God's Name, but with the new magic of science. The influence, if any, of the Golem legend on Mary Shelley's novel *Frankenstein* has yet to be established, although several studies have attempted to find a link between the two. For additional accounts of the Golem, see Schwartz, *Tree of Souls*, pp. 279–284.

69. **The Werewolf (Eastern Europe)**

From *Shivhei ha-Besht* by Dov Baer ben Samuel, edited by Samuel A. Horodezky (Berlin, 1922).

This is probably the most famous story of the young Ba'al Shem Tov, demonstrating his faith, wisdom, supernatural abilities, and courage all in one tale. The only other well-known werewolf tale in Jewish lore is "The Rabbi Who Became a Werewolf," from *The Ma'aseh Book* no. 228. One unusual aspect of the present tale is that it involves a double transformation: An evil spirit takes possession of a sinful woodcutter, turning him into an evil sorcerer. He then transforms himself into the werewolf, who attacks the children led by the Ba'al Shem Tov because their singing is so pure that Satan fears that it might hasten the coming of the Messiah. This theme is one of the most prominent in Hasidic literature. Basically, there are two ways to hasten the coming of the Messiah: One is to use kabbalistic formulas and holy names to force the Messiah to come (as portrayed in "Helen of Troy," p. 236), and the other is to bring the Messiah by a faith so strong, the Messiah could not resist the call. This tale is in the latter category. Satan's fear that the singing of the children might induce the Messiah to come establishes that the soul of the Ba'al Shem Tov, even as a young man, was so holy that it was a worthy adversary to Satan and could even shake the heavens.

70. **A Combat in Magic (Eastern Europe)**

From *'Adat Tzaddikim*, compiled by M. L. Frumkin (Lemberg, Poland, 1877). An oral variant, which does not involve the Ba'al Shem Tov, is found in *Sheva Havilot Zahav*, IFA 2030, collected by Dvora Fus, from her parents, Kalman and Esther Lipkind, translated into Hebrew by Israel Rosenthal, edited and annotated by Otto Schnitzler (Haifa, 1969). A variant concerning Rabbi Yoel Ba'al Shem, involving an evil midwife who takes the form of a cat, is found in Ayzik-Meyer Dik, *Alte Yidische Zagen Oden Sippurim* (Vilna, 1876).

This tale type, that of the rabbi-sorcerer engaged in magical combat with an evil wizard, is found in many variants in Jewish lore. The earliest such combat is that of Moses and the magicians of Pharaoh. In the medieval period such tales often involve Rabbi Adam, who is drawn into magical combat with various opponents. See "The Magic Mirror of Rabbi Adam," p. 86. The most famous such story recounts how a Jewish wizard from beyond the River Sambatyon defeated the terrible Black Monk. See "The Black Monk and the Master of the Name," in Schwartz, *Miriam's Tambourine*, pp. 335–348. Note that there is a strong element of illusion in the combat, with the flaming animals of the wizard vanishing when they reach the enchanted circle the Ba'al Shem Tov. The Ba'al Shem Tov demonstrates similar illusionary powers in "The Beckoning of the Besht" in Schwartz, *Lilith's Cave*, pp. 180–182. A similar use is made of a magic circle in "The Bride of Demons," p. 233, making this a popular motif.

The first part of the present tale tells of the Watch Night, the night before the circumcision, when a child was believed to be in danger from Lilith, who would try to strangle it. Lilith was believed to come as a black cat, the same form taken by the evil sorcerer. The Ayzik-Meyer Dik variant also concerns a Watch Night and a black cat. In *Sefer Hasidim*, no. 465, a witch is described as turning herself into a cat. There it is said that if such a cat receives a blow from someone, the witch will die unless she manages to get bread and salt from the one who struck her. This, then, can be seen as a Lilith-type tale about a child-strangling witch that has been recast in the context of a magical combat between sorcerers. Such combining of tale types is characteristic of folklore in general and Jewish folklore in particular.

71. The Perfect Saint (Eastern Europe)

From *Sippure Ma'asiyot*, by Reb Nachman of Bratslav (Ostrog, Russia, 1816).

Reb Nachman of Bratslav tended to see sexual desire as the temptation of the *Yetzer Hara*, the Evil Impulse. At the same time, not even the greatest sages could overcome lust, as recounted in several talmudic tales, such as one in which Rabbi Akiba sees a naked woman in a tree and climbs up after her. When he is halfway there, the woman turns into Satan, who says: "Were it not that it is said in heaven to respect Rabbi Akiba and his teachings, your life would have come to naught" (*B. Kid.* 81a). A parallel legend is told about Rabbi Meir, who glimpsed a naked woman on the other side of a river, jumped in, and proceeded across, getting halfway there before she turned into Satan, repeating the same warning given to Rabbi Akiba (*B. Kid.* 80a).

Because Reb Nachman's tales usually have a strong personal dimension, this tale seems to indicate an awareness that sexual desire cannot be escaped and may have been intended as a subtle confession that he himself may have engaged in a misguided attempt to do so. See I. L. Peretz, "The Hermit and the Bear," in *Selected Stories by I. L. Peretz* (New York: Schocken Books, 1975), pp. 34–39, which has a similar theme that may have been inspired by Reb Nachman's tale.

72. The Bridegroom Who Vanished (Eastern Europe)

From *Hiyo Haya Ma'aseh*, edited by H. B. Ilan-Bernik (Tel Aviv, 1945).

Some folktales are perpetuated by being told on specific occasions. This tale was traditionally told to bridegrooms on the day of their wedding. It is a warning tale that serves to explain and justify the custom (*minhag*) that on the day of the wedding, the groom is not allowed to be left alone.

In this story, no one notices when the groom wanders outside, where he is met by the spirit of his dead friend (or possibly a demonic figure so disguised in order to lure him away—this latter reading might seem more appropriate). Joining his friend for a few hours, lost in the complexity of their talmudic debate, time flies and one hundred and thirty years pass before the groom finally returns—although to him it seems but a single day. In providing such a warning, this tale reinforces the restrictive limits on a bridegroom. In fact, one can well imagine that this tale was told to such bridegrooms while waiting for the ceremony to begin, as a way of warning them not to take any risks in that dangerous time. Why is that time particularly dangerous? Because the jealousy of the demons is said to be at its peak at such times.

Other tales, such as "The Other Side," p. 283, and "Yona and the River Demon," p. 287, reinforce the warning not to go to the river on certain nights of the week. See "The Elusive Diamond" in Schwartz, *Lilith's Cave*, pp. 117–119, for another example of a warning tale that affirms a custom, in this case the Kurdish dictum that women who have given birth must not leave home for forty days. A secondary reading can also be found in the present tale, a subtle jibe at the excessive withdrawal of certain talmudic students from the world in their attempts to totally immerse themselves in the Torah. For other tales about the dangers facing those about to wed, see "The Beast," p. 249, and "The Other Side," p. 283.

This tale also closely echoes the famous talmudic tale about Honi (*B. Tan.* 23), who is said to have slept seventy years. Indeed, the tale about Honi is the likely inspiration of Washington Irving's "Rip Van Winkle." (See Irving's *The Sketch Book of Geoffrey Creyon, Gent.*, 1820.) In the case of Honi, he sees an old man planting a carob tree, which takes seventy years before it bears fruit. Honi make an impudent comment about how the man will not live to see its fruit, and shortly afterward he falls asleep nearby and wakes up seventy years later. Then the first thing he sees is a full-grown carob tree, bearing fruit. He learns from those nearby that the grandson of the man who had planted the tree lives there, and thus discovers that he has slept for seventy years. Such talmudic motifs are often reworked in later Jewish folktales and Hasidic lore. The moral drawn may change, however, as in this case, where Honi is guilty of impudence toward an old man, and the bridegroom has opened himself to danger from demons. A variant of this theme, set in the time of the Temple, is found in *Stories from the Rabbis* by Abram S. Isaacs pp. 202–211. Here the bridegroom sleeps seventy years (instead of one hundred and thirty) and awakens after the destruction of the Temple.

73. The Lost Melody (Germany)

From *Me-Otsar Genazai* by Hayim Dov Armon Kastenbaum, edited by Alter Ze'ev Wortheim (Tel Aviv, 1932). From the memory of Haym Dov Armon Kastenbaum, who heard this story from his grandmother.

Jewish folk tradition includes the belief that the dead pray in the synagogue at night. Rabbi Abraham hears his name called as he passes a synagogue at night.

When he goes inside he encounters the ghost of a cantor who has died. The cantor teaches Rabbi Abraham a melody the cantor created, although he died before he had a chance to play it for anyone else. In this way the lost melody is recovered.

This is an unusual ghost tale, where instead of having the intention of creating fright, the purpose of the ghost is to convey a melody that would otherwise have been lost for good. The high regard for such melodies come across clearly, and the purpose of th e story is both to reaffirm the existence of a spirit world alongside our own as well as to indicate that connections between the living and the dead still take place. For another ghost tale, see "The Dead Fiancée," p. 265.

74. **The Demon of the Waters (Eastern Europe)**

From *Otzar ha-Ma'asiyot*, edited by Reuven ben Yakov Na'ana (Jerusalem, 1961).

This tale, collected orally in Israel from Russian immigrants, still retains its historical kernel. The precise details about the names of those involved and the details of the location suggest that it is based on an actual incident in which a woman fell into a river from the broken stairway of a *mikveh*. The shock of this fall likely caused her to lose her mind, leading those around her to conclude that she was no longer the same person and that her place had been taken by a river demon.

If these assumptions are correct, this tale provides insight into the formation of such tales and the ways in which mental illness was interpreted in supernatural terms. Note that the woman's daughter attempts to convince her father that the true cause of the mother's personality transformation was his usurping the mill, which indicates that the fall in the *mikveh* might have been preceded by extreme stress, and that the combination of the two might well have resulted in the kind of dissolution of personality described in this tale.

"The Demon of the Waters" closely follows the pattern of the tales of dybbuk possession. Whereas the dybbuk takes possession of a person, who then speaks with its voice, here the personality transformation is so great that the wife and the demon who takes her place are identified as two separate beings. When the wife departs, the demon of the water arrives; when the demoness leaves, the wife returns. However, if the wife and the demoness are regarded as the same person, then the wife's return signifies the return of sanity.

How does the man in this story bring catastrophe down on his family? He makes two fatal errors. First, he refuses to let his son marry the other man's daughter. Since they were destined to be wed, this puts him in opposition to fate. Further, the man triggers disaster when he spurns the warning of the Saba Kaddisha Mishipoli. This story is part of the cycle of stories about him, and as such it is strongly hagiographic.

For another tale about a river demon, see "Yona and the River Demon," p. 287. This story also suggests the motif of the demonic double, as found in "The Other Side," p. 283. See "Demonic Doubles" in Schwartz, *Tree of Souls*, p. 130. See "The Dybbuk in the Well," p. 290, for an interesting variant, where a woman almost falls into a well, and becomes possessed by a dybbuk. For background about the belief in water demons, see T. Canaan, *Haunted Springs and Water Demons in Palestine* (Jerusalem: Palestine Oriental Society, 1922).

75. **The Underwater Palace (Eastern Europe)**

From *Der Golem: Jüdischer Märchen and Legenden aus dem alten Prag* (German), edited by Eduard Petiska (Wiesbaden, 1972). An oral variant about a drowning man who is saved by the Queen of the Sea is IFA 8831, collected by Ronit Bronstein from Moni Tivoni of Egypt. There are many oral variants of the episode of the midwife, including IFA 8140, collected by Yifrah Haviv from Moshe Aharon from Bukhara, and IFA 8902, collected by Dvora Dadon-Vilek from her mother Heftziba Dabon from Morocco. A variant on the theme of a maiden and a demon in a palace beneath the sea is IFA 6057, collected by Zalman Baharav from David Hadad of Libya. In this oral tale, however, the demon is portrayed in completely negative terms. Another interesting variant is "The Dybbuk in the Well," p. 290.

The present tale combines two basic tale types found in Jewish lore. One type is marriage with demons. The other type is a tale in which a *mohel* or midwife is called upon to go to the land of the demons to perform a circumcision or deliver a child. For the best known version of the story of the *mohel* see *Kav ha-Yashar* by Tsvi Hirsh Kaidanover (Frankfurt, 1903). The type of tale involving a midwife is one of the most popular collected from various Middle Eastern sources and exists in dozens of variants in the IFA. The theme of marriage with demons is also found in many variants. To the best of the editor's knowledge, this is the only Jewish tale in which these two tale types have been combined. It is also interesting to observe the tone of this tale, which is upbeat. This is in contrast to most other tales on the theme of marriage with demons. They inevitably end on a disastrous note, but here the demonic husband does not seem threatening and the human wife seems happy, if somewhat lonely, in the palace beneath the sea. Such underwater palaces are often found in Jewish folklore. See "The Palace beneath the Sea" in Schwartz, *Miriam's Tambourine*, pp. 315–334. Leviathan, the king of the deep, is supposed to live in such a palace. All of the midwife tales have an element of a test in them—if the midwife can resist eating anything or accepting any gifts while in the land of the demons, she will be permitted to leave; if she accepts anything, she will be forced to stay. In all of the variants of this tale, the midwife is warned of the fact that accepting anything would force her to remain there. (This test echoes the theme of the Greek myth of Persephone, who is forced to remain in the underworld six months because she ate six pomegranate seeds.) Thus these midwife tales have elements of fear and danger while the midwife remains in the land of the demons, but once she emerges there is an inevitable reward, in which something of little value, such as garlic or coal, is transformed into gold, as happens here. For an important discussion of the midwife theme in this tale, see "Is There a Jewish Folk Religion?" by Dov Noy in *Studies in Jewish Folklore*, edited by Frank Talmage (Cambridge, Mass.: Association for Jewish Studies, 1980), pp. 273–286.

MYSTICAL TALES

76. **The Cottage of Candles (Afghanistan)**

IFA 7830, collected by Zevulon Kort from Ben Zion Asherov. A variant is found in *Ha-Na'al ha-Ktanah* (Tel Aviv, 1966), edited by Asher Barash. Another variant, about a cave in which there are bottles of oil, where a person lives until the oil is exhausted, is IFA 8335, collected by Moshe Rabi from Hannah Haddad, in *Avotanu Sipru* (Jerusalem, 1976). An Arab variant of "The Cottage of Candles" can be found in *Folklore of the Holy Land* by J. E. Hanauer (London: Duckworth, 1907), pp. 176–188. Here the old man in the cottage is identified as the Angel of Death.

For a discussion of this tale, see the Introduction, p. 18.

77. The Cave of Shimon bar Yohai (Babylon)

From *B. Shab.* 33b. This legend is also found in *Beit ha-Midrash*, edited by A. Jellinek (Jerusalem, 1938), 4:22; *Pesikta de-Rab Kahana*, edited by Solomon Buber (Lyck, 1860), 88b; and *Koheleth Rabbah* 10:8. The account is amplified in *Zohar Hadash, Ki tavo* 59c–60a. The legend about the finding of the *Zohar* is from the introduction to *Or ha-Levanah* 1, edited by Abraham Azulai, published in 1816.

This key legend from the Talmud inspired a series of kabbalistic legends about the talmudic sage Shimon bar Yohai. According to this legend, Bar Yohai spent thirteen years in a cave, hiding from the Romans, who had condemned him. Moshe de Leon, who lived in Spain in the thirteenth century, claimed to have discovered the text of the *Zohar*, written by Rabbi Shimon bar Yohai in the second century, who was said to have written it during the years spent in hiding in the cave. However, modern scholars, especially Gershom Scholem, have demonstrated that the *Zohar* was actually the creation of Moses de Leon, with possible assistance from his circle of mystics. The *Zohar* is a mystical commentary on the Torah, but it also contains many legends about Shimon bar Yohai and his disciples. The portrayal of Shimon bar Yohai in the *Zohar* became the model of the master for later sages, especially the Ari. And the Ari became the archetype of the master for later rabbis, such as Shalom Sharabi and the Ba'al Shem Tov. So an imagined portrayal of a master by Moshe de Leon led to a real-life emulation of the model.

78. A Kiss from the Master (Israel)

IFA 612, collected by S. Arnest of Israel.

Rabbi Shimon bar Yohai, a talmudic sage who lived in second-century Palestine, is the hero and reputed author of the *Zohar*, the central text of Jewish mysticism, although modern scholars have concluded that the book was actually written or edited by Moses de Leon in thirteenth-century Spain. Building on the portrait of Shimon bar Yohai found in the Talmud, later texts, especially the *Zohar*, include many legends in which Bar Yohai demonstrates great mystical knowledge and powers. One of the earliest post-talmudic stories about him is found in *Ecclesiastes Rabbah* 10:10:

> One of the disciples of Rabbi Shimon bar Yohai forgot what he had learned and went weeping to the cemetery. After this Rabbi Shimon bar Yohai appeared to him in a dream and said: "When you throw three pebbles at me I will come to you." The disciple went to a dream interpreter, who told him to repeat each lesson three times and Rabbi Shimon would come to him, and he would no longer forget what he had learned. This turned out to be true. Every time he repeated the lesson three times, Rabbi Shimon came to him and his memory was preserved.

What this midrashic tale suggests is that the spirit of Rabbi Shimon bar Yohai returned in the form of an *ibbur*, literally an impregnation, a positive kind of possession in which the spirit of a great sage who has died is bound to one of the living in order to increase the man's wisdom and faith. This kind of spirit possession is known as metempsychosis, and is regarded as a blessing. In contrast, there is possession by a dybbuk, where the evil spirit of one who has died takes possession of one of the living, and must be exorcised. The presence of an *ibbur* was regarded as a great blessing by Jewish mystics, especially those of Safed in the sixteenth century, while the same mystics strove greatly to exorcise dybbuks from those who were possessed by them. However, accounts of dybbuks, such as "The Widow of Safed," were widespread in this period, while tales of possession by *ibburs* are rare and are found only among mystical tales.

"A Kiss from the Master" is a fascinating oral variant of this midrashic tale. It was collected orally in the city of Safed, not far from the tomb of Shimon bar Yohai in Meron. This story and several others demonstrate that the tales about the great mystics of Safed are still being told there. In the story, the spirit of Shimon bar Yohai comes in a dream to a man uneducated in the Torah. The spirit kisses him, and afterward the man discovers that he has become a master of the Torah, possessed with the spirit of Bar Yohai. It is characteristic of these tales that the possession by the *ibbur* is not permanent, but is triggered by something, such as the study of a sacred text, or, as in the case of "The Tefillin of the Or ha-Hayim," the wearing of tefillin.

The concept of the *ibbur* is suggested in *Zohar* 2:100b: "The Supernal Holy King does not permit anything to perish, not even the breath of the mouth, which emerges into the world as a new creation." Possession by an *ibbur* should be distinguished from *gilgul*, the transmigration of souls. In the latter, the soul of a person who has died is reincarnated in the body of a person born later. In the case of an *ibbur*, the soul of a sage who has died fuses with the soul of one who is living, and this mystical transformation is temporary.

One of the primary characteristics of Jewish literature is that the earlier texts serve as models for the later ones, as can be seen in these two stories about Rabbi Shimon bar Yohai, separated in time by well over a thousand years. Certainly, in the case of the later mystical tales, it is almost always possible to find a prototype in the early rabbinic texts. In general, these tales are a natural outgrowth of the Aggadah, the legendary material of the Talmud, just as the mystical commentary in the *Zohar*, the central text of the Kabbalah, often seems to be built on earlier midrashic commentary. The difference is that the rabbinic commentary is primarily legal or legendary, while that found in the *Zohar* is chiefly mystical. So too are the tales found in the *Zohar* of a mystical nature. In them Bar Yohai and his disciples see signs that reveal God's intentions, speak with an angel in the form of a rock, meet saints from the Other World, ascend to the celestial Academy, and read the book that Adam was once given by an angel.

The links between the classic rabbinic tales and those of kabbalistic, Hasidic, or folk origin also reveal how the later rabbis sought their personal models in the lives of the earlier sages. The primary models were the talmudic sages Rabbi Akiba, Rabbi Ishmael the High Priest, Rabbi Yohanan ben Zakkai, and Rabbi Shimon bar Yohai. Of these, the most extensive legendary tradition is that surrounding Bar Yohai. It is this legendary model, especially as found in the *Zohar*, that transformed Bar Yohai into the foremost archetype of Jewish mystics.

Both tales about the spirit of Shimon bar Yohai recount how someone who had forgotten or lacked knowledge received it miraculously from the intercession of the spirit of the rabbi. Both incidents also occur in dreams, making the two clear variants, despite the fact that they are separated by about 1,300 years. However, it is also understood in both cases that their new knowledge derives from the spirit of Bar Yohai that possesses them in the form of an *ibbur*. From a psychological perspective, the *ibbur* represents the inner being that emerges to guide a person through a difficult time of transition. The fact that the presence of the *ibbur* must be triggered in some way indicates that the presence of this inner being only emerges when it is required by internal or external circumstances. The oral variant therefore makes explicit what is implicit in the midrashic tale—that the presence of the spirit of Bar Yohai makes their knowledge possible.

Another ghostly appearance of Shimon bar Yohai occurs in "The Dancing of the Ari," where he appears at the Lag ba-Omer celebration of Rabbi Isaac Luria and dances with him. See "The Dancing of the Ari" in Schwartz, *Tree of Souls*, pp. 303–304.

For another example of an *ibbur* tale, see "The Tefillin of the Or ha-Hayim," p. 357, and the accompanying note. The motif of an untutored man suddenly becoming filled with knowledge is sometimes found in other sources. According to *Shalshelet ha-Kabbalah*, for example, Rabbi Menachem ben Benjamin Recanati was once an ignorant man who miraculously attained wisdom.

79. **The Angel of Forgetfulness (Syria)**

IFA 7198, collected by Amnon Shiloach from Abraham Massalton of Syria. A variant of this tale is found, in a much condensed version, in *Shivhei ha-Ari*, edited by Shlomo Meinsterl (Jerusalem, 1905). Other variants are found in *Sefer Peri Etz Hayim* 361 by Hayim Vital (Salonika, 1793) and in *Nagid Umezave* by Y. Zemah (published in 1798). The original legend of Miriam's Well is found in *B. Ta'anit* 9a and *B. Shabbat* 35a. The oral version of this tale collected by the IFA is by far the most extensive.

The primary disciple of Rabbi Isaac Luria, the Ari, was Rabbi Hayim Vital. Indeed, because the Ari did not commit his teachings to writing, it is the writings of Hayim Vital in *Etz Hayim* and other books that have preserved the teachings of the Ari. It is interesting to note that the writings of other disciples of the Ari are often at odds with the interpretations of Hayim Vital, and Vital's objectivity can easily be called into question because of his elevated view of himself and his destiny. Nevertheless, it is Vital's interpretation that has been traditionally accepted as the authentic version of the teachings of the Ari.

At the time the Ari arrived in Safed, Vital lived in Damascus and was himself known as a master of the Kabbalah. He was therefore reluctant to come to Safed to become a disciple. This tale recounts the powers used by the Ari to reach Hayim Vital and make him understand that it was his destiny to become the Ari's disciple. The Ari's powers include invoking the Angel of Forgetfulness, who causes Hayim Vital to forget his mystical knowledge. Vital finally recognizes this as a sign that he needs to approach the Ari, to restore his memory. The Ari takes Vital out in a boat on the Sea of Galilee, and draws water from Miriam's Well for him to drink. This does restore Vital's memory and at the same time creates a permanent bond between the two. The legend of Miriam's

Well recounts that God gave the Israelites an enchanted well of pure water in honor of the virtues of Miriam, sister of Moses, and that this well followed them in the wilderness. For another tale drawing on this legend, see "The Wandering Well" in Schwartz, *Gabriel's Palace*, pp. 250–251.

Note that the Ari uses the tomb of Rabbi Meir Ba'al ha-Ness as a guide in locating Miriam's Well. This revered tomb, which has many miracles linked to it, is reputed to be that of a Rabbi Meir who vowed never to lie down until the Messiah came, and was buried upright. (In Jewish folklore Meir Ba'al ha-Ness is sometimes identified with the talmudic sage Rabbi Meir. But they were almost certainly two separate figures living at two different periods.) Thus the Ari draws on the miraculous power of both this tomb and Miriam's Well to restore Hayim Vital's memory. This tale was collected from a Syrian Jewish immigrant, showing that the oral tradition about the Ari and Hayim Vital continued to exist there at least until recently, a heritage of the period when Hayim Vital and other Jewish mystics lived in Damascus.

The novelist Steve Stern alludes to this story in the title of his novel *The Angel of Forgetfulness.*

80. **A Vision at the Wailing Wall (Palestine)**

From *Shivhei ha-Ari* in *Sefer Toledot ha-Ari,* edited by Meir Benayahu (Jerusalem, 1987), pp. 228–230; *Emek ha-Melekh* by Naftali Hirsh ben Elhanan (Amsterdam, 1653), 109b; *Kav ha-Yashar* by Tsvi Hirsh Kaidanover (Frankfurt, 1903), chap. 92, p. 124; *Or ha-Yashar* by Meir ben Judah Loeb Poppers ha-Kohen (Jerusalem, 1964); *Hemdat Yamim* by Nathan Benjamin Halevi (Venice, 1763) 2:4a; *Iggerot Eretz Yisrael* by Abraham Ya'ari (Ramat Gan, 1971), pp. 205–206; *Iggerot mi-Tzefat,* by Simcha Asaf in *Kovetz al Yad* 3 (Jerusalem, 1939), pp. 122–123; *Midrash Tehillim* 11:3; and *Exodus Rabbah* 2:2.

This mythic tale derives from the city of Safed in the sixteenth century. It is included in the last of three letters written from Safed by Solomon Shlomel of Dresnitz in 1607 to his friend in Cracow. Together these three letters form the text of *Shivhei ha-Ari,* the first collection of tales about the great Jewish mystic Rabbi Isaac Luria. Additional volumes of tales about the Ari appeared later, including *Sefer Toledot ha-Ari* and *Iggerot Eretz Yisrael.*

This famous tale has a number of biblical and rabbinic precedents. The final words that the *Shekhinah* speaks to Rabbi Abraham come directly from Jeremiah 31:17. They are the words God speaks to console Rachel, weeping for her children (Jer. 31:14–16).

There is also a strong echo of Jeremiah's vision of Mother Zion in Jeremiah 15:9, which is developed in *Pesikta Rabbati* 26:7. Mother Zion is likely an early incarnation of the *Shekhinah.* See "Mother Zion," in Schwartz, *Tree of Souls,* pp. 46–47. The assumption that the *Shekhinah* could still be found at the Western Wall, despite the destruction of the Temple, is found in rabbinic sources such as *Midrash Tehillim* on Psalms 11:3 and *Exodus Rabbah* 2:2, and in Rabbi Moshe Alshekh on Lamentations 1:1–2.

Although this story demonstrates the prophetic wisdom of the Ari, the real focus of the story is on one of his disciples, Rabbi Abraham ben Eliezer ha-Levi Berukhim. Rabbi Abraham was born in Morocco in 1519 and came to Safed some fifty years later, where he was first a follower of Rabbi Moshe Cordovero

(1522–1570) and later became a disciple of the Ari. Rabbi Abraham was an important figure among the mystics of Safed, and Hayim Vital, the primary disciple of the Ari, described him in his autobiography, *Sefer ha-Hezyonot*, as someone who could move others to repentance (Jerusalem, 1954, p. 130). Vital, who firmly believed in *gilgul*, the transmigration of souls, also appears to have viewed Rabbi Abraham as the reincarnation of Elijah the Prophet.

In most versions of this story, there is no mention of Rabbi Abraham performing the midnight vigil of crying out in the streets because of the exile of the *Shekhinah*. But some variants of this famous tale, such as that in *Kav ha-Yashar*, add this important detail at the beginning of the story, giving new meaning to the Ari's directive for Rabbi Abraham Berukhim to seek out the *Shekhinah* at the Kotel. Devotion to the midnight vigil indicates that Rabbi Abraham was seeking the *Shekhinah* before the Ari sent him on his quest. In this view, the Ari, well aware of Rabbi Abraham's longing for the *Shekhinah*, simply directed him to seek out the *Shekhinah* in the right place—at the Kotel, the last retaining wall of the Temple Mount in Jerusalem, which was her home in this world.

This tale lends itself to multiple interpretations. From the traditional perspective, the Ari has remarkable powers that enable him to peer into the heavenly ledgers to determine the fates of his followers. These fates have been written in either the Book of Life or the Book of Death. (See "The Book of Life and the Book of Death" in Schwartz, *Tree of Souls*, p. 289.) While this ability to read in the heavenly ledgers is rare, it is not unheard of. In *B. Berakhot* 18b, there is a reference to a pious man who remained in the cemetery on Rosh ha-Shanah and there learned the decrees to be issued in heaven during the coming year.

Or, the Ari may simply have recognized Rabbi Abraham's profound need to encounter the *Shekhinah* after years of performing the midnight vigil and therefore sent him to find her.

Or, from a modern psychological perspective, the Ari has perceived that Rabbi Abraham faces a midlife transition. If he continues on his present path, he is shortly going to meet his death. That is to say, Rabbi Abraham's life has reached a dangerous transition, and in order to survive it, he must undertake an extraordinary task. Therefore the Ari sends him on a quest to find the *Shekhinah* in the logical place where she could be found—the Wailing Wall, the remnant of her former home in the Temple in Jerusalem. In giving Rabbi Abraham this quest, the Ari functions virtually as a therapist, sending Rabbi Abraham on a journey to wholeness, to plead for mercy from the *Shekhinah*, who is identified in the Kabbalah as the Bride of God. Once he reaches the Wall, Rabbi Abraham has dual visions of the *Shekhinah*, encountering her both as a grieving old woman and as a radiant bride, and afterward he is a new man, who through this visionary experience rediscovers his lost anima and reintegrates his feminine side.

Rabbi Abraham's visions of the *Shekhinah* can be recognized as both mythic and archetypal, very close to the purest vision of Jung's concept of the anima, the symbolic feminine aspect of every man. That is why he is able to live for another twenty-two years, one year for each letter of the Hebrew alphabet, representing a whole new cycle of his life.

The version in *Kav ha-Yashar* also makes changes in Rabbi Abraham's vision of the *Shekhinah*. Here, when he raised his eyes, he saw the shape of a woman on top of the Wall, instead of emerging from the Wall. Upon seeing Her, Rabbi Abraham fell upon on his face, cried and wept, "Mother! Mother! Mother Zion!

Woe to me that I see you thus." (It is presumed that She is wearing mourning garments.) Further, when Rabbi Abraham faints, the feminine figure puts her hand on his face and wipes away his tears. This identification of the *Shekhinah* with Mother Zion directly links this story with that of Mother Zion in *Pesikta Rabbati* 26:7.

Central to understanding this tale is the concept of the *Shekhinah.* See Schwartz, *Tree of Souls,* pp. xlvii–l and 47–63. The two appearances of the *Shekhinah* that Rabbi Abraham envisions at the Wall, that of the old woman in mourning and of the bride in white, are the two primary aspects associated with her. She appears as a bride or queen or lost princess in some texts and tales and as an old woman mourning over the destruction of the Temple in others. In "A Vision at the Wailing Wall," she appears in both forms. Thus he sees both aspects of the *Shekhinah,* her aspect of mourning and her joyful aspect, making his vision of the Shekhinah complete.

There is much to learn from this tale about how to read rabbinic tales to discover the psychic truths at the core of them. First, however, it is necessary to learn how to interpret their symbolic language. Identifying the *Shekhinah* with the anima is the first step toward translating this language into an archetypal framework. A similar vision of the *Shekhinah* is recounted by Rabbi Levi Yitzhak of Berditchev. See "A Vision of the Bride" in Schwartz, *Gabriel's Palace,* pp. 245–246.

For more background to this important tale, see the Introduction, pp. 15–17. Also see "The Metamorphosis of Narrative Traditions: Two Stories from Sixteenth Century Safed" by Aryeh Wineman, and "The Quest for Jerusalem" by Howard Schwartz.

81. **Gathering Sparks (Palestine)**

From *Sefer ha-Hezyonot* by Rabbi Hayim Vital (Jerusalem, 1914).

There are many accounts of mysteries revealed by the Ari at the tombs of various famous rabbis, especially the tomb of Rabbi Shimon bar Yohai, the key figure of the *Zohar.* Here the Ari reveals the mystery of the Shattering of the Vessels and the Gathering of the Sparks. This was the last of the great myths to enter Judaism. See Schwartz, "The Shattering of the Vessels and the Gathering of the Sparks" in *Tree of Souls,* pp. 122–124.

In many ways the myth of the Ari prefigures the Big Bang theory. In both accounts there is an explosion at the beginning of time, and in both, the universe as we know it comes into existence. And there are even earlier rabbinic descriptions of the creation of the world that strongly prefigure this theory, such as the following: "When the Holy One, blessed be He, created the world, it started to expand in all directions. It could have gone on expanding forever. However, at a certain point, God stopped the expansion by calling out 'Enough!'" (*B. Hag.* 12a).

The myth of the Ari can be seen as a reworking of the messianic myth. Indeed, the description of the restored world that will come about when all the sparks have been gathered and all the broken vessels restored is virtually identical to that envisioned in the messianic age. The widespread and powerful response to the Ari's myth influenced the messianic expectations that led to the debacle of the false messiah Shabbatai Zevi and left a deep imprint on Hasidism.

82. The Tzaddik of the Forest (Palestine)

From *Sihot Hayim* (Piotrkow, 1904). Also included in *Sefer ha-Ma'aysiot* 2:41–44, edited by Mordecai Ben Yehezkel (Tel Aviv, 1929).

This story is of particular interest because it concerns a virtually unknown hidden saint, Shimon Pilam, who lived in the time of the Ari. While mysterious figures, some human, some divine, are often found in the tales linked with the circle of the Ari, there is no mention of Shimon Pilam, although he is described as living in the same area of Safed at the same time as the Ari. This is not surprising in that Shimon Pilam works completely in secret, performing *tikkun olam*, repair of the world. These secret workings are characteristic of hidden saints, who rarely come in contact with others.

However, this tale may also indicate that there were other mystical circles active in Safed whose history is virtually unknown, and that this tale emerges out of one of these circles. It is also possible that this is a later legend that was intentionally set in the period of the Ari. In any case, this rather extensive tale describes the wonders performed in the forest by the hidden saint, and how the guards of the forest each managed to have children with his blessing.

The theme of the hidden saint is first found in the Talmud and recurs in virtually every phase of postbiblical Jewish literature, where these hidden saints are identified as the *Lamed-vav Tzaddikim*. There are said to be thirty-six of these righteous ones in every generation, generally hidden from the world. Shimon Pilam's dominant characteristic is his hiddenness. The miracles he accomplishes are done without witnesses, except for God. No one knows he is one of the hidden saints. This fits in entirely with the hidden nature of the *Lamed-vav Tzaddikim*. See "The Thirty-six Just Men" in Schwartz, *Tree of Souls*, p. 397.

At the same time, Shimon Pilam's objectives are a precise expression of Lurianic Kabbalah. He hopes to raise enough falling sparks to restore the shattered vessels recounted in the myth of the Ari. For more on this seminal myth, see "The Shattering of the Vessels and the Gathering of the Sparks" in Schwartz, *Tree of Souls*, pp. 122–124.

It is very interesting that the final episode of this tale is a distinct variant of "The Finger," p. 227, as well as "The Demon in the Tree," in Schwartz, *Lilith's Cave*, pp. 98–100. Those tales concern the theme of marriage with demons. In "The Finger" a young man about to be wed slips his ring over a finger sticking out of the ground and finds himself wed to a corpse, who comes back to life. In "The Demon in the Tree," a boy playing hide-and-seek accidently puts his ring on the finger of a demoness that is sticking out of a tree and after that the demoness considers herself his wife. It is possible that this story was expressly created to echo "The Finger," since that is a story in *Shivhei ha-Ari*, the first collection of tales about the Ari.

In the story about Shimon Pilam, one of the guards is reminded of a distant episode when, as a young man, he put his ring on the finger of a carving of a hand at the base of a tree, and discovers many years later that this caused him to be wed to a demoness, who has been slaying his infant sons. Shimon Pilam tells the man how to divorce her, and he does, and after that his newborn sons survive. The carving on the tree has distinct pagan overtones, recalling the tree worship linked to the Canaanite goddess Asherah. For more on this subject, see *The Hebrew Goddess* by Raphael Patai (Detroit, Mich.: Wayne State University Press, 1991) and *Did God Have a Wife? Archaeology and Folk Religion in Ancient Israel* by William G. Dever (Grand Rapids, Mich.: Eerdmans, 2005).

83. **The Angel of the Mishnah (Palestine)**

From *Maggid Mesharim* by Joseph Karo (Amsterdam, 1704).
Also *Shivhei ha-Ari,* compiled by Shlomo Meinsterl (Jerusalem, 1905).

Among the sages of Safed, there are several accounts of an angelic spirit known as a *maggid* speaking through them. These spirits come into existence out of deep study of a particular text. One possible explanation for the phenomenon of the *maggid* is the talmudic statement "From every utterance that goes forth from the mouth of the Holy One, blessed be He, an angel is created" (B. Hag. 14a). Since man was created in the image of God, these angelic spirits come into being from the words spoken by the sages in their study of one of the sacred texts. They then appear for that person after that text has been read several times, three being the usual number. These spirits served to teach divine mysteries to those they spoke through and who were witness to the words spoken. The most famous case is that of Rabbi Joseph Karo, the author of the *Shulhan Aruch,* which codified Jewish law. Thus, as indicated by the title of Zvi Werblowsky's study, *Lawyer and Mystic,* Karo was a mystic with a practical side. Karo's *maggid* identified itself as the angel of the Mishnah. Karo kept a journal of the teachings of this spirit, *Maggid Mesharim.* There also are several accounts of those who were present when the *maggid* spoke. This kind of positive possession resembles that found in the accounts of possession by an *ibbur,* except that an *ibbur* is the spirit of a sage who has died, and a *maggid* is an angelic spirit. Both *ibbur* and *maggid* accounts are associated with a particular book or a specific object, such as *tefillin.* See, for example, "A Kiss from the Master," p. 329, and "The Tefillin of the Or ha-Hayim," p. 357.

84. **Gabriel's Palace (Germany)**

From *Sefer ha-Ma'aysiot,* edited by Mordecai ben Yehezkel (Tel Aviv, 1929). Ben Yehezkel attributes the story to oral tradition.

The tradition about a celestial Torah grows out of *B. Pesahim* 54, where the Torah is described as one of seven things created before the creation of the world, based on the verse *The Lord made me at the beginning of his way* (Prov. 8:22). The legend of the thirteen Torahs derives from *Peirat Moshe* in A. Jellinek, *Beit ha-Midrash* 122–123 (Jerusalem, 1938). Here it states that Moses wrote all thirteen Torahs on the day he had been told he would die, as a means of preventing the Angel of Death from taking him, since the Angel is forbidden to take a person while he is studying the Torah. (This is similar to the legend of King David and the Angel of Death in *B. Shab.* 30a. Here the Angel of Death has to create a diversion to lure David away from his studies, so that he can take his soul.) The best of the Torahs that Moses wrote was brought by an angel into heaven. The requirement to read the Torah from a written text on the Sabbath is stated in *Tanhuma Buber Vayyera* 6. It is also hinted at in *B. Megillah* 32a. An unrelated folktale about Rabbi Meir's imprisonment is found in *Ma'aseh Nissim* (Yiddish), compiled by Jeptha Yozpa ben Naftali (Amsterdam, 1696), story no. 14. Here Rabbi Meir's body remains inside his prison cell for another fourteen years after his death, after the guard sent to remove it dies as he puts the key in the lock. Finally a righteous Jew is able to enter the cell and remove the body, which has not decayed, and transport it to a Jewish grave.

This story is a legend linked with the extended imprisonment of Rabbi Meir ben Baruch of Rothenburg, the leader of German Jewry in the thirteenth century. He was a great legalist, the author of more than one thousand responsa, and the most respected German Jew of his time. Rabbi Meir was captured and imprisoned because of his resistance to the decree of the German emperor Rudolf I that the possessions of Jews were the property of the empire and could be taxed as the emperor willed. This decree unleashed a vast exodus of German Jews, a movement led by Rabbi Meir. The emperor used the capture of Rabbi Meir to try to force the Jews to agree to the view that they were serfs of the treasury. Rabbi Meir continued to resist this view and remained imprisoned for the rest of his life. In characteristic legendary form, the harsh conditions of his confinement gave birth to this legend about him receiving a celestial Torah. (See "The Cave of Shimon bar Yohai," p. 327, where the thirteen years Shimon bar Yohai spends in a cave hiding from the Romans result in the creation of the *Zohar.*) In this variation of the legend of the celestial Torah, the heavenly Torah is said to have been one of those inscribed by Moses, who, according to this legend, wrote thirteen Torahs, one for each of the twelve tribes, and the thirteenth, which was taken up into Paradise and used by the angels. The angel Gabriel delivers this Torah to Rabbi Meir and lets it remain with him until he succeeded in making a perfect copy of it. The fate of this copy is a miracle tale in itself, as Rabbi Meir is said to have put it in a casket and lowered it into the Rhine, where it floated until it reached the Jews for whom it was intended as Rabbi Meir's final legacy.

85. **Rabbi Naftali's Trance (Eastern Europe)**

From *Sipurei Ya'akov* no. 7, edited by Rabbi Yakov Sofer (Dobrornill, 1864). A variant is found in *Sippurim Mi-she-kvar* (Haifa, 1986), no. 27.

In this tale, Rabbi Naftali Katz of Posen uses his great mystical powers to find the groom who has abandoned the daughter of a wealthy follower. It involves an extraordinary effort, for it turns out that the groom is no longer in this world. Rabbi Naftali demonstrates his mastery of soul travel, first circling the globe, searching for the wayward groom, then descending into Gehenna to find out his fate and setting up a meeting between the living and the dead. This follows the pattern of stories about holy men descending into hell, including Jewish tales about the Messiah descending into Gehenna, and Christian stories about Jesus making such a descent.

At its core, this is a story about the dilemma posed by *agunot*—abandoned wives, whose husbands refused to give them a *get*, a bill of divorce. According to Jewish law, these abandoned wives cannot remarry without a *get*, unless two witnesses testify that he is no longer living. Likewise, women whose husbands died in faraway places, who had no way to prove they were widows, were not permitted to remarry. This has caused tremendous difficulties for women whose husbands abandoned them or refused to give them a *get*. The only other alternative was for these women to receive written consent to remarry from one hundred rabbis or, as in this tale of Rabbi Naftali, have someone resort to supernatural methods. The apparent slaying of the groom by the soldier makes it possible for the two witnesses to testify that the groom is dead, which is the legal requirement for an *agunah* to remarry.

This story underscores the difficulties posed by *agunot* even among the rich, as even a rich father is unable to obtain a *get* for his daughter. Without that bill of divorce, she could not remarry. It is true that Rabbi Naftali seems reluctant to act, waiting thirteen years. The caution that Rabbi Naftali demonstrates indicates the kinds of dangers associated with out-of-body experiences. But once he decides to take action, Rabbi Naftali demonstrates vast powers over the forces of the supernatural. For this reason the story must also be recognized as a hagiographic tale about the greatness of Rabbi Naftali Katz.

This story draws on the lore about Gehenna. For more about the angel Samriel, who guards the gates of Gehenna, see "The Gatekeeper of Gehenna" in Schwartz, *Tree of Souls*, pp. 240–241. Only those condemned to Gehenna are permitted entry there, so that Rabbi Naftali has to convince Samriel to admit him. For another story about a descent to Gehenna, see "The Messiah in Hell," in Schwartz, *Tree of Souls*, p. 241.

The variant of this tale found in *Sippurim Mi-she-kvar* is very interesting. Instead of Rabbi Naftali Katz, the wonder working is done by a water carrier who is understood to be one of the hidden saints. The water carrier covers the eyes of the father with a handkerchief and takes him out into the desert, using kabbalistic magic. There the dead man appears first as a cloud of dust and then as part of an army marching through the desert. In this version, the dead husband does not resist admitting that he was the woman's husband, and thus makes it possible for the rabbi and the father to serve as two witnesses confirming that the husband who abandoned her is dead.

86. **The Spirit of Hagigah (Italy)**

From *Menorat ha-Ma'or* by Yitzhak Abohav (Mantua, 1573). The earliest edition was published in Constantinople in 1514. A variant of this tale is found in *Ma'aseh Buch* (Yiddish), no. 247, compiled by Jacob ben Abraham of Mezhirech (Basel, 1601).

Jewish lore asserts that there is an angel or spirit for every sacred text. In this tale, a man who devotes himself to a single tractate of the Talmud, *Hagigah*, has the spirit of that book, taking the form of a woman, mourn for him after his death. This tale confirms the notion that heaven delights in the study of the sacred texts, and in this case, because of the man's devotion to *Hagigah*, that spirit takes a particular interest in him and ensures that he is properly mourned after his death. The choice of *Hagigah* as the tractate that is the focus of his study indicates the importance of that text to the subject of Jewish mysticism. Many of the key mystical legends of the Talmud, including those concerning the four who entered Paradise, are found in *Hagigah*. Indeed, in *The Merkavah in Rabbinic Literature* (New Haven: American Oriental Society, 1980), chapter 3, pp. 64–105, David Halperin refers to the cluster of mystical tales in tractate *Hagigah* beginning with 14b as the "Mystical Collection." This suggests that the man who studied *Hagigah* was involved in some kind of mystical contemplation, and in this context the appearance of the spirit of Hagigah is an appropriate mystical response to his lifelong study of this mystical text. *Hagigah* means celebration, and sounds like a woman's name, creating a feminine personification. Note that the personification of Hagigah is identified as a spirit, not an angel. Nevertheless, the linkage of a spirit with a text strongly echoes the appearance of the angelic *maggid* who comes to Joseph Karo and speaks through him. See "The Angel of the Mishnah," p. 339. And because of his love for the *Zohar*, the guardian angel of Reb Pinhas of Koretz was said to have been the angel of the *Zohar*. See "The Angel of the *Zohar*" in Schwartz, *Gabriel's Palace*, p. 212. There is also a tradition of the Angel of the Torah. From these examples it is clear that there was an accepted belief that each great sacred text had its own angel or spirit guardian, or, alternately, the angel or spirit was a personification of the book itself.

This tale also echoes some of the personification of Mother Zion found in *Ecclesiastes Rabbah* and other texts, as well as the *Shekhinah* as a woman in mourning at the Kotel, the Western Wall in Jerusalem. See "Mother Zion" in Schwartz, *Tree of Souls*, p. 46, and "A Vision at the Wailing Wall," p. 333.

87. **The Ladder of Prayers (Eastern Europe)**

From *Midrash Ribesh Tov*, edited by Lipot Abraham (Kecskemet, Hungary, 1927), and *Or ha-Hokhmah* by Uri Feivel ben Aaron (Korzec, 1795); and *Shivhei ha-Besht*, by Rabbi Dov Baer ben Samuel, edited by Samuel A. Horodezky (Berlin, 1922), no. 42.

This Hasidic tale builds on the talmudic story of Rabbah bar bar Hannah's discovery of the golden dove. See "The Golden Dove," p. 188. The Ba'al Shem Tov's failure to capture this dove makes this one in a long line of tales about why the Messiah hasn't come. Dozens of other such tales record lost opportunities to bring about the messianic era, or attempts to force the Messiah's hand, and hasten the End of Days. The most famous such tale is "Helen of Troy," p. 236, about the attempt to Rabbi Joseph della Reina to force the End of Days. For another example of a failed attempt to bring the Messiah, see the talmudic tale "Forcing the End," in Schwartz, *Gabriel's Palace*, p. 496. Here the failure is attributed to the Ba'al Shem Tov's Hasidim, who fail to provide the spiritual support needed for this great endeavor, as symbolized by the collapse of the ladder of prayers. That makes this one more tale about why the Messiah has not come.

This tale of a heavenly ascent, and virtually the entire body of rabbinic, kabbalistic, folk, and Hasidic lore, exists in a mythological framework. The ladder of prayers the Ba'al Shem Tov ascends was surely inspired by the heavenly ladder in Jacob's dream. It is, perhaps, the very same ladder. Ascending this ladder, the Ba'al Shem Tov enters Paradise, a mythological realm with its own order, its own geography, its own history, and its own inhabitants—not only God and the angels but the Bride of God and the Messiah as well. It is understood that the Messiah is waiting for the sign to be given that the time has come for the messianic era. All the same, many traditions of Jewish mysticism are focused on how to hasten the coming of the Messiah, secrets that the Ba'al Shem Tov knows well.

In addition, this tale draws on a rich tradition of tales about heavenly ascent, from the ascent of Elijah in a fiery chariot (2 Kings 2:11) to the famous tale of the four who entered Paradise in *B. Hagigah* 14b. See "The Four Who Entered Paradise" in Schwartz, *Tree of Souls*, pp. 173–174. Indeed, "The Ladder of Prayers" is a direct descendant of the story of the four sages, which dates from around the second century. However, there is an important difference—while the four sages primarily seek greater knowledge and experience of the divine, the Ba'al Shem Tov seems focused on hastening the coming of the Messiah.

A variant of this tale is found in *Shivhei ha-Besht* (no. 42), the earliest collection of tales about the Ba'al Shem Tov:

> The Messiah once came to the Ba'al Shem Tov and said: "I make my home in a heavenly palace known as the Bird's Nest. Except for me, no one has ever entered there. If only you were to travel there and open that gate, redemption would surely come to Israel. I don't know whether or not you will succeed in opening the gate, but I heard God's voice saying to me, 'What can I do for you, since I must fulfill your wish?' "

This brief account about the Messiah speaking to the Ba'al Shem Tov is attributed to Rabbi Menahem Nahum of Chernobyl (1730–1797). Here the Messiah strongly hints to the Ba'al Shem Tov that he can bring about the messianic era—and set the Messiah free from his waiting—by making his way to the heavenly Garden of Eden and opening the gate to the secret abode of the Messiah, known as the Bird's Nest. Further, the Messiah suggests that God will look favorably on the efforts of the Ba'al Shem Tov, because God feels that He must fulfill the Messiah's wish—which is to initiate the messianic era. Thus, in this brief tale, the Messiah not only gives the Ba'al Shem Tov the key hint of how this can be done, but also strongly suggests that the time is right.

88. **The Tree of Life (Eastern Europe)**

From *Shivhei ha-Besht* by Rabbi Dov Ben Samuel, edited by Samuel A. Horodezky (Berlin, 1922). The myth of the Tree of Life is expanded in *Midrash Konen* in *Otzar Midrashim*, edited by Y. D. Eisenstein (New York, 1915), p. 255.

The quest to reach Paradise is echoed in many tales about the Ba'al Shem Tov. Sometimes this takes the form of a heavenly ascent, as in the previous story, "The Ladder of Prayers," or "Unlocking the Gates of Heaven," in Schwartz, *Gabriel's Palace*, p. 205, while in other tales the Ba'al Shem Tov takes his disciples on a mystical journey, known as *Kfitsat ha-Derekh*, the Leaping of the Way. Here the wagon in which they ride suddenly begins to move at great speed, traveling through time and space. This time they journey to the Garden of Eden, where the Ba'al Shem Tov leads his Hasidim closer and closer to the Tree of Life. However, he does not reveal their true location to them, nor his goal, and little by little the Hasidim become fascinated with what they encounter along the way. By the time the Ba'al Shem Tov reaches the Tree of Life, he is alone.

The legend most strongly echoed here is that of the four sages who entered Paradise. In that sense, a strong parallel can drawn between the Ba'al Shem Tov and Rabbi Akiba, who entered Paradise and returned in peace. Note that the earthly paradise and the heavenly paradise are known by the same term,

Gan Eden. This lends ambiguity as to exactly where the Ba'al Shem Tov has brought them—is it the mythological Garden of Eden of Genesis, or is it the heavenly Paradise? And should the Tree of Life be understood as the very tree of Genesis, or in symbolic terms, the Torah, since a popular proverb identifies the Torah with the Tree of Life: *It is a tree of life to those who cling to it* (Prov. 3:18), where it is universally understood to refer to the Torah. Both the mythical and symbolic readings seem appropriate. In this sense, the tale serves as an allegory about how the master tries to lead his disciples to the hidden treasures of the Torah.

89. **The Enchanted Island (Eastern Europe)**

From *Sipurei Tzaddikim* (Cracow, 1886).

Wolf Kitzes was one of the major early disciples of the Ba'al Shem Tov, and he was one of the most fascinating and complex figures in the circle of the Ba'al Shem Tov. His role as the Ba'al Shem Tov's shofar blower brought him legendary status, and there is a handful of important tales in which he plays a central role. Here he misses the chance to bring messianic redemption, as occurs in many other tales. See, for example, "The Ladder of Prayers," p. 350. In another variant of this story, Wolf Kitzes encounters Abraham, and they have a similar dialogue, with the same results. "The Enchanted Island" is also an example of an illusion tale. For other examples, see "The Enchanted Journey," p. 82, and "The King's Dream," p. 92.

There is a famous parable attributed to the Ba'al Shem Tov about a palace of illusion, which focuses on the nature of illusion. This parable is found in *Keter Shem Tov* by Aaron of Apt (Zolkiev, 1784), p. 87, as well as in *Degel Machane Ephrayim*, compiled by Moses Hayim Ephraim of Sudikov (Jerusalem, 1963):

> A great and powerful king who had mastered the secrets of illusion built a palace of many chambers that actually did not exist. But to all who approached it, the mirage seemed real. So too did the king surround the palace with obstacles, so that the way to reach it was fraught with danger.
>
> A wide river encircled the palace grounds, whose waters ran deep and were too wild to be crossed by boat. And only those who found some way to form a bridge could reach the palace. And even those few who managed this feat found themselves lost in a maze of garden paths that branched off in every direction. (It was said that a man could spend his days lost in that labyrinth.) And of the handful who ever found their way through the forking paths, further obstacles remained: seven walls, each impenetrable and with its own locked gate. And at each gate a guard was stationed, who had been commanded not to permit anyone to pass who could not reply correctly to a riddle. And even those who were clever at riddles and succeeded in reaching the third or fourth gate were usually turned back before they reached the seventh gate, for each succeeding riddle was more difficult. And in the unlikely event of anyone actually reaching the palace itself, his long quest was not complete, for the palace contained a great many chambers, and only one of them was that of the king. So it was that in all the years since the king had brought the palace into being, only one prince was said to have succeeded in reaching the door of the chamber of the king. At last there was a wise and righteous man who meditated on this matter and thought to himself: How is it possible that this merciful king, who has given

> all his subjects such great abundance, should hide himself and conceal his face? Perhaps all of these obstacles are only an illusion, created to test the perseverance of those who would approach him. And then, for the first time ever, the sage stepped directly into the river, without attempting to build a bridge across it. And at that instant the waters vanished, along with the labyrinth and the seven walls and seven gates, and the inner chamber of the king was revealed.

This parable is a commentary on a line of the Torah: *And I shall surely hide and conceal my face* (Deut. 31:18). The notion of illusion that stands behind it illustrates the concept of *ahizat enayim*, which can he translated as mirage, sleight of hand, or illusion. But behind the mirage that is this world stands God, who is eternal. In this allegory the king represents God, who has set up the world as a diversion and test. Those who recognize its true nature are then permitted to discern the true nature of God's existence, which is a far greater reward. Note the resemblance of the Ba'al Shem Tov's parable of illusion to the portrait of heaven found in the *Hekhalot* texts and other sources. The parallel is quite striking, as the system of symbols is virtually the same. A modern echo is found in Franz Kafka's famous parable "Before the Law," from *The Trial*. See "Before the Law" in Schwartz, *Tree of Souls*, pp. 179–180.

90. **Lighting a Fire (Eastern Europe)**

From *Knesset Israel* 13a, edited by Reuven Zak (Warsaw, 1866).

This is an exceptionally important Hasidic tale, in which Rabbi Israel of Rizhin mourns the loss of some essential mythic element that has been lost in his generation, and all that they have received is a story, but that is enough. The story itself is an advocate for the power of stories to sustain a tradition even if everything else is lost.

The source of this tale is a collection of tales about Rabbi Israel of Rizhin, which firmly places him in the line of the key Hasidic rabbis. In the original version of this legend, the Ba'al Shem Tov has a wax candle made and affixes it to the tree to light. This is a strange custom with no direct Jewish precedents, and probably for this reason most of the extensive retellings of this tale, including the present one, have described the Ba'al Shem Tov as lighting a fire, without specifying what kind of fire it was. Of course, candle lighting is commonly done by Jews every Sabbath, and the lighting of a *yahrzeit* candle is used to commemorate the death of a relative. But affixing a candle to a tree seems to have pagan overtones. According to Professor Dov Noy of Hebrew University, the lighting of candles was done for those who were sick, with the wick of the candle measured by the base of the tomb of a highly regarded sage or saint. This tale stresses the importance of the intention of the heart. Even though much of the ritual is lost, it is effective because the intention is true. This tale also emphasizes a common theme in Jewish lore: that the ancients knew a great deal more than the generations that followed. For an additional discussion of this tale, see *Kabbalah* by Moshe Idel (New Haven: Yale University Press, 1988), pp. 270–271 and p. 397, notes 92–94. Noting that in the original version the candle is lit to cure an only son, a pious young man who is very ill, Idel identifies the candle as a substitute for the soul of the son, according to the verse *The soul of man is the candle of God* (Prov. 20:27). He also identifies the tree as symbolizing the Tree of Souls. By affixing the candle to the tree and lighting it, he is affirming the boy's link to the Tree of Souls and thus to life. Thus the Ba'al Shem Tov is seen as the preeminent master, and each subsequent generation is a little less able to follow in his footsteps. Nevertheless, the tale stresses that it is worthwhile to retain whatever survives of the original tradition, and this in itself will be found to suffice. Such tales on the theme of how the earlier generations were greater than the later ones are common in Jewish literature. See *Jewish Preaching 1200–1800: An Anthology*, edited by Marc Saperstein (New Haven: Yale University Press, 1989), p. 425. A Hasidic tale on a very similar theme is that of Rabbi Levi Yitzhak of Berditchev's "The King Who Loved Music," from *Toledot Aharon*, compiled by Aaron of Zhitomir (Lemberg, 1864), as follows:

> There once was a king who loved music. Therefore he asked the finest musicians in the land to come to the palace at sunrise each morning to play for him. This suited the king well, as he was an early riser, but some of the musicians were not. Recognizing this, the king saw to it that those who arrived on time were given an extra reward, and that those who arrived even earlier, before sunrise, received a double reward. Nevertheless, it was not the reward that motivated the musicians to play for the king, but their love and respect for him and their mutual delight in music. For the musicians greatly loved to perform together, and the king loved to hear their music.
>
> These musicians served the king for many years, but in time they grew old and died, and the sons of the musicians sought to take their places. But unlike their fathers, they did not want to play out of respect for the king or love of music, but were intent only on the reward. Nor were they masters of their instruments, for although their fathers had sought to train them to be musicians, they had failed to practice, and as a result they had never acquired the art of making beautiful music. Needless to say, the music they played was harsh and offensive to the king's ears. Still, out of respect for their fathers, he did not send them away or replace them. Instead the king remained patient in the hope that they would eventually improve. And so it was that some of them did recover the love of music that had sustained their fathers, and they arrived even earlier to practice in a quiet corner and remained after the others had departed so that they might hone their skills. The king recognized these efforts and was pleased. And at last the day came when these few musicians formed the core of a new orchestra that played flowing melodies. True, their music did not attain the perfect harmony of their fathers, but it still sufficed to bring joy to the king, and thus he received it with favor.

This tale of Rabbi Levi Yitzhak is an allegory about prayer, and of the importance of *kavvanah*, or spiritual intensity, in praying. The king, representing God, derives great pleasure from the harmonies attained by the musicians, representing devout Jews who arrive shortly after sunrise each day to pray together. The generational gap between fathers and sons, which has grown even wider in our time, can be traced, according to Rabbi Levi Yitzhak, to the failure to retain the spiritual intensity of prayer. But this parable is more optimistic than "Lighting a Fire" in that it holds out the possibility that an effort on the part of the later generation will eventually raise them up almost to the level achieved by their fathers.

91. The Tefillin of the Or ha-Hayim (Palestine)

From *Sefer Segulat Moshe* by Moshe ben Naftali Hertz Hoffstein (Spring Valley, N.Y., 1974). Also found in *Toledot Rabbenu Hayim ben Attar,* edited by Reuven Margarliot (Lemberg, 1904). Also in *Otzar ha-Ma'aysiot,* edited by Reuven ben Yakov Na'ana (Jerusalem, 1961), vol. 2, pp. 87–88. Also in *Sefer ha-Ma'aysiot,* edited by Mordecai Ben Yehezkel (Tel Aviv, 1929), vol. 2, pp. 330–332. Additional variants are found in *Pe'er Layesharim* (Jerusalem, 1881). There also are oral variants of this tale, including IFA 9669, collected by Ephraim Haddad from Shimon Swissa, and IFA 12353, told by Nissim Malka of Morocco.

By their nature, tefillin are purely sacred objects, and it is natural that they are the focus of many Jewish folktales. "The Tefillin of the Or ha-Hayim" is the most famous of these tales. It demonstrates possession by an *ibbur,* the spirit of a departed sage that fuses with the spirit of a living person to strengthen him spiritually. Most commonly, in the tales of an *ibbur,* this spirit is present only when a sacred item such as the tefillin are worn. This kind of possession by the spirit of a sage can be contrasted with possession by a dybbuk, the spirit of an evil person who takes over the body of a living person. For an example of this latter kind of tale, see "The Widow of Safed," in Schwartz, *Tree of Souls,* pp. 228–230. The Moroccan oral version of this tale adds the following legends about the Or ha-Hayim's death:

> Rabbi Hayim ben Attar left the world on the fifteenth of Tammuz 1743 in Jerusalem. And all the great scholars of Israel and abroad mourned his death. There is a tradition among the Sephardim that at the time the Or ha-Hayim died, Rabbi Jacob Abulafia was completing his prayers. He leaned his head on the table for a long time, and when he stood up, he said in deep sorrow: "Rabbi Hayim ben Attar has just left this world, for I myself accompanied his soul to the gate of *Gan Eden.*" Also, the Ba'al Shem Tov knew by *Ruah ha-Kodesh,* the holy spirit, that Rabbi Hayim ben Attar had died. It was at the beginning of the third meal of the Sabbath, right after he said the blessing, that he told the students with him that "The western candle has blown out." But they did not understand what he meant, and at the end of the Sabbath, when the students asked him about it, he said: "Our rabbi, Rabbi Hayim ben Attar, blessed be he, is gone, and he is from the western countries, therefore he is called the 'western candle.' " And when the students asked him how he knew this, he answered, "There is *kavannah* in washing the hands to eat that can only be revealed to one in a generation. And that was our rabbi, blessed be he."

This enigmatic reply suggests that the Ba'al Shem Tov learned of the death while washing his hands before eating on the Sabbath, for now that the Or ha-Hayim had died, the secret of the washing of the hands had been revealed to him, as the successor to the Or ha-Hayim in that generation. Another oral variant, IFA 1892, collected by S. Arnst, records that the Ba'al Shem Tov felt the death of Hayim ben Attar from a distance, and he stopped singing the *niggun* he had been singing on the Sabbath.

92. The Angel of Friendship (Eastern Europe)

Based on *Midrash Pinhas* by Rabbi Pinhas of Koretz (Warsaw, 1876).

This haunting legend of the Angel of Friendship is one of the best known in Hasidic lore. For Reb Pinhas of Koretz the angel symbolizes the love and affection that grow up between two friends. But the angel's continued existence depends on them, and on how often they renew their friendship. If they do not, the angel dies. This tale grows out of the talmudic tradition that "Every day ministering angels are created from the fiery stream, and utter song, and cease to be" (*B. Hag.* 14a). The theme of the transformation of the angels is a common one in kabbalistic and Hasidic lore. The key passage behind the belief in imperfect angels is *Mishnah Avot* 4:2: "The reward for a good deed is a good deed, and the reward for a transgression is a transgression." Rabbi Hayim Vital offers the kabbalistic reinterpretation of this passage in *Sha'arei Kedushah* (Aleppo, 1866), where he writes that "The diligent study of the law and the performance of the divine commandments brings about the creation of a new angel. This serves as an explanation for the existence of the *maggidim*, the angelic figures who are said to visit sages and bring them heavenly mysteries." Joseph Karo, author of the *Shulchan Aruch*, was famous for being visited by such a *maggid*. See "The Angel of the Mishnah," p. 339.

A discussion of the transformation of evil angels into good ones is also found in the teachings of Reb Pinhas of Koretz in *Midrash Pinhas*: "Every good deed turns into an angel. But if the deed is imperfect, so is the angel. Perhaps it will be mute. What a disgrace to be served in Paradise by such an angel. Or it might have an arm or leg missing. And these imperfections can only be repaired by the repentance of the one who brought the imperfect angel into being." This kind of repair is known as *tikkun*, and strongly echoes the mystical cosmology of the Ari, where every good deed is said to raise up a fallen spark. This strange notion about a defective angel is also found in "The Blind Angel," p. 367.

Another source that is echoed here is found in *Ma'aysiot Noraim ve-Na'alim* (Cracow, 1896), concerning Rabbi Yehezkel of Prague. He was said to have stated that "the angels that are found in the upper world were created by the deeds of the tzaddikim." Note that Reb Pinhas has the angel that comes into being as a result of friendship, or, by implication, love, function as a symbolic child. This expands the circumstances for the creation of an angel to include angels created by human interaction.

93. **The Underground Forest (Eastern Europe)**

From *Ma'aysiot ve'shichot Tzaddikim* (Warsaw, 1881). Also found in *Sefer ha-Ma'aysiot*, edited by Mordecai Ben Yehezkel (Tel Aviv, 1929), vol. 4, p. 228.

This tale presents Reb Pinhas of Koretz in the role of Jewish conjurer. He sends the student in the story into a world of illusion, requiring a great struggle, which appears to last for years, then breaks the illusion and reveals that only a short time has passed. King Solomon is the model for the conjurer in these illusion tales in "The Beggar King," p. 57, a talmudic tale about King Solomon's efforts to recover his throne from Ashmodai, the king of demons. Many such tales are found concerning the late medieval wonder-worker Rabbi Adam. See "The Enchanted Journey," p. 82, and "The King's Dream," p. 92, as well as "The Enchanted Palace" in Schwartz, *Miriam's Tambourine*, pp. 245–249.

There are other examples of rabbis who function as conjurers. The best known are King Solomon and Rabbi Judah Loew of Prague, creator of the Golem. Other famous Jewish conjurers include Rabbi Naftali Katz, the Ba'al Shem Tov, and Rabbi Elimelekh of Lizensk. See "Rabbi Naftali's Trance,"

p. 344, "The Ladder of Prayers," p. 350, and "A Bowl of Soup" (Introduction, p. 13).

Dreams play a crucial role in this story. Reuven goes to Koretz because his father tells him in a dream to do so. Here dreams are treated with great respect, showing that they continued to be viewed as prophetic, much like the dreams that Joseph interpreted.

94. **Reb Nachman's Chair (Israel)**

Collected by Howard Schwartz from Matti Megged. The dream is recorded in *Sippurim Hadashim* in *Hayey Moharan* by Rabbi Nathan of Bratslav, edited by Reb Nachman Goldstein of Tcherin (Lemberg, 1874).

The account of the chair is widely told in Bratslaver circles, and the reassembled chair can be found next to the Ark in the Bratslaver synagogue in Meah Sha'arim in Jerusalem. As to whether or not Reb Nachman actually stated that he would always remain among his Hasidim, this is a somewhat controversial matter. According to some accounts, Reb Nachman did not state this directly, but when it appeared that he had died, Rabbi Nathan, his scribe, cried out: "Rebbe! Rebbe! To whom have you left us?" Reb Nachman then lifted up his head with an expression that said, "I am not leaving you, God forbid" (*Yemey Moharnat* 44a). Other Bratslav accounts record Reb Nachman as having said a few days earlier that he would always remain among them. In any case, the Bratslavers firmly believe that it was Reb Nachman's intention to always remain their rabbi, and he is still recognized as such to this day. For another account of the intervention of Reb Nachman's spirit into the lives of his followers, see the Introduction, p. 22, about a letter from the world to come.

Note that the motif of the chair being broken apart and then reassembled has strong echoes of the cosmological myth of the Ari about the Shattering of the Vessels and the Gathering of the Sparks. (See "The Shattering of the Vessels and the Gathering of the Sparks" in Schwartz, *Tree of Souls*, pp. 122–124.) There is a parable of Reb Nachman's, "The Tale of the Millstone," from *Sipurei Ma'aysiot Hadashim* (Warsaw, 1909), which presents a dilemma to which the wise prince finds a creative solution, much like that of the Bratslavers with Reb Nachman's chair:

> A king once sent his son abroad to be educated. The prince was gone for several years, and when he returned he was well versed in all branches of knowledge. On his return the king informed him that he wished to test his wisdom. He showed his son a great millstone, of immense size, and told him that he wished for him, and for him alone, to bring that millstone into the palace and bear it up to the palace attic. The prince was astonished at this request, for the millstone was so large that it would require a regiment of soldiers to lift it, and even they would have to struggle. How could he do such a task on his own? It seemed impossible. For several days the prince sat dejectedly on the millstone, trying to think of a way to move it. He consulted all of the branches of knowledge he was familiar with, but none seemed to offer any clue. Just when the boy was about to go to his father and confess his inability to perform the task, he saw a squirrel open a large nut and break it into many pieces. Then the squirrel carried the pieces one by one into its nest. Suddenly inspired, the prince took a hammer and began to pound at the millstone until he had broken it into a multitude of little pieces. Then he carried the pieces, one by

one, into the palace attic, and at last he was able to present himself to the king and declare that the task had been completed. Then the king knew that his son had indeed become wise and was worthy of becoming his heir.

It seems possible that this parable was brought up in the discussions about what to do about Reb Nachman's chair, too precious to leave behind. Indeed, the story does seem to contain a hint of how to proceed from Reb Nachman himself. See *Midrash Tehillim* 6:3 for the likely source of this parable.

95. **The Soul of the Ari (Eastern Europe)**

From *'Ateret Tif'eret* (Bilgorai, Poland, 1910). A variant can be found in *Sefer ha-Ma'aysiot*, edited by Mordecai ben Yehezkel (Tel Aviv, 1929), who attributes it to oral tradition. There are many other variants of this tale, including those in *Sihot Tzaddikim* (Warsaw, 1921) and *Esser Kedoshot* (Petrakos, 1906).

This tale draws on many now-familiar mystical motifs and presents them in a unique fashion. Reb Zevi Hirsch of Zhidachov finds a precious glowing stone in his cupboard, a gift from heaven. This clearly recalls the legend of the *Tzohar*, the glowing stone containing the primordial light, which God gave to Adam and Eve upon their expulsion from Eden. This initiates a long chain of legend in which the glowing stone comes into the possession of every major figure from Noah to Abraham to Moses. See "The *Tzohar*" in Schwartz, *Tree of Souls*, pp. 85–88.

In the present tale Reb Zevi Hirsch fasts to find out why he has received the mysterious gift, although it is clearly a heavenly reward, not unlike the leg of a golden table received by Rabbi Haninah ben Dosa in "The Golden Table." (See Schwartz, *Gabriel's Palace*, p. 58.) In this way Reb Zevi learns that he can either keep the glowing stone, and he and his descendants will become rich, or else he can give it up and instead the soul of the Ari will become fused with his own. This latter option closely resembles that of possession by an *ibbur*, where the spirit of one who has departed fuses with the soul of a living sage. See "The Tefillin of the Or ha-Hayim," p. 357. This leads to a student of Reb Zevi's overhearing a voice other than that of the rabbi discussing a passage of the *Zohar*. This voice is later identified as that of the Ari, and the student understands that the Ari was teaching Reb Zevi. This kind of speech closely resembles that of the *maggidim*, the spirits who come to scholars and speak through them, as happens with Rabbi Joseph Karo in "The Angel of the Mishnah," p. 339. Thus the link between Reb Zevi and the soul of the Ari seems to be a combination of the *ibbur* and the *maggid*.

When Reb Zevi returns the glowing jewel by casting it into heaven, there is an echo of the famous talmudic legends of the High Priest returning the keys of the Temple and of Rabbi Haninah ben Dosa praying that the leg of a golden table be returned to heaven. See "The Hand of God" in Schwartz, *Tree of Souls*, p. 426, and "The Golden Table," in Schwartz, *Gabriel's Palace*, p. 58.

96. **The Blind Angel (Eastern Europe)**

From *Admorei Chernobyl*, edited by Yisrael Yakov Klapholtz (B'nai Brak, 1971).

This tale grows out of the period of Hasidic decadence, when the succession of the Hasidic masters was determined on the basis of family rather than knowledge and leadership. At this time many rebbes became very affluent. Rabbi Mordecai of Chernobyl was a son of Rabbi Menachem Nahum of Chernobyl, the founder of the Twersky dynasty. This tale was clearly intended to justify Rabbi Mordecai's wealthy lifestyle, and to refute the appearance of avarice by demonstrating that the silver menorah was not really of material importance to the rabbi but had deeper spiritual meaning. Note that Rabbi Mordecai has been able to see into the future, learning that the rich man will need the merit of giving away his precious silver menorah in order to guide his blind angel into Paradise. Because Rabbi Mordecai lights the menorah on Hanukah, it can be assumed to have been a *hanukiah*, a modified menorah for use during Hanukah. For another tale of future vision, see "The Tale of the Kugel," p. 371. The notion of an imperfect angel is found in the tales and writings of Reb Pinhas of Koretz. See "The Angel of Friendship," p. 359, and the accompanying note.

The commandment to use a menorah is found in Numbers 8:1: *And the Lord spoke unto Moses, saying: "Speak unto Aaron, and say unto him: When thou lightest the lamps, the seven lamps shall give light in front of the candlestick."* The mystical aspects of the menorah in this tale suggest the even more symbolic interpretation of the menorah found in Reb Nachman of Bratslav's tale "The Menorah of Defects," from *Sipurei Ma'aysiot Hadashim* (Warsaw, 1909) as follows:

> Once a young man left his home and traveled for several years. After he returned, he proudly told his father that he had become a master in the craft of making menorahs. He asked his father to call together all the townsmen who practiced this craft, that he might demonstrate his unrivaled skill for them. That is what his father did, inviting them to his home. But when his son presented them with the menorah he had made, not everyone found it pleasing. Then his father begged each and every one to tell him the truth about what they thought of it. And at last each one admitted that he had found a defect in the menorah. When the father told his son that many of the craftsmen had noted a defect, the son asked what the defect was, and it emerged that each of them had noted something different. What one craftsman had praised, another had found defective. And the son said to his father: "By this have I shown my great skill. For I have revealed to each one his own defect, since each of these defects was actually in he who perceived it. It was these defects that I incorporated into my creation, for I made this menorah only from defects. Now I will begin its restoration."

This parable of Reb Nachman's has been subjected to various interpretations. Since the menorah is a traditional symbol of the creation of the world in seven days, with the center light representing the Sabbath, the craftsman in the tale may be seen to represent God, and the defects those of the world, with all its imperfections. The craftsman may also be seen to represent the rebbe, who must reveal the defects of his Hasidim to them, so that they may begin the process of *tikkun* or restoration.

97. A New Soul (Eastern Europe)

From *Froyen-rebbeyim un berihmte perzhenlikhkeyten in poylen* (Yiddish) (Warsaw, 1937).

One of the strangest and most fascinating episodes of Hasidic history was the emergence of Hannah Rochel Werbermacher, the Maid of Ludomir, as a rebbe.

This tale describes her transformative experience, in which she believed that she had received a new soul, and after that took on some of the rituals of men, including the wearing of a tallit and tefillin, and was eventually recognized as possessing great knowledge and wisdom, and began to function as a rebbe. This lasted until her marriage, arranged by Rabbi Menachem Mendel of Chernobyl, which brought this period of her life to an end. In her later life she moved to the Holy Land, where legend has it that she participated in an attempt to hasten the coming of the Messiah, as described in this tale.

Jewish lore has many stories about wise daughters who secretly listen in on the teachings of the Torah. See, for example, "The Donkey Girl" in Schwartz, *Miriam's Tambourine*, pp. 202–208. I. B. Singer's famous story "Yentl the Yeshivah Boy" is about such a young woman, who disguises herself as a student and joins the yeshivah. See *The Collected Stories* (New York: Farrar, Straus, & Giroux, 1982), pp. 149–169.

98. **The Tale of the Kugel (Eastern Europe)**

Collected by Rabbi Zalman Schachter-Shalomi from Reb Avraham Paris.
A variant can be found in *Legends of the Hasidim*, edited by Jerome R. Mintz (Chicago: University of Chicago Press, 1968), pp. 392–395.

This is a fine example of an illusion tale, where many years seem to pass, but in fact the whole experience takes place in an hour or two. It is possible to trace this genre of tale from rabbinic lore to medieval Jewish folklore, kabbalistic tales, and other Hasidic models. For other examples of illusion tales, see "The Beggar King," p. 57, "The Enchanted Journey," p. 82, and "The King's Dream," p. 92.

This tale portrays Rabbi Menachem Mendel I of Lubavitch as having great powers of illusion, as well as the powers to show a man a vision of the future path he will take. Here a man sees what his life would be like if he were to divorce his wife for not having any children. He experiences the time as if it were real—as if he were actually living out his alternate life. But when he emerges from the vision, very little time has passed. This is another example of the rebbe as wonder worker, in the model of the Ba'al Shem Tov and Reb Elimelech of Lizensk.

Rabbi Menachem Mendel was the author of *Zemach Tzaddik* (1870–74), a book of responsa, in honor of which he was known as the Zemach Tzaddik. He was the grandson of Rabbi Shneur Zalman, founder of the Habad movement.

99. **The Ocean of Tears (Eastern Europe)**

Collected by Howard Schwartz from Rabbi Shlomo Carlebach. A variant of this tale is found in *Sippurei Hasidim*, edited by Shlomo Yosef Zevin (Tel Aviv, 1964).

Rabbi Shlomo Carlebach often told this tale about the Kotzker Rebbe, whom he greatly admired. Rabbi Abraham Joshua Heschel wrote a famous book about the Kotzker Rebbe, *A Passion for Truth*. As the title indicates, the Kotzker Rebbe was devoted to finding truth, while his closest friend, Reb Yitzhak Kalish of Vorki, was devoted to loving-kindness. In this story Reb Yitzhak has deep bonds with both his son and his best friend. After Reb Yitzhak died, both survivors expected him to make contact with them from Heaven. When he does not, the Kotzker Rebbe starts to worry about him, even though he is no longer living.

A popular theme in Hasidic tales concerns a vow made between two friends, where the first to depart this world promises to contact the other. It is possible that there was such a vow between Reb Yitzhak and the Kotzker Rebbe. This puts a different perspective on the Kotzker Rebbe's heavenly journey, for since he knows that Reb Yitzhak would never break a vow, he is concerned about the fate of his soul. He decides to seek out Reb Yitzhak in heaven, and the story recounts his journey through the palaces of heaven, as well as a mythic encounter with the Ocean of Tears.

One of the primary themes of this story is the strong bonds between father and son and between friends that transcend death. This leads the Kotzker Rebbe to take the extraordinary step of making his heavenly ascent. In doing so, the Kotzker Rebbe is taking part in a tradition of heavenly journeys that includes such journeys by Adam, Enoch, Abraham, Isaac, Jacob, Moses, and, of course, Elijah. In addition, there was an early Jewish sect, dating from the second century BCE to the eighth century CE, known as the Hekhalot sect, who were devoted to heavenly journeys. *Hekhalot* means "palaces," and refers to the palaces of heaven. The Hekhalot texts, such as *Hekhalot Rabbati* and *3 Enoch,* describe such heavenly journeys in great detail. No one is certain of their intended purpose. They may have been accounts of mystical journeys, or they may have been intended to serve as guidebooks of ascent.

The great reward awaiting the righteous whose souls ascend on high at the time of their death is the palaces of heaven. Here the great figures of Jewish history each have a palace of their own. The Kotzker Rebbe visits four of these palaces, those of Rashi, Maimonides, Moses, and Abraham. It is Abraham who reveals where Reb Yitzhak can be found.

The ending of the story strongly implies that Reb Yitzhak has confronted God over the suffering of Israel. Reb Yitzhak has taken a vow to remain at the Ocean of Tears to remind God of Jewish suffering, and to refuse, in effect, his heavenly reward. As the story ends, the confrontation is ongoing.

There are other examples of rabbis who turned down their heavenly rewards. Reb Nachman of Bratslav is believed by his followers to have given up his place in heaven to remain in this world looking after them. This has given rise to many stories about encounters with Reb Nachman's wandering spirit. See "Reb Nachman's Chair," p. 364. Also, see "The Soul of the Ari," p. 366, where Rabbi Zevi Hirsh turns down one heavenly reward in favor of another.

Shlomo Carlebach's version of the story is clearly linked to Reb Yitzhak's son Mendele, clearly noting that he was named after Rabbi Menachem Mendel of Kotzk. However, another version of this tale exists, which does not attribute the story to Mendele, but to his brother, Rabbi Yakov David of Amshinov. This reflects a split in Reb Yitzhak's Hasidim about which of his sons should be regarded as his successor, with each side claiming to be connected with this legend about Reb Yitzhak. Here is the other version of the story:

> On a visit to Kotzk, Reb Yakov David of Amishinov complained to the Kotzker Rebbe that he had not seen his father since his soul had taken leave of this world. "You will see him," the Kotzker Rebbe told him. And indeed, while he was still in Kotzk, Reb Yakov David entered the rebbe's study and told him that he had seen his father. "Where did you see him?" the rebbe asked. "I saw him standing by a river," said Reb Yakov David, "leaning on his staff." "That river," said the Kotzker Rebbe, "flows from the tears of Israel." (*Sippurei Hasidim,* edited by Shlomo Yosef Zevin [Tel Aviv, 1964])

Note that this version of the story attributes the vision of Reb Yitzhak to Reb Yakov David, not to the Kotzker Rebbe. But the identification of the river as flowing from the tears of Israel is attributed to the Kotzker Rebbe. Thus, instead of a heavenly journey, Reb Yakov David has a vision of his father in the Kotzker Rebbe's home. Since this tale was important not only for Reb Yitzhak's followers but for those of the Kotzer Rebbe as well, it seems likely that the generally accepted version is that told by Shlomo Carlebach, with the Kotzker Rebbe playing a more extensive role.

100. **The Dream Assembly (United States)**

Collected by Howard Schwartz from Rabbi Zalman Schachter-Shalomi.

This is the only contemporary tale of Hasidic origin included here. Drawing on the model of Reb Nachman of Bratslav, who used stories as a method of teaching his Hasidim, Rabbi Zalman Schachter-Shalomi, founder of the Renewal Movement in Judaism, told a series of tales, based on his life and imagination, about a fictional Reb Zalman from the city of Zholkiev, city of the modern Reb Zalman's birth. These stories, set in the nineteenth century, have been collected in *The Dream Assembly*, selected and retold by Howard Schwartz (Nevada City, Calif.: Gateways, 1990).

In the title story, Reb Zalman's Hasidim discuss the true purpose of *davvening*—prayer. Each perceives a different purpose. When they ask Reb Zalman to resolve the question, he directs them, instead, to meet him in a dream. Miraculously, that night they all dream of meeting in an orchard, reminiscent of the famous tale of the four sages who entered *Pardes*—literally an orchard or garden, but also identified in mystical literature as Paradise. See "The Four Who Entered Paradise" in Schwartz, *Tree of Souls*, pp. 173–174. Here Reb Zalman gives them an impossible assignment: to create a living bird, where each of them is responsible for creating one part of it. Again, through great concentration and intensity (*kavannah*) the Hasidim succeed in this task, and the story ends with the song of the bird echoing as they awake.

This story, essentially a parable, is about the necessity of collaboration. The living bird they create represents the kind of miracle that can take place through collective prayer. Each prays on his own, but they also pray together. Singly, none of the Hasidim is capable of such a miraculous creation, but together, guided by Reb Zalman, they bring the imaginary bird to life. Reb Zalman's inspiration for this story was the tradition that before Reb Elimelech of Lizensk passed away, he willed something of himself to each of his four major disciples.

To the Apter Rav he gave his mouth (the power of oration); to the Seer of Lublin he gave his eyes (the power of prophecy and insight); to the Maggid of Kozhnitz he gave his heart (the power of deeper understanding); and to Reb Menachem Mendel of Riminov he gave his brain (the power of reasoning and mastery of knowledge).

The messianic implications of this story should not be overlooked. The bird suggests the golden dove whose nest is close to the palace of the Messiah. See "The Golden Dove," p. 188, and "The Ladder of Prayers," p. 350, and the accompanying notes. Creating the miraculous bird and bringing it to life represents the kind of *kavannah* required to bring the Messiah.

APPENDICES

A Note on the Sources

The one hundred stories included here come from a wide range of postbiblical Jewish sources, including the Talmud, the midrashic collections, kabbalistic sources, medieval Jewish folklore, Hasidic tales, and tales collected in the modern era by YIVO, the Israel Folktale Archives, and other oral sources. These stories have also been drawn from many countries. See Appendix C for a list of the countries of origin of these tales.

In retelling these tales, the editor has been inspired by the models of I. L. Peretz, who retold many of the tales collected by his friend, the ethnologist S. Ansky; of the Grimm Brothers, who recognized the need to retell the tales they collected; and of Italo Calvino, who established the modern standard for retelling in his classic *Italian Folktales.* As often as possible, Calvino located at least three variants of the tales he included, and drew on all of them in the versions he published. Here, too, multiple variants have been sought out and drawn on in as much as possible. These variants are especially important in the case of the orally collected tales, which have often been preserved in fragmentary condition.

At the same time, the editor has approached the issue of retelling much like a tailor—if the story was received in good condition, only minimal changes have been made; but if the story is fragmentary or unfinished (as in the case of Reb Nachman's tantalizing fragment "A Garment for the Moon"), the editor has reimagined the story in order to complete it.

These one hundred tales have been selected from more than 350 tales the editor has included in his previous collections. Most have been drawn from *Elijah's Violin & Other Jewish Fairy Tales, Miriam's Tambourine: Jewish Folktales from Around the World, Lilith's Cave: Jewish Tales of the Supernatural,* and *Gabriel's Palace: Jewish Mystical Tales.* In addition, a few choice tales have been included from the editor's books of stories for children, including *The Diamond Tree, The Sabbath Lion, The Wonder Child, Next Year in Jerusalem, A Journey to Paradise,* and *The Day the Rabbi Disappeared.* "The Dream Assembly" is from *The Dream Assembly: Tales of Rabbi Zalman Schachter-Shalomi.* In addition, this collection includes two previously unpublished tales, "The Dybbuk in the Well" and "The Groom Who Was Destined to Die on His Wedding Day."

To give the reader a sense of the sources drawn on in this collection, Appendix A provides the general sources. Detailed sources for each tale are found in the Sources and Commentary section. It is interesting to note that a little more than a third of the stories (37) come from oral sources, demonstrating the importance of this most recent stratum of Jewish folklore.

Appendix B provides a list of story cycles—that is, stories in which key figures such as Abraham, Moses, King Solomon, the Ari, or the Ba'al Shem Tov appear. Note that the Queen of Sheba appears with two identities. In one, she is the clever queen who challenges King Solomon ("The Maiden in the Tree," "A Palace of Bird Beaks") and in the other she is closely identified with Lilith ("The Queen of Sheba," "The Water Witch").

Appendix C lists the stories included by country of origin. Note that there is almost an even breakdown of Ashkenazi tales (from Eastern Europe) and Sephardic tales (from the Middle East), demonstrating that Ashkenazi and Sephardic folk traditions are equally important in Jewish tradition.

Appendix D lists specialized tale types—stories about angels, creating a living being, divine tests, dreams, enchanted places, ghost stories, journeys to a city of immortals, journeys to heaven or hell, magical combat, magical creatures, magical healing, magical objects, magical spells, marriage with demons, possession by dybbuks, possession by *ibburs,* visions, and witches. These are popular motifs in Jewish folktales, and some of them, such as possession by dybbuk and by *ibbur,* are unique to Jewish tradition.

Appendix E is a tale type index, based on the system of Antti Aarne and Stith Thompson, eds., *The Types of the Folktale: A Classification and Bibliography,* 2nd rev. ed. (Helsinki: Suomalaisen Thedeakatemia, 1961). This is the primary method of folktale classification, in which the tale type index is structured according to narrative genres and arranged according to themes. The alternate system of classification is a motif index, also formulated by Stith Thompson. See *Motif Index of Folk Literature* (Bloomington: University of Indiana Press, 1955–1958), 6 vols. Some scholars have continued to add new Jewish classifications based on specific Jewish versions of the broader types. (The placement of asterisks in the AT number derives from the scholars who created the Jewish subtypes listed.) These include Dov Noy, Heda Jason, and Reginetta Haboucha. According to Aarne and Thompson (identified with the abbreviation AT before the first letter or number of each tale type), specific Jewish tale types are marked with an asterisk (Jason and Noy-Schnitzler) or with two asterisks before the number (Haboucha).

Appendix A

Sources of the Stories

The Talmud

The Beggar King
The Cave of Shimon bar Yohai
The Golden Dove
King Solomon and Ashmodai
The Witches of Ashkelon

The Midrash

The Princess in the Tower
The Three Tasks of Elijah
The Water Witch

Kabbalistic Sources

The Angel of the Mishnah
The Finger
Gathering Sparks
The Tzaddik of the Forest
A Vision at the Wailing Wall

Medieval Jewish Folklore

An Apple from the Tree of Life
The Bride of Demons
The Cave of King David
The Cellar
The Charm in the Dress
The City of Luz
The Demon Princess
Gabriel's Palace
The Golem
The Haunted Violin
Helen of Troy
The Homunculus of Maimonides
The Knife
Leaves from the Garden of Eden
The Maiden in the Tree

Miriam's Tambourine
The Other Side
The Queen of Sheba
Rabbi Naftali's Trance
The Speaking Head
The Spirit of Hagigah
The Underwater Palace

Hasidic Sources

The Angel of Friendship
The Blind Angel
The Boy Israel and the Witch
The Dead Fiancée
The Enchanted Island
The Enchanted Journey
A Garment for the Moon
The Goat Whose Horns Reached to Heaven
The King's Dream
The Ladder of Prayers
Lighting a Fire
The Lost Princess
The Magic Mirror of Rabbi Adam
A New Soul
The Perfect Saint
The Pirate Princess
The Prince and the Slave
The Prince Who Thought He Was a Rooster
The Prince Who Was Made of Precious Gems
The Soul of the Ari
The Souls of Trees
The Tefillin of the Or ha-Hayim
The Treasure
The Tree of Life
The Underground Forest
The Water Palace
The Werewolf

Orally Collected Tales

The Angel of Forgetfulness
The Beast
The Bird of Happiness
The Bridegroom Who Vanished
The Cave of Mattathias
The Cottage of Candles
The Demon of the Waters
Drawing the Wind
The Dream Assembly
Elijah's Violin
The Exiled Princess

A Flock of Angels
Gabriel's Palace
The Golden Mountain
The Golden Tree
The Groom Who Was Destined to Die on His Wedding Day
The Hair in the Milk
Katanya
A Kiss from the Master
Lilith's Cave
The Lost Melody
The Magic Wine Cup
Milk and Honey
The Mute Princess
The Ocean of Tears
A Palace of Bird Beaks
The Princess and the Slave
Reb Nachman's Chair
The Sabbath Lion
The Staff of Elijah
The Sword of Moses
The Tale of the Kugel
The Twelve Golden Calves
The Wonder Child
The Wonderful Healing Leaves
The Wooden Sword
Yona and the River Demon

Appendix B
Story Cycles

Stories of Abraham
King Solomon and Ashmodai
Miriam's Tambourine
The Ocean of Tears
The Sacrifice (Introduction, p. 4)
Summoning the Patriarchs (Introduction, p. 2)

Stories of the Ari (Rabbi Isaac Luria)
The Angel of Forgetfulness
Gathering Sparks
The Soul of the Ari
A Vision at the Wailing Wall

Stories of the Ba'al Shem Tov
A Combat in Magic
The Enchanted Island
The Ladder of Prayers
Lighting a Fire
The Tree of Life
The Werewolf

Stories of Elijah
The Angel of Forgetfulness
The Beast
The Cave of Shimon bar Yohai
Elijah's Violin
Helen of Troy
Katanya
The Staff of Elijah
The Three Tasks of Elijah

Stories of King David
The Cave of King David
King Solomon and Ashmodai

Stories of King Solomon
An Appointment with Death (Introduction, p. 7)

The Beggar King
King Solomon and Ashmodai
The Maiden in the Tree
A Palace of Bird Beaks
The Princess in the Tower

Stories of the Kotzker Rebbe
The Goat Whose Horns Reached to Heaven
The Ocean of Tears

Stories of the Maharal (Rabbi Judah Loewe)
The Golem
Summoning the Patriarchs (Introduction, p. 2)

Stories of Maimonides
The Homunculus of Maimonides
The Ocean of Tears

Stories of Moses
The Ocean of Tears
The Princess and the Slave
The Sword of Moses

Stories of Rabbi Adam
The Enchanted Journey
The King's Dream
The Magic Mirror of Rabbi Adam

Stories of Rabbi Elimelech of Lizensk
A Bowl of Soup (Introduction, p. 13)
The Woman in the Forest (Introduction, p. 9)

Stories of Rabbi Shimon bar Yohai
The Cave of Shimon bar Yohai
A Kiss from the Master

Stories of Reb Nachman of Bratslav
The Angel of Losses (Introduction, p. 21)
A Garment for the Moon
The Lost Princess
The Perfect Saint
The Pirate Princess
The Prince Who Thought He Was a Rooster
The Prince Who Was Made of Precious Gems
The Princess and the Slave
Reb Nachman's Chair
The Souls of Trees
The Treasure
The Water Palace
The Wooden Sword

Appendix C
Countries of Origin

Afghanistan
The Cottage of Candles
The Wooden Sword

Babylon
An Appointment with Death (Introduction, p. 7)
The Beggar King
The Cave of Shimon bar Yohai
The Golden Dove
King Solomon and Ashmodai
The Witches of Ashkelon

The Balkans
Drawing the Wind
Yona and the River Demon

China
The Twelve Golden Calves

Eastern Europe
The Angel of Friendship
The Angel of Losses (Introduction, p. 21)
An Apple from the Tree of Life
The Blind Angel
A Bowl of Soup (Introduction, p. 13)
The Boy Israel and the Witch
The Bridegroom Who Vanished
The Cave of King David
The Cave of Mattathias
The Cellar
The City of Luz
A Combat in Magic
The Dead Fiancée
The Demon of the Waters
The Enchanted Island

The Enchanted Journey
The Exiled Princess
A Garment for the Moon
The Goat Whose Horns Reached to Heaven
The Golem
The Homunculus of Maimonides
The King's Dream
The Ladder of Prayers
Leaves from the Garden of Eden
Lighting a Fire
The Lost Princess
The Magic Mirror of Rabbi Adam
The Maiden in the Tree
Milk and Honey
Miriam's Tambourine
A New Soul
The Ocean of Tears
The Other Side
The Perfect Saint
The Pirate Princess
The Prince Who Was Made of Precious Gems
The Prince and the Slave
The Prince Who Thought He Was a Rooster
Rabbi Naftali's Trance
Reb Shmelke's Whip (Introduction, p. 12)
The Sacrifice (Introduction, p. 4)
The Soul of the Ari
The Souls of Trees
The Speaking Head
Summoning the Patriarchs (Introduction, p. 2)
The Tale of the Kugel
The Treasure
The Tree of Life
The Underground Forest
The Underwater Palace
The Water Palace
The Werewolf

Egypt
The Beast
Elijah's Violin
The Wonder Child

Ethiopia
The Groom Who Was Destined to Die on His Wedding Day

Germany
The Bride of Demons
The Cellar
The Charm in the Dress

Gabriel's Palace
The Haunted Violin
The Knife
The Lost Melody
The Queen of Sheba

India
The Golden Tree

Iraq
The Bird of Happiness

Italy
The Dybbuk in the Well
The Spirit of Hagigah

Kurdistan/Iraqi Kurdistan/Turkish Kurdistan
A Flock of Angels
The Hair in the Milk
The Sword of Moses
The Wonderful Healing Leaves

Morocco
The Golden Mountain
The Princess and the Slave
The Sabbath Lion

North Africa
The Demon Princess

The Orient
The Water Witch

Palestine/Israel
The Angel of Forgetfulness
The Angel of the Mishnah
The Finger
Gathering Sparks
Helen of Troy
A Kiss from the Master
The Princess in the Tower
Reb Nachman's Chair
The Tefillin of the Or ha-Hayim
The Tzaddik of the Forest
A Vision at the Wailing Wall

Romania
The Staff of Elijah

Syria
The Angel of Forgetfulness
The Magic Wine Cup

Tunisia
Lilith's Cave
The Three Tasks of Elijah

Turkey
Katanya

United States
The Dream Assembly

Yemen
The Mute Princess
A Palace of Bird Beaks

Appendix D

Specialized Tale Types

Angels

The Angel of Forgetfulness
The Angel of Friendship
The Angel of the Mishnah
The Blind Angel
A Flock of Angels

Creating a Living Being

The Golem
The Homunculus of Maimonides
The Mute Princess

Divine Tests

The Cottage of Candles
Miriam's Tambourine

Dreams

The Cave of Mattathias
The Dream Assembly
The Haunted Violin
The Lost Melody
The King's Dream
The Knife
The Souls of Trees
The Treasure
The Twelve Golden Calves

Enchanted Places

The Cave of Shimon bar Yohai
The Cottage of Candles
The Enchanted Island
The King's Dream
The Tree of Life
The Underground Forest
A Vision at the Wailing Wall

Forcing the End (Hastening the End of Days)

The Ladder of Prayers
Helen of Troy

Ghost Stories

The Dead Fiancée
The Haunted Violin
The Lost Melody

Journeys to a City of Immortals

An Appointment with Death (Introduction, p. 7)
The Cave of King David
The City of Luz

Journeys to Heaven or Hell

The Ladder of Prayers
The Ocean of Tears
Rabbi Naftali's Trance

Lilith

The Bride of Demons
The Cellar
The Hair in the Milk
The Other Side
The Queen of Sheba
The Woman in the Forest (Introduction, p. 9)

Magical Combat

A Combat in Magic
The Werewolf

Magical Creatures

The Goat Whose Horns Reached to Heaven
The Golden Dove
Katanya
The Sabbath Lion

Magical Healing

An Apple from the Tree of Life
Leaves from the Garden of Eden
The Wonderful Healing Leaves

Magical Objects

The Angel of Forgetfulness
The Cottage of Candles
Reb Nachman's Chair
Reb Shmelke's Whip (Introduction, p. 12)
The Soul of the Ari
The Staff of Elijah
The Tefillin of the Or ha-Hayim

MAGICAL SPELLS
A Bowl of Soup (Introduction, p. 13)
The Boy Israel and the Witch
The Charm in the Dress
A Flock of Angels
The Golden Mountain
The Golem
The Magic Mirror of Rabbi Adam
The Prince Who Was Made of Precious Gems
Summoning the Patriarchs (Introduction, p. 2)
The Water Palace
The Wonder Child

MARRIAGE WITH DEMONS
The Bride of Demons
The Cellar
The Demon Princess
The Finger
The Other Side
The Queen of Sheba
Yona and the River Demon

POSSESSION BY DYBBUKS
The Dybbuk in the Well

POSSESSION BY *IBBURS*
The Angel of the Mishnah
A Kiss from the Master

QUESTS
The Angel of Forgetfulness
An Apple from the Tree of Life
The Bird of Happiness
The Beggar King
The Blind Angel
The Cave of King David
The Cave of Mattathias
The City of Luz
The Cottage of Candles
The Dead Fiancée
The Dream Assembly
Elijah's Violin
The Enchanted Island
A Garment for the Moon
The Golden Dove
The Golden Mountain
The Golden Tree
The Golem
Helen of Troy

King Solomon and Ashmodai
The King's Dream
A Kiss from the Master
The Ladder of Prayers
Leaves from the Garden of Eden
Lighting a Fire
The Lost Princess
Miriam's Tambourine
The Mute Princess
The Ocean of Tears
The Pirate Princess
The Prince and the Slave
The Princess and the Slave
Rabbi Naftali's Trance
Reb Nachman's Chair
The Sabbath Lion
The Speaking Head
The Staff of Elijah
The Sword of Moses
The Tale of the Kugel
The Three Tasks of Elijah
The Treasure
The Tree of Life
The Twelve Golden Calves
The Underground Forest
The Underwater Palace
A Vision at the Wailing Wall
The Water Palace
The Wonderful Healing Leaves

THE THIRTY-SIX JUST MEN (*LAMED-VAV TZADDIKIM*)
An Apple from the Tree of Life
The Golden Mountain
The Prince Who Was Made of Precious Gems
The Tzaddik of the Forest

WITCHES
The Boy Israel and the Witch
The Water Witch
The Witches of Ashkelon

Appendix E

Tale Type Index

I. Animal Tales (AT 1–299)

Tale Type	Tale
156A The Faith of the Lion	The Sabbath Lion
156*B Woman as Midwife of Snake (of Cat, of Demon)	The Underwater Palace
178*C The Slaughtered She-Goat	Milk and Honey
298 Contest of Wind and Sun	A Garment for the Moon

II. Ordinary Folk Tales (AT 300–1199)

Tale Type	Tale
304 The Hunter	The Mute Princess
306A Heavenly Maiden Sought	The Angel of Friendship
	The Angel of the Mishnah
	The Spirit of Hagigah
	A Vision at the Wailing Wall
310 The Maiden in the Tower	The Princess in the Tower
312C Devil's Bride Rescued by Brother	The Bride of Demons
**313D Lovers Overcome All Obstacles	The Princess in the Tower
313H Flight from the Witch	The Water Witch
325 Apprentice and Ghost	The Homunculus of Maimonides
325** Sorcerer Punished	The Charm in the Dress
	The Magic Mirror of Rabbi Adam
327A Hansel and Gretel	The Water Witch
327G The Boy at the Devil (Witch's) House	The Boy Israel and the Witch
329 The Mirror	Lilith's Cave
332A Visit to the House of the Dead	The Cottage of Candles
365 The Dead Bridegroom Carries Off His Bride	The Finger
	The Tzaddik of the Forest
365B Young Men, Who Lie in these Graves, Come Dance with Us	The Finger
382 Quest to the Devil	The Lost Princess
405 Jorinde and Joringel	The Witches of Ashkelon
407*B (Andrejev) King-maiden	The Lost Princess
409A Enchanted Girl Disenchanted	Elijah's Violin

Tale Type	Story
400 The Man on a Quest for His Lost Wife	The Lost Princess
410 Sleeping Beauty	The Wonder Child
412 The Maiden with a Separable Soul in a Necklace	The Wonder Child
**415 The Supernatural Wife Subsists on a Single Lentil	Katanya
424* Youth Wed to a She-Devil	The Cellar The Demon Princess The Finger Helen of Troy The Other Side The Tzaddik of the Forest The Woman in the Forest (Introduction)
425 The Search for the Lost Husband	The Pirate Princess
425C Beauty and the Beast	The Bridegroom Who Vanished
425*Q Marvelous Being Woos Princess	Elijah's Violin
452A Sister Rescued from Devil	The Prince Who Was Made of Precious Gems
452D* Parents as Birds	The Witches of Ashkelon
460*C The Fortune of the Greater Fool	The Princess and the Slave
461A The Journey to the Deity for Advice	The Princess and the Slave
465A The Quest for the Unknown	The Underground Forest
465C A Journey to the Other World	The Ladder of Prayers Milk and Honey Miriam's Tambourine The Ocean of Tears
466** The Journey to Hell	Rabbi Naftali's Trance
468 The Princess on the Sky-Tree	The Goat Whose Horns Reached to Heaven
470* The Hero Visits the Land of the Immortals and Marries Its Queen	The Demon Princess
470B The Land Where No One Dies	An Appointment with Death (Introduction) The Cave of King David The City of Luz
471 The Bridge to the Other World	The City of Luz
471A* The Trip to Hell	Rabbi Naftali's Trance
476** Midwife in the Underworld	The Underwater Palace
476** Midwife to Demons	The Underwater Palace
480 The Spinning Woman by the Spring	The King's Dream
503 The Gifts of the Little People	The Three Tasks of Elijah
506** The Grateful Saint	Rabbi Nachman's Chair

506*C Dead and Elijah the Prophet as Helpers	The Lost Melody
508 The Bride Won in a Tournament	The Bride of Demons
510 Cinderella	The Exiled Princess
512B The Ghost Is Avenged	The Dead Fiancée
517 The Boy Who Learned Many Things	The Cave of Shimon bar Yohai
	A Kiss from the Master
	The Tefillin of the Or ha-Hayim
550 Search for the Golden Bird	The Bird of Happiness
	The Golden Dove
551 Sons on a Quest for a Wonderful Remedy for Their Father	An Apple from the Tree of Life
	The Golden Tree
	Leaves from the Garden of Eden
	The Sword of Moses
	The Wonderful Healing Leaves
555 The Fisherman and His Wife	The Cellar
	The Queen of Sheba
576B The Magic Knife	The Knife
577 The King's Tasks	The King's Dream
559-I (Andrejev) The Dumb Princess	The Mute Princess
612-II The Three Snake-Leaves	The Homunuculus of Maimonides
653*B The Suitors Restore the Maiden to Life	The Mute Princess
676 Open Sesame	The Golden Mountain
*677 (Andrejev) In the Underwater Kingdom	The Underwater Palace
	The Water Witch
681 Years of Experience in a Moment	The Beggar King
	The Enchanted Island
	The Enchanted Journey
	The King's Dream
	The Tale of the Kugel
	The Underground Forest
700 Tom Thumb	Katanya
705*A (Boggs) The Banished Wife or Maiden	The Exiled Princess
708 The Wonder-Child	The Wonder Child
709 Snow White	The Wonder Child
725 The Dream	The Cave of Mattathias
	The Dream Assembly
	The Lost Melody
	The Souls of Trees
	The Treasure
	The Twelve Golden Calves

Tale Type	Tale
726* The Dream Visit	The Dream Assembly
*730B Miraculous Rescue of a Jewish Community from Mob's Attack	A Flock of Angels
	The Golem
*730E Blood Libel: He Who Keepeth Israel Doth Neither Slumber nor Sleep	The Golem
*730K Rabbi Shows King, in a Mirror, His Unfaithful Wife's Doings	The Magic Mirror of Rabbi Adam
759 God's Justice Vindicated	The Blind Angel
*776 Miscellaneous Divine Rewards	The Angel of the Mishnah
	The Goat Whose Horns Reached to Heaven
	Katanya
	The Soul of the Ari
	The Spirit of Hagigah

III. Religious Tales (AT 750–849)

Tale Type	Tale
759 God's Justice Vindicated (The Angel and the Hermit)	King Solomon and Ashmodai
**771 Letters of the Hebrew Alphabet	Gathering Sparks
774A Peter Wants to Create a Man	The Golem
	The Homunuculus of Maimonides
776 Miscellaneous Divine Rewards	The Bird of Happiness
	The Enchanted Island
	Gabriel's Palace
	A New Soul
	The Soul of the Ari
**776A The Ordeal by Fire	Lighting a Fire
779 Miscellaneous Divine Rewards and Punishments	The Dream Assembly
	The Souls of Trees
**780E Justice by Supernatural Means	The Cottage of Candles
788 The Man Who Was Burned Up and Lived Again	A Kiss from the Master
**792 Impossible Tasks Imposed Because of Refusal to Desecrate the Sabbath	The Sabbath Lion
797* The Devil Tries to Pass for Jesus	The Beggar King
803 Solomon Binds the Devil in Chains in Hell	King Solomon and Ashmodai
810 The Snares of the Evil One	The Queen of Sheba
	The Werewolf
813 A Careless Word Summons the Devil	The Lost Princess
824 The Devil Lets the Man See His Wife's Unfaithfulness	The Magic Mirror of Rabbi Adam

**832A The Three Books of Wisdom	An Apple from the Tree of Life
	The Prince Who Was Made of Precious Gems
	The Tzaddik of the Forest
839*A The Hermit and the Devils	The Perfect Saint
839*C Miraculous Rescue of a Person	Drawing the Wind
841*A Letter to God	Milk and Honey

IV. Romantic Tales (AT 850–999)

881A Abandoned Bride Disguised as a Man	The Pirate Princess
888* The Faithful Wife	The Water Palace
910*M Do Not Believe a Gentile Even Forty Years After His Death	The Knife
920 The Son of the King (Solomon) and the Smith	The Prince and the Slave
922 The Shepherd Substituting for the Priest Answers the King's Questions	A Combat in Magic
	The Three Tasks of Elijah
922*C Jews Requested to Answer Questions or Perform Tasks	The Magic Wine Cup
	Summoning the Patriarchs (Introduction)
922*D Poisoning Contest	A Bowl of Soul (Introduction)
	Reb Shmelke's Whip (Introduction)
923 Love Like Salt	The Exiled Princess
926 Wisdom of Solomon	A Palace of Bird Beaks
	King Solomon and Ashmodai
926A The Clever Judge and the Demon in the Pot	The Demon of the Waters
930A The Predestined Wife	The Maiden in the Tree
	The Princess in the Tower
	The Underground Forest
930*A Fate Foretold as Punishment	The Maiden in the Tree
930*D Fated Bride's Ring in the Sea	The Magic Wine Cup
930*E Rabbi's Son Marries King's Daughter	The Exiled Princess
	The Princess in the Tower
930*G Black Slave Marries King's Daughter	The Princess and the Slave
930*H Failure of the Man Who Wants to Play God	The Maiden in the Tree
930*K Solomon's Daughter Marries a Bastard	The Princess in the Tower

Tale Type	Story
934B The Youth to Die on His Wedding Day	The Beast
	The Groom Who Was Destined to Die on His Wedding Day
934*B The Man Destined for the Jaws of a Wolf	The Beast
934E The Magic Ball of Thread	The Cottage of Candles
	The Golden Mountain
934*G Rescue of Boy Fated to Die on His Wedding Night	The Groom Who Was Destined to Die on His Wedding Day
936* The Golden Mountain	The Golden Mountain
	The Lost Princess
*955-II (Andrejev) The Woman-Robber	The Pirate Princess
975* The Exchanged Children	The Prince and the Slave
*981-I (Andrejev) Tales of Talking Birds	The Boy Israel and the Witch
	A Palace of Bird Beaks
*997 Remember Whence You Come	An Apple from the Tree of Life
	The Bird of Happiness
	The Wooden Sword

V. Tales Concerning Stupid Ogres (AT 1000–T 1199)

Tale Type	Story
1160 The Ogre in the Haunted Castle	The Speaking Head
1162* The Devil and Children	The Werewolf
1168 Various Ways of Expelling Devils	A Combat in Magic
	The Dybbuk in the Well
	The Hair in the Milk
1168A The Demon and the Mirror	Lilith's Cave
1332* Forgetfulness Causes Useless Journey	The Angel of Forgetfulness

VI. Amusing Stories and Anecdotes (AT 1200–1999)

Tale Type	Story
1476B Girl Married to a Devil	The Bride of Demons
	The Demon of the Waters
	Yona and the River Demon
1543C* The Clever Doctor	The Prince Who Thought He Was a Rooster
1645 The Treasure at Home	The Treasure
1699* The Coffin-Maker	The Haunted Violin
1736A Sword Turns to Wood	The Wooden Sword

Glossary

All the following terms are in Hebrew unless otherwise noted.

Aggadah (pl. *Aggadot*): The body of non-legal Jewish teachings, often in the form of legends; specifically those found in the Talmud and Midrash.

agunah (pl. *agunot*): A woman who is forbidden to remarry because her husband has abandoned her without a divorce or has possibly died, but without leaving proof that this has occurred.

ahizat enayim: Creating an illusion; conjuring or sleight of hand.

akedah: The binding of Isaac by Abraham on Mount Moriah (Gen. 22).

Aravot: The highest realm of heaven.

Ashmodai: The king of demons.

Avraham Aveinu: Lit., "Our father Abraham."

Azazel: A demonic figure, similar to the Devil, said to live in a desert canyon.

Bar Mitzvah: A ceremony recognizing the transition into adulthood of a thirteen-year-old Jewish boy.

bashert (Yiddish): A person's destined spouse.

Beit Din: A rabbinic court convened to decide matters of the law.

birkat ha-mazon: The blessing after meals.

b'rit: Lit., "covenant"; the circumcision given to male Jewish children on the eighth day after birth. The complete term is *b'rit milah*, or "covenant of the circumcision."

challah: Bread baked for Sabbath and holidays, which is often braided.

dybbuk: The soul of one who has died that enters the body of one who is living and remains there until exorcised.

Emet: Truth.

Gan Eden: The Garden of Eden.

Gehenna: The place where the souls of the wicked are punished and purified; the Jewish equivalent of hell.

Gemara: The core text of the Talmud, attributed to Rabbi Judah ha-Nasi.

get: A bill of divorce.

gilgul: Reincarnation; the transmigration of souls; metempsychosis.

Golem: Lit., "shapeless mass"; a creature, usually in human form, created by magical means, especially by use of the Tetragrammaton. The best-known legends are connected with the Golem created by Rabbi Judah Loew of Prague to protect the Jewish community against the blood-libel accusation.

Haggadah: Liturgical text read at the Passover seder that reflects upon the Exodus from Egypt.

Hagigah: A tractate of the Talmud that contains many episodes of a mystical nature.

Hasid (pl. *Hasidim*): Lit., "a pious one"; a follower of Hasidism, a Jewish sect founded by the Ba'al Shem Tov. Hasidim are usually followers of a charismatic religious leader, known as their rebbe.

Havdalah: Lit., "separation"; the ceremony performed at the end of the Sabbath, denoting the separation of the Sabbath from the rest of the week that follows.

Hekhalot: Lit., "palaces"; refers to the visions of the Jewish mystics of the palaces of Heaven. The texts describing these visions and the ascent into Paradise are known as Hekhalot texts.

ibbur: The spirit of a dead sage that fuses with a living person and strengthens his or her faith and wisdom; a positive kind of possession, the opposite of possession by a dybbuk.

Kabbalah: Lit., "tradition," "that which is received"; the primary system of Jewish mysticism; or, the texts setting forth that mysticism. A kabbalist is one who masters this wisdom.

Kabbalat Shabbat: Ceremony for welcoming the Sabbath Queen.

Kaddish: The prayer for the dead.

kavannah: Lit., "intention"; the spirit or intensity that is brought to prayer and other rituals, without which prayer is an empty form.

ketubah: A Jewish wedding contract.

kiddush: Blessing over wine.

kiddush levanah: Blessing of the moon.

Kotel ha-Ma'aravi (generally known as the Kotel): The Western Wall; the western retaining wall of the Temple Mount in Jerusalem, also known as the Wailing Wall.

Lag ba-Omer: Festival that falls between Passover and Shavuot.

Lamed-vav Tzaddikim: The thirty-six just men who are said to be the pillars of the world.

L'Hayim: Lit., "To life"; a traditional Jewish toast.

Lilith: Adam's first wife and later the queen of demons, the incarnation of lust, and a child-strangling witch.

maggid (pl. *maggidim*): A preacher who confines his talks to easily understood homiletics, such as the Maggid of Dubno. Also, a revelatory spirit invoked by the study of a sacred text.

Maharal: Acronym for Rabbi Judah Loew of Prague.

mashal: A parable.

matzah: Unleavened bread eaten during Passover.

menorah: A seven-branched candelabrum, described in the Bible. There is a special menorah, known as a Hanukiah, for the use of the festival of Hanukah, which has nine branches—one to be lit on each night and one to be used for the lighting of the others.

Messiah (Heb. *Mashiah*, lit., "anointed one"): The redeemer who will initiate the End of Days.

met: Dead.

Metatron: The highest angel, who was once the human Enoch; sometimes described as a "lesser Yahweh."

mezuzah (pl. *mezuzzot*): Lit., "doorpost"; a piece of parchment on which is written the prayer that begins "Shema Yisrael" (Hear, O Israel). It is affixed to the right doorpost of a Jew's home in accordance with the biblical injunction of Deuteronomy 6:9.

midrash (pl. *midrashim*): A method of exegesis of the biblical text; also refers to the body of post-biblical Jewish legends as a whole, while an individual rabbinic legend is known as a midrash.

mikveh: The ritual bath in which women immerse themselves after menstruation has ended. It is also used occasionally by men for purposes of ritual purification, and for conversions.

minhag: A local custom.

minyan: A quorum of ten men necessary to hold a prayer service.

mitzvah (pl. *mitzvot*): A commandment; one of the 613 commandments listed in the Torah. A *mitzvah* has also taken on the meaning of a good deed.

Moshe Rabeinu: Lit., "Moses our teacher."

mumser (Yiddish): Lit. "bastard"; derogatory term usually spoken in anger.

Nahash ha-Kadmoni: The primal serpent, one manifestation of the powers of evil; primarily a kabbalistic concept derived from the encounter of Eve and the serpent in Genesis.

nerot neshamah: Soul candles, lit on the *yahrzeit* (anniversary) of a person's death.

niggun: A melody, usually Hasidic, sung without words.

pilpul: The small points of the law.

Rambam: Acronym for Moses ben Maimon, or Maimonides.

reb (Yiddish): A term meaning "rabbi," used by the Hasidim to address each other.

rebbe (Yiddish): The term used for Hasidic leaders and masters; a Yiddish form of "rabbi."

Rosh ha-Shanah: The Jewish New Year, which takes place on the first day of Tishrei. Tradition says that the world was created on Rosh ha-Shanah.

Rosh Hodesh: The holiday celebrating the new moon.

Ruah ha-Kodesh: The Holy Spirit.

seder: A ritual meal served on Passover, which is accompanied by the reading of the Haggadah, which recounts the Exodus from Egypt.

sefirot: Ten emanations through which the world came into being, according to kabbalistic theory.

sendak: The person who has the honor of holding the child during the *b'rit* (circumcision) ceremony.

Shabbat: The Sabbath.

Shalom Aleikhem: Poem recited or sung on the Sabbath evening welcoming the angels. "Shalom aleikhem" is also a greeting, meaning "Peace be unto you." The traditional response is "Aleikhem shalom."

Shamir: A tiny creature in Jewish folklore that can cut through anything. King Solomon used it to capture Ashmodai, the king of demons.

shammash: Lit., "servant"; the beadle of a synagogue.

She'elat Sefer: A method of divination in which a sacred text is opened at random and a passage is pointed to, which is understood to be the reply to the question.

Shekhinah: Lit., "to dwell"; the Divine Presence, usually identified as a feminine aspect of the Divinity, which evolved into an independent mythic figure in the kabbalistic period. Also identified as the Bride of God and the Sabbath Queen.

Shema: The central prayer in Judaism from Deuteronomy 6:4–9. It is read every morning and evening.

shofar: The ram's horn that is ritually blown on the High Holy Days.

shohet: A kosher butcher.

siddur: Prayerbook.

sofer: A scribe.

shtetl: A small town with a large Jewish population in pre-Holocaust Central and Eastern Europe.

sukkah (pl. *sukkot*): A booth or hut built with its roof covered with vegetation, in which Orthodox Jews take their meals during the seven days of Sukkot.

tallit: A prayer shawl.

Talmud: The second most sacred Jewish text, after the Bible. The term "Talmud" is the comprehensive designation for the Mishnah and the Gemara as a single unit. There are Babylonian and Jerusalem Talmuds, which have different Gemaras commenting on the same Mishnah. The material in the Talmud consists of both Halakhah (law) and Aggadah (legend); in addition, there are discussions of philosophy, medicine, agriculture, astronomy, and hygiene.

Tammuz: A month of the Jewish religious calendar, corresponding very roughly to July.

Targum (pl. *Targumim*): Lit., "translation," early Jewish translations of the Bible into Aramaic.

tefillin: Phylacteries worn by men over the age of thirteen during the daily morning prayers (except Shabbat).

tekhelet: A blue dye. Even in ancient times there was uncertainty about its precise shade and how it was made. Numbers 15:38 includes an injunction for the use of *tekhelet*: *Speak to the Israelite people and instruct them to make for themselves fringes on the corners of their garments throughout the ages; let them attach a cord of blue to the fringe at each corner.*

teraphim: Idols used as household gods in biblical times. Rachel stole Laban's *teraphim* (Gen. 31:19).

Tetragrammaton: Greek for "four letters"; the four-letter ineffable Name of God: YHVH. The true pronunciation is believed to have been lost, and the knowledge of it is believed to confer great power. According to one tradition, only one great sage in each generation knows the true pronunciation of the Tetragrammaton.

tikkun: Lit. "repair"; restoration and redemption; in kabbalistic usage, of a soul, or of the cosmos.

tikkun olam: Repair of the world.

Torah: The Five Books of Moses. In a broader sense, the term refers to the whole Bible and the Oral Law. And in the broadest sense, it refers to all of Jewish culture and teaching.

tzaddik (pl. *tzaddikim*): An unusually righteous and spiritually pure person; specifically, a designation for a Hasidic rebbe.

Tzohar: Legendary jewel given to Adam and Eve as they were expelled from the Garden of Eden, and hung by Noah to illuminate the ark.

Ushpizin: Seven patriarchal figures who are said to come as guests to the sukkah during Sukkot.

yahrzeit (Yiddish): The anniversary of the death of a close relative.

Yahweh: One of the two primary biblical names of God (the other is *Elohim*).
yeshivah: School for talmudic and rabbinic studies.
Yetzer ha-Ra: The Evil Inclination.
Ziz: A giant mythical bird.
Zohar: The Book of Splendor; the primary book of Kabbalah, the body of Jewish mystical texts.

Bibliography of Original Sources

Adat Tzaddikim, edited by M. L. Frumkin (Rodkinson). Lemberg, Poland, 1864.

Admorei Chernobyl, edited by Yisrael Yakov Klapholtz. B'nai Brak, 1971.

Alpha Beta de-Ben Sira, edited by M. Steinschneider. Berlin, 1858.

Alte Yidische Zagen Oden Sippurim (Yiddish), edited by Ayzik-Meyer Dik. Vilna, 1876.

Al Tomar Noash by Yifrah Haviv. Haifa, 1966.

'Asarah Sippurei 'Am mi Bukhara by Jacob Pinhasi. Jerusalem, 1978.

'Ateret Tif'eret. Bilgorai, Poland, 1910.

Avot ha-Kadosh by Meir ben Ezekiel ibn Gabbai. Jerusalem, 1991.

Avotanu Sipru, edited by Moshe Rabi. Jerusalem, 1976.

Babylonian Talmud (Aramaic).

Be'er ha-Hasidut, edited by Eliezer Steinmann. Tel Aviv, 1960.

Beit ha-Midrash, edited by A. Jellinek. Jerusalem, 1938.

Be-Yeshishim Hokhma by Hanina Mizrahi. Haifa, 1967.

Degel Machane Ephrayim, compiled by Moses Hayim Ephraim of Sudikov. Jerusalem, 1963.

Der Dibek by S. Ansky. Written in 1914, first performed in 1920.

Der Golem: Jüdischer Märchen und Legenden aus dem alten Prag (German), edited by Eduard Petiska. Wiesbaden, 1972.

Dos Bukh fun Nisyoynes (Yiddish), edited by Israel Osman. Los Angeles, 1926.

Eder ha-Yekar in *Samuel Abba Horodezky Jubilee Volume*, edited by Zalman Rubashov (Shazar). Tel Aviv, 1947.

Edot Mesaprot, edited by Avraham Shatal. Jerusalem, 1969.

Em la-Binah, edited by Yekutiel Kamelhar. Lemberg, 1909.

Emek ha-Melekh by Naftali Hirsh ben Elhanan. Amsterdam, 1653.

Eretz ha-Hayim, edited by Hayim Liebersohn. Przemysl, Poland, 1926.

Esser Kedoshot by Y. Y. Berger. Piotrkov, 1910.

Froyen-rebbeyim un berihmte perzhenlikkeyten in poylen (Yiddish). Warsaw, 1937.

Hadre Teman, edited by Nissim Binyamin Gamlieli. Tel Aviv, 1978.

Hag La'am, edited by Eliezer Marcus. Jerusalem, 1990.

Ha-Glima shel Mullah Avraham by Moshe Nehmad. Haifa, 1966.

Ha-Ilan she-Safag Dema'ot, collected by Ya'akov Avitsuk, edited by Dov Noy. Haifa, 1965.

Ha-Havtakha she Nitkayma by Rachel Seri. Haifa, 1968.

Ha-Kamea ha-Kadosh, edited by Aliza Shenhar. Haifa, 1968.

Ha-Na'al ha-Ktanah, edited by Asher Barash. Tel Aviv, 1966.
Ha-na'ara ha-Yefefiya u-Sheloshet Benei ha-Melekh, edited by Dov Noy. Tel Aviv, 1965.
Hayay Moharan, Lemberg, 1874.
Hibbur Yafe min ha-Yeshua by Nissim ben Ya'akov ibn Shahin. In *Otzar Midrashim,* edited by Y. D. Eisenstein. New York, 1915.
Hibbur Yafe min ha-Yeshua, edited by H. Z. Hirschberg. Jerusalem, 1970.
Hiyo Haya Ma'aseh, edited by H. B. Ilan-Bernik. Tel Aviv, 1945.
Hodesh Hodesh ve-Sippuro 1961, edited by Dov Noy. Haifa, 1962.
Hodesh Hodesh ve-Sippuro 1968–1969, edited by Edna Cheichel. Haifa, 1969.
Hodesh Hodesh ve-Sippuro: 1974–1975, edited by Dov Noy. Haifa, 1975.
Iggeret Sod ha-Ge'ullah by Abraham ben Eliezer ha-Levi. Jerusalem, 1519.
Jerusalem Talmud.
Kav ha-Yashar by Tsvi Hirsh Kaidanover. Frankfurt, 1903.
Kehal Hasidim, compiled by Aharon Valden. Warsaw, no date.
Kehillot Yehudei Kurdistan, edited by Abraham Ben-Jacob. Jerusalem, 1961.
Keter Shem Tov by Aaron of Apt. Zolkiev, 1784.
Kibud Em by Malka Guter. Haifa, 1969.
Knesset Israel, edited by Reuven Zak. Warsaw, 1886.
Le Bestiaire du ghetto: Folklore tunisien (French), edited by J. Vehel and Ryvel (Raphael Levy). Tunis, 1934.
Likkute Ma'asiyot, edited by Yisrael ben Sasson. Jerusalem, 1909.
Livnat ha-Sappir, edited by Joseph Angelino. Jerusalem, 1913.
Ma'aseh Buch (Yiddish), no. 247, compiled by Jacob ben Abraham of Mezhirech. Basel, 1601.
Ma'aseh me-ha-Hayyat (Yiddish). Vilna, 1908.
Ma'aseh Nissim, edited by S. B. Huzin. Baghdad, 1890.
Ma'aseh Nissim (Yiddish), edited by Jeptha Yozpa ben Naftali of Worms. Amsterdam, 1696.
Ma'aseh Ta'atulim, edited by S. Rubin. Vienna, 1887.
Ma'aseh Yerushalmi, edited by Yehuda L. Zlotnik. Jerusalem, 1946.
Ma'asiyot me-Tzaddik Yesode 'Olam, edited by Lazar Schenkel. Podgaitsy, Russia, 1903.
Ma'asiyot U'Meshalim, in *Kokhavei Or,* edited by Rabbi Abraham ben Nachman of Tulchin. Jerusalem, 1896.
Ma'aysiot ve'shichot Tzaddikim. Warsaw, 1881.
Ma'assiyot me-Tzaddik Yesode 'Olam. Podgaitsy, Russia, 1903.
Ma'assiyot Noraim ve-Niflaim. Cracow, 1896.
Maggid Mesharim by Joseph Karo. Amsterdam, 1704.
Mekhilta de-Rabbi Ishmael, edited by J. Z. Lauterbach. Philadelphia, 1933–1935. 3 volumes.
Menorat ha-Ma'or by Yitzhak Abohav. Mantua, 1573.
Me-Otsar Genazai by Hayim Dov Armon Kastenbaum, edited by Alter Ze'ev Wortheim. Tel Aviv, 1932.
Meshal ha-Kadmoni by Isaac Ibn Sahula, edited by Yisrael Zemora. Tel Aviv, 1952.
Michtav Mi-Rebbe Nachman by Rabbi Yisrael Ber Odesser. Jerusalem, 1984.
Midrash Aseret ha-Dibrot, edited by A. Shapira. Jerusalem, 2005.
Midrash Konen, in *Otzar Midrashim,* edited by Y. D. Eisenstein. Jerusalem, 1969.

Midrash Mishlei, edited by Solomon Buber. Vilna, 1893.
Midrash Pinhas by Pinhas of Koretz. Warsaw, 1876.
Midrash Ribesh Tov, edited by Lipot Abraham. Kecskemet, Hungary, 1927.
Midrash Tanhuma, edited by Solomon Buber. Vilna, 1891.
Min ha-Mabu'a by Eliezer Marcus. Haifa, 1966.
Mora'im Gedolim, edited by Y. S. Farhi. Warsaw, 1909.
Nifla'ot Maharal, edited by Yudel Rosenberg. Piotrkow, 1909.
Nifla'ot ha-Tzaddikim. Piotrkow, 1911.
Nishmat Hayim by Menashe ben Israel. Amsterdam, 1650.
Noraot Anshe Ma'aseh. Warsaw, no date.
Nozat ha-Zahav, edited by Moshe Attias. Haifa, 1976.
Ohel Elimelech, edited by A. S. B. Michelson. Parmishla, 1870.
Ohel Shem. Bilgorai, 1910.
Or ha-Hokhmah by Uri Feivel ben Aaron. Korzec, 1795.
Oseh Pele, edited by J. S. Farhi. 3 vols. Livorno, 1902.
Otzar ha-Ma'asiyot, edited by Reuven ben Yakov Na'anah. 3 vols. Jerusalem, 1961.
Otzar Midrashim, edited by Y. D. Eisenstein. New York, 1915.
Pe'er Layesharim. Jerusalem, 1881.
Pe'er Mi-kedoshim. Lemberg, Russia, 1864.
Petirat Rabbenu ha-Kadosh mi-Belz. Lemberg, 1894.
Pesikta de-Rav Kahana, edited by Solomon Buber. Lyck, 1860.
Pirke de-Rabbi Eliezer. Venice, 1544.
Revue des Etudes Juives, vol. 35. Paris, 1897.
Rosinkess mit Mandlen: Aus der Volksliterature der Ostjuden (Yiddish), edited by Immanuel Olsvanger. 2nd ed. Basel, 1931.
Savta Esther Mesaperet by Esther Weinstein. Haifa, 1964.
Sefer ha-Ma'asiyot, edited by Mordecai ben Yehezkel. 6 vols. Tel Aviv, 1929.
Sefer Hasidim by Rabbi Judah the Pious, edited by Yehuda Wistynezki. Berlin, 1891.
Sefer Hezyonot by Rabbi Hayim Vital. Jerusalem, 1914.
Sefer Ma'aseh Nissim, edited by Pinhas David Braverman. Jerusalem, 1966.
Sefer Ma'or ve-Shemesh by Yehuda ben Avraham Koriat. Livorno, 1839.
Sefer Or Yesharim, edited by Moshe Hayim Kleinmann. Warsaw, 1884.
Sefer Peri Etz Hayim by Haim Vital. Saloniki, 1793.
Sefer Segulat Moshe by Moshe ben Naftali Hertz Hoffstein. Spring Valley, N.Y., 1974.
Sefer Sippure Kedushim, edited by Gedalyah Nigal. Jerusalem, 1977.
Sefer Toledot ha-Ari, edited by Meir Benayahu. Jerusalem, 1987.
Shalshelet ha-Kabbalah by Gedalyah ibn Yachya. Venice, 1587.
Sha'arei Kedushah by Hayim Vital. Aleppo, 1866.
Sheva Havilot Zahav by Dvora Fus, edited by Otto Schnitzler. Haifa, 1969.
Sheva Sippurei 'Am by Miriam Yeshiva. Haifa, 1963.
Sheva Sippurei 'Am mi-Borislaw by F. Sider. Haifa, 1968.
Shishim Sippurei Am, edited by Zalman Baharav. Haifa, 1964.
Shivhei ha-Ari by Shlomo Meinsterl. Jerusalem, 1905.
Shivhei ha-Besht by Rabbi Dov Baer ben Samuel, edited by Samuel A. Horodezky. Berlin, 1922.
Shiv'im Sippurim ve-Sippur, edited by Dov Noy. Jerusalem, 1964.

Shiv'im Sippurim ve-Sipur mi-Pi Yehudei Luv, edited by Dov Noy. Jerusalem, 1967.
Shomrim Ne'emanim by Zvi M. Haimovits, edited by Dov Noy. Haifa, 1976.
Sihot Hayim. Piotrkow, 1904.
Sihot Moharan, in *Hayey Moharan* by Rabbi Nathan of Bratslav. Lemberg, 1874.
Sihot Tzaddikim. Warsaw, 1921.
Sippur Rabbi Yosef della Reina by Shlomo Navarro. Safed, Warsaw, 1905.
Sippurei Am mi-Sanok, collected by Samuel Zanvel Pipe, edited by Dov Noy. Haifa, 1967.
Sippurei 'Am Yehudim me Hungariah, edited by G. Bribram. Haifa, 1965.
Sippurei Am, Romanssot, ve-Orehot-hayim shel Yehudei Sefarad by Max Grunwald, edited by Dov Noy. Jerusalem: Folklore Research Center, 1982.
Sippurei Dibuk b'Sifrut Yisrael, edited by Gedalyah Nigal. Jerusalem, 1983.
Sippurei Emunah ve-Musar by A. Stahl. Haifa, 1976.
Sippurei Hasidim, edited by Shlomo Yosef Zevin. Tel Aviv, 1964.
Sippurei Ma'asiyot by Reb Nachman of Bratslav. Ostrog, Russia, 1816.
Sippurei Ma'aysiot Hadashim. Warsaw, 1909.
Sippurei Tzaddikim. Cracow, 1886.
Sippurei Ya'akov, edited by Yakov Sofer. Dobromil, 1864.
Sippurim: Eine Sammlung Jüdischer Sagen, Märchen und Geschichten für Völkerkunde, edited by Wolf Pascheles. Prague, 1847.
Sippurim Hadashim by Rabbi Nathan of Bratslav, edited by Nachman Goldstein of Techerin. Lemberg, 1874.
Sippurim mi-Pi Yehude Kurdistan, edited by Dov Noy. Jerusalem, 1966.
Sippurim Mi-she-kvar, edited by Aliza Shenhar. Haifa, 1986.
Sippurim Niflaim, edited by Samuel Horowitz. Jerusalem, 1935.
Sippurim: Prager Sammulung Jüdischer Legenden in Neuer Auswahl und Bearbeitung, edited by Wolf Pascheles. Vienna and Leipzig, 1921.
Tarat, Tarat: Sipurei Am mi-Pi Yehudei Etiopia, edited by Tamar Alexander and Amla Einat. Tel Aviv, 1996.
Toledot Aharon, compiled by Aaron of Zhitomir. Lemberg, 1864.
Toledot Rabbenu Hayim ben Attar, edited by Reuven Margarliot. Lemberg, 1904.
Tsava'at Av by Yehoshua Ben Zion. Haifa, 1969.
Tzefunot ve-Aggadot by Micha Joseph Bin Gorion (Berditchevsky). Tel Aviv, 1957.
Vayehi ha-Yom by Hayim Nachman Bialik. Tel Aviv, 1934.
Yalkut Shimoni, edited by Shimon Ashkenazi. Frankfurt, 1687.
Yiddishe Folkmayses (Yiddish), edited by Y. L. Cahan. Vilna, 1931.
Yiddisher Folklor (Yiddish), edited by Y. L. Cahan. Vilna, 1938.
Zikaron Tov. Piotrkow, 1892.
Zohar (*Sefer ha-Zohar*). Vilna, 1894.
Zohar Hadash. Amsterdam, 1701.

ISRAEL FOLKTALE ARCHIVES (IFA) LIST

IFA 107, collected by Heda Yazon from Yeffet Shvili of Yemen.
IFA 280, collected by Zvi Moshe Haimovitch from Josef Shmuli of Basra, Iraq.

IFA 532, told by Dov Noy of Poland.
IFA 612, collected by S. Arnst of Israel.
IFA 708, told by Dvora Fus from the shtetl of Lewdow near Vilna, Lithuania.
IFA 779, collected by Devora Fus from her mother, Esther Lipkind, of the shtetl of Lewdow, near Vilna, Lithuania.
IFA 966, recorded by Nehamah Zion from Miriam Tschernobilski of Israel.
IFA 1071, collected by Issachar Ben Ami from Friha Susan of Morocco.
IFA 1892, collected by S. Arnst of Israel.
IFA 2030, collected by Dvora Fus, from her parents, Kalman and Esther Lipkind.
IFA 2558, told by Azriel Zaid of Romania.
IFA 2607, collected by Reuven Na'ana from an unknown Israeli Sefaradi from Turkey.
IFA 2675, recorded by Zvi Moshe Haimovitch from Shaul Ephraim of Egypt.
IFA 3145, collected by Zevulun Kort from Eliyahu Yarkone of Afghanistan.
IFA 3911, collected by Jacob Avitsuk from Shlomo Alozh.
IFA 4563, collected by Zalman Baharav from Yakov Chaprak.
IFA 4859, told by Esther Mikhael of Iraqi Kurdistan to her granddaughter, Esther.
IFA 5842, collected by Rachel Seri from her mother, Yona Seri of Yemen.
IFA 6057, collected by Zalman Baharav from David Hadad of Libya.
IFA 6405, collected by Ilana Zohar from her mother, Flora Cohen of Egypt.
IFA 6414, collected by Yakov Laseri from his father, Machlouf Laseri.
IFA 6432, collected by A. Rabi from Avner Azolai of Morocco.
IFA 6602, collected by Zvi Chaimovitz from Zion Sayda of Iraq.
IFA 6628, collected by Moshe Rabi from Avraham Etia.
IFA 7198, collected by Amnon Shiloach from Abraham Massalton of Syria.
IFA 7248, from *Sippurei Am Misanuk*, collected by Samuel Zanvel Pipe.
IFA 7830, collected by Zevulon Kort from Ben Zion Asherov.
IFA 8129, collected by Lili David from Rachel ha-Rambam of Persia.
IFA 8133, collected by Ilana Zohar from her mother, Flora Cohen of Egypt.
IFA 8140, collected by Yifrah Haviv from Moshe Aharon of Bukhara.
IFA 8161, collected by Zvi Haimovitz from Yitzhak Sasson of India.
IFA 8335, collected by Moshe Rabi from Hannah Haddad.
IFA 8831, collected by Ronit Bronstein from Moni Tivoni of Egypt.
IFA 8900, collected by Moses Gad from Sarah Gad of Turkey.
IFA 8902, collected by Dvorah Dadon-Vilek from her mother Heftziba Dabon from Morocco.
IFA 9586, collected by Haya ben-Avraham from Daniel Sigauker of India.
IFA 9669, collected by Ephraim Haddad from Shimon Swissa.
IFA 10125, collected by Ofra Elias from her mother Rachel Elias.
IFA 11165, collected by Avraham Keren from Yitzhak Isadore Feierstein of Poland.

IFA 11306, collected by Nissim Binyamin Gamlieli from Yehoshua ben Yoseph David of Morocco.
IFA 12353, told by Nissim Malka of Morocco.
IFA 13479 and IFA 13480, collected by Dvora Vilet from Juliet Ya'akovlaba, who heard the stories from her mother, Ada Kavka, born in Baku, Caucas.

Selected English Bibliography

Aarne, Antti, and Stith Thompson, eds. *The Types of the Folktale: A Classification and Bibliography.* 2nd rev. ed. Helsinki: Suomalaisen Thedeakatemia, 1961.
Abelson, Joshua. *The Immanence of God in Rabbinical Literature.* New York: Macmillan, 1912.
———. *Jewish Mysticism: An Introduction to the Kabbalah.* New York: Hermon, 1981.
Abrahams, Israel. *The Book of Delight and Other Papers.* New York: Jewish Publication Society, 1912.
———. *Jewish Life in the Middle Ages.* Philadelphia: Jewish Publication Society, 1896.
Agnon, S. Y., ed. *Days of Awe.* New York: Schocken, 1948.
———, ed. *Present at Sinai: The Giving of the Law.* Philadelphia: Jewish Publication Society, 1994.
———. *Twenty-one Stories.* New York: Schocken, 1970.
Alexander, Philip. "The Talmudic Concept of Conjuring ('*Ahizat Einayim*') and the Problem of the Definition of Magic (*Kishuf*)." In *Creation and Re-Creation in Jewish Thought,* edited by Rachel Elior and Peter Schafer (7–26). Tubingen: Mohr Siebeck, 2005.
Alexander, Tamar. "Folktales in Sefer Hasidim." *Prooftexts* 5 (1985): 19–31.
———. "Saint and Sage: The 'Ari' and Maimonides in Folktales." *Jerusalem Studies in Hebrew Literature* 13 (1992): 29–64.
———. "Theme and Genre: Relationships between Man and She-demon in Jewish Folklore." *Jewish Folklore and Ethnology Review* 14 (1992): 56–61.
Alexander, Tamar, and Elena Romano, eds. *Once Upon a Time—Maimonides: Traditional Hebrew Tales.* Lancaster, Cal.: Labyrinthos, 2004.
Alexander-Frizer, Tamar. *The Heart Is a Mirror: The Sephardic Folktale.* Detroit, Mich.: Wayne State University Press, 2007.
Alter, Robert, and Frank Kermode. *The Literary Guide to the Bible.* Cambridge: Harvard University Press, 1987.
Anderson, George K. *The Legend of the Wandering Jew.* Providence, R.I.: Brown University Press, 1965.
Ansky, S. *The Dybbuk and Other Writings,* edited by David G. Roskies. New York: Schocken, 1992.
Applefeld, Aharon, ed. *From the World of Rabbi Nahman of Bratslav.* Jerusalem: World Zionist Organization, 1973.

Aptowitzer, Victor. "Asenath, the Wife of Joseph: A Haggadic Literary-Historical Study." *Hebrew Union College Annual* 1 (1924): 239–306.

Ariel, David S. *The Mystic Quest: An Introduction to Jewish Mysticism.* Northvale, N.J.: J. Aronson, 1988.

Aron, Milton. *Ideas and Ideals of the Hassidim.* New York: Citadel, 1980.

Aryeh, Isaiah, and Joshua Dvorkes, eds. *The Baal Shem Tov on Pirkey Avoth.* Jerusalem: Jewish Academy Publications, 1974.

Ausubel, Nathan, ed. A *Treasury of Jewish Folklore.* New York: Crown, 1948.

Bader, Gershom. *The Encyclopedia of Talmudic Sages.* Northvale, N.J.: J. Aronson, 1988.

Baer, Yitzhak. A *History of the Jews in Christian Spain.* 2 vols. Philadelphia: Jewish Publication Society, 1961.

Bakan, David. *Sigmund Freud and the Jewish Mystical Tradition.* Princeton, N.J.: Van Nostrand, 1958.

Bamberger, Bernard J. *Fallen Angels.* Philadelphia: Jewish Publication Society, 1952.

Band, Arnold J., trans. *Nahman of Bratslav: The Tales.* New York: Paulist Press, 1978.

Barash, Asher. A *Golden Treasury of Jewish Tales.* Tel Aviv: Massadah–P.E.C. Press, 1965.

Baring-Gould, Sabine. *Curious Myths of the Middle Ages.* Mineola, N.Y.: Dover, 2005.

Bar-Itzhak, Haya. *Jewish Poland: Legends of Origin: Ethnopoetics and Legendary Chronicles.* Detroit, Mich.: Wayne State University Press, 2001.

Bar-Itzhak, Haya, and Aliza Shenhar. *Jewish Moroccan Folk Narratives from Israel.* Detroit, Mich.: Wayne State University Press, 1993.

Baron, Salo, W. "Medieval Folklore and Jewish Fate." *Jewish Heritage* 6:4 (1964): 13–18.

———. *A Social and Religious History of the Jews.* 2nd ed. 17 vols. New York: Columbia University Press, 1952–1983.

Bazak, Joseph. *Judaism and Psychical Phenomena.* New York: Garrett, 1967.

Beer, M. "Regarding the Sources of the Number of the 36 Zaddiqim." *Annual of Bar-Ilan University, Studies in Judaica and the Humanities* 1 (1963): 172–176.

Ben Zion, Raphael. *The Way of the Faithful: An Anthology of Jewish Mysticism.* Los Angeles: Haynes, 1945.

Ben-Ami, Issachar. *Saint Veneration among the Jews in Morocco.* Detroit, Mich.: Wayne State University Press, 1998.

Ben-Ami, Issachar, and Joseph Dan, eds. *Studies in Aggadah and Jewish Folklore.* Jerusalem: Folklore Research Center, 1983.

Ben-Amos, Dan. "Jewish Folk Literature." *Oral Tradition* 14:1 (1999): 140–274.

———. "Jewish Folklore Studies." *Modern Judaism* 11:1 (1991): 11–66.

———. "On Demons." In *Creation and Re-Creation in Jewish Thought,* edited by Rachel Elior and Peter Schafer (27–37). Tubingen: Mohr Siebeck, 2005.

———. "Talmudic Tall Tales." In *Folklore Today: A Festschrift for Richard M. Dorson,* edited by L. Degh, H. Glassie, and F. J. Oinas (25–44). Bloomington: Indiana University Press, 1976.

Ben-Amos, Dan, ed., and Dov Noy, consulting ed. *Folktales of the Jews: Tales from the Sephardic Dispersion.* Vol. 1. Philadelphia: Jewish Publication Society, 2006.

———. *Folktales of the Jews: Tales from Eastern Europe.* Vol. 2. Philadelphia: Jewish Publication Society, 2007.

Ben-Amos, Dan, and Jerome Mintz, trans. and eds. *In Praise of the Baal Shem Tov [Shivhei ha-Besht]: The Earliest Collection of Legends about the Founder of Hasidism.* Bloomington: Indiana University Press, 1970.

Ben-Sasson, H. H., ed. A *History of the Jewish People.* Cambridge: Harvard University Press, 1976.

Ben-Zvi, Itzhak. *The Exiled and the Redeemed.* Philadelphia: Jewish Publication Society, 1957.

Bension, Ariel. *The Zohar in Moslem and Christian Spain.* New York: Hermon, 1974.

Berger, Abraham. "The Literature of Jewish Folklore." *Journal of Jewish Bibliography* 1 (1938–1939): 12–20, 40–49.

Bergman, Simcha, trans. *Likutey Moharan by Reb Nachman of Breslov.* 11 vols. Jerusalem: Breslov Research Institute, 1986–1990.

Bettan, Israel. *Studies in Jewish Preaching.* New York: Hebrew Union College Press, 1948.

Bettelheim, Bruno. *The Uses of Enchantment: The Meaning and Importance of Fairy Tales.* New York: Knopf, 1976.

Bialik, Hayim Nachman. *And It Came to Pass: Legends and Stories about King David and King Solomon.* New York: Hebrew Publishing, 1938.

Bialik, Hayim Nahman, and Yehoshua Hana Ravnitzky. *The Book of Legends, Sefer ha- Aggadah: Legends from the Talmud and Midrash.* New York: Schocken, 1992.

Bilu, Yoram. "Dybbuk and Maggid: Two Cultural Patterns of Altered Consciousness in Judaism." *AJS Review* 21:2 (1996): 341–366.

———. "The Moroccan Demon in Israel: The Case of 'Evil Spirit Disease.'" *Ethos* (1980): 24–39.

———. "The Taming of the Deviants and Beyond: An Analysis of *Dybbuk* Possession and Exorcism in Judaism." In *Spirit Possession in Judaism,* edited by Matt Goldish (41–72). Detroit, Mich.: Wayne State University Press, 2003.

———. *Without Bounds: The Life and Death of Rabbi Ya'aqov Wazana.* Detroit, Mich.: Wayne State University Press, 2000.

Bin Gorion, Micha Joseph (Berditchevsky). *Mimekor Yisrael: Classical Jewish Folktales.* 3 vols. Bloomington: Indiana University Press, 1976. Abridged and annotated ed., prepared by Dan Ben-Amos, Bloomington: Indiana University Press, 1990.

Birnbaum, Salomo. *The Life and Sayings of the Baal Shem.* New York: Hebrew Publishing, 1933.

Bloch, Abraham P. *The Biblical and Historical Background of the Jewish Holy Days.* New York: Ktav, 1978.

Bloch, Chayim. *The Golem: Legends of the Ghetto of Prague.* New York: Rudolf Steiner Publications, 1972.

———. "Legends of the Ari." *Menorah Journal* 14 (1928): 371–384, 466–477.

Bokser, Ben Zion, trans. *Abraham Isaac Kook: The Lights of Penitence, the Moral Principles, Lights of Holiness, Essays, Letters and Poems.* New York: Paulist Press, 1978.

———. *From the World of the Cabbalah.* New York: Philosophical Library, 1954.

———. *The Jewish Mystical Tradition.* Northvale, N.J.: J. Aronson, 1981.

———. *The Talmud: Selected Writings.* New York: Paulist Press, 1989.

Braude, William G., trans. *The Midrash on Psalms (Midrash Tehillim).* 2 vols. New Haven: Yale University Press, 1959.

———. *Pesikta Rabbati: Discourses for Feasts, Fasts and Special Sabbaths.* 2 vols. New Haven: Yale University Press, 1968.

Braude, William G., and Israel J. Kapstein, trans. *Pesikta de-Rab Kahana: R. Kahana's Compilation of Discourses for Sabbaths and Festal Days.* Philadelphia: Jewish Publication Society, 1975.

———. *Tanna Debe Eliyyahu: The Lore of the School of Elijah.* Philadelphia: Jewish Publication Society, 1981.

Brauer, Erich. *The Jews of Kurdistan,* edited by Raphael Patai. Detroit, Mich.: Wayne State University Press, 1993.

Bregman, Marc. "The Darshan: Preacher and Teacher of Talmudic Times." *Melton Journal* 4 (1982): 3, 19, 26.

———. "Joseph Heinneman's Studies on the Aggadah." *Immanuel* 9 (1979): 58–62.

———. "Past and Present in Midrashic Literature." *Hebrew Annual Review* 2 (1978): 45–59.

Breslauer, S. Daniel. *Martin Buber on Myth: An Introduction.* New York: Garland, 1990.

Brinner, William M., trans. and ed. *An Elegant Composition Concerning Relief after Adversity by Nissim ben Jacob ibn Shahin.* New Haven: Yale University Press, 1977.

Broznick, Norman M. "Some Aspects of German Mysticism as Reflected in the *Sefer Hasidim.*" M.A. thesis, Columbia University, 1947.

Buber, Martin. *Hasidism and Modern Man.* New York: Horizon, 1958.

———. *The Legend of the Baal-Shem.* New York: Schocken, 1969.

———. *The Origin and Meaning of Hasidism.* New York: Horizon, 1960.

———. *Tales of Angels, Spirits and Demons.* New York: Hawk's Well Press, 1958.

———. *The Tales of Reb Nachman.* New York: Horizon, 1956.

———. *Tales of the Hasidim: Early Masters.* New York: Schocken, 1947.

———. *Tales of the Hasidim: Later Masters.* New York: Schocken, 1948.

———. *The Way of Man: According to the Teaching of Hasidism.* London: Routledge, 2002.

Burchchard, C. "Joseph and Asenath." In *The Old Testament Pseudepigrapha* 2, edited by James H. Charlesworth (177–247). Garden City, N.Y.: Doubleday, 1985.

Burton, Richard F., trans. *The Book of the Thousand Nights and Night.* 10 vols. London: Burton Club, 1885.

———. *Supplement to the Book of the Thousand Nights and a Night.* 6 vols. London: Burton Club, 1886–1888.

Bushnaq, Inea. *Arab Folktales.* New York: Pantheon Books, 1986.

Buxbaum, Yitzhak. *Jewish Spiritual Practices.* Northvale, N.J.: J. Aronson, 1990.
———. *Jewish Tales of Holy Wisdom.* San Francisco: Jossey-Bass, 2002.
———. *Jewish Tales of Mystic Joy.* San Francisco: Jossey-Bass, 2002.
———. *The Light and Fire of the Baal Shem Tov.* New York: Continuum, 2006.
———. *Storytelling and Spirituality in Judaism.* Northvale, N.J.: J. Aronson, 1994.
Campbell, Joseph. *The Hero with a Thousand Faces.* Princeton: Princeton University Press, 1975.
———. *The Masks of God: Occidental Mythology.* New York: Penguin, 1964.
———, ed. *Myths, Dreams, and Religion.* Dallas: Spring Publications, 1988.
Canaan, Taufik. *Haunted Springs and Water Demons in Palestine.* Jerusalem: Palestine Oriental Society, 1922.
Carlebach, Shlomo. *Lamed Vav: A Collection of the Favorite Stories of Rabbi Shlomo Carlebach,* compiled by Tzlotana Barbara Midlo. Jerusalem: Israel Bookshop, 2004.
Chabon, Michael. *The Amazing Adventures of Kavalier & Clay.* New York: Picador USA, 2000.
Chajes, J. H. *Between Worlds: Dybbuks, Exorcists, and Early Modern Judaism.* Philadelphia: University of Pennsylvania Press, 2003.
Charles, R. H., ed. *The Apocrypha and Pseudepigrapha of the Old Testament.* 2 vols. Oxford: Clarendon, 1913.
Charlesworth, James H., ed. *The Old Testament Pseudepigrapha.* 2 vols. Garden City, N.Y.: Doubleday, 1983–1985.
Cohen, A. *Everyman's Talmud.* New York: Schocken, 1975.
Cohen, Arthur A., and Paul Mendes-Flohr, eds. *Contemporary Jewish Religious Thought.* New York: Scribner, 1987.
Coleridge, Samuel Taylor. *Selected Poetry and Prose,* edited by Elisabeth Schneider. 2nd ed. New York: Holt, Rinehart and Winston, 1951.
Covitz, Joel. *Visions of the Night: A Study of Jewish Dream Interpretation.* Boston: Shambhala, 1990.
Crews, Cynthia. "Judeo-Spanish Folktales in Macedonia." *Folklore* 43 (1932): 193–224.
Daiches, Samuel. *Babylonian Oil Magic in the Talmud and in the Later Jewish Literature.* London: H. Hart, 1913.
Dan, Joseph. "The Beginnings of Jewish Mysticism in Europe." In Cecil Roth, ed., *The Dark Ages: Jews in Christian Europe* 711–1096. New Brunswick: Rutgers University Press, 1966, 2: 282–290.
———. *Binah: Studies in Jewish History.* 2 vols. New York: Praeger, 1985, 1989.
———. "The Desert in Jewish Mysticism: The Kingdom of Samael." *Ariel* 40 (1976): 38–43.
———. *The Early Kabbalah.* New York: Paulist Press, 1986.
———. "Five Versions of the Story of the Jerusalemite." *Proceedings of the American Academy for Jewish Research* 35 (1967): 99–111.
———. *Gershom Scholem and the Mystical Dimension of Jewish History.* New York: New York University Press, 1988.
———. "Samael, Lilith and the Concept of Evil in Early Kabbalah." *AJS Review* 5 (1980): 17–40.

———. *The Teachings of Hasidism.* New York: Behrman, 1983.

———. *Terafim: From Popular Belief to a Folktale.* In *Studies in Hebrew Narrative Art through the Ages,* edited by Joseph Heinemann and Shmuel Werses. *Scripta Hierosolymitana* 27 (1978): 99–106. Jerusalem: Magnes Press, 1978.

———. *Three Types of Ancient Jewish Mysticism.* Cincinnati: University of Cincinnati, 1984.

Dan, Joseph, and Frank Talmage, eds. *Studies in Jewish Mysticism.* Cambridge, Mass.: Association for Jewish Studies, 1982.

Danby, Herbert. *The Mishnah.* Oxford: Oxford University Press, 1933.

David, A. "R. Gedalya ibn Yahya's *Shalshelet Hakabbalah* ('Chain of Tradition'): A Chapter in Medieval Jewish Historiography." *Immanuel* 15 (1981–1982): 85–96.

Davidson, Gustav. *A Dictionary of Angels.* New York: Free Press, 1967.

Davidson, Isadore, trans. *Sepher Shaashim: A Book of Mediaeval Lore by Joseph ben Meir ibn Zabara.* New York: Jewish Theological Seminary, 1914.

De Lange, Nicholas. *Apocrypha: Jewish Literature of the Hellenistic Age.* New York: Viking, 1978.

Delumeau, Jean. *History of Paradise: The Garden of Eden in Myth and Tradition,* translated by Matthew O'Connell. New York: Continuum, 1995.

Dever, William G. *Did God Have a Wife? Archaeology and Folk Religion in Ancient Israel.* Grand Rapids, Mich.: Eerdmans, 2005.

Dobh Baer of Lubavitch. *On Ecstasy.* Chappaqua, N.Y.: Rossel Books, 1963.

Dorfman, Yitzchak. *The Maggid of Mezritch.* Southfield, Mich.: Targum, 1989.

Dresner, Samuel H. *Levi Yitzhak of Berditchev: Portrait of a Hasidic Master.* New York: Shapolsky, 1986.

———. *The Zaddik: The Doctrine of the Zaddik According to the Writings of Rabbi Yaakov Yosef of Polnoy.* New York: Abelard-Schuman, 1974.

Duling, D. C. "Testament of Solomon." In *The Old Testament Pseudepigrapha,* edited by J. H. Charlesworth (1: 977–982). Garden City, N.Y.: Doubleday, 1983.

Eberhard, Wolfram. *Folktales of China.* Chicago: University of Chicago Press, 1965.

Einhorn, David. *The Seventh Candle and Other Folk Tales of Eastern Europe.* New York: Ktav, 1968.

Ekstein, Rudolf. "Dreams and Fairy Tales." *Dreamworks* 4 (1984): 130–136.

Elbaz, Andre E. *Folktales of the Canadian Sephardim.* Toronto: Fitzhenry & Whitehead, 1982.

Eliach, Yaffa, ed. *Hasidic Tales of the Holocaust.* New York: Oxford University Press, 1982.

Elior, Rachel and Peter Schafter, eds. *Creation and Re-Creation in Jewish Thought: Festschrift in Honor of Joseph Dan.* Tubingen: Paul Mohr, 2005.

Epstein, I., ed. *The Babylonian Talmud.* 18 vols. London: Soncino, 1935–1952.

Epstein, M. *Tales of Sendebar.* Philadelphia: Jewish Publication Society, 1967.

Fine, Lawrence. "Benevolent Spirit Possession in Sixteenth-Century Safed." In *Spirit Possession in Judaism*, edited by Matt Goldish (101–123). Detroit, Mich.: Wayne State University Press, 2003.

———. *Physician of the Soul, Healer of the Cosmos: Isaac Luria and His Kabbalistic Fellowship*. Palo Alto: Stanford University Press, 2003.

———. *Safed Spirituality: Rules of Mystical Piety: The Beginning of Wisdom.* New York: Paulist Press, 1984.

Finkel, Avraham Yaakov, trans. *Ein Yaakov: The Ethical and Inspirational Teachings of the Talmud.* Northvale, N.J.: J. Aronson, 1999.

———. *Sefer Chasidim: The Book of the Pious.* Northvale, N.J.: J. Aronson, 1997.

Finkelstein, Louis. *The Jews: Their History, Culture, and Religion.* 3rd ed. 2 vols. New York: Harper, 1960.

Fishbane, Michael. *Biblical Interpretation in Ancient Israel.* Oxford: Clarendon, 1985.

———. *The Garments of Torah: Essays in Biblical Hermeneutics.* Bloomington: Indiana University Press, 1989.

Fleer, Gedaliah. *Reb Nachman's Fire: An Introduction to Breslover Chassidus.* New York: Ohn MiBreslov, 1975.

———. *Reb Nachman's Foundation.* New York: Ohn MiBreslov, 1976.

Forbes, T. R. *The Midwife and the Witch.* New Haven: Yale University Press, 1966.

Fox, Samuel J. *Hell in Jewish Literature.* Northbrook, Ill.: Whitehall, 1972.

Franck, Adolphe. *The Kabbalah: The Religious Philosophy of the Hebrews.* Hyde Park, N.Y.: University Books, 1940.

Frankel, Ellen. *The Classic Tales: 4000 Years of Jewish Lore.* Northvale, N.J.: J. Aronson, 1989.

Frazer, James G. *Folklore of the Old Testament.* 3 vols. London: Macmillan, 1918.

Freedman, H., and Maurice Simon, eds. *Midrash Rabbah.* 10 vols. London: Soncino, 1939.

Friedlander, Gerald, trans. *Pirke de Rabbi Eliezer.* New York: Hermon, 1965.

Friedman, Irving, trans. *The Book of Creation.* New York: Samuel Weiser, 1977.

Gaer, Joseph. *The Legend of the Wandering Jew.* New York: Mentor Books, 1961.

Gaster, Moses, ed. *Studies and Texts in Folklore, Magic, Medieval Romance, Hebrew Apocrypha and Samaritan Archeology.* 3 vols. New York: Ktav, 1971.

Gaster, Moses. *The Chronicles of Jerahmeel.* New York: Ktav, 1971.

———. *The Exempla of the Rabbis.* New York: Ktav, 1968.

———, trans. *Ma'aseh Book of Jewish Tales and Legends.* 2 vols. Philadelphia: Jewish Publication Society, 1934.

———. *Studies and Texts: In Folklore, Magic, Medieval Romance, Hebrew Apocrypha and Samaritan Archaeology.* 3 vols. New York: Ktav, 1971.

Gaster, Theodor H. *The Dead Sea Scriptures.* 3rd ed. Garden City, N.Y.: Anchor, 1976.

———. *The Holy and the Profane: Evolution of Jewish Folkways.* New York: W. Sloane Associates, 1955.

———. *Myth, Legend and Custom in the Old Testament.* New York: Harper & Row, 1969.

Gerould, G. H. *The Grateful Dead: The History of a Folk Story*. Urbana: University of Illinois Press, 2000.

Gersh, Harry. *The Sacred Books of the Jews*. New York: Stein and Day, 1968.

Gety, L. J. "Maidens and Their Guardians: Reinterpreting the 'Rapunzel' Tale." *Mosaic* 30:2 (1997): 37–52.

Ginsburg, Christian D. *The Kabbalah: Its Doctrines, Development, and Literature*. London: Longman, Green, Longman, Roberts, & Green, 1920.

Ginsburg, Elliot K. *The Sabbath in the Classical Kabbalah*. Albany: State University of New York Press, 1989.

Ginzberg, Louis. "Jewish Folklore: East and West." In Ginzberg, *On Jewish Law and Lore* (61–73). Philadelphia: Jewish Publication Society, 1955.

———. *The Legends of the Jews*. 7 vols. Philadelphia: Jewish Publication Society, 1909–1938.

———. *On Jewish Law and Lore*. Philadelphia: Jewish Publication Society, 1955.

Glatzer, Nahum N. *A Jewish Reader*. 2nd ed. New York: Schocken, 1961.

———. *The Judaic Tradition*. Boston: Beacon, 1969.

Goitein, S. D., ed. *From the Land of Sheba: Tales of the Jews of Yemen*. New York: Schocken, 1947.

Goldin, Judah, trans. *The Fathers According to Rabbi Nathan*. New York: Schocken, 1974.

———, ed. and trans. *The Living Talmud*. Chicago: University of Chicago Press, 1957.

———. *The Song at the Sea*. New Haven: Yale University Press, 1971.

———. *Studies in Midrash and Related Literature*. Philadelphia: Jewish Publication Society, 1988.

Goldish, Matt., ed. *Spirit Possession in Judaism: Cases and Contests from the Middle Ages to the Present*. Detroit, Mich.: Wayne State University Press, 2003.

Goldsmith, Arnold L. *The Golem Remembered:* 1909–1980. Detroit, Mich.: Wayne State University Press, 1981.

Goldstein, David. *Jewish Folklore and Legend*. London: Hamlyn, 1980.

Gonen, R. *To the Ends of the Earth: The Quest for the Ten Lost Tribes*. Northvale, N.J.: J. Aronson, 2002.

Goodblatt, C. "Women, Demons and the Rabbi's Son: Narratology and 'A Story from Worms.'" *Exemplaria* 12 (2000): 231–253.

Goodenough, Erwin R. *By Light, Light: The Mystic Gospel of Hellenistic Judaism*. New Haven: Yale University Press, 1935.

———. *Jewish Symbols in the Greco-Roman Period*. 13 vols. New York: Pantheon, 1953–1968.

Gore, Norman C., trans. *Tzeenah U-Reenah: A Jewish Commentary on the Book of Exodus*. New York: Vantage, 1965.

Gottesman, Itzik Nakhmen. *Defining the Yiddish Nation: The Jewish Folklorists of Poland*. Detroit, Mich.: Wayne State University Press, 2003.

Gottlieb, Freema. *The Lamp of God: A Jewish Book of Light*. Northvale, N.J.: J. Aronson, 1989.

Gratus, Jack. *The False Messiahs*. London: Gollancz, 1975.

Graves, Robert, and Raphael Patai, eds. *Hebrew Myths: The Book of Genesis*. Garden City, N.Y.: Doubleday, 1964.

Green, Arthur, trans. "Bratslav Dreams." *Fiction* nos. 1 and 2 (1983), 185–202.

———, ed. *Jewish Spirituality*. 2 vols. New York: Crossroad, 1986.

———, trans. *Menahem Nahum of Chernobyl: Upright Practices, The Light of the Eyes*. New York: Paulist Press, 1982.

———. "The Role of Jewish Mysticism in a Contemporary Theology of Judaism." *Shefa Quarterly* 1:4 (1978): 25–40.

———. *Seek My Face, Speak My Name: A Contemporary Jewish Theology*. Northvale, N.J.: J. Aronson, 1992.

———. *Tormented Master: A Life of Rabbi Nahman of Bratslav*. University: University of Alabama Press, 1979.

Greenbaum, Avraham, trans. *Garden of the Souls: Rebbe Nachman on Suffering*. Jerusalem: Breslov Research Institute, 1990.

———, trans. *Reb Nachman's Tikkun: The Comprehensive Remedy (Tikkun Haklali)*. Jerusalem: Breslov Research Institute, 1984.

———. *Under the Table and How to Get Up: Jewish Pathways of Spiritual Growth*. Jerusalem: Tsohar, 1991.

Grimm, Jacob, and Wilhelm Grimm. *The Complete Fairy Tales of the Brothers Grimm*, translated and edited by Jack Zipes. New York: Bantam, 1987.

Gruenwald, Ithamar. *Apocalyptic and Merkavah Mysticism*. Leiden: E. J. Brill, 1980.

Haboucha, Reginetta. *Types and Motifs of the Judeo-Spanish Folktales*. New York: Garland, 1992.

Hadas, Moses, trans. *The Book of Delight by Joseph Ben Meir Zabara*. New York: Columbia University Press, 1932.

Haddawy, H., trans. *The Arabian Nights*. New York: Norton, 1990.

Halkin, Hillel. *Across the Sabbath River: In Search of a Lost Tribe of Israel*. Boston: Houghton Mifflin, 2002.

Halperin, David J. *The Faces of the Chariot: Early Jewish Responses to Ezekiel's Vision*. Tubingen: J. C. B. Mohr, 1988.

———. *The Merkabah in Rabbinic Literature*. New Haven: American Oriental Society, 1980.

Hammer, Reuven. *The Jerusalem Anthology: A Literary Guide*. Philadelphia: Jewish Publication Society, 1995.

———, trans. *Sifre: A Tannaitic Commentary on the Book of Deuteronomy*. New Haven: Yale University Press, 1986.

Hanauer, J. E. *Folk-Lore in the Holy Land: Moslem, Christian and Jewish*. London: Duckworth, 1907.

Handler, Andrew, trans. *Rabbi Eizik: Hasidic Stories about the Zaddik of Kallo*. Rutherford: Fairleigh Dickinson University Press, 1978.

Harris, Monford. "Dreams in Sefer Hasidim." *Proceedings of the American Academy for Jewish Research* 31 (1963): 51–80.

Hasan-Rokem, Galit, ed. *Web of Life: Folklore and Midrash in Rabbinic Literature*, translated by B. Stein. Stanford: Stanford University Press, 2000.

Hartman, Geoffrey H., and Sanford Budick. *Midrash and Literature*. New Haven: Yale University Press, 1986.

Heinnemann, Joseph, and Dov Noy, eds. *Studies in Aggadah and Folk Literature*. Jerusalem: Magnes, 1971.

Heinnemann, Joseph, and Shmuel Werses, eds. *Studies in Hebrew Narrative Art throughout the Ages*. Jerusalem: Magnes, 1978.

Heschel, Abraham Joshua. *The Circle of the Baal Shem Tov: Studies in Hasidism.* Chicago: University of Chicago Press, 1985.

———. *The Earth Is the Lord's: The Inner Life of the Jew in East Europe.* New York: H. Schuman, 1950.

———. *God in Search of Man: A Philosophy of Judaism.* New York: Farrar, Straus, & Cudahy, 1955.

———. "The Mystical Element in Judaism." In *The Jews: Their History, Culture, and Religion,* edited by Louis Finkelstein (932–953). 3rd ed. 2 vols. New York: Harper, 1960.

———. *The Sabbath: Its Meaning for Modern Man.* New York: Farrar, Straus, and Young, 1951.

Hilton, James. *Lost Horizon.* New York: W. Morrow, 1933.

Himmelfarb, Martha. *Ascent to Heaven in Jewish and Christian Apocalypses.* New York: Oxford University Press, 1993.

———. *Tours of Hell: An Apocalyptic Form in Jewish and Christian Literature.* Philadelphia: Fortress, 1983.

Hirschman, Jack, trans. *The Book of Noah.* Berkeley, Calif.: Tree, 1975.

Hoffman, Edward. *The Way of Splendor: Jewish Mysticism and Modern Psychology.* Northvale, N.J.: J. Aronson, 1989.

Holden, Lynn. *Forms of Deformity.* Sheffield, England: JSOT Press, 1991.

The Holy Scriptures According to the Masoretic Text. Philadelphia: Jewish Publication Society, 1955.

Hsia, R. Po-chia. *The Myth of Ritual Murder: Jews and Magic in Reformation Germany.* New Haven: Yale University Press, 1988.

———. "Witchcraft, Magic, and the Jews in Late Medieval and Early Modern Germany." In *From Witness to Witchcraft: Jews and Judaism in Medieval Christian Thought,* edited by J. Cohen (419–433). Wiesbaden: Harrasowitz, 1996.

Hundert, Gershon David, ed. *Essential Papers on Hasidism: Origins to Present.* New York: New York University Press, 1991.

Hurwitz, Siegmund. *Lilith—The First Eve: Historical and Psychological Aspects of the Dark Feminine.* Einsiedeln, Switzerland: Daimon, 1992.

Idel, Moshe. *Ascension on High in Jewish Mysticism.* Budapest: Central European University Press, 2005.

———. *Golem: Jewish Magical and Mystical Traditions on the Artificial Anthropoid.* Albany: State University of New York Press, 1990.

———. "The Journey to Paradise: The Jewish Transformations of a Greek Mythological Motif." *Jerusalem Studies in Jewish Folklore* 2 (1982): 9–16.

———. *Kabbalah: New Perspectives.* New Haven: Yale University Press, 1988.

———. *Language, Torah, and Hermeneutics in Abraham Abulafia.* Albany: State University of New York Press, 1989.

———. *The Mystical Experience in Abraham Abulafia.* Albany: State University of New York Press, 1988.

Isaacs, Ronald H. *Ascending Jacob's Ladder: Jewish Views of Angels, Demons, and Evil Spirits.* Northvale, N.J.: J. Aronson, 1998.

———. *Divination, Magic, and Healing: The Book of Jewish Folklore.* Northvale, N.J.: J. Aronson, 1998.

Jackson, H. M. "Notes on the Testament of Solomon." *Journal for the Study of Judaism* 19:1 (1988): 19–60.

Jacobi, Margaret. "Serach bat Asher and Bitiah bat Pharaoh—Names Which Became Legends." In *Hear Our Voice: Women Rabbis Tell Their Stories*, edited by Sybil Sheridan. London: SCM Press, 1994.
Jacobs, Louis. "The Doctrine of the 'Divine Sparks' in Jewish Sources." In *Studies in Rationalism, Judaism & Universalism; in Memory of Leon Roth*, edited by Raphael Loewe (87–114). New York: Humanities Press, 1966.
———. *Hasidic Prayer.* New York: Schocken, 1973.
———. *Hasidic Thought.* New York: Behrman House, 1976.
———. *Holy Living: Saints and Saintliness in Judaism.* Northvale, N.J.: J. Aronson, 1990.
———. *Jewish Ethics, Philosophy and Mysticism.* New York: Behrman House, 1969.
———. *Jewish Mystical Testimonies.* New York: Schocken, 1977.
———. *Seeker of Unity: The Life and Works of Aaron of Starosselje.* New York: Vallentine Mitchell, 1966.
Jacobson, David C. *Modern Midrash: The Retelling of Traditional Jewish Narratives by Twentieth Century Hebrew Writers.* Albany: State University of New York Press, 1987.
Janowitz, Naomi. *The Poetics of Ascent: Theories of Language in a Rabbinic Text.* Albany: State University of New York Press, 1989.
Jason, Heda. *Folktales of the Jews of Iraq: Tale-Types and Genres.* Or Yehuda, Israel: Babylonian Jewry Heritage Center, Research Institute of Iraqi Jewry, 1988.
———. "Types of Jewish-Oriental Oral Tales." *Fabula* 7 (1965): 115–224.
———. *Types of Oral Tales in Israel.* Part II. Jerusalem: Israel Ethnographic Society, 1975.
Johnson, M. D. *Life of Adam and Eve* (and *Apocalypse of Moses*). In *The Old Testament Pseudepigrapha*, edited by James Charlesworth. Garden City, N.Y.: Doubleday, 1983–85.
Jones, S. S. *The Fairy Tale: The Magic Mirror of Imagination.* New York: Twayne, 1995.
Jung, C. G. *The Archetypes and the Collective Unconscious.* 2nd ed. Princeton: Princeton University Press, 1968.
Jung, Leo. *Fallen Angels in Jewish, Christian and Mohammedan Literature.* Philadelphia: Dropsie College, 1926.
Kafka, Franz. *The Complete Stories.* New York: Schocken, 1971.
———. *Parables and Paradoxes.* New York: Schocken, 1961.
———. *The Trial.* New York: Schocken, 1953.
Kaplan, Aryeh, trans. *The Bahir.* New York: S. Weiser, 1979.
———. *Chasidic Masters.* New York: Moznaim, 1984.
———. *Gems of Reb Nachman.* Jerusalem: Breslov Research Center, 1980.
———. *Innerspace.* Jerusalem: Moznaim, 1990.
———. *Jewish Meditation: A Practical Guide.* New York: Schocken, 1985.
———. *The Light Beyond: Adventures in Hasidic Thought.* New York: Maznaim, 1981.
———. *The Living Torah: The Five Books of Moses.* New York: Maznaim, 1981.
———. *Meditation and Kabbalah.* York Beach, Me.: S. Weiser, 1982.
———. *Meditation and the Bible.* New York: S. Weiser, 1978.

———, trans. *Outpouring of the Soul: Reb Nachman's Path in Meditation.* Jerusalem: Breslov Research Center, 1980.

———, trans. *Reb Nachman's Stories (Sippurey Ma'asioth): The Stories of Reb Nachman of Breslov.* Jerusalem: Breslov Research Center, 1983.

———. *Sefer Yetzirah: The Book of Creation.* York Beach, Me.: S. Weiser, 1990.

Kasher, Menahem M., ed. *Encyclopedia of Biblical Interpretation.* 9 vols. New York: American Biblical Encyclopedia Society, 1955.

———. *The Western Wall.* New York: Judaica Press, 1972.

Katz, Steven T. *Jewish Ideas and Concepts.* New York: Schocken, 1977.

Kaufman, William E. *Journeys: An Introductory Guide to Jewish Mysticism.* New York: Bloch, 1980.

Kern-Ulmer, Brigitte. "The Depiction of Magic in Rabbinic Texts: The Rabbi and the Greek Concept of Magic." *Journal for the Study of Judaism* 27:3 (1969): 289–303.

———. "The Power of the Evil Eye and the Good Eye in Midrashic Literature." *Judaism* 40 (1991): 344–353.

Kirsch, James. "The Zaddik in Nachman's Dream." *Journal of Psychology and Judaism* 3, 4 (1979): 227–234.

Kitov, Eliyahu. *The Book of Our Heritage.* 3 vols. Jerusalem: "A" Publishers, 1970.

Klapholtz, Yisroel Yaakov. *Stories of Elijah the Prophet.* 4 vols. B'nai Brak, Israel: Pe'er Hasefer Publishers, 1978.

———, ed. *Tales of the Baal Shem Tov.* 5 vols. Jerusalem: Pe'er Hasefer Publishers, 1970–1971.

———, ed. *Tales of the Heavenly Court.* 2 vols. B'nai Brak, Israel: Pe'er Hasefer Publishers, 1982.

Klein, Aron, and Jenny Machlowitz Klein, trans. *Tales in Praise of the Ari (Shivhei ha-Art) by Shlomo Meinsterl.* Philadelphia: Jewish Publication Society, 1970.

Klein, Isaac. A *Guide to Jewish Religious Practice.* New York: Jewish Theological Seminary of America, 1979.

Klein, Michele. *A Time to Be Born: Customs and Folklore of Jewish Birth.* Philadelphia: Jewish Publication Society, 1998.

Kluger, Rivkah Scharf. *Satan in the Old Testament.* Evanston: Northwestern University Press, 1967.

Koén-Sarano, Matilda, ed. *Folktales of Joha: Jewish Trickster,* translated by D. Herman. Philadelphia: Jewish Publication Society, 2003.

———. *King Solomon and the Golden Fish: Tales from the Sephardic Tradition,* translated by Reginetta Haboucha. Detroit, Mich.: Wayne State University Press, 2004.

Koltuv, Barbara Black. *The Book of Lilith.* York Beach, Me.: Nicholas-Hayes, 1986.

Kugel, James L. *In Potiphar's House: The Interpretive Life of Biblical Texts.* San Francisco: HarperSanFrancisco, 1990.

———. *Traditions of the Bible: A Guide to the Bible as It Was at the Start of the Common Era.* Cambridge: Harvard University Press, 1998.

Kuyt, Annelies. "Hasidut Ashkenaz on the Angel of Dreams. A Heavenly Messenger Reflecting or Exchanging Man's Thoughts." In *Creation and Re-Creation in Jewish Thought,* edited by Rachel Elior and Peter Schafer (147–163). Tubingen: Mohr Siebeck, 2005.

Kvam, Kristen E., Linda S. Schearing, and Valarie H. Ziegler, eds. *Eve and Adam: Jewish, Christian, and Muslim Readings on Genesis and Gender.* Bloomington: Indiana University Press, 1999.

Lachower, Fischel, and Isaiah Tishby, eds. *The Wisdom of the Zohar: An Anthology of Texts,* translated by David Goldstein. 3 vols. New York: Oxford University Press, 1989.

Lachs, Samuel T. "The Alphabet of Ben Sira: A Study in Folk Literature." *Gratz College Annual of Jewish Studies* (1973): 9–28.

Lamm, Norman, trans. "The Letter of the Besht to R. Gershon of Kutov." *Tradition* 14:4 (Fall 1974): 110–125.

Landis, J. C., ed. and trans. *The Dybbuk and Other Great Jewish Plays.* New York: Bantam, 1966.

Langer, Jiri. *Nine Gates to the Chassidic Mysteries.* New York: Behrman House, 1976.

Langton, Edward. *Essentials of Demonology: A Study of Jewish and Christine Doctrine, Its Origins and Development.* New York: AMS Press, 1982.

Lassner, J. *Demonizing the Queen of Sheba: Boundaries of Gender and Culture in Post-biblical Judaism and Medieval Islam.* Chicago: University of Chicago Press, 1993.

Lauterbach, Jacob Z., trans. *Mekilta de-Rabbi Ishmael.* 3 vols. Philadelphia: Jewish Publication Society, 1935.

———. *Studies in Jewish Law, Custom, and Folklore.* 3 vols. New York: Ktav, 1968.

Lehrman, S. M. *The World of the Midrash.* London: T. Yoseloff, 1961.

Leslau, Wolf, trans. *Falasha Anthology.* New Haven: Yale University Press, 1979.

Leslie, D. D. *The Survival of the Chinese Jews: The Jewish Community of Kaifeng.* Leiden: Brill, 1972.

Levin, Meyer. *Classic Hassidic Tales.* New York: Penguin, 1975.

Levner, J. B. *The Legends of Israel.* London: J. Clarke, 1946.

Levy, I. J., and R. L. Zumwalt. "The Evil Eye and the Power of Speech among the Sephardim." *International Folklore Review* (1987): 75–81.

Liebes, Yehuda. *Studies in the Zohar.* Albany: State University of New York Press, 1993.

Locks, Gutman G. *The Spice of Torah-Gematria.* New York: Judaica Press, 1985.

Lorand, Sandor. "Dream Interpretation in the Talmud." *International Journal of Psychoanalysis* 38 (1957): 92–97.

Maccoby, Hyam. *The Sacred Executioner: Human Sacrifice and the Legacy of Guilt.* London: Thames and Hudson, 1982.

Mahdi, M., ed. *The Thousand and One Nights (alf layla wa-layla): From the Earliest Known Sources.* 3 vols. Leiden: E. J. Brill, 1984–1994.

Manger, Itzik. *The Book of Paradise.* New York: Hill and Wang, 1965.

Marcus, Ivan G. "The Recensions and Structure of *Sefer Hasidim.*" *Proceedings of the American Academy for Jewish Research* 45 (1978): 131–153.

Marcus, Jacob R. *The Jew in the Medieval World.* Philadelphia: Meridian, 1960.

Matt, Daniel C., trans. *The Zohar,* Pritzker edition. 3 vols. Stanford: Stanford University Press, 2004–2007.

Meltzer, David. *The Secret Garden: An Anthology in the Kabbalah.* New York: Seabury, 1976.

Metzger, Bruce M., ed. *The Apocrypha of the Old Testament.* New York: Oxford University Press, 1965.

Millgram, Abraham E. *An Anthology of Medieval Hebrew Literature.* New York: Abelard-Schuman, 1961.

———. *Jerusalem Curiosities.* Philadelphia: Jewish Publication Society, 1990.

———. *Jewish Worship.* Philadelphia: Jewish Publication Society, 1971.

———. *Sabbath: The Day of Delight.* Philadelphia: Jewish Publication Society, 1944.

Mintz, Jerome R., ed. *Legends of the Hasidim: An Introduction to Hasidic Culture and Oral Tradition in the New World.* Chicago: University of Chicago Press, 1968.

Muhawi, Ibrahim, and Sharif Kananna. *Speak, Bird, Speak Again: Palestinian Arab Folktales.* Berkeley: University of California Press, 1989.

Muller, Ernst. *History of Jewish Mysticism.* Oxford: Phaidon, 1946.

Musaph-Andriesse, R. C. *From Torah to Kabbalah: A Basic Introduction to the Writings of Judaism.* New York: Oxford University Press, 1982.

Mykoff, Moshe, ed. *The Breslov Haggadah.* Jerusalem: Breslov Research Center, 1989.

———, trans. *Once upon a Tzaddik: Tales of Rebbe Nachman of Breslov.* Jerusalem: Breslov Research Center, 1989.

Nachman of Breslov. *The Aleph-Bet Book: Reb Nachman's Aphorisms on Jewish Living (Sefer Hamiddot).* Jerusalem: Breslov Research Center, 1986.

Nadich, Judah, ed. *Jewish Legends of the Second Commonwealth.* Philadelphia: Jewish Publication Society, 1983.

Nagarajan, Nadia Grosser. *Jewish Tales from Eastern Europe.* Northvale, N.J.: J. Aronson, 1999.

———. *Pomegranate Seeds: Latin American Jewish Tales.* Albuquerque: University of New Mexico Press, 2005.

Nahmad, H. M. A *Portion in Paradise and Other Jewish Folktales.* New York: W. W. Norton, 1970.

Nathan of Breslov. *Advice (Likutey Etzot).* Jerusalem: Breslov Research Center, 1983.

———. *Tzaddik (Chayey Moharan): A Portrait of Reb Nachman.* Jerusalem: Breslov Research Center, 1987.

Neubauer, A., and A. Cowley, eds. *Catalogue of the Hebrew Manuscripts in the Bodleian Library.* 2 vols. Oxford: Clarendon, 1886–1906.

Neugroschel, Joachim. *The Dybbuk and the Jewish Imagination: A Haunted Reader.* Syracuse: Syracuse University Press, 2000.

———, ed. *Yenne Velt: The Great Works of Jewish Fantasy and Occult.* 2 vols. New York: Cassell, 1976.

Neusner, Jacob. *First Century Judaism in Crisis: Yohanan ben Zakkai and the Renaissance of Torah.* New York: Ktav, 1982.

Neusner, Jacob, and William Scott Green, eds. *Origins of Judaism: Religion, History, and Literature in Late Antiquity.* 20 vols. New York: Garland, 1990.

Newman, Louis, and Samuel Spitz. *The Hasidic Anthology: Tales and Teachings of the Hasidism.* New York: Bloch, 1963.

———. *Maggidim and Hasidim: Their Wisdom.* New York: Bloch, 1962.
———. *The Talmudic Anthology: Tales and Teachings of the Rabbis.* New York: Behrman House, 1945.
Nigal, Gedalyah. *Magic, Mysticism, and Hasidism: The Supernatural in Jewish Thought.* Northvale, N.J.: J. Aronson, 1994.
Noah, Mordecai Manuel, trans. *The Book of Yashar (Sefer ha-Yashar).* New York: Hermon, 1972.
Noy, Dov. "Eighty Years of Jewish Folkloristics: Achievements and Tasks." In *Studies in Jewish Folklore,* edited by F. Talmage. Cambridge, Mass.: Association for Jewish Studies, 1980, 1–11.
———. "Folklore." *Encyclopedia Judaica,* vol. 6. New York: Keter, 1971, 1374–1410.
———, ed. *Folktales of Israel.* Chicago: University of Chicago Press, 1963.
———. "Is There a Jewish Folk Religion?" In *Studies in Jewish Folklore: Proceedings of a Regional Conference of the Association for Jewish Studies Held at the Spertus College of Judaica, Chicago May 1–3, 1977,* edited by Dov Noy and Frank Talmage (273–286). Cambridge, Mass.: Association for Jewish Studies, 1980.
———, ed. *Moroccan Jewish Folktales.* New York: Herzl Press, 1966.
———. "Motif Index of Talmudic-Midrashic Literature." Ph.D. dissertation, Indiana University, 1954.
———. "The First Thousand Folktales in the Israel Folktale Archives." *Fabula* IV (1961): 99–110.
———. "What Is Jewish about the Jewish Folktale?" Foreword to *Miriam's Tambourine: Jewish Folktales from around the World,* edited by Howard Schwartz (xi–xix). New York: Free Press, 1986.
O'Hara, John. *Appointment in Samarra.* New York: Modern Library, 1953.
Ozick, Cynthia. *The Puttermesser Papers.* New York: Vintage, 1998.
Parffit, Tudor. *The Lost Tribes of Israel: The History of a Myth.* London: Weidenfeld & Nicholson, 2002.
Patai, Raphael, ed. *Arab Folktales Palestine and Israel.* Detroit, Mich.: Wayne State University Press, 1998.
———. "Exorcism and Xenoglossia among the Safed Kabbalists." *Journal of American Folklore* 91 (1978): 823–835.
———, ed. *Gates to the Old City: A Book of Jewish Legends.* Detroit, Mich.: Wayne State University Press, 1981.
———. *The Hebrew Goddess.* 3rd ed. Detroit, Mich.: Wayne State University Press, 1991.
———. *Man and Temple in Ancient Jewish Myth and Ritual.* 2nd ed. New York: Ktav, 1967.
———, ed. *The Messiah Texts.* Detroit, Mich.: Wayne State University Press, 1979.
———. *On Jewish Folklore.* Detroit, Mich.: Wayne State University Press, 1983.
Patai, Raphael, Francis Lee Utley, and Dov Noy, eds. *Studies in Biblical and Jewish Folklore.* Bloomington: Indiana University Press, 1960.
Peretz, I. L. *The Book of Fire.* New York: T. Yoseloff, 1959.
———. *In This World and the Next.* New York: T. Yoseloff, 1975.
———. *Peretz,* translated by S. Liptzin. New York: Yiddish Scientific Institute, 1947.

———. *Selected Stories*, edited by Irving Howe and Eliezer Greenberg. New York: Schocken, 1975.

Petuchowski, Jakob J. *Our Masters Taught: Rabbinic Stories and Sayings*. New York: Crossroad, 1982.

Pick, Bernard. *The Cabala: Its Influence on Judaism and Christianity*. La Salle, Ill.: Open Court, 1974.

Piontac, Nechemiah, ed. *The Arizal: The Life and Times of Rabbi Yitzchak Luria*. New York: Mesorah, 1969.

Prager, Moshe. *Rabbi Yisroel Baal-Shem-Tov*. New York: Torah Umesorah Publication, 1976.

Pritchard, J. B, ed. *Solomon and Sheba*. London: Phaidon, 1974.

Propp, V. *Morphology of the Folktale*. 2nd rev. ed. Austin: University of Texas Press, 1968.

Prose, Francine. *Judah the Pious*. New York: Atheneum, 1973.

Pye, Faye. "A Brief Study of an Hasidic Fairy Tale." *Harvest: Journal for Jungian Studies of the Analytical Psychology Club* 21 (London) (1975): 94–104.

Rabinowicz, Harry M. A *Guide to Hassidism*. New York: T. Yoseloff, 1960.

———. *Hasidism: The Movement and Its Masters*. Northvale, N.J.: J. Aronson, 1988.

———. *The Slave Who Saved the City and Other Hasidic Tales*. New York: A. S. Barnes, 1960.

Rabinowitsch, Wolf Zeev. *Lithuanian Hasidism*. New York: Schocken, 1971.

Rader, Benzion, ed. *To Touch the Divine: A Jewish Mysticism Primer*. Brooklyn, N.Y.: Merkos L'Inyonei Chinuch, 1989.

Rapaport, Samuel. A *Treasury of the Midrash*. New York: Ktav, 1988.

Raphael, Simcha Paull. *Jewish Views of the Afterlife*. Northvale, N.J.: J. Aronson, 1993.

Rapoport-Albert, Ada. *Hasidism Reconsidered*. London: Vallentine Mitchell, 1996.

———. "On Women in Hasidism." In *Jewish History: Essays in Honor of Chimen Abramsky*, edited by Ada Rapoport-Albert and Steven Zipperstein (495–525). London: Halban, 1988).

Rappel, Yoel. *Yearning for the Holy Land: Hasidic Tales of Israel*. New York: Adama Books, 1986.

Rappoport, Angelo S. *The Folklore of the Jews*. London: Soncino, 1937.

———. *Myth and Legend of Ancient Israel*. 3 vols. New York: Ktav, 1966.

Reimer, Jack. "Franz Kafka and Reb Nachman." *Jewish Frontier* 28:4 (1961): 16–20.

Reps, Paul. *Zen Flesh, Zen Bones*. Garden City, N.Y.: Doubleday, 1961.

Robinson, James M. *The Nag Hammadi Library*. 3rd rev. ed. San Francisco: Harper & Row, 1988.

Rosenbaum, Thane. *The Golems of Gotham*. New York: Perennial, 2003.

Roskies, David G. *A Bridge of Longing: The Lost Art of Yiddish Storytelling*. Cambridge: Harvard University Press, 1995.

Rosman, Moshe J. *Founder of Hasidism: A Quest for the Historical Ba'al Shem Tov*. Berkeley: University of California Press, 1996.

Ross, Dan. *Acts of Faith: A Journey to the Fringes of Jewish Identity*. New York: St. Martin's, 1982.

Rossoff, Dovid. *Safed: The Mystical City.* Jerusalem: Sha'ar Books, 1991.

Roth, Cecil, ed. *The Dark Ages: Jews in Christian Europe* 711–1096. Vol. 2 of *World History of the Jewish People.* New Brunswick: Rutgers University Press, 1966.

Roth, Cecil, and G. Wigoder, eds. *Encyclopedia Judaica.* 16 vols. Jerusalem: Keter, 1972.

Rothenberg, Jerome, Harris Lenowitz, and Charles Doria, eds. A *Big Jewish Book.* Garden City, N.Y.: Anchor, 1978.

Rubenstein, Jeffrey L., trans. *Rabbinic Stories.* Mahwah, N.J.: Paulist Press, 2002.

Rubin, R. "Y. L. Cahan and Jewish Folklore." *New York Folklore Quarterly* 11 (1955): 34–45.

Rudaysky, David. *Modern Jewish Religious Movements.* 3rd ed. New York: Behrman House, 1979.

Ruderman, David B. *Kabbalah, Magic, and Science: The Cultural Universe of a Sixteenth-Century Jewish Physician.* Cambridge: Harvard University Press, 1988.

———. *A Valley of Vision: The Heavenly Journey of Abraham ben Hananiah Yagel.* Philadelphia: University of Pennsylvania Press, 1990.

Rush, Barbara. *The Book of Jewish Women's Tales.* Northvale, N.J.: J. Aronson, 1994.

Rush, Barbara, and Eliezer Marcus, eds. *Seventy and One Tales for the Jewish Year: Folk Tales for the Festivals.* New York: A.Z.Y.F., 1980.

Sabar, Yona. "Childbirth and Magic: Jewish Folklore and Material Culture." In *Cultures of the Jews: A New History,* edited by David Biale (671–722). New York: Schocken, 2002.

———. *The Folk Literature of the Kurdistani Jews: An Anthology.* New Haven: Yale University Press, 1982.

Sadeh, Pinchas. *Jewish Folktales.* New York: Doubleday, 1989.

Safran, Bezalel, ed. *Hasidism: Continuity or Innovation?* Cambridge: Harvard University Center for Jewish Studies, 1988.

Saperstein, Marc. *Decoding the Rabbis: A Thirteenth-century Commentary on the Aggadah.* Cambridge: Harvard University Press, 1980.

———. *Jewish Preaching* 1200–1800*: An Anthology.* New Haven: Yale University Press, 1989.

———. "The Simpleton's Prayer: Transformation of a Motif in Hebrew Literature." *Judaism* 29:3 (1980): 295–304.

Schachter, Zalman M. *Fragments of a Future Scroll.* Germantown, Pa.: B'nai Or Press, 1975.

———. *Wrapped in a Holy Flame: Teachings and Tales of the Hasidic Masters.* San Francisco: Jossey-Bass, 2003.

Schachter, Zalman M., and Edward Hoffman. *Sparks of Light: Counseling in the Hasidic Tradition.* Boulder, Colo.: Shambhala, 1983.

Schachter-Shalomi, Zalman Meshullam. *Spiritual Intimacy: A Study of Counseling in Hasidism.* Northvale, N.J.: J. Aronson, 1991.

Schafer, Peter. *The Hidden and Manifest God: Some Major Themes in Early Jewish Mysticism.* Albany: State University of New York Press, 1992.

Schauss. H. *The Jewish Festivals: History and Observance.* New York: Schocken, 1938.

Schechter, Solomon. *Studies in Judaism: Essays on Persons, Concepts, and Movements of Thought in Jewish Tradition.* New York: Meridian, 1970.

Schochet, Elijah Judah. *Animal Life in Jewish Tradition: Attitudes and Relationships*. New York: Ktav, 1984.

Schochet, Jacob Immanuel. *The Great Maggid: The Life and Teachings of Rabbi Dov Ber of Mezhirech*. Brooklyn, N.Y.: Kehot, 1974.

———. *Mystical Concepts in Chassidism*. Brooklyn, N.Y.: Kehot, 1979.

———. *The Mystical Dimension*. 3 vols. Brooklyn, N.Y.: Kehot, 1990.

———. *Rabbi Israel Baal Shem Tov*. Toronto: Lieberman's Publishing House, 1961.

Scholem, Gershom. *Jewish Gnosticism, Merkabah Mysticism and Talmudic Tradition*. New York: Jewish Theological Seminary, 1960.

———. *Kabbalah*. New York: Quadrangle/New York Times, 1974.

———. *Major Trends in Jewish Mysticism*. New York: Schocken, 1964.

———. *The Messianic Idea in Judaism and Other Essays on Jewish Spirituality*. New York: Schocken, 1971.

———. *On Jews and Judaism in Crisis: Selected Essays*. New York: Schocken, 1976.

———. *On the Kabbalah and Its Symbolism*. New York: Schocken, 1965.

———. *On the Mystical Shape of the Godhead: Basic Concepts in Kabbalah*. New York: Schocken, 1991.

———. *Origins of the Kabbalah*. Philadelphia: Jewish Publication Society, 1987.

———. *Shabbatai Zevi: The Mystical Messiah*. Princeton: Princeton University Press, 1973.

———. *Zohar: The Book of Splendor*. New York: Schocken, 1963.

Schram, Peninnah. *Jewish Stories One Generation Tells Another*. Northvale, N.J.: J. Aronson, 1987.

———. *Stories within Stories: From the Jewish Oral Tradition*. Northvale, N.J.: J. Aronson, 1987.

———. *Tales of Elijah the Prophet*. Northvale, N.J.: J. Aronson, 1991.

Schrire, T. *Hebrew Magic Amulets: Their Decipherment and Interpretation*. London: Routledge & Paul, 1966.

Schurer, Emil. *The Literature of the Jewish People in the Time of Jesus*. New York: Schocken, 1972.

Schwartz, Dov. *Studies on Astral Magic in Medieval Jewish Thought*. Leiden: E. J. Brill, 2005.

Schwartz, Howard. "The Aggadic Tradition." In *Origins of Judaism*, edited by Jacob Neusner (vol. 1, part 3, 446–463). New York: Garland, 1990.

———. *The Day the Rabbi Disappeared: Jewish Holiday Tales of Magic*. New York: Viking, 2000.

———. *Elijah's Violin & Other Jewish Fairy Tales*. New York: Harper & Row, 1983.

———. *The Four Who Entered Paradise*. Northvale, N.J.: J. Aronson, 1995.

———. *Gabriel's Palace: Jewish Mystical Tales*. New York: Oxford University Press, 1993.

———. *Gates to the New City: A Treasury of Modern Jewish Tales*. New York: Avon Books, 1983.

———. *Invisible Kingdoms: Jewish Tales of Angels, Spirits, and Demons*. New York: HarperCollins, 2002.

———. *A Journey to Paradise & Other Jewish Tales*. Jerusalem: Pitspopany, 2000.

———. "Jewish Tales of the Supernatural." *Judaism* 36:3 (1987): 229–351.
———. *Lilith's Cave: Jewish Tales of the Supernatural.* New York: Harper & Row, 1988.
———. "Mermaid and Siren: The Polar Roles of Lilith and Eve." In *Reimagining the Bible: The Storytelling of the Rabbis* (56–67). New York: Oxford University Press, 1998.
———. *Miriam's Tambourine: Jewish Folktales from Around the World.* New York: Free Press, 1986.
———. "The Mythology of Judaism." In *The Seductiveness of Jewish Myth: Challenge or Response,* edited by S. Daniel Breslauer (11–25). Albany: State University of New York Press, 1997.
———. *Next Year in Jerusalem: 3000 Years of Jewish Stories.* New York: Viking, 1996. [Reprinted as *Jerusalem of Gold: Jewish Stories of the Enchanted City.* Woodstock, Vt.: Jewish Lights, 2003]
———. "The Quest for Jerusalem." In *Judaism* 46:2 (1997): 208–217.
———. "The Quest for the Lost Princess." In *Opening the Inner Gates: New Paths in Kabbalah and Psychology,* edited by Edward Hoffman (20–46). Boston: Shambhala, 1995.
———. "Reb Nachman of Bratslav: Forerunner of Modern Jewish Literature." In *Judaism* 31 (1982): 211–224.
———. *Reimagining the Bible: The Storytelling of the Rabbis.* New York: Oxford University Press, 1998.
———. *Tree of Souls: The Mythology of Judaism.* New York: Oxford University Press, 2004.
Schwartz, Howard, and Barbara Rush. *The Diamond Tree: Jewish Tales from Around the World.* New York: HarperCollins, 1991.
———. *The Sabbath Lion.* New York: HarperCollins, 1997.
———. *The Wonder Child & Other Jewish Fairy Tales.* New York: HarperCollins, 1996.
Schwarzbaum, Haim. *Jewish Folklore between East and West: Collected Papers,* edited by Eli Yassif. Beersheva: Ben-Gurion University of the Negev Press, 1989.
———. "The Hero Predestined to Die on His Wedding Day." *Folklore Research Center Studies* (1974): 223–252.
———. *Studies in Jewish and World Folklore.* Berlin: Walter de Gruyter, 1968.
Segal, Alan F. *Life After Death.* New York: Doubleday, 2004.
———. *The Other Judaisms of Late Antiquity.* Atlanta, Ga.: Scholars Press, 1987.
———. *Paul the Convert: The Apostolate and Apostasy of Saul the Pharisee.* New Haven: Yale University Press, 1990.
———. *Rebecca's Children: Judaism and Christianity in the Roman World.* Cambridge: Harvard University Press, 1986.
———. *Two Powers in Heaven: Early Rabbinic Reports about Christianity and Gnosticism.* Leiden: E. J. Brill, 1977.
Segal, S. M. *Elijah: A Study in Jewish Folklore.* New York: Behrman's Jewish Book House, 1935.
Seymour, St. John D. *Tales of King Solomon.* London: Oxford University Press, 1924.

Shah, Idries. *Tales of the Dervishes: Teaching-stories of the Sufi Masters.* New York: Dutton, 1969.

Sharot, Stephen. *Messianism, Mysticism, and Magic: A Sociological Analysis of Jewish Religious Movements.* Chapel Hill: University of North Carolina Press, 1982.

Shenhar, Aliza. "Concerning the Nature of the Motif 'Death by a Kiss' (Motif A185.6.11)." *Fabula* 19 (1978): 62–73.

———. "The Jewish Oicotype of the Predestined Marriage Folktale: AaTh930*E (IFA)." *Fabula* 24 1/2 (1983): 43–55.

Sherwin, Byron. *The Golem Legend: Origins and Implications.* Lanham, Md.: University Press of America, 1985.

———. *Mystical Theology and Social Dissent: The Life and Works of Judah Loew of Prague.* Rutherford: Fairleigh Dickinson University Press, 1982.

Shulman, Yaacov David. *The Chambers of the Palace: The Teachings of Rabbi Nachman.* Northvale, N.J.: J. Aronson, 1993.

———, trans. *The Return to G-d: Based on the Works of Rabbi Nachman of Breslov and His Holy Disciples (Derech Hatshuvah).* Brooklyn: Keren hadpasah di-Haside Breslav, n.d.

Silver, Daniel Jeremy. *The Story of Scripture: From Oral Tradition to the Written Word.* New York: Basic Books, 1990.

Silverman, Dov. *Legends of Safed.* Jerusalem: Judah L. Magnes Museum, 1991.

Singer, Isaac Bashevis. *The Collected Stories.* New York: Farrar, Straus, & Giroux, 1982.

———. *Selected Short Stories of Isaac Bashevis Singer.* New York: Modern Library, 1966.

Singer, Sholom Alchanan. *Medieval Jewish Mysticism: Book of the Pious (Sefer Hasidim).* Northbrook, Ill.: Whitehall, 1971.

Soloveitchik, Hayim. "Three Themes in the Sefer Hasidim." *AJS Review* 1 (1976): 311–357.

Spector, Sheila A. *Jewish Mysticism: An Annotated Bibliography on the Kabbalah in English.* New York: Garland, 1984.

Sperber, Daniel. *Magic and Folklore in Rabbinic Literature.* Ramat-Gan: Bar-Ilan University Press, 1994.

Sperling, Harry, and Maurice Simon, eds. *The Zohar.* 5 vols. London: Soncino, 1931–1934.

Spiegel, Shalom. *The Last Trial.* New York: Pantheon, 1967.

Steinman, Eliezer. *The Garden of Hasidism.* Jerusalem: World Zionist Organization, 1961.

Steinsaltz, Adin. *Beggars and Prayers.* New York: Basic Books, 1979.

———. *The Essential Talmud.* New York: Basic Books, 1976.

———. "The Losing of the Princess: An Interpretation." *Ariel* 35 (1974): 65–70.

———. *The Thirteen Petalled Rose.* New York: Basic Books, 1980.

Steinschneider, Moritz. *Jewish Literature from the Eighth to the Eighteenth Century with an Introduction on Talmud and Midrash.* New York: Hermon, 1965.

Stern, David. *Parables in Midrash: Narrative and Exegesis in Rabbinic Literature.* Cambridge: Harvard University Press, 1994.

Stern, David, and Mark Jay Mirsky, eds. *Rabbinic Fantasies: Imaginative Narratives from Classical Hebrew Literature*. Philadelphia: Jewish Publication Society, 1990.

Stone, Michael E. *Scriptures, Sects and Visions: A Profile of Judaism from Ezra to the Jewish Revolts*. Philadelphia: Fortress, 1980.

———, trans. *The Testament of Abraham: The Greek Recensions*. New York: Society of Biblical Literature, 1972.

Stone, Michael E., and Theodore A. Bergren. *Biblical Figures Outside the Bible*. Harrisburg, Pa.: Trinity Press International, 1998.

Strack, Hermann L., and G. Stemberger. *Introduction to the Talmud and Midrash*. Minneapolis: Fortress, 1992.

Swan, C., and W. Hooper, eds. and trans. *Gesta Romanorum: Or, Entertaining Moral Stories*. New York: Dover, 1959.

Talmage, Frank, ed. *Studies in Jewish Folklore*. Cambridge, Mass.: Association for Jewish Studies, 1980.

Tanakh: A New Translation of the Scriptures. Philadelphia: Jewish Publication Society, 1985.

Thieberger, Frederic. *The Great Rabbi Loew of Prague: His Life and Work and the Legend of the Golem*. London: East and West Library, 1955.

Thompson, R. Campbell. *Semitic Magic: Its Origins and Development*. London: Luzac, 1908.

Thompson, Stith. *The Folktale*. New York: Holt, Rinehart & Winston, 1946.

———. *Motif-Index of Folk-Literature: A Classification of Narrative Elements in Folktales, Ballads, Myths, Fables, Mediaeval Romances, Exempla, Fabliaux, Jest-Books and Local Legends*. Rev. ed. 6 vols. Bloomington: Indiana University Press, 1955–1958.

Tishby, Isaiah. "Gnostic Doctrines in Sixteenth-Century Jewish Mysticism." *Journal of Jewish Studies* 6 (1955): 146–152.

———, ed. *The Wisdom of the Zohar: An Anthology of Texts*. 3 vols. New York: Oxford University Press, 1989.

Tolkien, J. R. R. *The Silmarillion*. Boston: Houghton Mifflin, 1977.

Townsend, John T. *Midrash Tanhuma*. Hoboken, N.J.: Ktav, 1989.

Trachtenberg, Joshua. *The Devil and the Jews*. New Haven: Yale University Press, 1943.

———. "The Folk Element in Judaism." *Journal of Religion* 22 (1942): 173–186.

———. *Jewish Magic and Superstition:* A *Study in Folk Religion*. New York: Behrman's Jewish Book House, 1939.

———. "The Lost Ten Tribes in Medieval Jewish Literature." Thesis, Hebrew Union College, 1930.

Tsalka, Dan. *On the Road to Aleppo*. Ra'annana, Israel: Even Hoshen Publishers, 1999.

Twersky, Isadore, and Bernard Septimus, eds. *Jewish Thought in the Seventeenth Century*. Cambridge: Harvard University Press, 1987.

Ulmer, R. *The Evil Eye in the Bible and in Rabbinic Literature*. Hoboken, N.J.: Ktav, 1994.

Unterman, Alan. *Dictionary of Jewish Lore and Legend*. London: Thames and Hudson, 1991.

———, ed. *The Wisdom of the Jewish Mystics*. New York: New Directions, 1976.

Urbach, Ephraim. "The Fable of the Three and Four of H. N. Bialik." *Ariel* 38 (1975): 31–49.

———. *The Sages: Their Concepts and Beliefs*. 2 vols. Jerusalem: Magnes, 1975.

Uther, H. J. *The Types of International Folktales: A Classification and Bibliography. Based on the System of Antti Aarne and Stith Thompson*. 3 parts. Helsinki: Suomalainen Tiedeakatemia, 2004.

Verman, Mark. *The Books of Contemplation: Medieval Jewish Mystical Sources*. Albany: State University of New York Press, 1992.

Vermes, Geza. *Post-biblical Jewish Studies*. Leiden: E. J. Brill, 1975.

———. *Scripture and Tradition in Judaism*. Leiden: E. J. Brill, 1961.

Vilnay, Zev. *Legends of Galilee, Jordan and Sinai*. Philadelphia: Jewish Publication Society, 1978.

———. *Legends of Jerusalem*. Philadelphia: Jewish Publication Society, 1973.

———. *Legends of Judea and Samaria*. Philadelphia: Jewish Publication Society, 1973.

Visotzky, Burton I. *Reading the Book: Making the Bible a Timeless Text*. New York: Anchor, 1991.

Von Franz, Marie. *Individuation in Fairy Tales*. Boston: Shambhala, 2001.

———. *Shadow and Evil in Fairy Tales*. Boston: Shambhala, 1995.

Wallach, Shalom Meir. *Haggadah of the Chassidic Masters*. Brooklyn, N.Y.: Mesorah, 1990.

Waxman, Meyer. A *History of Jewish Literature*. 6 vols. New York: T. Yoseloff, 1960.

Weiner, A. *The Prophet Elijah in the Development of Judaism: A Depth-Psychological Study*. London: Routledge & Kegan Paul, 1978.

Weinreich, Beatrice Silverman. "The Prophet Elijah in Modern Yiddish Folktales." Master's thesis, Columbia University, 1957.

———, ed. *Yiddish Folktales*. New York: Pantheon, 1988.

Weinreich, Uriel, ed. *The Field of Yiddish: Studies in Yiddish Language, Folklore, and Literature*. New York: Linguistic Circle of New York, 1954.

Weinreich, Uriel, and Beatrice Silverman Weinreich. *Yiddish Language and Folklore: A Selective Bibliography for Research*. The Hague: Mouton, 1959.

Weinstein, Roni. "Kabbalah and Jewish Exorcism in Seventeenth-Century Italian Jewish Communities: The Case of Rabbi Moses Zacuto." In *Spirit Possession in Judaism*, edited by Matt Goldish (237–256). Detroit, Mich.: Wayne State University Press, 2003.

Weiss, Joseph. *Studies in Eastern European Jewish Mysticism and Hasidism*, edited by David Goldstein. London: Litmann Library, 1985.

Werblowsky, R. J. Zwi. *Joseph Karo: Lawyer and Mystic*. Philadelphia: Jewish Publication Society, 1977.

———. "Some Psychological Aspects of the Kabbalah." *Harvest: Journal of the Analytical Psychology Club of London* (London) 3 (1956): 77–96.

Werblowsky, R. J. Zwi, and Geoffrey Wigoder. *The Encyclopedia of the Jewish Religion*. New York: Massadah, 1967.

Werthheim, Aaron. *Law and Custom in Hasidism*. Hoboken, N.J.: Ktav, 1992.

Wiesel, Elie. *Sages and Dreamers: Biblical, Talmudic, and Hasidic Portraits and Legends*. New York: Summit Books, 1991.
———. *Somewhere a Master: Further Hasidic Portraits and Legends*. New York: Summit Books, 1982.
———. *Souls on Fire: Portraits and Legends of Hasidic Masters*. New York: Random House, 1972.
Wieseltier, Leon. *Kaddish*. New York: Knopf, 1998.
Wineman, Aryeh. *Beyond Appearances: Stories from the Kabbalistic Ethical Writings*. Philadelphia: Jewish Publication Society, 1988.
———. *The Hasidic Parable*. Philadelphia: Jewish Publication Society, 2001.
———. "The Metamorphosis of Narrative Traditions: Two Stories from Sixteenth Century Safed." *AJS Review* 10: 2 (1985): 165–180.
———. *Mystic Tales from the Zohar*. Princeton: Princeton University Press, 1998.
Winkler, Gershon. *Dybbuk*. New York: Judaica, 1980.
———. *The Golem of Prague*. New York: Judaica, 1982.
———. *They Called Her Rebbe*. New York: Judaica, 1992.
Wisse, Ruth S., ed. *The I. L. Peretz Reader*. New York: Schocken, 1990.
Yassif, Eli. *The Hebrew Folktale: History, Genre, Meaning*. Bloomington: Indiana University Press, 1999.
———. *Jewish Folklore: An Annotated Bibliography*. New York: Garland, 1986.
———. "The Medieval Saint as Protagonist and Storyteller. The Case of R. Judah ha- Hasid." In *Creation and Re-Creation in Jewish Thought*, edited by Rachel Elior and Peter Schafer (179–191). Tubingen: Mohr Siebeck, 2005.
Yourcenar, Marguerite. *Oriental Tales*. New York: Farrar, Straus, & Giroux, 1985.
Zangwill, Israel. *The Master*. New York: Harper & Brothers, 1897.
Zeitlin, Solomon. "Dreams and Their Interpretation from the Biblical Period to the Tannaitic Time: A Historical Study." *Jewish Quarterly Review* 66 (1975): 1–18.
Zenner, Walter P. "Saints and Piecemeal Supernaturalism among the Jerusalem Sephardim." *Anthropological Quarterly* 38 (1965): 201–227.
Zevin, S. Y. A *Treasury of Chassidic Tales on the Torah*. 2 vols. New York: Artscroll, 1980.
Zimmels, H. J. *Magicians, Theologians and Doctors*. London: Goldston, 1952.
Zimmer, Heinrich. *Myths and Symbols in Indian Art and Civilization*. New York: Pantheon, 1946.
———. *Philosophies of India*. New York: Pantheon, 1951.
Zinberg, Israel. A *History of Jewish Literature*. 12 vols. New York: Ktav, 1974–1978.
Zipes, Jack. *Why Fairy Tales Stick: The Evolution and Relevance of a Genre*. New York: Routledge, 2006.

Credits

Some of these stories have been selected from the following collections edited by Howard Schwartz: *Elijah's Violin & Other Jewish Fairy Tales* (Harper & Row, 1983), *Miriam's Tambourine: Jewish Folktales from Around the World* (Free Press, 1986), *Lilith's Cave: Jewish Tales of the Supernatural* (HarperSanFrancisco, 1987) and *Gabriel's Palace: Jewish Mystical Tales* (Oxford University Press, 1994).

The following stories also have been included in this collection:

"The Water Witch," "Katanya," "A Palace of Bird Beaks," and "The Prince Who Thought He Was a Rooster" from *The Diamond Tree: Jewish Tales from Around the World*, selected and retold by Howard Schwartz and Barbara Rush (HarperCollins, 1991). Copyright © 1991 by Howard Schwartz and Barbara Rush. Used by permission of the authors.

"The Sabbath Lion" from *The Sabbath Lion*, selected and retold by Howard Schwartz and Barbara Rush (HarperCollins, 1992). Copyright © 1992 by Howard Schwartz and Barbara Rush. Used by permission of the authors.

"The Wonder Child" from *The Wonder Child & Other Jewish Fairy Tales*, selected and retold by Howard Schwartz and Barbara Rush (HarperCollins, 1996). Copyright © 1996 by Howard Schwartz and Barbara Rush. Used by permission the authors.

"An Apple from the Tree of Life" from *A Journey to Paradise & Other Jewish Tales*, selected and retold by Howard Schwartz (Pitspopany Press, 2000). Copyright © 2000 by Howard Schwartz. Used by permission of the author.

"A Flock of Angels," "Drawing the Wind," "The Souls of Trees" and "The Magic Wine Cup" from *The Day the Rabbi Disappeared: Jewish Holiday Tales of Magic*, selected and retold by Howard Schwartz (Viking, 2000; Jewish Publication Society, 2003). Copyright © 2000 by Howard Schwartz. Used by permission of the Jewish Publication Society.

"The Lost Melody," "Yona and the River Demon" and "The Demonic Double" from *Invisible Kingdoms: Jewish Tales of Angels, Spirits and Demons*, selected and retold by Howard Schwartz (HarperCollins, 2002). Copyright © 2002 by Howard Schwartz. Used by permission of the author.

"The Bird of Happiness" and "Milk and Honey" from *Jerusalem of Gold: Stories of the Enchanted City* (Jewish Lights Publishing). Copyright © 1996 by Howard Schwartz. $18.95 + $3.96 s/h. Order by mail or call 800–962–4544 or on-line at www.jewishlights.com. Permission granted by Jewish Lights Publishing, P.O. Box 237, Woodstock, VT 05091.

Index